Andrew Johnson and Reconstruction

ANDREW JOHNSON

AND RECONSTRUCTION

By Eric L. McKitrick

OXFORD UNIVERSITY PRESS
NEW YORK • OXFORD

Oxford University Press

Oxford   New York   Toronto
Delhi   Bombay   Calcutta   Madras   Karachi
Petaling Jaya   Singapore   Hong Kong   Tokyo
Nairobi   Dar es Salaam   Cape Town
Melbourne   Auckland

and associated companies in
Berlin   Ibadan

Library of Congress Cataloging-in-Publication Data

McKitrick, Eric L.
Andrew Johnson and Reconstruction/Eric L. McKitrick.
p.   cm.
Reprint. Originally published: Chicago: University of Chicago
Press, 1960.
Bibliography: p.
Includes index.
ISBN 0-19-505707-4 (pbk.)
1. Reconstruction. 2. Johnson, Andrew, 1808–1875. 3. United
States—Politics and government—1865–1877.   I. Title.
E668.M156   1988
973.8'1'0924—dc19   88-23509

2   4   6   8   10   9   7   5   3
Printed in the United States of America

For

E. S. M.

Contents

Contents

Contents

Part One: **1865**

Andrew Johnson:
The Case Reopened

One of the most notable reversals of sentiment toward a high public figure ever to be brought about in this country has been the rehabilitation of Andrew Johnson's historical reputation as seventeenth President of the United States. Nowadays when President Johnson's memory is invoked, it is with few traces of the odium that surrounded him during the climactic years of his own lifetime and that persisted for nearly two generations after his death. With judgment no longer inflamed by the passions of a former age, a number of our scholars over the past thirty years have decently refurbished the picture of Lincoln's successor. Their devotion and care, tinged with belated remorse, have produced a setting in which we may now see the unfortunate man in the light of justice and reason.[1]

Andrew Johnson, having assumed the executive chair in the spring of 1865 upon the assassination of Abraham Lincoln, had in the summer and fall of that year put into effect a policy for the political reconstruction of the defeated Southern states, the outlines of which for the most part had been laid down by Lincoln himself. Despite some indications in the beginning that Johnson's attitude toward the South might be a harsh one, his policy turned out to be quite otherwise. Such was its mildness, such was the generosity with which amnesties were made available, and such was the simple efficiency with which civil

---

[1] This attitude has given unity to a whole cycle of writing on Johnson, most of it appearing within the space of a single decade: Howard K. Beale, *The Critical Year, 1866: A Study of Andrew Johnson and Reconstruction* (New York: Harcourt, Brace, 1930), George F. Milton, *The Age of Hate: Andrew Johnson and the Radicals* (New York: Coward-McCann, 1930); Robert W. Winston, *Andrew Johnson, Plebeian and Patriot* (New York: Henry Holt, 1928); Claude G. Bowers, *The Tragic Era: The Revolution after Lincoln* (Boston: Houghton Mifflin, 1929); Lloyd Paul Stryker, *Andrew Johnson: A Study in Courage* (New York: Macmillan, 1929); and James G. Randall, *The Civil War and Reconstruction* (Boston: D. C. Heath, 1937). The point of view represented in these works has, in turn, had immeasurable influence upon nearly everything else on the period that has since been written.

governments could once more be set up in those states, that the policy gave every promise of the South's rapid reincorporation into the political life of the nation as a whole. Its initial reception in the North was not unfavorable. Many Northern newspapers—probably a good majority of them—commended the President for the energy with which he had approached his inherited task, counseled patience, and urged that his policy be given a fair trial.

Widely organized opposition to the President would have been difficult to identify in the summer and fall of 1865. Yet the extraordinary fact is that in a matter of weeks after the opening of Congress in December, Johnson's relations with an increasingly radical House and Senate had deteriorated; by the spring of 1866 his position as leader of the Union party[2] had become meaningless; and by the fall elections of that year his influence in the country at large had all but collapsed. In March, 1867, Congress took reconstruction into its own hands. So complete was this collapse, so profound the breach between Congress and the President, and so general the contempt and hatred in which the latter had come to be held, that the famous impeachment brought against him during his last year in office—the only attempt of its kind ever made so far in our history—could actually come within a single vote of succeeding.

All this makes the eventual rescue of Johnson's reputation the more remarkable. His personal honor has now been vindicated and placed beyond question. The violent attacks made upon him, the charges—by Republican politicians—of incompetence, drunkenness, and even of immorality, have all been discredited by the work of twentieth-century historians. His diligence and administrative capacities were, as we now know, unusual. President Johnson may now be seen as a man of undoubted personal integrity and firm principle who was slandered intemperately by his fellow citizens. Today's portrait of him actually contains touches of the heroic.

And yet the very effort to revise our historical perspective on Andrew Johnson, and the great intensity which has gone into it, may have produced results that have not turned out to be, in the fullest sense, "balanced" after all. History may in the end require that more than one kind of justice be done toward any man who happens to have

---

[2] The "Union" party had represented the wartime effort of the Republicans to form an all-party coalition. Despite numbers of notable Democratic recruits, however, the core of the Union party was made up of Republicans, and the organization was Republican throughout—a fact which the regular Democrats stressed on every possible occasion. The terms "Union" and "Republican" were used interchangeably in the early years of reconstruction, and will be so used throughout the present work.

occupied for a time the supreme position of prime mover in our political society and who has also incurred the supreme rebuke which that society can accord him. The rescuing of a damaged reputation is, in principle, a humane and laudable work. But one does this in a relatively narrow personal setting: the victim's honor is restored while his principal enemies are banished in shame and confusion. Historical justice may exact a more complicated settlement than that, when it must deal with a man who has held great power, who has allowed his power to be stripped from him, and who has let his enemies be numbered in the millions. One comes back to the things the defendant was tried for in the first place by his own contemporaries and to the question of why he should have fallen from grace at all. The satisfaction of his personal honor might be conceded with relative willingness, and one could still be a long way from satisfied on these larger questions. The personal drama in which Andrew Johnson is pitted against Thaddeus Stevens and Charles Sumner and their followers provides too limited a scope for what one wants to discover, or rediscover, about the crisis in national government which occurred in 1866. While the two positions at stake in the bitter struggle between Johnson and the radicals are spelled out in primarily personal terms, as in a morality play, something is sacrificed in the way of dramatic soundness: the play is produced without a setting.

There is a structural aspect here which does not seem to have been accorded anything like full legitimacy in past work done on the subject. This is the aspect of the political party as institution. We have come to assume, for instance, that the behavior of many thousands of men in 1866 was animated by "mere partisan politics." But if the whole subject were reopened, it might make a great deal of difference to assume that there is really nothing "mere" about party loyalty in American politics and that for 1866 in particular the scope and implications of such partisanship had become so prodigiously extended as to render the very notion of "partisanship," in its ordinary acceptance, temporarily meaningless.

The Republican party, though it had been in office only a little over four years, had by 1865 undergone an experience which had conferred attributes of a virtually organic nature upon it. For those men to whom it had afforded careers—indeed, for all those who had become in one way or another identified with the party in the course of its short life—the connection had acquired a multitude of meanings of more than ordinary profundity. In 1860 the Republican party, a half-dozen years after coming into being, had won a national election. In the very act of its assuming power, a national crisis, long in the making, had been precipitated. The party nonetheless had subsequently organized a government, built up its own bureaucracy and civil service, cast its lines into all the Northern states, recruited armies, and smashed the rebellion. Its leader had suffered martyrdom. Out of all this an institution had been created, something that now had a life of its own.

One may not consider the "life" of such a structure without also assuming a set of vital structural needs which must somehow be fulfilled if such life is to be sustained—needs whose denial might be compared metaphorically to the denial of oxygen and nourishment. It is possible, in certain connections, to think of them as existing quite apart from particular individuals and particular policies. So far as the Republican party was concerned, these needs, in less than a year after the rebellion's end, appeared to be threatened from both within and without. Something of a "threat," of course, is aimed at any party on the occasion of almost any election. And though, in assessing institutional behavior, it is worthwhile to take such a threat seriously at any time, it is especially important to recognize that the election of 1866 was no ordinary election. The influence of the Republican party had extended itself in circles so unusually wide by that time, and the things the party represented had become so manifold, that great numbers of Northern families found themselves concerned in the most vital and basic way with its institutional well-being.

The historian's reappraisal of the Johnson administration has been a reaction both against the personal indignities suffered by President Johnson and against the character of reconstruction as it was eventually inaugurated by Johnson's congressional opponents along lines differing so vastly from those advocated by the President. It is natural to connect the one with the other—and it is thus rather hard to avoid the conclusion that of the two policies it was Johnson's which contained the greatest long-range wisdom and which best seemed to serve the interests of the country at large.

Still, the question remains: what came in between? What was there about the speed and completeness of Johnson's collapse that renders such a version of "wisdom" almost beside the point? There must have been, in Johnson's policy and in the manner in which it was promoted, a challenge so basic and so widely felt that considerations of morality, wisdom, or the "interests of the country" temporarily lost a great deal of their ordinary meaning.

Here it will be necessary to summarize briefly the leading facts, so that they may later serve as points of reference.

By May, 1865, Andrew Johnson had decided that the initial problems of reconstruction—of re-establishing civil governments in the rebellious states and preparing those states to resume their normal functions in the Union—might best be handled, not by calling a special session of Congress, but by a continued exercise of executive powers. His first major step was taken on May 29. On that day he issued two proclamations, one of which laid down the terms whereby individual Southerners at large might obtain amnesty. This was done under the authority of the President's pardoning power. In the other, which he issued in his capacity as commander-in-chief of the armed forces, he appointed a provisional governor for North Carolina and authorized him to establish a government there, thus setting postwar reconstruction on its way. He was shortly to issue similar proclamations for six other states.[3] Lincoln himself had acted by proclamation at moments when he preferred, at least temporarily, not to be hampered by the more cumbersome process of acting jointly with Congress. Here was a problem sufficiently analogous to those which Lincoln had faced, together with a precedent sufficiently recent, that Johnson's step did not at the time seem unwarranted. Although the country was no longer in a state of war and although there were some doubts as to the appropriateness of launching so deeply important a project as reconstruction except by closely united executive-legislative procedure, generally speaking there was at first very little serious objection to the President's action. His was simply the opening step, not necessarily challenging any basic principle. It was generally supposed that his purposes and those of Congress would prove, in due course, to have been more or less in harmony throughout.

Indeed, the proclamations in themselves were not such as to afford undue grounds for misgiving. The amnesty policy, in addition to its general provisions, contained qualifications which guaranteed, at least

[3] The proclamation appointed William W. Holden, a North Carolina Unionist, as provisional governor. Other such proclamations, of virtually identical wording, named William L. Sharkey for Mississippi on June 13; James Johnson for Georgia and Andrew J. Hamilton for Texas on June 17; Lewis E. Parsons for Alabama, June 21; Benjamin F. Perry for South Carolina, June 30; and William Marvin for Florida, July 13. The proclamations are printed in James D. Richardson, *A Compilation of the Messages and Papers of the Presidents* (Washington: Bureau of National Literature and Art, 1908), VI, 312–16, 318–31. The other four states of the erstwhile Confederacy—Arkansas, Louisiana, Tennessee, and Virginia—already had "restored" governments of sorts, and these were considered far enough along in the process of reconstruction as not to require the appointment of provisional governors.

in principle, that large categories of former participants in the rebellion would come under individual scrutiny before being granted full pardon. Nor did the other proclamation—the one for North Carolina, which was to serve there and elsewhere as the basis for presidential reconstruction—foreclose the possibility of reasonable guarantees and safeguards for the future loyalty of any state governments that might be set up in the South. Federal agencies were re-established there, and the provisional governor was directed to appoint civil officers, state and local, giving preference to loyal people. A constitutional convention was to be called which would amend the state's organic law in conformity with the results of the late conflict. Properly construed, this implied a warning that certain conditions would have to be met before such states and their reconstructed governments could be considered for full recognition by federal authority. Presumably the Executive would make these conditions clear and explicit by private correspondence. The provision most open to question was the one directing that the convention—or the legislature that would later be elected—should prescribe the state's qualifications for voting and officeholding. Considerable sentiment existed in the North favoring suffrage, in some qualified form, for the newly freed Negroes;[4] and thus the wide individual discretion which this part of the proclamation allowed to a former slave state may not have been the most effective way of promoting such an aim. And yet here, too, the possibility of informal pressure remained theoretically open. Only the radical extremists of the Republican (or Union) party showed immediate signs of alarm.

There is a sense in which it could be said that "reconstruction" proceeded with remarkable smoothness during the summer, fall, and early winter of 1865. Numerous observers, taking note of Southern conditions immediately after the collapse of the Confederacy, commented upon the widespread sense of shock, amounting virtually to apathy, exhibited by the people of that region. With little notion of what to expect from the conqueror, the majority of the population was immersed in the dull awareness of defeat. It was thus hardly an extravagance to report that they "accepted the situation"; nothing could be more unanimous than this very point, in dozens of such reports; and to add, as General Grant did in his, that it was "in good faith," was almost a *non sequitur:* it scarcely mattered. Submission to force was complete and beyond question; no tendency to further rebellion could

[4] A sentiment recognized by both Lincoln and Johnson in messages to the governors of Louisiana and Mississippi. See below, pp. 56 ff.

be discerned anywhere; and the most dominant and definite of political desires—insofar as they existed at all—was the desire for speedy reunion. The functions of local government were resumed, and delegates to conventions were chosen, mainly without incident.

After the conventions had done their work—voiding the prewar ordinances of secession, abolishing slavery, and repudiating the rebel state debt—regular elections were held in the course of which were chosen state governors, state legislatures, and members of Congress. By late fall these legislatures had been organized and were in session. When a legislature had ratified the Thirteenth Amendment, the President would as a rule retire the state's provisional governor, and the elected governor would assume the full exercise of his duties. At this point—although Federal garrisons would not immediately be withdrawn—the former rebel states were, so far as the President was concerned, in full and legitimate operation. It was thus that by the end of 1865 all these states, with the exception of Texas, had been "reconstructed" and were, in Johnson's opinion, entitled once more to full rights of representation in the federal Congress.

There was, however, another sense in which the process had been anything but satisfactory. Once it had become certain that the Southerners were not to suffer wide-scale reprisals and that summary punishment was not to fall upon their leaders, another kind of uncertainty had apparently been allowed to invade their minds; they were not precisely sure what was now expected of them. There was a margin of doubt wide enough that they were encouraged to experiment with the spirit of the requirements. A sense of decision in complying with these requirements was lacking in all the conventions; the irritable Northern observer was struck by a legalistic tendency of delegates to quibble, to split hairs, and to indulge themselves in the luxury of hedging. Some states would not nullify secession, but "repealed" it; others would not abolish slavery straight out, but for the record's sake simply acknowledged, in effect, its destruction by force of arms. Two of them—Mississippi and South Carolina—failed altogether to repudiate their Confederate debt before adjourning, which evoked agitated messages of remonstrance from the President. Mississippi actually refused to ratify the Thirteenth Amendment.

There had been other annoyances. The provisional governor of South Carolina had made a speech in July in which he had said, among other things, that Lincoln's death had not been the calamity for the South that many had imagined—a statement which produced a very unfortunate impression. In August, Mississippi's provisional governor, scarcely four months after the close of hostilities, had begun organizing local militias, on the grounds that they were necessary for the preservation of law and order. Although the federal commander in the state had immediately ordered a stop to all such activity, his orders were countermanded by Johnson himself; Johnson, in his anxiety to avoid friction between his provisional governor and his military commander, had discriminated between them in such a way as to anger and humiliate the latter and had permitted initiatives and prerogatives to the former which a Northern public could not yet view without hostility and suspicion. It was thus that the South—perhaps in spite of itself—was contributing, item by item, to a malaise which threatened to undermine the North's initial disposition to support, experimentally, presidential reconstruction.

By early winter two sets of developments had progressed enough to provide the North with a major focus for bitterness. One involved Southern intentions toward the masses of newly freed Negroes; the other had to do with the character of the men being elected to public office in the Southern states. Legislation defining the rights of "persons of color" was already under way in several of these states, and the "black code" of Mississippi had been substantially completed. Though the Mississippi code guaranteed certain basic civil rights (to sue and be sued, to make contracts, and to acquire property), the severe restrictions which it placed upon landownership, labor arrangements, and testimony in the courts, together with its rigorous definitions of vagrancy, were widely denounced as a savage effort to fling the Negro back into that very state of slavery from which he had so recently been lifted. Similar codes in South Carolina and Louisiana would evoke similar anger, and those of other states would seem less severe only by contrast. The right to vote, even on the most limited terms, had of course everywhere been placed quite out of the question. It is true that most of the high ideals of wartime had centered upon the sanctity of the Union, and those, on the other hand, which had to do with emancipation—and with the consequences which might follow from it—had always remained in vaguer form. Yet those ideals, such as they were, now appeared suspended in the limbo of unreality. Men who had felt them with passion now saw themselves cheated of even a token fulfilment; others who had shared them but nominally still saw them, or thought they saw them, flaunted contemptuously by a people who had temporarily forfeited any right to a hand in the settlement of such grave matters.

As for political rights in Congress, the Southern people apparently supposed that they were now entitled without qualification to all that they had once enjoyed. Their presumptions seemed all too clearly written in the records of the men they sent to represent them. Waiting to be seated, as the Thirty-ninth Congress assembled in December, were an inordinate number of Confederate military officers and former members of the Confederate Congress. Here was a bizarre dramatization of the serious difficulties now obstructing the speedy reconciliation which had been so widely assumed, earlier in the year, to be both possible and desirable.

It was in Congress during the preliminaries to the opening of business in December, 1865, that the Northern reaction was given its first sharp expression. After the Clerk of the House, by prearrangement, had omitted from his roll call the names of the Southern members-elect, extremists of the Republican party immediately assumed the leadership in forming a Joint Committee of Fifteen to pass on the qualifications of the new claimants. Thaddeus Stevens, its most energetic member, made it clear that his committee intended to make the most extensive and unhurried deliberations, not only upon membership, but also upon the entire question of reconstruction and the adequacy of the President's policy. The implications of that policy, in short, were already thought to be sufficiently grave as to call for a minute reappraisal, down to the very fundamentals. Meanwhile, the ex-Confederate states would be kept waiting indefinitely for readmission.

Concurrently, legislation was prepared for the purpose of insuring a firmer degree of federal political control in the South and for strengthening the position of the masses of colored freedmen. The first of such measures was the Freedmen's Bureau Bill, originating in the Senate under the sponsorship of Lyman Trumbull of Illinois. By its terms the Freedmen's Bureau—the federal agency most directly concerned with the affairs of displaced Negroes—was to have its jurisdiction widened, its powers strengthened, and its life extended. Another, the Civil Rights Bill, was an even more direct response to the "black codes"; it forbade discrimination between citizens on grounds of race or color and represented an effort to assert jurisdiction for the federal government over matters which, owing to the looseness of presidential policy, had been improperly allowed to pass by default to the recently rebellious states.

It was mainly in connection with this legislation that any possibility of compromise was finally withdrawn. The President himself removed all remaining doubts by making the break open and explicit. Senator

Trumbull, a man of moderate preferences and in Lincoln's time a consistent supporter of the administration, had tried to design both bills in such a way as to provide some common ground tolerable to both the President and the radicals; he had read the bills to Johnson and assumed that the President had found them acceptable. His chagrin, therefore, was considerable when on February 19 Johnson without warning vetoed the Freedmen's Bureau Bill, saying that he could not reconcile its provisions "with the words of the Constitution." Three days later Johnson, in a passionate and semi-impromptu speech, told his audience of the indignities he had suffered at the hands of the radicals, naming and denouncing those who he thought were planning to wreck his policy. The speech was generally regarded in the press as intemperate. Then, on March 27, he vetoed the Civil Rights Bill, also on the ground of doubtful constitutionality, and it was at this point that the President was abandoned by most of the Northern journals which had hitherto supported his policy.

While the Freedmen's Bureau Bill had failed, by several Senate votes, to be re-enacted after the veto, the Civil Rights Act became law after repassage in both houses. A second Freedmen's Bureau Act, later in the session, was passed, vetoed, and successfully repassed. In June, 1866, the momentous Fourteenth Amendment to the Constitution—which Johnson advised the Southerners not to ratify—was completed and sent out to the states. This Amendment—a long step toward Negro suffrage—designated Negroes as citizens entitled to security of life, liberty, and property; it specified penalties of reduced representation for former slave states who withheld the franchise from such citizens; it denied state and federal officeholding privileges to persons who had broken oaths of loyalty to the Constitution in order to support the rebellion; and it forbade any state to invalidate the federal debt or to validate the Confederate debt. It thus represented a major definition of emergent congressional policy on reconstruction.

With such a total impasse as now existed between the legislative and executive branches of the government, in the sense of effective dealings with each other, the critical and decisive character of the forthcoming fall elections of 1866 was everywhere recognized. The radicals, on the assumption that every measure of importance would have to be repassed over a presidential veto, required majorities comfortably in excess of two-thirds. For them it was thus not merely a question of victories but of overwhelming victories. On the other hand, if the moderate supporters of the President were to be put on anything like a decisive footing, the entire character and complexion of both houses would require the most drastic alterations.

Two events of the pre-election period served to dramatize the true hopelessness of Johnson's position. One was the so-called National Union Convention, held in August in Philadelphia for the purpose of rallying support to the President's cause. The conglomerate pattern of political elements represented there made it impossible for the gathering to do more than issue a statement of principles; the political energy, commitment, and power required to form a new party or to force the major parties to some new accommodation in Johnson's interest, were not available at Philadelphia. The convention may have been a demonstration of protest, but it was also a demonstration of impotence. The other event was Johnson's two-and-a-half-week speaking tour in defense of his policy, from August 28 to September 15, during which the President, face to face, as it were, with "the people," was showered with abuse and ridicule, to which he retorted with much indiscreet and foolhardy word-bandying. The few shreds of dignity which still clung to the presidency were thus torn away in the course of this disastrous "Swing around the Circle," and the bankruptcy of the President's role, insofar as it depended upon popular support, was made visible before the entire country. The November elections resulted in overwhelming majorities for the radicals.

The end of presidential reconstruction came on March 2, 1867. On that day three acts of Congress were passed which brought executive power to the lowest point it has ever reached before or since. The Reconstruction Act voided the legality of all existing governments in the formerly seceded states,[5] placed the South as a whole under military rule, and specified that no state could "reconstruct" itself and become re-eligible for representation in Congress without the enactment of full Negro suffrage and wide-scale disfranchisement of ex-Confederate leaders. The Army Appropriation Act contained a section severely limiting the President's function as commander-in-chief: military orders were to be issued only through the General of the Army, who could not be transferred from Washington without his own or the Senate's consent. The Tenure of Office Act forbade the President to remove civil officers without the consent of the Senate.

Such, in its essentials, had been the course of reconstruction from May 29, 1865, to March 2, 1867. And now, with reconstruction fully

[5] With the exception of Tennessee, readmitted July 24, 1866, after having ratified the Fourteenth Amendment.

in congressional hands, the Executive could in no further sense be seen as a leader in the formation of federal policy, but only as an obstacle to it. It was in this role that Johnson incurred the final act of Republican wrath. On February 24, 1868, the House of Representatives resolved to impeach him.

How Andrew Johnson threw away his own power both as President and as party leader, how he assisted materially, in spite of himself, in blocking the reconciliation of North and South, and what his behavior did toward disrupting the political life of an entire nation will form the subject of this book.

Chapter

2

A Democratic
Society
Emerges
from
Total War

I PUBLIC FEELING: "WAR HATRED" VERSUS
"BACK TO NORMAL"

It is part of the post–Civil War legend that the ruthless quality of Southern reconstruction was the outgrowth of hatreds
carried over from wartime and interminably prolonged. The legend in
its gross form is accurate enough; the Northern people have ultimately acknowledged that they did not really know how to adminis-
ter their great victory once they had got it, and that on the whole they
managed it badly. This admission must itself stand as part of the
legend; the North, for three generations, has had something on its
conscience which will probably never be exorcised. But inasmuch as
reconstruction, in the form which it finally took, was not inaugurated
until two years after the moment of victory, there remains the question of how fully the case is covered by depending on the notion of
"war hatreds" alone to explain it.[1] Was there perhaps a conspiracy,

[1] The basic study on the resumption of peaceful pursuits after the Civil War—a process which took so extraordinarily long to complete—is Paul H. Buck, *The Road to
Reunion, 1865–1900* (Boston: Little, Brown, 1937); see esp. chap. i ("Victory"), pp.
3–25. This work, unique of its kind, is painstaking, thorough, and indispensable for an
understanding of the problems of reconciliation. The slow nature of the reunion process
(the book covers a thirty-five-year period) is, however, taken more or less for granted,
which means that the author has not asked himself whether real alternatives were present at war's end for launching the process in a direction different from that which it
in fact took. He did not, of course, have the benefit of World War II and its aftermath
as a test of what really great differences were possible in achieving an emotional settlement between two former enemies. If, however, one should assume that such alterna-

somewhere along the way, to manipulate and aggravate those hatreds? But if so, why did the movement take so long to mature and how could a political society which embraced a population of over twenty million have been "manipulated" so successfully?

If there had been a strong desire in the North, born of the passions of war, to punish the South, then it would seem that the most auspicious time to harness such passions ought to have been the very moment of victory. Yet victory itself, at least for the victor, functions powerfully as a solvent for hatreds, if we may judge from the nation's wars in the twentieth century. How is it, then, that for so many years after the Civil War there was a malignancy of feeling toward the late enemy not experienced in the wake of the two world wars, even while the enemies of the fratricidal conflict partook of a spiritual and cultural rapport not shared with later enemies of the Republic? It is conceivable that this malignancy was not entirely a matter of "war hatreds." There may have been other feelings besides those growing specifically out of war, and it may have been the victory, as much as the war, that engendered them. The nature of that victory would come to seem, as time went on, very different from what it had seemed at the beginning.

The experience of total victory, in a total war which has successfully made the ultimate claim upon the resources, energies, and loyalties of a whole people, is an experience which Americans have actually undergone only three times in all their history. It is the kind of thing that, in the memory of a people, has acute point but not much breadth; memory leaves too little room for it between the war time and the postwar time, between the unrelieved hate of the one and the deepening oblivion of the other. The quality of feeling in that interim time, as one tries now to grasp at it, seems an intense surge of the undefinable—something of war, something of peace—so full and yet so transient as to repel any effort to give it limits and a character of its own.

Two notions come to mind as one tries to re-create the sense of an American society moving from war to peace. One of them, to be sure, is "war hatred"; the other is "back to normal." After each of the two world wars of this century, Americans have experienced a "back to normal" urge which has been all but irresistible, even to the point—

---

tives did exist and that the painful slowness of post–Civil War reunion was not necessarily foreordained and inevitable after all, then the story would have to be organized somewhat differently. Less emphasis would be placed on the "long slow healing" aspect; one would tend instead to shift the emphasis to the conditions of 1865, the very first year after the war, and assign them great critical importance. Part One of the present work represents such an effort.

someone was always there to say—of fatuous imprudence. At the close of our Civil War, however, if such an impulse toward peace and oblivion existed, it was shortly to be submerged in something very like its opposite. Here, then, is a kind of suspended balance: on the one hand, vindictiveness and hate; on the other, magnanimity, forgiveness, and peace. That the latter theme should prevail seems natural and normal, but perhaps not inevitable.

There is still something in the interim moment of consummation and solvency that should not be allowed to slide out of view too soon: a great sea of undifferentiated emotion, long since set in turmoil by all the hopes and fears and agonies of war, and long since having passed the bounds of ordinary guidance and control. This deep emotional submersion of all society appears to be not only an inevitable feature of a democratic war but actually a functional necessity for the full prosecution of such a war.[2] What becomes of it when the war is over? How does the sea of feeling calm itself? What is the principle of prediction? It is not entirely in the power of the victor to settle such a question. Here the conquered, for all the completeness of his subjugation, seems to retain rather more initiative than might at first be imagined.

The people of the North received the news of Lee's surrender much in the way that the Armistice of 1918 and the German and Japanese capitulations of 1945 would be received years later—with spontaneous upheavals of relief, joy, and thanksgiving. "The sun in his course on this blessed tenth of April, 1865, beholds a Union restored, inseparable, indivisible, eternal!" One hundred thousand people were said to have thronged the streets of Chicago on that day,

[2] Tocqueville, in one of his shrewdest predictions on the behavior of democratic nations, guessed that a democracy, though reluctant to begin a war, and though faltering in the war's initial stages, would ultimately fight it with irresistible determination and energy. "When a war has at length, by its long continuance, roused the whole community from their peaceful occupations, and ruined their minor undertakings, the same passions which made them attach so much importance to the maintenance of peace will be turned to arms. War, after it has destroyed all modes of speculation, becomes itself the great and sole speculation, to which all the ardent and ambitious desires that equality engenders are exclusively directed. Hence it is that the selfsame democratic nations which are so reluctant to engage in hostilities, sometimes perform prodigious achievements when they have taken the field." Alexis de Tocqueville, *Democracy in America*, trans. Henry Reeve (Cambridge: Sever & Francis, 1863), II, 341. Democratic war would tend, by this logic, toward total involvement. The moral as well as the physical resources of the nation would eventually be organized in support of the war effort, and the conflict itself would readily take on the quality of a great crusade, fought by all society for the preservation of its principles. Some of our wars, of course, have not required this total commitment. But for those that have, Tocqueville's predictions retain an essential soundness.

and the *Tribune* reported with awe the tremendous manifestation of feeling. "Nothing like it has ever been witnessed in our streets. . . . It seemed as if the fountains of the great deep were broken up and poured forth their floods."[3]

This emotion appears to have been directly tied to the energy which had sustained the war effort itself:

It was like the steam of a giant locomotive, being blown off when it reached the end of its journey. It was that pent-up power that propelled the engine. The tumultuous raptures of yesterday was the sudden letting loose of the feeling which for four years has nerved the heart of the people to fight on and to hold out and when the first born fell, to send to the battle the second and the third born. It was this unconquerable spirit in the common people to save their Union, unconditionally, which won the contest.[4]

Inherent in that first swell of thanksgiving, and held in unsteady suspension, were two distinguishable themes. One was the theme of peace: the binding-up of wounds, the resumption of normal pursuits, and magnanimity toward the beaten enemy. The chord had already been touched by President Lincoln in his Second Inaugural, and echoes were sounded once more with the fall of Richmond and the collapse of the Army of Northern Virginia. "Let us not forget, in our rejoicing," counseled Postmaster-General Dennison amid the tumult of Washington on the tenth, "that, as freely as we have poured out our treasure and copiously as has been shed the blood of our sons and brothers in the defense of the government, they would have availed nothing but for the Divine favor which has enlightened our darkest hours . . . ; and we can well afford to be magnanimous."[5]

There was, however, a second theme, without which the first would not have had much meaning. This was the sterner note of justice and security: ". . . let it be carefully borne in mind," continued the Postmaster-General, "that the only magnanimity we can further exercise must be that which will secure to the nation permanent peace and universal freedom." This motif, emphasizing safeguards for the fruits of victory, assumed a sudden urgency a few days later with the assassination of the President, an event which thousands in their distraction took as a sign that magnanimity and leniency would be inadequate as the sole keynote for a policy toward the vanquished rebels.

And yet the "back to normal" urge, though chastened and qualified, continued to diffuse itself and gain headway. By the first of June, a number of things had happened to nurture this more peaceful senti-

---

[3] Chicago *Tribune*, Apr. 11, 1865.

[4] *Ibid.*   [5] *Ibid.*

ment and bring it to some form of initial maturity. There were the continued surrenders of the rebel armies, a process which was complete and final with the capitulation of Kirby Smith on May 26. No guerrilla warfare materialized thereafter. There was the death of Booth and the speedy launching, on May 10, of military trials for the other conspirators. The summary quality of this proceeding was muted by a certain official defensiveness; the sessions of the court were made semi-public, and they were accompanied by daily reporting of the testimony. There was the capture of Jefferson Davis on May 10, and although Davis was to remain a prisoner for two years, the sentiment for making an example of him was never resolute enough to command wide popular support.[6] Even less determination could be mobilized for the punishment of Robert E. Lee. Moreover, there were the stories of devastation that were begining to filter up from the stricken South—stories not without their effect upon Northern sympathies, judging from the frequency with which they were being printed by early summer.[7] Finally, there was the grand review of the Armies of the East and West at Washington, where for two days, on May 23 and 24, the great rank and file of the defenders of the Republic paraded in their ultimate and seasoned glory, thence to disperse forever. The catharsis of demobilization was under way. "We want true union and concord in the quickest possible time," announced the Springfield *Republican*, "and by such means as will make these blessings perpetual. Are these ends to be gained by reproaches and invectives; by prolonging the spirit and the evils of war after the war itself has terminated?"[8]

President Johnson meanwhile, through proclamations and the exercise of executive power, was launching his program of reconstruction. For the public this represented, among other things, further progress in clearing the air. It was not so much that it was either a good policy or a bad one; the plan was not ostentatiously punitive; at the same time, there were aspects of it that certainly exceeded in sternness the

[6] Thaddeus Stevens, who thought that the punishment of individuals was a waste of time and whose own emphasis was on the reconstruction of governments, actually offered to defend both Davis and Clement C. Clay when it became known that the administration was planning to prosecute them for complicity in the murder of Lincoln. Horace Greeley, in June, 1866, offered to sign a bond for Davis. These stories are in Robert L. McElroy, *Jefferson Davis: The Unreal and the Real* (New York: Harper & Bros., 1937), II, 560–61; and Richard N. Current, *Old Thad Stevens* (Madison: University of Wisconsin Press, 1942), p. 212.

[7] E.g., there is a great deal of material in the *Nation* during this period from correspondents traveling in the South, and destruction forms a major theme in it.

[8] Springfield (Mass.) *Weekly Republican*, June 10, 1865.

Lincoln proclamation of eighteen months before. And Johnson's own phrase, "Treason is a crime and must be made odious," still rang in Northern ears. The important thing now was that someone had taken charge of the problem, and a little of the urgency and burden of speculation and debate had been lifted. Reconstruction had at least been set in motion. The result was that by mid-June the two themes—peace, normality, and leniency on the one side, and security, justice, and guarantees for future loyalty on the other—were more or less in a state of balance. The wide range of expectations which together these themes represented could, for the time being, unite in a "trust-Johnson" sentiment which was widespread and generally shared. We tend now to forget the extent of Johnson's initial support. Among the leading journals, such support comprised every shade of Unionist sentiment, from the Midwest's formidable Chicago *Tribune* to the New York *Herald*, and including all three of the great New York Unionist dailies, the *Times*, the *Herald*, and the *Tribune*—not to mention such leading weeklies as *Harper's* and the *Nation*.[9] It is important in any

---

[9] Editorially, the most hard-bitten of the great Unionist dailies of the country was probably the Chicago *Tribune*, whose columns were not noted for their sentimentality toward the South. Yet even the *Tribune* had been a leading supporter of Lincoln, the man of mercy; the *Tribune*, moreover, was only too willing that peaceful pursuits be resumed in return for a change in the rebellious spirit of the South. "If this reaction," it declared in an editorial of April 8, "shall be spontaneous, hearty and in good faith, the path to Union will be cleared of its only formidable obstacle." The New York *Tribune*, however, stigmatized by so many writers of recent years as incorrigibly radical, was anything but that, in the spring and summer of 1865, with regard to the question of clemency and forgiveness. Scarcely a trace of vindictiveness is to be found in its editorial columns throughout all this time, and the paper would not hear of executing Davis or any other Southern leader. "The Southern mind is now open to kindness," it declared on April 14 (a sentiment which it continued to express after the tragedy of Lincoln's assassination), "and may be magnetically affected by generosity. Let assurance at once be given that there is to be a general Amnesty and no general Confiscation. This is none the less the dictate of wisdom because it is also the dictate of mercy." The New York *Times*, on the other hand, whose moderation on all questions, then and now, is legendary, was at first all for hanging Davis and treating the Southern people with stern justice. "So far as their *civil rights* and *franchises* are concerned, they are today practically as much outside the pale of the Federal Constitution as the people of Russia. They are subject to military rule only" (May 5). And yet this notion was counterbalanced elsewhere in the *Times* by the note of magnanimity. "Their courage [it said on June 12] . . . has been our enemy, but hereafter it is to be our friend." And further: "It is not for us to poison the wound we have inflicted on their pride, nor to stab, with insulting blows, the dead body of their ambition." The most interesting case of all is that of the New York *Herald*, whose zeal by midsummer in promoting Southern restoration put that journal well out on the fringes of Unionist opinion. Yet the *Herald*, in the spring of 1865, was full of hot words on rebel punishment and many times expressed itself in favor of Negro suffrage in some form (on the latter point, indeed, all these journals in principle agreed during this early period). Said the *Herald* on April 22: "All the conspirators of the South, responsible as the contrivers or managers of this prostrate rebellion, whether as confederate-rebel rulers or local leaders, would do well

diagnosis of Johnson's subsequent downfall not to belittle the fact that virtually every Republican paper in the country, including those later to be designated as "radical," was initially on the President's side. Even the most extreme of these journals would remain with him for a number of months, and the majority would not fully sever connections until early in 1866.

Still, returning to the idea of a balance of themes inherent in post-victory feeling and inherent to all intents and purposes in the President's policy, it is well to note that a balance is by nature something uneasy and precarious. So it was with this one. The "back to normal" side was legitimate and real for the great masses of the Northern public. But the qualifications and *caveats*—the other side of the balance—included items so formidable and so complex that no prelude to such a subject as reconstruction would be properly completed without some further consideration of them. Here the implications of "security" and "justice" are not fully covered by the concept of "war hatred"—or, as it was later called, the waving of the bloody shirt.

II "SYMBOLIC REQUIREMENTS"

By the end of the summer and fall of 1865 an uneasy conviction had spread throughout most of the North that somehow the South had never really surrendered after all. This was hardly a "rational" persuasion in the ordinary sense: the evidence was overwhelming that the Southerners had had their fill of fighting. There was no way in which the military security of the North was in the least threatened; the Southern armies had fully dispersed; no legitimate forum for the expression of Southern sentiment, not one of the agencies of government, state or local, showed the least inclination to rebel further against the authority of the United States. And yet Northern feeling, well before the meeting of Congress could give it any clear leadership, had already become noticeably poisoned with fear and suspicion.

Of course, there were many men in the North of violent radical

---

to quit the country without delay. This advice is the best that we can now do for them in the way of charity."

The point of this hasty survey is to illustrate the oscillation of sentiment—not always consistent—within the Union ranks, between the themes of mercy and sternness, up to the time of Johnson's launching of presidential reconstruction. It can be said, further, that Johnson's initial promulgations of policy did something to "jell" these diverse feelings and hold them in a temporary state of balance. This seems borne out by the willingness of all these papers, representing every conceivable facet of Unionist opinion, to offer the President their support. It might also be added (though this is somewhat ahead of the story) that all of them ultimately deserted him.

proclivities who would have been quite willing that sectional bitterness be prolonged until such time as thoroughgoing changes might be effected in Southern society. But it would be difficult, this early, to locate any such group of men sufficiently well organized, and exerting enough general influence and authority throughout the North at large, to have manufactured such asperities themselves. Indeed, these feelings were neither focused nor organized; they were pervasive, they seemed to ooze from everywhere, and they invaded the repose of weary men who would have given much to be rid of them. Charles Sumner, to be sure, wrote letters to his friends all summer long, tirelessly sounding the alarm. But Charles Sumner was hardly the tribune of the Northern people and never had been; if the Northern people had a tribune at this time, it was still Andrew Johnson. Probably this phenomenon of feeling did not have much direct connection with the work of individual Northern or Southern leaders. It may actually have had more to do with the meaning of victory itself, and with the peripheral meanings that hover about the notion of surrender.

Centuries ago, men gave much thought and effort to the problem of bringing a kind of *de jure* sanctity to the *de facto* brutality of conquest in war. They were oppressed by the realization that, right or no right, it was in the nature of war that the conqueror was somehow not to be thwarted from having his will in the end. Many of the things written by the commentators upon the ancient laws of war were therefore based on the implicit question of why, in fact, this had to be. Though the victor ought to use prudence in his exactions and temper his demands with mercy, the arbitrary inequity of "might makes right" flowed from the very nature of conquest. The victor in any war emerges from his conquest preoccupied with a whole set of requirements, and in his hour of triumph he is in the supreme position to insist upon their fulfilment. Both victor and vanquished desire peace and a return to peaceful occupations. But the conqueror's conception of peace is of a far more sweeping character than that of the conquered: the latter expects nothing, the former expects all. He requires a kind of total security; his idea of "peace" is a function of his sense of security.

These barbaric thoughts of a former age are implicit, for example, in the writings of Grotius, who assures the conqueror that he "is entitled to impose ANY terms upon the conquered, who is now placed, by the external laws of war, in a situation to be deprived of every thing, even personal liberty or life, much more then, of all his property, either of a public or private kind." But now that the conqueror knows his rights to be absolute, he should in practice observe limits: "... *as far as security allows*, it is always laudable to incline to moderation and clemency. Sometimes even circumstances may require such a line of conduct and the best conclusion of any war is that, which reconciles all contending claims by a fair adjustment, and a general amnesty. The moderation and clemency to which the vanquished appeal, are by no means in abolition but only a mitigation of the conqueror's absolute right."[10]

Such principles have their shortcomings as international jurisprudence.[11] But although they have little to tell us about the right and the good, there has been many a garbled insight into men's psychic needs hidden away in the old categories of political economy, philosophy, and law. Here we seem to have a glimpse of certain "spiritual" requirements with which men have perennially emerged from battle, and of the appropriate behavior which may follow upon their satisfaction. Let the conqueror feel that his victory and dominion—and therefore his security—are absolute, so that the granting of clemency, if it suits his pleasure, may itself be absolute.

This "security" concept has a significance that goes beyond the gross fact of physical conquest and disarming of the enemy. There are deeper requirements: the victor needs to be assured that his triumph has been invested with the fullest spiritual and ceremonial meaning. He must know that his expenditures have gone for something, that his objectives have been accomplished, and that the righteousness of his principles has been given its vindication. The assurances must be accorded him in terms that go well beyond the physical and objective; he must have ritual proofs. The conquered enemy must be prepared

---

[10] Hugo Grotius, "On Good Faith between Enemies," in *The Rights of War and Peace*, trans. A. C. Campbell (London: M. W. Dunne, 1901), p. 399; italics added. Grotius' original treatise was published in 1625. Most of the classical treatises on international law (including the rights of conquest), beginning with the fourteenth-century *De bello, de repraesalis et de duello* of Giovanni da Legnano, have been handsomely republished both in photographic reproductions of the originals and in translation, under the auspices of the Carnegie Endowment for International Peace. The series title is "Classics of International Law," ed. James Brown Scott (Oxford: Clarendon Press, 1911——).

[11] They were attacked and discredited by Locke and, following him, by the writers of the Enlightenment. Rousseau quotes the Marquis d'Argenson in support of his own attack on Grotius: "Learned researches upon public right are often only the history of ancient abuses; and it is lost labor to take the trouble to study them too much." See Jean Jacques Rousseau, *The Social Contact*, trans. Rose M. Harrington (New York: G. P. Putnam's Sons, 1893), p. 5. The value of such writings as those of Hobbes and Grotius certainly does not lie in their adequacy as law and right but rather in their refracted descriptions of men's actual behavior in situations where different sets of values (such as clemency and security) appear at loggerheads.

to give symbolic satisfactions as well as physical surrender; he must—in some way appropriate to his customs and his culture—"act out" his defeat.[12] This properly done, with satisfying gestures, the conditions are created wherein peace and clemency, if they are to obtain at all, will have their most auspicious setting. The foolish doubts which may still congest the victor's mind regarding the completeness of his victory—and which may cloud his impulses toward mercy, if he has any—could thereby be swept away at the very outset.

War being what it always has been—a species of ritual slaughter—there is much reason to think that the ceremonial requirements of earlier days still find some echo in those of more modern and enlightened warfare. Our war with Japan, judging from the results, affords considerable proof of the point.[13] What is one to think, then, coming upon an instance in which the passions, hatreds, and suspicions of war have not been swept away at all but seem to have been unduly and abnormally prolonged? It may be that in such a case the victor has had his "security"—in this enlarged, symbolic sense—withheld from him. His principles may never have been vindicated at all; he may have wrested the enemy's arms from him, but nothing more: perhaps no rituals of submission were performed to satisfy his deeper needs. Something of this sort seems to have been involved between North and South in 1865. In this case, the psychic fulfilments needed for a proper transition from war to peace were experienced by no martial sovereign but by an entire people. It is here that the quality of total commitment in a modern, democratic war becomes of particular importance.

The Civil War could in a way be called the most democratic of all our wars—conceivably the most democratic war of all time. The *levée en masse* was not the feature which made it so; many another culture has had that. The war was democratic in a kind of total, political sense: it was carried on within an intensely democratic political culture, and its democratic and its political features are impossible to separate. Unlike our foreign wars, this one had to be prosecuted and promoted—"campaigned for," as it were—almost as an expanded political platform. Consequently the sense of a "cause" (vital to any war) was not to be imposed by remote authority. The cause

[12] It was thus, for instance, that the victory processions of ancient times would include the enemy chieftains, followed by files of captives loaded with chains, who would at the appropriate moment throw themselves upon the clemency of the conquering sovereign.

[13] See below, pp. 33–35.

had to be something whose effectiveness, from both without and within the individual citizen, depended to a remarkable degree on its being voluntarily assumed. The moral coercions flowed not from the fiat of the state but from consensus in the community. Such coercions, of course, are the hardest of all to resist, for no one can really personify their source: they emanate, in the ultimate sense, from "the people."[14] The principles that justify such a war must thus strike very deep. They must be strong enough and safe enough to be carried about in the individual's own conscience throughout all vicissitudes, and they must constantly be refreshed, renewed, and re-created by a process essentially political in nature.

The consequences of this democratic quality in our Civil War can be illustrated in a number of ways. There was a very intimate relationship, for instance, between battles and elections. Throughout the war, the political prospects of almost anyone running for major state and federal offices depended upon the military situation. It was more imperative than ever in wartime that the government remain sensitive to public feeling; both state and federal administrations had to carry the population with them in order to prevent being hamstrung, in their conduct of the war, by the elections. Military campaigns had to be "ratified," in effect, at the polls. Conversely, the administration party's success, or lack of it, was one fairly dependable criterion for judging how things were going in the field.[15]

[14] We may imagine a counter-instance in the loyal Austrian peasant of 1914 being conscripted into the imperial army. "The powers above," he might have said, "tell me that I must go and do my duty; therefore, of course, I must." This is in the tradition of authority, acceptance, and obedience. The same tradition can also be one of revolution and mutiny: there is something removed from the community scene, yet something focused and personified in the heads of the state, that can specifically be resisted. Indeed, there have been thousands of cases, among our own European immigrant forebears, where such resistance to military authority has been a matter of great pride. And yet in our own military tradition, such as it is, there are no such themes, either of implicit acquiescence to authority or of revolt. The conviction that our military enterprises are just and righteous does not flow automatically from on high. At the same time, one does not point with pride to an ancestor who evaded duty in any of our wars. Where, then, are the coercions? They emanate, in a special sense, from ourselves. Nobody, for instance, wants very much to be drafted for military service, but the sanctions are hard to "mutiny" against; they come not so much from the President as from "a local board composed of your neighbors." The principle of "conformity," for all its odium, is a democratic concept (the odium is itself symptomatic of the individualistic as well as the mass themes of democracy); "conformity" does not, in any case, mean the same thing as "obedience to authority." It means conformity to standards that one has one's own part in maintaining, if only negatively, and that would collapse if substantial numbers of one's friends and neighbors refused to support them.

[15] This connection between battlefield success and success at the polls may be tested by noting that the two lowest points of the war for the North coincided with ebb tides in the fortunes of the Union party. In 1862, after the abortive Peninsular cam-

Another feature of the war was that of full and constant communication. There were few aspects of the war's military progress—the location of troops, their disposition, the attributes of their commanders, and so on—which were not most of the time a matter of general knowledge. An extraordinary amount of information was carried simply by men going back and forth on furlough, and since units were made up geographically rather than at random, news of the regiment would be cherished at home by the entire community. Above all, there were the newspapers. One has only to follow for a week or two the reports, the dispatches, and the maps in the wartime files of any leading daily to be convinced that this was the best-reported war in history.[16] Hand in hand with this pitch of awareness and sensitivity to every development in the military situation, so fully diffused among the entire population, went the widest latitude for criticism of the war effort.[17] Principles, objectives, and dedication to the cause would have been put to the sternest of tests amid so minute a process of communication. The commitments, to survive such a process and retain their vitality and meaning, would have had to reach great depths in the popular soul.

Even the procurement of troops depended, in a way that would

---

paign and Second Bull Run, the Democrats won extensive victories which included the governorships of New York and New Jersey. They made similar inroads in the legislatures and congressional delegations of Ohio, Pennsylvania, Illinois, and Wisconsin. Republican Governor Oliver Morton was faced with an antiwar majority in the Indiana legislature, against which his heroic efforts to maintain his state's troops in the field have become part of the wartime legend. See William B. Hesseltine, *Lincoln and the War Governors* (New York: Alfred A. Knopf, 1948), pp. 265–71; also Kenneth Stampp, *Indiana Politics during the Civil War* (Indianapolis: Indiana Historical Commission, 1949), pp. 179–85, and William Dudley Foulke, *Life of Oliver P. Morton* (Indianapolis: Bowen-Merrill, 1899), I, 203 ff. The second low point for the Union party came in the summer of 1864 with the desperate and apparently fruitless bloodletting of Grant's army in Virginia. Seldom had Lincoln's political future looked so dark. His subsequent success at the polls, and in effect the administration's mandate to continue the war, were directly related, as everyone knows, to Sherman's capture of Atlanta and the victories of Sheridan and Farragut. The people did, of course, have a clear alternative: they could have voted for the "peace plank" of the Democratic party.

[16] For much interesting material on the fiercely competitive efforts of the New York dailies to outdo each other both in the completeness of their war coverage and in the speed with which they got their stories before their readers, see Bernard A. Weisberger, *Reporters for the Union* (Boston: Little, Brown, 1953); and Louis M. Starr, *Bohemian Brigade* (New York: Afred A. Knopf, 1954).

[17] "Despite great provocation there was no Espionage Act and no Sedition Act during the Lincoln administration. During a time when disloyalty was widespread and defiant, the anti-Lincoln and anti-Union organs were, as a rule, left undisturbed; and the continuous stream of abuse which the opposition papers emitted was in itself a standing evidence of the fact that liberty of the press, even to the point of license, did exist." James G. Randall, *Constitutional Problems under Lincoln* (New York: D. Appleton, 1926), p. 508.

never again be so direct, upon the maintenance of these principles and commitments as justification for re-enlistment. The nucleus of the Union army in 1864 was composed of veterans who had enlisted in 1861 and whose three-year terms were then running out. Only persuasion could keep them in; they could not be conscripted. Yet nearly three-fourths of them did re-enlist; to the end, only about 6 per cent of the Union troops would be brought in by the draft. The 1864 re-enlistment of three-year volunteers was thus in effect a ratification, by the army itself, of the war and its principles.[18]

The most important point of all, in considering the democratic, shared quality of this war and its effect on the sense of dedication necessary to prosecute it, is the aspect of sacrifice. There is no very precise way to measure dedication, but there is a rough way of indicating its ultimate test. The people had to be convinced, and to convince themselves, that the cause for which their sons were fighting was worth sacrifices that would go well beyond the experience of any other generation of Americans, before or since. The Union casualty rate was between six and seven times heavier than the comparable percentage of American losses in the Second World War.[19] It is well and just that war should be pronounced the most depraved and useless of all modes of human enterprise. But there are special times when such a judgment is better withheld than uttered. Not much is gained in telling a people that the ordeal from which they have just emerged is without moral meaning; nor does one ever say these things to a Gold Star mother. Once the sacrifice is made, the principles themselves,

[18] "Union armies in the Civil War did not sign up for the duration. They enlisted by regiments, and the top term was three years. This meant—since the hard core of the United States Army was made up of volunteers who had enlisted in 1861—that as the climactic year of 1864 began, the army was on the verge of falling apart. Of 956 volunteer infantry regiments, as 1863 drew to a close, 455 were about to go out of existence because their time would very soon be up. Of 158 volunteer batteries 81 would presently cease to exist.

"There was no way on earth by which these veterans could be made to remain in the army if they chose not to stay. If they took their discharges and went home—as they were legally and morally entitled to do—the war effort would simply collapse." Bruce Catton, *This Hallowed Ground* (New York: Doubleday, 1956), p. 317. "Astoundingly, 136,000 three year veterans re-enlisted. They were the men who had seen the worst of it—men who had eaten bad food, slept in the mud and the rain, made killing marches, and stood up to Rebel fire in battles like Antietam and Stone's River, Chickamauga and Gettysburg—and they had long since lost the fine flush of innocent enthusiasm that had brought them into the army in the first place." *Ibid.*, p. 318.

[19] In round figures, Union casualties have been estimated at 360,000 deaths from all causes, out of a population of about 20 million. American losses in World War II came to 384,000 deaths from all causes, from a population of 135 million. This is a comparison of 1.8 per cent to 0.28 per cent. A casualty rate in World War II comparable to that of the Civil War would have required nearly 2.5 million deaths.

despite the corrosions and disillusionments of time, become in some way consecrated. They become, like the young man in death, incorruptible.

The meaning of victory, then, would be to declare all the ideals successful. The nation had told itself that, with victory, the war principles would be vindicated, and now, with the collapse of the rebellion, they were presumably vindicated and secured beyond all question. The logic of military events, at least, would appear to have made them so. As for just what these principles were, it was not that easy to say. The fundamental thing about them was not their precision, for they had none; it was rather their pervasiveness and depth. Lincoln, as poet, had given them their fittest expression at Gettysburg. The basic symbol was that of the Union, whose sub-theme was freedom. The poet himself had become a sacrifice, and it was now required of the beaten enemy that he pay some form of homage to the symbol. The thing could not be fully consummated with the surrender of the Confederate army. It was somehow necessary that the South go a little farther in acting out its defeat, though no one had much of a notion as to just when the curtain should be allowed to fall. But among the millions of witnesses there would have to be at least a consensus of sorts that the effort had been made—and that reunion had been accepted with appropriate and satisfying ritual gestures. Peace on the battlefield must be followed by a willingness to bring peace to the Northern mind.

There were no precedents at all for the case of two American communities facing each other in the attitudes of victory and defeat. In the North, men talked of "guarantees," knowing that they did not quite mean guarantees for their homes and firesides. They longed for "reassurances," but knowing the courage of the men who had fought them, they hardly expected abject and groveling servility. On "reconstruction," some form of which was universally anticipated, there were many variations of opinion and much muddled reasoning in matters of both procedure and principle. But they did want something in the way of satisfaction; they wanted a security that was more than military. In the things they said, it is possible to make out at least some pattern of consistency.

For one thing, the fire-eating "secesh" style in Southern manners would have to be repudiated and discredited. There must be some transcendent assurance, willingly given by all of society, not only that the South was "loyal" in the passive sense, but also that the act of secession was somehow wrong. No blood sacrifice was asked. Nothing really overwhelming was demanded—but the notion of "repentance" kept recurring like a leitmotif.[20] Meanwhile those who had been active secessionists should be "firmly ostracised for the time being,"[21] and "excluded from all participation in political affairs,"[22] so that they might have leisure to reflect upon their errors.

We hold that repentance, a repentance not to be repented of, should go before absolution and perfect pardon. We believe in the conversion of sinners, but we are slow to believe in instantaneous conversions. Let fruits meet for repentance be first brought forth, and then let the repentant prodigals be restored to the rights of sonship and brotherhood, and not before.[23]

Directly related to this need for some visible and articulate rejection of secessionism was the requirement that Southern Unionists be given some kind of security for having been Unionists. Not only must they receive protection, but upon them should fall the responsibility of forming the postwar governments.

The reorganization of the several Southern States' governments must necessarily be exclusively entrusted to men who have played no active parts in the rebellion, who besides being against it originally, have at no time and in no manner given it the countenance of their willing support.[24]

The Unionist position must now in some way be redefined as "right." No doubt practical considerations would render an utter revolution in leadership impossible; perhaps it would sooner or later be realized that there were not so many Southern Unionists as one had initially thought and that the South's best men had been rebels. But at least the new values of postwar Southern society should to some extent be

---

[20] "Let them take their own time in coming in to supper. We can stand it as long as they can; and besides, we can rely upon the repentance of men who have been cured of their folly upon empty stomachs and cool reflection." New York *Herald*, May 3, 1865.

[21] Washington *Evening Star*, June 12, 1865.

[22] *Illinois State Journal*, May 29, 1865. "But there are, and long will be, bad men in every Southern State, who are filled with the most rancorous hate of the government, and whose whole study hereafter will be how to do it injury. All such men can be shut out of Congress by the very stringent oath of allegiance which is now required before allowing a seat in either body. But they should also be precluded so far as possible, from all eligibility to State offices, and from the elective franchise. A State ruled by such men would become a nest for hatching new treason." New York *Times*, May 5, 1865.

[23] *Nation*, I (Oct. 19, 1865), 485.

[24] Washington *Evening Star*, June 12, 1865.

imparted by the men who had been loyal and Unionist throughout; society should accord them some kind of meaningful honor.

In the third place, it was of great symbolic importance that the masses of Southern Negroes, especially the ex-soldiers,[25] be conceded full protection in their newly conferred freedom. Slavery and its appurtenances should be fully repudiated. The new society must be based on a system of free labor which would include the ex-slave's freedom to work where he pleased, physical security in his comings and goings, and fair treatment in all matters pertaining to legal rights. The period of victory's immediate aftermath coincided with the period of least pessimism in Northern minds over this entire question. This was the time when the North's sense of responsibility for the freedmen was at its maximum, and the question had a moral clarity then that was later to disintegrate when the issue of Negro suffrage became a political football in partisan battles.

This sense of responsibility flowed from two sources, both full of coercion for the Northern conscience. Emancipation had become one of the war principles and was now an accomplished fact whose rightness had been sanctioned by victory. The Negro population, moreover, represented a strong salient of loyalty to the Union. "It is the duty of the government," asserted the *Illinois State Journal* of Springfield, "not only to protect its friends among the white population of the South, but to maintain the rights of the freedmen also, who have been solemnly clothed with the privileges of citizenship."[26] But although the prime responsibility for this protection and security should lie with the federal government, it must somehow be morally certified by the South itself. It was not simply that the Southern constituent assemblies were being asked to ratify the new emancipation amend-

[25] "From first to last there were 178,975 Negroes in the United States Volunteer army, and of this number 36,847 were killed, wounded, and missing. They participated in four hundred and forty-nine battles, and served in nearly every military department of the United States Army. Besides this large military force there were at least one hundred and fifty thousand Negro laborers in the Quartermaster and Engineering departments." George W. Williams, *A History of the Negro Troops* (New York: Harper & Bros., 1888), p. 324.

[26] May 29, 1865. This thought (the Negro as a responsibility, implied in both emancipation and the Negro's own loyalty) was elaborately discussed in a New York *Times* editorial of May 5, 1865, entitled "The Points To Be Secured before Reconstruction." "Some security," the *Times* insisted, "must be provided for the freedmen of the South. They have been unswervingly loyal to the government from the beginning of the rebellion, and that alone is enough to entitle them to its special protection. However, the government, for its own purposes, made them what they are, and it therefore is bound to take care that emancipation shall be a blessing to them, and not a curse. The fulfillment of these duties is really the hardest difficulty, the very gordian knot of reconstruction."

ment. The North was really concerned with how the thing would be done. Northerners wanted to see it acted out, and to judge its style.[27]

Finally, there were expectations, vague but palpable, regarding the reception of Northerners in Southern communities. Such expectations could not be announced in any manifestoes, but they were there. "A reunion of hands and hearts" was a note sounded surprisingly often in the immediate post-victory period. This did not necessarily represent a simple willingness to forgive and forget. It is rather that one may, reading a little between the lines, think of such a sentiment as yet another function of victory. The Northern conquest should be, among other things, a conquest of hands and hearts. "There must be a change of heart": the victor was coming, and he would have to be welcomed. The North had besieged the South with arms and she had submitted; the South, now in her defenseless, "feminine" entity, had no further right to repel the North, should the North now assume the role, as it were, of suitor. The South would henceforth be disarmed in all ways: not only was she to receive armies of occupation, of whose authority there was to be no question, but a new era of hospitality to Northern immigrants, Northern enterprise, and Northern ideas was about to be inaugurated.[28]

Before considering how these requirements were responded to, let us experiment briefly with a kind of analogy. In many ways, the German and Japanese occupations in 1945 may constitute a bad parallel for the post-surrender situation that followed the Civil War. But in at least one limited respect the parallel, such as it is, can be enlightening. It seems to show that there is such a thing as "symbolic" needs and that their fulfilment does make a great difference in the quality of feeling that will characterize the postwar behavior of former enemies toward each other. The analogy can show nothing

[27] "They [the delegates to the Southern state conventions] will signify unconditional submission to the Union—they will surrender slavery, by ratifying the constitutional amendment providing for its abolition, and last, but not least they will adopt such measures toward the freedmen—their recent slaves—as will guarantee them full protection in their persons and the enjoyment, prospectively, if not at once, of all their political rights. If, on the other hand, the Southern people are not yet prepared to accept the position of faithful citizens under a Government, which is not only founded upon common ideas of National sovereignty and unity, but under which all men shall be, in the spirit of the Declaration, free and equal, that fact will doubtless be manifested, not only in a failure to do the things above specified, but in the display of a hostile temper which will betray the treason lurking in their souls." *Bureau County* (Ill.) *Republican*, Oct. 5, 1865.

[28] As the *Nation* put it, "They must deal better with . . . the stranger that may be within their gates, than they have ever yet done. . . ." I (Oct. 19, 1865), 485.

specific about which ceremonial affirmations of defeat may be peculiarly proper but simply that the need for them exists. These requirements were fulfilled so automatically and so completely after World War II that they never constituted a problem for us; this in itself may be a good reason for making a point of it, and for suggesting that the point is applicable to more than one war.

Societies with a long tradition of accommodating themselves to power will have acquired, in the course of things, a deep knowledge of power in all its forms and meanings. They will know, for example, how to recognize superior power and how to appreciate and respond to it when they meet it. They will have little need of instruction on the requirements of a conqueror, and even less need of being told that he has them. Such societies, schooled in the ways of power, will know by instinct the cleanest ways of liquidating defeat; they will recognize, as a matter of self-interest, that when the requirements are met, the willingness (whatever its limits) of the conqueror to be merciful, to grant clemency, forgiveness, and oblivion, is at its maximum. So there is a sense in which the ancient law of conquest, to the extent that it makes the matter explicit, need not be thought of as entirely inhumane. It is here that our experience of victory in World War II seems particularly illuminating.

Those who participated in the last stages of the offensive against Germany in 1945, and subsequently in the occupation, will remember their surprise at the total collapse of all forms of resistance, civilian as well as military. The lack of sullenness on the part of the population was most remarkable; respect and deference, bordering on the obsequious, to the occupying power was everywhere in evidence. Before long there was even a willingness by the Germans themselves to try, and to convict, their own "war criminals." In the light of their supposedly arrogant ways, the people at large showed an amazing spirit of accommodation to the presence of our army; and the friendliness of the women was especially notable.[29]

---

[29] Here is one point (among several) at which it is important not to let the analogy get out of hand. It is true that the overpowering and occupying of one country by another has both figuratively and literally all sorts of "sexual" overtones. But on the more literal level, the community morals of nineteenth-century America, even under conditions of fullest hospitality, would not have allowed anything like the freedom that existed between American soldiers and the women of post–World War II Germany. And yet that need not banish the parallel altogether. Allowing for the differences in mores, one can still ask what happened, in the South of 1865, to the *ad hoc* society that seems to spring up on the spot, in all times and places, whenever there are young people. The fact was that in 1865 not even the normal and accepted gradings in relationship between men and women were sanctioned by Southern society vis-à-vis the Northern occupying force—and here it was the women themselves who made the law.

And yet all this pales before the tableau that was acted out, in virtually pure form, by the Japanese. The chronology of the first year's occupation of Japan, taken in sequence through the pages of one of the news magazines, will evoke renewed amazement at the week-by-week story of how all the horror and loathing of the Japanese, and all the wartime hatreds, simply melted away. Before the first landings, early in September, 1945, the Americans were filled with misgivings. Perhaps we as a nation had been tricked in our decision to retain the Emperor. We were outnumbered, as General MacArthur later put it, "a thousand to one." There seemed no reason why the Japanese, with an undefeated army of several million—many of whom would shortly be unemployed brigands—could not carry on underground activity indefinitely. The troops were given dire warnings against the women: ". . . they have been taught to hate you. . . . The Geisha girl . . . may entice you only to poison you."[30]

Meanwhile, the peacemaking government decreed the banishment of autocracy and the inauguration of democracy, all of which was legalized by the Diet, while the *Nippon Times* pronounced the death of the old order and called for all haste in the work of building the new. Coming ashore was "like a veteran's dream of victory" for the tautly apprehensive Americans. Advance detachments were smothered with attentions which included turtle soup, roast beef, cold beer, and beds with clean linen sheets. A sign on a factory roof read, "Three cheers for the U.S. Navy and Army." The arrival of the conqueror was as extravagantly heralded in the newspapers as had been the early victories of the imperial forces. Three weeks later in the United States it was being reported, with bated optimism, that "the big news from Japan was what had not happened." Not a single demonstration of enmity had occurred; on the contrary, the people were giving every evidence of sincere accommodation and submission.[31]

Almost immediately, the Japanese repudiated their militarist leadership, and even before the official war criminal lists were prepared, the Japanese themselves were suggesting names for them. They reacted with unfeigned symptoms of guilt to the stories of atrocities to American prisoners, published in their own newspapers, and asked to set up their own courts for the punishment of those responsible.[32]

In October, General MacArthur "decreed revolution," which in-

30 *Time*, Aug. 27, 1945, pp. 27–29.

31 *Ibid.*, Sept. 3, 1945, p. 28; Sept. 10, 1945, pp. 28–29; Sept. 24, 1945, p. 21.

32 *Ibid.*, Sept. 10, 1945, p. 29; Sept. 17, 1945, p. 27; Sept. 24, 1945, p. 22; Nov. 19, 1945, p. 31.

volved the most sweeping changes in Japanese life: full civil liberties, free speech and free thought, release of political prisoners, abolishment of all totalitarian powers, the inauguration of democratic government, the organization of labor, and the dissolution of the zaibatsu, or great family business combines. "Japanese officialdom bowed low, smiled, and consented," and a new cabinet was formed by Baron Shidehara, one of the few surviving prewar liberal leaders. New parties sprang into existence, and the general election which was held in the spring brought 27 million voters to the polls. With Olympian understatement, the Supreme Commander pronounced it "satisfactory."[33]

The Japanese eagerness to please was manifested in a hundred ways. The Tokyo theater featured such plays as Drinkwater's *Abraham Lincoln* and Lillian Hellman's anti-Fascist *Watch on the Rhine*. With the decrees of female equality came an influx of women into politics; there was a flood of new business for the divorce courts; and the Emperor himself asked for an American woman tutor for the crown prince. The first contingent of Navy wives was welcomed at the pier by a delegation of Japanese women announcing their desire to learn American ways. The popular songs became heavily American in style; the efforts at Americanization extended even to the underworld.[34] On the anniversary of Hiroshima's destruction a tremendous "Peace and Reconstruction Festival" was joyously staged by the city's boosters.[35] And finally, nothing was half so well suited to softening the asperities of war as the way in which the girls of Japan welcomed their American suitors. It was necessary at one point for General Eichelberger, in the interests of propriety and good military order, to issue a directive against "public displays of affection."[36]

After one year, the progress report on occupation could sum up a great success, from anyone's viewpoint. The Japanese had magnificently acted out all that was required of them;[37] the symbolic satisfac-

[33] *Ibid.*, Oct. 1, 1945, p. 28; Oct. 15, 1945, p. 29; Apr. 22, 1946, p. 32.

[34] *Ibid.*, Feb. 25, 1946, p. 50; July 1, 1946, p. 50; Apr. 1, 1946, p. 32; May 6, 1946, p. 35; Sept. 9, 1946, pp. 59–60; July 1, 1946, p. 25; Apr. 29, 1946, p. 48; June 24, 1946, p. 35. Giichi Matsuda, boss of the Matsuzakaya gang, tried to get his followers to wear Western-style sack suits and pursue more democratic and progressive business methods. When an outraged henchman assassinated Matsuda, the latter's widow was elected as the first woman gang chief ever known in Japan.

[35] *Ibid.*, Aug. 19, 1946, p. 36. A child whose mother and sister had been killed by the bomb said to a *Time* correspondent: "American soldier good. American number one." *Ibid.*, July 15, 1946, p. 38.

[36] *Ibid.*, Apr. 1, 1946, p. 25. A few months later, however, the military authorities were issuing phrase books with hints on "sweet talk." *Ibid.*, July 15, 1946, p. 38.

[37] "Last September MacArthur came to a Japan whose people were imprisoned in feudalism and superstition, whose cities were ashen ruins, whose militarist traditions

tions of occupation had changed everything between the two peoples. With our Oriental enemies of over a generation, there now existed something closer to a "union of hands and hearts" than any American, in the bitter days of Bataan, Corregidor, and Guadalcanal, could very well have imagined.[38]

To expect from the conquered South any such behavior as that just described would have been grotesque. It would have been not only impossible but probably undesirable; it might conceivably have undermined a more permanent objective, that of remaking two peoples into one. Indeed, neither side had more than the dimmest idea of what was proper under the circumstances: Americans had never been conquered before, had never really known authority, had had no real experience or appreciation of power, in either the active or the passive sense, and no instinct was sharp enough to warn of the behavior appropriate to any given instance of it. Such things lay outside the realm of anyone's experience. So the South could not in the truest sense submit, not really knowing how, and that was the way things had to be. But there would still have to be a price: the North still realized—dimly, perhaps, but somehow—that something was missing.

---

had no place for such concepts as defeat and war guilt. The Supreme Commander's first job was to destroy what was left of Japan's war potential. But he said: 'I am not concerned with how to keep Japan down but how to get her on her feet again.'

". . . By last week the U.S. imprint was strong on Japan. Japanese girls strolled hand in hand with G.I.s beside the imperial moat. Children played with toy models of American 'jeepu'; women copied U.S. fashion. In Tokyo a special school taught U.S. slang, and cinema fans queued up to see Hollywood movies (biggest hit: *Tall in the Saddle*, a Western). In geisha houses, the girls gaily crooned *You Are My Sunshine*.

"The Japs, long used to following the leader, followed American democracy in much the same spirit as they accepted U.S. jazz. When MacArthur ordered them to hold an election, 27 million of them trooped to the polls. They organized Western-style political parties and prepared to accept a Western-style constitution. When they were ordered to cease worshiping their Emperor as a god, they willingly obliged." *Ibid.*, Sept. 2, 1946, p. 27.

[38] It is being argued that the experience of victory, together with the appropriate tokens of acquiescence, constitutes the most effective—and indeed the indispensable—ritual catharsis for the liquidation of prior hatreds. A final example of its profundity, before leaving the point, might come out of a few comparisons between American attitudes toward wartime "friends" and toward defeated enemies. In 1898, after the close of hostilities in Cuba, our hearts went out to the gallant Spaniards, whose submission was perfect, while we quickly perceived what an unsavory lot our friends, the suffering Cuban rebels, had been. On this point see Walter Millis, *The Martial Spirit* (New York: Literary Guild, 1931), pp. 363–64. (The same thing, of course, happened in the Philippines.) In Europe, our unsteady friendship for the French and Russians in World War II paled beside the real warmth which developed in our feelings for the prostrated Germans. And in Asia our relationship with our wartime friends, the Chinese, has become odious in every way conceivable.

As the North waited, first in expectancy and then in deepening mortification, it began to dawn on the people that they were being somehow cheated of all the truly meaningful satisfactions of their victory. The South "accepted the situation," but this, as Northerners came to realize, was an idiomatic phrase brought into being especially for the purpose; it covered, with a special nicety, military defeat and no more.[39] As the reports came in, it began to appear that the deeper gratifications, even in their mildest form, could never be accorded by the erstwhile enemy.

Representative James Garfield of Ohio, by the fall and early winter of 1865, was one of the numerous public men receiving letters from the Southern states, with details of the political activities going on there, and it was made clear to him that in none of these states could the late enemy help glorying in his secessionism. "The 'secesh' ticket in this county was elected throughout," wrote Joseph R. Putnam from Huntsville, Alabama.[40] L. A. Sheldon, a conservative Northern businessman, wrote from New Orleans that "politically the state is in the

[39] This point was explained by E. O. Dunning to the Joint Committee on Reconstruction. *Report of the Joint Committee on Reconstruction*, 39 Cong., 1 sess., Part II, "Virginia, North Carolina, South Carolina," p. 48.

Of all the groups in society, however, that element closest to the full ritual requirements of war appears perennially to be the military. The ceremonial of surrender made its deepest impression on those who actually participated in it—namely the armies—and those Southerners most convinced of defeat, and of the need for performing the gestures appropriate to it, were the Confederate soldiers. This should be taken mainly, of course, as a matter of degree, since no one class in a democratic society can be expected to remain aloof very long from the moral coercions of the rest of society. But the attitude was still noticeable enough, in the first six months or so following the war, that any number of otherwise critical Northern observers made a point of commenting on it, simply to emphasize the recalcitrance of Southern society at large. "Indeed," wrote Whitelaw Reid, "nothing was more touching, in all that I saw in Savannah, than the almost painful effort of the rebels from Generals down to privates, to conduct themselves so as to evince respect for our soldiers. . . ." *After the War: A Southern Tour* (London: Sampson Low, Son, & Marston, 1866), p. 156. Sidney Andrews wrote, "I found it almost everywhere true in Georgia and the Carolinas that the best citizens of to-day are the Confederate soldiers of yesterday." "Three Months among the Reconstructionists," *Atlantic Monthly*, XVII (Feb., 1866), 242. Conversely, the Union armies constituted the most conservative class in all Northern society, so far as further exactions on the South were concerned. This is not fully explained simply by saying that the soldiers had had their fill of war and its horrors and now wanted to end it once and for all. The point is rather that the armies had participated in a very profound and compelling experience which was denied the respective civilian populations—the experience of surrender. The ceremony had, of course, opposite meanings for the opposing participants, but for a moment it brought them spiritually very close together. It prepared the Southern soldier for submission, the Northern soldier for magnanimity. But then, the meaning of such an occasion has to be tremendously enlarged and extended for the civilian who could not be there, or for the man whose son was sacrificed in order that it might take place. That is why, for full satisfaction, the gestures of surrender could not end with Appomattox.

[40] Joseph R. Putnam to James Garfield, Nov. 10, 1865, Garfield MSS, Library of Congress. Putnam was a Union soldier whose regiment, stationed at Huntsville, was about to be mustered out.

hands of the men who voted her out of the Union."[41] "In a word," declared James Atkins, writing from Atlanta,

the control of everything down here is in the hands of the thoroughly disloyal. At a distance I felt a great sympathy for the people here: now that I am here and know how the pulse of the people beat, I have lost a great portion of my sympathy. The people have suffered terribly and are in a pitiable condition for the most part. Nevertheless all their sympathy is with those who distinguished themselves in behalf of the Confederacy. Men are advocated for such virtues openly. . . .[42]

Conversely, Southern Unionists found, even after the South's defeat, that their Unionism not only conferred no moral status whatever in their home communities but actually made their very existence intolerable there. The first test occurred in Virginia, where a large number of local elections, held late in May and early in June, brought solid rebel victories. "There is no security here for such men as me," flatly declared J. E. Brush of Norfolk,[43] and James H. Clements assured Charles Sumner that "if the Rebels continue to have the same privileges as now appears to be the policy to give them in this State, God help the Union men."[44] "The real Union men of this state," lamented G. W. Welker of North Carolina, "are but few and are so situated that they must look abroad for aid. . . . We entreet Congress never to place us again under the power of the men who betrayed us, plundered us & oppressed us."[45] It was observed by Sidney Andrews

[41] L. A. Sheldon to Garfield, Nov. 21, 1865, Garfield MSS.

[42] James Atkins to Garfield, Dec. 7, 1865, Garfield MSS. Atkins was a federal office-holder in the Department of Internal Revenue.

[43] J. E. Brush to Sumner, June 9, 1865, Sumner MSS, Harvard College Library. "The undersigned is a Native of this Town, but left immediately after hostilities commenced destined for the City of Memphis with high hopes of being able to reach the Federal lines, but failed, was in Memphis 26 months, was there when the city was captured, absent from my family that length of time, 9 months of which did not hear from them. . . . Was born and reared here, but have bitter enemies because of the decided stand which I took and the liberal opinions which I now entertain. Many things I could tell you about [conditions] here provided I could get a hearing from you or some other influential man in the Congress of the U. States."

[44] James H. Clements to Sumner, June 11, 1865, Sumner MSS. Clements, who called himself "simply a Mechanic," had left Portsmouth, Virginia, at the outbreak of the war in order to join the Union Forces. "I hope sir," he said to Sumner, "you will excuse the freedom I take in addressing you, but sir the interest I feel in my future welfare and that of my family justifies me in calling on the rulers of my country."

[45] G. W. Welker to Thaddeus Stevens, Dec. 2, 1865, Stevens MSS, Library of Congress. Another North Carolina Unionist, who signed himself only "Union," summarized for Stevens the result of the recent congressional election in his district:

" 'I cannot take the oath, if I would' & (defiantly) 'I would not, if I could.' Stubbs.

" 'I cannot take the oath.' Speed.

" 'I can honestly and truthfully take the oath, having never done any thing inconsistent with it except *involuntarily* under military or mobocratic coercion.' Bond.

"The result was—Stubbs 2783, Speed 2013, Bond 450!!! Speed and Stubbs won simply

that "In Barnwell and Anderson districts, South Carolina, official records show the murder of over a dozen Union men in the months of August and September. . . ."[46] And Gillet Watson wrote imploringly to Thaddeus Stevens from Richmond: "We represent the loyal people of this section, many of whom have fought and bled, and lost their all in defence of the stars and stripes. Are these men to be turned over to an excited and infuriated mob, by the U.S. Representatives?"[47]

Meanwhile, whatever illusions the North may have cherished regarding the future of the Southern Negro began to dissolve. The ideals of emancipation and free labor, as well as the hope of an incorruptible Unionist bulwark (which required at least some form of citizenship), faded before the reports. Even the most sanguine Northerner became heavy-hearted at what he read and heard. "As for your niggers," said a Virginia ex-colonel to Whitelaw Reid, "you've got 'em on your hands. They won't work, unless you force them to it, and they'll steal rather than starve. You even talk about giving them suffrage! There are no words to express the infamy of such a proposition. This is a white man's government, and must be kept so till the end of time."[48] "Three-fourths of the people," wrote Sidney Andrews,

assume that the negro will not labor, except on compulsion; and the whole struggle between the whites on the one hand and the blacks on the other hand is a struggle for and against compulsion. The negro insists . . . that he shall be free to come and go as he pleases; the white insists that he shall come and go only at the pleasure of his employer. . . . I did not anywhere find a man who could see that laws should be applicable to all persons alike; and hence even the best men held that each State must have a negro code.[49]

---

on the hope, that the oath would be repealed. Let Congress do that, & the seats from the South will be occupied by the 'Secesh,' the Unionist in the South forever proscribed by them & the Group in constant danger from their plots & intrigues." "Union" to Stevens, Nov. 27, 1865, Stevens MSS.

[46] Andrews, "Three Months among the Reconstructionists," p. 238. "I spent the months of September, October, and November, 1865," Andrews wrote, "in the States of North Carolina, South Carolina, and Georgia. I travelled over more than half the stages and railway routes therein, visited a considerable number of towns and cities in each State, attended the so-called reconstruction conventions at Raleigh, Columbia, and Milledgeville, and had much conversation with many individuals of nearly all classes."

[47] Gillet Watson to Stevens, Dec. 5, 1865, Stevens MSS. Watson was chairman of the Union League of Virginia. "Sir," wrote a Louisiana correspondent of Nathaniel P. Banks, "the present Legislature boast on the streets that they intend to *ostracise* all so called loyal men to the United States Government by giving them no private or public employment, & thus force them to leave the State for more agreeable quarters." J. P. Henderson to Banks, Nov. 26, 1865, Banks MSS, Essex Institute.

[48] *After the War,* p. 318.

[49] "Three Months among the Reconstructionists," p. 243.

Such a movement, indeed, was well under way by December. The hitherto circumspect *Nation*, confronted with the codes of South Carolina, Alabama, and Mississippi, was appalled at these "disgraceful statutes." "Such are some of the open manifestations of the mood of 'our Southern brethren' in circumstances when they would have been tempted to make a show at least of complete acquiescence in the will of their magnanimous conquerer."[50]

Finally, in receiving her triumphant conqueror, the South was unable to tender even the civilly measured hospitality that accompanies a forced submission.[51] Northerners with plans for emigration were chilled to discover that their arrivals were openly discouraged[52] and that there were no guarantees, except for the presence of federal troops, that they were even safe in their persons.[53] But what really

[50] *Nation*, I (Dec. 28, 1865), 806.

[51] Sidney Andrews, who did more listening than talking and therefore got into less trouble than many Northern travelers, reported that he had had much less to complain of than most of his fellow Yankees. Yet there were numerous snubs and humiliations at hotels and boarding houses; "at one house in South Carolina," he noted, "when I sought accommodations for two or three days at a boarding-house, I was asked by the woman in charge, 'Are you a Yankee or a Southerner?' and when I answered, 'Oh, a Yankee, of course,' she responded, 'No Yankee stops in this house!' and turned her back upon me and walked off. In another town in the same State I learned that I was the first Yankee who had been allowed to stop at the hotel since the close of the war." "Three Months among the Reconstructionists," p. 237. This was easily the most commonly shared experience of Northern travelers. It even extended to the military. General Grant's aide, Cyrus Comstock, at New Orleans with the General's party, laconically wrote in his diary for February 5, 1866: "Saw Gen. Baird. Says feeling in Nov. & Oct. was very bad, that officers were insulted at St. Charles, that officers wives at St. Charles table were not waited on and that on remonstrances being made were told they were not desired there as it might affect the custom of the house." Diary of Cyrus B. Comstock, Feb. 5, 1866, Library of Congress.

[52] "At the time I am writing, the owners of property in Richmond are holding it at such high rates as to repel Northern purchasers. Letters from that city say, the residents have determined to sell no property to Northern men, when they can possibly avoid it." Thomas W. Knox, *Camp-Fire and Cotton Field: Southern Adventure in Time of War* (New York: Blelock, 1865), p. 497. "One of our firm, Jos. Glenn," wrote Richard Smith (of the Cincinnati *Gazette*) to James Garfield, "has been travelling in Miss. and Louisiana for some time and bought a cotton plantation, which he now regrets. He says that if the troops are withdrawn Northern men could neither live nor travel there. . . ." Smith to Garfield, Jan. 14, 1866, Garfield MSS.

[53] John Murray Forbes declared that "if you withdraw the army, and give back the local government to the Governors and Mayors and Magistrates and Constables who have been fighting us, any northern man who wishes to emigrate south must either cut out his tongue and his conscience, or provide himself with an India rubber neck and a ball proof jacket!" Forbes to N. M. Beckwith, Aug. 6, 1865, Carl Schurz MSS, Library of Congress. "It follows, of course," wrote Sidney Andrews in milder vein, "that safety of person is not assured. Very likely one might travel through every county of either State without harm; but any Union man must expect to hear insulting words; and any Northern man is sure to find his principles despised, his people contemned, and himself subjected to much disagreeable contumely; while any man hold-

must have struck the Northerner to the heart, in all the flush and pride of his victory, was the implacability of the Southern women. The women, far from performing for their people any of the gentler rites of peace, were the bitterest of all. "A day or two ago," wrote Carl Schurz from Savannah, "a Union officer, yielding to an impulse of politeness, handed a dish of pickles to a Southern lady at the dinner-table of a hotel in this city. A look of unspeakable scorn and indignation met him. 'So you think,' said the lady, 'a Southern woman will take a dish of pickles from a hand that is dripping with the blood of her countrymen?' "[54] The Northern and Southern hands were not to join, even over the sour formality of a dish of pickles.

In no case were specific violations of the Confederate surrender involved in any of these stories. It was the protocol of defeat for an entire people that had been violated, a protocol whose spirit and overtones could hardly be specified in any articles of surrender. Under the circumstances, there may have been very little help for it: there were no cues in the national experience to follow in setting matters to rights once they had gone awry. But whatever the cause, there were poisons in the Northern bosom by December, 1865, that had not been there in May. In one sense they had been carried

ing and openly advocating even moderately radical sentiments on the negro question, stands an excellent chance, in many counties of Georgia and South Carolina, of being found dead some morning,—shot from behind, as is the custom of the country. Of course the war has not taught its full lesson till even Mr. Wendell Phillipps can go into Georgia and proclaim 'The South Victorious.' " *The South since the War, As Shown by Fourteen Weeks of Travel and Observation in Georgia and the Carolinas* (Boston: Ticknor & Fields, 1866), p. 385.

[54] Carl Schurz, "Letters from the South, No. 4," July 31, 1865, Schurz MSS. "As we rode through the city," wrote Grant's aide at Charleston, "I saw several who called themselves ladies make faces at the Yankee officers with us. It is useless to say they are only women—they express openly what their husbands & brothers feel but do not show." Diary of Cyrus B. Comstock, Dec. 1, 1865. Even President Johnson's emissary, Benjamin Truman—whose report was specifically designed to present Southern conditions sympathetically—corroborated other witnesses on this point. "There is a prevalent disposition not to associate too freely with northern men," Truman wrote, "or to receive them into the circles of society; but it is far from insurmountable. Over Southern society, as over every other, woman reigns supreme, and they are more embittered against those whom they deem the authors of all their calamities than are their brothers, sons and husbands." *Senate Executive Documents,* 39 Cong., 1 sess., No. 43, "Report of Benjamin Truman," p. 6. Here Truman was assuming that with the melting of that insignificant barrier, all would be changed. He little appreciated the formidability of the women: they did *not* melt. Joseph LeConte of Columbia, South Carolina, writing of the later reconstruction period, said that the men of Columbia were very cordial to the officers stationed there, "but the ladies were inexorable." "I became quite friendly with some of the officers," he wrote, "but I could never induce my wife to invite one of the gentlemen to the house for a social meal." *Autobiography of Joseph LeConte,* ed. William D. Armes (New York: D. Appleton, 1903), pp. 236–37.

over from a long, costly, and bitter war. But something had now been added, a new malaise, created not so much by war as by peace. It had been a most irregular peace, very uncertainly managed, a peace whose quality was quite different from anything that had been expected. Many were saying, by early 1866, that the wartime principles were now tarnished, the fruits of victory soured, and the sacrifices rendered meaningless; there seemed little left to show for the overwhelming moral commitment which the war had once represented. The moral victory which the North imagined itself to have won had come to nothing.

Although the above themes may tell us something important about the new turn in sectional feeling that occurred in the latter half of 1865, they still make up only a part of the story. The Southerners in the beginning could hardly have been so blind to their own deepest interests; nor could Northerners have been quite so muddled about what they required of the South. Still other things were involved during that summer of 1865, among them the fact that the most important channels of communication between the North and the South were not really open. The United States government, whose most authoritative agency at this time was the Republican party, was not in full functioning for the settlement of Southern problems, nor would it be until the end of the year. No one, meanwhile, could be expected to know how much difference this made; nor was it clear to what extent President Johnson considered himself the spokesman of that agency. Each of the interested parties had quite different notions on this point. Indeed, the entire period—the summer and fall of 1865— might be seen from a later viewpoint as a season of self-delusion on nearly all sides. So if Southerners misconceived the accuracy with which the Northern will was being communicated to them, there remains the question of how much of this was properly their responsibility. Other explanations must be sought, more perspectives established, further trial balances struck.

Chapter

3

The State
of Parties,
1865

I THE REPUBLICAN PARTY AND THE MORALITY OF THE CIVIL WAR

In the North, the Civil War was prosecuted within a peculiarly political framework, and the public commitment to the Union war effort was suffused with a deeply moral quality. Attention has been called to both these points in the previous chapter. For a full appraisal of the party situation in 1865, these two aspects—the political and the moral—should now be brought a little closer together.

The Civil War was not, politically, a "bipartisan" war in anything like the sense that would be true of the two world wars. Circumstances required that it be waged as a party war. Despite the initial flush of bipartisan patriotism generated by such men as Stephen A. Douglas, it was to become in its course a Republican war, and the victory, when finally achieved, turned out to be in effect a Republican victory. The Democrats themselves did little to contest it.[1] Even the change of party

---

[1] By contrast, in the fall elections of 1918 the Republican party contested, with decisive results, President Wilson's insinuations that the war had been peculiarly a Democratic concern. Likewise, in World War II, the extent of Republican partisanship over the war consisted in promises to prosecute it more vigorously than the administration —rather than less, as had been the case with the Democrats in the Civil War. Of course thousands of officers and men in the Union armies came from Democratic families. It was in their organized character as a political party, however, that the Democrats and their political leaders voluntarily renounced the initiative in campaigning for a fully victorious conclusion—thus forfeiting their claim, which would otherwise have been substantial, to share in the credit for the final victory. Lincoln himself made a point of this in a conversation with Hugh McCulloch shortly before the end of the war. " 'I am here,' said Mr. Lincoln, in one of the last conversations I had with him, 'by the blunders of the Democrats. If, instead of resolving that the war was a failure, they had resolved that I was a failure and denounced me for not more vigorously prosecuting it, I should not have been reelected, and I reckon that you would not have been Secretary of the Treasury.' " Hugh McCulloch, *Men and Measures of Half a Century: Sketches and Comments* (New York: Charles Scribner's Sons, 1900), p. 162.

names, from "Republican" to "Union," that took place in many states
turned out to be less a sign of bipartisanship than of a greatly
broadened base for the original Republican party. It was not clear in
the beginning, of course, that these efforts at coalition-making would
all contribute to one result, the Republicans' ultimate ascendancy. The
war may actually be seen in two clear political phases, whose dividing
point was the 1862 elections. Before that, the war was a popular-front
"fusion" enterprise whose keynote was defense of the Union. But after
1862 the parties pulled ever farther apart in their very conception of
the war. The contrast was marked not only by the Republicans' growing emphasis on emancipation as well as on total victory but also by
the Democrats' deepening commitment to peace. The result was an
extraordinarily close connection between the war principles and the
Republican party, a fact which now requires some spelling out. How
had this happened? How had so full a share of the country's energy,
power, and moral authority drifted within the sphere of a political
party?

For a brief period following the firing on Sumter, there
had been an almost revolutionary sense of unity as former political
enemies sank their differences in pledges of support for Lincoln and
the flag. Democratic opposition to war preparations ceased abruptly.
The concept of "War Democrat" was born in the furious energy of
Douglas, who, after his conference with Lincoln, toured the Northwest and addressed the legislatures of Ohio, Indiana, and Illinois with
pleas for support of the administration. Both parties were then, in
effect, war parties. Douglas had set the tone: "There can be no neutrals
in this war, *only patriots—or traitors!*"[2]
During this early Unionist phase, many Democrats were willing to
join new political coalitions whose primary object was promotion of
the war effort. It was possible in the beginning to do this without
feeling any inherent conflict with ultimate loyalty to the Democratic
party. There would merely be a temporary suspension of normal partisanship. The terms of the coalition varied from state to state. In Ohio
—a doubtful state with a strong prewar Democratic establishment—
one of the first of the "Union" organizations was set up in 1861 with
David Tod, a former Democrat, as its candidate for governor. In Iowa,
on the other hand, the Republicans were strong enough to keep the

[2] Wood Gray, *The Hidden Civil War: The Story of the Copperheads* (New York:
Viking Press, 1942), pp. 51–59.

party name and insist on setting the terms for any Democrats wishing to join them.[3]

But it soon became clear to the Democrats that with an end of partisanship it was *their* party that suffered. The Cincinnati *Enquirer* complained that "No More Party" meant in effect "No More Democratic Party." Self-preservation required that the party foster a certain amount of discontent over the war, and accordingly the regular Democatic organizations began to experiment with varying techniques and degrees of opposition. The formula typically included support of the war, but it was qualified more and more heavily as time went on by the insistence that the war be waged "constitutionally"—without undue enlargement of executive powers.[4] It was under these altered sanctions, especially after the military disappointments of the spring and summer of 1862, and the announcement of emancipation in September, that Lincoln's administration came in for torrents of abuse. It was charged with incompetence, abolitionism, and tyrannical exercise of arbitrary power. This stepping-up of opposition, coinciding with handsome Democratic gains in the fall elections, seemed to legitimize for the Democratic party a clear new line: criticism of the administration bordering on outright opposition to the war itself. This was the turning point at which the party made, in effect, its decision to turn the war over to the Republicans, to let them bear the responsibility for the drawn-out failure which at that time seemed all too likely.[5]

From here on, the "peace" aspect of Democratic principles gained ascendancy within the party, and overwhelmingly so in the Midwest. This had two very important meanings. One was that in state after state the "Peace Democrats" would dominate the party organizations; the other was that "War Democrats" in many of those same states, with nowhere to go, had to make decisions which would be critical for their own future political careers.

The Democrats now became, in effect, the "Copperhead" party of the wartime legend, and their attempts to discredit the Union war effort took on a more positive quality. In Illinois, former Democratic governor John Reynolds insisted, in December, 1862, that force be abandoned in the North's efforts to restore the Union. Clement L.

---

[3] *Ibid.*, pp. 59–63; Eugene H. Roseboom, *The Civil War Era, 1850–1873*, Vol. IV of Carl Wittke (ed.), *History of the State of Ohio* (Columbus: Ohio State Archaeological and Historical Society, 1944), pp. 391–92.

[4] Gray, *Hidden Civil War*, pp. 63–65.

[5] *Ibid.*, pp. 103–8, 115–17; Arthur C. Cole, *The Era of the Civil War, 1848–1870*, Vol. III of C. W. Alvord (ed.), *Centennial History of Illinois* (Springfield: Illinois Historical Commission, 1919), pp. 297–99.

Vallandigham, the ultra-Copperhead of Ohio who was now coming into his own, declared in January, 1863, that the South could never be conquered and advised young men not to volunteer. In the same month the Indiana legislature, dominated by Democrats, passed a resolution withholding war funds until the Emancipation Proclamation should be revoked. The legislators of Indiana further demanded a six months' armistice and tried to remove control of the militia from Governor Morton's hands.[6] Leading Democratic newspapers in the Midwest, by January, 1863, were openly opposing the war; some actually encouraged desertion on the grounds that the soldiers had been deceived about the war's true purpose, which was no longer union but abolition. The high point of this phase was Vallandigham's candidacy for the Ohio governorship in 1863, the threat of which, from the administration's viewpoint, could hardly be overemphasized. Only the military victories of Gettysburg and Vicksburg served to blunt it. Lincoln, anxiously awaiting the Ohio election returns, fervently wrote, "Glory to God in the Highest. Ohio has saved the Union," when the news finally came that John Brough had beaten Vallandigham by 100,000 votes.[7]

Great numbers of War Democrats, meanwhile, could no longer stay with their party, and they found themselves, in case after case, with no choice but to come into the Union fold—this time for good. Here is the point at which the "Union" name takes on great importance. It is sometimes said that the Union party of 1864 and 1865 was not the old Republican party of 1860, that the "Union" designation was substituted in order to emphasize support of the war and to minimize the antislavery overtones of prewar Republicanism, and that consequently the party's character changed so much in the course of the war that it was in effect no longer the same party at the end.[8] But strengthening a prior structure with new tissue is not at all the same as creating a new structure, and in this case a new organizational structure did not come into being when party names in the various states began to change. The organizational nucleus was there already, and the organization was Republican; the charter members, the men who

---

[6] Gray, *Hidden Civil War*, pp. 115–20, 131; William B. Hesseltine, *Lincoln and the War Governors* (New York: Alfred A. Knopf, 1948), p. 313; William Dudley Foulke, *Life of Oliver P. Morton* (Indianapolis: Bowen-Merrill, 1899), I, 213–38; Stampp, *Indiana Politics*, pp. 179–85.

[7] Donald B. Sanger, "The Chicago Times and the Civil War," *Mississippi Valley Historical Review*, XVII (March, 1931), 567. Roseboom, *Civil War Era*, p. 421; Gray, *Hidden Civil War*, pp. 133, 151–53.

[8] See William A. Dunning, "The Second Birth of the Republican Party," *American Historical Review*, XVI (October, 1910), 56–63.

gave the organization its temper and *élan*—were by definition "primitive Republicans." And the change back to "Republican" again, after the war, was not a "second birth" but simply another change of name, not dissimilar to the wartime change from "Republican" to "Union."

It is true that the importance of "Union," as an emblem for drawing in those new voters and local politicians who may have been repelled by the antislavery note, was considerable. But it should be repeated that there were two "Unionist" phases in the career of the administration party. It was in the early phase, before emancipation, that the emphasis on non-partisan coalitions and minimizing of antislavery were most critical. It was after emancipation, however, that the Union party made its greatest gains. By 1863 and 1864, the decision on slavery had long since been made, and those who came in at that time did so with open eyes. It is hard to imagine many men having by then been really "duped."

Here the important thing was the meaning, for a professional politician, of making a change in party loyalties. Making such a change may well involve the most important decision of a man's career, a decision not lightly taken and not arrived at without great soul-searching. It was such a decision that thousands of War Democrats faced in 1863, and it can be imagined that any device that might have smoothed the transition would have been gratefully embraced. The "Union" label was widely in use in the various states by 1863, and it was officially adopted by the national organization in the presidential campaign of 1864. There must be points at which semantic niceties, though "fooling" nobody, are still vital to self-respect; perhaps this was one of them. The "Union" symbol, in place of "Republican," might be thought of as a mechanism for easing the strains in the process whereby a Democrat who had no choice became a Republican. Thus in such a case, say, as that of Matt Carpenter of Wisconsin, and many others like him, the transition would go from "Democrat" to "War Democrat," to "Union," and eventually to "Republican."[9] If the "Union" symbol could serve this function for professionals, one can well think what it must have done for several million voters.

[9] Carpenter was at first very reluctant to join the Republicans. He supported the war and the administration, but remained with the Democratic party. It was not until the fall of 1863, when the Democrats nominated a candidate for governor who openly praised slavery and put the responsibility for the war on Northern Republicans, that he decided he had to leave the party. His first thought was to try to organize a third party that would be neither Copperhead nor abolitionist, but in the end he threw his support to the Union party and campaigned for Lincoln in 1864. In the Grant era, a few years later, we see him as a stalwart of the Republican party. E. Bruce Thompson, *Matthew Hale Carpenter: Webster of the West* (Madison: State Historical Society of Wisconsin, 1954), pp. 64–83, 148 ff.)

Thenceforth the regular Democratic party lost all remaining claim to the war as a positive program to which it might appeal for support. This fact was formally ratified at the national convention of 1864. The eastern leaders of the party, who were neither so warlike as their already-bolted western brothers nor yet such Copperheads as the regular Democrats of the West, tried vainly in committee to keep a peace plank out of the platform. But when the plank was introduced on the floor, it was greeted with roars of approval. The national Democratic party was thus committed—and at a time when military matters once more looked very dark. Meanwhile the administration party was being officially baptized, on a national scale, as the "Union party."[10] While that party officially assumed more "conservative" colors, it was becoming, as everyone knew, less and less so in actual fact.

Our particular concern with the parties begins with the period following the war's close, the spring and summer of 1865. It should be noted, however, that the positions which the parties then occupied had been overwhelmingly set by the events of late 1864, following the Union's final new low which had been reached that summer. By then had come the dazzling reversal of fortune which included the victories of Sherman in Georgia and Sheridan in Virginia, the revelations of a giant Copperhead plot in the Midwest (in which prominent Democrats were implicated), and, finally, the triumphant re-election of Lincoln behind the united support of a party grown by then to gigantic proportions. As the war drew to its close, the Union party had become so large that *Harper's Weekly* by February, 1865, could actually say: "We are at the end of parties."[11]

The deepening popular commitment to the Union war effort had thus taken on a political meaning; the Republican, or Union, party had accumulated a tremendous fund of moral capital. The war, in a sense that went much beyond ordinary national undertakings and ordinary party projects, was their war; the war principles were their pinciples; and, should those principles once more seem in any way endangered, there was every likelihood that the people's loyalty to them would be linked without question to support of the party. Never was loyalty to a party more fully and automatically identified with

[10] Gray, *Hidden Civil War*, pp. 172–74, 183–84; Alexander Flick, *Samuel Jones Tilden: A Study in Political Sagacity* (New York: Dodd, Mead, 1939), pp. 147–49; Stewart Mitchell, *Horatio Seymour of New York* (Cambridge, Mass.: Harvard University Press, 1938), pp. 366–72; see also Dunning, "Second Birth," p. 57.

[11] George F. Milton, *Abraham Lincoln and the Fifth Column* (New York: Vanguard Press, 1942), pp. 306–8; Gray, *Hidden Civil War*, pp. 197–98; *Harper's Weekly*, IX (Feb. 25, 1865), 114.

consensus on matters of public morality—never until the days of the Solid South, which represented the reverse end of the same process.

What were the prospects which now faced the parties in the peace-time setting of 1865? The future would hinge almost completely on the question of a policy for the defeated South. On that question, the parties would once more be driven very far apart, and at the same time each would achieve a considerable degree of internal solidarity. Such solidarity was to be apparent very soon in the case of the Democrats; with the Republicans it would take somewhat longer. The Republican party, being much the larger, and with its extremes thus separated by a greater distance, would have to move more slowly in coming to a definition of its middle ground. Another reason for the initially tentative quality of the Republicans' position on reconstruction was that the position of their nominal leader, the new President, was itself by no means free from ambiguities.

II RECONSTRUCTION AS CONSTRUED FROM THE PROCLAMATIONS

It has come to be assumed that the reconstruction policy which President Johnson eventually tried to carry out was, from the first, fully self-evident in his proclamations of May 29, 1865, and that one needed only to read the texts to discover exactly what that policy was. Yet neither the behavior of political parties nor the texts of the proclamations quite bear out this assumption; to thousands, the policy was not at all self-evident. We do more or less know that by May 29, when the two proclamations—the one on pardon and amnesty, and the other on provisional government for North Carolina—were issued, the President's intentions on the general subject of reconstruction had become fairly well fixed in his own mind. But it is very important to recall that this was not generally known at the time. Indeed, a good deal more tentativeness was read into executive plans than actually existed. There was thus a certain leeway for interpretation which may not have been warranted, as one sees from later developments, but which seemed to be encouraged by the President's somewhat lonely and taciturn habits. For a majority, this ambiguity was not to be fully dissipated for another eight or nine months. Not only might men differ over the wisdom of the policy; they could even differ over what it meant. Some were less quick to see its full implications than were others, and the very fact that there was for a time more than one way of interpreting the policy holds the key to much that is politically significant in the remaining half of 1865.

Three major subjects were dealt with in these proclamations. One was amnesty and pardon, a second was restoration of state governments to the Union, and the third, qualifications for officeholding and suffrage in the lately rebellious states.

The Amnesty Proclamation of May 29, which superseded those issued by President Lincoln in 1863 and 1864,[12] conferred "amnesty and pardon, with restoration of all rights of property, except as to slaves," to all direct or indirect participants in the rebellion who should take a properly registered oath to support all the laws of the United States, including those with reference to emancipation. Fourteen classes of persons were excluded from its benefits, among them being those former rebels whose taxable property was worth more than $20,000. The latter provision gave to the edict a note of sternness which Lincoln's proclamations had not contained, and the setting-forth of other exceptions—persons who had treated prisoners unlawfully, and persons then under civil or military confinement "for offenses of any kind"—appeared to provide assurances that ways would be kept open for punishing the most flagrant forms of treason. All such cases required direct individual applications to the President for pardon and were to be decided on their merits. The conditions of amnesty and pardon, then, as here set forth, constituted on the whole the least exceptionable and the least controversial of these three subjects.

The second major problem—that of how states were to be restored to the Union—was covered in the proclamations on reconstruction, the first of which was that for North Carolina. Here again, the language was sufficiently general that the spirit and intention, together with the mode of implementation, would have to emerge in practice before anything like a full and fair appraisal of the plan would be possible. The President appointed a provisional governor (named in the proclamation) whose duty it would be, "at the earliest practicable period," to arrange for a convention whose delegates would be chosen by the loyal people of the state. He was to have the assistance and co-operation of the military commander of that department. This convention would amend or alter the state's constitution, and it would have the authority

to exercise within the limits of said State all the powers necessary and proper to enable such loyal people of the State . . . to restore said State to its constitutional relations to the Federal Government and to present such

[12] Richardson, *Messages and Papers*, VI, 310–14, 213–15, 218. Lincoln's amnesties were primarily designed to undermine the Confederacy, that of March 26, 1864, being issued especially to prevent prisoners of war from claiming the rights of amnesty simply by taking an oath. See also below, chap. 6.

a republican form of State government as will entitle the State to the guaranty of the United States therefor and its people to protection by the United States against invasion, insurrection, and domestic violence. . . .

That the President looked to the ultimate restoration of these states could not be doubted. But then so did nearly everyone. The really important question was, how soon? There was ample ground, within the meaning of the text, for keeping the states out indefinitely. Or, the wording made it just as conceivable that the states might be fully reconstructed, that the dislocations of war might be rectified and the poisons of rebellion fully purged, before the year was out.

The third question dealt with in the reconstruction proclamations was that of officeholding and suffrage. It was at this point that a sudden glint of light could be said to have fallen across Johnson's plans and purposes, illuminating them for the hypercritical eye. But then no one could be certain. The voters who chose delegates to the conventions were to qualify under the state's laws of 1860, though they were also required to have taken the amnesty oath. This may not have been a sufficient guarantee against reimposition of the old status quo; still, without detailed and uniform prior understandings, any arrangements at that point other than those specified would probably have been tied up in such sheer mechanical detail as to delay immeasurably the process of constitutional revision. Actually the real sticking point, if there should be one, was that

the said convention, when convened, or the legislature that may be thereafter assembled, will prescribe the qualification of electors and the eligibility of persons to hold office under the constitution and laws of the State. . . .

It was here that any control over the questions of rebel disfranchisement and Negro suffrage, however they might in the end be decided, could very possibly pass out of federal hands once and for all. The Democrats, of course, would not in the least have objected to such an arrangement, but the Unionist would have had his second thoughts. From his viewpoint it might not be wise, this early, to eliminate the possibility of some federal discrimination in these matters. A good many strains had already been placed on the Constitution by Johnson's predecessor in waging the war; Johnson's own proclamations were exerting more; and the Constitution would probably not be stretched a great deal farther should the government retain for itself some say as to who should and who should not vote in the former rebel states.

And yet even this difficulty was one which a reasonable man might have seen as less real than theoretical. The Southern conventions, though the proclamations did not say so, would certainly be getting their cues directly from the President with regard to those enactments which would or would not be considered satisfactory, prior to any kind of restoration. A wide discretion would be retained; strong private pressure would be put upon the governors before, during, and after the conventions as Johnson, testing the winds of public opinion, would doubtless keep the Southerners accurately informed on how their proceedings were being viewed by the country at large. It could be assumed that Johnson during this period would not knowingly allow the rebel states to develop pretensions which would mobilize Northern Union sentiment en masse against them. Discretion and statesmanship would consist in guarding against all occasions for hostile feeling, so that an unprecedented set of problems might be managed with as little further upset as possible. As for Negro suffrage, most Union spokesmen and newspapers were already saying—and echoes of this were heard even in the South—that at least some token form of it was inevitable. There could be no more satisfying spectacle of Southern good faith, after all, than that of the states voluntarily enfranchising certain classes of their colored citizens. This would certainly be preferable to having the thing forced on the states by federal coercion. If all else failed, there was an ultimate guarantee. The undenied right of Congress to judge of its own membership, and thus to refuse seats to any who should not be deemed properly members, gave Congress a final veto on anything that the Southern states, before their final restoration, might do.[13]

President Johnson's program, then, as first revealed, seemed to provide ample ground upon which a wide diversity of opinions might meet and across which a middle-of-the-road position might be traced. The "middle of the road," that is, could be found if one were at all sure where the road itself lay.

History has not actually left us a very clear picture of the political landscape of 1865. The later triumph of radical recon-

---

[13] This line of reasoning was spelled out quite fully by the New York *Times* (June 15, 1865): "But it must not be forgotten that these enabling proclamations, and official appointments, are not final acts. A great deal has been said about the danger that the elections will be carried by those who are still inimical in spirit to the National Government. . . . Even so moderate, and liberally disposed, a man as Senator Sherman has expressed, in a speech just delivered, the fear of this in the strongest terms. We admit that there would be no security against this, if all the old constitutional powers were now to be restored *fully* and finally to the states. . . . But there is still a further protection, and one quite independent of the action or will of President Johnson. By the constitution each branch of Congress is made the exclusive judge of the qualifications of its own members."

struction in 1867, being in so many ways the high point of the entire postwar decade, has come to dominate every historical image that we have formed of the period as a whole. Somehow everything that happened from the end of the war now seems as though it ought to fit into a pattern of steady and logical progression toward the notorious consummation of 1867. For instance, during the six months from the end of May to December, 1865, there was not much purposeful organized political activity; yet we still tend to suppose that this six-month period must have been one of busy preparations within the Republican party for what was to come, with the Democrats standing more or less passively by. The evidence, however, does not quite warrant such a picture. If anything, it should be reversed, with the Democrats at the outset playing the more active role, and the Republicans the more passive.

The Democrats in mid-1865 had begun applying names to the Republicans which did not as yet fit, ascribing to them plans which they had not as yet laid, and predicting consequences which very few Republicans at this early date wanted to incur. The more "radical" these alleged designs might be made to appear, the greater of course would be the advantage that would accrue to the minority party. That many of these extreme predictions would ultimately come true gives them now an air of clairvoyance which at the time they did not really possess. Later reconstruction was hardly inherent in the Republican party policy of 1865; the Republicans during these months did not as yet have a policy. Most of them still assumed that whatever they might later evolve in the way of policy could be worked out quite satisfactorily within the pattern laid down by President Johnson.

So if we have unduly taken for granted a certain tightness and clarity of party positions here, it is to some extent historical hindsight that has coerced us into it. Taking another figurative look across the political countryside—say, on an early summer evening in 1865—we are struck to discover that the party battalions are not camped in quite the military order that later history has led us to expect. The Democratic bivouacs seem animated by a certain amount of bustle, but the far more numerous Republicans, disposed about the landscape in almost negligent array, do not really have the look of troops girding for fresh warfare. There are some stirrings of restlessness; a few of their scouts are out skulking in the twilight; but that is about all. Thinking ahead to the scenes that would be enacted a year hence, one could almost say that the field looks downright peaceful.

III THE RADICAL REPUBLICAN: THE MEANING
OF "RADICALISM"

The concept of "radicalism" is one with which the
history of the Civil War and reconstruction has played vexing tricks.
The term "radical" is, and was, legitimate enough. It was freely used
in the war years and even more freely in the era that followed; most
men had a fairly good idea what they meant when they used it, and
in a rough and ready way they recognized a radical when they saw
one. It once signified little more than the extreme position on any
given issue, one which men could and did move in and out of with
surprising ease.[14] Last year's "radical" could readily become this year's
"moderate," and vice versa.

Instead, we have subsequently come to picture a resolute band of
men, with set fanatical purposes ranging from abolition to protective
tariffs, moving abreast through an entire era. The radicals, according
to one historian,

steadily grew in power from the days when Garrison was ostracized and
Lovejoy murdered, until in 1867 they controlled Congress. A few earnest
men with fanatical perseverance had conquered a nation. With success the
objectives broadened, but Thad Stevens and Ben Wade led the same movement in 1867 that Lovejoy and Garrison had served thirty years earlier.[15]

Another writer says that after a four-year struggle with Lincoln this
revolutionary cabal then proceeded to turn upon Andrew Johnson:

Once again the Jacobins faced a hostile president. Once again they knew
they must fight the battle of reconstruction. But they felt no misgivings,
only a fierce joy. They had conquered Lincoln, they would conquer Johnson. With a grim confidence, they entered the savage years of the tragic
era.[16]

[14] This is essentially the reasoning of David Donald, in a recent essay which has
brought a strong note of good sense into this problem and has done much to check
the growth of an elaborate demonology. In "The Radicals and Lincoln," Professor
Donald deals with the Civil War phase of the radical myth. He fastens upon the
alleged relationship of men and principles and shows how difficult it is to draw a clear
line between a "radical" and a "conservative" policy on the waging of the war. The
radical position on one issue did not necessarily imply the radical position on any
other, and one looks in vain for the same men from issue to issue. See David Donald,
Lincoln Reconsidered: Essays on the Civil War Era (New York: Alfred A. Knopf,
1956), pp. 103–27.

[15] Howard K. Beale, *The Critical Year: A Study of Andrew Johnson and Reconstruction* (New York: Harcourt, Brace, 1930), p. 51.

[16] T. Harry Williams, *Lincoln and the Radicals* (Madison: University of Wisconsin
Press, 1941), p. 384. In this work it is assumed that an ultimate objective of the radical
"plan" (Negro suffrage, etc.) was to bring the South under a kind of economic vas-
salage to the powers of Northern industrial capitalism. "Thus a Southern bourgeoisie
would displace the ruling landed aristocracy, to make doubly sure that in the nation

One might imagine, then, that despite a general haziness elsewhere on the political scene the radical Republican of 1865 would have been a man with a perfectly clear sense of who he was and what he wanted. He was presumably a strong advocate of Negro suffrage; he wanted the Southern states excluded indefinitely from the Union; and he had already become the enemy of Andrew Johnson. Actually, however, the vagueness of all these issues was still so extensive that it permeated not only the party at large but the party's extreme fringes as well. Thus in trying to characterize the chronological pocket formed by the summer and fall of 1865, one must be governed by the fluid side, rather than the rigid side, of the "radical" concept. Radicalism was not then the focused affair that it later became; nor will it quite do to suppose that the "real" radicals were simply in hiding, a "hard core" of plotters waiting to throw off the mask and take over the country.[17]

There were certainly "radicals" in 1865, quite enough for us to require a special category for them. But they were radical for different objects and for different reasons; they should not be endowed with too much retroactive solidarity or sense of group purpose. We find no program, no unity, no "grim confidence," and certainly no "fierce joy." For anything more than a kind of irritable confusion, the evidence is extremely sketchy.

We do have a few letters—hardly more than notes—exchanged between Charles Sumner and Thaddeus Stevens.[18] Much has been made of them, but they contain little sign of a strategy. Stevens and Sumner between them hardly made a battalion, or even a platoon; they were not even in full agreement with each other; and no real predictions as to what would eventually be done about reconstruction could have been made from what either of these men said during this period. Nothing ever came of Stevens' confiscation schemes, and from Sumner's constant note of justice to the Negro no one could have foreseen

---

the forces of industrial capitalism would retain the favored position they had won in 1860." *Ibid.*, p. 9; for a similar viewpoint see Beale, *Critical Year*, pp. 229–30; and James G. Randall, *The Civil War and Reconstruction*, p. 748.

[17] Except in the sense, of course, that there is always someone, somewhere, who is plotting to take over the country.

[18] The extant letters of this period in 1865 from Stevens to Sumner are in the Sumner MSS at Harvard, and their rather meager contents are well known, having been quoted many times in print. Their dates are as follows, together with page references to full or partial quotations in Beale, *Critical Year*, Milton, *Age of Hate*, and Current, *Old Thad Stevens:* June 3 (Beale, pp. 63–64; Current, p. 211); June 14 (Beale, p. 64; Milton, p. 217; Current, p. 211); Aug. 17 (Beale, p. 64; Current, p. 213); Aug. 26 (Beale, p. 73; Milton, p. 227; Current, p. 214); Oct. 7 (Current, p. 217); and Oct. 25 (Beale, p. 67; Current, p. 218). There is one note from Sumner to Stevens, Aug. 20, 1865, Stevens MSS, Library of Congress (Beale, p. 67; Current, p. 214).

carpetbaggery. Sumner wrote letters everywhere, whose principal theme was "Alas! Alas!" But not much that is specifically practical shows up in either the letters or the replies. A clear and unquestionably radical voice heard at this time was that of Henry Winter Davis. Davis was a man of unusual talent but a man who would be dead within six months. In Boston there was a great deal of pro-Negro suffrage activity among upper-class philanthropic and humanitarian groups during the summer, but this does not appear to have had much direct connection with "radical" political strategy.[19] The Democratic newspapers applied the term "radicals" to the entire Republican party (just as Southerners would later apply it to all carpetbaggers) and accused them of plots to attack the President and subvert his policy. But a good many "radicals" kept reassuring themselves and one another, well into 1866, that Johnson stood upon sound Union principles. Meanwhile they attacked the Democratic party bitterly for scheming to get their President away from them.

With the issues of Negro suffrage, exclusion of the Southern states, and opposition to President Johnson, we come about as close as is possible to the issues that define "radicalism" for the summer of 1865. But that is still not very close. None of them, for this period, has more than a provisional usefulness.

Negro suffrage.—If the question were confined to what should be done in the South, it would be safe to say that a good majority of the entire Republican party favored some form of Negro suffrage. The

[19] Amos Abbott Lawrence wrote to President Johnson on July 1: "Some of the N. York newspapers have asserted that the recent meetings at Faneuil Hall and elsewhere are called by men of extreme views, to create an opposition to yrself and yr. administration. I will take the opportunity to assure you from my own personal knowledge that the reverse of this is the case. The discussion was started, & has been carried on with great propriety, by some of the best legal minds here, and the opinion is becoming fixed that under a republican govt. there should never be any disfranchisement owing to race. Many think that the higher the standard of qualifications required of the electors, the better it will be for all.

"All understood what yr position is, & some of its difficulties, & are desirous to support you in carrying out a doctrine which lays at the foundation of our govt. The fact that the negro vote of the Southn. States would be cast in sympathy with the old aristocracy does not alter this principle: & it may perhaps induce the latter to adopt it at a future time." A. A. Lawrence, Letterbook, July 1, 1865, Lawrence MSS, Massachusetts Historical Society. Both the Springfield *Republican* (July 1) and the Boston *Advertiser* (July 17) protested that the Faneuil Hall meetings had been managed by men of respectable and conservative views. It might be added that one of the leading spirits in the dissemination of Negro suffrage literature was George L. Stearns, proprietor of the *Advertiser*, who was at the same time a strong supporter of Andrew Johnson. The campaign strategy of the Republican party all through this period was probably more embarrassed than aided by the work of the Boston reformers. One wonders, indeed, whether this activity might not best be considered primarily as a kind of moral rearmament, rather than as political strategy per se. For an opposing view, see Beale, *Critical Year*, pp. 68–69.

party had, of course, its doctrinaires. There were those who promoted the issue primarily on grounds of principle: such men as Chief Justice Salmon P. Chase, Representative George W. Julian, Wendell Phillips, B. Gratz Brown, Horace Greeley, Carl Schurz, and Charles Sumner. There were others who saw Negro suffrage as a possible device for establishing some sort of Republican foothold in the South: Senators Jacob Howard, Benjamin F. Wade, and Henry Wilson, General Benjamin F. Butler, Representative George S. Boutwell, and former Representative Henry Winter Davis. Where "principle" left off and "expediency" began (or vice versa) would be difficult to determine. Unionists who lived in the South were already beginning to see that without Negro suffrage their own positions would be intolerable. There, the governing instinct was that of self-preservation.

Whatever the "motive," few suffrage advocates really had universal Negro suffrage in mind. They tended toward either a specific set of qualifications for Negro voters or a formula known as "impartial suffrage," which meant only that whatever the qualifications might be, they should apply equally to both races. This could come to much or little; it could mean almost anything and thus nothing in particular, so that together these positions represented something that a very wide range of temperaments could share in the months following the war's end. For example, both President Lincoln and President Johnson had suggested extending the vote to Negroes who could read and write, who had served in the army, or who had property. Among those who favored such a plan were the radical Senator Howard, the radical Chicago *Tribune*, and Horace Greeley's New York *Tribune*—even though, as Greeley put it, the plan "would probably not, for the present, enable one negro in a hundred—perhaps not one in five hundred—to vote."[20] "Give the emancipated negroes of the rebel states . . .

[20] "Now you are about to have a convention which among other things will probably define the elective franchise. I barely suggest for your private consideration whether some of the colored people may not be let in, as for instance the very intelligent and especially those who have fought gallantly in our ranks." Lincoln to Michael Hahn, Mar. 13, 1864. *Collected Works of Abraham Lincoln,* ed. Roy P. Basler (New Brunswick: Rutgers University Press, 1953), VII, 243.

"If you could extend the elective franchise to all persons of color who can read the Constitution of the United States in English and write their names, and all persons of color who own real estate valued at not less than two hundred and fifty dollars, and pay taxes thereon, you would completely disarm the adversary and set an example the other States will follow." Johnson to William L. Sharkey, Aug. 15, 1865, *Senate Executive Documents,* 39 Cong., 1 sess., No. 25, "Telegraphic Correspondence between the President . . . and the Provisional Governors," p. 229.

"We have never doubted that to the negro who had done his duty as a soldier in the Union army, the negro who could read and write, and the negro who had demonstrated his fitness to take care of himself by the acquisition of property, should have the ballot put into his hands. . . ." Chicago *Tribune,* June 20, 1865. On Howard, see below, p. 338; the New York *Tribune* editorial appeared on June 6, 1865.

the right to vote along with the whites," demanded the "conservative" New York *Herald*. "There need be no fear that this concession will lead to negro social equality."[21]

Carl Schurz insisted that "if any qualification can be found, applicable to both races . . . , such qualification would in that respect be unobjectionable."[22] Even Sumner was not at first prepared to demand unqualified suffrage. "What I especially ask is impartial suffrage," he was saying as late as February, 1866; ". . . I simply insist that all shall be equal before the law. . . . Education also may, under certain circumstances, be a requirement of prudence. . . ."[23] The old abolition crusader William Lloyd Garrison, on the other hand, was not a Negro suffrage advocate at all; nor, indeed, was Thaddeus Stevens.[24] At the same time, there were actually Southern conservatives who would have been quite willing to grant the freedmen a qualified—but impartial—suffrage.[25]

There were, however, substantial numbers of Northerners who could anticipate Negro suffrage in the South with perfect equanimity but who would not have promoted the same thing in the North with anything like the same enthusiasm. Here it was perfectly possible to keep two distinct sets of feelings in solution. On the one hand, a good majority of Unionists required visible proofs that their victory in war had made a difference, and since emancipation had become one of the war aims, a logical and fitting justice would require that political rights of some sort be conferred upon those former slaves most qualified to exercise them. This was taken very widely for granted immediately after the war. On the other hand, color prejudice in some form, in the

21 New York *Herald*, May 3, 1865. The *Herald*, Johnson's strongest supporter among the public prints, soon dropped this line, doubtless because Johnson himself showed no enthusiasm for it.

22 *Senate Executive Documents*, 39 Cong., 1 sess., No. 2, "Report of Carl Schurz on the States of South Carolina, Georgia, Alabama, Mississippi, and Louisiana," p. 43. See also above, n. 19.

23 *Congressional Globe*, 39 Cong., 1 sess., p. 685. "I wrote to Sumner," confided Francis Lieber to Senator Morgan of New York in October, 1865, "imploring him not to make the negro suffrage in any way a test question in Congress, because the thing is plainly impossible at present (I believe we could have got at one time [a] reading and writing test for *all*, had the chief [executive] insisted on [it] . . .)." Lieber to E. D. Morgan, Oct. 6, 1865, Morgan MSS, New York State Library.

24 Edward L. Pierce, *Memoir and Letters of Charles Sumner* (Boston: Roberts Bros., 1894), IV, 229. Stevens thought that Negro suffrage was inexpedient as a political issue in the North; moreover, as an instrument for governing the Southern states as conquered provinces, it struck him as rather inefficient. He appears, for example, to have sabotaged any effort to put Negro suffrage into the 1865 Pennsylvania Republican platform; moreover, in April, 1866, it was Stevens, as much as anyone, who scuttled the Negro suffrage guarantee in Robert Dale Owen's plan for a constitutional amendment. Stevens to Sumner, Aug. 26, 1865, Sumner MSS. See also below, chap. 11.

25 See below, pp. 209–10.

North as well as in the South, was all but universal. Republican politicians in the various Northern states were only too aware of this fact, and were not overly anxious to run afoul of it. The seemingly double standard implied in all this was probably not so very sinister, since there was little at that stage of things that anyone could do to change it, but it certainly made for ambiguity. At this soft spot the Democrats struck with all their might, making a political issue out of something that did not at first have the controversial sharpness that it later took on.

It was the resumption of partisan politics in the postwar setting that precipitated these two sets of feelings out of solution—justice to the Southern freedman as a national aim, and color prejudice as a local liability. For the Democrats, this prejudice was hardly a problem; it was in fact their greatest asset. All they needed to do was to keep it alive and exploit it in every way they could. Of all the aspects of reconstruction, the issue of Negro suffrage was the one upon which they could with clearest assurance take the initiative and catch the Republicans on their exposed flank. In this they had a fair degree of success. The Republicans were denounced as the "nigger party," and the fact that only six Northern states allowed the Negro to vote was thrown in their faces: the Republicans were at once fanatics and hypocrites.[26] Were the people really willing, demanded the Democrats, to enact universal suffrage?

The returning soldiers, to whom much of this was addressed, proved anything but hospitable to Negro voting. Three states, Connecticut, Wisconsin, and Minnesota, held elections in which amendments for extending the franchise equally to both races were referred to the people, and in all three elections the question was lost.[27] Republican conventions were held in ten Northern states during the summer and fall; the platforms of five included resolutions favoring equal suffrage; in the other five, such resolutions were omitted.[28] In short, as long as

[26] In five of these states (Maine, Vermont, New Hampshire, Massachusetts, and Rhode Island), no legal distinction was made on grounds of color. In the sixth (New York) colored citizens, to be voters, had to own a freehold worth $250. There is a summary of the state suffrage laws in the *Tribune Almanac for the Years 1838 to 1868 Inclusive* (New York: The Tribune, 1868), II (1866), 46–48.

[27] *The American Annual Cyclopaedia and Register of Important Events of the Year 1865* (New York: D. Appleton, 1869), V, 304, 577, 823 (hereafter cited as "*American Annual Cyclopaedia, 1865*"). The Wisconsin state Supreme Court, however, subsequently decided that Negroes had been given the franchise in a constitutional amendment ratified in 1848. *Ibid.*, p. 823.

[28] The states in which Republican resolutions were passed expressing favorable sentiments toward Negro suffrage were: Maine, Vermont, Massachusetts, Iowa, and Minnesota. Such resolutions were omitted in New York, New Jersey, Ohio, Pennsylvania, and Wisconsin. *Ibid.*, pp. 441, 523, 535, 577, 610, 614–15, 685, 692–93, 813, 822.

it remained a matter of Southern policy, there was little objection
anywhere in the Union party to the enactment of qualified suffrage;
but let it be forced to the test of consistency with Northern practice
and local prejudice, and a budding consensus would tend to break in
two. The result was a political hot potato.

Yet even after all this is taken into account, the fact remains that
Negro suffrage of some sort constituted a strong and widely held
position not confined to radicalism.[29]

Exclusion of the Southern states.—The search for a criterion by
which to identify radical sentiment in 1865 leads to still another possibility. This is the notion that the full benefits of restoration should,
under congressional authority, be withheld from the Southern states
for some indefinite period. But that is not much of a criterion either,
since it could be applied to virtually the entire Union party. There
were certain points upon which agreement throughout the party was
so broad that it could be more or less assumed. One such point was
that normality meant a restored Union, and the sooner this could be
brought about with safety (whatever that might mean), the better.
A second, however, was that readmitting the states immediately was
unthinkable; it was first necessary for Congress to deliberate. The
third point was implicit. Naturally Congress had the power to deliberate, and to make any decisions which might seem proper, on matters
of such universal concern. These notions were certainly challenged,
but not from within the party; the challenge was thrown down by the
Democats.

Within the broad formula of temporary exclusion and federal supervision there was much diversity of sentiment, from the mild to the
vindictive, even among those whom history has designated as radicals.
If the South were to be "punished," would the punishment apply to
individuals or to states? One "conservative" New York newspaper,
the *Times,* breathed hotly for the hanging of traitors; meanwhile the
"radical" New York *Tribune* repudiated punishment of individuals
and urged that all policy be characterized by conciliation and human-

---

[29] The most extreme test of this question for the Northern voter was whether he
wanted Negro suffrage in his own state's constitution. There are two ways of apprais-
ing the voting figures for the elections in which this test was made in 1865. One way
would be simply to observe that in two out of three cases the impartial suffrage
amendment was defeated by a comfortable margin. The other would be to note that
the numbers of those who favored such an amendment (though not in the majority)
were more than substantial. The figures are as follows:

Connecticut (Oct. 2, 1865)		*Wisconsin* (Nov. 7, 1865)		*Minnesota* (Nov. 7, 1865)	
Against	33,489	Against	55,591	Against	14,840
For	27,217	For	46,588	For	12,170
Majority	6,272	Majority	9,003	Majority	2,670

ity.[30] Ben Wade talked of "humiliating and destroying the influence of the Southern aristocracy";[31] Chandler, Stevens, and other extremists spoke in much the same vein. But just how the "humiliating" would be done was another matter. Wade called for reprisals against Confederate leaders (President Johnson's lurid language to the same effect was what had created Wade's initial enthusiasm for him);[32] Stevens and Winter Davis were strongly opposed to any such punishments. The concern of Stevens and Sumner was for states rather than individuals, but here their objectives diverged markedly. "State Suicide," for Charles Sumner, meant federal authority to impose Negro suffrage and guarantee equal rights; "Conquered Provinces," for Thaddeus Stevens, meant a thorough confiscation of Southern property and a revolutionizing of Southern society.[33] Military government, he thought, was a far more efficient way to accomplish this than Negro suffrage. Scarcely anyone in the Republican party, radical or otherwise, took Stevens' confiscation schemes seriously, or would then or later have anything to do with them.

If radicals were unanimous on the principle of excluding the South, so also were Republicans at large. But such a spirit of unanimity was little more than a negative spirit. It was not so much that they had a specific object for keeping the states indefinitely out; mainly it was a matter of general anxiety that those states might be let back in too soon.[34] Most Republicans, with or without vindictive feelings, took for granted that it was not prudent and not in the country's best interest to have Southerners participating just yet in national political affairs; nor was there any point at all, a mere matter of months after the war's close, in handing such a free bonus to the Democats. That view could be expressed quite as succinctly by a moderate as by a radical. "We all know," wrote the conservative Senator James W. Grimes of Iowa to one of his friends,

that the Democratic party desire and intend to coalesce with the returned rebels from the South. By that means, if they can succeed in distracting the supporters of the Government and secure a few Northern States, they hope to obtain control of the Government, and then will follow the as-

[30] New York *Tribune*, Apr. 11, 13, 1865; New York *Times*, Apr. 12, 16, May 5, June 5, 1865.

[31] Wade to Sumner, July 29, 1865, Sumner MSS.

[32] George W. Julian, *Political Recollections, 1840 to 1872* (Chicago: Jansen, McClurg, 1884).

[33] See below, chap. 5.

[34] "The great fault," Jacob Howard wrote to Sumner, "is *too great hastiness to* bring back the rebel states." June 22, 1865, Sumner MSS.

sumption of the rebel debt, the restoration of slavery under a less odious name, and the return of the leaders of the rebellion to power.[35]

Opposition to the President.—A final criterion to use in the effort to say what "radicalism" consisted of in the summer and fall of 1865 might be the early appearance of strong anti-Johnson feeling within the Republican party. Such feeling would presumably have sprung from the perception that Johnson, with his proclamations, had fore-stalled and undermined the freedom of action which Congress required but could not exercise until it met in December. Yet the May 29 proclamations were not quite the automatic danger signals to most Republicans—even to most radicals—that we now tend to think they were. The important thing was not what the proclamations said, so much as how, and in what spirit, they might be administered; this could only be determined by waiting to see what happened. The Chicago *Tribune*, for one, was quite willing to wait and see. When the proclamations were published, the *Tribune* observed that the President "does not disappoint public expectation," even though the door to a limited Negro suffrage had not been left as widely open as might have been hoped.

But throughout the North there will undoubtedly be a reasonably unan-imous, if not complete acquiescence in the line of policy that the President, in the exercise of his patriotic discretion, has adopted. There is, we believe, profound confidence in the sincerity of his anti-slavery opinions, and no man can deny to him the possession of full and accurate knowledge of the actual condition of the black man of the South, including his fitness and unfitness to be suddenly, after a life of bondage, invested with the rights and privileges, the responsibilities and duties of citizenship.[36]

Much the same sentiment was expressed by the New York *Tribune*:

Whether a safer, juster rule might or might not have been indicated, all good citizens must desire that the result should be general satisfaction, harmony and content. This country has had quite enough of internal strife, alienation and feud: its necessities no less than its interests demand the earliest and fullest establishment of concord, unity and fraternal sym-pathy.[37]

There were those, indeed, whose suspicions were excited almost at once. But their number seems to have been rather overestimated. The outright critics of President Johnson in the summer of 1865, even among men professing the most radical doctrines, were surprisingly

[35] Grimes to E. H. Stiles, Sept. 14, 1865, in William Salter, *The Life of James W. Grimes* (New York: D. Appleton, 1876), p. 280.

[36] Chicago *Tribune*, May 31, 1865.

[37] New York *Tribune*, June 20, 1865.

few; those who did criticize presidential reconstruction did so reluctantly; and such criticism almost never took the form of public attacks on the President. It would be misleading, moreover, to think of the President's enemies as simply lying low; most of his enemies did not as yet exist. Charles Sumner was certainly one of the early critics—though it was anxiety rather than malice that animated him; nor did Sumner yet suppose himself so fully alienated as to rule out another effort, made late that fall, to reach an understanding with the President.[38] George Julian claimed, years later, to have distrusted Johnson since well before the May 29 proclamations[39] (which would have made him virtually the original anti-Johnson man); yet Julian's influence was of a limited sort, and he seems to have communicated with almost no one of importance during those summer months. James M. Ashley, the arch-radical of Ohio who would eventually sponsor the resolution to impeach Johnson, told the people of Toledo in June: "In the interview I had with him . . . I formed the belief that the president desires earnestly to carry out the wishes of the Union men of the country."[40] Among the earliest and sharpest public criticisms of the President was that of Wendell Phillips; Phillips' words, however, were deplored even by men who shared his views on suffrage.[41] Carl Schurz, though at first alarmed by the North Carolina proclamation (a copy of which the President had shown him in advance), continued to assume throughout most of the summer that Johnson's mind remained open.[42]

[38] Pierce, *Memoir and Letters of Charles Sumner*, IV, 250–51, 267–68. An examination of Sumner's papers for this period seems to show that the Massachusetts senator did not succeed in rousing his correspondents to anything like the pitch of alarm which he himself felt.

[39] Julian, *Political Recollections*, p. 262.

[40] Springfield *Weekly Republican*, June 24, 1865.

[41] Speech to New England Anti-Slavery Convention, May 31, New York *Tribune*, June 1, 1865. Horace Greeley wrote a disapproving editorial two days after the speech. In October, George William Curtis of *Harper's Weekly* wrote sarcastically to Charles Eliot Norton, "Wendell Phillips, I hear, is coming to tell us that the rebels have conquered and that twice two this time make only three." The Springfield *Republican* compared Phillips unfavorably to Jefferson Davis: "Davis is a man of more courage and character; he has not only talked repudiation and treason; he has acted both." New York *Tribune*, June 2, 1865; Curtis to Norton, Oct. 15, 1865, Curtis MSS, Harvard College Library; Springfield *Weekly Republican*, June 10, 1865.

[42] It was with this assumption that Schurz undertook, at Johnson's invitation, his tour to investigate conditions in the South. The two men had been on good terms at Nashville during Johnson's military governorship, and Johnson on one occasion had put in a good word for Schurz with President Lincoln. They became alienated, however, after the Sharkey-Slocum affair in Mississippi and Johnson's frigid reception of Schurz upon the latter's return to Washington. *Speeches, Correspondence, and Political Papers of Carl Schurz*, ed. Frederic Bancroft (New York: Putnam's Sons, 1913), I, 258–76.

As for Thaddeus Stevens, he apparently never had very high hopes for Johnson's policy, though even he thought it well to caution Sumner: "While we can hardly approve of all the acts of the government we, must try to keep out of the ranks of the opposition."[43] Henry Winter Davis by mid-June was likewise taking a dim view of that policy. Davis expressed his fears publicly in a Fourth of July oration —adding, however, that he hoped they were without basis. Meanwhile such men as George Boutwell, Henry Wilson, and Jacob Howard were still expressing faith in the President.[44] Ben Wade and Ben Butler both lost their early confidence, though apparently not until some time in July, while from their kindred spirit, Zach Chandler, no word of censure against the latter's old comrade, Johnson, would be heard until the following year.[45] Large numbers of the old Boston anti-slavery circle, now promoting Negro suffrage, were at this time benevolently pro-Johnson.[46] Secretary of War Edwin Stanton, of later notoriety in the impeachment crisis, would continue to labor in behalf of harmony between Congress and the Executive well into 1866.

[43] Stevens to Sumner, Aug. 17, 1865, Sumner MSS.

[44] George S. Boutwell, *Speeches and Papers Relating to the Rebellion and the Overthrow of Slavery* (Boston: Little, Brown, 1867), pp. 378–79, and *Reminiscences of Sixty Years in Public Affairs* (New York: McClure, Phillips, 1902), II, 103–4; J. M. Howard to Sumner, July 26 and Nov. 12, 1865; Henry Wilson to Sumner, Sept. 9, 1865. These men were by no means ardent Johnsonites, but they continued to support him publicly on the "experiment" formula (see below, pp. 76–80). Howard wrote to Sumner on July 26: "Be mild with *Johnson*. I think—at least hope, his policy merely *experimental* till Congress shall meet. 'Twas *Lincoln's* lead." And on November 12: "I still have hope—confidence—that Mr. Johnson will stand with us. *There is no other place for him*." Sumner MSS.

[45] Before the May 29 proclamations both Wade and Butler had apparently been well pleased with Johnson. As late as June 30, Gideon Welles said in his diary that Wade, though dissatisfied, was "mollified and disinclined to disagree with the President." A letter to Sumner of July 29, 1865, however, makes Wade's disillusionment plain. Exactly how Butler felt about Johnson can only be conjectured from two letters exchanged between him and Wade in mid-July, wherein both express feelings of gloom but neither refers directly to the President. *Diary of Gideon Welles* (Boston: Houghton Mifflin, 1911), II, 438; Benjamin F. Butler, *Private and Official Correspondence* (privately issued, 1917), V, 617, 641. On the other hand, Butler was still assuring his fellow Republicans in September that Johnson's policy could be supported as "experimental." New York *World*, Oct. 2, 1865. See also Wilmer C. Harris, *Public Life of Zachariah Chandler, 1851–1875* (Lansing: Michigan Historical Commission, 1917), pp. 86–87.

[46] "It seems to me strange," wrote George William Curtis to Richard Henry Dana after Dana's vigorous "Grasp of War" speech at Faneuil Hall in June, "that your critics . . . do not see that the President is substantially acting upon the principle of the public safety which you lay down." July 13, 1865, Dana MSS, Massachusetts Historical Society. (See also below, chap. 5, n. 11.) William Henry Channing said very much the same thing. ". . . I agree with you entirely," he wrote, "in your estimate of President Johnson. He has not the shadow of a shade of a purpose to betray the cause of freedom. Let us stand by him and uphold his hand & so at once impel & guide him onward. He deserves it." Channing to Dana, July 13, 1865, *ibid.*

There were not many men whose suspicions of the President's plans, this early, were in pointed enough form to be expressed to others. Although such a group of anti-Johnson radicals existed, the setting in which these men might communicate with one another was so imperfect that it would almost be a mistake to think of them, at this time, as constituting a "group" at all. It was summer; Congress was not in session; Congress, as a sounding board and medium of communication on matters of national policy, was probably much more sensitive than the newspaper, the telegraph, or the writing of letters between politicians. There was not even much to write about; very little that was happening was of such a nature that it could not be read more than one way. The precise state of feeling throughout the party at large was still imperfectly known. There had as yet been few formal expressions of it, except through editorials and—later in the summer—the platforms of the Republican state conventions. The keynote of all such expressions was party unity and the importance of harmony with the President. Everyone agreed to that much, and if some were disturbed by afterthoughts, there was as yet no clear way of deciding what should be made of them. The party's leadership, on the question of reconstruction, had simply had no chance to organize itself; aside from fundamentals, no one was very sure just what the rest thought. As Jacob Howard put it, *"we can't tell till we get together & talk the thing over."*[47]

It was thus primarily suspicion, rather than a sense of purpose, that bound the early radicals together. Charles Sumner, who had conferred with the President a number of times before the latter issued his first proclamations, had gone home to Boston secure in the thought that on the subject of suffrage "there was [as he wrote to Chase] no difference between us."[48] Sumner was thus mortified when he read in the proclamation that such matters would apparently be left to the states. He flew to his writing desk and began imploring everyone to "help save the President."[49] It was not so much the ques-

[47] Howard to Sumner, July 26, 1865, Sumner MSS. Italics added. There is no denying that a certain malaise with regard to Johnson had pervaded the Republican party by December (see below, pp. 179–84); but it is important not to overrate this. It was not the same as sharp and purposeful opposition. Johnson could have made it evaporate at any time before then, and for some time afterward, with a word or a gesture.

[48] Sumner to Chase, July 1, 1865, Chase MSS, Pennsylvania Historical Society; Sumner to Wade, Aug. 3, 1865, Wade MSS, Library of Congress; Pierce, *Memoir*, IV, 245–46, 248 ff.

[49] Sumner to Chase, July 1, 1865, Chase MSS.

tion of what *was* to be done as the uneasy feeling that something ought to be done. "Is it possible," wrote Thaddeus Stevens on June 3, "to devise any plan to arrest the government in its ruinous course?" Wade wrote to Sumner: "I regret to say, that with regard to the policy resolved upon by the President I have little consolation to impart. To me, all appears gloomy. . . ." "I trust," wrote Henry Winter Davis, "you are not as I am in despair."[50] If these men had anything in common beyond what might be attributed to Republicans in general, it amounted to little more than marginal personal situations and idiosyncratic personal commitments—and not all of the same kind, either —which located them where they would be the first to have their nerves touched by one or another of the President's sayings and doings[51] There was almost a chance quality about these men, and a random unity at best. They were not members of a hard phalanx, but out-riders—skirmishers watching for shapes in the darkness and listening for noises in the underbrush. They perceived things, or thought they did, but about all they could signal to each other was simply that something was wrong.

There was to come a time, indeed, when the whole party would begin moving toward positions which only its early extremists once occupied, and in the three general directions just indicated: toward Negro suffrage, indefinite exclusion, and anti-Johnsonism. But this is

[50] Stevens to Sumner, June 3, 1865, Wade to Sumner, July 29, 1865, Davis to Sumner, June 20, 1865, Sumner MSS. Davis before his death may momentarily have changed his mind about Johnson, judging from a hint conveyed by J. M. Howard. "I learnt that Winter Davis has written [Wade] that he is getting more & more reconciled to Johnson & urges him [Wade] to forbear all attacks." Howard to Sumner, Nov. 12, 1865, Sumner MSS.

[51] An example might be found in the case of Henry Winter Davis, a man of conservative antecedents, whose radicalism was a direct function of his anomalous position as a border-state Republican. Davis was an extremely attractive and gifted man whose principal political liability was the precarious footing which he had in his home state of Maryland, despite the fact that by 1864, when he was defeated for re-election, he had become the most popular member of the House of Representatives. He was thus so located at war's end that his mind was prepared to strike immediately for what seemed the only alternative, both for himself and for his party: the creation of a substantial Negro electorate.

It is a pity that the materials on Henry Winter Davis are so slight. He was a man of extraordinary persuasive talents (his rhetorical style reads grandly, even today) who was literally cut down in his prime, meeting death by pneumonia in December, 1865. See William E. Dodd's article in *Dictionary of American Biography*, V, 119–21; *Speeches and Addresses Delivered in the Congress of the United States and on Several Public Occasions*, ed. J. A. J. Creswell (New York: Harper & Bros., 1867); and Bernard Steiner, *Life of Henry Winter Davis* (Baltimore: John Murphy, 1916). There is a moving description of Davis' funeral in the diary of Chief Justice Chase, who was one of the pallbearers (Chase MSS); Gideon Welles comments disapprovingly on Davis and on the impressive memorial service held for him in the House of Representatives. Welles, *Diary*, II, 438.

a long way from saying that these men "caused" such a movement, or even influenced it very much, except in a kind of *post hoc propter hoc* connection. Even Thaddeus Stevens' function in these later battles would be that of a day-to-day tactician, not basically that of a planner, and many men whom history would come to call "radicals" were not in this early group at all. If there were to be a real prime mover, a "causal agent," such a role would have to be played by the one man—Andrew Johnson—whose behavior was critical in anything and everything the party did.

What was it, then, that set the "radical" legend on its way? Once more a major clue might be found in the very necessities of political partisanship. For the Democrats, it would be of immense advantage if such a hard core of radical plotters could be postulated and then identified, and the Republican party be exhibited to the country as shot with fanaticism and disunity. The strategy was almost too perfectly made to order. The Democrats would brand the entire Republican party as the "radical" party and then select the most obvious, idiosyncratic, and most odious symbols of that party's depravity: *this* was the party that could shelter such men as these, and these were the men who were conspiring to shackle the South, fasten Negro suffrage upon the country, and ruin the President. Even now, Democratic newspapers declared, these efforts were cracking the party itself into factions. Less than a fortnight after Johnson's proclamations, the Philadelphia *Age* announced:

> It is now evident that a radical conspiracy has been entered into to embarrass the administration of President Johnson. The point of attack selected is his position upon the reconstruction and negro-suffrage question. Chief Justice Chase has abandoned his duties and is addressing mixed audiences of whites and blacks in the Southern States, upon this theme. Senator Sumner is contributing, as his share of the work, orations and letters. Wendell Phillips is openly declaring that strife and repudiation are preferable to such a settlement of the difficulties as is presented in the President's North Carolina proclamation.[52]

The New York *World* rejoiced that "the Republican party . . . as all men see, is splitting into factions on the reconstruction question, [and] on the negro suffrage question. . . ." "It does not matter that the breach is not declared," charged the Chicago *Times* in predicting that war would be made on the President. "Every intelligent observer knows that the party of the Sumners and Wades is marshaling its forces for assault, at the first moment of the meeting of congress, against the president's policy of restoration." On September 9 the

---

[52] Philadelphia *Age*, June 10, 1865.

Times announced "that President Johnson is not on the same train with the republican party, but is moving against it from an opposite direction, and that there will be a collision. This will involve the 'smashup' of the party."[53] The Democrats were of course predicting that which they most desired to see.

IV   THE DEMOCRATS AND RECONSTRUCTION

The results of the 1864 elections, combined with the triumphant outcome of the Civil War, had placed the fortunes of the Northern Democratic party at the lowest ebb to which they had sunk in many years. This turn of affairs, occurring in the last year of the war—during which time the party had staked its future on peacemaking—had made it possible, as we have seen, for the Republicans to garner all the immense moral fruits of the Union victory. At a critical turning point, the Democrats had more or less consciously turned over the responsibility for the war to Lincoln's party, thus divesting themselves, as it later turned out, of the credit for the war's successful conclusion. It was thus understandable that by the summer of 1865 the "Copperhead" aspect should have become irrevocably stamped upon the Democratic party at large.

At war's end, the Democrats had a minority in Congress of less than a third, and a Democratic administration in only one of the Northern states.[54] Thus, looking at the party's position simply in terms of its own institutional well-being, it is not difficult to see that the true policy for the future was marked out with bright simplicity. From the viewpoint of both practical results and viable issues, everything depended on restoring the Southern states just as quickly as possible. There was probably not a single Democratic newspaper, not a Democratic politician, not one Democratic organization in any state, that

---

[53] New York *World,* July 18, 1865; Chicago *Times,* July 12, Sept. 9, 1865.

[54] The 1864 elections had greatly increased the Republican majorities. Whereas in the House of Representatives the balance had stood at about three to two in the 38th Congress, the new House, with a Republican gain of over thirty seats, showed a preponderance of well over three to one. In the Senate, where smaller numbers meant that a greater difference could be made by the switching of a few votes, there was less security for the Republicans even though their preponderance, in percentage terms, was greater. There, the ratio of Republicans to Democrats in the 38th Congress was about three to one; in the 39th, four to one. These ratios would of course be altered by the scattering of quasi-independents—the "Americans" and "Old Whigs" of the 38th Congress, and the "Johnson Republicans" of the 39th—depending on which way they voted on any given issue. For the critical issues, this latter group would be at the disposal of the Democrats. See James G. Blaine, *Twenty Years of Congress: From Lincoln to Garfield* (Norwich, Conn.: Henry Bill, 1884), I, 316, 500–501, II, 118–20; also *Tribune Almanac,* 1865, p. 18, 1866, pp. 24–25. The only state government still in Democratic hands in 1865 was New Jersey, and the fall election would bring a Republican administration to that state also.

failed to recognize this instantly.[55] The party stood as a unit, according to the Indianapolis *Sentinel,* for the "immediate restoration of the late rebel States to their former relations to the general Government. . . ."[56] The National Democratic Committee asserted on July 3 that the great host of Democrats—who would have swept the previous election had it not been for certain "extraneous influences"—was still organized and ready to act. The address continued: "Add to these the numbers then estranged [meaning the Democrats in the Confederate states] by causes now obsolete, and there can be no doubt that . . . the majority will be overwhelmingly with us."[57] And (more pointedly) from the New York *World:* "RESTORATION—OUR PRIME POLITICAL NECESSITY."[58]

Dovetailing with this "prime political necessity" was the fact that no set of principles emitted by the Democratic party could include positive claims of credit for the war's success. The appeal would have to be pitched on at least three planes. One was that of the Constitution: strict construction and states' rights. Besides inexcusable extravagance in waging war, the federal government had flouted the Constitution in letter and spirit by augmenting its own powers and invading the liberties of individuals. With regard to states' rights, according to Democratic party policy, the only "state right" not now existing in full vigor was the right to secede. "This and this alone," insisted the Detroit *Free Press,* "has been decided by the war, and it is the voice of the nation which declares it. But in no particular has the status of the States, or the rights reserved to the States by the constitution been altered or impaired, and every right they have ever been entitled to, they can still demand and exercise." The states, consequently, had never legally been out at all. "The Democratic party," asserted the Philadelphia *Age,* "always contended that these States were not, except in a revolutionary sense, out of the Union."[59]

On another plane, it was necessary to stir men's prejudices. The like-

[55] Every Democratic state convention held that summer had a "restoration" plank in its platform. The Ohio resolution may serve as an example:

"*Resolved,* That their ordinances of secession being void, the so-called seceded States are in the Union as States, and are therefore entitled to all the reserved rights of the States, and to their due representation in Congress, and to vote at future elections of President and Vice-President; and any attempt of the General Government, or any department thereof, to deprive them of these rights, would be an assault upon the rights of every State in the Union, and an effort to overthrow the Government ordained by the Constitution." *American Annual Cyclopaedia, 1865,* V, 685.

[56] Indianapolis *Sentinel,* July 22, Sept. 4, 1865.

[57] "Address of the National Committee to the Democracy of the United States," quoted in Detroit *Free Press,* July 12, 1865.

[58] New York *World,* July 15, 1865.

[59] Detroit *Free Press,* June 11, 1865; Philadelphia *Age,* June 14, 1865.

liest way to dissolve any potential consensus on the Negro suffrage question was simply to invoke white supremacy. To the extent that Republicans looking at the South may have inclined to see their party's safety dependent on Negro enfranchisement, so, inversely, did it seem vital to the Democrats that such enfranchisement be at all costs denied. "The supremacy of the White race" was a doctrine shared by all Northern Democrats.[60]

On still a third level, the appeal was directed to the loftier sentiments of magnanimity and forgiveness toward the South. Few reached quite the delicacy of feeling on this point that was attained by Charles Mason, chairman of the Democratic National Committee:

> The erring members of our political family [he wrote] are now anxious to resume their wonted places in the social circle. Let them be welcomed as was the prodigal son in the parable and received back with all their rights and privileges unabridged. Let the promptings of resentment or revenge meet no favor from those who may perhaps feel that they need some forgiveness themselves. Let statesmanship and not childish animosities control our conduct.[61]

The keynote, in short, must be forgiving and forgetting.

The people of the country had seen President Johnson take hold of the problem of reconstruction, which was evidence at least that something was being done. Nor did it appear that any doors were as yet irrevocably closed against Republican hopes. But for those Republicans most sensitive to the various possible alternatives, the policy could not very well have brought much certainty. At the same time, that which to Republicans meant uncertainty was to the Democrats an undreamed-of and providential boon. They would have nothing at all to lose by exploiting the promise which Johnson's policy seemed to hold forth to them. Just as the extreme radicals reacted to it in accordance with their worst fears, so those fears, turned inside out, corresponded exactly with the best hopes of the entire Democratic party.

The proclamations were received by the Democrats with unconcealed glee, and it was not long before their newspapers were giving the President fulsome assurances of support. "His recent proclamation

---

[60] The formula is quoted from the 1865–66 prospectus of the Democratic Indianapolis *Sentinel*, Sept. 4, 1865. Cf. also the resolution passed in the Vermont Democratic state convention on June 27, 1865: "That believing, with the immortal Douglas, that the Government of the country was organized for, and should be controlled by, the white race therein, and that the good of all will be promoted by confining the right of suffrage to the white citizens thereof, we are unalterably opposed to conferring the right of suffrage upon the ignorant negroes of the country." *American Annual Cyclopaedia, 1865*, V, 812.

[61] Detroit *Free Press*, July 12, 1865.

regarding reconstruction in North Carolina," announced the Cincinnati *Enquirer* on May 31, "shows that Mr. Johnson has set his foot down against permitting the negroes having anything to do with putting the State governments into operation." Of the seceded states, the Philadelphia *Age* exclaimed, "President Johnson says they *never were out*, thus fully endorsing our position. . . ."[62] Within two weeks the Detroit *Free Press* was pointing out how much more cheerfully Johnson was being supported everywhere by Democrats than by Republicans—insisting, however, that the Democrats were animated by no crass motives ("They are the eagles of the nation, soaring far above the scramble for government pap") and affirming, "This support is given purely on principle."[63] But when the Republican press began taunting the Democrats about their true designs, some of the Democratic newspapers coolly abandoned all pretenses. "The more strongly the Democracy are charged with southern sympathies," declared the New York *World*, "the less surprise ought to be felt by their accusers, that they wish to strengthen their party by the aid of Southern votes." Then turning the taunt against the Republicans, the *World* demanded, "Why *should* they [the Republicans] approve a policy which is certain, if successful, to bring their political opponents into power?"[64]

Democratic politicians, with fresh hopes and a new lease on life, were stimulated into activity. Numbers of them began calling upon the President and coming away very agreeably impressed. Congressman Adam Glossbrenner of Pennsylvania assured Jeremiah Black (though with "few details that ought to be given in a letter") that his impressions were "most comfortable as to the condition of things, politically, in and around the White House."

The faces in the ante-chamber of the President look very much as they would if a Democratic administration were in power. There was the old Quaker Congressman, Sykes of New Jersey—and Skelton, of the same

[62] Philadelphia *Age*, June 9, 1865.

[63] Detroit *Free Press*, June 10, 1865.

[64] New York *World*, Sept. 11, Sept. 12, 1865. The *Enquirer* also baited the Cincinnati *Gazette* in more or less the same tone: "The Southern States are all in the Union, *they have never been out*, 'they could not secede.' They will be represented both in the Senate, in the House, on the Bench, in the Cabinet, in the Army, in the Navy, and in foreign Courts. Yes, Mr. *Gazette*, all these things are fast coming, and you and your fanatical party will like your tory ancestors, be banished from power for at least a century." Cincinnati *Enquirer*, Sept. 2, 1865. Earlier the *Enquirer* had replied to the Cleveland *Herald*: "Now if the editor . . . really supposes that the Democratic leaders are studious to conceal the fact that they desire to bring their party into power in the State and in Congress, he must certainly be a very remarkable individual. . . . We shall . . . be compelled to confess that thus far the *Herald* is correct in its conjectures, though we fail to see the acuteness which it imagines itself to have displayed in making its discovery." *Enquirer*, July 7, 1865.

state—and George W. Jones, of Tennessee, with a pardon in his pocket—Senator Harris of N.Y. and Senator Browning, of Tenn., both said to be entirely with the President on negro suffrage in the reorganized or reorganizing states—and scores of others who are "of us."

The feeling in Washington, Glossbrenner reported, was "that every prominent Democrat who can do so ought to call promptly upon the President." Charles Mason, emerging from "a long and very satisfactory interview with the President," urged the same course upon Black, saying, "I believe he is strongly inclined to return to the true fold," and, "He is outspoken on the subject of State rights & old fashioned democracy." Mason also wrote his impressions to George Jones, former Democratic governor of Iowa, who in turn reported them to former President James Buchanan:

Judge Chs. Mason late Comssr. of Patents writes me from Washn. under date of the 22nd inst, that he & other demc. friends had had an interview with the Prest, & that Orr of S. Carolina late Speaker H.R., Gov Perry & others, also, had & that they all came off much gratified at the views expressed by the Chief Magistrate, who said that "this country never could be governed, successfully, except by the democratic party & that he (J) was then as he always had been & as he intended to continue to be a democrat & nothing else." Judge Mason thinks that "we should not, indeed, that *we cannot afford* to quarrel with the President."[65]

The Blair family, cut adrift from the Lincoln administration, had by this time virtually returned to the Democratic party. They were now busily cultivating the President, besieging him with advice, and seeking to solidify Johnson sentiment, in the hope of mending their own political fortunes. "If we support the President," wrote Montgomery Blair to Jeremiah Black, "in his great aim to restore the Union & the Constitutional representation of the South we shall have the Govt. as it was with all its checks and balances. Hence I make little account of . . . Joe Holts or Edwin Stantons or Wm. H. Sewards even[,] compared to the great measure of securing a restored representation of the people who will make short work of these worthies & call them to a dread account for their doings too."[66] The New York chiefs, Samuel J.

[65] A. J. Glossbrenner to Jeremiah Black, June 23, 1865, Mason to Black, June 14, 1865, Black MSS, Library of Congress; G. W. Jones to Buchanan, July 30, 1865, Buchanan MSS, Pennsylvania Historical Society.

[66] M. Blair to J. Black, Aug. 5, 1865, Black MSS. The Blairs were, as most students of this period know, mighty intriguers. From the letters preserved in the Johnson and Blair collections we cannot pretend to specify in precise detail the extent of their designs at this time, but there are certain general lines that can be made out: (1) that they labored to get Frank Blair appointed as Secretary of War (which would of course have required Johnson to get rid of Stanton); (2) that all three of the Blairs, now as Democrats, had attached themselves to Johnson's orbit, just as Francis P., Senior, had

Tilden, Dean Richmond, and Samuel L. M. Barlow, were all in direct or indirect touch with Montgomery Blair and were quickly convinced of the great wisdom of supporting Johnson. "We want to say to the President earnestly and frankly," wrote Barlow to Blair, "that the whole party is today a Johnson party."[67] John Van Buren, another New York leader, also publicly announced his support in a letter to the Grand Sachem of the Tammany Society.[68] Barlow disclaimed any designs upon the federal patronage, or any intention by the New York Democracy of suggesting new cabinet members. All he hoped was that the Democrats might "suggest those who *should not* be appointed" and that Johnson would not use the patronage (especially that of the Custom House) *against* the Democrats.[69] In any event, the support of the New York Democratic convention in September was not extended blindly, for Blair was turning Barlow's letters over to the President, and prior to the writing of the resolutions (which was done in the office of the *World*), Tilden had called upon Johnson and "returned satisfied."[70]

Meanwhile Johnson himself was receiving letters from Democrats everywhere, letters which contained not only assurances of support but also broad hints that he might as well, in view of his policy, abandon all pretense of staying with the Republicans and return to his old Democratic brethren. "The old Democracy of this region," wrote Congressman John Hogan from St. Louis, "not only acquiesce [in], but fully endorse, your course." It was a course, as Hogan understood it, "for bringing back the Southern States, with as much of the man-

---

done to Andrew Jackson's a generation before; (3) that they had ready access to Johnson (they had in fact been his hosts at their Silver Spring, Md., estate); and (4) that Montgomery Blair felt he knew enough to give assurances to his political associates concerning the President's intentions (as he did to Mason in the case of the military commissions). Montgomery's close working with the New York Democratic organization, and the fact that a good number of the letters he received from its leaders ended up in Johnson's hands, may not indicate anything sinister. But it does seem to show that these men were by no means in the dark as to each other's plans and aims. Letters in the Johnson collection in the Library of Congress, in addition to those cited below, which bear on this relationship are: S. L. M. Barlow to M. Blair, June 15, 1865; M. Blair to Johnson, June 16, 1865; F. P. Blair, Sr., to M. Blair, June 22, 1865; F. P. Blair, Sr., to Johnson, Aug. 1, 1865; T. G. Pratt to Johnson, Aug. 21, 1865.

[67] S. L. M. Barlow to M. Blair, July 24, 1865, Johnson MSS.

[68] New York *World*, July 6, 1865.

[69] S. L. M. Barlow to Thomas G. Pratt, Aug. 17, 1865, Barlow to Pratt, Aug. 21, 1865, Barlow to M. Blair, Sept. 11, 1865, Johnson MSS.

[70] Barlow to M. Blair, Sept. 11, 1865, Johnson MSS. "If half of what we hear is true," wrote the Albany correspondent of the Democratic New York *Sunday Mercury*, "certain Democratic leaders occupy relations with the President entirely too intimate to suit the party that elected him." Quoted in New York *Tribune*, Aug. 28, 1865.

hood of the people retained, as is possible," and it was being carried out "with you—a Democrat—in the lead." D. A. Ogden, a Democratic politician of upstate New York, wanted to know

whether it is possible with your antecedents, your confirmed political principles, to fraternize with the Republican party and its federal tendencies. The Democratic party is your life long party and now is the time to lead it, to give effect to its great and good principles, and to bring about yourself and administration a power which will ensure and render success certain.

"The Democracy of the North," advised the old Jacksonian, Duff Green, "look to the South to reinstate them in power." Johnson's best hopes of re-election lay in exploiting this fact: "If you so act, towards the South, as to command their confidence and support you will carry the Democratic party and unite the North West and South in your support and secure an overwhelming majority."[71]

Johnson's course, then, gave great cheer to Democrats everywhere. This was particularly true of those who, during the war, had left least doubt about their peace sentiments. With grand understatement, Lewis D. Campbell of Ohio informed Johnson: "Bitter as have been the Butternuts here, the most intelligent of them declare their purpose to sustain your administration if it moves on as it has commenced."[72] Three days after Campbell's letter was written, the most distinguished "Butternuts" of the state assembled in high spirits at the Democratic party convention. The intrepid Vallandigham was chosen to preside; Allen G. Thurman headed the Committee on Resolutions; and the main address was delivered by George H. Pendleton. The party's objectives were stated and restated many times during the proceedings. Foremost among them, as Vallandigham announced, was restoration, and all the speakers invoked the Constitution to show that "the ordinances of secession were invalid for every purpose." "He who tells you," proclaimed Vallandigham, "that he is against the return or restoration of

[71] John Hogan to Andrew Johnson, June 19, 1865, D. A. Ogden to Johnson, July 25, 1865, Duff Green to Johnson, June [?], 1865, Johnson MSS.

[72] L. D. Campbell to Andrew Johnson, Aug. 21, 1865, Johnson MSS. "Butternut" was one of the synonyms used in the Middle West for "Copperhead." The Copperhead New York *Daily News*, organ of the brothers Benjamin and Fernando Wood, said of the President in an editorial entitled "Andrew Johnson's Opportunity": "The Democracy wait with open arms to receive him into their councils, and to inscribe his name upon their banners as one of their co-workers in the great revolution that is at hand. He is sure of their earnest and united support in carrying out a policy that aims at the full and immediate restoration of the Southern States . . . , and with that support, he can laugh defiance at Radical cabals and intrigues. That he intends to break away from Black Republican influences is a foregone conclusion in the minds of those who have had opportunities to read his purposes. . . ." Quoted in New York *Tribune*, Sept. 2, 1865.

the seceded states to the Union for five, ten, fifteen, thirty years, or any indefinite period, is a disunionist, and ought to be denounced as such." A second aim was to denounce Negro suffrage, which everyone did, and the party's nominee for governor, General George W. Morgan, gave the convention a seething white-supremacy oration, similar to one he had delivered a few weeks earlier at a Fourth of July celebration, at which time he had proved that the Declaration of Independence had not made all men free and equal. General Morgan urged this as the theme for a reconciliation between civilian Democrats and those who had served in the army: the latter had gone forth "to sacrifice life and limb in defense of the Constitution and Union, but not of the nigger." Appropriate to these objectives were sentiments of charity and kindliness toward the South. "Magnanimity is good policy," said the standard-bearer, "in peace and in war, and a party incapable of magnanimity is unworthy of being trusted with power."[73]

The great hope, restoration, with its sub-themes—the Constitution strictly construed, white supremacy, and magnanimity to the ex-Confederates—were all embodied in the platform, together with the recognition that support of Johnson was essential to their fulfilment. As Pendleton told the delegates that evening:

President Johnson has done well in this, that he recognizes the powers of the States over the question of suffrage; that he appoints as Provisional Governors the citizens of the States, and not superserviceable patriots from Ohio or Massachusetts—that he desires the States to resume their relations to the Federal Government as soon as possible, and to be represented in both Houses of Congress—and on those points I desire to give him a cordial and hearty approval.[74]

On those same points, every Democratic convention, in every state where one was held that year, also gave to President Johnson a "cordial and hearty approval." For Johnson, beyond all question, was proving a godsend to them. "It is hardly a superstitious fancy," wrote the industrious Mason, "which regards him as having been specially ordained for this great and glorious mission. The designs of Heaven begin now to be visible throughout."[75]

[73] The proceedings of the convention were fully reported in the Cincinnati *Enquirer*, Aug. 25, 1865. The *Enquirer* in this same number printed choice excerpts from General Morgan's Fourth of July oration, delivered at Mt. Vernon, Ohio, on Negro inferiority. The most important of the Ohio convention's resolutions may also be found in *American Annual Cyclopaedia, 1865*, V, 685-86.

[74] Cincinnati *Enquirer*, Aug. 25, 1865.

[75] "Address of the National Committee to the Democracy of the United States, July 3, 1865," quoted in Detroit *Free Press*, July 12, 1865.

Such were the circumstances in which the prospects of the Democrats had taken—or so it seemed—such a sudden and unexpected turn for the better. From their viewpoint, the President had imparted a strong note of legitimacy to the party's principles. Yet the final balance, so far as principles went, was not really in their favor after all. It is true that the Negro-suffrage implications of the Republican position had given the Democrats something vulnerable to probe. But in other respects the latter could not be said to have held the moral initiative. Republican principles could be personified and objectified in ways that touched the experience of a nation in agony: the boys in blue, the flag, the Union, and the martyred Lincoln. The shrines and memorials that came to be erected at every crossroads village were symbols of sacrifice that the Democrats could not claim; politically, the vacant chair and the empty room upstairs were beyond their reach. The military and political fortunes of war had made all these symbols invulnerable and had delivered them into Republican custody. It was this that had made political and moral authority so inseparable and had committed them so fully into Republican keeping.

The enemy had likewise been personified, objectified, and given a political being; and here again the Democrats' position was essentially a defensive one. The enemy lived on in the image of the rebel slaveholder and now gained new malignancy from the stories of unrepentant secessionism. But the enemy would also be embodied, unavoidably, in the followers of the Democratic party. Secessionist principles had come to be identified with the local Copperheads; community after community, in the Middle West especially, had been torn apart by the presence of these people, and bitterness would continue to smolder for many years. So even the protocol of magnanimity, the note of forgiving and forgetting, so far as the Democrats took the initiative in invoking it, was sure to be struck off key; its very origin was self-discrediting. All this was bound to affect the appeal of the Democratic party.

Thus it must have been rather hard for the Unionist of, say, the Ohio Valley to keep reading in the Cincinnati *Enquirer* that the war had been a waste of money. Union men were as ill-disposed as anyone, there or elsewhere, toward the thought of intimate social and political transactions between themselves and colored men. But their receptivity to the notion of Negro rights might still have reached whatever maximum was possible as they listened to Vallandigham proclaiming Negro inferiority, on the one hand, and denouncing white men's loss of personal liberty, on the other. Conversely, their feelings of generosity toward the late enemy could not have been much quickened by the honeyed words of the *Enquirer:*

There is, thank God! however, another organization, a great and mighty party which . . . does remember the past with pleasure, surveys the present with sorrow and regret, and is endeavoring to make the future bright and cheerful to our unfortunate and depressed countrymen. . . . They have no taunts for the unfortunate, no derision for the fallen, and no exultation over any portion of our people. In this hour of darkness and gloom, so oppressive and saddening to our Southern brethren, we should remember that magnanimity is always the accompaniment of the patriot and christian.[76]

The first test of the Democrats' appeal was the fall elections of 1865, in which they sustained heavy losses everywhere.[77]

V   THE "MODERATE UNIONIST" AND JOHNSON'S
SOUTHERN "EXPERIMENT"

There was a considerable body of Republicans in good standing—pillars of the party and high in its councils—who were recognized generally as men tending by nature and practice toward the conservative solution of almost any given problem. Their "moderation" at this time, fully recognized as such, consisted in the advocacy of temperance and compromise, the deploring of excess, and, most specifically, the readiness to support and stand by President Johnson in his work of reconstruction. Prominent among them were Senators Lyman Trumbull of Illinois, James W. Grimes of Iowa, William Pitt Fessenden of Maine, Edwin D. Morgan of New York, William M. Stewart of Nevada, and John Sherman of Ohio. In the House of Representatives were James Garfield, John Bingham, and Rutherford B. Hayes of Ohio, James G. Blaine of Maine, Henry L. Dawes of Massachusetts,

[76] Cincinnati *Enquirer*, July 1, 1865.

[77] Gubernatorial elections were held in eight states, with the Republican candidate winning in every case, as follows: Maine: Samuel H. Cony re-elected over James Howard, 53,449 to 31,117; Massachusetts: Alexander H. Bullock defeated Darius N. Couch, 69,912 to 21,245; Vermont: Paul Dillingham defeated Charles N. Davenport, 27,586 to 8,857; New Jersey: Marcus L. Ward defeated Theodore Runyon, 67,522 to 64,731; Ohio: Jacob D. Cox defeated George W. Morgan, 223,633 to 193,697; Wisconsin: Lucius Fairchild defeated Harris C. Hobart, 58,332 to 48,330; Iowa: William M. Stone re-elected over Thomas H. Benton, 70,445 to 54,070; Minnesota: W. R. Marshall re-elected over Henry M. Rice, 17,335 to 13,864. In New York, the highest office contested was that of Secretary of State, and Francis Barlow (R) defeated Henry W. Slocum (D) for that office, 300,254 to 272,793. The Republicans similarly won the auditor-generalship in Pennsylvania, J. F. Hartranft defeating W. W. H. Davis, 238,-400 to 215,740. Elections for county officers and state legislatures in Illinois, Indiana, Kansas, and California all resulted in substantial Republican majorities. See *American Annual Cyclopaedia, 1865,* V, under the states named; also *Tribune Almanac,* 1866, pp. 53–63.

and Elihu Washburne of Illinois, to mention only several—all of whose conservatism at this period was quite above reproach. Other warm supporters of the President and advocates of moderation were governors John Andrew of Massachusetts and Oliver P. Morton of Indiana. In the President's cabinet—occupying middle ground between Stanton on the one hand and Welles, McCulloch, and Seward on the other—were Postmaster-General William Dennison, Secretary of the Interior James Harlan, and Attorney-General James Speed, whose loyalty to the President was unimpeachable. There were public men in other capacities who tendered the President their support: there was Henry Ward Beecher, pastor of Plymouth Church, Brooklyn, and there were such influential publishers and editors as Samuel Bowles of the Springfield *Republican*, George L. Stearns of the Boston *Advertiser*, John W. Forney of the Philadelphia *Press*, Charles A. Dana of the Chicago *Republican*, George William Curtis of *Harper's Weekly*, and E. L. Godkin of the New York *Nation*, to name only the most prominent.

The views of these men were very diverse. At first some, like Oliver Morton, opposed Negro suffrage, though most of them were firm believers in some form of suffrage, several very emphatically so. There was little agreement on the precise nature and extent of the President's powers, though all assumed that the final say on reconstruction rested with Congress. On this point, most of them made known their opinions in terms that were unmistakable. As for restoration of the Southern states and admission of the Southern members-elect, most of them in principle looked to as early a restoration as was decently possible—some sooner, some later. Not one of these men, however, felt that it was proper or safe, as yet, to admit Southerners to seats in the United States Congress.

There were certain general points upon which this group—representing the great majority of the party in 1865—was fully united. One was their settled intention to "preserve the fruits of victory": to exact guarantees (whatever form they might take) of security and future loyalty from the Southern states, before restoring them to full status in the Union. Another point of consensus was their determination that the solidarity, power, and predominance of the Republican party should be maintained with the utmost energy. The final ground which they all occupied was their provisional willingness—as the wisest and most reasonable mode of approaching these objectives—to support President Johnson. But since every single one of them would eventually turn against him, perhaps the really basic question is how the Republican party could ever have supported Johnson at all. The answer must somehow be found in the lengths to which parties as a whole have been willing to go, and the breadth of the formulas which they have been willing to accept, on those occasions when party unity is at a very special premium. Here was just such an occasion, and a formula was ready at hand. It was a kind of rug under which many divergent hopes and fears and conflicting views could for a time be swept, and in the name of unity it was invoked again and again. The formula was this: the President's policy *"is, after all, but an experiment."*[78]

Conceiving Johnson's work on reconstruction between sessions of Congress as "experimental" enabled hosts of Republicans to calm their misgivings, and those of others, with the thought that the presidential mind was being deliberately kept open and that final decisions of policy were being held in suspension. Held also in suspension, therefore, could be the widest range of expectations, and as long as men could be persuaded to think of the policy as an "experiment" (to be readily abandoned if unsatisfactory), neither Negro suffrage nor exclusion of the South nor, indeed, the most rigid policy of military occupation need have been considered incompatible with support of the President.[79] "I don't intend," wrote Charles A. Dana, "to be a party to any arrangement of the Southern States which shall leave justice out of view." He continued:

Loyal negroes must not be put down, while disloyal white men are put up. But I am quite willing to see what will come of Mr. Johnson's experiment. And I think it desirable to keep with him as far & as much as possible. I don't want to see the Democrats coming back into power through any unnecessary quarrel among ourselves.[80]

Or, as John Murray Forbes wrote to N. M. Beckwith:

My great hope lies in Pres. Johnson's stubborn democracy. I have full faith in his hatred of the slave aristocracy; and if he finds that under his experiment the oligarchy rears its head and begins to grasp the reins of power, I look to see him promptly resume the military power, and hold it

[78] "If it fails, it will not be the fault of the President; and he will then be at liberty to pursue a sterner policy, and the people will sustain him in it." Hugh McCulloch to Charles Sumner, Aug. 22, 1865, Sumner MSS.

[79] "Still, we are not sorry the president is trying the experiment. . . . It may succeed. There may be more loyalty at the South than many are willing to admit. And if it fails, it is not the final or only method. Congress meets next winter, and can ratify or overthrow the president's plan as it pleases. But is it not well to treat the South with confidence and give the people thus a chance to come back to their allegiance with as few trammels as possible? . . . Mr. Johnson deserves our support, as the president we have selected, till it is evident that his experiment fails to accomplish the desired end." Springfield *Weekly Republican*, July 1, 1865.

[80] Charles A. Dana to Sumner, Sept. 1, 1865, Sumner MSS.

until we can be sure of some other reconstruction than the old aristocratic one.[81]

Even in the face of deepest doubts, Republicans clung doggedly to the concept of "experiment" as their sanction for refraining from open opposition. Lot M. Morrill, in his efforts to calm Sumner, conceded:

> The Prest. is trying to demonstrate his theory of "restoring states.". . .
> It will fail of course. There is consti[tutional] revolution & Negro insurrection in it. Nobody approves it.
> Still, it is but an experiment—let him try it. That I think is the feeling.

And yet from the very beginning, everything depended on the President's real intentions. "If the North Carolina project of Prest. Johnson is a finality & not an experiment," wrote George Hoadly to William Henry Smith one week after the proclamation was issued, "I am ready to quit supporting him with my vote, & go out into the cold once more."[82]

The Democrats, of course, could not fail to be touched on their own exposed nerve by the reiteration of the "experiment" formula. They sensed that the Republicans' maintenance of party harmony depended on constant reinvocation of that formula, and they struck back, almost by instinct, to disparage it. When Benjamin F. Butler told the Massachusetts Republicans on September 14 that Johnson regarded his policy as an experiment, the New York *World*, whose editor had himself conferred with the President and claimed to know his views, declared: ". . . we assert as positively as if we were speaking in his behalf that he does not regard his plan as 'an experiment' in any such sense as that in which General Butler uses the term."[83] Congressman Robert

---

[81] J. M. Forbes to N. M. Beckwith, Aug. 6, 1865, Schurz MSS, Library of Congress. Boutwell and Howard, both radicals, were willing to suspend judgment on Johnson for this reason. It was only under such a formula as "experiment," of course, that one could be both a Johnson supporter and a Negro-suffrage man. Jacob M. Howard, in a letter telling Sumner of his feeling that the Johnson policy was "experimental," also added: "I can only speak for myself & colleague: we are for negro suffrage." Boutwell. Speech at Weymouth, Mass., July 4, 1865, in *Speeches and Papers*, pp. 378–79; Howard to Sumner, July 26, 1865, Sumner MSS. On August 12, Simon Cameron of Pennsylvania urged an audience of serenaders to aid and encourage Johnson "until he shall have developed a policy, the result of his mature reflection." Cameron assumed that the procedure then in effect was not really a "policy" at all. Philadelphia *Ledger*, Aug. 11, 1865, quoted in New York *World*, Aug. 12, 1865.

[82] L. M. Morrill to Charles Sumner, July [n.d.] 1865, Sumner MSS; George Hoadly to William Henry Smith, June 5, 1865, Smith MSS, Ohio Historical Society. Hoadly was a Cincinnati judge; Smith was Secretary of State of Ohio and a prominent figure in the Republican party there. He later became president of Associated Press.

[83] New York *World*, Oct. 2, 1865. John Forney's support of Johnson on that basis was similarly belittled. "So far from the present reconstruction policy having always been acknowledged as Andrew Johnson's platform, it is not so recognized by the Radical leaders even now, but on the contrary, they affect to call it an experiment and

Schenck of Ohio made a speech at Chillicothe on August 16 in which he too said, after talking with the President, that the latter "regarded the local governments set up in the rebellious states as temporary experiments, simply to give the people an opportunity to show whether they will develop the right spirit and policy necessary for a full restoration to their proper position in the government."[84] Montgomery Blair was furious. "You yourself know that Schenck's speech was a lie from the beginning to the end," he wrote to Jeremiah Black. "Johnson told you in my presence that his action in relation to reconstruction was not an *experiment* to be abandoned but [was] based on the constitution to which he was sworn to adhere!"[85]

There was also a miscellaneous group of apparently moderate Republicans who did not quite fit the "moderate" description just given but whose position was sufficiently anomalous (or would shortly become so) that one is not entirely sure where else to put them. A small but conspicuous number of men nominally attached to the party showed, to all intents and purposes, the attributes of a "conservative" position but at the same time did not appear to maintain that position in a conservative way at all. They would ultimately go to extreme lengths—to the point of cutting most of their party connections—in support of their principles. The distinguishing feature of these men's position was a determination to support President Johnson on a ground very similar to that occupied by the Democrats: the ground that the Southern states had never legally been out, that their rights—including that of fixing suffrage—thus remained unimpaired, and that they should be readmitted just as quickly as possible.

An almost doctrinaire quality was imparted to these men's position by the fact that their manner of maintaining it was only in the remotest sense geared to the requirements of the Republican party. Actually, the support of President Johnson by either party at this time assumed

the experiment a failure, and are using almost superhuman exertions to make him change it, declaring that he cannot carry it out without destroying the party that elevated him, both politically and morally." Detroit *Free Press*, Sept. 29, 1865; see also New York *World*, June 21, 1865. The Indianapolis *Sentinel*, in an October 6 editorial headed "Not an Experiment," declared flatly: "Never was there a greater delusion than that President Johnson looks upon his restoration policy as an experiment."

84 New York *World*, Aug. 21, 1865.

85 M. Blair to J. Black, Aug. 31, 1865, Black MSS. John A. McClernand, the Illinois Democratic leader, complained to Johnson's son-in-law about the Republicans' tactics. "Already, they are skirmishing against him: and how are they doing it? Notoriously, by disparaging everything he does as an 'experiment.' . . ." McClernand to David Patterson, Oct. 12, 1865, Johnson MSS.

a state of contingency: the implicit understanding that if such support should become a political liability it would have to be abandoned. But for this other position, this peculiar hybrid brand of "moderation," the primary basis was rigid and unadulterated principle: a fixed constitutionalism that showed little willingness to recognize the problem's having a political dimension at all.

Among the men who might have been described in this way—men who seem, for one reason or another, to have fallen out of touch politically in the "party" sense—were Gideon Welles, Secretary of the Navy; Hugh McCulloch, Secretary of the Treasury; Edward Bates, the retired Attorney-General; Charles Francis Adams, Minister to Great Britain; Preston King, Collector of the Port of New York; Thomas Ewing, former senator and once a cabinet appointee of General Harrison; William Tecumseh Sherman, the hero of Georgia and the Carolinas; former Senator Orville H. Browning; and William H. Seward, Secretary of State and no longer *persona grata* in the New York Republican organization. In the Senate, of all the Republicans who might have held such a position, only three actually did: James R. Doolittle of Wisconsin, Edgar Cowan of Pennsylvania, and James Dixon of Connecticut.

There seems, in this position, to have been a certain touch of the bureaucratic. There seems to have been the impulse, when confronted with a difficulty of magnitude, to reach for the simplest set rule that would cover the case. The rule here was the Constitution. The testy Welles, bedeviled over the matter of Negro suffrage, asserted in his diary that "those who urge this doctrine would subvert the Constitution" and "violate the reserved and undoubted rights of the States."[86] It seemed that a premium was being placed on certainty; there was a longing to get matters set, an abhorrence of clutter—as when McCulloch in a burst of irritability told Sumner, even before Congress had convened and begun its deliberations on reconstruction, that the business of the Treasury and the security of the public credit would be unsettled by continued agitation over that subject.[87] A similar impulse might have been discerned as far back as May in Sherman's terms to Johnston; the general's impatience upon that occasion with the meddling of politicians became notorious. In terms of policy, such a position—unlike that of most Republicans—was anything but a matter of "wait and see"; it was rather an urge to see doubts removed, to have the President, navigating only by the Constitution, get on with the

[86] Welles, *Diary*, II, 324 (June 27, 1865).

[87] McCulloch to Sumner, Aug. 16, 1865, Sumner MSS.

reconstruction process as speedily as possible. An attitude of this sort could enable a man to take a stand, in his search for certainty, and adhere to it without feeling the necessity for compromise. Not only could he become impervious to pressure; he could attain heights of almost religious intensity in his devotion to principle.

The most pervasive aspect of this position was actually not so much the "bureaucratic" as simply the non-political. It seemed to involve a man's willingness, still in defense of principle, to wear his political obligations lightly and to kick over the traces rather than cloud the fundamentals with unwonted complexity. "As there must and will be parties," wrote Welles, "they may as well form on this question, perhaps, as any other. It is centralization and State rights."[88] There was the latent conviction, as with Doolittle in Wisconsin, that the people, for all the howls from the "organization," would in the end certify the right thing. Thus Doolittle, by opening fire on the radicals in the Wisconsin state convention and on the stump, would put his party organization and his own political clientele under the severest strains in the late summer and fall of 1865.[89] But willingly or not, once a man had lost touch with his political moorings, it became relatively easier for him—even despite long experience—to anchor himself instead to principles and theory. It was not so much that political "expediency" could get in the way of "principle" but rather that whenever popular demands and party requirements lost their effectiveness as a check on his thinking, any man's safeguards against rigidity and dogma could be

[88] Welles, *Diary*, II, 324 (June 27, 1865).

[89] "Never, in my judgment," wrote one of Doolittle's friends to him, "was there a more unreasoning and unreasonable clamor than that now made by many of the press of the state, touching the action of the late convention [at which the committee on resolutions, of which Doolittle was chairman, threw out a Negro suffrage resolution]—and also touching yourself personally." C. L. Sholes to Doolittle, Sept. 20, 1865, Johnson MSS. "The howling against me of which he speaks," commented Doolittle in passing this letter on to Johnson, "is . . . because I attended our late Union Convention was chairman of the Committee on resolutions which sustain your course and policy, and especially because I opposed resolutions of the minority condemning your policy of reconciliation. I am going into the fight. The great mass of our people will sustain you. The democratic party in their resolutions endorse your policy. . . ." Doolittle to Johnson, Sept. 23, 1865, Johnson MSS. "The neglect of the Convention to speak out on the great questions," wrote one of the delegates, ". . . was owing principally to the pernicious influence of Senator Doolittle, who labored diligently among the members, not only to accomplish that result, but also to suppress debate. There has been a Mass State Convention held since . . . which was large and enthusiastic, and adopted among others, the resolutions, laid on the table at the other convention." Byron Paine to C. Sumner, Oct. 7, 1865, Sumner MSS. Doolittle, in his strict constitutionalism, declared publicly on October 9 that if Delaware and Kentucky did not ratify the Thirteenth Amendment, the right of those states to maintain slavery would still exist inviolate. "These are the words of Senator Doolittle of Wisconsin," wrote the editor of the Whitewater *Register* on October 13, "and not of Senator Hammond, of S. Carolina."

immensely lowered. The doughty Charles Francis Adams, away across the Atlantic, was determined to stick to *his* dogmas on reconstruction. But he also recognized that there would have to be a price: he could never promote them politically.[90]

At any rate, these moderates—"doctrinaire moderates," they might almost be called—in 1865 began displaying signs that came to set them well apart from the rest of their party. There was a strong antipathy to radicals and a vigorous willingness to attack them, calling constant attention to the actual or potential cleavage between the radicals' views and their own. (There was no such cleavage among the Democrats.) There was a readiness to praise Democrats for their support of Johnson's policy, and to think of that support as actually available in some way for a special Union Republican position. A united Republican party figured less prominently in their thinking than did the question of pure doctrine. All of this seems very clear, for example, in the impassioned letters of Dixon and Doolittle to the President.[91] It was not so clear to Doolittle, however, as it was to the rest of his party, that every word he uttered in his speechmaking that fall would serve just that much more to reduce his influence everywhere.[92]

Here, then, was a special stand that would become fully identifiable by 1866, though it probably did not emerge quite so soon as the others. It would not become fully apparent until later that the only political matrix within which such a position could make sense was the Democratic party. But that would run up against still another "principle": these men could never associate with Copperheads, any more than with radicals. It was, or would become, a peculiarly suspended and isolated position, for the Democrats could no more repudiate their Copperheads than the Republicans could their radicals. All this would

[90] See below, p. 419.

[91] E.g., Doolittle to Johnson, Sept. 9, 23, and Oct. 10, 1865, Dixon to Johnson, Aug. 24, Sept. 26, Oct. 8, 16, 1865, Johnson MSS. Dixon admitted that there was an element in the Republican party, "not without influence," that did not approve of Johnson's policy, though the Democrats, he observed with satisfaction, were entirely with the President. But upon the "immense majority of the entire people" Dixon dwelt with something approaching transfiguration: "They thank God that he has inspired you thus to act. Their enthusiastic gratitude to you would move your feelings, could you see and appreciate it . . . , nothing that I have ever seen has equalled it, and I do not hesitate to say that to-day you are . . . the most popular President since the days of Washington." *Ibid.*, Oct. 8. These men's passion for "states' rights," which quite transcended self and party, was equaled only by their passion against Republican radicals. In short, party partisanship was almost entirely lacking in them; they said very little against the Democrats.

[92] "Doolittle I see," wrote Thaddeus Stevens on October 7, "is playing the fool as usual." Sumner MSS. See also above, n. 89, and below, chap. 12, n. 65.

eventually have its test in the summer of 1866 with the National Union movement. Still, the position was already in the making in the summer and fall of 1865. It was reflected in these men's determination to support Johnson through thick and thin, come what might—a support based not so much upon an appraisal of its usefulness to the party as simply upon the conviction that it was right. Perhaps it is only in terms of this variant version of "moderation" that one can come to appreciate the political personality of Andrew Johnson himself.

Andrew Johnson, Outsider

The man who succeeded Lincoln, who thought of himself as following in Lincoln's footsteps and carrying out Lincoln's designs, was a lone wolf in almost every sense of the word. He was a man of undoubted ability. Indeed, the order which he brought to the administration of the executive office was in sharp relief to the clutter of Lincoln's time. But the only setting in which Andrew Johnson's powers could become fully engaged was one in which the man would be battling against great odds. The only role whose attributes he fully understood was that of the maverick, operating out on the fringe of things. For the full nourishment and maximum functioning of his mind, matters had to be so arranged that all the organized forces of society could in some sense, real or symbolic, be leagued against him. In such array they could be overborne by the *un*organized forces of whom he always imagined himself the instrument—an assault whose only rhythm was measured out, as it were, by the great heartbeat of the people. These were the terms in which the battle of life had its fullest meaning for Andrew Johnson.

It is often said of Johnson, with much truth, that his plebeian origins bred in him a fierce and independent spirit. One does not, however, think of Lincoln in any such way. One does not say that *his* plebeian origins bred in him "a fierce and independent spirit." Why is this? Had Johnson come of poorer "poor white" stock than Lincoln—had his struggle been a harder one? It would certainly seem so; and yet these things are relative and not easy to measure. We know that Johnson eventually became a man of means and a slaveowner; it does not generally occur to us, on the other hand, to describe the Lincolns' circumstances as more than comfortable. We also know that for nearly thirty years prior to the presidency, Johnson had enjoyed, to all intents and purposes, the highest honors in the public gift—legislator, governor, representative, and senator, whereas Lincoln had only served in the Illinois legislature and gone to Congress for a single term. The key to the contrast between the two men does not seem to be "success" in any objective measure; it lies rather in the way success was conceived. For Johnson, personal fulfilment had long since come to be defined as the fruit of struggle—real, full-bodied, and terrible—against forces specifically organized for thwarting him. Not so for Lincoln. Johnson, all his life, had operated as an outsider; Lincoln, in most of his worldly dealings, and temperamentally as well, was an insider.

The early life of Andrew Johnson was an incredible struggle against grinding destitution that reads like a chapter first of Dickens and then of Horatio Alger, with perhaps a dash of Al Capp. His father, a good-natured porter at Casso's tavern in Raleigh, North Carolina, had lost his life rescuing two drunken gentlemen from an icy stream when Andrew was only three. Andrew's mother, an amiable but rather ineffectual woman known as "Polly the Weaver," apprenticed him to a tailor at fourteen when she could no longer support him. He had no formal education. After a time the young man ran away and hid out while his furious master advertised a reward for his capture. Eventually Andrew, his mother, his ne'er-do-well brother Bill (of "black hair, eyes, and habits"), and his sometime-acquired impecunious stepfather, all headed west over the mountains with their cart. They landed at Greeneville, Tennessee. There Andrew set up a tailor shop, practiced the rudiments of reading, and at nineteen married a wife who taught him to write. Eliza McCardle had a little education but no family connections whatever, being the orphaned daughter of a shoemaker. (Here one thinks, in contrast, of Lincoln's marriage to Mary Todd, the daughter of an aristocratic family with excellent connections.) Through scrimping and hard toil, Johnson bit by bit acquired a home, a new tailor shop, a brick store in Greeneville, and a comfortable farm. He practiced debating with the young men of the town, and in time held several local offices.[1]

In spite of numerous signs that he was really getting on quite decently in the world, the matter of class and social acceptance churned sourly in Andrew Johnson's vitals. His father, the happy menial, had never questioned his meager lot in life; that poor soul had gone to his reward without ever having thought much about the mysteries of

---

[1] The material for this portrait is largely drawn from Robert W. Winston's *Andrew Johnson: Plebeian and Patriot* (New York: Henry Holt, 1928). This work, while erratic in its scholarship, has at least the merit of a sympathetic approach to its subject on the level of human biography rather than political doctrine—not the case with George F. Milton's more ambitious biography (*The Age of Hate*), in which Andrew Johnson, the man, is all too seldom seen.

"class" at all. Andrew thought of nothing else; his own struggle to rise consumed and obsessed him. Grimly ambitious, he brooded over the wrongs, real and imaginary, which were thoughtlessly foisted upon him by his social betters, and out of his inner world of suspicious fantasy he evolved an extravagant credo of plebeian democracy and honest toil. Once, after a snub from one of the Greeneville gentry, he raged: "Some day I will show the stuck-up aristocrats who is running the country. A cheap purse-proud set they are, not half as good as the man who earns his bread by the sweat of his brow."[2] With a dogged masochism, he never ceased to harp publicly on his own humble origins; he was still doing it on the occasion of his inaugural as Vice-President. Even as governor of Tennessee, Johnson on one occasion insisted on cutting out a coat for a judge, a former blacksmith who had made a shovel for him; he accompanied the gift with an open letter proclaiming that "the main highway and surest passport to honesty and useful distinction will soon be through the harvest field and the workshop."[3] Throughout it all, Johnson remained inordinately fastidious in matters of dress. One wonders what he must have thought, in later years, of the slovenly habits of the Great Emancipator.

Politically, Johnson's plebeianism served him wonderfully well in the fundamentalist atmosphere of the East Tennessee upcountry. Long hours of cultivating his voice in the solitude of his shop had made him a superb speaker. From the stump he would conjure up the spirit of Old Hickory; he would revive, in order that he might scourge, the ancient and terrible threats of tyranny and Federalism; he could call forth, as Mencken would later say of Bryan in that same country, all the dread "powers and principalities of the air." The simple mountaineers were deeply impressed by his philippics, and they would shiver in appreciation as his words rang through the valley in the gathering twilight.[4] They said of him, as he thundered out his harsh paeans to equal-

---

[2] Winston, *Andrew Johnson*, p. 38. "Andrew Jackson, the pioneer and planter," wrote Thomas P. Abernethy, "was never possessed of class consciousness. Andrew Johnson, the tailor, never escaped it." *From Frontier to Plantation in Tennessee* (Chapel Hill: University of North Carolina Press, 1932), p. 357.

[3] Winston, *Andrew Johnson*, p. 83.

[4] "As Mr. Johnson grew warm and hurled the terrible thunder of his wrath against the old Federalists," wrote a contemporary, "the shouts sent up by the Democracy could be heard far and wide among the surrounding hills. As he pictured the old Federal party in fearful colors, and pathetically entreated the people to stand firm upon the Constitution, his hearers would huddle closer together, as if for mutual protection, and plant their feet more firmly upon the ground. . . . It was usually nearly night when the crowd dispersed. . . . When night overtook them on their homeward way, in the bewildered condition of their intellects, they recalled dim images of 'blue lights and black cockades,' and in every dark wood they feared to see these monsters, whatever they were, confront them!" Oliver P. Temple, *Notable Men of Tennessee* (New York: Cosmopolitan Press, 1912), pp. 373–74.

ity, "Old Andy never went back on his raisin'." But there was no merriment in Johnson's performances. Unlike Lincoln, he had none of that humor which comes from an appreciation of the ever altering, shimmering complexity of things. "He was dead in earnest," says his biographer, "and he believed with his soul every doctrine he announced."[5]

Johnson's conception of political life was one which had the merit of great simplicity, and in the loosely organized political setting of East Tennessee it was one which could be exploited with overwhelming personal success in the advancement of a career. Politics for Andrew Johnson was essentially a matter of principles that had to be defended rather than of a party organization that had to win elections. He was a Democrat but never really a party man.

Because of his unwillingness to cooperate with political parties or organizations, Johnson in Congress waged but a guerilla warfare—a warfare sometimes inside the Democratic party and sometimes outside. Always, however, he stood upon the old platform, equal distribution of government favors, equal treatment of rich and poor, farmer, laborer, mechanic, manufacturer or what not. A strict interpretation of the Constitution and an observance of its letter had now become his guiding principle.[6]

There was such a direct and immediate quality about Johnson's successes on the stump that he could hardly fail to construe re-election as a persuasive test of personal merit owing nothing to "the interests." His constituency sent him back year after year. In such circumstances it was perhaps only natural that he should never feel pressed to put a very high premium on party responsibilities. He was willing, time and again, to break with the organization on any pretext; indeed, much of his career was occupied in fighting it. It is hard to picture Lincoln, on the other hand, with either the taste or the talent for political operations conceived in such terms. Lincoln could not imagine working without his party connections.

It was perfectly in character for Johnson, at the drop of a hat, to "go to the people." Such was the nature of his constituency, combined with the simple values which he represented, that not only was the direct appeal successful time after time, but Johnson's own experience, in the process, could develop and sustain in him an almost religious sense of "the people." If the people did wrong, it was the fault of their conniving leaders. His inaugural as governor in 1853 saw him transfigured with the Democratic faith. On that occasion, he delivered an

[5] Winston, *Andrew Johnson*, p. 62.

[6] *Ibid.*, p. 52.

apocalyptic speech which was received with much amusement by the Whigs and anti-Johnson Democrats but which was greatly approved by the common folk. He dwelt upon the coming "divinity of man," likened the "voice of the people" to the "voice of God," and declared: "It will be readily perceived by all discerning young men, that Democracy is a ladder, corresponding in politics to the one spiritual which Jacob saw in his vision; one up which all, in proportion to their merit, may ascend. While it extends to the humblest of all created beings, here on earth below, it reaches to God on high. . . ."[7]

The texture of Johnson's mind was essentially abstract. Concrete problems never had the power to engage his interest that "principles" had;[8] the principles of equal rights, local self-rule, states' rights as well as Union, and strict constitutionalism had served him through all vicissitudes and had taken on mystic powers with the passage of the years. Faced with a crisis that had no parallels in his past experience, he would have found it next to impossible to imagine that the moral rules which had guided him in his youth should not suffice him then.

Despite Johnson's tendency to boast, he was not a person who had real confidence in his intellectual powers. For a public man, he was obsessed with himself to a degree that exceeded the normal, and most of his speeches, no matter what else they dealt with, may be read as demands for personal vindication and personal approval. Unlike Lincoln, whose "humility" was sustained by the odd arrogance of a superior man's self-knowledge, Johnson lacked assurance. He tended to hesitate in full realization of his own shortcomings. At bottom, general rules were an easy substitute for concrete thinking; confronted with a difficulty, Johnson's mind searched instinctively for such rules in order that it might once more close itself and be at rest. He was not really capable of intellectual courage until after he had made up his mind, and once he had, he would do anything rather than undergo the agony of further doubts. It was a peculiar kind of courage (if such it was): "He could bear insult, personal danger, obloquy; but he could not yield his point."[9] In contrast, there is a downright blitheness about Lincoln's last speech, in which he said that bad promises were better broken than kept. Lincoln was never unprepared, should matters of

[7] Oliver Temple observed, "I doubt if Mr. Johnson could ever have gotten many to locate in this empyreal commonwealth." *Notable Men*, p. 382.

[8] The major exception (if such it could be called) was Johnson's identification with homestead legislation, which he promoted for many years with a simple monotony and an evangelical intensity ("free land for free laborers") not unlike that of Bryan for free silver.

[9] Howard K. Beale, *The Critical Year*, p. 26.

great moment seem to make it necessary, to redefine something as a "bad promise."

The final stage of Johnson's career, culminating in his rise to the ultimate power, was launched with a characteristic act of dissociation. In 1860 and 1861, with superb disdain for his own personal safety, Johnson—then a senator—defied the secessionists of Tennessee. True to the principles of the sainted Jackson (for whom he had been named),[10] he defended the Constitution and the Union with bitter devotion until no drop of hope for his state was left. He was loyal to the end, and when Tennessee went out, Andrew Johnson stayed on as the loyal senator from a disloyal state—he "could not yield his point." When the Union armies precariously occupied certain parts of the state in 1862, Lincoln asked Johnson to go to beleaguered Nashville as military governor; Johnson hesitated not an instant. For three years, amid unbelievable anxieties and dangers, through nightmares of uncertainty, Johnson stood at his post, playing the role of the outsider under the most heroic circumstances. It was his finest hour; and it was for this that Lincoln in 1864 picked him for his Vice-President.

Johnson had certainly earned his reward. But there was a difficulty which nobody thought much about at the time and the embarrassments of which would not really become apparent until well after Johnson's accession to the presidency itself. The man had no real connections with the party organization which had placed him there, nor would he ever recognize any. There was little in his past that had given him any preparation for the role of party leader—a role whose essence Abraham Lincoln had understood in his bones.

Might any general predictions have been made as to the future course of the man who took the oath as President on April 15, 1865? What were the prospects for a man whose career had been successful on such a basis as Andrew Johnson's? He had never played his chances on the conservative side. He had played them on the margin—but he had always won. The role of the outsider had formed the political personality of this man; it was a role based on essentially non-political behavior, and it had been played through thirty years of politics—thirty years in the thick of things. It was a role to which he was now committed beyond choice, and it was not an asset to a man who had become President of the United States. The social outsider, the political outsider, and now the outsider who had power: such had been the stages of Johnson's rise, and it was not a background that augured well for political sensitivity or for "moderation," institutionally defined.

[10] His full name was Andrew Jackson Johnson.

Johnson was temperamentally and sociologically a "radical," whereas the insider, in our politics, has perennially found it very difficult to be that kind of "radical": he is weighted down by too many connections. To be a good freebooter, one must somehow—like Andrew Johnson—carry as few connections as possible.

Johnson's policy on reconstruction, despite the hopes of the Republican party, were, after all, fully consistent with all his past habits, and they should not have occasioned (and probably did not occasion) any surprise to men who really knew those habits.

In justice to Johnson, it would be well not to be misled by "evidence" that the President, in the summer and fall of 1865, was somehow edging toward his ancient Democratic associations. He was temperamentally incapable of "selling out" in that sense. It was true that Democrats, emerging from interviews, found his conversation much more to their liking on matters of reconstruction than did Republicans who discussed similar questions with him. But this satisfaction was based upon the President's principles, which the Democrats soon saw as those most conducive to their own political prospects. And yet for Johnson himself, those doctrines were not really conceived in party terms at all. To all such considerations he seemed oblivious.

Johnson's stand appears to have been settled in his own mind fairly early. Indeed, it was he who, with Representative Crittenden, had produced the resolutions of 1861 which declared that the war objectives should be restricted to defense of the Constitution and the Union and that "as soon as these objects were accomplished the war ought to cease." "I hope," he wrote to Montgomery Blair in 1863, "that the President will not be committed to the proposition of States relapsing into territories and held as such."[11] When John A. Logan called upon Johnson to discuss reconstruction on May 31, 1865, the President was said to have declared: "General, there's no such thing as reconstruction. These States have not gone out of the Union. Therefore reconstruction is unnecessary."[12]

Flushed with passion, Johnson had exclaimed, in the celebrated audience with Wade and others on April 16, the day after Lincoln died, "Treason must be made infamous and traitors must be impoverished."[13] Then, in view of a pardoning policy which became progressively

[11] Edward McPherson, *The Political History of the United States . . . during the Period of Reconstruction . . .* (Washington: Philp & Solomons, 1871), p. 199.

[12] Chicago *Republican,* quoted in Cincinnati *Enquirer,* July 7, 1865.

[13] George W. Julian, *Political Recollections,* p. 257.

milder as the months went on, many have supposed that a major shift of intention occurred in the President's mind sometime between his inauguration and the early summer. This softened attitude is attributed variously to the counsels of Secretary Seward, the intrigues of the Blairs, and the blandishments of Southern ladies seeking pardons for their husbands. It is not unlikely that the President derived a certain pleasure from the position in which he found himself vis-à-vis these ladies; to be able to confer his boon upon them could hardly have failed to be a source of some satisfaction. In any case he could be, for all his obstinacy, a forgiving man. We can easily imagine, moreover, his constitutional convictions being fortified in lengthy talks with the Blairs at Silver Spring. But in the long run Johnson made his own decisions, and the really critical aspect of his reconstruction policy—the constitutional relations of the states to the Union—had probably hardened for him, and thus ceased to vex his mind, early in the war.

The states, then, had never been out of the Union at all, and the constitutional right of the state to regulate its own internal concerns had never ceased to exist in all its vigor. The abstractness of such a dogma, in view of Johnson's willingness to use pressure (however erratically he may have exerted it) in getting the states to ratify the Thirteenth Amendment and repudiate their debt, never seemed to occur to him. He somehow had to convince himself—and apparently did—that these things were being done "voluntarily." Nor could his laissez-faire attitude on Negro suffrage fail to strike him as both fair and logical. It was true that, under such a policy, Negro suffrage would in all likelihood be ruled out, but there the inscrutable will of the Fathers (as he saw it) left him no choice. And so with the admission of the Southern representatives: it was the *constitutional* thing to do, regardless of consequences.

Such were the President's views, doubtless fully articulated by the time he issued his May 29 proclamations. He still held them when Congress met in December, 1865, six months later. He would defend them, against merciless abuse, in his "swing around the circle" the following year. And in December, 1866, those principles would remain doggedly unaltered. In his message to Congress at that time he serenely announced:

Upon this question, so vitally affecting the restoration of the Union and the permanency of our present form of government, my convictions, heretofore expressed, have undergone no change, but, on the contrary, their correctness has been confirmed by reflection and time.[14]

[14] Richardson, *Messages and Papers*, VI, 488.

Reconstruction
as a Problem
in
Constitutional Theory

If the historians' rehabilitation of President Johnson has blurred for us the political dimension of reconstruction, that is nothing to what it has done to our sense of reconstruction as a constitutional problem. A question which at one time had real meaning and depth on theoretical grounds alone seems no longer to be taken with much seriousness. We know all about Johnson's own extreme reverence for the Constitution; there was never any doubt of the man's almost hypnotic determination to follow what he conceived as its spirit and letter. From this we would conclude that the constitutional side of the matter remained more or less self-evident, that the constitutional position on reconstruction was Johnson's position, and that other viewpoints—though perhaps viable in other ways—were not entitled, except through painful casuistry, to be considered on constitutional grounds at all. But the apparent matter-of-factness of this conception is not historically justified. It dates back not much further than the last generation.

There were actually four or five different theoretical positions on reconstruction, and numerous variations and combinations of those; all were carefully developed and perfectly arguable, and the point of departure was in all cases the Constitution. Probably few authorities in constitutional law, if pressed, would even be willing to argue flatly that Johnson's position was the correct one. There were certain logical weaknesses in it, to say nothing of practical difficulties, which these other theories did much to remedy. For that matter, the Supreme Court's own conception of reconstruction diverged very markedly from that of the President. Although the justices themselves were not unanimous on the true word, none of them found the Johnson theory admissible as proper constitutional doctrine.

Still, the fact remains that reconstruction as a problem in theory has been out of vogue for some time and no longer has the vitality that it once had. Its elimination may have been one of the special requirements (though not necessarily recognized as such) in the work of redeeming Andrew Johnson's political reputation. Most of the writing done on this period over the past generation has assumed not only that Johnson's position was the "constitutional" one but also that the other arguments were in themselves meaningless—that they were really blinds for programs essentially political (or even economic) in nature. Here, Professor Beale is quite emphatic:

Lawyers and Congressmen, true to form, made lengthy speeches on matters of constitutionality, for this gave them an air of erudition, and satisfied the legalistic conscience of their constituents. Nevertheless constitutional discussions . . . determined nothing. They were pure shams.
. . . But for all the heat and bombast of their enunciation, these constitutional arguments were mere justifications of practical ends. Except the men who made political capital out of them, few cared about constitutional niceties.[1]

Styles change, and so do objects of preference. Still, there is something arbitrary and self-denying in the assumption, now more or less tacit and orthodox, that the constitutional side of reconstruction may safely be passed over with no more than perfunctory notice.[2] There

---

[1] Howard K. Beale, *The Critical Year*, pp. 147, 150.

[2] The two principal studies of the Johnson era which have been made in the past generation—Beale's *Critical Year* and G. F. Milton's *Age of Hate*—both ignore reconstruction as a constitutional problem. This is also generally true of J. G. Randall's *Civil War and Reconstruction*. Other works specifically on Johnson himself—forming, with these others, a group all written within a very few years of one another—consistently overlook this dimension of reconstruction. Robert W. Winston, Johnson's very temperate biographer, pictures the President as ready if necessary to "die defending the Constitution" (the assumption being that if the Constitution had any defender, it was Johnson). Winston, *Andrew Johnson*, p. 346. Claude Bowers, much less temperate, makes this gesture to the constitutional aspect of reconstruction: "The Constitution was treated as a doormat on which politicians and army officers wiped their feet after wading in the muck." *The Tragic Era* (Boston: Houghton Mifflin, 1929), p. v. Lloyd Paul Stryker's *Andrew Johnson: A Study in Courage* (New York: Macmillan, 1929), likewise assumes Johnson's position to have been so fully correct in all ways as to remove the entire subject from serious controversy. There is a reluctance, even in the texts on constitutional history, to deal with reconstruction as a matter of theory. Andrew McLaughlin, with a certain respect for earlier traditions of scholarship, takes the theories up very briefly in his *Constitutional History of the United States* (New York: D. Appleton-Century, 1935); on the other hand, C. B. Swisher's *American Constitutional Development* (Boston: Houghton Mifflin, 1943), in other ways a much more exhaustive book, does not discuss them on their merits at all, treating the whole question

might be good reasons for taking up these questions all over again, in something of the same spirit in which they were examined by Burgess and Dunning around the turn of the century—on their merits.[3] It would bring back before us something that has been all but forgotten in the passage of time—the fact that Andrew Johnson was by no means the only man who cared immensely about the Constitution. Although men and parties were experiencing difficulties and strains utterly without precedent, men could not even think seriously about public matters in any idiom from which the Constitution had been eliminated. They may have been no less determined that such difficulties should be solved and such strains alleviated, but they themselves were aware that the alternatives for doing so were hardly limitless.

Thus it would not be wise to assume hypocrisy, claptrap, and sham as a formula for explaining any problem of this magnitude. There were, to be sure, political needs. But had there been no such needs, we would have no problem; it is this very fact that gives the constitutional dimension such great importance. It would be misconceiving the nature of the Constitution to suppose that it was brought into being in the first place for any other reason than the most pressing of political needs. And needs do change—such is the major stimulant under which the Constitution has grown, in its application and meaning. Moreover, constitutional discussion did form an indispensable part of the framework within which men thought in the nineteenth century. Although our political system had developed by then a whole lore of its own, and special ways of responding to problems, we still cannot ignore the legal idiom in which so much of this thinking found expression. Faced with new political requirements, men were still much concerned over the question of how the Constitution would square with them.

Suppose, in the process, that the outlines of the Constitution should undergo alterations. It had certainly happened before; it would be fresh evidence of the instrument's adaptability to change. Less clear,

---

as essentially a battle between the Executive and the Legislative. In two other texts, Homer C. Hockett, *The Constitutional History of the United States* (New York: Macmillan, 1939), and Alfred H. Kelly and Winfred A. Harbison, *The American Constitution* (New York: W. W. Norton, 1948), the subject is treated only in a very perfunctory way.

[3] It is remarkable to note how much more important such matters were assumed to be fifty or so years ago. They were dealt with in some detail in such works as William A. Dunning, *Essays on the Civil War and Reconstruction* (New York: Macmillan, 1898); John W. Burgess, *Reconstruction and the Constitution* (New York: Charles Scribner's Sons, 1902); and Walter L. Fleming, *Civil War and Reconstruction in Alabama* (New York: Columbia University Press, 1905).

however, would be the essentially dual way in which the Constitution seems to have functioned even in times of fluidity: it adjusts; at the same time, it resists. The Constitution is not only a substantive charter, with a flexibility which allows rearrangements; it is also a powerful abstraction, inherently conservative in nature—a philosophical balance wheel, as it were, that operates against real upheaval and renders the idea of such upheaval repugnant to men's habits of thought. The permissive attributes which the Constitution may at times assume are meaningless apart from its inhibitive attributes, and the same principle is true in reverse. Few steps may be taken in public policy, in times of change or in times of stability, without the Constitution's standing between each of those steps as a challenge and as a difficulty. The Constitution will grant terms, but men must stop and ask for them; there is no passing on without such terms. It is thus one thing to predict that the political arrangements of a people emerging from such an experience as the Civil War were bound to undergo change; it is another to remember that there were still checks on men's minds. This fact was of no small importance at a time when great masses of peaceable men were disposed to revolutionary action.

The scholars of the past have recognized, in general, five distinct theoretical positions on reconstruction. Despite the great variety both in the positions themselves and in the purposes which were associated with them, one is struck by at least two general features in them as a group. One is the fact that their proponents all accepted the Constitution as the central "given" with which their purposes must all somehow make terms. The other is contained in the numerous and intricate ways in which these theories were all related. This in itself says much about the Constitution as an item in the public conscience, especially since there was nothing at all in it that came even close to anticipating such a problem as reconstruction.

Two basic questions had to be settled. What had the war done to the rebellious states? And what was the new relation of those states—or districts—to the federal government? In taking up the theories wherein solutions were sought, we might think of such theories, figuratively, as the strokes of a pendulum. Let it be imagined that such a pendulum was swinging back and forth in shortening arcs, measuring the alternatives as they narrowed, and coming to rest at what men might recognize as acceptable federal policy to fit these new and unprecedented conditions.

I THE "SOUTHERN" THEORY

       The first of these doctrines, known as the "Southern" theory, was the one best suited for whatever hopes the South may have had for an easy peace. There is a symmetry about its argument that must have had its attractions. The South's attempt to exercise "state sovereignty," as implied in the pretended right of secession, had been snuffed out by war. The crude fact of war had given sure proofs that secession could not physically take place, and that the federal Union was indeed indissoluble and indestructible. The North had itself defined this attempt as a rebellion of individuals, implying that there was no thought of interfering with the true and undoubted rights of states; the North had waged war for the avowed purpose of suppressing such rebellion and had been successful. Therefore all must now submit once more to the authority of the Constitution. With the end of war, all affairs should revert to their pre-existing condition: individuals might be guilty of treasonable acts against the United States, but the states themselves, as governmental and territorial entities, had by definition all the same rights and duties as before. All that remained, therefore, was the adjustment of certain unreal conditions which had resulted from the imaginary separation. The officers of the states, for example, should now take oaths to support the Constitution; arrangements should be made to send representatives back to Congress; and federal agencies—treasury, postal, and judiciary—should be re-established as quickly as possible.[4]

Here, in view of the new condition of things, was a very radical theory, comparable in reverse to what the Confederacy had staked its life for. Several of the rebel governors took steps, after Lee's surrender, to call their legislatures together for the purpose of offering submission and making terms—hoping that this might be the basis on which the war would be liquidated. It is hard to say whether they really expected, in their hearts, that the North would go along with such a gesture. Undoubtedly, in their state of shock many Southerners could have persuaded themselves of almost anything. But certainly there was nothing to lose by trying. Actually, the most famous exponent of the "Southern" theory was not a Southerner at all; it was General Sherman himself. Sherman's terms to Johnston, as embodied in their agreement of April 18, were squarely based on just this conception of the rebellion. Sherman, unaware of Lincoln's explicit orders to Grant on this

---

[4] Dunning, *Essays*, pp. 101–3; Fleming, *Civil War and Reconstruction in Alabama*, pp. 333–34.

subject,[5] not only proposed to let the armies disperse with all their equipment (to be stored in their state capitals); he also presumed to undertake, on his own authority, the most sweeping commitments on the subject of reconstruction. There would be a general amnesty; the existing state governments would be recognized by the President; the people would be guaranteed, insofar as possible, all their political and property rights (except for slaves); and no citizens would be molested by reason of the late war, so long as they lived in peace and obeyed the laws.[6]

Sherman imagined that he had done the right thing; indeed, the logic alone of the theory had much to recommend it. Moreover, he knew that Lincoln had intended no bloody work in the punishment of traitors. He never understood the immediate and spontaneous uproar in the Northern press.[7] But Grant, upon reading Sherman's dispatch, needed no consultation with anyone to realize that "it could not possibly be approved."[8] The agreement was, in fact, repudiated; even President Johnson could not accept so extreme a view of reconstruction. A similar view was later pressed upon Johnson by B. F. Moore, a citizen of North Carolina, before preparations for setting up a provisional government in that state were complete. The President would not hear of it.[9]

One thing, then, was settled. Reconstruction on this basis was ruled out; even the hero of Atlanta could not be allowed to try it. A clear test had been made, and a set of limits established for the guidance of all: a simple return to *status quo ante* was not acceptable. There was a kind of reverse radicalism in so abrupt a claim for turning back the clock—a special extremism in the thought that the Constitution somehow did not apply to anything that had happened between Sumter and Appomattox.

[5] "[The President] instructs me to say that you are not to decide, discuss or confer upon any political question; such questions the President holds in his own hands and will submit them to no military conferences or conventions." This command was issued March 3, having been dictated by Lincoln to the Secretary of War—though for some reason no copy was forwarded to Sherman. *The Collected Works of Abraham Lincoln*, ed. Roy P. Basler (New Brunswick: Rutgers University Press, 1953), VIII, 330.

[6] William T. Sherman, *Memoirs* . . . (New York: D. Appleton, 1889), II, 356–57.

[7] Months later Sherman was still grasping at signs that his policy was being seen at last as the true one. "You will observe," he wrote to his brother late in 1865, "that Mr. Johnson is drifting toward my terms to Johnston. He cannot help it, for there is no other solution." W. T. Sherman to John Sherman, Nov. 4, 1865, *The Sherman Letters: Correspondence between General and Senator Sherman from 1837 to 1891*, ed. Rachel Sherman Thorndike (New York: Charles Scribner's Sons, 1894), p. 257.

[8] *War of the Rebellion: Official Records*, Ser. I, Vol. XLVII, Part III, p. 265.

[9] J. G. de Roulhac Hamilton, *Reconstruction in North Carolina* (New York: Columbia University, 1914), pp. 106–7.

II "CONQUERED PROVINCES"

Another theory equally extreme, in the long run equally inadmissible, and sharing certain of the same features as the Southern theory turned inside out, was that of Thaddeus Stevens. The germ of it first found expression in August, 1861, barely four months after the war had begun; it had become fully developed by 1863; and, after a speech at Lancaster, Pennsylvania, in September, 1865, the "conquered province" views of Thaddeus Stevens were widely publicized throughout the country.[10]

Not only did the Constitution have no application to the events of 1861–65 (as was also the case with the Southern theory), but the acts of the Southern states had so shattered the Constitution—in its application to themselves—that they could no longer claim any rights under it. To treat the war as a "rebellion" would be to twist the Constitution into grotesque shapes and make a travesty of it; the instrument should not be required to undergo such strains. For example, if "rebellion" were the only category in which to place the conflict, the sole reprisals would have to be through trials of individuals for treason. They would be mockeries of justice. Jefferson Davis could not constitutionally be tried for treason in Pennsylvania, for he had committed no treason there; he had committed it in Virginia. And yet only through prearranged judicial murder could Davis be convicted in Virginia by a "jury of his peers." Nor would it be proper, Stevens insisted, under the full restoration of the Constitution, for anyone—either Congress or the President—to do any reconstructing: "What reconstruction is needed?" But there must be reconstruction. The circumstances which had made necessary so great an expenditure of blood and treasure must now be altered beyond recognition.

[10] It is sometimes claimed that the burning of Stevens' Caledonia iron works by the Confederates in 1863 had a great deal to do with his hard views on Southern reconstruction. Those views, however, had been formed by Stevens early in the war; the idea that rebellion had broken the Southern states' constitutional bonds, making them subject to the law of nations, was expressed by him in a debate on the first Confiscation Act in 1861. The matter was debated again in January, 1863, at which time Stevens said, "we have the right to treat them as we would any other provinces that we might conquer." The elections of 1863 brought forth a public speech, in which the "conquered provinces" doctrine was repeated, this time more formally. His remarks in the House on January 22, 1864, on the relations of the seceded states to the Union were, as he said, "but repetition." His position was given its most complete utterance in another public speech, at Lancaster on September 6, 1865. See *Congressional Globe*, 37 Cong., 1 sess., p. 414 (Aug. 2, 1861); *ibid.*, 37 Cong., 3 sess., pp. 239–40 (Jan. 8, 1863); Lancaster *Intelligencer*, Sept. 17, 1863; *Cong. Globe*, 38 Cong., 1 sess., pp. 317–18 (Jan. 22, 1864). The Lancaster speech of September 6, 1865, is printed in the New York *Tribune*, Sept. 11, 1865; Richard Current, in *Old Thad Stevens*, pp. 214–16, quotes extensive excerpts from it; and there is a copy in the Stevens MSS, Library of Congress.

In a full *de facto* sense, Stevens argued, the rebellious states *were* out. They had waged war on the North, and the North on them; they had done all the things that a belligerent in war can do, and they had been treated, in virtually all ways, as an alien enemy. For such a condition of things the Constitution was quite unprepared. The victorious North could only treat these erstwhile states, which had succeeded in removing the Constitution from themselves and thus were states no longer, as conquered provinces according to the law of nations. The lives and property of the inhabitants were at the mercy of the victors, who could do anything they pleased with them.[11] Stevens insisted that the Southern social system would have to be remodeled, and this would require an extensive program of confiscation. As territories, these states would have their governments supervised by Congress, as provided for in the Constitution. When fit to re-enter the Union, they might apply for readmission as new states.[12]

The "conquered provinces" theory, in the stark form which Thaddeus Stevens gave it, could not really command much general support in the North. True, the argument would not have been quite comprehensible without the Constitution functioning in some sense as its mooring post—but for most men's comfort the particular emphasis that Stevens gave, not only to wartime but to postwar treatment of the South, had stretched the bonds of the Constitution fearfully far. The very phrase, "conquered provinces," was not one which most Northerners could pronounce without a sense of awkwardness. Leading

[11] Such also, in effect, was the "Grasp of War" doctrine of Richard Henry Dana. Dana made a widely circulated speech on this subject at Faneuil Hall in June, 1865, in which he made the same assertions as Stevens regarding the Confederacy's exercise of *de facto* belligerent powers and the federal government's subsequent right to exact any guarantees it thought necessary. He said, "Let the states make their own constitutions, but the constitutions must be satisfactory to the Republic, and . . . by a power which I think is beyond question, the Republic holds them in the grasp of war until they have made such constitutions." He also insisted (unlike Stevens) that satisfactory constitutions and a republican form of government should include Negro suffrage. Richard Henry Dana, Jr., *Speeches in Stirring Times and Letters to a Son* (Boston: Houghton Mifflin, 1910), pp. 243–59.

[12] "In reconstruction, therefore, no reform can be effected in the Southern States if they have never left the Union. But reformation *must* be effected; the foundation of their institutions, both political, municipal, and social, *must* be broken up and *relaid*, or all our blood and treasure have been spent in vain. This can only be done by treating and holding them as conquered people. Then all things which we can desire to do, follow with logical and legitimate authority. As conquered territory Congress would have full power to legislate for them; for the territories are not under the Constitution except so far as the express power to govern them is given to Congress. They would be held in a territorial condition until they are fit to form State Constitutions, and ask admission into the Union as new States. If Congress approve of the Constitutions, and think they have done works meet for repentance they would be admitted as new States." Address by Thaddeus Stevens, Sept. 6, 1865, Stevens MSS.

publicists, such as Horace Greeley, John Forney, and dozens of others, were scandalized, moreover, at what Stevens wanted to do with private property. Beyond any doubt, they expressed the convictions of a vast majority of the Northern people.

And yet from a Southern viewpoint the Stevens theory was by no means, in principle, so farfetched. Indeed, it had its attractions for a Southerner like Fleming, who was remarkably fair in dealing with it. Without the confiscatory overtones, and administered with statesmanship, the "conquered provinces" notion could very well be offered as most in line with the facts and as best suited not only to the South's deepest interests but also to its logical scruples. For the South had, in a sense, succeeded in breaking the Constitution; it had set up its own government; it had waged organized war.[13] The Southern Confederacy was desperately beaten, and many a Southerner, especially the military man, was not at all squeamish about saying so. The social and political arrangements of the South were in a state of great confusion. No matter which way things went, there was every likelihood that such confusion would be exploited by the most dubious elements of Southern society. In such circumstances there might seem to be something almost clean about an outright military government. Interminable treason trials, for one thing, would then be both unnecessary and absurd (if "treason" had any meaning as a concept, then a whole society was "guilty"); and conceivably a season of order under the federal military would provide the most impersonal kind of setting in which rebuilding might be got under way and relief be found from all the unhinging griefs and passions of the struggle.

Still, both the "Southern" theory and the "conquered provinces" theory were out of the question as being too radical. They were too far removed from the reach of the Constitution, as most men thought of it; most men, radical Republicans included, sensed the violence inherent in Stevens' thinking and were repelled by it. This pendulum-stroke, in other words, was slowed down and dragged back by a combination of political and constitutional conservatism.

III THE PRESIDENTIAL THEORY

Andrew Johnson thought of himself as a "strict constructionist," and in most respects his constitutional views were, in-

---

[13] "Stripped of its violence, Stevens's theory was probably the correct one from the point of view of public law. It was more in accord with historical facts. It recognized the great changes wrought by war in the structure of the government. It was frank, explicit, and practical. Unfortunately, the statesmanship necessary to carry to success such a plan was entirely lacking in its supporters." Fleming, *Civil War and Reconstruction in Alabama*, p. 340.

deed, conceived in terms that were uncompromising. But he also recognized that the extreme Southern notion of reconstruction would not do, and between that conception and his own there were certain marked distinctions. He did say that the states had never for one moment been outside the Union, and that when restoration was complete, they would be states in every sense as before, with none of their "reserved" rights in any way impaired. But he also claimed that the officers of those states, in exercising power under a "right" that had never existed—the so-called right of secession—had been treasonable and insurrectionary. It was under the pardoning power that the President could at this point assume extensive authority in the rebalancing of things. Indeed, through this power he, the President, became the sole authority on reconstruction; no other was needed. He could withhold pardon while new governments—or, more properly, new sets of officers whose loyalty was not in doubt—were being installed in the rebellious states. Meanwhile the states themselves, though not dead, remained "asleep"—in a condition, as it were, of suspended animation—and the President would in this interim, through the appointment of provisional governors, supervise the performance of certain acts prerequisite to their full functioning. With these satisfactorily accomplished, he would, still under the pardoning power, breathe the full breath of the Constitution into the states. Thereupon they would be fully "awake" in all senses, and in full possession of the rights they had had before, which included among others that of regulating the franchise.[14]

But the very dogmatism with which Johnson insisted on the strict constitutionality of one side of his program left the other side of it exposed to a certain amount of not unjustified criticism. There were inconsistencies which both the "Southern" and the "conquered provinces" advocates were equally quick to point out. "How absurd," exclaimed Thaddeus Stevens, "his interfering with the internal regula-

[14] Johnson's first expression, as President, of his constitutional views on secession and reconstruction appears to have been made on April 21, 1865, in reply to compliments tendered him by a delegation of Indiana citizens headed by Governor Oliver P. Morton. In his remarks, the President referred to his position as "heretofore well known," and he saw "no cause to change it now." "Some are satisfied," he said, "with the idea that States are to be lost in territorial and other divisions; [and] are to lose their character as States. But their life-breath has only been suspended. . . ." Frank Moore, *Speeches of Andrew Johnson* (Boston: Little, Brown, 1865), p. 483; see also George W. Julian, *Political Recollections*, pp. 260–62. The full doctrine, summarized above, in which Johnson outlined his conception of the executive function in restoring this "life-breath," was given in his first Annual Message of December 4, 1865. Richardson, *Messages and Papers*, VI, 353 ff.

tions of the States, and yet consider them as '*States in the Union.*'"[15] Walter Fleming, a scholar who did much around 1900 to present the South's case to the nation, said largely the same thing. "For a firm believer in the rights of states," Fleming wrote of Johnson, "he took strong liberties with them while restoring their suspended animation."[16] As the President discussed his plan to appoint a provisional governor in North Carolina with various prominent citizens of that state, B. F. Moore, of the more irreconcilable wing (W.W. Holden, leader of the "moderate" faction, was the man Johnson ultimately appointed as governor), was shocked and appalled at the plan. He declared that Johnson had no constitutional power to carry it out. He said that the state could be led back "with a silken thread" and urged that its legislature be permitted to take charge of the business of calling a convention and managing the restoration. Johnson replied, doubtless with prudence, that he could not afford to risk it.[17] Were he to recognize the legislature, he would, by the very act of legitimizing it, abdicate all further control over the state's affairs. Such was the impasse into which his own logic had brought him.

Looming always behind the idea of a "presidential theory" on reconstruction is of course the shadow of Abraham Lincoln. In this realm, the realm of the theoretical, Lincoln must forever remain something of a shadow. But this very aspect of indeterminacy should itself tell us something about the theoretical clothing of Lincoln's words and deeds and give us clues to the differences, if any, between his and his successor's conception of how the Constitution might or might not apply to the problem of reconstruction. In private life Andrew Johnson, the tailor of Greeneville, had made it a point of pride to give his customers "a good snug fit," and it seemed to be in much the same spirit that he measured the cloth of the Constitution to everything he did in public life. For Lincoln, on the other hand, wartime experience had taught him that the constitutional "fit" of certain things he did must be rather loose and free. He could not afford, at any rate, to sew himself up in his own reasoning.

The strains which were placed upon the Constitution by Lincoln and his government—thinking now of the instrument only in its inhibitive character—have been commented upon so many times that to

---

15 Stevens to Sumner, June 14, 1865, Sumner MSS.

16 Fleming, *Civil War and Reconstruction in Alabama*, p. 338.

17 Hamilton, *Reconstruction in North Carolina*, pp. 106–7.

do more than mention them would be simply to rehearse the familiar.[18] The government found itself forced, for some purposes, to regard the war as an insurrection, so that it might take advantage, in practical policy, of the many legal consequences which would flow from its own role as sovereign in suppressing domestic rebellion. At the same time it was necessary to pretend, for still other purposes, that the United States was engaged in war with an alien enemy, so that the government might claim certain "rights" accruing to a status of belligerency. The Constitution was forced—or, shall we say, found itself not unprepared—to meet this dilemma in the *Prize Cases*, and in effect to absorb it.[19] A majority of the Supreme Court on that occasion found that the country was engaged in something that had a dual nature—a war as well as an insurrection; the federal government thus "sustained the double character of a belligerent and a sovereign, and had the rights of both."[20]

As the time approached when reconstruction would be a problem faced in every Southern state and in the South at large, as well as a problem that involved many Southern individuals figuring prominently in the rebellion, it is with difficulty that we picture Lincoln deliberately renouncing the advantages inherent in this essentially dual concept of war and insurrection. On the one hand, his role as the fountainhead of mercy gave him the useful power to extend or withhold pardon to or from individuals for treason. On the other hand, as head of a national state dealing with an enemy once powerful—an

[18] "He carried his executive authority to the extent of freeing the slaves by proclamation, setting up a whole scheme of state-making for the purpose of reconstruction, suspending the *habeas corpus* privilege, proclaiming martial law, enlarging the army and navy beyond the limits fixed by existing law, and spending public money without congressional appropriation. [Etc.]" James G. Randall, *Constitutional Problems under Lincoln* (New York: D. Appleton, 1926), p. 514. "In all this extension of governmental power there was a noticeable lack of legal precision. A tendency toward irregularity may be observed as a characteristic of the period, in military and civil administration, in legislation, and in legal interpretation." *Ibid.*, pp. 515–16. But Professor Randall adds: "In a legal study of the war the two most significant facts are perhaps these: the wide extent of the war powers; and, in contrast to that, the manner in which the men in authority were nevertheless controlled by the American people's sense of constitutional government." *Ibid.*, p. 522.

[19] "All persons residing within this territory," wrote Justice Grier in the majority opinion, "whose property may be used to increase the revenues of the hostile power are, in this contest, liable to be treated as enemies, though not foreigners. They have cast off their allegiance and made war on their Government, and are none the less enemies because they are traitors." *Prize Cases* 2 Black 674 (1863).

[20] *Miller v. United States*, 11 Wallace 306–7 (1870). "The conflict was defined as both a public war and a rebellion, with the result that in Southern territory the United States claimed both belligerent and municipal powers. Many bootless and mystifying discussions resulted from this acceptance of two inconsistent viewpoints." Randall, *Constitutional Problems*, p. 516.

enemy bound in the course of things to become a power again—he might, in his search for a settlement, have recourse to a whole range of political, and even diplomatic, devices. Two levels of effort would be necessary in order to retain these potential advantages, and there is reason to suppose that Lincoln was quite conscious of both, though fully aware that neither was simple. At one such level, the looseness of any and all plans had to be preserved with much care; all policy must be protected from rigidity. At the other, it was important to discourage excessive theoretical talk, to suppress the distinctions and inconsistencies of "duality" as much as possible, in order that an essentially murky problem be prevented from taking on too much theoretical precision. This discipline—if such it may be called—of practical flexibility and theoretical vagueness was imposed so successfully, at least on himself, that we are by no means sure what Lincoln did want, except in a general direction, regarding policy on reconstruction. We may even suspect that he was anything but sure himself. His final acts form a striking sequence in the behavior of a man still making up his mind.

Back in 1863, when Lincoln's first general moves toward reconstruction had contained objectives of an immediate military as well as an ultimately peacetime character, he had taken particular pains to emphasize the fluid quality of those moves. The closing words of his "Ten Per Cent Plan" proclamation of December 8 were: ". . . while the mode presented is the best the Executive can suggest, with his present impressions, it must not be understood that no other possible mode would be acceptable." In July, 1864, he gave as one of his reasons for not approving the Wade-Davis reconstruction bill his reluctance "to be inflexibly committed to any single plan of restoration"; and the same theme, with variations, was developed in his address to the seranaders on April 11, 1865:

. . . so great peculiarities pertain to each State, and such important and sudden changes occur in the same State, and withal so new and unprecedented is the whole case, that no exclusive and inflexible plan can safely be prescribed as to details and collaterals. Such exclusive and inflexible plan would surely become a new entanglement.

The President also reminded his audience on that occasion that he had "distinctly protested that the Executive claimed no right to say when or whether members should be admitted to seats in Congress from such States." Nor was he opposed, he remarked, to the principle of breaking bad promises.[21]

[21] *Collected Works*, VII, 56, 433, VIII, 399–405.

The other theme of this last public speech, in addition to that of flexibility of practice, was on the particular role which should be assigned to theory. This too is a repetition of something many times quoted, "the question whether the seceded States, so called, are in the Union or out of it." It is often repeated simply as a kind of wry cracker-barrel caution against making the mind giddy with undue philosophizing. But what is not fully self-evident is a specific warning not to formalize a problem that had not yet crystallized—a plea just to refrain from talking about it too much.

> . . . I [myself] have *purposely* forborne any public expression upon it. As appears to me . . . any discussion of it, while it thus remains practically immaterial, could have no effect other than the mischievous one of dividing our friends. As yet, whatever it may hereafter become, that question is bad, as the basis of a controversy, and good for nothing at all—a merely pernicious abstraction. We all agree that the seceded States, so called, are out of their proper practical relation with the Union; and that the sole object of the government, civil and military, in regard to those States, is to again get them into their proper practical relation. I believe it is not only possible, but in fact, easier, to do this, without deciding or even considering, whether those States have ever been out of the Union, than with it.[22]

The humanity of Lincoln's intentions toward the defeated South and his desire for an early restoration are well known. Those intentions might easily be translated into theoretical and constitutional terms not unlike those in which Johnson developed his own views on reconstruction. But Lincoln's own unwillingness to do the translating should not pass without notice. The North Carolina proclamation, it is known, was very similar to one which had been discussed at Lincoln's last cabinet meeting.[23] Whether he would have issued the same one for all the other states, as Johnson did, we cannot of course know. But there is, again, some importance in Lincoln's odd aversion to committing himself and his acts to theory: it might become peculiarly convenient for him to consider the states as having been both "in" and "out"—out for some purposes and in for others. After the restoring was done, men could then discuss the matter in any constitutional terms which might by that time appear most proper and most orthodox.

In any event, during the last two weeks of Lincoln's life he operated,

---

[22] *Ibid.*, VII, 402–3. Italics added.

[23] The proclamation had actually been prepared by Secretary of War Stanton. Welles, *Diary*, II, 281, 301; Charles H. McCarthy, *Lincoln's Plan of Reconstruction* (New York: McClure, Phillips, 1901), p. 458.

with regard to the case of Virginia, at both levels. After the evacuation of Richmond, his equivocal dealings there with Judge John A. Campbell, the Confederacy's erstwhile assistant secretary of war, gave rise to a certain amount of misunderstanding which has not been fully cleared up to this day. But from the very nature of the balance which Lincoln was trying to maintain in his own mind, such ambiguity would probably still exist even if we knew for certain all that the two men said to each other. Lincoln wanted to let Campbell carry out his plan for assembling the Virginia legislature, which would in turn take that state out of the war and avoid a final major battle. He even issued orders to his commander at Richmond sanctioning such a meeting, even though he already had a "Virginia" government operating at Alexandria which he recognized *de jure* while its *de facto* power was nil. Campbell might be expected, of course, to construe as much legitimacy into the idea of a "legislature" as circumstances permitted; Lincoln, on the other hand, would make the maximum possible use of these men's moral authority over their own constituents, while reserving somewhere in his mind the legal fiction that they had only "acted as" a legislature ("so-called"), that they were simply a group of influential gentlemen. But when he got back to Washington he found that none of his cabinet approved of the scheme anyway, whereupon he repudiated it and countermanded his own orders. Judge Campbell, as may be imagined, supposed himself to have been left somewhat in the lurch.[24] General Sherman, moreover, who knew something of what was going through Lincoln's mind during this period but who could hardly appreciate the full deviousness of that mind, may possibly be excused for the political blunder which he himself committed less than a week after Lincoln's death.[25]

A strict constitutional definition of the states' condition could hardly have been construed with any finality out of these goings-on. Nor could such a definition, at that time, have failed to be anything but an embarrassment to Lincoln, who was still experimenting with alternatives and trying to keep them in suspension. Abraham Lincoln,

[24] This episode is described in James G. Randall and Richard N. Current, *Lincoln the President: Last Full Measure* (New York: Dodd, Mead, 1955), pp. 353–59; Lincoln's order to General Weitzel on April 6 is in the *Collected Works*, VIII, 389; and the two countermanding telegrams of April 12, *ibid.*, pp. 405–7. Campbell's side of the story is told in "Papers of Hon. John A. Campbell—1861–1865," *Southern Historical Society Papers*, N.S. IV, 61–74 (October, 1917). See also Welles, *Diary*, II, 279–80.

[25] I.e., the surrender arrangements with Johnston. Not only had Sherman not received a copy of Lincoln's March 3 order to Grant; he had apparently not heard of Lincoln's revoking the April 6 order to Weitzel either. Welles, *Diary*, p. 296.

himself a lawyer, was certainly as competent as anyone to construe the Constitution, probably more so than his successor; nor could his reverence for the Constitution, and all it represented, have been any less deep than that of the man who followed him. But the President's primary relation to the Constitution, Lincoln seems to have assumed, was a political and not a judicial one; it was not to the advantage of his political mobility, at a time of breakup and rapid change in all relationships, to take on the additional role of constitutional preceptor. The President's base of operations was a political base, and it would take more than conflicts of inclination, or a desire for constitutional clarity, to induce him to stray very far from it. His advisers, his government, his party—it was from these, not from the Constitution, in any immediate functioning sense, that his power must be drawn.

Abraham Lincoln did not have much luck, of course, in trying to keep other men from theorizing; it was something they had to do, and it is well in the long run that they did. But the most that they got from him, in the way of clues on reconstruction, was mildness of intention and ambiguity of theory. Those who hoped that Johnson's policy in 1865 was conceived as an "experiment" would have had little to sustain them had it not been for Lincoln's example—an example not of precision but of indeterminacy.[26]

Whatever may have been President Johnson's virtues, he was at least no experimenter: once the minimum conditions had been fulfilled, the constitutional logic would be set implacably in motion. If for any reason the Southern representatives were then denied admission, the wheels would by definition be stopped. Johnson would subsequently assert, in his vetoes of the Freedmen's Bureau and Civil Rights bills, that among his reasons for disapproving such legislation was the fact that Congress had refused to allow the Southerners to

[26] E.g., *Harper's Weekly*: "But President Johnson is doing what President Lincoln did: he is feeling his way." IX (July 1, 1865), 402. "Like his great predecessor, he has no way but the people's way. . . ." *Ibid.*, IX (Dec. 23, 1865), 802. See also above, chap. 3, n. 44. By April, 1866, *Harper's* was chiding Johnson for his stubbornness and saying that part of Lincoln's greatness lay in the very fact that he seldom had his mind made up. *Ibid.*, X (Apr. 14, 1866), 226. Comparing the two, George Julian, who did little to conceal his antipathy toward Lincoln, found himself forced to much the same sort of preference between two evils that had caused Hamilton to prefer Jefferson over Burr, on the grounds of his being a temporizer. "It was forgotten in the fever and turbulence of the moment," he wrote, "that Mr. Lincoln, who was never an obstinate man, and who in the matter of his Proclamation of Emancipation had surrendered his own judgment under the pressure of public opinion, would not have been likely to wrestle with Congress and the country in a mad struggle for his own way." Julian, *Political Recollections*, p. 256.

take their seats.[27] As long as such refusal persisted, in short, no legislation touching Southern conditions could properly be considered as constitutional. Why, then, had the President taken a hand in the process at all? He knew, somehow, that certain prerequisite acts had to be performed. But he was simply setting up the conditions, or so he imagined, under which they might be performed "voluntarily."

As soon as the full drift of Johnson's policy was clear, his course very quickly became acceptable to most Southerners and to most Northern Democrats. By the same token, it became anathema to the great majority of the party of which Johnson was nominally the head. He had so defined his position that the power to set matters going was exclusively his, whereupon the new officers and legislatures, once elected, were automatically out of his control. There were great difficulties, both theoretical and practical, in this position. The mixed logic, simply on its merits, had much in it that was dubious when maintained on rigid constitutional grounds. But the most acute difficulty, the really practical one, might best be characterized as political. The President's narrow insistence, balanced only on the pardoning power, that he be conceded full authority over a matter of the most vital interest to Congress and people, and against the deepest convictions of a majority of both, did not augur well for the success of his administration. Indeed, to give notice as a matter of principle—when the peacetime precedents for it existed nowhere—that Congress and the nation be excluded from participating in such vital decisions, could not have failed to strike thousands of the President's well-wishers as the gravest folly.

A by-product of all this, as everyone knows, would shortly be a

---

[27] "The Constitution imperatively declares . . . that each State *shall* have at least one Representative, and fixes the rule for the number. . . . It also provides that the Senate of the United States *shall* be composed of two Senators from each State, and adds with peculiar force 'that no State, without its consent, shall be deprived of its equal suffrage in the Senate.' . . . At the time, however, of the consideration and the passing of this bill there was no Senator or Representative in Congress from the eleven States which are to be mainly affected by its provisions. . . . As eleven States are not at this time represented in either branch of Congress, it would seem to be . . . [my] duty on all proper occasions to present their just claims to Congress. . . . It is hardly necessary for me to inform Congress that in my own judgment most of those States, so far, at least, as depends upon their own action, have already been fully restored, and are to be deemed as entitled to enjoy their constitutional rights as members of the Union." Richardson, *Messages and Papers*, VI, 403–5.

Johnson took another thrust at this same point the following month in his veto of the Civil Rights Bill. Therein he said that if Negroes were not already citizens, it was a "grave question" whether it would be "sound policy" to make them so, "when eleven of the thirty-six States are unrepresented in Congress at the present time." *Ibid.*, p. 406. The first veto was delivered on February 19, 1866, the second on March 27.

bitter struggle for power between the executive and legislative branches of the government. But it would be quite misleading to say that the "purpose" of the struggle was to settle this balance of powers, or to assume that the conflict would necessarily have occurred on some other grounds if not over reconstruction. The primary question was what to do with the Southern states, and that question had assumed so acute an importance that men's minds were temporarily disposed toward measures going much beyond the normal in order that it might be settled. Had harmony on that single issue prevailed, it is quite conceivable that the great shocks which were later sustained by the system of checks and balances would never have occurred.

IV "STATE SUICIDE"

To some extent the reconstruction doctrine of Charles Sumner may be thought of as the return stroke of the pendulum. It embodied certain features of the presidential plan, though it also resembled the "conquered provinces" theory—for its own prospects, perhaps, a little too much so. Still, it was somewhat less extreme than the latter theory. Sumner first proposed "state suicide" as a formula for reconstruction in a series of Senate resolutions on February 11, 1862. Constitutionally, he argued, it was impossible to remove United States territory from the jurisdiction of the federal government. But the attempt on the part of the inhabitants to do so, though constitutionally inoperative and void, was both an act of treason and a disruption of normal constitutional relations so extreme that it had extinguished all rights of the entity as a state. The state, that is, had through its inhabitants performed an act of suicide: ". . . the State becomes, according to the language of the law, *felo de se.*"[28]

Thus, although the United States retained jurisdiction and control in all former states where this had occurred, such control must be exercised as over territories. Under the Constitution this could only be done by Congress. Congress would "proceed to establish therein republican forms of government under the Constitution." Though state lines would presumably remain intact (they did not necessarily remain so under the Stevens theory), the suspension of political statehood automatically terminated "those peculiar local institutions which, having no origin in the Constitution, or in natural right independent of the Constitution, are upheld by the sole and exclusive authority of

[28] *Works of Charles Sumner* (Boston: Lee & Shepard, 1880), VI, 301–5; *Cong. Globe*, 37 Cong., 1 sess., pp. 736–37 (Feb. 11, 1862).

the State." Here Sumner specifically referred to the institution of slavery. These territories might only come back to statehood by fulfilling conditions which Congress should find compatible with a republican form of government. To these conditions Sumner, in later elaborations, added Negro suffrage—basing it upon the Declaration of Independence.[29]

This theory came very close in substance to what many men wanted. Its outlines were straightforward; and whatever the specific conditions of readmission might finally be, they need not have been Sumner's conditions in order to be imposed within Sumner's framework. The suspension of state functions was not so drastically conceived as it had been by Stevens; indeed, it was not at all unlike the Johnson conception, except that it was more specific than the latter, less provisional and more orderly, and defined for what it was. It made many connections not only with the *de facto* state of affairs but also with the Constitution itself.[30] In its total impact, however, there were still difficulties, principally of tone. The "suicide" metaphor, while apt enough (suicide may be "illegal," but a man can find ways to accomplish it),

[29] Sumner's basic position was laid down in his 1862 resolutions. In further development of his views, he prepared a speech for delivery later in that session, but having no good occasion to give it, he published it instead as an article in the *Atlantic Monthly*, XII (October, 1863), 507–29, under the title "Our Domestic Relations: Power of Congress over the Rebel States." Here the combined wisdom, precedents, and authorities of all ages were invoked to support and enlarge greatly upon his original premises; and it included the picturesque statement, "The whole broad Rebel region is *tabula rasa*, or 'a clean slate,' where Congress, under the Constitution of the United States, may write the laws." *Works*, VII, 534. This general notion of the states' abdication, by self-destruction, of their constitutional rights was argued by Sumner in the Senate on various subsequent occasions; e.g., on the admission of a senator from Arkansas, June 13, 1864; on the ratification of a constitutional amendment by rebel states, February 4, 1865; and on the representation of Virginia in the Senate, February 17, 1865. *Ibid.*, IX, 1–24, 233–35, 266–68.

Negro suffrage was specifically urged by Sumner, as one of the prerequisites for readmission, in his remarks in the Senate in February, 1865, on the Louisiana provisional government. *Ibid.*, IX, 311–23. By September, 1865, Sumner's views on both Negro suffrage and the constitutional relations of the seceded states were well known. Both lines of doctrine were more or less combined (though the latter, often repeated, had now come to be taken for granted in his public utterances) in a speech given on September 14, 1865, before the Massachusetts state Republican convention at Worcester. This speech, together with the 1862 resolutions, may be taken as Sumner's counterpart, for his theory, of Stevens' September speech at Lancaster for his. *Ibid.*, IX, 441–77.

[30] Another "state suicide" advocate was Orestes Brownson, who said, "The rebellion, in a word, kills the whole State and everything dependent on it. Whether the State be revived and permitted to return to the Union depends entirely on the good pleasure of the Federal authority." *Brownson's Quarterly Review*, III (April, 1862), 201–2. He also developed it in his *American Republic: Its Constitution, Tendencies & Destiny* (New York: P. O'Shea, 1866), pp. 277–347.

was still somewhat extravagant, and extravagant metaphors do not often find their way into constitutional doctrine. Moreover, the association of the theory with Charles Sumner himself, with the unnaturally ardent views on suffrage which the man's very name stood for, made other men shy away from it. Besides, the senator's habit of festooning his arguments with endless precedents and quotations on classical subjects touched often on the bizarre and filled his colleagues with ennui whenever he spoke.[31] The "state suicide" theory of reconstruction, for reasons that were not so much substantive as qualitative, was received by most men as being quite doctrinaire.

Where would the pendulum come to rest? What were the requirements for a fully satisfactory constitutional formula? The picture would probably have to be blurred somewhat, and the doctrine even made a little dull. One of Sumner's correspondents wondered whether it would not be possible to put in a little of everything. Let the states be "thrice dead—once by abdication—once by forfeiture and once by becoming the subjects of conquest under the sanction of the law of nations."[32] This sort of thing might well be considered as the mere urge to play with words in order to camouflage what was going to be done anyway. It was that, but not "merely" that. It was absolutely necessary to theorize; this was what had always been done in the past when change was in the offing. But by the same token, theory must be dulled and softened in such a way that men might see themselves as doing what they were in fact doing: trying to think conservatively about something that was in all ways an extreme situation. In finding sanctions for doing what an overwhelming majority of the dominant party wanted done—simply to have the Southern states held out awhile —it was necessary to keep at a minimum the dramatic and lurid aspects of change which all knew was inevitable. "Their feelings and instincts," as Burgess put it, "required a principle of reconstruction which, at the same time that it did not recognize secession as having any validity for the shortest moment, yet regarded the 'States' in which it was attempted, as having thereby become something other than 'States' of the Union, and as requiring the assent of Congress to

[31] "The infirmity in Mr. Sumner's theories of reconstruction," wrote a fellow senator many years later, "came from the great exuberance of his learning. He ransacked history, ancient and modern, for precedents growing out of civil wars. But these precedents all antedated the American Constitution. . . . Under our system there can be no suicide of a State." John B. Henderson to Charles H. McCarthy, Aug. 21, 1901, quoted in McCarthy, *Lincoln's Plan of Reconstruction*, p. 495.

[32] John Y. Smith to Sumner, Aug. 11, 1865, Sumner MSS, Harvard College Library. Smith edited the *Argus* of Madison, Wisconsin.

the rightful resumption of that status."[33] This can all be seen as "mere sham"; but though viewing the thing in such a light may be the simplest way, it is not necessarily the only way.

V THE SOLUTION: SHELLABARGER'S "FORFEITED RIGHTS" THEORY

On January 8, 1866, Samuel Shellabarger of Ohio, a man of rather scholarly aspect, delivered a speech in the House of Representatives on the subject of reconstruction. The circumstances were not of the best. He was embarrassed by the one-hour rule; he was interrupted and had to bandy words over legal authorities (he had, however, painstakingly looked them all up in advance); he overran his time; one of his colleagues kindly moved that the time be extended; and in his race with the clock he was obliged to omit various sections of the discourse which he had so laboriously prepared. Thus the clarity of his argument was probably not all that it could have been and he had later to do a certain amount of explaining just what he had meant. Despite all this, his ideas appear to have been well received, and he was congratulated upon them later by various important persons, including the Chief Justice. In fact, Samuel Shellabarger's theory ultimately became, in one form or another, the majority position on reconstruction.

It was very little different from the Sumner theory, though perhaps a little less clear; Burgess, indeed, lumped the two together. "There is no doubt," he wrote, "that the Sumner-Shellabarger theory of Reconstruction was correct. The only question was how exacting Congress would be in realizing it."[34] Secession was void, according to Shellabarger's doctrine; no state ever was or could be out of the Union. A "state," however, had more than one character. It was a territorial entity with its inhabitants, and in that character it could not be altered.

I will not inquire whether any subject of this Government, by reason of the revolt, passed from under its sovereignty or ceased to owe it allegiance, nor whether any territory passed from under that jurisdiction, because I know of no one who thinks that any of these things did occur. I shall not consider whether, by the rebellion, any State lost its territorial character or defined boundaries or subdivisions, for I know of no one who would obliterate these geographical qualities of the States.[35]

[33] Burgess, *Reconstruction and the Constitution*, p. 59.

[34] *Ibid.*, p. 61.

[35] *Cong. Globe*, 39 Cong., 1 sess., p. 142.

It might be noted that under the Stevens theory such boundaries could be eliminated; even in Sumner's there were no absolute guarantees against it.

But a state must also be considered in another character, that of a "body politic" with powers of government—an entity long recognized both in constitutional law and in the law of nations. After the rebellion, states in this character could not be considered in the same relation to the federal government as before: ". . . such States and their people ceased to have any of the rights or powers of government as States of this Union. . . ."[36]

What was to be done? Shellabarger did not say anything specific on this, except that the key would be found in the constitutional obligation "to guaranty to each State a republican form of government." The implication of this phraseology was that a state could be a state and still be capable of having lapsed from a republican form of government.[37] This corresponded to the "suspended animation" features of Johnson's and Sumner's theories, and, in addition, like those of Sumner and Stevens, located the power to reconstruct in Congress. Here Shellabarger quoted the language of the Court in *Luther* v. *Borden*, wherein Chief Justice Taney had said,

Under this article of the Constitution it rests with Congress to decide which government . . . is the established one, for as the United States guaranties to each State a republican government, Congress must necessarily determine what government is established in a State before it can decide whether it is republican or not.[38]

Whatever the proofs that might be required to settle this question ("is it safe, and are they fit?"), there was at least no disputing the right of Congress, under the Constitution, to take jurisdiction and decide. "This," asserted Burgess, "was sound political science and correct constitutional law."[39]

Shellabarger maintained that his position was really the most conservative of all, and such was the basis on which he promoted it. This

[36] *Ibid.*, p. 142.

[37] "It is absolutely self-evident," Shellabarger explained afterward, "that here a thing is still looked at as, and called 'a state' which has no government or no republican one—else why talk about giving or guaranteeing to each 'STATE' a republican gov. if there could be no Constitutional possibility as a state having lost such government & why talk about guaranteeing a thing which could not possibly be other wise than continue to be." A state in its geographical entity, in other words, can live to be reconstructed in its character as a body politic. Samuel Shellabarger to James Comly, [Jan. 20, 1866], Comly MSS, Ohio Historical Society.

[38] 7 Howard 1, 42 (1849).

[39] Burgess, *Reconstruction and the Constitution*, p. 60.

assumption may seem a little odd. But the setting was by that time one in which Democratic strict-construction states'-rights doctrine had been ruled out a priori; meanwhile a good many hot words were being poured forth about conquered provinces, the law of nations, and even the possibility that the Constitution might, for this problem, be disregarded altogether. That same setting, therefore, was one in which Shellabarger's words could be received with considerable favor by men looking for middle ground. In a letter to his friend James Comly, Shellabarger praised a speech made on January 19 by Representative Henry C. Deming of Connecticut, which took ground not dissimilar to his own. However, Shellabarger said, "he may go the length of Stephens [*sic*] as to these states being mere territories & he requires guarantees I do not." "By the way," he added, comfortably, "I think you will find that my positions are conservative in contrast with the aggregate opinions of both branches of Congress."[40]

Such, also, was the viewpoint of Chief Justice Salmon P. Chase. The Chief Justice had already outlined the same position in a letter to the Cincinnati *Commercial* in 1865. He held

that no State has ever been withdrawn from the Union or from the authority of the National Government by any such acts or ordinances [of secession]; but each State, with its former boundaries & with its entire population remains, in the Union & subject to its Constitutional authority as before attempted secession.

But it does not follow that the *entire* population of a rebel State remains in the same condition or in the same relations to the nation & the National Government.[41]

Chase's purpose in making the point at this time—he added that there was no reason in law why the work of reorganization was necessarily bound by the state's pre-existing laws—was to promote a favorite design of his, Negro suffrage. But aside from this, his was not essentially a radical position.[42] It found its way into the majority side (and the conservative side) of a Supreme Court decision several years later. It was Chase himself who wrote the opinion.

The problem, in *Texas* v. *White*, was whether a loyal state government of Texas might recover some United States bonds alleged to have

[40] Shellabarger to Comly, [Jan. 20, 1866], Comly MSS.

[41] "To the Proprietors of the 'Commercial,'" [1865], Chase MSS, Pennsylvania Historical Society.

[42] Radicalism on a single issue, as with Chase, can do strange tricks with what we see of a man's personality as refracted through that one subject. But the Sherman brothers (for example), who were nothing if not "conservative," appreciated Chase's own essentially conservative nature, aside from his peculiar views on suffrage; moreover, they thought he would make a good President. See *Sherman Letters*, pp. 293, 295, 299.

been improperly alienated by the disloyal government of Texas for the purpose of furthering the rebellion. But the weightier problem, so far as the Court was concerned, was whether it could take jurisdiction at all. Someone had to decide whether Texas had or had not *ceased* to be a state by reason of rebellion, before it could be known whether Texas could or could not be a party to an original suit before that Court. The same reasoning and the same conclusions on that point formed the basis of the majority opinion as set forth in brief by the Chief Justice in 1865 and at greater length by Representative Shellabarger early in 1866.

The state of Texas (and thus, by implication, all the so-called Confederate states) had never terminated its obligations as a state in the Union, for it had entered into an indissoluble relation to the United States, an act which was final. Thus the ordinance of secession "and all the acts of her legislature intended to give effect to that ordinance, were absolutely null."[43] (It was on this basis that the Court thought Texas entitled to bring suit.) However, said the Court, it by no means followed that because the state remained in this sense a "state," its relations to the Union had remained unaltered while in rebellion. "All admit that, during this condition of civil war, the rights of the State as a member, and of her people as citizens of the Union, were suspended." After the suppression of the rebellion, it became the duty of the federal government to re-establish the broken relations, and, for doing so, "authority was derived from the obligation of the United States to guarantee to every State in the Union a republican form of government."[44]

In locating the power to carry out this guaranty clause, Chase invoked the precedent of *Luther* v. *Borden* (as Shellabarger had done), saying that it was "primarily a legislative power, and resides in Congress." "The action of the President," he added, "must, therefore, be

[43] *Texas* v. *White*, 7 Wallace 726 (1869). As Chase prepares this position, his rhetoric very perceptibly alters in rhythm. It assumes a loftiness which evokes (perhaps consciously) the cadences of Marshall himself: "The Union of the States never was a purely artificial and arbitrary relation. It began among the Colonies, and grew out of common origin, mutual sympathies, kindred principles, similar interests, and geographical relations. It was confirmed and strengthened by the necessities of war, and received definite form, and character, and sanction from the Articles of Confederation. By these the Union was solemnly declared to 'be perpetual.' And when these Articles were found to be inadequate to the exigencies of the country, the Constitution was ordained 'to form a more perfect Union.' It is difficult to convey the idea of indissoluble unity more clearly than by these words. What can be indissoluble if a perpetual Union, made more perfect, is not?" *Ibid.*, 724–25.

[44] *Ibid.*, 727–28.

considered as provisional, and, in that light, it seems to have been regarded by Congress."[45] Reconstruction, in short, fell under the guaranty clause, and the determination of whether or not that clause's conditions were met must be considered (as the earlier Court under Taney had also considered it) primarily a political question.

Justice Grier, speaking for himself and two other dissenting justices, wanted to go much further and base the constitutionality of the matter on *de facto* grounds entirely, looking first at what the rebel state had done and then at what Congress had done. "This is to be decided as a *political fact*, not as a *legal fiction*." On those grounds it would be discovered that Texas (and by implication every other rebel state) was in fact a state no longer and was entitled to no such rights as were now being claimed for it.

Is Texas a State, now represented by members chosen by the people of that state and received on the floor of Congress? Has she two senators to represent her as a State in the Senate of the United States? Has her voice been heard in the late election of President? Is she not now held and governed as a conquered province by military force?
. . . I can only submit to *the fact* as decided by the political position of the government; and I am not disposed to join in any essay to prove Texas to be a State of the Union, when Congress have decided that she is not. It is a question of fact, I repeat, and of fact only. *Politically*, Texas is not *a State in this Union.*[46]

The argument was clean and simple, and facts were indeed facts. But the facts had been placed at a very great distance from the Constitution—too great for the taste of the majority justices. They said, in effect, no: we must balance fact and *law*. Here, apparently, was the point at which the pendulum had come to rest.

Constitutional matters may make for a certain stuffiness; it may even be fortunate that such matters have a way of protecting themselves against flamboyancy and sparkle. Stuffiness and rigidity, however, do not have to come to the same thing. Treating the Constitution as something immaculate and apart can bring great perplexity when it comes to such a problem as reconstruction. Reconstruction was hardly one of those Gordian knots that could be cut by a clean judicial blade. There is a good case for saying that the Shellabarger-Chase approach to reconstruction, so far as theory was con-

---

[45] *Ibid.*, 730.

[46] *Ibid.*, 738–39. The other two dissenting justices, besides Grier, were Swayne and Miller.

cerned, was in a full sense the conservative one. In the working-out of such a position, an adjustment of political needs to the Constitution, and vice versa, was going on in a large way just as it had always gone on in smaller ways—in recognition that the nature of that instrument was elastic, not brittle, as certain of the other theories had appeared to presume. At the same time, the Constitution was not something that could be stretched infinitely.

All matters of public policy must necessarily have a constitutional dimension, for the Constitution is by definition the supreme law. But there are in practice relatively few such matters that the Constitution can decide in advance. There are occasionally problems of such magnitude that the Court itself must simply look to the principle of majority rule as the key to their ultimate settlement.[47] Here was a case in which the Republican party, now the all-powerful arbiter of political decisions, backed by crushing Northern majorities and opposed by a stubborn Executive, was bound to have its way and impose its will. But had men suddenly lost their willingness to be kept in rein by the concept of the Constitution? Given needs which had somehow come to be defined as imperative, was the effort to settle them conservatively still possible? Here was a test, in the form of a choice among various theoretical alternatives.

One alternative, which was never taken, would have been a fresh start—a real shattering of the mold, an abandonment altogether of the Constitution as a hampering factor in men's decisions. The choices might then have been widened to make possible the greatest variety of action against the conquered states. Meanwhile the Court, arbiter of the supreme law, would by definition have been cut adrift from that traditional function, preserved intact from its traditional responsibilities, a mere spectator to revolutionary doings. It would be well to think of that alternative along with the others in reflecting, as commentators sometimes do, on the "weakness" of the Court in reconstruction. For there were men who, in their less guarded moments, blurted out that so far as they were concerned the country *was* in a state of revolution and that the Constitution had nothing to do with the case.

Instead, the idea of constitutional Union, for all the upheaval of those years, would ultimately come to supersede every other senti-

[47] The doctrine of political questions has proved indispensable to the Court on many occasions, though even here (as in *Texas* v. *White*) there can be both a more extreme and a less extreme interpretation of it. On this doctrine see Charles G. Post, Jr., *The Supreme Court and Political Questions* (Baltimore: Johns Hopkins Press, 1936), esp. pp. 15–27, 38–46, 109–12.

ment. For it was always the *idea*, as well as the charter itself, that was needed to complete the full essence of a Constitution. It worked both ways; the Constitution, under great stress, still retained both its elasticity and its toughness. We tend to think of the twelve years of reconstruction, while the instrument made its adjustments, as an eternity. But there may be no paradox in supposing that one of the very things that made it seem so was ingrained constitutional scruples and that without those scruples it might have lasted much, much longer.

Reconstruction
as a Problem
in Policy

Just as reconstruction was a problem with a theoretical dimension, so also was it a problem in actual policy. The theoretical part had been called into being because it seemed vitally important at the time to define in legal terms the occasion which had made reconstruction necessary and to discover the constitutional basis upon which it should rest. But to work out that aspect of it was still to make no more than the barest beginning. Beyond providing a few general directions, constitutional theory could be of next to no help in the mapping of specific policy.

The ultimate objective was not really "reconstruction," nor was it exactly "restoration" either; it was a combination of both: reunion.[1] It was both an institutional problem and a problem of individuals. The government must of course have its reckoning with individuals; loyalty which had been corrupted by rebellion must be recaptured and purified. But in addition there was an institutional side not to be got at by any amount of individual "purification." The Union and Confederate governments had in fact represented two quite distinct institutional structures which must now be knit back into one. Individual oaths in themselves had no power to accomplish this. Individuals could truthfully forswear all inclination to rebel against the authority of a central government, and this is in a practical sense was all that the central government could ask them, as individuals, to do. But loyalty was a much subtler thing than that; the other requirements, whatever they

---

[1] "Reconstruction" was the term most people used, both then and since, so it would probably be less misleading to continue using it here than to try to establish a new one. It is by and large a more accurate term than "restoration," which is associated rather too closely with the limited conception of reunion and its requirements embodied in the "Southern" and "presidential" constitutional theories.

might be, would have to be exacted on quite a different plane. Allegiance had not simply been withdrawn from the government, thence to operate in some anarchic limbo of "rebellion"; it had been given positively to another government. The ties which this entity had represented were so profound, so intimate, and so complex, that men and women behaving in any kind of group capacity could not but continue, in spite of themselves, to be in some way governed by them. This part would require an institutional settlement, in effect an understanding with what remained of the Confederacy itself, if true reunion were not to be held in the shadow of these prior loyalties for many years thereafter. This could not be accomplished if the Confederacy were simply defined out of all existence with the collapse of the rebellion.

In the previous chapter, reference was made to the peculiar footing of "duality" upon which the federal government had to face certain legal problems incident to waging the Civil War. The seceded states had to be regarded as "out" for some purposes and "in" for others. Institutionally they were "out"; they had combined to form a hostile government against which the United States found itself making war. With regard to individual allegiance, however, it was necessary to say that they remained "in"—that their populations, as individuals never ceasing to owe loyalty to the United States, were in a state of treasonable rebellion. Constitutional theory had had to accommodate itself somehow to this paradox; so also would policy. This paradox—of "outness" as well as "in-ness," of reunion as both an institutional and an individual problem—would make for inconsistencies and contradictions at every step of the way.

Some of these inconsistencies have continued to baffle all efforts to trace the full logic of reconstruction policy, if such it had, and to connect it with the logic of the Civil War. Three difficulties in particular seem never to have been satisfactorily settled. One of them is the question of how dependable was the actual experience of wartime reconstruction as a guide for peacetime policy. From all indications, the value of that experience was extremely limited. It represented no more than a holding operation in both the "individual" and "institutional" senses. For anyone concerned with the problem—Benjamin Wade, Henry Winter Davis, Abraham Lincoln himself—it was painfully difficult, while still immersed in the setting of wartime, to project what peacetime policy ought to be and to anticipate all the complications it would raise. "Harshness" versus "mildness" would not necessarily furnish the only key to this problem.

A second difficulty has had to do with the apparent discontinuity between the reconstruction activities, which bordered on outright brutality, of Andrew Johnson as military governor of Tennessee, and the almost perfunctory policy of the same man as President of the United States in reconstructing the entire South. A final difficulty, directly related, is raised by the seeming inconsistency of President Johnson's pardoning policy. That policy was in the beginning quite strict. Its strictness, however, collapsed with mystifying suddenness, and by the fall and winter of 1865 the President was issuing pardons in great profusion.

Taken altogether, these things add up to a problem of formidable dimensions, possibly the most difficult to understand of all those which the history of reconstruction has left for us. What was there, simply in the halting of the war, that caused such an overturning of conceptions on peacetime reunion? Why did it become, at that point, an entirely new problem? The key, to repeat, does not seem to lie in the difference between "harshness" and "mildness." The key, if there is one, is more likely to be found in the dual "institutional-individual" nature of the problem, and in the numerous logical paradoxes which it created for practical policy—paradoxes many of which were never reconciled at all.

I AMBIGUITIES OF WARTIME RECONSTRUCTION

The limited experience of "reconstructing" disloyal states in wartime had been rather uniformly discouraging. The efforts of President Lincoln to set up loyal governments in three of the Confederate states—more properly, in parts of them—would have been hard to describe for most purposes as anything but failures. These efforts had been made under Lincoln's so-called Ten Per Cent Plan[2] as portions of Louisiana, Arkansas, and Tennessee had come under Union control in the course of military operations, with special expedients being resorted to in the case of Virginia. So limited, however, was the participation which these governments could command among the local citizenry, so narrow the support on which they rested, and such was the general disfavor in which they were held, that these establishments were all but powerless to perform any of the real functions

---

[2] The "Ten Per Cent" proclamation issued December 8, 1863, unlike Johnson's two separate ones of May 29, 1865, combined amnesty and reconstruction in the same paper. Amnesty was offered to all but certain excepted classes who were willing to take an oath of allegiance to the Union; it was further proclaimed that whenever 10 per cent of the voters qualified under the 1860 laws, having taken such oath and not violated it and having taken steps to establish a government, "such government shall be recognized as the true government of the State. . . ." Lincoln, *Collected Works*, VII, 53–56.

which a government must exercise in order to be called a government. Lincoln himself was painfully aware of all this when he urged, on April 11, 1865, that the Louisiana experiment be given a further try. Even the Tennessee effort, despite the heroic labors of Governor Andrew Johnson, had represented little more than a desperate struggle to survive in an angry sea of disloyalty.[3]

When the state of Arkansas was opened to Union invasion following the fall of Vicksburg to Grant's army in 1863, there were plausible grounds for Lincoln's hope that the state might successfully be redeemed as a loyal and functioning part of the Union. Its citizens in 1861 had been generally pro-Union in sentiment, and in March, a few weeks before the firing on Sumter, an election of convention delegates to consider the question of secession had returned a sound Union majority. It was not until Lincoln's call for volunteers to suppress the rebellion that Arkansas shifted its allegiance to the Confederacy. Even then, however, the Confederate grip was never too firm, and Unionist elements became restless as early as 1862 when Grant began his operations in the West. The capture of Little Rock in September, 1863, two months after Vicksburg, seemed to open the way for redemption. The President accordingly gave much encouragement to local efforts at reconstruction, and on January 4, 1864, a convention met at Little Rock to prepare a new state constitution. In reality, however, this convention was little more than a splinter. Less than half of the state's fifty-seven counties were in any way represented, and from those that were, the delegates had been chosen by methods so irregular that it was impossible to arrive at any standards of accreditation. Considering the wild informality of the proceedings, it is surprising that the subsequent vote on ratifying this "constitution"—

[3] Besides the separate state studies cited below, two general works on this subject of wartime reconstruction are available. Both were written around the turn of the century: Eben Greenough Scott, *Reconstruction during the Civil War in the United States of America* (Boston: Houghton Mifflin, 1895); and Charles H. McCarthy, *Lincoln's Plan of Reconstruction* (New York: McClure, Phillips, 1901). The Scott book, being primarily a strict-construction exercise in constitutional argument, contains very little factual narrative, though it is distinguished by unusual literary grace. McCarthy's is much more comprehensive and thus more generally satisfactory. Neither work attempts to make any connection between the Lincoln and Johnson policies. McCarthy points out that the conditions under which they were initiated were so different that in many respects the two were not even comparable. He suggests not only that the Lincoln policy, though full of defects, was inherently amenable to change but also that the differences between Lincoln and Congress on reconstruction in 1864 were not so great as the heated debates of the time lead one to think. Be that as it may, an interesting thing about both of these books is that they were written at a time before historians had begun feeling pressed to think of the Johnson plan as a necessary consequence of the Lincoln plan, or to take the identity of the two for granted.

a vote numbering about one-fourth of the qualified electorate of 1860 —was as large as it was.[4] State officers were also elected at that time, and Isaac Murphy was chosen as the loyalist governor. The new legislature, hoping for more support and more converts, did not want to go the length of disqualifying all but "original" Unionists. Of the two senators whom it sent to Washington, one had actually voted for secession. Both were refused seats.[5]

On the face of it, things had by no means looked unfavorable for reconstruction in Arkansas. But numbers alone gave little clue to the actual working strength of the Unionist factions there. The center of energy, initiative, and moral authority could not be said to have rested anywhere in their midst. The allegiance of the truly influential and substantial men, even in Arkansas, still lay with the Confederacy. The Unionist government established in 1864 was unable to keep order without the help of the military and, until the Confederate surrenders in 1865, could maintain its very existence only under the most wretched difficulties. Its fortunes were hardly improved by the ending of hostilities. While the regime struggled through the spring and into the summer of 1865, men of prominence were appealing to President Johnson to dispense with Murphy—a "lump of stupidity and imbecility"—and to give the state a provisional government like those established elsewhere by proclamation. The new President refused to unseat the incumbent group. This wartime cabal, however, would be summarily ejected in the course of things by the people of Arkansas.[6]

[4] It was estimated that in 1860 there had been some 54,000 voters. Thus under the "Ten Per Cent Plan" of President Lincoln only 5,400 voters would have been required for a bona fide election. Actually, the result was announced as 12,177 for ratification, with only 226 against, which enabled the Unionists to claim a great victory. Thomas S. Staples, *Reconstruction in Arkansas, 1862–1874* ("Columbia University Studies in History, Economics and Public Law," Vol. CIX [New York: Longmans, Green, 1923]), p. 41.

[5] The fight in the legislature over the election of William Fishback, one of the two senators, is a good illustration of the force that worked to demoralize and divide the Unionists in all the reconstructing states. It was the problem of what degree and manner of accommodation should ultimately be made to the returning ex-Confederates, even while the Confederates were being legally defined as traitors. But the more new men the Unionists could bring into their government, logically the more popular support it would have. At the same time, every such instance of widening the base would serve that much more to set the original "hard-shell" Unionists apart from the rest and make for fragmentation within the group as a whole. Fishback was a man of some ability, but he had been a Confederate and a secessionist, only later becoming discouraged with the Confederate cause. A bitter minority opposed the election of any but original and unconditional Union men, but by this time Fishback's friends had cornered the votes of a majority in the legislature. Consequently the speaker of the House, upon his refusal to sign Fishback's certificate of election, was removed. *Ibid.*, p. 62.

[6] Murphy saw his entire wartime government voted out from under him by ex-Confederate "conservatives" in the late summer elections of 1866. *Ibid.*, pp. 108–9.

The Unionist predicament in Louisiana was even more painful than in Arkansas; in Virginia it was downright ludicrous. Efforts at reconstruction in Louisiana were confined to the New Orleans area, which had been brought under Federal control by the exploits of Farragut in the spring of 1862. Yet it was not until February, 1864, and only after tremendous efforts by the military authorities to round up enough voters to meet Lincoln's "Ten Per Cent" conditions, that an election of state officers could be held. Michael Hahn and J. Madison Wells were named governor and lieutenant governor, respectively. A legislature was elected in September, 1864, under a new constitution which had been produced earlier in the year; a delegation to Congress was also chosen, though Congress subsequently refused to seat its members.[7] One of the senators was Hahn, and the governorship was assumed by Wells in March, 1865. The Unionists' smallness of number had meanwhile proved a chronic factor of demoralization; rent by internal factions, moreover, they provided little in the way of a rallying point for the mass of citizenry.[8] The state was governed for the most part through proclamations issued by the military. By war's end J. Madison Wells, a devious old trickster, stood as the quintessence of what Unionism had produced and could offer to the people of Louisiana. By then the 1864 constitution (which, like those of the other "reconstructed" states of wartime, had disqualifying sections on voting and officeholding) was all but devoid of support. Before long Wells would be calling for Negro suffrage to salvage an impossible political position.[9]

[7] Wartime representation in Congress from these states was generally discouraged, but practice was not entirely consistent. In December, 1862, an election of congressmen was held in Louisiana and those chosen were actually seated by the House, though they occupied their seats for only a few weeks until the end of the session. Except for this very brief interlude, neither Louisiana nor Arkansas had any representation in Congress during wartime. The "restored" government of Virginia had a partial representation; Tennessee had members in the House of Representatives and one senator, Andrew Johnson (until 1862), in the Thirty-seventh Congress, but none in either house in the Thirty-eighth.

[8] One might imagine that small numbers would at least make for internal solidarity, if nothing else, among the Unionists; but—as in Arkansas—such was not the case. In the election of February 22, 1864, there were three different tickets of candidates, each claiming to represent some form of "Unionism." The "purer" these men were in their Unionism, the more marginal and non-indigenous did they seem to be as Louisianans. The ticket most acceptable to the military authorities in this election contained only one man who was neither a native of a Northern state nor of a foreign country. John R. Ficklen, *History of Reconstruction in Louisiana (through 1868)* ("Johns Hopkins University Studies in Historical and Political Science," Vol. XXVIII, No. 1 [Baltimore: Johns Hopkins Press, 1910]), p. 61 n.

[9] Wells had managed to get himself re-elected in 1865 under the new constitution but only through the most assiduous cultivation of ex-Confederate elements whose

The loyalist "government" of Virginia was simply a legal fiction, set up in order that it might "consent" to the formation of West Virginia at the begining of the war. Though this queer little establishment was "recognized" by the Union government, the area which it controlled did not extend much farther than the environs of Alexandria, just across the Potomac from Washington, together with parts of a few counties within the Union lines. Yet Francis H. Pierpoint, the "governor," was recognized by President Johnson in a proclamation of May 9, 1865, as the true governor of Virginia. He too, like Wells in Louisiana and Murphy in Arkansas, had little influence and would thus find it virtually impossible to function as a real executive officer.[10]

The likeliest of the states in which attempts were made at wartime reconstruction was the state of Tennessee. There, the combination of a substantial Unionist element and an early Union invasion produced conditions which were about as promising for redemption as could be expected in a state which had actually seceded and joined the Confederacy. And yet even with these optimum conditions, the effort to create a loyal nucleus of official authority which could exercise real influence and operate in the odor of legitimacy fell far short of satisfactory. The operations of Grant on the Cumberland and the Tennessee early in 1862, and the capture of Nashville by Buell in February of that year, opened up large parts of central and western Tennessee to Union control. It was in such circumstances that Lincoln

---

actual trust of him was at best no more than provisional. The personal benefits of this policy proved extremely short-lived when the voters, and the legislature itself, began systematically disposing of Wells's appointees in 1866. Wells thus found himself more and more obliged to look for radical support. *Ibid.*, pp. 146–47, 159. See also below, chap. 13.

[10] There is a good account of the West Virginia movement in James G. Randall, *Constitutional Probems under Lincoln*, pp. 433–76, and a more condensed one, also very useful, in the same author's *Civil War and Reconstruction*, pp. 329–37. (On the various spellings of Pierpoint's name, see *ibid.*, p. 334 n.) See also Charles H. Ambler, *A History of West Virginia* (New York: Prentice-Hall, 1933), pp. 311–34.

Just as had been the case in both Arkansas and Louisiana, the governor's henchmen were voted out by the assembly in 1866. Like Wells, Pierpoint had the impossible task of trying to carry water on both shoulders. When he made an effort to conciliate the ex-Confederates by proposing that the disfranchisement clause of the 1864 Alexandria constitution be revoked, he brought upon himself the wrath of his wartime Unionist associates. But then when he later tried to compromise with the radical Unionists and Northern Republicans by urging Negro suffrage and ratification of the Fourteenth Amendment, whatever standing he had gained with the ex-Confederates and conservatives of the state simply evaporated. Hamilton J. Eckenrode, *The Political History of Virginia during the Reconstruction* ("Johns Hopkins University Studies in Historical and Political Science," Vol. XXII, Nos. 6–8 [Baltimore: Johns Hopkins Press, 1904]), pp. 32–34, 45, 51, 66, 104.

sent Andrew Johnson to Nashville to try his hand at reconstruction.

Johnson arrived there on March 12, 1862, and from that time until his departure in February, 1865, he made a variety of attempts to mobilize native Union sentiment, virtually all of which resulted in humiliation and disappointment. The first test of public opinion was an election on May 22 for circuit judge which Johnson permitted to be held in Nashville. The victor was a man who had been openly disloyal, and the Governor promptly had him clapped into jail, announcing the appointment of his Unionist opponent.[11] Johnson, hoping at first to encourage loyalty through the taking of oaths, very soon found it necessary to make use of arbitrary arrests and reprisals as a matter of standard policy and to depend on the military to keep order. An election for congressmen held in two af the districts on December 29, 1862, was broken up by one of Forrest's cavalry raids. This was probably fortunate, since the Unionist sentiment in those districts was so uncertain that one of the Unionist candidates had to flee the state in order to avoid assassination.[12]

Bragg's evacuation of Chattanooga in September, 1863, revived Lincoln's hopes for Tennessee's reconstruction, and he urged Johnson once more to attempt the installation of a loyal government; once more they were both filled with chagrin by the fiasco of Rosecrans at Chattanooga-Chickamauga. By 1864, however, the state had been all but cleared of regular Confederate military forces, and Johnson ordered an election of county officers for March 5, 1864. But the test oath which he prescribed for voters was so sweeping that no honest ex-Confederate could take it, and the Governor's prestige declined severely in the wake of the farcical election which followed. A Union convention, meeting in September, 1864, with Johnson himself prompting from the wings, devised another test oath which effectively excluded the growing body of McClellan supporters in the state.[13]

The state of Tennessee did not get anything like a full government until April, 1865. A constitutional convention which met in January had amended the constitution to abolish slavery and nullify secession; it also provided for a general election at which a legislature and new governor were to be chosen. None but known "unconditional union" men, and those taking the oath used in the previous presidential elec-

---

[11] Clifton R. Hall, *Andrew Johnson, Military Governor of Tennessee* (Princeton: Princeton University Press, 1916), pp. 48–49.

[12] James W. Patton, *Unionism and Reconstruction in Tennessee* (Chapel Hill: University of North Carolina Press, 1934), pp. 37–38; Hall, *Andrew Johnson*, p. 90.

[13] Hall, *Andrew Johnson*, pp. 119–23, 139–46, Patton, *Unionism*, pp. 43–48. See also below, p. 141.

tion, could vote. The election was held on March 4, and again the vote was mortifyingly light. The successful candidate for governor was the flamboyant and sulphurous William G. Brownlow, "fighting parson of the Southern highlands." He was inaugurated on April 5, 1865, as successor to Andrew Johnson, now Vice-President. In the end he too, like Wells, would be brought to see the need for Negro suffrage in order to maintain himself.[14]

In one sense, the lesson taught by these various efforts was the lesson of failure. The Unionists in these states were essentially marginal people, a group which in no way included the South's recognized leaders. The moral orbit of the community had in virtually all cases continued to encircle with full assurance the Confederate cause. But given the limited setting of wartime, this lesson was not a completely negative one, nor was the illogic of "Ten Per Cent" necessarily a sufficient ground for abandoning the effort. For Lincoln's purposes, the "Ten Per Cent" formula may have supplied an ample margin.

A test of alternatives came with the controversy over the Wade-Davis bill in the summer of 1864, the reconstruction measure to which Lincoln applied his famous pocket veto. The bill's principal sponsors, Benjamin F. Wade and Henry Winter Davis, were hardly noted for feelings of tenderness toward the South. But having passed both houses of Congress, the bill must at least be considered something which embodied important aspects of majority sentiment at that time. It was a very rigid bill, specifically designed as a counter-response, among other things, to Lincoln's "Ten Per Cent Plan"—about which few could find a really good word to say.[15] The Wade-Davis bill attempted to establish a clear and precise formula for reconstruction and to let the Southerners know exactly where they stood. A provisional gover-

[14] Hall, *Andrew Johnson*, pp. 157–75. For an absorbing account of Brownlow's personality, as well as his career, see E. Merton Coulter, *William G. Brownlow, Fighting Parson of the Southern Highlands* (Chapel Hill: University of North Carolina Press, 1937). An excellent monograph on Tennessee reconstruction is Thomas Alexander, *Political Reconstruction in Tennessee* (Nashville: Vanderbilt University Press, 1950); this work does not deal, however, except in summary, with the events of wartime reconstruction. The most complete account of the war phase is the work by Hall, cited above; it is a fine study, complete, exhaustive, and very well written. For the character of Johnson, it contains many insights not to be found in later works.

[15] "Congress gave it the cold shoulder, for it was looked upon as a clear usurpation of powers which belonged to that body alone; and the people did not welcome it, for it came to them 'in shapeless gear'; it was a stranger to them, and a stranger with no attractive nor even propitious demeanor. Democrats and Republicans joined in one cry, that it was a creature unknown to the Constitution, and both, as if inspired with the same motive, fell upon it, stripped it of its raiment, and lashed it in mockery through the world." Scott, *Reconstruction during the Civil War*, p. 273.

nor for each state would be appointed by the President and confirmed by the Senate, and reconstruction itself could not begin until military resistance in the state had been crushed, and only after a majority—more than 50 per cent—of the voters qualifying under the laws of 1860 were known to be loyal. The test of such loyalty would be willingness to swear an oath of allegiance, and this in turn was to be determined in the course of a universal enrolment of voting-age males. Steps might then be taken to have an election for a constitutional convention, whereupon a more rigid test of loyalty went into effect. No one could vote or be a delegate who could not swear the "ironclad oath" to the effect that he had never been disloyal—that he had neither borne arms against the United States nor held state or Confederate office under the rebel government.[16] The constitution of the state must thereupon be altered to include three amendments on disfranchisement, emancipation, and repudiation of the rebel debt:

FIRST. No person who has held or exercised any office, civil or military, except offices merely ministerial, and military offices below the grade of colonel, state or confederate, under the usurping power, shall vote or be a member of the legislature, or governor.

SECOND. Involuntary servitude is forever prohibited, and the freedom of all persons is guaranteed in said state.

THIRD. No debt, state or confederate, created by or under the sanction of the usurping power, shall be recognized or paid by the state.[17]

The amended constitution must subsequently be ratified by a majority of the "ironclad" electorate.

This procedure was not at all unlike that being followed, or about to be followed in Tennessee under the grim encouragement of Andrew Johnson—who at that time was just as hard a man as anyone in Congress, Ben Wade and Winter Davis not excepted.[18] If tenderness to-

16 This was the federal test oath, first required of federal officeholders by an act of Congress of July 2, 1862, and subsequently included in various other federal legislation. *U.S. Statutes at Large*, XII, 502.

17 Richardson, *Messages and Papers*, VI, 223–26.

18 The Nashville constitutional convention which was called by Johnson in January, 1865, was a strictly "ironclad oath" affair. Among the constitutional amendments it proposed, was one enfranchising Negro soldiers, though this was finally rejected in committee (Wade-Davis did not contain such a provision either); and the referendum on its other amendments was to involve only ironclad voters—even more "ironclad," it might be added, than under the federal test oath (see below, p. 141, for a description of the Tennessee oath). The legislature to be elected under the new constitution (under duly ironclad conditions) was empowered to fix voting qualifications. This it proceeded to do with a wholesale disfranchising law—all under the vigorous leadership of Johnson's personally sponsored ironclad governor, William G. Brownlow. See Alexander, *Political Reconstruction in Tennessee*, pp. 28–32, 71–76.

ward the South was what was wanted, there was little of it to be found at a period of some of the war's worst bloodletting.[19]

Indeed, what was at stake between the Wade-Davis and Lincoln plans cannot be fully appreciated within the criteria of hardness or softness. Lincoln would not have been averse to having Wade-Davis applied in any place where there was a chance of its success, and we are not necessarily bound to picture the President chuckling and winking when he said so.[20] Nor was Lincoln's resistance directed simply against an effort by Congress to seize the initiative in reconstruction; he had already recognized the practical authority of Congress in that sphere.[21] He was resisting encroachment on his own military powers. He had experimented with a number of war measures, reconstruction among them, and he wanted very much to retain his freedom to keep on experimenting; that would have had to be abandoned under the new plan. But there may have been something more in Lincoln's instinct to shy away from Wade-Davis, something not unconnected with the notion that reconstruction had both its "individual" and its "institutional" aspects.

The primary element in the Wade-Davis reasoning was *individual* loyalties, not very subtly conceived. The net would be thrown wide, but it would catch only men, not institutions; allegiance would literally be squeezed out of each man through subjugation and oaths, and, whatever new institutions of government emerged from the process, such government would have had to be purified by a kind of super-oath: pure governments would follow from pure men.[22] Corrupted

[19] In the Wilderness–Cold Harbor campaign of May and June, 1864, Grant's army had lost approximately 55,000 men.

[20] See below, p. 132.

[21] E.g., "If Louisiana shall send members to Congress, their admission to seats will depend, as you know, upon the respective Houses, and not upon the President" (Lincoln to N. P. Banks, Aug. 5, 1863). "And for the same reason it may be proper to further say that whether members sent to Congress from any State shall be admitted to seats, constitutionally rests exclusively with the respective Houses, and not to any extent with the Executive" (Proclamation of Amnesty and Reconstruction, Dec. 8, 1863). "I distinctly said that this was not the only plan which might possibly be acceptable; and I also distinctly protested that the executive claimed no right to say when, or whether members should be admitted to seats in Congress from such States." (Last Public Address, Apr. 11, 1865). *Collected Works*, VI, 364–65; VII, 56; VIII, 399–405.

[22] The very same principle, of course, would guide the municipal reform movements of the Progressive Era nearly a half-century later. Similar difficulties arose in each case from ignoring as illegitimate (and therefore as "unreal") certain vital institutional functions not to be understood simply with reference to individuals. Such functions were performed in the one case by "treasonable" Confederate governments, and in the other by "corrupt" urban machines.

loyalty, on the other hand, would be made permanent and irreversible through constitutional interdict against voting and officeholding by those who had been leaders in rebellion. Government, in short, must rest upon a very special definition of individual virtue and must at the same time be certified by majority rule. It was assumed that a government, to mean anything, must be based upon majorities, and this assumption would have been quite correct if majority rule had been the only thing at stake. On that basis, of course, Lincoln's governments had all been miserable failures.

Over against all this was the conception of "Ten Per Cent," whose primary assumption must certainly be something other than "majority rule." Such a government as that set up on the basis of 10 per cent of a state's qualified voters willing to offer future allegiance must of course balance on certain pretenses. Under the conditions of war it was necessary to pretend that such a government was *the* legal government and to claim as many sanctions for it as possible—all the while in full awareness that it was really anything but *the* government. Tacitly it must be recognized that there was in fact another government, and that a majority of the people were loyal to it. The logic of Wade-Davis insisted on one government; "Ten Per Cent" was an intermediate concept which recognized the existence of two. In view of the wartime setting, it is understandable that perfectly honest men should have been exasperated at this twilight notion, never made explicit, whose logic was almost impossible to discover amid the necessities of mortal struggle.

But that was just the very trouble with Wade-Davis: it was a plan for peacetime reconstruction, conceived under desperate wartime conditions and not flexible enough for either. "Ten Per Cent" was conceived as something in between, a kind of bridge from wartime to peacetime, which might be liquidated if new conditions should supersede it. For the time being it made good sense as a war measure. With such a government, coupled with the offer of individual amnesties, Lincoln had a device which might be used to subvert the Confederacy and bore into its foundations. He was apparently quite willing to recognize that the Confederacy was a fully functioning institution, and though its legitimacy could never be admitted for an instant, nevertheless the behavior of a majority in each state could not be assessed with accuracy without assuming that other institutional sanctions did in fact exist, hedged about, for that majority, by all the incidents of legitimacy. The best he could do, therefore, was to set up a counter-institution—not to replace the dominant one but to undermine it. A "Ten Per Cent" government was a competing symbol of legitimacy, an organized alternative expression of loyalty, about which minority groups might coalesce. These groups might grow, and they might not, but whatever was to be done about them afterward, it was at least necessary to do something for them now. They must be protected and "institutionalized" as much as the circumstances allowed, and for this, all that was needed—indeed, all that was possible—was "Ten Per Cent."

The struggle over Wade-Davis was not seen by Lincoln primarily as a struggle between one plan and another; it was just that he wanted his own plan let alone. He did not like to use the veto, and opposing the majority will was not to his taste. For him, it was simply an effort to retain alternatives, and in his proclamation of July 8, 1864, explaining his attitude on the bill, he said as much, to this effect, as he dared. The paper has been described as "a rather eccentric proclamation,"[23] but there is little reason for not taking the President more or less at his word:

. . . while I am (as I was in December last, when, by proclamation, I propounded a plan for restoration) unprepared by a *formal* approval of this Bill, to be inflexibly committed to any single plan of restoration; and while I am also unprepared to declare, that the free-state constitutions and governments, already adopted and installed in Arkansas and Louisiana, shall be set aside and held for nought, thereby repelling and discouraging the loyal citizens who have set up the same . . . nevertheless, I am fully satisfied with the system of restoration contained in the Bill as one very proper plan for the loyal people of any State choosing to adopt it. . . .[24]

He did not want to be bound, in short, to any one plan, nor was he willing to renounce either the advantages, the multiple implications, or the vagueness of "Ten Per Cent."

How this plan could be graded into the conditions of peacetime, Lincoln was hardly prepared to say, though he obviously thought that the transition might be better cushioned by his plan than by the other. Presumably he wanted a species of loyalty that meant something, and he appears to have been quite cautious about putting loyalty to such rigid tests that he would get nothing at all. The subscribing of oaths was a way of recapturing one side of a man's loyalty: his loyalty to what must for the time remain rather an abstraction—the United States. This was the easier part. But the other side, the concrete, the truly "institutional" side that would live on and keep its power in habit and memory—what were the ways of getting at that? Perhaps it could

[23] Randall, *Civil War and Reconstruction*, p. 700.
[24] *Collected Works*, VII, 433–34. Italics added.

only be done through the men of real influence, the men who held the true keys to "legitimacy" in any Southern community. It would require more than a "Ten Per Cent Plan," but then Wade-Davis would kill it altogether. Should the whole South suddenly surrender, neither plan would fully do. Yet "Ten Per Cent" would be easier to start from than nothing—and easier to liquidate, conversely, than 51 per cent.

After all this is said, the fact still remains that Lincoln did not live to face the problem of what to do with the "Ten Per Centers" after the coming of peace. These men—Murphy, Wells, Brownlow, Pierpoint, and their followers—were not exactly a prepossessing lot. Even Lincoln, with all his political acumen, may have deceived himself as to just how easily a transition could be effected through them. Johnson simply acknowledged the existence of these regimes and permitted them to keep on functioning, and there is certainly evidence that Lincoln had been prepared to do the same. In Johnson's hands, at any rate, such a policy did much to perpetuate a murky and poisonous political atmosphere in all of those states.

The Union government's dilemma, though it seems not to have been fully recognized at the time, was that with the very arrival of peace, the "Ten Per Centers" had automatically fulfilled and terminated their function. A stable reunion could never be effected under the leadership and moral aegis of these men—or, more properly, without the men whose leadership really counted in these states. At the same time the Murphys and the Wellses could hardly be thrown to the wolves. The government, however, in the very act of legitimizing them, in effect abandoned them, and thus committed itself to a policy fraught with demoralizing consequences for the entire business of reunion.

An alternative to these painful extremes can only be guessed at. Suppose that the British, in the 1770's, had succeeded in suppressing the rebellion of the American colonies. We should find it difficult to imagine them placing their reconquered subjects under the charge of the American Tories, much as they may have wished to cherish and reward the men who had remained loyal to the mother country throughout. Purposeful understandings would certainly have been required for their physical and moral protection. Yet any new arrangement, for ultimate success and stability, would somehow have had to be graded back through the very institutional loyalties represented by such leadership as that of John Adams, Thomas Jefferson, and George Washington.

II   JOHNSON'S EMERGENCE FROM MILITARY
GOVERNOR TO PRESIDENT

Many historians have wondered how the same man who served as military governor of Tennessee could seem to behave so differently, within a matter of weeks, as President of the United States. As military governor, Andrew Johnson had not hesitated to manipulate his Unionist creatures with an insensitivity that partook of the brutal. He could compose resolutions to be passed at their meetings, putting his own words into the mouths of others, and then later pretend to listen with surprised gratification while his own sayings and praise of himself were solemnly read back to him.[25] He was hated throughout the state for his dictatorial ways and for his stolid readiness to use force on any occasion. With a certain obtuseness, he would insist on the most impossibly proscriptive oaths. So thoroughly highhanded was his course throughout that he came under heavy criticism from his contemporaries; he was accused of wilfully delaying the establishment of civil government in Tennessee long after it had become a full possibility.[26]

But why, then, did Andrew Johnson as President seem such a changed man? He had probably done in Tennessee—for all his crudity —about what had to be done. Why should he not put into effect over the entire South policies in some way consistent with those which he had himself followed in Tennessee, and which he himself had seen as absolutely necessary there? How is one to account for his willingness, as President, to allow the South the widest kind of leeway in the resumption of political life, with only the most nominal kind of scrutiny into matters of vital concern for substantial portions of the Northern public? Indeed, some of the most extreme elements of the opposition to Johnson as President in the summer of 1865 would gladly have settled for a policy throughout the South exactly like the one which he, Andrew Johnson, had followed in Tennessee as military governor.

[25] The man whose chore it was to read as his own the prefabricated resolutions prepared for a mass meeting in April, 1864, has left an account of the affair. Brownlow was supposed to have done the reading, but having temporarily lost his voice, he suggested that Oliver P. Temple, another prominent Unionist leader, present them instead, which the latter did. Johnson listened with great interest to his own resolutions and announced that they met with his full and hearty approval. "No doubt," says Temple, "the resolution which declared that the meeting had 'full confidence in the integrity and patriotism of Andrew Johnson, Military Governor of the State,' did meet with his approval and gave him great pleasure!" Temple, *Notable Men of Tennessee*, p. 409.

[26] *Ibid.*, pp. 410–12.

In any effort to discover the reasons for Johnson's seemingly drastic shift of policy so soon after assuming the presidency, some attention should certainly be given to the series of personal shocks which he underwent during this period, coinciding exactly with the staggering changes which had been brought about everywhere by the collapse of the rebellion. The full impact of all this might very plausibly have served to shake him loose with extraordinary effectiveness from the state of mind in which he had operated in wartime Tennessee. It might also have made Johnson peculiarly amenable to the kinds of influence which happened to surround him during his initial period of adjustment to the newly transformed world of affairs in peacetime Washington.

In the first place, the military governorship of Tennessee, whose political requirements were starkly simple, may have given Andrew Johnson a preparation for the presidency which was not only very limited but quite the wrong kind. He was assuming a role which had demanded almost extrasensory political adjustments on the part of his predecessor throughout,[27] and at a time when the Emancipator's own mind had become painfully tentative over the approaching problems of peace and reconstruction. Johnson was stepping into a complex situation which called for both delicacy and a sense of scope, neither of which was among his most prominent virtues. It was as though a pugnacious regimental commander had suddenly been called to the rear to take charge of a whole army, just when the entire strategy was taking on a multitude of new and more intricate requirements. Here the experience of the firing line might well have functioned not as an asset but as a bewildering liability. For all the bulldog courage which acompanied it, that experience had a quality of simplicity which put a high premium on reflex and a very indifferent one on thought.

At any rate, things were changing everywhere by March and April, and the changes must have made the gap between epochs in Johnson's personal situation seem the wider. His removal from Nashville to Washington, coming when it did, was a transit between two different universes. He had been in full command in Tennessee until the day he

---

[27] E.g., Lincoln's perception of the uncertain state of unity in his party, as the 1864 nominations approached, had made him willing at one point to have Benjamin F. Butler as his vice-presidential candidate. He also saw the advisability, in September of that year, of conciliating the radical wing by dropping Montgomery Blair from his cabinet. See also David Donald's essay, "A. Lincoln, Politician," in *Lincoln Reconsidered*, pp. 57–81.

left, February 25, 1865, to assume the vice-presidency.[28] Yet as it turned out, he would be meeting something less than a hero's welcome; he was advancing not to receive greater honors but to be heaped with unexpected shame. He arrived in Washington desperately ill with typhoid. Then the oversized glass of brandy which he took to fortify himself for the ceremonies, followed by the befuddled harangue which he babbled forth upon taking the inaugural oath, made an episode mortifying for all present.[29] Clothed in humiliation before the elite of the Republican party (indeed, before the entire country), alone in the nation's capital and far from his family, Johnson was given solace and shelter by the Blairs, who took him to their country seat at Silver Spring, Maryland. There he remained at least a week for recuperation, reflection, and doubtless some long conversations with his assiduous hosts.[30]

Shortly thereafter, in giddy succession, came the utter breakdown of the rebellion against which he had fought so long, the assassination of Lincoln, and his own elevation to the supreme power. A distinguished cabinet headed by Secretary of State Seward and a triumphant army led by Grant, the hero of Vicksburg and Appomattox, were now his to command. Their combined wisdom was at his disposal. His enemies, the treasonable Southern aristocrats, were now laid low, represented only, it might seem, by their female relatives coming to beg his clemency. The intriguing Blairs, whose political fortunes could only be mended in the setting of a "soft" Southern policy—Seward, already rather isolated politically—the magnanimous Grant, splendidly above all faction—the Southern ladies: to the new President who had so recently been given the cold shoulder by a massed array of Republican dignitaries, all such influences might well have added up to something irresistible.

These things, severally and singly noted by many writers, must clearly have their place in explaining the course of behavior assumed by President Johnson. But there remain certain difficulties. A rather striking feature of Johnson's personality was the fact that, unless his

[28] Johnson had actually left an interregnum there; it was not until the day of his own inauguration as Vice-President on March 4 that his successor, Brownlow, would be elected governor of Tennessee, and the latter would not be installed until April 5. Meanwhile the secretary of state, Edward H. East, acted as governor *pro tempore*.

[29] "I'm a-goin' for to tell you—here to-day; yes, I'm a-goin' for to tell you all, that I'm a plebeian! I glory in it; I am a plebeian! The people—yes, the people of the United States have made me what I am; and I am a-goin' for to tell you here to-day—yes, to-day, in this place—that the people are everything." William E. Smith, *The Francis Preston Blair Family in Politics* (2 vols.; New York: Macmillan, 1933), II, 327–28.

[30] *Ibid.*, pp. 327–30.

mind had been strongly disposed in their direction already, he was all but impervious to the "influence" of others. To an almost abnormal degree he was a man who made up his own mind. Moreover, this may be another of those points at which historical hindsight has tended somewhat to foreshorten our vision. Strictly speaking, Johnson did not "change" quite that suddenly, or even that radically. It might even be argued that in a basic sense he never "changed" at all. But at least it should be as important to discover a principle of continuity and consistency in Johnson's behavior as to try accounting for the discrepancies.

It is not entirely fanciful to say that the basic line of Andrew Johnson's reconstruction policy derived, with a curious kind of consistency, not from Abraham Lincoln but from Benjamin F. Wade. Originally fellow members of the Committee on the Conduct of War, Wade and Johnson in wartime had many rather vindictive attributes in common. Their essentially one-dimensional conception of individual loyalty, as seen in their respective activities of 1864, was practically identical. The high point of rapport between the two men was reached the day after Lincoln died. As they stood there face to face, Wade was thrilled to the depths by Johnson's thundering "Treason must be made infamous and traitors must be impoverished!" In that moment, each man's sense of the rebellion as a problem of corrupted loyalties, to be liquidated through individuals, was very much the same—and at bottom it never really changed. At the same time, a sense of the institutional side of rebellion and reconstruction was in both cases virtually nonexistent.

Subsequently the two men's interpretation of what had happened to those individual loyalties, and their feelings on what should be done about them, would of course diverge very markedly. Here the fact that one of them was a transplanted New Englander now representing Ohio, and that the other came from seceded Tennessee, made all the difference. The theme of personal vindication in Johnson's career—in this case vindication as a Tennessean—would be of tremendous importance. But it is still conceivable that in the narrowly individual, noninstitutional conception of loyalty which they shared, and which neither would quite abandon, there was more room for violent fluctuation in policy than had ever been inherent in the ambivalent and oscillating sayings and doings of Abraham Lincoln.

Johnson's entire notion of his own personal integrity, as seen in his course throughout the war, depended on his believing that it was he and not the disloyal secessionists who had all along represented the "real" Tennessee. It was terribly important for him to believe that he had proved this as military governor, demonstrating both his own rightness and the error of secession. True, he ought to have been able to see that he had never actually reconstructed Tennessee. But he could not have left at a moment more critical for deceiving himself to the contrary, or for shutting his eyes to all the things that yet remained undone. As the time drew near for him to go, he was exceptionally anxious that his work be regarded as a success and that his efforts at reconstruction be taken as complete and sufficient. "All is now working well," he had telegraphed to Lincoln on January 13, 1865, "and if Tennessee is now left alone, [she] will soon assume all the functions of a state according to the genius and theory of the government."[31]

Johnson had certainly discovered for himself the terrible difficulty of coercing a hostile state. But the circumstances all seemed to warrant his persuading himself that the hostility was "unnatural," that the true heart of the people had merely been lured elsewhere, and that the people, "his" people, had been unnaturally coerced into doing wrong. This was what could justify for him a policy of force, of counter-coercion, in the first place; "unreal" conditions warranted "unreal" methods. All would fall right in the end, after the eerie spell was broken.[32] Meanwhile the symbols of coercion and countercoercion remained always there before him; Confederate guerrillas infested the state down to the very end,[33] and Johnson in turn was bulwarked by the only protection which in cold fact really mattered—the Union military. But what if both these forces had suddenly been removed, so that Johnson might see for himself where the state's "natural" loyalties lay? How did the democratic, the truly "popular" sentiment stand—and how much room was there in it for *him*? It was Brownlow, not Johnson, who had to stay and face that problem.

Parson Brownlow's dilemma was that of the wartime Unionist who saw Unionism drastically redefined with the war's termination, which

---

[31] *War of the Rebellion: Official Records*, Ser. III, Vol. IV, p. 1050.

[32] E.g., Johnson's speech to the Nashville constitutional convention on January 12, 1865, in which he argued for immediate action despite the questionable legitimacy of its proceedings: "Suppose you do violate the law," he said; "if by so doing you restore the law and the constitution, your consciences will approve your course, and all the people will say, amen!" Hall, *Andrew Johnson*, p. 168.

[33] Brownlow's concluding promise, in accepting his nomination as governor on January 9, 1865, was: "God being my helper, if you will send up a legislature to re-organize the militia and pass other necessary laws, I will put an end to this infernal system of guerrilla fighting in the state, in East, Middle and Western Tennessee, if we have to shoot and hang every man concerned." *Ibid.*, p. 172.

now in effect made "Unionists" of everyone. What was he to do at the sight of the returning host, full of men willing to take any oath of allegiance to the Union just so that they might vote once more and throw him out? Brownlow would conclude that the only way to resolve this dilemma was through stringent disfranchisement and, ultimately, Negro suffrage. But let us just imagine that his and Johnson's positions had been reversed, that Brownlow had been elected Vice-President, and Johnson had remained behind as a "Ten Per Center." It would not be hard to picture the behavior of each man as being just the opposite from what it in fact was. With no inconsistency, Brownlow as President could have followed the same policy as Johnson did (as it was, he remained a Johnson supporter until 1866);[34] at the same time there is no reason why Andrew Johnson, as peacetime governor of Tennessee confronted with the difficulties that Brownlow faced, might not very quickly, and in all ways, have become just as hot a radical as Brownlow.

That of course was not the way things went, and meanwhile Johnson's constitutional principles—the dogma that the states were never really out—could be maintained inviolate from start to finish. In other words, the organized and institutional side of the rebellion had never been real to him for an instant. What animated him instead was on the one hand his mystic vision of "the people," and on the other hand a bizarre sense of conspiracies and plots. A good many of Johnson's queer notions about the world of affairs and relationships were of course shared in some way by most of the American people. This was a highly individualistic culture, whose modes of thought were essentially non-institutional and whose automatic instinct, then and since, has been to think of all modes of organization in an idiom of suspicion even while accepting them. But in these things there are degrees and degrees. It is quite likely that in the true "outsider," the man whose career has been given much of its meaning through siege upon organized society, such notions can take on exaggerated, grotesque, and uncompromising forms.

The secession movement had been a gigantic plot. Johnson's ancient demon, the aristocrats, had been responsible for duping and corrupting the people. "You know perfectly well," he declared to a delegation of Virginians in 1865, "it was the wealthy men of the South who

---

[34] The two were on excellent terms all through 1865; it was not until the Freedmen's Bureau veto in February, 1866, that Brownlow began having misgivings about Johnson. The open break came in late spring over the Fourteenth Amendment. During most of this time Brownlow, like most other Tennesseans, had been strongly anti-Negro suffrage. Coulter, *Brownlow*, pp. 279, 286, 289-93, 308-12.

dragooned the people into Secession." As President he was thus still repeating the things he had believed while still in the thick of things back in Tennessee. "Many humble men, the peasantry and yeomanry of the South," he had announced in 1863, "who have been decoyed, or perhaps driven into the rebellion, may look forward with reasonable hope for an amnesty. But the intelligent and influential leaders must suffer."[35]

The rebellion, then, had been a conspiracy of aristocrats. Johnson had of course come up in the world since the days of his youth when he had burned with class envy. By the 1850's he was on reasonable terms with a number of the Tennessee slaveholding gentry and could at least make discriminations between good and bad aristocrats. It was now primarily the secessionist aristocrats, in their character as rebel conspirators, who filled him with fury. If the rebellion could only be ended, however, the aristocrats would by definition be brought to their knees, and the "unnatural" force which kept the conspiracy organized would by definition be removed. Then the true voice of the people could once more ring forth. If only the aristocrats would then say they were sorry, his own vindication would be perfect. Repentance! How he would have savored that, in the dark days when the chivalry still rode high in their pride! How sweet would any words of contrition have sounded in his ears! How little would he have settled for, how much would he have forgiven, just to hear the *words!*

Words: it may be in just this sense that we are to understand Johnson's intense preoccupation with oaths. It was as though there were something occult in them; conspiracies were somehow bound and unbound by oaths, as by charms and spells, if cunningly contrived. The "oath" theme that recurs throughout Johnson's military governorship is quite striking, and Johnson's conjurations in this realm seem to have exceeded the normal. "He seems to have had great faith," observed a Tennessee contemporary who knew him, "in the efficacy of oaths."[36]

Johnson felt that Lincoln's 1863 Amnesty Oath was not stringent enough, and for the March, 1864, elections he himself devised a far more exacting one which came in for much bitter criticism. Judging from Johnson's own oath, we may imagine that he felt the Lincoln oath to be not only too mild but also too flat. The enriched oath, in which the swearer must "ardently desire" the success of Union arms

[35] Winston, *Andrew Johnson, Plebeian and Patriot,* p. 273; Hall, *Andrew Johnson, Military Governor,* p. 102.

[36] Temple, *Notable Men,* p. 412.

and the defeat of Confederate power, was supposed to turn men aside from Confederate predilections and "bind them unequivocally to the Union party."[37] For good measure, all officials and judges of election then had to take a special oath themselves, swearing that the voters had all duly sworn to *their* oath. The subsequent vote was extremely sparse. The people's repugnance to the oath may have been due not simply to its "stringency" but also to the way in which it offended a man's modesty. But the Governor was at it again in the fall, this time contriving an oath to discourage men from voting for McClellan. In this one, equally mouth-filling, the voter would "sincerely rejoice" in the triumph of the Union armies, and "cordially oppose all armistices and negotiations" (such as were promoted by the Chicago "Peace Platform"); and should it be discovered that he had not actually believed in the solemn words, he would be subject to punishment.[38] The Nashville *Press*, Johnson's supporter earlier in his governorship, now ridiculed him over the whole business of oaths. The *Press* told its readers to take any oath Johnson might prescribe, for all the meaning it could have:

He may construct a new or additional oath—he may even require folks to swear that they love him for his candor and humanity and disinterested patriotism, and "ardently desire" that he shall be perpetual dictator of Tennessee—they can still take it in the same sense they offer to the other—the sense of void nothingness.[39]

After the rebellion had been terminated, the conspiracy was broken. Of course a heavy residue of sinfulness still lingered on; many times during the following summer Johnson would intone the dire words, "Treason is a crime and must be made odious." He would now strike everywhere for the sinner's conscience; more than ever it was a matter of individuals. Both Ben Wade and Andrew Johnson in April, 1865, had panted for punishment and the making of individual examples. But perhaps already their sense of the depth and permanence of the sin had begun to diverge. It may already have become something like "original sin" for the one versus the power of conversion for the other—of eternal damnation as against redemption through repentance and oaths. On this point the pardoning policy of Johnson as President might eventually fall to pieces without his ever quite realizing it, but he still had, and would continue to have, "great faith in the efficacy of oaths."

[37] Hall, *Andrew Johnson*, pp. 114, 119–20.

[38] *Ibid.*, p. 145.   [39] Quoted in *ibid.*, p. 122.

III   THE EXECUTIVE PARDONING POLICY

Some of the confusion which still hangs over the initial stages of reconstruction may be traceable to a distinction which existed, but was not always fully acknowledged, between the reconstruction of states and the reconstruction of individuals. In most men's minds these two things were never entirely separated. In a practical sense the primary concern of the Republican party at large had by the fall and winter of 1865 come to be centered upon the problem of a policy toward the Southern states as governmental entities. But a major share of President Johnson's attention had meanwhile been devoted to problems of amnesty and pardon for individuals, which undoubtedly had much to do with preventing the question of reconstruction as a whole from taking on the clarity which it otherwise might have had during this period.

It took a majority of Northern Unionists some time to realize that Johnson had never regarded the other side of reconstruction with anything like the seriousness which they thought it deserved, whereas the emphasis which the President gave to his pardoning policy may have imparted to that policy an undue importance which it ought not to have had. Matters were further confused by the signs of disintegration which the Executive pardoning policy itself began eventually to show and which brought down upon the President a certain amount of criticism. From one viewpoint, much of this criticism may have been justified; from another, it was curiously and ironically unfair. Johnson took the pardon seriously enough; yet as a matter of practical consequence the pardon was far less important as an instrument of reconstruction than either Johnson or his critics imagined. The policy began breaking down for mechanical reasons inherent in the very magnitude of the task which the President had assigned to himself. It collapsed completely when the laissez-faire side of his reconstruction policy—the constitutional dogma that the states had never been out—became endangered by it.

With the outbreak of the Civil War, there had been little doubt that the rebellion fell squarely under the constitutional and statutory definition of treason, a crime for which the law specified the penalty as death. But it was also generally recognized that for treason on such a mass scale, punishment would have to be conceived in terms somewhat more practicable than those of mass executions. The Confiscation Act of July 17, 1862, represented in this sense a major adjustment. It established, in addition to its other provisions, three important principles relative to the crime of treason. The first made death only the most extreme of a range of punishments for that crime; the second recognized a broad category of offenses which bordered on treason but which would not as a rule be considered as partaking directly of it; and the third confirmed the President's power of pardon as applicable on a mass scale in the proclaiming of general amnesties. President Lincoln did not wish to avail himself of this power until the favorable fortunes of war should promise it some effectiveness in persuading waverers to resume their former loyalties. Eventually, though individual pardons had been granted before that time, the first general amnesty was announced in Lincoln's proclamation of December 8, 1863. In that proclamation—the prototype of later ones by President Johnson—full pardon was offered to all those who, except for certain classes of participants, were willing to resume their allegiance to the United States and take an oath to that effect. Presumably those of the excepted classes, should they too desire pardon, would have to make special application for it.[40]

It was upon this broadened conception of Executive power that Johnson's own pardoning policy was based, and the principles of Johnson's amnesties were similar to those of Lincoln. Although Johnson did in fact issue four proclamations of amnesty and pardon, the first one, that of May 29, 1865, was by far the most important. Whereas Lincoln's had contained only six excepted classes (a seventh was added in his supplementary proclamation of March 26, 1864), Johnson's specified fourteen such classes. This was what required such an unusual number of special pardons in addition to the general amnesty. The second amnesty, proclaimed September 7, 1867, would virtually bring the business of special pardoning to an end. Up to that time about 13,500 individual pardons had been issued, with about 150,000 persons still under some kind of disabilities. Now, with only three general classes of exceptions remaining under the new amnesty (the "twenty thousand dollar" exception was one of those removed), only about three hundred ex-Confederates still remained beyond the pale. The third amnesty, that of July 4, 1868, left all but a very few—Davis, Breckinridge, Lee, Buckner, and a few others—still unpardoned. Finally, in a Christmas proclamation at the end of 1868, Johnson granted "unconditionally and without reservation, to all and to every person, who di-

[40] Jonathan T. Dorris, *Pardon and Amnesty under Lincoln and Johnson* (Chapel Hill: University of North Carolina Press, 1953), pp. 4–8, 29–36.

rectly or indirectly, participated in the late insurrection or rebellion a full pardon and amnesty for the offense of treason against the United States. . . ."[41]

Congress, in its subsequent clash with the President on reconstruction, did not by any means wipe out the benefits of the presidential pardon. Those benefits, however, were profoundly modified by the Fourteenth Amendment and the Reconstruction Acts. Although the ordinary civil and property rights restored by the presidential pardon remained unimpaired, together with immunity from prosecution for treason, such rights did not necessarily include those of officeholding and franchise. Where these two rights had been removed by congressional action, it followed that only Congress could restore them, and the law so specified. Thus it was necessary for Congress to have an amnesty policy of its own. By special bills, several thousand ex-Confederates were amnestied between 1868 and 1872, in response to the various exigencies of congressional reconstruction. The sweeping General Amnesty Act of May 22, 1872, restored full political privileges to all but a few hundred.[42]

Although the pardoning policies of Johnson and Lincoln did in certain formal respects resemble each other, in a more fundamental sense the two are not even comparable. The quality of "mercy" inherent in each could hardly tell us much; it is in the nature of any pardon that it should be an instrument of mercy. The important thing is that the one operated in wartime, the other in peacetime; and in these two settings, so vastly different, the pardon would be used for markedly different purposes. For Lincoln, pardoning was to be employed primarily as a war measure; it should be an instrument for weakening the will of the Confederacy and encouraging desertion and surrender. He had used it with caution, waiting for the time when optimum use might be made of whatever effectiveness it had. He was rather less willing than Johnson himself, at that same period, to make liberal use of the pardon.[43] By the time Johnson was President, the pardon was of course no longer a weapon of war. It now became an

[41] *Ibid.*, pp. 108–12, 339–61; Richardson, *Messages and Papers*, VI, 310–12, 549, 655–56, 708.

[42] The special acts continued through the succeeding generation, though with dwindling frequency as old campaigners passed from the scene. A few unpardoned ones must still have remained by the 1890's though their names are now unknown. On June 8, 1898, the last of them were restored to the full rights of voting and officeholding when President McKinley placed his signature upon the final congressional General Amnesty Bill. Dorris, *Pardon and Amnesty*, pp. 362–92.

[43] *Ibid.*, pp. 21–22.

instrument of reconstruction, and, so far as he was concerned, it was the only instrument.

By late 1865, Johnson would be heavily criticized for the wholesale issuance of special pardons to those not included in the general amnesty. It is true that by the fall and winter he had begun to issue pardons very profusely. Due justice, however, should be done to the record of the spring and summer; the President proceeded with almost painful caution all during that period, and in those months very few pardons were actually granted. The criticism would doubtless have lost much of its force had only the same number of pardons been somewhat more evenly distributed over the same period of time. If Johnson's pardoning policy were to be questioned, it would have to be questioned not for its strictness or liberality, its harshness or its mildness, but rather for its very purpose. What did Johnson expect to accomplish with it? The problem would involve the value of the pardon as an adjunct to general policy; it was a question of just what could and could not be done with it to effect the government's more general ends.

On the one hand, there were inherent limits to the effectiveness of the pardon, no matter what extrinsic ends might be conceived for it: once a man was pardoned, he was pardoned; by the discharge of a formality he was by definition released from further dependency upon government favor. Moreover, from the government's own standpoint there was a limit to the degree of scrutiny any individual might receive, in view of the thousands of other applicants demanding like attention. On the other hand, for the person who received it, a pardon was anything but an insignificant item. It guaranteed him immunity from prosecution for treason; it restored, presumably, his political privileges; even more basically, it left him once more in the full enjoyment of his property rights, with immunity from confiscation; and it enabled him to transact business, make contracts, and—if his livelihood were from the law—to practice in the courts. Thus the grantor of this boon was by no means without power, should he know how to appraise with accuracy both the possibilities and the limits of that power. Such power, if not pressed beyond its capacities, could conceivably be used to some advantage as a fulcrum for other policy.

It could hardly be said that President Johnson was not impressed with the gravity of the problem. *"Treason is a crime and must be made odious"*: here was the leitmotif of all his utterances on the subject of disloyalty as he turned to the mountainous task of pardoning. It was natural, in view of Johnson's conviction that reconstruction rested basically on the pardoning power, that he should not have taken the business lightly. His initial notion was that he could make careful discriminations among individuals, based upon separate judgments of each individual's misdoings. As he brooded over the cases, however, he soon found himself, as might be expected, mired down in work. The more bloodthirtsy aspect of his zeal for punishment soon spent itself amid the practical perplexities of what to do in the case of any given "traitor" among the thousands and thousands, and of exactly how his crime differed in infamy from that of any other. The President must have decided fairly early that the traitors, as a matter of basic policy, would have to be forgiven. But this did not in any way alter the requirement that treason must be made odious; there must still be remorse. Johnson admitted, in an interview with George L. Stearns on October 3, that he did not really expect to deny pardon to many of the excepted classes; ". . . but," he declared, "I intended they should sue for pardon, and so realize the enormity of their crime."[44]

The basic act of repentance was thus the act of asking for pardon. As the applications piled up, there was accordingly much reading matter for the President; these testaments of "remorse" would often run to many pages. Perhaps having decided that there would be no real reprisals he felt it only proper that the wrongdoers should at least be kept in a certain amount of suspense. Thus relatively few pardons were issued in the early months of Johnson's presidency. Meanwhile a number of high Confederate civil officers were kept in confinement. The President was most reluctant to let them go, even though he had no specific idea about what should be done with them, beyond allowing them time to ponder their misdeeds. During this period Johnson received lengthy memorials for the release of these men and heard entreaties (sometimes accompanied by tears) from women who had taken up their cause.[45]

With the approach of the fall, however, everything apparently began breaking down. With the mounting flood of applications, the President found himself subject to the most intense pressures. The Southern elections, upon which he depended to set civil governments in motion, were at hand; and the possibility that numbers of unpardoned men might be elected to office promised embarrassments for his entire program. There was much criticism, from his own well-wishers, of the throngs of pardon-seekers that choked his anterooms

[44] McPherson, *Reconstruction*, p. 49.

[45] Dorris, *Pardon and Amnesty*, pp. 244–77, 284–86, and *passim*.

daily; and he was being urged at the same time to set up a pardon board so that he himself might be released from the more routine aspects of the business. With characteristic stubbornness he refused to do this. But he did have to make certain concessions to the sheer physical magnitude of his task. He did it by relaxing his standards; he permitted himself to depend on various informal channels for the expediting of pardons (though he denied this; perhaps he never fully admitted it even to himself); he turned over a portion of the work to his provisional governors; and, finally, he did hire an extra man to act as pardon clerk—a Southerner who had been, according to the head of the Secret Service, a Confederate colonel.[46] Pardons thereupon began issuing from the executive offices in great numbers, under circumstances which could not help placing the President's policy in a very unfortunate light.[47]

Especially notorious was the activity of pardon brokers, both men and women, who had some sort of access to the President and who were selling their services to applicants for the latter's clemency. Johnson was greatly annoyed by the stories which circulated about these characters and denied having assisted knowingly in such traffic. But when General L. C. Baker, who was charged with security precautions, attempted to restrain the activities of a certain Mrs. Cobb, he was roundly rebuked by the harassed President for his meddling.[48] Then came the odd spectacle of pardons being turned out to Southerners whose title to them seemed to rest on no special ground other than that they had been, or were about to be, elected to office. The total result, so far as the public could see, was a sudden rash of pardons being granted for rather questionable reasons. The Northern people had meanwhile been watching the Southern conventions and had found much that was unsatisfactory in their behavior. They had seen Southerners who might better have maintained a decent inactivity being triumphantly chosen to public office; some of the would-be congressmen, despite federal law, were unable to take the test oath;[49] and the Southern legislatures had already begun passing the notorious

---

[46] *Ibid.*, pp. 139–40; Lafayette C. Baker, *History of the United States Secret Service* (Philadelphia: L. C. Baker, 1867), p. 691.

[47] Dorris, *Pardon and Amnesty*, pp. 140–42.

[48] Baker, *Secret Service*, pp. 589–691. Most pro-Johnson narratives have a tendency to discredit the veracity of Baker's story. On the other hand, Mr. Dorris, though himself primarily sympathetic to Johnson, is reluctant to accept the view that Baker was dishonest. *Pardon and Amnesty*, pp. 146–51.

[49] McPherson, *Reconstruction*, pp. 107–9.

"black codes." In the light of all this, the President's pardoning policy became unduly vulnerable to dissatisfied criticism.

The Executive pardoning policy broke down not so much because the President suddenly "turned soft" but rather because he himself had given the pardon far too much importance in the first place. It was so unwieldy that circumstances which were bound in any case to have a sapping effect on the policy could now knock it away entirely, leaving the President with the appearance of having no alternative resources. Beneath all this was something quite fundamental to Johnson's entire conception of reconstruction. The institutional side of the rebellion, as we have seen, had always been most unreal to him, whereas the individual side was probably rather simpler than he thought. The easy things and the difficult things which the war had left in its wake were thus to a certain extent reversed in Johnson's mind. The re-establishing of individual loyalty to the abstraction of "Union"—for all Johnson's concern over "repentance"—could be effected with relative ease, in the sense that men might be counted on not to take up arms again in rebellion. But Johnson was very reluctant to see that the whole idea of "loyalty" had institutionalized itself in a manner not to be dissipated by formulas of repentance: it was something that had established its claims in ways which could not be got at simply by acting through individuals. The rebellion, that is, had imposed itself upon all those things in Southern life to which a man was truly loyal, at depths to which mere words could never reach: the intricate systems of expectation which governed men's relationships with each other, which bound families together, and which regulated the affairs of communities.

True, men themselves had in some way to be reconstructed. But there had to be some workable connection between that sort of "reconstruction" and the larger problem of realigning the polity of states and local communities with that of the nation itself. It would be necessary to work from many directions at the task of persuading two sections to become one people again, when in their hearts and in literal fact they had been two. There was a political dimension to this; the matter of relationships between state and federal institutions was much more complex than the simple question of individual allegiance. But Johnson's basic dogma here was, "The states never were out." For him, relationships on this level had not really been altered; they had simply been interrupted, and thus the "real" ones were those existing prior to the abnormalities of the rebellion. On the "institutional" level,

therefore, the measures necessary for full resumption of normal relationships could seem quite simple and quite perfunctory.

The individual level of the problem, consequently, was much more
real to Johnson. "Treason is a crime and must be made odious"—this
was his other dogma. True, the intensity and passion of it underwent
much erosion. But what did not change, from the days of his military
governorship through his presidency, was the focus upon individuals
and the conviction that it was somehow at this level that reconstruction was to be effected. This was what enabled Johnson to conceive
the pardoning power and the reconstructing power as one and the
same. The basic test, after all, was repentance. Had he achieved repentance? What better evidence did the once-reviled military dictator
of Tennessee have, for the vindication of himself and the principles
he stood for, than the heaps of petitions now before him, from the
very revilers who were presently craving his pardon? In a sense the
main question was simply, how long would he relish them before acting?[50] Meanwhile, however, his basic dogma—that the states had never
been out—was coming to be menaced by his own slowness on pardons.
Circumstances thus made it necessary to curtail the period of repentance, if both sides of the logic were to be preserved. The President did
this so abruptly that the cooling waters of mercy became a boiling
torrent.[51]

What Johnson never did do with the pardoning power
was to use it consciously as a mode of communication. The "remorse"
aspect was probably rather fanciful; the benefits of Executive pardon
were tangible enough that in most cases a man's failure to experience
inner stirrings of repentance would still not have deterred him from

[50] Describing a midsummer day at the White House in 1865, Whitelaw Reid wrote:
"Sundry gentlemen woud be greatly obliged if they could be handed their pardons
now. The President was not quite ready; they were made out and lying on the table,
but he wasn't just prepared to deliver them yet. 'Were not the cases decided?' 'Oh,
yes, it was all right; they would get their pardons in due time.'
" 'They're not quite enough humiliated yet,' whispered an official onlooker." *After
the War*, p. 307. See also above, p. 146.

[51] By late fall, the pardon was sufficiently easy to come by that men who did not
even need pardons had apparently begun applying for them and putting them to uses
for which they were never intended—such as the improvement of personal credit
ratings. "President Johnson is pardoning all the rebels here," complained a Unionist of
Henrico County, Virginia, "and . . . men are getting pardoned who was never worth
twenty thousand dollars in their life but want to take advantage of the northern men to
borry money on account of their receiving pardon, but dont trust them that [is] all I
have to say upon that subject." Martin M. Lipscomb to Schuyler Colfax, Dec. 1, 1865,
Justin S. Morrill MSS, Cornell University.

applying as a matter of routine. The pardoning power, all told, was important but not quite so vital for the government's primary purposes as many of Johnson's critics—including Ben Wade—imagined, and the extent to which it could be abused was probably narrower than many of them would have recognized.

As an auxiliary tool, however, carefully adjusted to an otherwise well-functioning policy of reconstruction, the pardon might have had its uses. The power to confer it might have assisted in putting Southern men of influence in touch with the presidential will and the presidential policy—assuming that the President's will was clear and that he had a policy. Through a sensitive touch on the conferring and withholding of pardon, standards might have been imposed upon the Southern elections which they did not in fact have and which might have saved the South from the worst embarrassments of Northern criticism. A little more manipulation (not unlike that which Johnson had practiced in Tennessee) might have helped to elect a more acceptable set of officers throughout the South than were actually elected. As it was, the President had apparently been caught unprepared for this problem, and instead of letting it be known well in advance that no one should be running for office who had not received a presidential pardon, he found it suddenly necessary to distribute batches of pardons to men *because* they had been elected to office. He was unprepared to make advance provisions for the cold-blooded but nicely adjusted discriminations which would have kept certain kinds of secessionists unpardoned until after a due number of elections. In allowing his provisional governors (very properly, in principle) to pass on pardon applications from their states, he did not furnish them with clear standards on what use they might make of their power in influencing the formation of satisfactory governments. In North Carolina, Governor Holden used it to improve his own political position, rewarding his friends and punishing his enemies with the pardon. On the other hand, Perry, the South Carolina governor, approved and forwarded to Washington every pardon application he received.[52]

An inference which we may draw from this "institutional-individual" duality in the realm of policy is that the primary need which existed all along was the need for a full settlement—a settlement not only with Southerners singly and at large, but somehow with the Confederacy itself. No one could be very sure just how to

[52] Dorris, *Pardon and Amnesty*, pp. 194–210, 138.

make such a settlement; but if it were not made, severe cramps might conceivably remain to obstruct the political life of the "restored" nation for many a year. Federal legislation would in all likelihood be required, and amendments would probably have to be written into the Constitution. But the really important things would have to be done in advance of all that, and perhaps not even publicly, to insure that the foundations for ultimate reunion might be made solid and sound. In the last analysis it takes two parties to make reunion, if only in order that both parties may share in the recognition that an understanding exists. The Confederacy had been smashed as an entity of warmaking and of government, but it lived on and kept its being in other ways. There was nothing "unreal" about its remaining a power in men's thoughts; and as long as it did, with twenty-two senators and several times that many representatives, the Confederacy under whatever name would retain its meaning and its potency. Besides, the men who had lent authority to it in the first place still retained the respect of their fellow citizens.

Still, the North must be satisfied. How was it to be managed? The peace must be an unbalanced peace, in that the North would present the terms, but to mean anything it could never *quite* be a dictated peace, a wholly unilateral settlement. The terms must be acceptable, the South must accept them, and the North must be convinced that they had been accepted. If this proved impossible, then reconstruction, restoration, or whatever else it might be called, was doomed from the first to failure.

Again, the shadow of Lincoln falls across the whole problem. The very scarcity of hints and clues which the shadow affords may be a clue in itself, the clue of indeterminacy. Lincoln's purposes were never made fully explicit, and their author apparently saw that it was not in his interest to make them so. He may well have realized that peacemaking had to have not only its formal but also its informal side and that while official acts were performed at the front door, unofficial ones must be taking place at the back. The President might have to be playing a variety of roles all at once, including the very shadowy one of go-between. "Unlike the case of a war between independent nations," Lincoln had said in his last speech, "there is no authorized organ for us to treat with." It was characteristic of the man to deny officially what would surely have to be done in fact, unofficially, just as he had denied legitimacy to the Confederate government while behaving as though its legitimacy were a fact for thousands of Southern men and women.[53] There was a whole category of things, in the business of peacemaking, that had to be done without saying that they were being done. *How* they were done might make all the difference between peace and no peace.

[53] According to Judge Campbell, at the time of the Richmond negotiations in April, 1865: " 'He deemed it important that that "very legislature" that had been sitting in Richmond should vote upon the question. That he had a government in Northern Virginia—the Pierpont Government—but it had but a small margin, and he did not desire to enlarge it.' " "Papers of Hon. John A. Campbell," *Southern Historical Society Papers*, N.S., IV, 69; see also above, chap. 5. This might be described as "double-dealing" both literally and figuratively.

Chapter 7

Peace
for the South

In viewing the South's emergence from the humiliation of defeat, and the South's efforts to face the problems of adjustment to Northern victory, one has a tendency to take for granted an undue amount of Southern intransigence and blundering. That such intransigence and blundering did occur is hardly to be denied: it was indeed this very fact that had come to dominate the mood of the North as Congress prepared to assemble in December, 1865.

And yet simply to take this for granted, without asking whether there may not have been very special and complex reasons—even "abnormal" reasons, if "normality" can have any meaning in such a setting—is possibly to do the South something less than justice. The things to be explained in Southern behavior during this period are really most extraordinary. Why did the Southerners—not ordinary men, but men in some sense officially and publicly situated—seem so utterly impervious to Northern public opinion? Why did they commit so many mistakes? Why did they quibble so, in their conventions, over points which substantively meant nothing but which to the North would mean the difference between their states' fitness and nonfitness to re-enter the Union? How is one to explain their almost brazen willingness to put forward so many of their most forthright secessionists for public office? What of their incredible black codes? Why should these men have disregarded so completely President Johnson's suggestion, made to all intents and purposes in good faith, that they grant the suffrage to a small and very highly qualified class of their colored freedmen? That step alone, so relatively easy compared with all they would have to undergo in later years, could beyond doubt have effected a revolution in Northern sentiment. It was hardly as though there were not men in the South—men fully identified with the Confederate cause—who saw the dangers in all this behavior and who occasionally called attention to them. Why were their warnings so completely ignored? True, there was certainly cause for the South's incapacity to satisfy some of the subtler requirements of Northern feeling. But why was the South unable to satisfy even the grossest ones?

One way to deal with this question would be simply to ask: what else could have been expected? There was little reason why the South should feel inclined to truckle to the North in any way at all, when the North had in literal truth broken its heart. How could the passions of war be expected to evaporate so soon from the wreck that now lay everywhere? Why should any man of pride accept Yankee notions about making voters out of slaves? Secession had been impossible, and tongues could say it, but could anyone's heart declare—after the flower of Southern youth had given everything for it—that secession had been really wrong? Was not the South at least to honor its heroes, as the North honored its own? Possibly what the South most needed was simply time—time for bitterness to soften, time for adjustment by slow degrees to the new order.

There is much to be said for this reasoning—but not quite everything. If there had ever been a time when the South was most painfully sensitive to Northern wishes, and most fully prepared to adjust to them, it was in those very months that immediately followed Lee's surrender. Between this fact and the South's gross misreading, later on, of all the North's desires, lies a great deal of unexplored ground. How closely, indeed, was the South kept in touch with those desires? What sort of communication was occurring between North and South during the summer of 1865, and how was it being guided?

I PRIDE AND SUBMISSION IN DEFEAT: THE BALANCE

There is hardly anything in the terrible legend of a mutilated South, silenced at war's end and torn with wrack and woe, that needs to be probed, questioned, or trifled with. The devastation, wherever else it lay, was in the people's hearts and would remain there forever.

Reference was made earlier to a precarious, ambivalent suspension of themes in the surge of Northern victory: the theme of stern retribution side by side with that of healing mercy. Something comparable, some reverse counterpart, might also have been found suspended in the gloom of Southern defeat. There, also, was a balance, something equally precarious, possibly too fragile in its passing quality to have been preserved in the legend. But it was there: a balance between bitterness and submission. There was bitter, intransigent hatred; there was also sensitive, alert submission; it is important to see that both themes were truly present before asking why the one should so soon have overwhelmed the other.

On the night of April 10, 1865, a Virginian lady, Judith McGuire, tending the Confederate wounded in a Richmond hospital, heard sounds of cannon in the distance, too regular for a bombardment. There were passers-by, and she called out in the darkness to ask what had happened. "A voice answered, as if from a broken heart: 'They say General Lee has surrendered.' We cannot believe it, but my heart became dull and heavy. . . ." On Good Friday, there were no church services. That evening Mrs. McGuire wrote in her diary: "An order came out in this morning's papers that the prayers for the President of the United States must be used. How could we do it?" Even as she sat down to write the words, the President, a hundred miles away, may have been taking his seat in Ford's Theatre. The last entry in the distracted woman's diary was that of May 4. "General Johnston surrendered on the 26th of April. 'My native land, good-night!' "[1] No Northerner might ever imagine such ache and grief; no Southerner, even, could give it adequate voice. "A feeling of sadness hovers over me now, day and night," wrote Mary Chesnut of South Carolina, "no words of mine can express."[2]

Out of the shock of defeat came hate, awful and implacable. "They've left me one inestimable privilege," an impoverished South Carolina innkeeper said of the Yankees, "—to hate 'em. I git up at half-past four in the morning, and sit up till twelve at night, to hate 'em."[3] John T. Trowbridge, a traveler from Massachusetts, passed through a little town in Virginia in the summer of 1865 and asked a perfunctory question or two of a young man he met there. "His almost savage answers," wrote the Northerner, "did not move me; but all the while I looked with compassion at his fine young face and that pendent idle sleeve. . . . His beautiful South was devastated. . . . 'Well may your thoughts be bitter,' my heart said, as I thanked him for his information."[4] But those least able to contain their bitterness were, after all, the women—they who, since long ago in 1861, could only wait and

[1] Judith W. McGuire, *Diary of a Southern Refugee during the War* (3d ed.; Richmond: J. W. Randolph & English, 1889), pp. 351–52, 355, 360.

[2] *A Diary from Dixie, As Written by Mary Boykin Chesnut*, ed. Isabella D. Martin and Myrta L. Avary (New York: D. Appleton, 1905), p. 390.

[3] John T. Trowbridge, *The South: A Tour of Its Battle-Fields and Ruined Cities . . .* (Hartford: L. Stebbins, 1866), p. 577.

[4] *Ibid.*, p. 72.

wait. "We are shattered and stunned," Mrs. Chesnut wrote in May, "the remnant of heart left alive within us filled with brotherly hate. We sit and wait until the drunken tailor who rules the United States of America issues a proclamation, and defines our anomalous position."[5]

The men, having been closer to the fight itself, were in certain ways spared some of the festering emptiness of its aftermath. The soldiers had tested the cause in the most direct, decisive, and convincing terms possible; and whatever the outcome, they could know that they had given their best. For them, amid all the desolation and ruin, the issue had at least been decided honorably. There seems to have been something curiously liberating, almost purifying, in this knowledge. Great numbers of the officers and men of the late Confederate army in those first months seemed to find genuine relief in avowing, as emphatically and straightforwardly as they could, that they were beaten. Such was the almost universal impression made upon Northern travelers during this period—the same ones to whom later Southern behavior would seem so odious. Most of them were greatly touched, and gave due recognition to what they saw and heard. "I tell you, sir," declared a Union general in Mobile to Whitelaw Reid early in June, "I tell you, they are behaving splendidly. In fact, sir, these Rebel soldiers are an honor to the American name." Reid further relates:

"You've whipped us," said one of their officers, with whom I had been carrying on a desultory conversation, "and you did the work thoroughly. I think too much of the bravery of our army and of my own honor to admit that we should have surrendered if we had *not* been thoroughly whipped."[6]

Indeed, of all the elements of Southern society, it seems to have been the military men (there were, of course, thousands of them; scarcely a family had failed to send someone) who were most willing and able to accept the results. "Next to the uncompromising Union men," Trowbridge wrote, "the most sincerely loyal Virginians I saw . . . were those who had been lately fighting against us." "The truth is," said a Confederate colonel to the same observer, "we have had the devil whipped out of us. It is only those who kept out of the fight that are in favor of continuing it. I fought you with all my might until we got whipped; then I gave it up as a bad job; and now there's not a more loyal man in the United States than I am."[7]

---

[5] *Diary from Dixie*, p. 390. [6] Reid, *After the War*, p. 206.

[7] Trowbridge, *The South*, p. 188. "For my part," wrote Sidney Andrews, "I wish every office in the State [South Carolina] could be filled with ex-Confederate officers. It is the universal testimony of every officer of our own troops with whom I have con-

For the South as a whole, then, the two themes of bitterness and submission must in some way be seen as distinct and separate. Of course the one would serve to limit the other. The South's humiliation, and the need to repair its shattered pride, would set bounds to whatever willingness it might have to accommodate itself to Northern demands. Much would also depend both on the nature of the North's requirements and on the manner in which they were communicated. No one would be more aware of all these limits, once they were fully defined, than the Southerners themselves; the Southerners might naturally be expected never to stop testing them, which in fact was just what happened. Whitelaw Reid did not deceive himself on this point; he saw that Southern spokesmen would ask for whatever they could get: ". . . the absolute right to State Governments, the old suffrage, and, in a word, the old *status* on everything, slavery only excepted. Yet, withal, there is a curious submissiveness about them, whenever there is talk of the power of the conquerors. The simple truth is, they stand ready to claim everything, if permitted, and to accept anything, if required."[8]

Why not reopen a question long closed, and assume a wide range of alternatives in what the South might be brought to do in response to the North's requirements? Suppose it were assumed that there was actually a period in which the problem still remained undefined, that there was still more than one way in which the thing might be spelled out, and that the North—and the North alone—would have to take the initiative in doing it. Why not also suppose that it was at this very time, the first months following the war, that the South's readiness and willingness to accommodate itself was at its maximum? Trowbridge, viewing the scene at first hand, would have made the case even stronger. "At the close of the war, the South was ready to accept

---

versed, from the commanding general down, as well as every Northern man two months resident in the State, that the late Rebel soldiers are of better disposition toward the new government, toward Northerners, toward progression, than any other class of citizens." *The South since the War*, p. 95.

[8] *After the War*, pp. 154–55. "I [have] been told by all Union men," wrote a friend of Lyman Trumbull after a sojourn at Mobile in December, "that after the surrender of the Reb. armies that the men returned perfectly quiet [,] came to union Southern and Northern men saying we don't know what is expected of us by the Government. But one thing is certain we are tired of war and desire above all things to return to the quiet pursuits of life and try to mend our fortunes as best we can, and cultivate a friendly feeling with all parts of the country once more. Now tell us how to do this." J. W. Shaffer to Trumbull, Dec. 28, 1865, Trumbull MSS, Library of Congress. According to Sidney Andrews, who was at the South Carolina convention in September, " 'The conqueror has the right to make the terms, and we must submit,' say dozens of men every where." *The South since the War*, p. 95.

any terms which the victorious government might have seen fit to enforce."⁹ Certainly the South's flexibility would never be any greater than it was then.

Everything would thus depend on clarity of communication. What picture would the South be given of the nature of the choices? How would the North's authority—and the location of that authority—be represented to the South? How might the North's requirements be conveyed to make for maximum compliance, with minimum abuse of either Southern pride or Southern willingness? Whatever version of these things the South might be given, it must represent the North's maximum effort to speak with one voice. The voice or voices which the South heard and acted upon would have to be those which echoed the undoubted consensus of Northern feeling, in order for the result to constitute peace and a settlement. It may be supposed that every satisfactory alternative was still more or less realizable within the May 29 proclamations of President Johnson.

What followed during the summer and fall, however, involved so complete a breakdown in communication between North and South that, to perfectly reasonable and intelligent men, the very same concrete events could carry vastly different meanings. So remarkable was this breakdown, so great a disparity of purposes did it embrace, and so wide a divergence of understanding was the result, that such developments must be looked at almost through three sets of eyes in order to be appreciated. The President saw them one way; the alert Northerner saw them another way; and the equally alert, perfectly responsible, perfectly sensible Southerner saw them in still another way.

II   THE PRESIDENT'S COURSE AS SEEN BY THE PRESIDENT

There was something unusually personal for Andrew Johnson about every public proceeding in which he himself in any way figured. Somehow personal success and personal vindication were forever being laid on the block. There should thus have been a great many reasons for his assuming, after the first anxious days of his presidency, that the fortunes of Andrew Johnson were indeed meant to be favored after all and that his uphill climb had truly reached its summit. Considering the state of things in Tennessee so short a time before, the way in which resistance there had so utterly ceased was nothing short of amazing. It would seem that Johnson had the right to make some association between Tennessee's submission and his own

⁹ Trowbridge, *The South*, p. 589.

work there. And he could not have failed to see, in the collapse of Confederate leadership there and everywhere, some oracular response to his own principles—his burning hatred of the aristocrats and his mystic faith in the masses.

But what must have been peculiarly coercive upon Johnson were the organized expressions of deference and support that now went beyond anything his own experience could have prepared him for. They came from everywhere. Members of the powerful Conduct of War Committee, with Senator Wade as their spokesman, waited upon Johnson on April 16, the day after his inauguration, and heartily voiced their full faith in him.[10] The very men who had turned from him in disgust six weeks before—for example, the exalted Senator Sumner—were now constantly seeking his counsel, deferring to him on matters of highest state, and according him all the marks of profound respect.[11] He was honored by delegations from the several states. From Illinois on the eighteenth came a group headed by Governor Oglesby, who praised the "splendor of your recent gigantic efforts to stay the hand of treason" and announced the "cordial, earnest, and unremitting purpose of our State to give your administration the strong support we have heretofore given to the administration of our lamented late President."[12] A party of dignitaries arrived from Indiana on the twenty-first, and the heroic Governor Morton likewise praised the new President and tendered him the state's support.[13] Similar delegations, with similar compliments, came from elsewhere. A group of Southern exiles came on the twenty-fourth; Johnson himself, but for his own charmed life, might have been of their number. Now he could thank them for their "regard and respect," and intimate to them that "the time is not far distant when our people can all return to their homes and firesides, and resume their various avocations."[14] He now had invitations from the highest Brahmin society of Boston. Amos Abbott Lawrence hoped that Johnson and his family might spend a few days at his summer home in Nahant, and Governor Andrew, on behalf of the Board of Overseers, invited the President

[10] Julian, *Political Recollections*, p. 257.

[11] Edward L. Pierce, *Memoir and Letters of Charles Sumner* (4 vols.; Boston: Roberts Bros., 1877–94), IV, 245.

[12] Frank Moore (ed.), *Speeches of Andrew Johnson . . .* (Boston: Little, Brown, 1865), pp. 466–73.

[13] *Ibid.*, pp. 481–84; Julian, *Political Recollections*, pp. 260–62; William D. Foulke, *Life of Oliver P. Morton*, I, 440–42.

[14] Moore, *Speeches*, pp. 477–81.

to assist at the Harvard commencement, receive an honorary degree, and be feted by the magnificos of New England's wealth and culture.[15]

Most satisfying of all was the succession of visits from parties of chastened ex-rebels. Here was proud South Carolina, the first state out, confessing on June 24, 1865: "We are defeated and conquered by the North, who are too strong for us." South Carolina was saying this to the onetime tailor, the runaway apprentice, the man of servile antecedents, assuring him of its "pledge of loyal support to the government," and daring to hope that he, the President now, would see fit to designate a governor who would execute his purposes in their state.[16] When extreme views on states' rights were expressed—as by Judge Moore of North Carolina—he could brush those views aside with even a touch of indulgence (such was his power now), and in so doing he would be supported by most of the Southerners themselves. It was *his* constitutional view of the problem—which he carefully explained to them—that must prevail.[17] For practical purposes, whatever he told them they accepted. He could even permit himself to say that he was "a better States rights man" than they were, and they would laugh obediently.[18] He was being given almost miraculous proof of how right he had been all along in his constitutional and states' rights convictions.

Johnson's rightness seemed further borne out as he performed his first presidential acts. Nothing he did met with any real resistance—certainly not the kind that he had known. Resistance back in Tennessee, from his earliest experience there, was something crude, fully vocal, and undisguised by ceremonial camouflage; it was something that one confronted head-on and overcame. But here, for some reason, there was nothing to overcome. By executive order on April 29, the President removed all restrictions on domestic and coastwise trade with the Southern states, and the blockade of Southern ports was lifted by proclamation on May 22. The President acted with vigor in regard to the conspirators in Lincoln's assassination; he directed on May 1

[15] A. A. Lawrence to Johnson, Letterbook, July 1, 1865, Lawrence MSS, Massachusetts Historical Society; John Andrew to Johnson, June 24, 1865, Andrew MSS, Mass. Hist. Soc. Johnson did not accept either of these invitations.

[16] New York *Times*, June 26, 1865. "From all the Southern delegations waiting upon him we have the same voice:—'We are beaten. We submit to the consequences of our defeat. . . . We are in your hands, Mr. President. We bow to your authority. We rely upon your justice and magnanimity. We accept your terms. We need your assistance, and we come to ask it, and to learn what we are to do." New York *Herald*, June 30, 1865.

[17] Hamilton, *Reconstruction in North Carolina*, pp. 106–7.

[18] New York *Times*, June 26, 1865. Interview with South Carolina delegation.

that they be tried by military commission; by proclamation on May 2 he offered rewards for the capture and arrest of Jefferson Davis and others, on the chance that they, too—as rumor had it—were somehow implicated. It soon became apparent that they had not been, but at least no stone was being left unturned. (Henry Wirz, the sinister commandant of Andersonville, would also be tried and sentenced by military commission later in the summer.) On July 5 it was ordered that the convicted conspirators—including the unfortunate Mary Surratt —be executed on the seventh. The President by executive order declared on May 9 that federal authority and federal agencies should be re-established in the state of Virginia; and on the twenty-ninth came the celebrated proclamation of amnesty, bristling with stern exceptions. On the same day, the reconstruction proclamation for North Carolina was issued.[19]

Meanwhile, under military supervision, order had been re-established with such ease everywhere that actual military occupation could even now be seen as a distinctly temporary expedient. So far as the main thing, reconstruction, was concerned, arrangements were being set up whereby the resumption of civil governments in the Southern states was an early possibility. The President's provisional governors would be just that: provisional; they would simply be there to manage the details of transition from the anarchy of defeat to the full self-government of restoration. (He preferred this word to "reconstruction.") The President let it be known privately, to the citizens who were to take part in this process, that their states should in general meet three requirements. They must repudiate the Confederate debt, nullify their ordinances of secession, and ratify the Thirteenth Amendment abolishing slavery. There was almost a clockwork quality in the smoothness with which all these things were set in motion. The Northern public, anxious that the world should see its government continue functioning without interruption despite the disaster of Lincoln's death, and thus equally anxious that its new President should succeed, hastened to praise everything he did. As for the Southerners, they were little disposed to question the justice which the President dispensed to them. Why should they?

There were certain annoyances. But they came from out on the fringes, from extremists at both ends of the scale, and they served only to highlight the great difficulties he had overcome and to define the

---

[19] Richardson, *Messages and Papers*, VI, 307–14, 333–38, 342–48. The trial of Wirz, who had been arrested in May, began on August 23 before a court presided over by General Lew Wallace and lasted for two months. The sentence of hanging, which was approved by President Johnson, was executed on November 10.

real range of his support. There were queer little notes (almost impossible to decipher) from Thaddeus Stevens: "Among all the leading men of the North with whom I have had intercourse I do not find one who approves of your policy. . . . Can you not hold your hand and wait the action of Congress and in the meantime govern them by military rulers?"[20] There were shrill noises from Sumner and his Boston abolitionist friends; these persons were demanding Negro suffrage at the top of their voices, and it was being said of them that they meant war on the President's restoration plans. Wendell Phillips in a speech on May 31 came very close to a direct personal attack.[21] There were apocalyptic forebodings from Winter Davis in a July 4 oration at Chicago; Davis, too, harped on Negro suffrage and ascribed certain principles to the President which the latter did not in fact hold, with the implication that no sane man could fail to see their full and undoubted wisdom.[22] Still, if this were "criticism," none of it ever quite came to the point. That is, it was not *personal*. Back in Tennessee when men attacked Andrew Johnson, they had been known to do it with threats of tar and feathers.[23]

The Negro suffrage ideologues had such men as Chase and Carl Schurz touring through the South, and they were not disposed to any very great optimism concerning the South's intentions toward the freedmen. The case of Major General Carl Schurz had given the President special cause for exasperation. Just before the issuance of the North Carolina proclamation, Schurz had come to see him, full of advice on how to proceed. One of his suggestions was that the President should "appoint a sensible and reliable person" to observe the execution of policy in the South and "to keep the Government advised of what is going on, etc."[24] Johnson intimated that he might

[20] Stevens to Johnson, July 6, 1865, Johnson MSS, Library of Congress.

[21] "He contended that . . . the reconstruction policy of the Administration, as set forth in the proclamation for the reconstruction of North Carolina, was absolute surrender of the helm of the Union into the hands of Alexander H. Stephens and his co-workers. Reconstruction on that basis was a practical fraud upon the people of the North. Every life and every dollar they had spent had been stolen from them. . . . Every man who supported the North Carolina proclamation was a Davis sycophant. Better, far better would it have been for Grant to have surrendered to Lee, than for President Johnson to have surrendered to North Carolina." New York *Tribune*, June 1, 1865. Phillips delivered another attack on the President in a Fourth of July address at Framingham, Massachusetts. Boston *Advertiser*, July 7, 1865.

[22] Davis, *Speeches*, pp. 564–84.

[23] Hall, *Andrew Johnson, Military Governor*, pp. 37–38.

[24] *Speeches, Correspondence, and Political Papers of Carl Schurz*, ed. Frederic Bancroft (New York: G. P. Putnam's Sons, 1913), I, 259. One may follow Schurz's entire Southern tour through his letters in *ibid.*, pp. 258–78.

consider asking Schurz himself to do this. The matter was then dropped, but Schurz reintroduced it himself in a lengthy letter to Johnson on June 6, and the upshot was that the General would visit the South and report to the President on conditions prevailing there. He left early in July.

Schurz in his peregrinations afforded the administration two distinct occasions for embarrassment. He took advantage of his official mission, while still on it, to publish a series of five long and extensive "Letters from the South" in a Boston newspaper which was itself editorially committed to Negro suffrage. The letters gave a picture of the Southern disposition toward the Negroes that was by no means rosy.[25] But the other matter was much the more serious; it involved Schurz's taking a hand in a quarrel between Johnson's provisional governor in Mississippi and the military commander in that state. Governor William L. Sharkey had issued a proclamation on August 19 which provided for the raising of militia companies in the various counties to preserve the peace and prevent disorders. The President, though not at first disposed to approve such a proceeding, changed his mind upon receipt of two urgently worded dispatches from the Governor, who assured him that the local forces were actually very badly needed. According to Sharkey the federal military was insufficient, and the presence of Negro troops was inflammatory to the people. Sharkey also reminded Johnson of an earlier promise to allow the raising of militias if circumstances required it. Meanwhile, however, Major General Henry W. Slocum, commanding the department of Mississippi, had on the twenty-fourth issued his subsequently famous General Order No. 22, which forbade any such activity as Sharkey contemplated— and which the latter had, in fact, already begun. This brought the tension between the Governor and General Slocum to an extremely high pitch.

It was at this point that Schurz, passing through Vicksburg, took a hand in the affair himself. In a dispatch to the President on August 29, he denounced the militia project and strongly pressed Johnson to uphold Slocum's position. By that time the President had decided that it was necessary to move swiftly and decisively. The footing of his provisional governor, being delicate anyway, was critical now and should be upheld and strengthened at every possible point. Accordingly, he sent off a brisk rebuke to Schurz, reminding him of the proper limits of

25 The five letters were dated July 17, 21, 25, 31, and August 8, 1865; they were printed in the Boston *Advertiser* on July 31, August 3, 5, 8, and 19. There are also copies in the Schurz MSS, Library of Congress.

his mission and pointedly "presuming" that Slocum would do nothing to interfere with Sharkey without consulting the government first. A copy of the same message went to Sharkey himself, and on September 2 a War Department order directed that Slocum revoke any order of his own whose effect may have been to countermand the Governor's August 19 proclamation.[26]

So much for Schurz. Although his dispatches and those of Chief Justice Chase may have been gloomy with regard to general conditions in the South, Johnson had other emissaries who were also reporting to him, and their reports were most encouraging. Harvey Watterson, who by arrangement with the President toured the South from early July through October, reported that all was going well and that the Southern states were loyal without exception. "Everyone considers it his first and highest interest to get the State in the Union, as the proper and only means of preserving liberty, and his hope is to accomplish it by heartily supporting and cooperating with the Executive. . . ." Watterson's observations on the use of Negro troops (that it had a bad effect on the citizenry and was therefore bad policy) would bear out the complaints of Sharkey; and as for Negro suffrage, it was well, all things considered, that the administration was staying away from that. "Your Administration is growing daily in the confidence of the people of North Carolina. The position that you are now understood to occupy in regard to negro suffrage is more than anything else doing the work."[27] (Johnson had prudently refrained from pressing suffrage.) Two other emissaries were equally reassuring to Johnson in his own growing estimate of himself and the wisdom of his policy. His faithful lieutenant, Benjamin C. Truman, was sent South in the fall, and Truman's subsequent report would represent the states of the late Confederacy as fully ready to resume their places in the Union.[28] General Grant himself—the inscrutable hero of the Union, now basking in the fullest glow of public admiration—undertook a brief tour of inspection late in November. There was a note of detached serenity in the General's words upon returning:

I am satisfied that the mass of thinking men of the South accept the present situation of affairs in good faith. . . . I was pleased to learn from the leading men whom I met, that they not only accepted the decision ar-

[26] *Senate Executive Documents*, 39 Cong., 1 sess., No. 26, "Provisional Governors," pp. 229–32. See also *Speeches, Correspondence . . . of Carl Schurz*, I, 258–78; and James W. Garner, *Reconstruction in Mississippi* (New York: Macmillan, 1901), pp. 96–103.

[27] Watterson to Johnson, Oct. 3, July 8, 1865, Johnson MSS.

[28] *Sen. Exec. Docs.*, 39 Cong., 1 sess., No. 43.

rived at as final, but, now that the smoke of battle has cleared away and time has been given for reflection, that this decision has been a fortunate one for the whole country.[29]

Thus the gloomy predictions, the harassment and occasional sniping from the radical side, could be classified for the most part as irresponsible, considering their source and considering also the apparent solidity of reports coming from men whose judgment he could really trust. Nor did the President fail to meet intransigence from the other side; persisting traces of obstinacy and irreconcilability from the Southerners themselves continued to give him moments of extreme irritation, occasionally of downright anxiety. But these notes simply served to punctuate, more than anything else, an otherwise wonderfully smooth-running Southern policy.

His governors went speedily to work, and their most immediate concern was the filling by appointment of local and state offices, so that the necessary functions of government at that level might once more be resumed. Many complaints thereupon began drifting north, to the effect that in numerous cases secessionists were being preferred to good Union men in the making of such appointments. These reports came to Johnson's attention, and by August 22 he felt it necessary to address a circular telegram concerning them to all his provisional governors. He did not ask whether they were true—indeed, he assured the governors, "I place no reliance in such statements"—but he did think they ought to know about them. Not all the replies were impeccable, there being, for instance, an undercurrent of truculence in that of Governor Perry of South Carolina, who asserted: "There were not a dozen decided Union men in the whole State at the commencement of the rebellion, and none of them have sought office." His own sympathies, Perry protested, were "with the Union men," but the mass of South Carolinians were, after all, now loyal and could be counted on to support the Union. "If I have ever given a preference over a pretended Union man, it was because I doubted his fitness and principles, as well as his Unionism."

The other replies, however, not only were more satisfactory, but most of them were fully reassuring, even enlightening. Holden of North Carolina was emphatic in declaring, "I have been very careful to prefer and to reappoint persons who were original Union men"; Sharkey was not quite so emphatic, but then his mind was occupied at that particular time with the Slocum affair and, everything considered, his reply that he had "endeavored to avoid the appointment or recom-

[29] *Ibid.*, No. 2, pp. 106–8.

mendation of secessionists" was quite acceptable; Hamilton in Texas called the alleged report, so far as it applied to his appointments, "a most unmitigated falsehood"; and James Johnson of Georgia assured the President, "I have uniformly given all preference to Union men in my recommendations." At the same time, with thousands of offices to fill (Holden alone had "some four thousand"), it would be folly to expect that untainted Unionists could in anywhere near all cases be found to occupy them.[30] The executive branch of the federal government was having its own troubles in making appointments to Southern post offices and revenue positions under the Treasury.[31] All told, if there had been anything to criticize in the reconstruction policies going on, this was the point at which such criticism was least relevant.

The next move of the governors was to arrange for the holding of conventions, so that their states might perform those acts of acceptance and adjustment which had been made necessary by the outcome of the war. The first convention was that of Mississippi; it met on August 14, and before its business was under way, the President telegraphed Governor Sharkey his expectations of what it would do. "I hope," he said, "that without delay your Convention will amend your State constitution abolishing slavery and denying to all future legislatures the power to legislate that there is property in man; also that they will adopt the amendment to the Constitution of the United States abolishing slavery." He also covered himself fully on Negro suffrage, suggesting (much in the manner of Lincoln in his message to Louisiana's Governor Hahn in 1864) that they could "with perfect safety" extend the franchise to the literate and property-holding freedmen and thus "set an example the other States will follow."[32] The results of this first test were not all that they might have been. The hints on suffrage were ignored, though that was more or less to be expected; at least the President himself had behaved correctly. Rather more vexing was the convention's failure to repudiate the state's war debt. Slavery was abolished, however (if not with the best of grace), and the convention did declare Mississippi's ordinance of secession "null and void."[33]

Alabama's convention, meeting on September 12, behaved much more sensibly and straightforwardly. The debt was repudiated, seces-

[30] *Ibid.*, No. 26, "Provisional Governors," pp. 221–22, 230, 234–35, 241–42, 244, 248, 258–59.

[31] Hugh McCulloch to Charles Sumner, Sept. 11, 1865, Sumner MSS, Harvard College Library; Hugh McCulloch, *Men and Measures*, pp. 227–32.

[32] "Provisional Governors," p. 229.

[33] *Ibid.*, pp. 71–73.

sion nullified, and slavery abolished. The convention adjourned on September 30, and the President indicated his satisfaction. "The proceedings of the convention have met the highest expectations of all who desire the restoration of the Union. All seems now to be working well, and will result, as I believe, in a decided success."[34]

South Carolina was in all ways the most exasperating. The President's annoyances with that state had begun fairly early. Benjamin F. Perry, his provisional governor, was hardly the man of tact that this particular state might well have used. Before his appointment, Perry (who had originally opposed secession but who had served the state as a judge in wartime) had made a speech on July 3 in which he had simply said all the wrong things, with the right things all in the wrong order. He had "deeply regretted" secession at the beginning. But then no one felt more bitterly "the humiliation and degradation of going back into the Union" than he did. But then, he said he knew he would be "more prosperous and happy in the Union than out of it." He did not think that Lincoln's death had been a great loss to the South. Andrew Johnson, on the other hand, was "a much abler and firmer man."[35]

The South Carolina convention assembled on September 13. The Governor apparently suffered from spells of obtuseness as to the tone and spirit in which its proceedings might most acceptably present themselves to the rest of the country, for there was much quibbling and hair-splitting among the delegates. The ordinance of secession was not nullified but "repealed." Since the slaves had been "emancipated by the action of the United States authorities," it followed that slavery could never be re-established in South Carolina.[36] As for Negro suffrage, Perry himself had made a point of saying in his message to the convention that even qualified suffrage would be "little less than folly and madness." He declared, ". . . this is a white man's government, and intended for white men only; and . . . the Supreme Court of the United States has decided [referring to the Dred Scott case] that the negro is not an American citizen under the Federal Constitution."[37] And finally, not only did Perry let the convention adjourn without repudiating the Confederate debt, but he had not even mentioned it in his message.

[34] *Ibid.*, p. 246.

[35] Benjamin F. Perry, *Reminiscences of Public Men, with Speeches and Addresses* (Greenville, S.C.: Shannon & Co., 1889), pp. 229–41.

[36] "Provisional Governors," pp. 173, 140–41.

[37] *Ibid.*, p. 124.

The President was in a sterner frame of mind when the North Carolina convention met on October 2. The secession ordinance was quickly and correctly declared "null and void," and two days later slavery was "forever prohibited" in North Carolina. But as soon as difficulty showed itself with reference to the rebel debt, Johnson wired a swift remonstrance: "Every dollar of the debt created to aid the rebellion against the United States should be repudiated finally and forever." And it was done.[38]

There was difficulty in Georgia, with undue word-bandying over secession and the abolition of slavery. But these matters were discharged, after a fashion; the real trouble—as with North Carolina—was over the debt. But, again, a presidential telegram produced the desired effect.[39] In the last of the conventions to meet in 1865, that of Florida (the Texas convention would not be held until March, 1866),[40] everything went off without a hitch, and everything that had been asked for was done.[41]

All told, Johnson probably had good reason to congratulate himself on the vast amount that had really been accomplished through these conventions, despite their occasional truculence. They had been, after all, popular assemblies, popularly elected, and they had conducted their own proceedings. All had been, in the last analysis, voluntary. There was surely many a bitter dose in what they had brought themselves to do (in response to the President's hints); and in this light it was remarkable that so few items of business actually remained undone. These could certainly be managed in the legislatures which were even then, along with the regular civil officers and representatives to Congress, in the process of being elected.

As for these elections, they proceeded on the whole with commendable orderliness, though it had to be admitted that here, too, the choices made were not in all cases the most admirable. In trying to pick suitable officials, the people showed a regrettable tendency to prefer their former Confederate leaders. So far as the state officers were concerned, this problem was almost inevitable, and it could in large measure be smoothed over by the hasty granting of pardons to successful candidates. And yet the President could hardly be expected in every case to give automatic indorsement to what had been done. He was not at

[38] *Ibid.*, pp. 28, 226–27, 38.   [39] *Ibid.*, pp. 236, 93.

[40] For details of Texas' delayed reorganization, see Charles W. Ramsdell, *Reconstruction in Texas* ("Columbia University Studies in History, Economics and Public Law," Vol. XXXVI [New York: Columbia University, 1910]), pp. 55–107.

[41] "Provisional Governors," pp. 259, 211–13.

all pleased, for instance, with the election of General Benjamin G. Humphreys as the regular governor of Mississippi. Many of the senators and representatives-elect were unable to take the federal test oath, and conceivably something might have to be done about modifying that oath before all obstacles would be removed from the resumption of Southern seats in Congress. The President did not fail to indicate to the Southerners his apprehension that they had not acted entirely in their own best interests here. "The results of the recent elections in North Carolina," he telegraphed to Governor Holden, "have greatly damaged the prospects of the State in the restoration of its governmental relations. Should the action and spirit of the legislature be in the same direction it will greatly increase the mischief already done and might be fatal."[42]

The "action and spirit" of these legislatures, when they began to meet, furnished the President with much encouragement, though here again not wholly unmixed with distress. Of particular interest to him was action on the Thirteenth Amendment. It was thus with satisfaction, not to say relief, that he received the news of its prompt approval by the various legislatures. Mississippi was the one exception; it flatly refused to ratify.[43] Of course there was nothing in the law or the Constitution compelling a state to ratify any constitutional amendment; besides, the approval of Alabama on December 2 completed the necessary two-thirds and enabled the Secretary of State to proclaim the Thirteenth Amendment as part of the law of the land.[44] But the President could not help regarding Mississippi's recalcitrance as something of a disappointment, after all his urgent suggestions.

A much more serious annoyance, however, was to come with the infamous "black codes." Few things could have been more inflammatory than the action of the Southern legislatures in passing these special laws for the governance of their colored population. It is true that emancipation had made necessary the conferral of certain basic civil rights upon the freedmen. All persons of color must now be accorded the right to hold property and make contracts; provision of some sort must be made permitting them to sue and be sued, and to give testimony (under certain conditions) in the courts; and they must be allowed to solemnize marriage and be protected in its rights and duties.

---

[42] *Ibid.*, p. 228.

[43] *Ibid.*, pp. 79–80. The other states ratified as follows: South Carolina, Nov. 13; North Carolina, Dec. 1; Alabama, Dec. 2; Georgia, Dec. 5; Florida, Dec. 27. Johnson found it necessary to put a bit of extra pressure on South Carolina. *Ibid.*, pp. 197–98.

[44] McPherson, *Reconstruction*, p. 6. Seward's certificate was issued Dec. 18, 1865.

But the apprenticeship and vagrancy laws which accompanied the bestowal of these rights were quite another matter, and not in any way entitled to be considered on the same plane with such rights. The enactments of Mississippi and South Carolina were, as might have been expected, the worst. They bore an uncomfortable resemblance, in the severity of punishments which they prescribed for vagrancy and the violation of labor contracts, to certain of the old slave codes.[45]

To a certain extent these laws may have been necessary; obviously the Southerners themselves had thought so. Emancipation had indeed left something of a legal void. Moreover, that section of the population which had so recently been in a state of slavery would probably present—in practice if not in theory—special problems in matters of police. And the Freedmen's Bureau, regarded as anything but a blessing in the South, could not continue indefinitely supervising labor contracts and performing for the Negro every manner of quasi- and extrajudicial functions. There was thus reason to believe that the Southerners really thought they were doing the right thing. It would be difficult for the President or anyone else looking at these codes to find anything downright illegal in them. Still, it was hard to gloss over a certain amount of plain folly; the Southerners at this particular point in their fortunes should have known better. This was just the sort of thing the hypersensitive and hyperfanatical radicals were sure to pounce on. Johnson would try to put the best face he could on it, but for the time being he was doubtless prudent in allowing the worst of the codes to be set aside by the military commanders.[46]

Despite the obstacles which had been put in his path, it was enough for the President to look out once more over the vast area of support which he enjoyed in order to judge what a success his policy must surely be. If a test were needed, what better one than the newspapers, spokesmen of the people? Even the "radical" papers, despite occasional rumblings, apparently adhered to the course he was following. The Chicago *Tribune* itself (the most extreme of the Republican journals whose editorial opinions received nationwide attention) hung on with at least the appearance of support. The *Tribune* at the very outset, upon the issuance of the first proclamations, had predicted that Johnson's policy would receive wide popular acceptance. This journal expressed reservations, as time went on, to both the seeming haste with which reconstruction was proceeding and the limited consideration

---

[45] The "black codes" are summarized in *ibid.*, pp. 29–44.

[46] Garner, *Reconstruction in Mississippi*, p. 119; Francis B. Simkins and Robert H. Woody, *South Carolina during Reconstruction* (Chapel Hill: University of North Carolina Press, 1932), p. 57; Eckenrode, *Virginia during the Reconstruction*, pp. 42–43.

being given to political rights for Negroes, but this was apparently balanced by the conviction (expressed on July 10) that there was "nothing which will justify us in condemning the spirit in which the President's measures were conceived and executed." On July 28 the *Tribune* credited Johnson with "a far-sighted policy" and commended the scope being given the Southern states "to display their latent patriotic devotion to the Union." In short, the President was *testing* them. Although the Chief Executive was being warned by September about the consequences of not keeping faith "with the men who elected him," the *Tribune* as late as November experienced a renewal of confidence, with the President's sterner line toward the Southern governors and legislatures. There was a good deal of dissatisfaction, by the time Congress met, with the way reconstruction was going, but the *Tribune* still felt great reluctance to make an actual break with the President.[47] That paper was probably the most outspoken and least cordial of all the major journals. The formidable eastern organs of radical Negro suffrage sentiment, *Harper's Weekly* and Horace Greeley's New York *Tribune*, continued throughout the year as supporters of Johnson. That the President's policy could draw praise even from the radical side was testified in even more direct and personal fashion. Major George L. Stearns of the Boston *Advertiser*—the very paper in which Schurz's "Letters from the South" had appeared—was most agreeably impressed by an interview which he had had with the President on October 3, and his published account of it was widely circulated.[48] It stimulated the influential Henry Ward Beecher, pastor of Brooklyn's Plymouth Church, to write Johnson on October 23:

I think I may assure you that the religious men of the North and West, are rapidly growing into a confidence in your patriotism, and wisdom, second only to that which they felt for Mr. Lincoln—a confidence which I am sure will increase. . . .
I am heartily thankful to you for that statesmanlike caution with which you touch the essential affairs of *States*. State sovereignty is a heresy but State-rights, is a reality of transcendent value. . . . Much as I desire to see the *natural* right of suffrage given to the freedmen, I think it would be attained at too great a price if it involved the right of the Federal Government to meddle with State affairs. . . . just how far to go, and where to stop, was the very test of statesmanship, and I think you have hit it exactly.
. . . I have not half expressed the great thankfulness which I feel that God has raised you up for such a crisis, endowed you with the ability and disposition, to save the nation, rather than yourself or any mere party.[49]

[47] Chicago *Tribune*, May 31, July 10, 28, Sept. 14, 15, 21, 23, Nov. 16, 1865.

[48] McPherson, *Reconstruction*, pp. 48–49.

[49] Johnson MSS.

It was naturally from the great moderate sector of Unionist opinion in the North that Johnson could draw his greatest comfort. Here he might rely upon such substantial journals as the New York *Times*, the Philadelphia *Press*, the Springfield *Republican*, and the New York *Herald*. Indeed, the *Herald* so faithfully publicized every detail of his policy, sustaining it with such consistent praise, that Johnson on October 6 was moved to address a special note to its editor, James Gordon Bennett, expressing his thanks for the latter's unsolicited support.[50] As for the great rank and file of the Union party, it was only necessary to read the resolutions of support that issued from every state convention held that year, to estimate the solidity of the Executive's position.[51]

Nor was this support confined only to the Union party—it was actually bipartisan. Even the Democrats were on Johnson's side. They were so overwhelmingly with him that it was almost embarrassing. But a reason could be found for that: "The Democratic party finds its old position untenable, and is coming to ours," as the President himself explained to Stearns.[52] Abraham Lincoln had certainly not been above drawing upon the Democrats for assistance; he had actually brought great numbers of them into his own party. It was good at least to know that they were there, in case Johnson should have to call upon them. The New York Democracy, to take a particular case, were being most co-operative.[53]

And support from the South itself: here was the truly glorious thing. Johnson, the renegade Southerner, was being praised everywhere in the Southern press: "The President is to us what the plank is to the shipwrecked mariner. We have nothing else to cling to in the Providence of God, to save us from being engulfed in the dark sea of Republican hatred and malice."[54]

[50] Don C. Seitz, *The James Gordon Bennetts, Father and Son: Proprietors of the New York Herald* (Indianapolis: Bobbs-Merrill, 1928), pp. 198–99.

[51] The resolutions of both parties, in states where conventions were held in the summer and fall of 1865, may be found in *American Annual Cyclopaedia, 1865*, entered under the states concerned.

[52] McPherson, *Reconstruction*, p. 48.

[53] John Van Buren, in a speech at Albany early in October, had actually gone so far as to "nominate" Johnson for reelection, a move which was delightedly seconded by the *World*: "The Democratic party would not only nominate him with alacrity and enthusiasm if the election were to take place now, but it is not at all improbable they *will* nominate him in 1868." New York *World*, Oct. 7, 1865. Similar expressions of support in the *World* all during this period, on behalf of the New York Democracy, are too numerous to cite. See also above, p. 72; and below, p. 197.

[54] Mobile *Register*, Sept. 2, 1865, quoted in Frank L. Owsley, "Contemporary Southern Opinion of President Johnson" (M.A. thesis, University of Chicago, 1917), p. 11.

I am not mistaken [wrote Harvey Watterson to Johnson from Columbus, Georgia] in the fact that a mighty revolution has been wrought in the minds and hearts of the Southern people in reference to the President. They were afraid that he would treat them with vindictiveness. Instead of that, he is all kindness. He says in words—and his acts attest their sincerity —"I entertain no personal resentments, enmities, or animosities to any living soul South of Mason's and Dixon's line, however much he may have differed from me in principle." A noble sentiment—worthy of the head of a great nation. It sent a thrill of admiration for the author through the entire South.[55]

A committee of citizens representing nine Southern states called on Johnson on September 11 (this, in its way, was a kind of climax). "They come, sir," said the courtly McFarland of Virginia, introducing them,

for the purpose of manifesting the sincere respect and regard they entertain for you, and to express their sincere determination to coöperate with you in whatever shall tend to promote the interests and welfare of our common country, and to say that they are as earnest now and faithful to their allegiance to the United States and to the Constitution of the Union as in the past, and that they have great confidence in your wisdom to heal the wounds that have been made, and in your disposition to exercise all the leniency which can be commended by a sound and judicious policy. They are assured, in doing this, of your desire and intention to sustain Southern rights in the Union of the United States.[56]

The President was overwhelmed at the demonstration: "I am free to say it excites in my mind feelings and emotions that language is totally inadequate to express." In the course of his reply to the Southern gentlemen, he could not resist exulting a bit in the immense personal vindication which the entire course of affairs had represented for him since he had first stood up for the Union:

I remember the taunts, the jeers, the scowls, with which I was treated. I remember the circle that stood around me, and remember the threats and intimidations that were freely uttered by the men who opposed me, and whom I wanted to befriend and guide by the light that led me; but feeling conscious in my own integrity, and that I was right, I heeded not what they might say or do to me, and was inspired and encouraged to do my duty regardless of aught else, and have lived to see the realization of my predictions and the fatal error of those whom I vainly essayed to save from the results I could not but foresee.

It need not have been surprising that the President, dissolved in the emotion of the occasion, should then somewhat effusively declare his

[55] Watterson to Johnson, Oct. 20, 1865, Johnson MSS.

[56] *American Annual Cyclopaedia, 1865*, p. 805.

deep reverence for the Constitution, his opposition to unduly concentrated federal power, his great love for the Southern people, and his intense desire to restore the full bonds of Union as early as possible.[57]

The President had, indeed, performed prodigious labors. With step after step bringing him ever nearer the goal as winter approached, he might well have pinched himself more than once. "We are making very rapid progress," he said to George Stearns, "—so rapid I sometimes cannot realize it. It appears like a dream."[58] The task would be virtually complete when the time came for Congress to assemble,[59] and Johnson's work would indeed be crowned if he might at that time view a House and Senate with the Southern seats once more occupied. There had, to repeat, been difficulties. But surely there was nothing, given the proper will and a really sincere regard for the Constitution, that should put any needless barriers to the great object of full restoration.

It would not be easy; the President was fully aware that the perversity of wilful men had already shown itself. As early as October the Clerk of the House, Edward McPherson, had announced his intention to omit the names of the Southern members-elect from his roll call. It was to be hoped, however, that resources would be available to the President of the United States for dealing with the irresponsibility of a clerk.[60]

Such, in essence, was Johnson's version of the major developments which had occurred from the spring up to the winter of 1865. There was much in this version that might be seen as reasonable and justified. But more important is the fact that Johnson's version was not the only possible version; it was probably not even the majority one. The Northern Unionist public, not necessarily swayed by passion and certainly not prepared to renounce its loyalty to the President, could still see all these things from a point of view quite different from his.

[57] *Ibid.*, pp. 805–6.

[58] McPherson, *Reconstruction*, p. 49.

[59] In December, Johnson began relieving his provisional governors and directing them to turn their states' affairs over to their elected successors, as follows: Holden, of North Carolina, Dec. 4; Sharkey, of Mississippi, Dec. 14; Parsons, of Alabama, Dec. 18; Johnson, of Georgia, Dec. 19; Perry, of South Carolina, Dec. 21; and Marvin, of Florida, Jan. 18, 1866.

[60] The President did, however, think it prudent to advise Perry that it was not necessary for the South Carolina members to present themselves until after Congress had completed its organization. "Provisional Governors," p. 256.

III   EARLY RECONSTRUCTION AS SEEN
IN THE UNIONIST NORTH

"Reunion" was in most men's thoughts, in some form,
but the notion was bound to be fairly complex still, at a time when hate
and death had been so recently a major fact of the national existence.
Much still depended on the signs, gestures, and omens coming out of
the South. Nor was it clear at the time that President Johnson could be
reading those signs and gestures in a manner substantially different
from that in which they were being read by the Northern public at
large.

It was not primarily a question of whether or not reunion should
occur, or whether the Southern states would or would not be readmitted to full status in the federal Union. Most men took for granted
that they would be and that such readmission was mainly a matter of
time. Nor did the issue of harshness or mildness occupy a place of predominance in the talk, for there was next to no agreement on what
federal policy should even look like. The North was still in the very
tentative stages of forming a preliminary attitude on the whole problem of reconstruction and Southern loyalty. To all intents and purposes, nobody had as yet decided anything; the Northern mind was
still very much open. An attitude, meanwhile, could only be formed
on the basis of things one saw and heard and read. It was certainly not
a question of supporting the President; still less was it a matter of
President versus Congress: that issue had not as yet been made, and it
was hardly to the interest of any Unionist to make it now or any time,
if it could be helped. Few doubted that Congress would have a great
deal to say on the whole question of reconstruction, or that a substantial portion of the time and energy of Congress throughout the entire
coming session would be devoted to the forming of policy on that
subject. The main question was still quite general: how was the South
behaving?

If there was an issue in the air, it was not between the President and
the Republican party but rather between Republicans and Democrats
over what the President's intentions really were. Republicans at large
could not bring themselves to believe that Johnson's purposes were
substantially at variance with their own; indeed, they could not afford
to believe it, with party unity at such a premium. There were only
two views of the Southern states' present relation to the federal government, according to *Harper's Weekly,*

one that of the late rebels themselves and the Northern Copperheads, which is, that the rebels in certain States having laid down their arms the States are by that fact restored to all their former rights and privileges . . . ; and the other that of the President and loyal men in all the States, which is, that they can resume their ancient position only by the consent of the Government and upon such terms as it may impose.[61]

The President and the South, in short, had not in any sense been combined into a single issue. Men thought of them on quite separate planes: support of the President was one thing, not as yet seriously questioned; the South and its readiness for full readmission was quite another. What made this attitude possible was again the "experiment" formula: the assumption that the President's policy was as yet indeterminate, and that the President, like everyone else, had as yet to see and assess the proofs. Were it otherwise, and had the President's policy in any way implied that delegations from the new governments should be admitted to Congress without further investigation, then "the whole country," as *Harper's* declared on September 30, "would have crackled in opposition to it."[62]

Under this "experiment" formula it would be possible to ignore a great many discrepancies of purpose which later—but only later—would become all too clear. Rather interesting in this connection is the queer exchange that took place between Johnson and Stearns a few weeks after their personal interview in October. Johnson had apparently called Stearns's attention to the latter's use of "reconstruction" in one of his published accounts of the conversation and emphasized that the term he himself had used was "restoration." Stearns, graciously conceding that he had probably misquoted the President, said: "Restoration was in your thought, Reconstruction in mine, hence the use of the word." A revealing passage then follows:

This seems to set *you* right, but the people do not regard it of consequence. They see in that letter a frank expression of your policy which gives them confidence in *you*, and in a determination that those states shall not be admitted to the full privileges of loyalty, until they give guarantees for further good behavior, by present good works, even if it takes time to accomplish it.[63]

Stearns was quite right. "The record of this remarkable conversation," exulted *Harper's*, "will be read with the utmost pleasure and satisfac-

[61] *Harper's Weekly*, IX (Nov. 25, 1865), 739.

[62] *Ibid.*, IX (Sept. 30, 1865), 610.

[63] George L. Stearns to Johnson, Nov. 13, 1865, Johnson MSS.

tion by those who voted for Andrew Johnson, who have never doubted his fidelity to the principles upon which he was elected, and who have, consequently, never faltered in their support of him,"[64]

The President's course, as men soon came to see, was most magnanimous. But where was the evidence, on the other hand, that the South actually deserved this generosity? One wondered, for instance, if such a bigoted legalist as Benjamin F. Perry represented the most loyal voice then issuing from South Carolina. It was hard to read Perry's cool words on Lincoln without seeing in them a scantily veiled contempt for all the sorrow of the Emancipator's martyrdom. Sharkey's activities in Mississippi were hardly more acceptable: here was the governor of a rebel state, actually raising armed forces once more, successfully defying the federal commander, and exulting publicly in his triumph. Nor could the public letters of Carl Schurz be taken simply as fabrications; whatever Schurz was known for, it was hardly for lack of scruple.

But the really disagreeable things came with the meeting of the southern conventions and legislatures. How could former rebels, now chastened and contrite, be capable of such insolent quibbling? It was "a white man's goverment," they said, "and intended for white men only"; and they actually invoked the still-smoldering Dred Scott decision to prove it. Would they allow that slavery was a thing of the past? Not with any clarity; not without the hope that they might be compensated for their "property." Would they regard secession as a nullity? Not without lofty circumlocution; let it be "repealed" in acquiescence to force, so that the memory of the Confederacy might remain unsullied. Would they be pleased to repudiate the debt which they had incurred in the service of treason? But the debt was "trifling," and the burden of its repudiation "would fall on widows and orphans." Here were men—some of whom, barely months before, had taken Union lives—now being allowed to meet under the protection of the United States Army and to work out their own salvation; they were being asked (not told) to perform the most perfunctory acts, the very minimal gestures that could have been required after the bloodiest of all rebellions; it was a miraculous chance, a reprieve beyond anything they themselves could have hoped for. And what were they doing with it? Quibbling, objecting, splitting hairs.

The New York *Herald* and the New York *Times*, both desperately anxious for Johnson's success, were kept squirming all through these

[64] *Harper's Weekly*, IX (Nov. 4, 1865), 690.

goings-on. The *Herald* thought Perry had been rather breezy about Negro suffrage:

He talks of the "radical republican party of the North," as if that party had no vote in Congress upon the acceptance of the work of his convention. He repeats the old exploded notions . . . that "this is the white man's government, intended for white men only"—notions which, since the deluge, are, even in South Carolina, utterly absurd and unmeaning nonsense. . . . We must say, moreover, to Governor Perry that the exclusion of the blacks from the benefits of the government does not enter in the programme of President Johnson.[65]

As the legislatures began meeting and putting up obstructions for ratifying the Thirteenth Amendment, the *Herald* was furious:

The inference is strongly suggested that this evasion can only be for the purpose, if possible, of securing the restoration of all the Southern States to Congress before the ratification of said amendment, and then, in default of its ratification, to re-establish slavery by State authority. Preposterous as this scheme may appear, how are we to know. . . ?[66]

The *Times* warned on November 7 that the Southern states had better see to the full protection of Negro rights, and if they did not do it, the North would, since the war had made this a federal responsibility. "The moment the South is seen to be doing this heartily and willingly, that moment it will be left in their hands, and all the 'fanatics' in the North could not take it out, if they would. But . . . *if the South will not do this, the nation* MUST."[67] The Chicago *Tribune*, in language more flamboyant, said substantially the same thing when the news of Mississippi's "black code" came out three weeks later:

We tell the white men of Mississippi that the men of the North will convert the State of Mississippi into a frog pond before they will allow such laws to disgrace one foot of soil in which the bones of our soldiers sleep and over which the flag of freedom waves.[68]

Now, they expected to be welcomed back into Congress as though nothing had happened. There they waited, while Black Republicans haggled and bickered. Among the penitents were four Confederate generals, five Confederate colonels, numerous Confederate congress-

[65] New York *Herald*, Sept. 21, 1865.

[66] *Ibid.*, Nov. 11, 1865.

[67] New York *Times*, Nov. 7, 1865.

[68] Chicago *Tribune*, Dec. 1, 1865. "In amending the criminal law of the State," wrote the *Times* correspondent from Columbia, South Carolina, on December 28, "these astute representatives succeeded in framing what might not inappropriately be styled a bloody code, and incorporated several provisions which will be upset and rendered inoperative either by the juries or the government." New York *Times,* Jan. 4, 1866.

men and members of Confederate legislatures, not to mention the
Honorable Vice-President of the Confederacy.[69] "The Northern
people," the *Times* announced crisply,

will not see with composure the wheels blocked by the insisting of these
Southern claimants to seats that the disposal of their cases shall be the first
business in hand. That decision ought not to be made without long deliberation. It, in fact, involves the whole question of reconstruction. The day
that the[y] . . . are admitted to their seats, reconstruction will be for all
practical purposes completely and irreversibly consummated. . . . A decision that is to carry with it such results should be formed with great caution, and only after the most conclusive proof that these States now possess a genuine loyalty, and are prepared to perform all their appropriate
duties. It will at best take much time to establish that proof.[70]

What was one to think of Andrew Johnson and his
role amid all this? Mr. Johnson, President of the United States, was a
man of solid patriotism deserving the prayers of all who loved the
Union. The presidency, through the fires of conflict and the sacrifice
of Lincoln, had added to itself greater claims to veneration than ever.
Johnson, risen from the people like his predecessor, was doing his best
to fill that role which had now become so awesome. The winter ahead
was sure to be full of trouble, and one might fervently hope that Congress—with extremists like Stevens and Sumner kindling tempers at
every step—would not be driven to a break with the President. What
would happen to the great Union party then? A reasonable man would
support the President until there was good cause for doing so no
longer; he would certainly remain loyal until it was absolutely clear
what the Chief Executive was up to.

But in loyalty there could still be many degrees of discrimination.[71]
There were actually a number of things that wanted explaining. Why
did the President, on the one hand, and the political leaders in one's
own district, on the other, seem to be talking in two such altogether
different languages? What did "reconstruction" mean, if the President
kept correcting everyone who uttered it, and said "restoration" in-

[69] McPherson, *Reconstruction*, pp. 107-9.

[70] New York *Times*, Dec. 1, 1865.

[71] During this period Joseph Barrett, an official of the Pension Office, wrote from
Washington: "I was struck by the remark of a good Republican friend here, who knew
Mr. Lincoln well, that he now went but little to the White House, and that it seemed
like going to a *stepfather*. We do not distrust President Johnson. We cordially sustain
him. But as to mere *personal* relations, how changed is the feeling! I have far less inclination than ever to think of an official position here as one to be made permanent."
J. H. Barrett to William Henry Smith, Oct. 21, 1865, Smith MSS, Ohio Historical Society.

stead? The leadership which the former Democrat of Tennessee was giving to Northern opinion could have been a great deal more helpful and satisfying than it actually was. One stuffy, cautious senator wrote to another in July: "What do you think of Andy's reconstruction schemes? It strikes me that matters are getting complicated, and that the rebels are having it all their own way."[72] Was Johnson really speaking for the people, or were the people having to speak for him? Men kept reassuring one another that the President meant this or that; but somehow Johnson himself always seemed to be saying something else—something that everyone kept hoping he did not mean at all. Men wanted at least a little clarity on the subject of Southern affairs, and from the very first they had not quite had it. It was almost as though Johnson were baffling their efforts to find proper standards by which to judge what was happening. This went on all summer long.

There came at last a time when men's talk concerning the presidency became blurred, almost furtive. Somehow it was necessary to express one's confidence by means of a kind of double-negative idiom: "Those who have counted upon the President's treachery to the principles upon which he was elected have reckoned without their host."[73] The triumphant Union party had met in state conventions everywhere throughout the North by late summer. The declarations of loyalty to their new President were, of course, all properly there. But some instinct was already at work to make them a little less than ringing and vibrant. Nobody could help noticing the quality of strain. The President's rabid partisan, Senator Doolittle, had pushed his own resolutions through the Wisconsin convention while shouldering aside expressions of a more qualified nature advanced by others. Through parliamentary aggressiveness he had got a majority for them, but the business left numbers of men in rather a sullen frame of mind.[74] Then there was the busy and garrulous Lewis D. Campbell, a strong Johnson man in Ohio; he, too, in his convention, had scrambled about seeing that the resolutions, especially the expressions of support to the President, would be just so. Gleefully he wrote to Johnson afterward: ". . . we *hived* the swarm of radicals and your policy was triumphantly approved. I hope

[72] William Pitt Fessenden to James W. Grimes, July 14, 1865, Fessenden MSS, Bowdoin College.

[73] *Harper's Weekly*, IX (Oct. 28, 1865), 674. Cf. also: "There is nothing in the acts or words of the President to justify the insinuation that he wishes to intrust the political power of the late rebel States exclusively to the class to which for his whole life he has been bitterly opposed." *Ibid.*, IX (Sept. 2, 1865), 546.

[74] See above, chap. 3, n. 89.

you found some comfort in that result."[75] But why should it be such hard work finding words to express the things that everyone was supposed to believe anyway? After the Pennsylvania gathering, Thaddeus Stevens observed with saturnine brevity: "Our views ('reconstruction' & confiscation) were embodied in our resolutions at Harrisburg, amidst much chaff." Sumner, meanwhile, was getting ready for the Massachusetts convention, and George L. Stearns wrote him with an air of some diffidence: "I hope you will . . . say all you conscientiously can in favor of the President."[76] "I am getting very tired of this state of not knowing exactly where we are," wrote George William Curtis to Charles Eliot Norton early in November. "It must soon end[,] for Johnson must express himself in his Message. I am very sure of his honesty. He will not 'sell us out.' "[77]

But why did the Copperheads keep praising Johnson so loudly? How much longer was it possible for the Unionist newspapers to push them off, claiming that their own grounds for supporting the President were much the sounder? This was an odd predicament: where was the great solidarity of Union triumph? Here was the New York *World*, gloating over an Executive policy which it boasted would soon restore the Democratic party to power and push the Black Republicans from office forever. The New York *Tribune* could only fume: "*The World* has no warrant for these calumnies on the President, and the future will show that the impudent attempt of his deadly foes to abduct and convert him to their base uses will recoil on their own heads."[78] One or another of the New York Democratic leaders—Van Buren, Richmond, Marble, or Tilden—seemed to be going down to chat with the President every other week. They all kept giving out rumors to the effect that Johnson was hoping "the Democratic party . . . may succeed at the coming election." The *Times* sounded desperate: "The insolence with which the Democratic leaders in this State claim the support of President Johnson is simply astounding."[79] Still, what exactly had been going on? How had the Democrats got the initiative? "We are not surprised," pleasurably observed the Copperhead Lancaster *Intelligencer*,

[75] L. D. Campbell to Johnson, Aug. 21, 1865, Johnson MSS.

[76] Stevens to Sumner, Aug. 26, 1865, Stearns to Sumner, Aug. 28, 1865, Sumner MSS.

[77] G. W. Curtis to C. E. Norton, Nov. 5, 1865, Curtis MSS, Harvard College Library. Curtis was editor of *Harper's Weekly*.

[78] New York *Tribune*, Sept. 13, 1865.

[79] New York *Times*, Oct. 5, 1865.

that the President's course in regard to the reconstruction of the Southern States should give greater satisfaction to the Democratic press than it does to the radical. It is much more in accordance with Democratic doctrine than with the fanatical creed and the crude political theories of the radical abolitionists.

What had made the victorious Republican party so vulnerable to this kind of talk? How long could Unionist sentiment be nourished on such slender gruel as Johnson gave it? How soon before it simply wore itself down, in its efforts to defend him? Could the President perceive no signs of demoralization among his supporters? Why did he make no move to rescue them in their growing embarrassment? "For God's sake," implored Joseph Medill, "move cautiously and carefully. Don't show so much eagerness to rush into the embrace of the '$20,000 rebels.' They will suck you like an orange and when done with you throw the peel away. Better stick to old friends who carried you into the White House than to exchange them for Copperheads & rebels who will garrote you after using you." Judge Ransom Balcom, writing to Johnson from upstate New York as "your sincere friend and a member of the Union Party that elected you," admitted that the Democrats' praise of the President made "the masses of the Union party feel as members of a Christian Church do when Sabbath breakers, whoremasters and gamblers praise their preacher."[80]

It could be that the North had become a little spoiled after four years of a party leader as sensitive as Lincoln had been to the various zephyrs of public opinion. It was perhaps unfair to expect that the overworked Johnson should ever develop all the knacks which came so easily to his predecessor. But there were cases in which it was not easy on any terms to be satisfied with the President's judgment. For instance, when he made his wishes known to the Southern states, why did he not give orders? What harm was there in telling the South a little more clearly what the North wanted? Why did he merely "hope" and "trust in God" that they would do this and that—why not just tell them? Then they would do it. On Negro suffrage: If Johnson really favored this, why not be plain about it? "He might have exacted this from every State at the South," declared the *Nation* late in November, "just as readily as he has exacted the repudiation of its war debt, and the adoption of the Constitutional Amendment."[81] Specifically on this matter of suffrage, President Lincoln, in his letter to Gen-

---

[80] Quoted in New York *World*, July 20, 1865; Medill to Johnson, Sept. 15, 1865, R. Balcom to Johnson, Jan. 2, 1866, Johnson MSS.

[81] *Nation*, I (Nov. 23, 1865), 646.

eral Wadsworth (now being widely publicized), had not seemed to think it would wreck the Constitution to lay down the law once in a while:

> You desire to know, in the event of our complete success in the field, the same being followed by a loyal and cheerful submission on the part of the South, if universal amnesty should not be accompanied with universal suffrage.
>
> Now, since you know my private inclinations as to what terms should be granted to the South in the contingency mentioned, I will here add, that if our success should be thus realized, followed by such desired results, I cannot see, if universal amnesty is granted, how, under the circumstances, I can avoid exacting in return universal suffrage, or, at least, suffrage on the basis of intelligence and military service.[82]

Or the affair of the Mississippi militia: should it really have been allowed to reach the point, however it was to be settled, where the President had to humiliate publicly and deliberately two Union major generals for doing what they had assumed to be their duty? Then there was the President's speech to the Southern delegation on September 11, hardly more than a week later. Certainly no one wanted to believe the things the Copperheads kept saying about him. But was this exactly wise, all this about "love, respect, and confidence," "forbearing and forgiving," "fraternal kindness," and the North's not being able to get along without the South, and all the rest? With quite the best will in the world, one winced. Wounds were still not fully closed; there was time; let there be some decent repose; the North could very well "get along without the South" for just a little while. For the moment it only brought new shrieks of glee from the New York *World*.[83]

And, indeed, what *was* the President's attitude on Negro rights? How much evidence was there that he had any positive intentions toward the freedmen, beyond leaving them to the mercies of Southern

---

[82] *Collected Works*, VII, 101–2. The date of this letter is unknown, but it appears to have been written early in 1864. It was first printed in the *Southern Advocate* of September 18, 1865, and widely reprinted in the North during that same month—e.g., it appeared in the New York *Tribune* September 26 and in the Chicago *Tribune* September 27.

[83] "It has been, for a while, the cue of the Radicals to pretend that the President regarded his policy as a doubtful experiment. . . . But a succession of significant acts has destroyed this hope. The letter of congratulations to the Mississippi Convention, the reversal of the military order arresting the organization of the state militia by Governor Sharkey, and though last not least, the noble, magnanimous, and confiding speech to the southern delegation, have convinced the Radicals that the policy of the President is fixed; that no choice is left them but open opposition. . . ." New York *World*, Sept. 18, 1865.

legislatures? Was it really Johnson who ordered the Mississippi black codes set aside, or was it the Freedmen's Bureau? Where was the thundering presidential denunciation which these laws deserved? The New York *Tribune* bravely insisted—as had Stearns and others—that Johnson favored Negro suffrage and all other rights, but more than one reader must have smiled. Greeley was known to incline a little to the fatuous. The Copperheads certainly spoke with a good deal more conviction than he could, when they toasted the President as the nation's chief defender of white supremacy. *Harper's* eagerly praised a passage in Johnson's address to the colored troops on October 10, in which he had said, "This is your country as well as anybody else's."[84] But the Cincinnati *Enquirer* had already reported, in italics, something else which the President was supposed to have said to the governor of Missouri: *"This is a country for white men, and by G——d, so long as I am President, it shall be a Government for white men."*[85]

All told, there was something reassuring to the Northern public about the approaching meeting of Congress, and one felt a promise of clarity in the winter air. A very able group of men would shortly gather in Washington, one of the ablest Congresses in many years. (The poet Whittier had just honored it with an Ode.)[86] The Copperheads were of course making an issue over Clerk McPherson and his roll call. But this was a matter of gravest policy, as McPherson and everyone else knew; the papers had been full of it for weeks, and there was scarcely a Union journal that questioned McPherson's stand. For that matter, it was hardly a "stand"; McPherson had no choice; the decision was not his to make because public consensus had already made it for him. In the circumstances, the Clerk would not have dreamed of taking such a thing into his own hands and inviting bedlam by calling the Southerners' names—and the Southerners, according to the circumspect New York *Times*, had not a right in the world to presume that he should:

[84] *Harper's Weekly*, IX (Oct. 28, 1865), 674; McPherson, *Reconstruction*, pp. 49–51.

[85] Cincinnati *Enquirer*, Sept. 30, 1865, referring to "a recent interview with Governor Fletcher," in which the President "repeated his convictions on that point with decided emphasis." The Jackson (Miss.) *News* during this period carried at its masthead: "This is a white man's country—President Johnson." Garner, *Reconstruction in Mississippi*, p. 94.

[86] John G. Whittier, "To the Thirty-Ninth Congress," *Nation*, I (Dec. 7, 1865), 714. In his Ode, the poet urged Congress ("O People-Chosen! are ye not / Likewise the chosen of the Lord . . . ?") to grant universal amnesty to the South and impartial suffrage to the Negro.

This high demand for an immediate return of the chairs that were kicked down is not humility. This impatient elbowing through the crowd to the clerk's desk for the chance to say who shall be Speaker is not humility. We venture to predict that the loyal Representatives will so conceive, and will with all due civility invite these gentlemen to keep the back seats in the lobby until they are sent for.[87]

Now, at last, it was possible for the executive and legislative branches of the government to take counsel with each other, to appraise the President's "experiment," and to perfect a policy which would be fully expressive of the entire country's wishes.

Such, in essence, was what Speaker Colfax said upon his arrival at Washington, in an informal speech which was cheering to hear and read, and which was heartily applauded all over the North. (A "bold and forcible speech," the *Times* had called it, "the subject of much congratulation here among the true supporters of the President.")[88] In it, there was praise of the President that fairly glowed with warmth and cordiality. There was at the same time the reassurance that nothing hasty would be done about admitting the Southern claimants: "The Constitution, which seems framed for every emergency, gives to each House the exclusive right to judge of the qualifications of the election-returns of its members, and I apprehend they will exercise that right." The Speaker briskly enumerated, in simple words, those precise items in Southern behavior[89] which gave him cause to think that the congressional policy on reconstruction would not be made in haste. ("The danger now is in too much precipitation.") He declared that not only had the government given the slave his freedom; it also meant to maintain that freedom. Mr. Colfax' closing words seemed exactly right:

Let us study unity in the light of unity, and I believe the executive and legislative departments of the government, when they compare views together, will cordially co-operate in this great work before us all, and so act that the foundations of our Union, wisely and patriotically reconstructed, shall be eternal as the ages, with a hearty acceptance by the South of the new situation.[90]

87 New York *Times*, Dec. 1, 1865.

88 *Ibid.*, Nov. 20, 1865.

89 He referred to the states' recalcitrance in ratifying the antislavery amendment, in repudiating their debt, and in nullifying secession (instead of "repealing" it, etc.); also to their proscription of Unionists and their failure to enact proper legislation for the freedmen.

90 New York *World*, Nov. 20, 1865; Willard H. Smith, *Schuyler Colfax: The Changing Fortunes of a Political Idol* (Indianapolis: Indiana Historical Bureau, 1952), pp. 221–26.

Here, from all signs, was at last the kind of talk that a majority of Northern Union men understood and wanted to hear. There seemed to be no real reason now why Congress and the President should not agree, at least on the fundamentals.

IV   THE REQUIREMENTS, AS THE SOUTH
SAW AND UNDERSTOOD THEM

It thus appears that within Union circles in 1865 there were at least two versions of reconstruction, and two interpretations of events in the South, and that it was not at all clear which version was the "official" version or even that there were two versions. An understanding on these matters between the President and the Union party seems to have been, to say the least, considerably less than perfect. And now, between the President and the South, were the understandings in this direction any clearer, any more perfect? This, to repeat, must be considered as a problem in communication, a problem in which "intransigence" does not really have to be one of the variables. It may be assumed that the Southerners, at their end, would strain to hear and assess correctly everything that was said to them before they acted: such were the stakes for the South that this communication process was one in which every syllable counted.

Over the whole question of liquidating the late conflict, everyone, including President Johnson, understood in some way that there had to be terms. The South would have to do things, and the North would have to say what they were. There was thus a sense in which the matter would be dictated. But that could not possibly be its only aspect; there must also be an element of negotiation, even though no Northern spokesman—least of all the President—could admit that "negotiation" in any formal sense would occur. Yet whatever it was called, Southern men of influence had in some way to be persuaded to promote the government's minimum purposes in the several Southern states. This the President seemed more or less to recognize. There were any number of ways, moreover, in which the South might be expected to think, react, and behave as a unit, just as it had under the Confederacy. Thus what was said to men of influence in one state, so far as the South as a whole was concerned, was said to all the rest. For the federal government, this could be both a liability and an asset.

The President, as spokesman for his government, back of which stood the Unionist North and all its sanctions of power, would have a leading role in bringing about an understanding. As go-between, he would have to perform both coercive and negotiating functions—

functions which were not fully separable but which might each be exercised to great advantage—in his efforts to get those with whom he communicated to do what had to be done. But just how was he to retain the maximum possible leverage inherent in his position? How was he to exploit both the coercive and negotiating aspects of his role with maximum effectiveness? He must not commit himself *personally*. Or rather, he must proceed as though, for the outcome of any given matter, it were quite irrelevant whether his own purposes were tender or stern. In the interest of whatever he wanted to accomplish, he must not weaken any of his sanctions of force or give away any of his immense bargaining power, either by revealing more of his private ambitions than might be pertinent to matters at hand or by letting it be presumed that his was the final decision on any of these matters. He must have room to reverse himself if necessary, and it must be understood that his own decisions might not all be acceptable to the people whom he represented. There must always be something in reserve: one more veiled threat, one more implied promise.[91] Such principles, of course, more or less hold for any game of persuasion in which the counters are neither all force nor all reason.

The President's task would obviously be very difficult. He would have to choose his words with care. No matter whom he might see fit to designate as *ad hoc* representatives for the South, he must assume that these men, anxious above all things for a settlement, would extract every morsel of meaning from what he said and did. Everything depended, for them, upon reading his communications through every shade of significance that they contained, parsing and construing them down to the last syllable; whatever freedom of movement they were to have, they would have to map their operating territory somewhere between his threats and his promises. And it would follow that whatever these Southerners did as a consequence of what he told them, he himself must be prepared to assume a large share of the responsibility, for good or ill.

An effort should in any case be made to see and hear things the way they saw and heard them. What did President Johnson actually communicate to the South during the spring, summer, and fall of 1865 with regard to the Northern will? What meanings was the South entitled to draw from these communications? What were the points

---

91 Although Roosevelt and Churchill, during World War II, found Stalin a hard bargainer, there was one advantage they did have over him: they could disclaim power of decision over certain matters simply by telling Stalin that—regardless of their own inclinations—their electorates would never accept such decisions. They knew, meanwhile, that *he* had the ultimate decision on everything.

which the South might construe as most significant, in its effort to define its own future and to understand the terms of the settlement?

The first thing the Southerners needed to know was which conceptual framework, among several possible ones, the North would use in defining the nature of reconstruction. They needed some notion of their own status, which was anything but clear; they had to have some indication of the kinds of actions that would be required of them and possibly even some cues to how they ought to behave. Even the most general nod in this direction, before anything at all was done, would clear the air tremendously. It would eliminate the need to dwell upon any number of alternatives, each equally conceivable and each requiring quite different sets of responses and different styles of behavior.

The President's first move here, after issuing his proclamations, was to invoke the Constitution. Not only were the principles of the Constitution self-evident, he told the South, but also, among the several versions of those principles that men might be tempted to consider, the self-evident version was his version. Every Southern delegation that visited the President was treated to discourses on the nature of the Constitution and states' rights. "A State cannot go out of the Union," Johnson announced to the South Carolinians before appointing a provisional governor for them, "and therefore none of them having gone out, we must deal with the question of restoration and not of reconstruction." He was "a better States rights man," he suspected, "than some of those now present," and proceeded to say why. Now that the rebellion had been suppressed it would be the policy, in line with constitutional principles, "not to restore the State Government through military rule, but by the people." (The gentlemen "seemed to be well pleased with the proceedings," according to report.)[92] The same thoughts were communicated to a large group of leading citizens from several Southern states later in the summer:

While I think that the rebellion has been arrested and subdued, and am happy in the consciousness of a duty well performed, I want not only you, but the people of the world to know, that while I dreaded and feared disintegration of the States, I am equally opposed to consolidation or concentration of power here, under whatever guise or name; and if the issue is forced upon us, I shall still endeavor to pursue the same efforts to dissuade from this doctrine of running to extremes. But I say let the same rules be applied. Let the Constitution be our guide.[93]

[92] New York *Times*, June 26, 1865.

[93] *American Annual Cyclopaedia, 1865*, pp. 805–6.

This, then, was Johnson's most general step toward letting the Southerners know where they stood: "Let the Constitution be our guide." They were thus encouraged—if not commanded—to think of reconstruction in its general nature as a constitutional and legal problem rather than primarily a political one, and this in itself must have relieved their minds of much uncertainty. Since constitutional thinking was quite congenial to the Southerners anyway, we may suppose that their submission to Johnson's views must have been more or less cheerful and that squaring their own hopes—full restoration—with those views could be managed with a minimum of strain. As for "behavior," it seemed to follow that the definition given to this very vague notion was also being narrowed to essentially legal rather than political terms; conceivably, in this closer setting, many of the overtones in behavior which might otherwise influence undisciplined popular passions would not be subjected to excessive scrutiny.

A major elimination of alternatives had been made. Yet the South needed to have its problem defined in still another way. Nobody had to be told that the South must adjust to Northern power, but the Southerner who eyed the North with any alertness, any sensitivity at all, would not have been satisfied very long to think simply of generalized and undifferentiated "power." He would have wanted to know more specifically where that power was located. To which aspect of Northern power must the South accommodate itself? Which centers of prerogative must be watched most carefully? If all must look to the Constitution as their guide, who then was the true guide to the Constitution? By whose authority, in short, would reconstruction proceed? The President said, in effect, to those most concerned not to misconstrue his meaning, "It shall proceed by my authority, and mine alone."

When Johnson made it known in a variety of ways that he considered reconstruction solely an Executive function, so far as federal authority was needed to set it going, he was performing an act of communication whose effects would be diverse and far-reaching. He enabled the Southerners—indeed, he compelled them—to fasten their attention upon himself with a peculiar sharpness, while they might at the same time selectively ignore many a potential anxiety-point which had now been defined for them as having but secondary importance. The power to which they had primarily to adjust was the Executive; so far as their position was concerned, the legitimate authority variously resident in Northern opinion and in the other branches of the federal government was all being duly expressed and represented to them through the Executive. Should there be new developments and complications, political or whatever, then the Executive might be expected, in the proper course of things, to give the South due indication of them.

Not only did the President define for the South all those legitimate areas of authority which he in his person might safely be taken to represent; he also let them know where the illegitimate areas were— areas of opinion and feeling from which he dissociated himself and which were thus not entitled to be counted in the eventual settlement. Through his own words, he gave to "radicalism" a definition which the Southerners had no choice but to take as official and formal. When Mississippi organized its convention, for example, Johnson's telegram to Governor Sharkey was so conspiratorial in tone that it probably could not have exerted much leverage for getting what he seemed to be asking; but to the South it had much value just for the substantial morsels of information that might be construed out of it. The President deprecatingly suggested that the convention might "with perfect safety" extend suffrage to certain heavily qualified classes of Negroes in such a way as would "completely disarm the adversary." The "adversary" was named: ". . . the radicals, who are wild upon negro franchise, will be completely foiled in their attempt to keep the Southern States from renewing their relations to the Union by not accepting their senators and representatives."[94] That is, there were men of evil intentions who were not nearly so well disposed as Johnson himself to permit a speedy restoration. On the other hand, given a reasonable circumspection, the presidential plan could be relied upon to provide the necessary protection. "There may be speeches published from various quarters," Johnson told the Southerners, "that may breathe a different spirit. Do not let them trouble or excite you, but believe that it is . . . the great object of the Government to make the union of these United States more complete and perfect than ever. . . ."[95] It was almost as though he had defined as "radical" all sentiment, present or potential, that should make any kind of objection to the course he himself had laid down. With such official certification, at any rate, the South might have been excused for a growing sense of reassurance:

It may safely be said [according to the Charleston *Daily Courier*] that the views of Sumner, Thad Stevens, Wilson, and some other Northern Radicals have been considered too unworthy to be seriously commented upon by members of the convention. It is well known that the sentiments of these gentlemen are extremely unpopular in the North.[96]

[94] *Sen. Exec. Docs.*, 39 Cong., 1 sess., No. 26, "Provisional Governors," p. 229.

[95] *American Annual Cyclopaedia, 1865*, p. 806.

[96] Charleston *Daily Courier*, Sept. 26, 1865, quoted in Simkins and Woody, *South Carolina during Reconstruction*, p. 42.

Along with Johnson's concept of the presidency as the reconstructing power, it was probably unavoidable that certain suppositions regarding the legislative branch, and the extent of its authority in such matters, should also be communicated to the South. On suffrage, he appears to have told Governor Perry with great emphasis, "It must be left to the Legislature of each State to decide who shall be allowed to vote in that State." He also said, as Perry reported to the people of South Carolina, "Any attempt on the part of Congress to control the elective franchise of a State would be an unwarrantable usurpation."[97] Johnson's message to Sharkey was only one of many in which the President expressed his conviction that the South would be entitled by winter, barring radical sabotage, to have its representatives in Congress. After the governors and conventions had done their work, all that the states needed to do, in their organized capacity as states, was to ratify the Thirteenth Amendment (though even that, apparently, could not be absolutely insisted on), in order to "make the way clear for the admission of senators and representatives to their seats in the present Congress."[98] This conviction was repeated before the entire country in the President's annual message. The right of Congress to judge of its own membership was admitted by the President, but he chose to construe that right in the narrow procedural sense: members were to be admitted or rejected on their individual qualifications, not on any other basis. In other words, Congress had legally nothing to say on reconstruction: the process was complete by the time the states could present delegations for admission, and thus the power to pass on qualifications of members-elect would be a power improperly and unconstitutionally usurped should Congress presume to use it as an instrument of reconstruction.

This angle of the case, to say nothing of the many other implications concerning the President's own vast prerogatives, was apparently accepted in full faith by the South. Herschel Johnson of Georgia, hearing of the embarrassments which might be made for the Southern delegations at the opening of Congress, thought that a splendid way to settle the thing once and for all would be for the President simply to issue a proclamation announcing that they *were* entitled to representation. "It would not only delight the Southern States," he wrote enthusiastically to Watterson, in a letter intended for the President's eyes, "but, in my judgment, it would be a stroke of masterly policy.

[97] Lillian A. Kibler, *Benjamin F. Perry, South Carolina Unionist* (Durham, N.C.: Duke University Press, 1946), p. 393. This speech (made at Greenville, S.C., Aug. 1, 1865) was published and was read with considerable interest throughout the country.

[98] Johnson to Sharkey, Nov. 1, 1865, "Provisional Governors," p. 233.

For being *constitutionally* qualified, no party in the North can be sustained who will advocate rejection."[99] One might almost think that men of judgment had been pushed into something of a fool's paradise when it became possible for them to demand, in answer to doubts about the President's power in this connection: "Hasn't he the army?"[100] The New Orleans *Picayune* thought that the President, to effect his full purposes, might actually require a military force during the first sittings of Congress—"but if so, the bayonets will be there!"[101]

It might still be supposed that the Southerners were acting not primarily upon the cues they were getting from the President but simply out of perversity and unreason. Yet somewhere between the feelings of their own people and the things the President told them, they were understandably, and perhaps correctly, working out for themselves the limits of the possible. Since their primary responsibility was after all the repairing of Southern fortunes, there was a sense in which they were hardly doing wrong by applying themselves with great care to the work of discovering just where their liberty of action lay. Again, communication should be considered the primary key to this, and it should be recognized that for their purposes the communication process was critical. The point may be illustrated by a specific case study.

Though the Sharkey-Slocum affair has already been mentioned in other connections, the most instructive aspect of the episode may perhaps lie in its character as a sequence in communication. All the correspondence is available; moreover, the significant items were published in the newspapers at the time, and public men not only in Mississippi but everywhere in the South were thus given a peculiar opportunity to scrutinize and assess for themselves a series of dispatches that could tell them much of what they most needed to know in charting their own course. Governor Sharkey, greatly desiring to muster local militias throughout the state of Mississippi, told the President of his wishes, but then, without awaiting a reply, on August 19 he proceeded to issue a proclamation authorizing them. Johnson in his reply of the twenty-first (unaware of the proclamation) advised Sharkey not to take this step—reminding him of the efforts being made "by the extreme men of the North" to thwart Southern restoration—but instead to call on General Slocum for any military assistance that might be

[99] H. Johnson to H. Watterson, Oct. 28, 1865, Johnson MSS.
[100] Reid, *After the War*, pp. 318–19.
[101] New Orleans *Picayune*, Oct. 5, 1865.

needed in suppressing disorder. Sharkey replied on the twenty-fifth, protesting that this would leave the state "in a helpless condition." "General Slocum," he said, "has no cavalry, and has not force enough to protect us. His negro troops do more harm than good when scattered through the country." Johnson, replying the same day, was still not disposed to accept Sharkey's view of the case but assured him that "the government does not intend to irritate or humiliate the people of the south, but will be magnanimous and remove the cause of your complaint at the earliest period it is practicable to do so."[102]

Meanwhile, on the twenty-fourth, Slocum issued his "General Order No. 22." He declared that such an organizing of the young men would create greater difficulites than it would solve and ordered all those so engaged to cease and desist. Sharkey now called for a showdown between himself and Slocum. He wired Johnson on August 30, in language of exceptional belligerence (considering the personage he was addressing), and resurrected his version of some matters apparently touched upon in a prior talk with the President: "In our last interview you distinctly stated to me that I could organize the militia to suppress crime if necessary." He further declared,

General Slocum has thought proper to issue an order to prevent any such organization, and to arrest those who attempt it. His chief reasons seem to be because I did not consult him. Here is a collision that must be settled, and it rests with you to do it. I wish to be able to vindicate myself when trouble comes, as we apprehend it will.[103]

It was two or three days before this that Carl Schurz, the President's special commissioner, had come upon the scene. Schurz's dispatch of the twenty-ninth to Johnson briefly but approvingly reported Slocum's order, and deplored what "would have been a fatal step," had it not fortunately been prevented. Johnson's first knowledge, then, of Slocum's order came not from Sharkey but from Schurz, and before he even received the Sharkey dispatch of the thirtieth (on the afternoon of the thirty-first) he had already sent his blistering telegram to Schurz, rebuking both him and Slocum:

I presume General Slocum will issue no order interfering with Governor Sharkey in restoring the functions of the State government, without first consulting the government, giving the reasons for such proposed interference. It is believed there can be organized in each county a force of citizens or militia, to suppress crime, preserve order, and enforce the civil authority of the State and of the United States, which would enable the

102 "Provisional Governors," pp. 229–31.

103 *Ibid.*, p. 231; *Sen. Exec. Docs.*, 39 Cong., 1 sess., No. 2, "Report of Carl Schurz," pp. 62–63; Slocum to Stanton, Aug. 25, 1865, Stanton MSS, Library of Congress.

federal government to reduce the army and withdraw, to a great extent, the forces from the States, thereby reducing the enormous expenses of the government. If there was any danger from an organization of the citizens for the purposes indicated, the military are there to detect and suppress on the first appearance any move insurrectionary in its character. One great object is to induce the people to come forward in the defence of the State and federal government. . . .

The main object of Major General Carl Schurz's mission to the south was to aid as far as practicable in carrying out the policy adopted by the government for restoring the States to their former relations with the federal government. It is hoped such aid has been given. The proclamation authorizing restoration of State governments requires the military to aid the provisional governor in the performance of his duties as prescribed in the proclamation, and in no manner to interfere or throw impediments in the way of consummating the object of his appointment, at least without advising the government of the intended interference.[104]

Johnson, when he received Sharkey's telegram the next day, sent an identical copy of this message to him. It may be imagined that the Governor was filled with the sweetest satisfaction. He moved quickly to take the fullest possible advantage of the dispatch, and asked Johnson if he might publish it. "It will do great good; it will soothe a troubled public mind, it will give implicit confidence in you." Johnson promptly granted the desired permission, and the whole affair with all its particulars was spread across the newspapers of North and South.[105]

Aside from the reaction which this episode produced in the North (to say nothing of its effect on Schurz and Slocum), it is important to consider what sort of enlightenment may have been given to Governor Sharkey himself, and to other persons in the South who were in any way concerned with public matters. The pertinent documents contained a wealth of what appeared to be the most official kind of information, and there were specific classes of inference that the South was fully entitled to draw. In the first place, Johnson was committed in the deepest personal way to a program of restoration, whose completion he was singularly impatient to see and with which he would brook no interference. In the second place, Johnson was convinced that whatever dangers to that program existed lay not in the South but in the North. Moreover, he felt his own position sufficiently correct, and sufficiently secure, that he could afford to move ruthlessly against any "radical"

---

[104] "Provisional Governors," p. 232; Schurz to Johnson, Aug. 29, 1865, Johnson to Schurz, Aug. 30, 1865, Schurz to Johnson, Sept. 1, 1865, Schurz MSS; Schurz to Stanton, Aug. 29, 1865, Stanton MSS; *Speeches, Correspondence . . . of Carl Schurz,* I, 269–70.

[105] "Provisional Governors," p. 232; Garner, *Reconstruction in Mississippi,* pp. 99–103.

meddling, even at the expense of sanctioning Southern actions whose propriety had by no means been settled in his own mind.[106] His sympathies appeared to be such that he was actually less tender of Northern feelings than of Southern: he had no wish "to irritate or humiliate the people of the south." To avoid it, he was quite willing to humiliate two of his own generals instead, and to do great damage to their effectiveness and influence, all with the fullest publicity. Furthermore, Johnson made it clear that already he regarded military occupation itself as an affair so strictly temporary that in any local conflict of jurisdiction he would be almost automatically predisposed in favor of the local civil authority: in short, he had more fully identified himself with the latter than with the former. And finally, in giving way before his provisional governor in the face of his own military commander and his own special envoy (who thereupon became no envoy at all), Johnson gave significant clues to the liberties with federal authority that Southern officials might take generally, without his insisting on anything to the contrary.

That this and other aspects of Executive communication added up to a consistent pattern in Southern expectations may be tested by another case study, this time a study in response. The New Orleans *Picayune*, which in June had soberly advised the young men of Louisiana, and indeed all classes of the population, to settle down and be good citizens, "yield to inevitable and invincible events," and against the blandishments of fanatics and demagogues to "oppose a manly and dignified scorn and contempt,"[107] seemed by September to be inhaling heady gusts of oxygen from every breeze that now blew from Washington. By then the *Picayune* was telling its readers that the President was "much exasperated at the attempts ... made to further goad the South—it being his sole aim and study to heal the breach and bring all into harmony again as quickly as possible."[108]

Political news from the North now brings a real note of buoyancy to the *Picayune*'s columns. Northern Democrats, in their efforts to capture the federal government, are receiving much encouragement from the President. Their opponents, on the other hand, "insist on keeping these States out of the Union ... until they comply with the

---

[106] There are military documents from the Northern District of Mississippi giving strong evidence that the "lawlessness" Sharkey complained of was primarily the work of roving bands of idle young whites—the very men he wanted to organize into militias. See esp. "Report of Carl Schurz," pp. 59–61, 68–70, 101–3; and Garner, *Reconstruction in Mississippi*, p. 104 n.

[107] June 24, 1865.   [108] Sept. 6, 1865.

will of their masters." "Against this Radical scheme," rejoices the *Picayune*, "the President is fully committed by his public acts, and more explicitly—if all accounts be true as we hear them—by his conversations with friend and foe. . . ." "Radicals," the paper announces on September 17, "will make no headway by threatening Andrew Johnson." On the President and Negro suffrage, the *Picayune*, with superior information, can laugh at the delusions of the hapless Greeley:

The Tribune is palming off a reported expression which Mr. Johnson is said to have made to "a prominent New Orleans journalist," that he was in favor of negro suffrage. Now the writer of this knows the "journalist" alluded to, and is well aware that President Johnson did make a remark that might be construed that way, but he made it with a wink of the eye and an expression of countenance that showed it was a joke. In fact, he gave it to be understood that he was not in earnest in the use of the observation, nor would he, of his own free will, advocate the policy of negro suffrage.[109]

As for stories in Northern papers about Southern bad behavior, the *Picayune* on September 27 takes great cheer from the reassurances given by the President to the Southern delegation that recently called upon him:

He said he did not believe the stories from Raleigh and elsewhere with reference to the "disaffection of the South": but, on the contrary, that he looked upon them as "pestilent and malignant utterances." For his part, "he had confidence in the professions of the Southern people and of their purpose to return to the Union upon the principles of the constitution." For himslf, he should adhere to that as the chart of his action, nor would he deviate one iota from it, unless there was urgent necessity to do so, which he did not believe would be the case.

What a shot was that at the Radicals!

What, now, of the radical schemes to keep the Southern states out of Congress? the *Picayune* asks itself on October 3. Has the President the power to suppress them? Yes: the plot will fail. "The President was fully aware of it three months ago, and at that early date he took measures for its discomfiture. His own plan for the restoration of the Union was deliberately formed, and he has carried it out, step by step . . . and he will carry it out fully. He knows the extent of his power, and he will use his power to the fullest extent. . . . The people of the South need have no fears. . . ."

The news of October 5 contains a report that the Freedmen's Bureau "will soon be smashed," since the President regards it "as far more

[109] Sept. 14, 19, 1865.

ornamental than useful." In the same report are further taunts at Greeley, who has attacked Governor Perry's message to the South Carolina convention.

The President, however, holds no such views . . . , and it is sufficient to know that he indorses the message of the Governor. Indeed he thinks that South Carolina is progressing bravely in the work of "restoration", and he cares not a snap of his fingers whether the Radicals like it or not! . . . President Johnson is backed by the people—by every man of them whose influence, friendship and labor are worth having; and he will be sustained to the fullest extent in his efforts to restore harmony and peace to the nation.

In another column the *Picayune* exults, "The President is laying blows on the Radicals thick and fast," and enumerates the evidence given by the President of his intentions toward the South, including his conferral upon the people of Mississippi "the right to have and bear arms, in the maintenance of a militia."

There is more cheering news from New York on October 14, this time based on the President's talk with Manton Marble, editor of the Democratic New York *World*:

The President . . . told Mr. Marble . . . that he was determined to stand or fall on his plan for the immediate restoration of the Union. He had staked the success of his administration on that plan, and not only this, but he staked his own present and future place in the history of the country upon it.

"Those who sustain me," added the President, "I will sustain. Those who oppose, I will oppose."

In his whole conversation with Mr. Marble, he persistently avowed himself a Democrat—as much today as ever. . . .

The *Picayune*'s main theme from here on is the President's heroic determination to have the Southern representatives admitted to Congress. Standing in the way, on the one hand, is a malignant and unnatural conspiracy. "On the other hand, President Johnson is determined that the Southern States shall be represented; and . . . neither he nor his friends are idle. They understand the game of the Radicals, and have quietly taken measures to thwart their designs."[110] "When the time comes," promised the *Picayune* on October 18, "he will out-manoeuvre all his adversaries, and carry out his policy triumphantly. He is perfectly confident of his ability to do this." By the twenty-eighth, it is being assumed that Johnson no longer maintains any real connections with the Republican party at all:

110 Oct. 14, 1865.

The steps which he has already taken since his succession to the Presidency, and particularly those which he has taken during the last two months, indicate plainly enough his abhorrence of the principles of the Republican party, and his fixed determination to conduct his administration upon conservative Democratic principles.

The Radicals, consequently, "can no longer conceal from themselves the unpleasant fact that it is hopeless for them to attempt any longer to influence him in the least degree, or to give direction to his administration."[111] Senators Doolittle and Cowan, in the coming Congress, will of course act with the Democrats and President Johnson. "The Republican party is, indeed, fast undergoing the process of disintegration. In a short time it will become extinct."[112]

As for Johnson himself, the *Picayune* has become convinced that with the prestige of the Executive office, the control of the military, and the overwhelming support of the North's plain people, the President holds at his fingertips power and influence equal to the most prodigious crises. Even his personal attributes are such that he can perform miracles of persuasion, actually winning over enemies. With a contemptuous allusion to his predecessor, the *Picayune* glowingly announces of Johnson:

Without ever indulging in low buffoonery; without finding it necessary to remember a "little story" in order to give point to his arguments, there is a weight in the latter that never fails to carry conviction with it, and there is an irresistible charm in his manner which often disarms enmity, and converts opponents into supporters of his policy.[113]

The Southerners could not know, of course, that whereas they were learning much about the President and his ambitions and intentions, they were at the same time being demoralized. The process of communication was in a positive sense revealing a great deal to them; the very same process, however, had a dark and negative side. There were matters of the most vital importance being concealed and obscured from them.

This negative aspect was somehow bound up with the President's failure—indeed, his refusal—to insist on terms. For all his assumption of prerogative, he would not put himself in the posture of an agent whose government required a specific settlement. Agents of no legal status—but agents nonetheless—awaited his pleasure, only too anxious to know the conditions under which they might bury their pretended "government" forever. That establishment was moribund, but it was still an entity of some kind and would remain so despite all legal fic-

[111] Oct. 28, 1865.   [112] Nov. 1, 1865.   [113] Nov. 11, 1865.

tions to the contrary until its affairs might with emphasis be liquidated once and for all. The South knew, in its way, as did the North, that such liquidation would have to occur rather more palpably and more visibly than by the mere waving aside of the war as an odd delusion which had really changed nothing. Virtually everything, in fact, had changed. Let it be called anything—rebellion, organized treason, or whatever—but let it be something, simply that men might lay hold of the thing and dispose of it: let it be settled. Andrew Johnson did much to baffle this impulse when he refused to specify clear terms, communicate them to the concerned parties, and then insist that they be met. "The President . . . said that as Executive, he could only take the initiatory steps to enable them to do the things which it was incumbent upon them to perform."[114]

Such was the position which Johnson had defined for himself that the whole process of reconstruction had to be called a voluntary one. True, there did have to be a "voluntary" aspect of this peacemaking. But conceivably to place so much of that responsibility on the defeated power as Johnson did, was to impose burdens beyond what the South was in a position to bear. It is in the nature of peace terms to a defeated enemy that they must partake, no matter how lightly, of the punitive; and there is something a little eerie about asking a helpless foe to prescribe his own penalties.

There would be terms, and there would not be terms. Johnson might hint to the Southerners of "things which it was incumbent upon them to perform," and yet deny that he was dictating to them. He could nod in a general way toward the kinds of acts which would be acceptable, but his own position—that all was being done through the free will of the people—denied him the resources, the graded standards, whereby he could say with assurance that such acts were or were not being performed acceptably. The free will of the people and the self-evident Constitution: here was something of a closed circle, a sacred grove wherein oracles might be consulted and from which omens might emerge, but nothing seemed to come out of it that resembled a hard and fast understanding among men of responsibility

Thus, while men might imagine they heard Andrew Johnson saying, "Let there be terms," what were they to think when he not only shrank from spelling out the terms, with that precision and assurance which a dazed people needed, but provided no sanctions against their being met or not met—nothing that he was ready to stand back of in

114 Interview with South Carolina delegation, June 24, 1865, New York *Times,* June 26, 1865.

the name of his government, nothing for which *he* was prepared to be responsible? The President had assumed immense powers while shunning others that properly accompanied them; and having taken his position, he depended not upon the North but on the South—an impotent, disorganized, and prostrate entity—to sustain him in it. Just how much—more than one Southerner, in his second thoughts, might have asked himself—did the President really comprehend of their dilemma? How much did he care? How much attention was the President really paying to the efforts they were making? Could it be that Johnson wanted his restoration project so badly, was he so anxious, so irritably impatient to get it over with, that in his preoccupation it did not too much matter in the meanwhile what they did?

In any case, it was almost as though Johnson were goading the Southerners into taking liberties even with the things they knew he wanted. The most notable of such instances were Mississippi's non-ratification of the Thirteenth Amendment and South Carolina's non-repudiation of the Confederate debt. Here again, nothing is so instructive as Johnson's own messages to the governors.

The pertinent sequence, in the case of Mississippi, is as follows:

Johnson to Sharkey, Aug. 15 [Hopefully]:
I hope that without delay your convention will amend your State constitution, abolishing slavery . . . also that they will adopt the amendment to the Constitution of the United States abolishing slavery.

Johnson to Sharkey, Aug. 21 [Still hopefully; perhaps if they do not care to do it one way, they might prefer the other]:
Your convention can adopt the amendment to the Constitution of the United States, or recommend its adoption by the legislature.

Johnson to Sharkey, Nov. 1 [Now wheedling; they still have not done it]:
It is all-important that the legislature adopt the amendment. . . . The argument is, if the convention abolished slavery in good faith, why should the legislature hesitate to make it part of the Constitution of the United States?
I trust in God that the legislature will adopt the amendment, and thereby make the way clear for the admission of senators and representatives to their seats in the present Congress.

Johnson to Sharkey, Nov. 17 [Downright plaintive; it would really be in their own interest to do this]:
Let the amendment to the Constitution of the United States abolishing slavery be adopted. . . .
I do hope the southern people will see the position they now occupy, and avail themselves of the favorable opportunity of once more resuming all their former relations to the government of the United States, and, in so doing, restore peace, prosperity, happiness, and fraternal love.

At no point does Sharkey, in any of his replies, acknowledge these hints. But on December 8 a copy of the legislature's committee report on the amendment, together with a resolution adopted December 2 regarding the same, is transmitted to the President:

The first and main section of the article has already been adopted by Mississippi, so far as her territory and people are concerned.

It was substantially . . . incorporated into the Satte constitution by the late convention. Now is it possible for the State by any act, or in any mode, conventional or otherwise, to change the status fixed by the convention?

. . . The second section is subject to more grave objections. It confers on Congress the power to enforce the article by "appropriate legislation." Slavery having been already abolished, there is really no necessity for this section, nor can the committee anticipate any possible good that can result from its adoption. On the contrary, it seems to be fraught with evils. . . .

If there be no danger now, the committee fear the time may come that the public mind might be influenced on this subject to the degree of endangering the reserved rights of the States.

The committee are also of the opinion that the present is not a propitious time to enlarge the powers of the federal government. The tendency is already too strong in the direction of consolidation. . . .

It would be unwise and inexpedient to open a subject which your committee had believed extinct, as themes for radicals and demagogues to use to the detriment of the best interests of the country. Mississippi cannot give her deliberate consent to leave open any question from which agitation can arise, calculated to disturb the harmony so happily being restored among the States and the people. . . .

Resolved, therefore, by the legislature of the State of Mississippi, That it refuses to ratify the proposed amendment to the Constitution of the United States.[115]

"There is nothing," announced the *Picayune* triumphantly, ". . . to confirm the view that President Johnson holds the ratification of the amendment to be an indispensable duty, and as a condition precedent to their restoration to their functions as States in the Union."[116]

In the case of South Carolina, the President addresses Governor Perry in general terms, as the convention is about to meet.

Johnson to Perry, Sept. 2:
I hope you will proceed with the work of restoration as rapidly as possible, and upon such principles as will disarm those who are opposed to

---

[115] "Provisional Governors," pp. 229–30, 233–34, 79–80.

[116] New Orleans *Picayune*, Nov. 19, 1865. Johnson's telegram of August 21 to Sharkey, sent just before the Mississippi convention adjourned, also contained congratulations on what had been done and expressed the hope "that your doings will set an example that will be followed by all the other States." This was the only part of the message that had meaning for Southerners in general. "He has thus declared this action sufficient for reinstatement." Charleston *Courier*, Sept. 12, 1865.

the States resuming their former relations with the federal government. This is all-important.

Either the President has not made the debt question clear, or Perry thinks he may safely ignore it, for the latter telegraphs on September 20, after the convention is finished, still not having repudiated the debt: "I hope the action of our convention is satisfactory." And three days later, on September 23, to the Secretary of State:

I am happy to have it in my power to inform you that the State convention of South Carolina have done well, and shown a perfectly loyal spirit throughout all their proceedings. . . .

. . . They have, in fact, carried out all of my recommendations which were important. . . .

I enclose you a copy of my message. [Perry in his message does not mention repudiation of the debt among the "recommendations" he deems it necessary to have carried out.]

At this point the Secretary of State takes up the correspondence, speaking for the President:

Seward to Perry, Nov. 10:

He [the President] observes with regret that neither the convention nor the State legislature has pronounced debts and obligations contracted in the name of the State for unconstitutional and even rebellious purposes to be void.

Seward to Perry, Nov. 20:

Upon reflection, South Carolina . . . would not care to come again into the councils of the Union incumbered and clogged with debts and obligations which had been assumed in her name in a vain attempt to subvert it. The President trusts that she will lose no time in making an effective organic declaration, disavowing all debts and obligations created or assumed in her name in aid of the rebellion.

Perry to Seward, Nov. 27:

Your telegram of the 20th instant was not received in due time, owing to my absence from Columbia. The convention having been dissolved, it is impracticable to enact any organic law in regard to the war debt. That debt is very small, as the expenditures of South Carolina were reimbursed by the confederate government. The debt is so mixed up with the ordinary expenses of the State that it cannot be separated. In South Carolina all were guilty of aiding the rebellion, and no one can complain of being taxed to pay the trifling debt incurred in his own account in perfect good faith. The convention did all that the President advised to be done, and I thought it wrong to keep a revolutionary body in existence and advised their immediate dissolution, which was done. There is now no power in the legislature to repudiate the debt if it were possible to separate it from the other debts of the State. Even then it would fall on widows and orphans whose estates were invested in it for safety.

Seward to Perry, Nov. 30:

I have the honor to acknowledge the receipt of your telegram of the 17th instant informing me that, as the convention had been dissolved, it was impossible to adopt the President's suggestion to repudiate the insurgent debt, and to inform you that while the objections which you urge to the adoption of that proceeding are of a serious nature, the President cannot refrain from awaiting with interest an official expression upon that subject from the legislature.[117]

Nothing at all, however, was done about the debt, and the Columbia *Phoenix* praised what everyone knew to be Perry's own stubborn opposition to any action on it. The *Picayune* had already predicted: "As the President, however, endorsed the action of Mississippi, so will he doubtless endorse also that of Alabama and South Carolina; and it matters not a straw whether the fanatics like the programme or not. Let them rave." Meanwhile Secretary Seward, in his message of December 23 relieving Perry, serenely took leave of the truculent provisional governor by saying: "It gives me especial pleasure to convey to you the President's acknowledgement of the fidelity, the loyalty and the discretion which have marked your administration."[118]

In the Mississippi election, Benjamin G. Humphreys, an unpardoned Confederate general, was a candidate for governor, and it was well known not only in Mississippi but all over the country that Johnson did not want him elected. But Humphreys would not withdraw, and he was subsequently elected. Johnson's reaction to this rebuff has been cited by one writer as an example of the President's firmness: "Humphreys was not recognized as Governor of Mississippi until Johnson saw fit to pardon him. . . . Johnson knew how to be firm when he chose."[119] It is unlikely, however, that anyone in Mississippi so construed it. Humphreys was elected on October 2, had himself inaugurated on the sixteenth, and was handed his pardon on the twenty-sixth.[120] Johnson's displeasure consisted in telling Sharkey (as, for that

[117] "Provisional Governors," pp. 249–50, 117, 123–26, 198–201.

[118] Kibler, *Benjamin F. Perry*, pp. 423–24; New Orleans *Picayune,* Oct. 11, 1865; "Provisional Governors," p. 47.

[119] Beale, *Critical Year*, p. 39.

[120] Garner, *Reconstruction in Mississippi*, pp. 94–96; Humphreys to Johnson, Oct. 26, 1865, Johnson MSS. It is likely that Humphreys knew well before this time that he was being pardoned. He received his pardon from Sharkey, rather than directly from Johnson, and it seems to have been the practice for the provisional governors to advertise lists of pardons pending their final receipt. According to Garner, Johnson "sent Humphreys a pardon in the first week in October"—a pardon which, if we are to believe evidence published later, was dated August 11. The correspondent of the Vicksburg *Herald*, having heard a rumor immediately after the election that Hum-

matter, he told all the others) that he was to remain as provisional governor until duly relieved; if the President really considered not recognizing Humphreys, it must have been awkward in the meanwhile to have to instruct Sharkey—as he did—to show certain presidential dispatches to the governor-elect. Sharkey was relieved on December 14 (sooner than any of the other governors except Holden) and told to turn over the state's affairs to Humphreys.[121] The Baton Rouge *Tri-Weekly Advocate* hooted at the New Orleans *Star* for advising men who had been prominent in the rebellion not to "force themselves upon the people":

> President Johnson has "forced" a number of men "prominent in the rebellion" into high positions since he became President. . . . The long and short of it is, this cry about men not running for office who have fought heroically for the past four years in a cause they loved, is all nonsense. . . . Their past bravery and their frank submission to the Government is the best guarantee of their future fidelity, a fact known and already recognized by the President.[122]

When it came to the black codes—so wrathfully denounced in the North and so often cited as the prime instance of Southern tactlessness—it might at least be said on behalf of the Southerners that not only had they received no hint from the President concerning the inadvisability of such codes but there was actually little evidence in Johnson's prior or subsequent behavior that he himself disapproved of them. There was even evidence that he considered the legislatures to have been quite within their rights. He had ample foreknowledge of what these legislatures were preparing to do. Governor Perry wired on October 29 that he had submitted to the South Carolina legislature "a code of laws on this subject, prepared by order of the convention." He thought it would be passed. Two days later he sent the President a copy of the convention journal, together with the proposed code in its entirety.[123]

In Mississippi, Governor-elect Humphreys, though not recognized by the President, immediately took over the duty of advising the legislature on laws regulating the freedmen. In his inaugural address on

---

phreys might not be recognized, checked with military headquarters and was assured that there was no intention of setting aside the election. This announcement was made in the *Herald* on October 4, and the New Orleans *Picayune* published the story on the eleventh. See also "Provisional Governors," p. 234; and *House Exec. Docs.*, 40 Cong., 1 sess., No. 32, "Additional Lists of Pardons," p. 71.

[121] "Provisional Governors," p. 47.

[122] Baton Rouge *Tri-Weekly Advocate*, Sept. 29, 1865.

[123] "Provisional Governors," pp. 119, 175–97.

October 16, published everywhere, he said that the Negroes should be protected in person and property, and should be compelled to fulfil their labor contracts. He also declared, "It is due to ourselves . . . to maintain the fact that ours is and it shall ever be a government of white men." He sent a message to the legislature on October 20, again urging the passage of a code. A committee had in fact already been working on the matter (as in South Carolina) since the convention, and its report was submitted a few days later, with a proposed series of laws.

While some of the proposed legislation may seem rigid and stringent to the sickly modern humanitarians, they can never disturb, retard or embarrass the good and true, useful and faithful of either race, . . . while the wayward and vicious, idle and dishonest, the lawless and reckless, the wicked and improvident, the vagabond and meddler must be smarted, governed, reformed and guided by higher instincts, minds and morals higher and holier than theirs. . . .

All these items received the fullest publicity.[124]

In each case, the governors supposed such legislation to be part of the process that would bring them closer to full restoration. They imagined that it would hasten the removal of the military, and particularly of the Freedmen's Bureau (strongly denounced by Humphreys in his message), by taking over the functions which the Bureau was currently performing. Both Perry and Humphreys said as much to their legislatures,[125] and even the President had uttered thoughts which might be construed as encouragement:

There is no concession required on the part of the people of Mississippi, or the Legislature, other than a legal compliance with the laws and Constitution of the United States, and the adoption of such measures giving protection to all freedmen and possession of property without regard to color, as will entitle them to assume their constitutional rights in the Federal Union.[126]

No sooner had the Mississippi code been passed than General O. O. Howard, head of the Freedmen's Bureau, took the initiative and telegraphed orders to his assistant commissioner on November 30 suspending much of the new code in that state. Similar action was taken a month later in South Carolina when General Sickles declared that state's entire code to be "null and void." But all that Johnson himself did was to refrain from reversing what his commanders had done, thus

[124] Garner, *Reconstruction in Mississippi*, pp. 111–19.

[125] *American Annual Cyclopaedia, 1865*, p. 586; Kibler, *Benjamin F. Perry*, p. 422; Simkins and Woody, *South Carolina during Reconstruction*, pp. 48–52; James L. Orr to Johnson, Dec. 23, 1865, Johnson MSS.

[126] Johnson to Humphreys, Nov. 17, 1865, *American Annual Cyclopaedia, 1865*, p. 585.

simply allowing the codes' non-enforcement. As a matter of fact, the governor of Mississippi immediately sent to Washington a committee of two, protesting Howard's action, and the committee was assured by the President that "none of the acts should be nullified except by courts of law."[127]

What had happened? Besides leading the South into realms of fantasy regarding the true location of Northern authority, the nature of majority sentiment, and the support which he himself could command for whatever policies he deemed proper, the President had at the same time thrown away most of the vast bargaining power with which he had started out. Having placed an extraordinary amount of faith in the non-coercive side of his role—a side which by definition put extra stress upon techniques of persuasion and negotiation—he had then proceeded to breach all the most basic principles of advocacy, diplomacy, and bargaining. As advocate for the plaintiff, he had in effect conspired with the defendant; as representative of a sovereign nation, he had cut himself off from the power of his government; as bargaining agent, he had kept shifting the terms of the bargain so that nobody could be sure what he was asking for. Even as judge, as mediator, as go-between—to whatever extent his role partook of those functions—he had got himself and his emotions openly involved in the claims of the one side, at the expense of those of the other. Such behavior would certainly have sabotaged the business of any courtroom, chancellery, or bargaining table; as for the affairs of an entire nation, the disruption which may have been effected there, and the extent of its consequences, can only invite speculation. That the primary victim of those consequences—the defeated South—should have been in any position to point out the President's errors, to resist them, or to aid him in repairing them, is a likelihood that cannot be taken with very great seriousness. For once the President's attitude had been fully revealed, the South, by the very nature of its position, could not for a minute afford to see things through eyes other than his.

But if the President had done disservice to Southern claims—to say nothing of Northern—in his negotiating character, it is just as conceivable in a curious way that from the coercive side of his role he may have done them even deeper mischief. To say that the problem had its negotiating aspects is most important, but it should never carry us too far from the primary thing, which was that the South had been

---

[127] Simkins and Woody, *South Carolina during Reconstruction*, p. 57; Garner, *Reconstruction in Mississippi*, p. 119.

defeated in war; no amount of words could talk away the fact that the South was being confronted by its conqueror. Nor was there any use pretending that the South was not in some sense being asked to pay; no fact, for the South, could have been more immediate. Thus no matter what the beaten enemy might be asked to do, no matter how little, it would be idle to imagine that he should derive the least pleasure from it—except for the relief, once it was done, of having it cleanly and honorably over with. Moreover, it is much to be doubted that there was any real mercy in telling the enemy that his punishment, especially if never made fully clear, must be undergone voluntarily—or much realism in expecting, on that basis, that he would go about it in any but a confused and afflicted state of mind. In those areas in which the South was, indeed, without choice, it was conceivably better to say so, and to order that the thing be done—coolly, sparing the Southern gentlemen those words about "forgiveness" and "fraternal love" which could not sound in their ears without some ring of mockery until a later, happier day. Some things are easiest to do when there is no choice at all.

On those rare occasions when President Johnson, in his dealings with the South, did come in any way close to laying down the law, those concerned responded immediately, almost with alacrity. Contrasted with the oddly inhibited character of most of the President's dispatches, there is something of the coiled spring in his message to Holden on the North Carolina debt:

Every dollar of the debt created to aid the rebellion against the United States should be repudiated finally and forever. The great mass of the people should not be taxed to pay a debt to aid in carrying on a rebellion which they in fact, if left to themselves, were opposed to. Let those who have given their means for the obligations of the State look to that power they tried to establish in violation of law, constitution, and the will of the people. They must meet their fate. . . . I repeat [etc.]. . . .

He spoke to Georgia in similar language, and in both cases the thing was done.[128] In Alabama, the relative ease with which the Executive wishes were carried out was doubtless due in some measure to the fact that there happened to be in Washington men of influence communicating those wishes to Governor Parsons in terms stronger and more precise than those used by the President himself.[129] In South Carolina, at the same time, Governor Perry's success in convincing the convention delegates that he could be counted on to represent reliably

[128] "Provisional Governors," pp. 226, 236.
[129] Thomas Sykes *et al.* to L. E. Parsons, Sept. 19, 1865, Johnson MSS.

to them what the President would and would not stand for was what gave him such extraordinary influence. Sidney Andrews, who was present at the time of the convention, wrote of Perry that

his position, in the peculiar circumstances of the hour, makes his word and wish of very unusual significance. . . . it is an almost every-hour occurrence, in the debates, that the question is asked, "Is that view approved by the Provisional Governor?" or that the remark is made, "I think we had better consult the Governor first." So it may be said that he is the leader of the Convention.[130]

Indeed, there were repeated occasions on which the Southerners themselves had to beg Johnson to make himself clear on a thing if he really wanted them to do it. A member of the South Carolina legislature wrote, regarding the unrepudiated debt: "Make the *requirement absolute*, the state will meet it." Indeed, Johnson's strong words to North Carolina and Georgia on that same subject were not forthcoming until the governors themselves, in each case, urged the President by telegraph to declare himself. Even in Tennessee, when difficulty arose in November over the enactment of a Negro testimony bill, the Tennessee secretary of state, recognizing that the bill would not pass unless the legislature were convinced that its failure to do so would have a bad effect on Tennessee's chances of readmission, implored the President to telegraph an "opinion" for his use in the matter. A question of some delicacy in Georgia was the election of United States senators. The preference in the legislature was for such men, prominent in the Confederacy, as Alexander Stephens and Herschel Johnson, and the election of a Unionist like Joshua Hill would only be possible through the express influence, unmistakably exerted, of the administration. Hill himself informed the President to this effect. "I tell you," a prominent man of Richmond said to Whitelaw Reid, "President Johnson can name his Senators and they will be straightway elected. He can say what he wants, the Virginia legislature, so-called, will register his edicts in legislative enactments."[131]

There was much evidence that men of influence in the South initially understood their own position a good deal more clearly than did the President. There was much quibbling in the early sessions of the Mississippi convention over abolishing slavery in the state constitution, and a series of resolutions was introduced by one of the ablest delegates, casting doubts upon the validity of emancipation. Three prom-

---

[130] Andrews, *The South since the War*, pp. 49–50.

[131] A. S. Wallace to Seward, Dec. 25, 1865, Johnson MSS; "Provisional Governors," pp. 81, 226, 236; A. J. Fletcher to Johnson, Nov. 20, 1865; Joshua Hill to Johnson, Dec. 20, 1865, Johnson MSS; Reid, *After the War*, p. 321.

inent judges, men of conservative views, thereupon took the occasion, one by one, to lay things on the line and remind the convention exactly where it stood, and in terms Johnson himself would never have dreamed of using. J. W. C. Watson reminded the delegates that they were a conquered people, that their freedom of action was impaired by the very circumstances under which they met, and that they had no right to dictate to Congress the terms of their readmission. "Gentlemen talk as if we had a choice," Judge Amos Johnston then declared, "but we have no choice, and it is no humiliation to admit it. The only course we can pursue is that dictated to us by the powers at Washington." Judge William Yerger spoke of the Northern people's determination not to be "trifled with." "As men of sense," he admonished them, "let us endeavor to remedy what we cannot alter, and gather together whatever may tend to palliate our misfortunes." The speeches made quite an impression on the convention, and by a large majority the resolutions were tabled forthwith.[132]

The "men of sense" whom Judge Yerger invoked had declined in influence by November, but there were enough of them, even then, who were appalled at the passage of the black code. The laws were denounced by some of the foremost newspapers of the state, including the leading one, the Jackson *Clarion*. The Columbus *Sentinel* said that the legislature had been controlled by

a hard and shallow-headed majority, that were far more anxious to make capital at home than to propitiate the powers at Washington. They were as complete a set of political Goths as were ever turned loose to work destruction upon a State. The fortunes of the whole South have been injured by their folly.[133]

Nowhere in the South, any time, could more than a tiny minority have been assembled to enact of its own free will even a qualified Negro suffrage. But it is important to note that things were still open enough in the summer of 1865, all through the South, that men of standing could discuss with surprising freedom even this subject as a possibility. Professor Fleming, writing in 1905, said that in Alabama political leaders talked a great deal about suffrage in 1865, and that

132 Garner, *Reconstruction in Mississippi*, pp. 87–90.

133 *Ibid.*, p. 116; Vernon L. Wharton, *The Negro in Mississippi* (Chapel Hill: University of North Carolina Press, 1947), pp. 89–90. J. H. Jones, a Confederate colonel and later a legislator and lieutenant-governor, wrote: "Looking back upon the methods by which that Legislature undertook to deal with the negro problem, one is amazed at such stupidity. . . ." "Reconstruction in Wilkinson County," *Publications of the Mississippi Historical Society*, VIII (1904), 156. There was similar sentiment in South Carolina; see Simkins and Woody, *South Carolina during Reconstruction*, p. 52.

even before the Reconstruction Acts, Negroes were allowed to vote in a few local elections.[134] General James L. Alcorn of Mississippi, one of the two senators elected by that state in 1865, was convinced that if the whites did not make the Negroes their friends through the franchise, their path would be "red with blood and damp with tears."[135] A few of the leading men in South Carolina felt that it would be wise and proper to enact a limited Negro suffrage; among them were A. Toomer Porter, Wade Hampton and his brother Christopher, Joseph LeConte, and Judge Edward Frost (who had headed the delegation that visited the President on June 24). "I insisted," wrote LeConte, "that the convention should adopt a franchise *without distinction of color*, but with a small educational and property qualification. My friends admitted the wisdom of the suggestion but said that it was impossible, as the leaders had not 'backbone' enough to propose it, and the people were not ready to indorse it."[136]

Here we may revert once more to the early aftermath of the surrender, with the themes it contained, and make a final effort to appreciate the crushing effects of defeat, the ruin which lay in all hearts and minds, the South's apprehension of unnamable penalties, and the mute petition of the South for any kind of settlement. "The months of May and June," wrote Whitelaw Reid, "were the chaotic period of the returning Rebel States. All men were overwhelmed and prostrated under the sudden stroke of calamity which the fewest number had anticipated." The theme of irreconcilability—of rage, bitterness, and hate—was mingled and balanced with that of submission, and of exposed sensitivity, and readiness to do what had to be done.

The first feelings were those of baffled rage. . . . Then followed a sense of bewilderment and helplessness. Where they were, what rights they had left, what position they occupied before the law, what claim they had to their property, what hope they had for an improvement of their condition in the future—all these were subjects of complete uncertainty. . . . They expected nothing; were prepared for the worst; would have been thankful for anything.

In North and South Carolina, Georgia, and Florida, we found this state of feeling universally prevalent. The people wanted civil government and

---

[134] Walter L. Fleming, *Civil War and Reconstruction in Alabama*, pp. 386–90.

[135] Wharton, *Negro in Mississippi*, p. 140. Alexander Stephens of Georgia was also an early exponent of qualified Negro suffrage; see C. Mildred Thompson, *Reconstruction in Georgia* (New York: Columbia University Press, 1915), p. 160.

[136] *Autobiography of Joseph LeConte*, ed. W. D. Armes (New York: D. Appleton, 1903), pp. 235–36; A. Toomer Porter, *Led On! Step by Step* . . . (New York: G. P. Putnam's Sons, 1898), p. 224; Simkins and Woody, *South Carolina during Reconstruction*, p. 41; Reid, *After the War*, pp. 288–89; *Nation*, I (August 17, 1865), 208; *ibid.*, I (Aug. 24, 1865), 238.

a settlement. They asked no terms, made no conditions. They were defeated and helpless—they submitted. Would the victor be pleased to tell them what was to be done?[137]

But things had apparently begun to happen when the President started imposing himself on Southern feelings. J. R. Dennett, much impressed by the orderly state of sentiment in South Carolina in midsummer (the people of that state having gone into the rebellion "more earnestly and honestly" than anywhere else, had acquiesced in their defeat "more honestly and promptly than any others"), thought it just possible by late August that a "reaction" may have occurred, "caused by the premature establishment of civil government, unsettling their minds, and interrupting a healthy progress of opinion."[138] Reid, who had been in the South from early May to midsummer, took another trip in November and found the people's temper much changed. "Yesterday they cringed for pardon at the feet of 'the boorish and drunken tailor' they had denounced; today they are harder to satisfy than ninety and nine just men who have no need of repentance."[139] About this time Johnson's own provisional governor in North Carolina, William W. Holden, wrote to the President in rather pathetic words that betrayed something close to a failure of nerve:

I regret to say that there is much of a rebellion spirit still in this state. In this respect I admit I have been deceived. In May and June last these rebellious spirits would not have dared to show their heads even for the office of constable; but leniency has emboldened them, and the Copperhead now shows his fangs. . . .

I communicate these corrections with regret. It may be that the policy of the government has been too lenient; or it may be that I have seriously erred in the discharge of duty, or that I was not the proper person for Provisional Governor. . . . I am ready and willing at any moment to retire from this position; and if you have the shadow of a wish that I should do so, I pray you as a friend to let me know it.[140]

Johnson had encouraged the Southern people to think of him as their protector against the Black Republicans of the North. He himself had so defined the picture for them, and such were the illusions he had given them of his power that even a year later, when any remnants of that power had all but collapsed, they could still look forward to the fall elections of 1866—which would actually bring Republican landslides—expecting a triumphant vindication for the President and

[137] Reid, *After the War*, pp. 295-96.

[138] *Nation*, I (Aug. 24, 1865), 238.

[139] Reid, *After the War*, p. 317.

[140] Holden to Johnson, Dec. 6, 1865, Johnson MSS.

themselves. Their shock may well have been all the worse, since they had come to know that the President would not use his power to coerce *them*. Meanwhile the President, all unwittingly, may have worked a still subtler mischief with the feelings of two whole peoples as they emerged from conflict. Standing in the ambiguous position which he had taken up between them, he had with the best of intentions cut himself off from the deepest needs of both. It may be supposed that these enemies, when the fight was over, wanted at least to respect each other, so that they might the more respect themselves for the exertions they had made, and to put aside their arms at least in the honorable knowledge of pride well served. This may be the point at which the "balm of time" idea is actually most relevant. A certain decent punctilio of reserve was needed, a due season of correctness and repose not to be interrupted by too many exhortations to "fraternal love" from a man whose title to the place he held could never be quite above doubt—a man whom neither North nor South, with all good will, could quite help regarding as an outsider. In such a setting as this, and with Johnson's special position vulnerable just on general principles, one can imagine that the President's resources might have been much augmented by a greater willingness to share his authority.

In the interests of the South's own pride, it might possibly have been as well that the basic terms of the settlement, if there was going to be one, should initially be concluded with a minimum of reference to the people—though for maximum success the parties to it would have had to be men whom the people trusted, men fully identified with the cause. The possibilities of secret diplomacy, if such it might be called, were about at an end by December, 1865. One of the reasons was that the presidential power, to which Southerners had been so ready to adjust earlier, was not being put to coercive uses. Since by winter this was more or less clear to all, the new power to which Southern political leaders were now having to adjust, in ever increasing degree, was the power of their own constituencies—that is, the will of the people. Democracy in such circumstances is of course the enemy of diplomacy. All this placed ever greater limits on these men's freedom of action, so limited already—a kind of freedom indispensable for complying with demands bound to be distasteful no matter what. Moreover, they needed sanctions of coercion at their backs, for their own protection, so that they might tell the people, as Judge Johnston told the Mississippi convention, "we have no choice, and it is no humiliation to admit it." Every "political Goth" (as the Columbus *Senti-*

nel might have put it) that came down from the Mississippi hills to sit in the legislature spelled that much less influence for the likes of Judge Johnston, Judge Yerger, and General Alcorn. And, finally, the President might denounce the secessionists of South Carolina and the abolitionists of Massachusetts as much as he chose,[141] but for all his talk, no real peace could be made until South Carolina and Massachusetts were, in some sense, brought face to face.

[141] "As a Tennessee politician, it had been necessary for him to denounce the 'Abolitionists and fanatics of the North;' to declare, in the stereotyped phrase of the stump, that he had equal hatred for the Secessionists of South Carolina and the Abolitionists of Massachusetts. They [pardon-seeking Southerners] asked him if he was going to let Massachusetts Abolitionists lead him now and control his Administration, while his own native South lay repentant and bleeding at his feet. He was ambitious, proud of his elevation, but stung by the sneer that after all he was only an accidental President." Reid. *After the War*, p. 305.

Massachusetts and South Carolina: An Imaginary Peacemaking

A kind of dualism has by now fastened itself upon our subject in all ways and places. It was probably inherent in the subject's very nature, involved as it is everywhere with divided loyalties, divided vision, and a divided people. So there may be no harm at this point in experimenting with still another kind of "duality," this time the duality between what did not happen and what did.

Into the "National Union" convention at Philadelphia, on August 14, 1866, walked two sets of delegates, one from Massachusetts and the other from South Carolina, arm in arm. James L. Orr, at the head of South Carolina's delegation, and General Darius N. Couch of Massachusetts led the procession. The convention had been gotten together to help mend an Executive position which was by then fast deteriorating, and the proceedings, being under the special sanction and encouragement of President Johnson, were thus watched by him with great care. Many of those present thought that the arm-in-arm entry of the Massachusetts and South Carolina delegates represented the fullest and most persuasive possible token of reunion. But *Harper's Weekly* pointed out, not without reason, that the scene could not be said to carry much meaning as long as Massachusetts was not represented elsewhere by the marginal men who presumed to represent it here. The presiding officer "knew perfectly well," *Harper's* declared, "that Massachusetts could enter his Convention only in the person of a man like JOHN A. ANDREW. If he staid away Massachusetts was not there." This was, among other things, *Harper's* implicit recognition that probably no one in Massachusetts was nearly so influential as the state's very remarkable ex-governor.[1]

Actually, there was a sense in which South Carolina was not there either. James L. Orr was recognized as the elected governor of that state, but in the election held the previous fall, his "opponent" had found it necessary to promote Orr's election in order to prevent his own, and even then the margin between them was only a few hundred votes. This opponent was Wade Hampton, easily the most popular man in South Carolina.

The men who were "not there" were the men who embodied the "real" Massachusetts and the "real" South Carolina. Why had the President and his friends not staged their drama of reunion—which, as all must have known, was itself not real—with such men as these for its principals? Assuming that the President, in his efforts to make peace, had truly been inclined to avail himself of the moral resources at his disposal in the "real" Massachusetts and the "real" South Carolina—how might he have done it? Obviously one cannot say; it may be guessed, however, that the scene would have been very different from the one that did occur. This one would have to be enacted at least a year earlier—in 1865, not 1866; it would have taken place privately, not publicly; and there would not have been anything very effusive about it—the principals would not have entered "arm in arm." But they might have left with an understanding, one that could serve as a model for similar understandings with all the ex-Confederate states—a settlement, as it were, with the Confederacy itself.

For one reason or another, no such settlement was ever made. We can do no more than guess what it might have been like. But what we can do is bring forth something of the real Massachusetts and the real South Carolina, in the persons of the men most fully authorized to speak for them, and see if they have anything to tell us in our "unreal" guessing. We cannot put down anything that did not happen; that would not be "history." But out of the stories of these two men, all of which *is* history, we may, if we wish, draw inferences. From these stories, the reader is asked to imagine his own settlement.

I   JOHN ANDREW, INTELLECTUAL

One of the most notable things about the Lincoln administration—and notably missing from that of Lincoln's successor—was the prominent role played in the realization of government policy

[1] *Harper's Weekly*, X (Sept. 1, 1866), 547.

by public men of standing and influence situated strategically through-out the country. This was particularly true of certain of the war governors, and much has been said of the highly intelligent use which Lincoln made of them. But the process was more intricate than a mere matter of "use." Although the affinities between Lincoln and the masses of the Northern people had already become legend before the Emancipator's death, and were ruefully commented upon more than once by his opponents, Lincoln himself had always seemed to under-stand the extent to which those affinities had to be mediated through regional leadership—through men of varying types upon whose ex-ample the people of so many diverse communities depended and through whom so many diverse needs were given voice. Thus Lincoln depended upon these spokesmen to assist in the carrying-out of na-tional policy, but it was hardly a simple matter of one-way manip-ulation. Their responsibility to the people was as great as his own; he may have had his requirements, but they too had theirs. The result was that each managed to exact a great deal from the other.

As men of character, energy, zeal, influence, and intelligence were brought into the war effort, these men themselves came to make a real difference, leaving their own impress upon the times, and it was some-thing beyond mere "yielding" and "giving way" on the part of the executive that made this possible. Their response to the administra-tion's needs was part of a process which worked reciprocally: these men were able to infuse energy into the government that was not previously there; they could be of great value in the setting of tone; they could exert pressures to which the administration was never in-sensitive; and thus they could make it do things it would not have done otherwise. In short, these men not only carried out government policy but actually did much to make it. So, although one convenient way to think of Lincoln's wartime trials is to picture him as hounded by radical pressures, it is by no means the only way. There should be some appreciation of those numerous pressures which were exerted responsibly, pressures which Lincoln himself recognized as legitimate: the endless political requirements that had to be taken seriously, and if possible satisfied, if such a mass undertaking as the Civil War were to be maintained from day to day. The same picture might look quite different if considered in the light of a certain unspoken understand-ing. Lincoln knew, despite wide gulfs of opinion between himself and them, that there were public men whose assistance he could not do without and still hope for success—all of which meant, as far as they in their turn were affected, that given the assumption of dependability in certain basic connections, the extent to which a man's personality and thought could then impinge upon public policy was considerable.

There was no better embodiment of this principle than John Andrew, war governor of Massachusetts. Andrew was the man who put the first troops in the field after the firing upon Sumter—the man who, throughout all of four years, never once seemed to stop moving. It is surprising that a great deal more has not been said about how very much the whole tone, the elan, the quality and character, the very success, of the Union war effort owed to this one man, who in terms of inspirational strategy was located so exactly right.

John Andrew and Abraham Lincoln were anything but intimate. Indeed, there was scarcely a moment throughout the war when the tension between the Capitol at Washington and the State House at Boston was not fairly tight. But it was a fine tension, salutary and productive, and the Union war effort proved much the better for it. Throughout it all, both Lincoln and Andrew understood, each with a curious kind of delicacy, the requirements of the other's public position. Something more came out of this than simply the success of Union arms. Each man in his way did something to help the other reveal himself in the accents and outlines of what other men would call greatness; each, for the other, contributed more than a little to that setting in which an individual personality, emerging from obscurity, might actually lay hold of events and change them. There was something oddly parallel, in fact, about the two men's careers. If Lincoln was the man of the times, the man of the people, the man of good will, in the style and idiom set by pioneer Illinois, then John Andrew in his turn incarnated all the same attributes in a very different idiom, that of the old Bay State.

John Albion Andrew, born in 1818 at Windham, Maine, was the son of the village storekeeper. His parents were both people of strong character who made exceptional efforts to see that their sons were educated. John attended Bowdoin in the 1830's, the period when Longfellow was teaching there. In 1837 he arrived at Boston in search of a career, very much the young man from the provinces. New England in those days was still a good deal what it had been from the beginning, a social, geographical, and cultural entity whose center was Boston. The other states were still, as they had always been, moral dependencies of Massachusetts; Boston was to John Andrew's Maine what it had been two decades earlier to Daniel Webster's New Hampshire, a beacon drawing the young men of talent from the hinterlands. Andrew read law with Henry Fuller and was admitted to the Suffolk bar in 1840. He was a man of sunny disposition but with great reserves of vitality—"a warm heart but a cool head," as Samuel Bowles said of him in later life.[2]

In view of the times, and considering the thin state of high culture prevailing even in New England, Andrew's strong intellectual powers were undoubtedly rescued from debilitation by his going straight into a life of affairs instead of dabbling self-consciously in what then passed for a life of thought. The man's mind operated with a special economy of its own. Not very responsive to abstractions, he was immensely responsive to the power of thought in relation to immediate problems, as it acted upon them and fastened itself about them. He had not been an exceptional student at Bowdoin—he appears to have been even a bit lazy—but his great sociability, his extraordinary facility with language, and the challenge he felt in the issues of the day, all made him an excellent debater. His law practice in the early days was modest. This was partly because much of his energy was funneled into "legal aid" problems—problems of legal assistance to people without money—and partly because he found the law, as a philosophical subject, somewhat dull. At the same time, Andrew had great powers as an advocate. His mind became fully engaged in the face of something specific, and he became a formidable trial lawyer.[3]

Like Lincoln, John Andrew found it hard to imagine working as an outsider. Individual satisfactions had little reality for him outside of a fairly complex social and institutional setting. He was much attracted by the Transcendentalists but was temperamentally unable to conceive of individual experience in quite the private purity that they did. His religious feeling, for instance, was not at all the same as that of Parker and Emerson (who attacked the church as an "ice-house, all external"); private experience for Andrew had none of the importance that a religious community had, knit together in the ceremonial of public worship which he loved. He was a member of James Freeman Clarke's congregation (it is interesting to note that Clarke was the most institution-minded of the Transcendentalist ministers); Andrew once had the occasion to say, pleading for congregational unity

[2] The major sources on Andrew's life and career are Henry Greenleaf Pearson, *The Life of John A. Andrew: Governor of Massachusetts, 1861–1865* (2 vols.; Boston: Houghton Mifflin, 1904), and the Andrew MSS at the Massachusetts Historical Society. Peleg W. Chandler, *Memoir of Governor Andrew, with Personal Reminiscences* (Boston: Roberts Bros., 1880), and Albert G. Browne, Jr., *Sketch of the Official Life of John A. Andrew . . .* (New York: Hurd & Houghton, 1868) are largely superseded by the Pearson work, though the former contains several of Andrew's addresses, and both have the text of the celebrated Valedictory Address of January 5, 1866.

[3] Pearson, *Andrew*, I, 15–22, 27–31.

in the face of a threatened schism, "I am not a come-outer. I am a stay-iner." As for the general question of ceremonial, there was something quite conscious and deliberate in Andrew's attitude here, something very different from the contempt expressed by the Transcendentalists for "vain pomps" and "empty forms." Ceremonial for John Andrew, not only in religion but in other institutional connections, was something to be appreciated not so much in terms of private satisfaction as in shared observance, in which men in the sight of other men gave deference to objects of common devotion, strengthening and reaffirming in the very process their sense of community with one another. Andrew understood with intuitive keenness this affirmative function of ritual observance, and years later, in solemn times, it was fostered with particular care by him as governor of the Commonwealth.[4]

Massachusetts had become by the 1840's the great cockpit of antislavery activity, and it never occurred to John Andrew—so finely attuned to the age—not to "go with his state." He was nothing if not a New Englander. His first entrance into politics came about the time of the Mexican War, and he associated himself with the antislavery groups then forming in New England, becoming a follower of Charles Sumner. He was subsequently on hand at the beginnings of the Republican party in Massachusetts. The fine zeal and fire of the political antislavery movement in the early fifties had no better embodiment than in such a man as Sumner; it was precisely at this time that men of Sumner's type could best serve as examples; it was then that men of his dedication, his purity of principle, and his singleness of aim were at their maximum effectiveness. The "Sumner theme" in Andrew's career might take on darker hues with the passing of time, but here it was at its brightest. And yet John Andrew could never be, even at the first, quite the man of principle that Sumner was; nor did his abolitionism ever have quite the baleful philosophical purity to be seen in that, say, of Henry Thoreau. The way Andrew used his energies in the John Brown affair was rather characteristic. Thoreau called meetings at Concord to proclaim the wrong of slavery and to bathe in the common guilt which Brown had tried to erase in blood; Andrew, in Boston and Washington, set about to save Brown's life. Although he, too, attended meetings and spoke at them with eloquence, Andrew's principal object was to organize legal assistance and to have Brown declared a victim of insanity, a thing which he had suspected of

[4] *Ibid.*, I, 31–39, 273–74.

Brown already. At the same time, Andrew's furious activity through-out the whole hopeless affair attracted much admiring attention.[5]

The first public office to which Andrew was elected came to him in 1857 when he went to the Massachusetts legislature. He was there one year, serving only a single term. But that one year was a critical one in the man's career. The new antislavery party had been somewhat sapped by the successes of the Know-Nothings, and Andrew gave it tremendous new energy and esprit, himself rising to unquestioned personal leadership in a remarkably short time. By 1860 men were saying that John Andrew was the most popular man in Massachusetts. In that same year he went to Chicago as a delegate to the Republican national convention. The Massachusetts delegation, with Andrew as spokesman, had been committed at first to Seward but changed its support to Lincoln after the third ballot; Andrew was one of the committee that subsequently went to Springfield to notify the prairie lawyer of his nomination. He came back favorably impressed. Later in the summer he himself was nominated for governor of his state, the invalided Sumner having given his candidacy some dramatic eleventh-hour assistance. The same election which made Abraham Lincoln President of the United States made John Andrew governor of Massachusetts. Andrew's election meant the political victory of antislavery in Massachusetts, just as Lincoln's election, in a dimmer way, meant the same thing to the nation at large.[6]

Few had ever seen such energy as that which animated the new governor from the moment of his inauguration. Andrew took office on January 5, 1861, ten days after the Charleston garrison had been concentrated in Fort Sumter, a month before the formation of the Confederacy at Montgomery, and two months before Lincoln assumed the presidency. From Washington, Charles Francis Adams kept Andrew posted on every move of the South (for nearly a century, Massachusetts in such times had had the services of an Adams); even on inauguration day Governor Andrew was putting his state on a war footing, having already sent couriers plunging through a snow-storm to other New England governors with messages urging that they do the same. The first major decision of the Lincoln administration was taken before it assumed office: no compromise with secession —and the clear voice of Massachusetts in pre-inauguration councils had had much to do with it. Andrew, really a born compromiser in prac-

[5] *Ibid.,* I, 40–47, 56–57, 96–111.

[6] *Ibid.,* I, 68–95, 111–29.

tice, understood that the moment had passed; he had been convinced earlier that the South would not secede, until a trip to Washington in December convinced him otherwise. But even in January, his response to Virginia's peace conference proposal was characteristic. Inclined at first to think that Massachusetts should have nothing to do with it, Andrew changed his mind at the last minute when Adams advised that failure to send commissioners might "confirm the charge of indifference which is much used against us." Sumner was profoundly offended at what he saw as Adams' willingness to subvert principle, and a lifetime friendship was thereupon broken; it is at this point, too, that the Sumner leitmotif in Andrew's life undergoes its first modulation. But Andrew wanted to be covered at both ends, and sent commissioners after all. At the same time he made very sure that they were "of the *right stamp.*"[7] He already knew, anyway, that the South was not turning back, and that secession meant war.

When the call for troops went out from the War Department, Andrew was the first of the governors to respond. Secretary Cameron wanted to send mustering officers to Boston; all Andrew wanted was his marching orders. The troops themselves had been ready for weeks. "Despatch received. By what route shall we send?" The first United States soldiers killed in Baltimore were members of the Sixth Massachusetts. Andrew became the man of action, personally overseeing an incredible range of detail as all energies were hurled into the stupendous work. His attention to particulars, his vitality, his sheer efficiency, left his associates panting. The Governor worked at all hours. He was everywhere, breathing inspiration and will into the people of the Commonwealth. From elsewhere in the North, it was as though a shower of sparks streamed forth day and night out of Massachusetts. Constituting himself, as one writer puts it, "unofficial secretary of war for New England," Andrew never hesitated to seize the initiative from others when he thought it necessary; he was constantly on the back of the War Department, lashing the unheroic Cameron with a hail of advice and suggestions. He told Cameron that the government should strengthen the defenses of Fortress Monroe and offered to send two regiments there himself. He advised protection for Harpers Ferry. He wanted an immediate increase in the arms output of the Federal arsenal at Springfield. He offered the results of experiments on a new projectile being carried on by his own staff. His impact upon the ad-

[7] W. D. Northend to William Bigler, Mar. 1, 1865, Bigler MSS, Pennsylvania Historical Society. Northend was a leader of the Democratic minority in the Massachusetts legislature in 1861, and he described in this letter how Andrew had given in. See also Pearson, *Andrew*, I, 154–56, 164.

ministration must have been quite overpowering; answering to the people for the progress of preparations must not have seemed nearly so formidable as answering to John Andrew. We see Cameron plaintively trying, late in May, to fend off the dynamic governor:

You will have no excuse to complain of the want of vigor in the prosecution of this expedition now on foot to suppress the rebellion in our Southern states. The whole power of the government, with all the resources of the Northern people united, will be used to settle the disturbing element for all time to come. I have no doubt of the result, and I feel that as the policy of the government develops itself to the public it will leave no doubt in your mind.[8]

President Lincoln himself may have felt similarly badgered a year later, for among his problems by then was that of what to do with General McClellan, commanding the Army of the Potomac. Among the leaders in the fight to get McClellan removed from that command was Governor Andrew of Massachusetts.

Such was Andrew's course throughout the war. Whenever Lincoln got into trouble with his own party, John Andrew would nearly always be in the forefront of the forces that were harassing him. But seldom was this energy irresponsibly expended. With the issue of emancipation, for instance: Andrew supported Frémont's emancipation order of August, 1861, but would not attack Lincoln when the latter repudiated Frémont. He remained silent until the spring of 1862 and then, despite his growing irritation at Lincoln's slowness, did what he could to build up emancipation sentiment, at the same time refraining from any assault upon the administration. Andrew was among the first to urge the use of Negro troops, and he later made his own Fifty-fourth Massachusetts a model regiment. The troops were carefully recruited from all over the North, and the Governor picked the officers himself, making sure that they came from the best antislavery families of Massachusetts. He took every precaution to see that the enterprise should be a success, which it was. (Indeed, for his repeated acts of personal kindness, the Governor won the devotion and loyalty of all the Massachusetts regiments; that in itself had much to do with the high élan shown by Massachusetts troops throughout the war.) By 1864 Andrew had doubts about the vigor of Lincoln's leadership and, as the nomination approached, would have preferred someone else. And yet when change did not prove feasible, Andrew threw all his support behind Lincoln's efforts for re-election. Mean-

[8] William B. Hesseltine, *Lincoln and the War Governors* (New York: Alfred A. Knopf, 1948), pp. 110–15, 148–50, 157–58, 167–68; Pearson, *Andrew*, I, 176–213 and *passim*. The quotation is from Hesseltine, p. 168.

while he worked tirelessly to prevent the least hint of negotiations, or anything short of total victory, from creeping into the Republican platform.[9]

In a word, John Andrew was always there to be reckoned with when policy was made at the national level, and he left his mark on it in overwhelming measure. Whenever there is occasion to wonder why Lincoln should have continued veering ever more in a "radical" direction, it should be remembered that the President was accommodating his course not simply to hotbloods and zealots but in a primary sense to the most dynamic wing of the Republican party. Those who gave the party that energy were men such as John Andrew, and there was nothing capricious about the way Lincoln trimmed his sails to the winds that blew hardest from such states as Massachusetts. For Lincoln knew that the "radical" tone set by the leaders in these states represented responsible sentiment, not to be sidetracked or belittled. There is in Andrew's case another reason for judging his course a responsible one, beside the fact that he acted with honor and intelligence always, voiced with fidelity the feelings of Massachusetts, and consistently delivered far more than his share to the Union effort. His experience with power (he was four times re-elected governor) had again and again taught him the meaning of conservative behavior—of respecting the limits of the possible—even while working in concert with "radical" policy. Samuel Bowles of the Springfield *Republican* had been quick to recognize this quality in Andrew, even amid the excitement of 1860: ". . . he may be hot and extreme in individual expression . . . but he feels keenly the responsibilities of power and follows kindly the conservatizing influences of position." "In respect to *principles*," Andrew himself asserted, "I am always *radical*. In respect to measures I am always conservative."[10] The beleaguered President himself could not have failed to perceive this in his loyal tormentor, the war governor of Massachusetts.

When the war ended, Andrew's mind was filled with thoughts of reconstruction. As for a proper policy, however, he would not reach a decision until after a due interlude of observation and reflection. He sensed that war and reconstruction were two problems of quite different nature; a mode of thought appropriate to the one must be altered quite deliberately to suit the other. The man's mind, ever attuned to the needs of the moment, perceived that moments did

9 Pearson, *Andrew*, I, 249–51; II, 1–10, 44–51, 71–121, 149–77.
10 *Ibid.*, I, 123–24; II, 321.

not pass so quickly now; it was not so pressing that the moment be seized before it flew away forever: there was *time*. That mind, with all its fine tautness of action, conflict, and swift decision, so responsive to all the demands of war, might now enter a mellower, a more ruminative phase. It could take hold of the more leisurely measured problems of peace and bring forth prodigies of refinement. It is at this point that John Andrew truly becomes the man of thought.

His every step was taken now with great caution and circumspection. Every utterance of any length (and there were few) would bear the deliberate marks of careful shaping for specific purposes. Andrew was conscious of his powers by 1865, fully aware of the distinction which he had brought to his own name and to that of his office. He knew that when he spoke, men everywhere in the nation listened with respect, and he would do nothing unbecoming to what he had made of his authority. Preparing to retire from the governorship at the end of the year, he had no wish for any immediate resumption of public service; but if it should appear that his influence might at some future time be of any value to the public or to the government, he would not want it already dulled by overuse. (He could not as yet know, of course, that the new government would never call upon him for anything.)

In one respect, the technique of Andrew's first step on reconstruction—his Faneuil Hall letter of June 19, 1865—was similar to that which had worked so well in his dealings with the Lincoln administration. It involved a balance, an expression of confidence and loyal support to the new President, combined with the unmistakable inference that there was anxious concern (for which he himself was prepared to vouch) over the possibility of a hasty reconstruction. Andrew had been invited to address a meeting which had been called for June 21 at Faneuil Hall, to deprecate "haste in receiving back the rebel states, before they have proved their loyalty," and to recommend the immediate extension of suffrage "to all friends of the Union irrespective of race or color." The Governor judiciously decided that it would not be convenient for him to attend and prepared a letter instead, suitable for reading before the assembly—and suitable, it need not be added, for publication throughout the country. He began by paying full deference to the objects of the meeting:

It is not my belief that in any one of the seceding states the time has yet arrived when its state government can be re-established with safety. Whether the white man only vote or whether the colored man also votes, I regard the movement at the present moment with inexpressible concern.

. . . Let us hold on to the power we now have to do right, to protect the loyal, to rebuild the state, to re-establish society, to secure the liberty of the people and the safety of the Union. Let it be used with parental kindness and in the temper of conciliation. But hold on to the power, and, in the fear of God let it be used. . . . I think the loyalty of the South needs time for concentration.

But the other half of the document gave it the balance which Andrew intended it should have, and it contained two principal thoughts. Suffrage was inevitable and right, and was therefore in no need of premature agitation. As for the judgment of the President himself, there was as yet no reason for deeming it other than sound:

. . . I think no reconstruction will be successful now, and, therefore, as a radical believer in the suffrage for all men of competent capacity, irrespective of color or national origin, I the less regret that colored men are not now permitted to vote in the South. I do not believe their voting would prevent the failure which seems most likely to result from these experiments, and we may be glad not to have them involved in the catastrophe. They will vote by and by. Their votes will be wanted just as their arms were wanted. . . .

I deeply deplore the necessity of raising of the general question of suffrage for colored men in the South thus early. I had hoped that the last vestige of heresy on that question might be first eradicated from New England, where it even now retains a foothold. . . . For one, however, I still hope and believe that there need be no strife nor angry debate. We have reached a point where temperate, philosophical, and statesmanlike treatment of grave questions has become easy, because it is of controlling and absolute necessity. . . .

Allow me to add—that in the end, although for the present it may seem otherwise to casual observation, I do not expect to find the deliberate judgment of the President, who is an able statesman and an honest patriot, differing with that of Massachusetts herself.[11]

Andrew's experiences in the summer and fall of 1865 supplied for his mind the elements still needed for a fully considered position on reconstruction. In New York and Washington during this period he had repeated occasion to meet and talk with a considerable number of planters and men of high position from the South. He was much impressed by their intelligence and reasonableness and was convinced of their willingness to deal justly with the emancipated Negro. He came to the conclusion that, for all the implacable energy with which they had carried on the rebellion, it was in the last analysis to men of this type that the North must look; it was to such hands as theirs that the North must in some way intrust the Southern end of reconstruction. Such a conclusion connected very logically in Andrew's mind

11 New York *World*, June 23, 1865; Pearson, *Andrew*, II, 263–65.

with an undertaking then being planned by himself and Frank Howe —an enterprise which combined business and benevolent purposes. Through the "American Land Company and Agency," organized in September, Andrew and his associates hoped to establish a brokerage house for Northern businessmen seeking to invest money in Southern agriculture, and to provide for hard-pressed Southern planters a source of needed capital for getting back into production. The latter function, together with the possibility of taking up idle cotton lands and disposing of them to Negroes and poorer whites, inspired Andrew for a time with high hopes that enough economic leverage might thus be organized to make a real difference both in rebuilding the South and in improving the condition of the freedmen. What all this added up to was the conviction, by then fairly well settled in his mind, that neither political nor economic reconstruction in the South could realistically be hoped for or undertaken without the good faith and participation of the South's most influential men.[12]

It is about at this point that the "Sumner theme" in Andrew's life undergoes virtual eclipse, never fully to re-emerge. One cannot say whether the coolness that fell upon them here could be called more his or Sumner's doing, though in any case there was nothing mean in it; it was a development long inherent in the two men's careers. Andrew's had reached something of a pinnacle; Sumner's moment of greatness now lay somewhere in the past. But more than anything else, here were two men who, though united in bonds of rectitude, were infinitely separated in mind and temperament. Their paths had merged, and in many ways had run parallel, during the intense antislavery times. Yet the circumstances which had formed them left very different marks.

Charles Sumner, having been reared in a Boston household of some refinement, was no child of the New England countryside and no real Yankee. At Harvard his diligence in study was unsurpassed, and such was his mastery of the classics of jurisprudence that Joseph Story once expressed the hope that his own professorship in that subject might some day fall to the young Sumner. As a practitioner of law, however, Sumner had little skill. His mind would often be diverted during the presentation of a case, and he would be drawn into speculative discourses bearing little upon matters at hand. He was primarily a literary jurist, with a deep penchant for the abstract. (Once in an article that dealt with the seven law journals then published in America, he took

---

[12] *Ibid.*, pp. 266–69.

up a dozen metaphysical pages on the occult properties of the number "seven.") In his late twenties he made a trip to England, visiting many distinguished houses and meeting many notable personages; he made many friends and enjoyed a great success. The English themselves were not quite sure why, for he had no wit, no small talk, no stories, and no brilliance of conversation. But his deportment was apparently grave and courteous; he made no mistakes, bore marks of cultivation, and was versed in the classics. Few Americans of that sort ever visited England in those days.[13]

He was a young man of spotless idealism, tall, of noble and inspiring mien. In 1845 he was asked to speak at a Fourth of July celebration, replete with the pageantry and military ceremonial appropriate to such an affair. He spoke in empyrean cadences of the vanity of arms and the wickedness of war, blissfully innocent of any wish to offend. He found his true calling at last in the crusade against slavery. Life itself gave him few joys; in principles he found all. The antislavery movement drew forth from Charles Sumner his maximum powers; of that which he had, he gave everything. He took part as a "Conscience Whig" in the Free-Soil campaign of 1848, and although he had no taste or liking for politics, he attracted wide attention through his zeal and attained prominence in spite of himself. He took no pleasure in being elected to Webster's Senate seat in 1851 and went to Washington inspired only by duty. There, he defied the slave power, as Carl Schurz observed many years later, "with an almost childlike audacity," throwing the Southern members into fits of rage. It may have been his classical but elephantine metaphors, as much as anything, that goaded Preston Brooks into beating him senseless with his cane after the "Crime against Kansas" speech in 1856. He was transfigured before the Northern public, however, in temporary martyrdom. Sumner's hatred of war was set aside with the outbreak of the rebellion. The nation had entered a holy war for universal rights, and while passion was at its hottest, Charles Sumner brought forth his recon-

[13] The material on Charles Sumner is very rich, thanks to Sumner's own meticulousness in the preservation of his papers, deposited at the Harvard Library, and to the efforts of his friend, literary executor, and biographer, Edward L. Pierce, whose *Memoir and Letters of Charles Sumner* (Boston: Roberts Bros., 1877–93), in four volumes, is still the standard work. The completeness plus the unusual scholarly apparatus which characterizes the Pierce biography have enabled it to outlast several subsequent efforts. It is shortly due to be superseded, however, by the eagerly awaited definitive work by David Donald, as yet, unfortunately, unavailable at the time of this writing. Carl Schurz, *Charles Sumner: An Essay*, ed. Arthur Reed Hogue (Urbana: University of Illinois Press, 1951), is full of insights. It should be added that Sumner's *Works* (15 vols.; Boston: Lee & Shepard, 1870–82) is, for completeness and care of annotation, likewise a model for its time.

struction doctrine, "state suicide." Once formulated, there was nothing that could happen before his eyes—even the coming of peace—to affect the doctrine or induce him to alter it.

Few Northerners really had much luck understanding Charles Sumner; to Southerners, he was beyond comprehension. History itself has been wanting in justice to the man. To select standards which do not somehow pass him by is difficult, even baffling. Much has been said, for instance, of Sumner's vanity—which was magnificent but not really very personal, not even too earthly in fact, for there was a naïve incapacity in him to envy others. His delight at praise of himself was so transparent as to be beyond suspicion. His dogmatism was so perfect that anyone could see what his theory of truth was: truth and right, once received, were changeless and ageless. He was so devoid of humor as to excite pity, as we pity one who has never known the qualities of sight, sound, color, or smell. All in all, the likeliest key to Charles Sumner may be that he was in all ways, and to a degree well beyond the understanding of ordinary men, a truly abstract person. With certain fleshly capacities withdrawn from him—abstracted, as it were, from his being—and with duty and honor, principle and rectitude, as his only remaining passions, the result of such a remarkable rearrangement of human attributes was a kind of prodigy. He could resist all the lures and byways which make most decisions so complicated and so cluttered; here, embodied in a man, was the meaning of "incorruptible." He had none of the sly subtlety that warns other men not to identify truth and justice too closely with their own personalities; in this respect Sumner was really quite simple and classical: there was little else that he *could* represent. Carl Schurz's tribute is the more affecting in that Schurz, in his estimates of others, was seldom disposed to extravagance:

His personal and official integrity stood so high above all suspicion that even the bitterest spirit of partisan hostility never dared to question it. Whatever criticism his constitutional doctrines or his views of policy may have called for, nobody ever doubted the sincerity of his convictions or the disinterestedness of his motives. Never was there a calculating thought in his mind as to how the utterance of his opinions might affect his fortunes as a public man. Without the slightest hesitation he would set his convictions of right and duty against any adverse current of sentiment in his party, or among his constituents, or even among his intimate friends. He would have considered it a desecration of his high office to descend to any of the arts of the demagogue or the wirepuller, for the purpose of strengthening his personal following; nor would he ever solicit any one to vote for him when his seat in the Senate was at stake. In every sense he towered grandly above the ordinary run of politicians.[14]

[14] Schurz, *Sumner*, pp. 80–81.

In short, Sumner having few of the personal needs that most men have, it was the more important not to trifle with those that remained: to trifle with Sumner's principles was to trifle with *him*. It was this, for instance, that made it not only possible but necessary for him on various occasions to renounce long-standing friendships. All of which has more than a little bearing on what was ultimately bound to come between Sumner and John Andrew. For by 1865 it had come down to the question, with neither of them quite realizing it, of which of the two was to speak for Massachusetts on reconstruction.

One wonders if Andrew knew, when he specifically attacked "state suicide"—as he had earlier in the year and would again later[15]—that it would be the beginning of the end with him and Sumner. "State suicide," in principle, did not depart drastically from the views he himself was shortly to offer. But we may suppose that Andrew was concerned somewhat less with principle than with style. He did know, as did everyone else, that principle, for Sumner, could not be altered by the developments of day to day (Schurz thought that Sumner, on questions of right and wrong, would rather consult the heroes of Plutarch than his own contemporaries); Andrew in 1865 was laboring to remove the theme of implacability from Massachusetts doctrines and to replace it with flexibility. A further stab for Sumner must have come on November 7 when Governor Parsons of Alabama spoke at the Union Club in Boston soliciting a loan for his state. Sumner's reply to Parsons was a declaration of the rigid terms which he thought should be imposed upon the South prior to readmission, whereupon Andrew, who was also present, came to Parsons' defense. The two men engaged in spirited debate. A note from Sumner a few weeks later is written in the third person and shows the chill that had by then fallen over the old association. We hear the last echo in a letter written the following year by Sumner to their mutual friend F. W. Bird. Schemes had by then been set afoot to press Andrew for Sumner's Senate seat, an episode in which both men acted with honor. Andrew would have no part in it, and Sumner, in his letter, reaffirms the affection and respect of many years and adds that he would be happy to stand aside should Andrew ever desire his place. That final effort must have consumed the last spark that still glowed, for that was about where matters came to rest between the two foremost statesmen of Massachusetts.[16]

We are thus brought to the full development of Andrew's thinking on reconstruction. Its outlines are to be found in one of his last letters to Sumner and in a letter to Hermann Bokum, both

---

15 Pearson, *Andrew*, II, 261, 277–78.   16 *Ibid.*, II, 272–76, 315–17.

written in November, 1865, while the Governor turned over in his mind the things he planned to say in his Valedictory, to be delivered the first week in January. To Sumner, he concedes the existence in the South of evil designs upon the Negro and declares that Northern influence and Northern ideas must surely be brought to bear upon Southern society. But he also insists, "The educated most enlightened and superior persons of the South have a strong tendency *now* toward the right side." As for the Freedmen's Bureau, Andrew regards it as an indispensable agency which must be strengthened and sustained to prevent demoralization among the Negroes (he had said as much to the President the week before). He restates the position he had taken in his Faneuil Hall letter on the readmission of congressmen—that such readmission should be deferred pending full reorganization and that confidence in the President's good intentions should prevail in the meantime, even though the latter's present "experiment" showed all signs of failure. Finally: "The right position for New England is one of friendliness, not of antagonism. In taking the latter we are defeated, —in the former we shall win."[17]

To Bokum, he is more specific on the problem of Southern leadership. "The most hopeful and reliable men I meet are the active men accustomed to business, owning plantations, men of education & culture, and Rebel officers of rank. Those have brains enough to understand and manliness enough to admit and accommodate themselves to the new position." These are the men whom the government will have to use, though they should be neither overworked nor tied down. The present leaders, not being the natural ones, are timid and do not enjoy the people's confidence. "And they must do what not even the best leaders *could* well do, with no *proper fire on their rear* to hold them up to the work; meanwhile the most important forces in Southern society are neutralized." It should be made clear to the true leaders just what the North requires, and what they themselves have to convince the Southern people of. "A rebel vote is the best of all, if it is only cast in the right way." If the people vote in the *wrong* way, "then they are not prepared in their minds for reconstruction."[18]

On January 5, 1866, John Andrew delivered his Valedictory Address on the occasion of his retirement from the governorship. The address was devoted entirely to the subject of reconstruction. The question we are bound to ask as we read this document today is: Why did Andrew's Valedictory not become one of the really eminent state

[17] Andrew to Sumner, Nov. 21, 1865, Sumner MSS; Pearson, *Andrew*, II, 273–75.

[18] Andrew to H. Bokum, Nov. 30, 1865, Andrew MSS; Pearson, *Andrew*, II, 270–71.

papers of the nineteenth century? It is certainly the work of a mind worth celebrating. Why is it not still quoted as one of the distinguished examples of political thought produced by Americans in response to crisis? The only answer, as we look forward to carpetbag reconstruction and backward to the North Carolina proclamation, is itself best phrased as a further question: What had happened to the setting in which a man of such influence in the war crisis should see his influence —and that of others like him—go for so little in the peace crisis? That would be just one more way of phrasing the leading question of the whole 1865–66 period of presidential reconstruction. Thus if we were disposed to imagine a different course, a clear alternative to that which was taken, John Andrew's Valedictory would have to constitute our primary text.[19]

The Valedictory deserves the closest analysis for what it contains and represents. In it, the retiring statesman brings all his experience and all his resources into the effort to discover anything that might exist, in the nation's experience and habits of self-government, which might in any way bear on problems essentially without precedent. It is not, for the times and for the purpose, a long document; nor are there many words in it that refer to or deal with eternal principles. But it does contain brief analyses, in succession, of every problem pertinent to the immediate subject. In it, the Governor considers the status of the Southern states, what those states should be required to do, the meaning of a "popular vote," the nature of leadership, Negro suffrage, who "the people" are, what the President's policy has been, and what should be done in case current measures be found inadequate.

On the legal condition of the revolted states, Andrew sets forth, in cleaner and more succinct language, what was later to reappear elsewhere as the Chase-Shellabarger theory of reconstruction.[20] Andrew's "theory" is in one sense a deprecation of theory, for in denying the more picturesque positions—"state suicide" and "conquered provinces"—on the one hand, and appropriating on the other hand some of their salient features, he both softens and absorbs most of the pertinent thought on reconstruction then extant, not excluding that of the President. The states did not commit suicide, nor did they become territories; the power to end their lives or to make them other than states does not reside either in the states themselves or in the national government, save by changing the Constitution. But their condition

[19] The text of the address is to be found in Chandler, *Memoir*, pp. 239–98, and Browne, *Sketch*, pp. 167–211.

[20] Cf. above, pp. 113 ff.

now is most assuredly not what it was. "They did not revert by their rebellion, nor by our conquest, into 'Territories.' They did not commit suicide. But they rebelled, they went to war; and they were *conquered*."

Who shall fix their status now, and by what authority? This would have been settled, had they prevailed in arms, by their own acts of secession and by something in the nature of a peace treaty. As matters stand, it is for the federal government to say. The authority for doing so is twofold: the laws and rights of war ("The first duty of the Nation is to regain its own *power*"), and the nation's constitutional guarantee to each state of a republican form of government. How shall we know when these things have been accomplished? The state of war will continue in some way

until a peaceful, loyal and faithful state of mind gains a sufficient ascendancy in the rebel and belligerent States, to enable the Union and loyal citizens everywhere to repose alike on the purpose and ability of their people, in point of numbers and capacity, to assert, maintain and conduct State Governments, republican in form, loyal in sentiment and character, with safety to themselves and to the national whole.

Until this is clear, some form at least of the Union's belligerent rights must remain. But the conditions should not be left to chance; they must not be ambiguous:

It is absolutely necessary . . . for the Union Government to prescribe some reasonable test of loyalty to the people of the States in rebellion. It is necessary to require of them conformity to those arrangements which the war has rendered, or proved to be, necessary to the public peace, and necessary as securities for the future. As the conquering party, the National Government has the right to govern these belligerent States meanwhile, at its own wise and conscientious discretion. . . .

Who shall be the arbiter? There is none, "save the people of the United States."

Such, at the outset, is Andrew's "theoretical" basis for reconstruction. Nowhere thus far has he referred to the Executive pardoning power; only once, later on, does he even mention it, and then only in passing. The pardoning of individuals is not considered more than a minor incident ("artificial rules"); it has little or nothing to do with the reconstructing of states. In short, Andrew would have said, in this first section, had he chosen to employ the terminology of "pardoning," that whatever the process were called, the whole North would have to "pardon" the whole South before there could be peace.

He then specifies exactly what he thinks the states should be required to do and what he thinks would satisfy the North. They should reform their constitutions,

1. Guaranteeing to the people of color, now the wards of the Nation, their civil rights as men and women, on an equality with the white population, by amendments, irrepealable in terms.
2. Regulating the elective franchise according to certain laws of universal application, and not by rules merely arbitrary, capricious and personal.
3. Annulling the ordinances of Secession.
4. Disaffirming the Rebel Debt, and
5. To ratify the anti-slavery amendment of the United States Constitution by their legislatures.

These conditions, Andrew thinks, should be ratified by a popular vote. By this he does not simply mean "what is termed the 'loyal vote' "; he is concerned with the "rebel vote," which he knows means a majority of the people. The war, for the South, was "a *great popular revolution*" which public opinion favored, to which the people gave all, and in which they acquitted themselves with courage. It will not do to set up distinctions between the people and their natural leaders, and to make one rule for rich rebels and another for poor rebels. The poorer and less powerful were just as disloyal, and hated Yankees and abolitionists just as ardently, as the richer and more powerful. True, there were exceptions. The Negroes were loyal to the Union, and their loyalty was based on the expectation of freedom (such freedom, thus, had to be included in the "loyal" idea "if the Union could be saved, or served, by it"). There were those, moreover, who were not prepared for the responsibility of war against the Union. ("But they were not the positive men. . . . The Revolution either converted them or swept them off their feet.") There were those whites, of course, who did stand fast throughout. All honor to them, asserts the Governor, but a distinction now between them and the rest could have little practical purpose: the North must proceed on the assumption that a majority of any popular vote would consist of men once disloyal. Andrew is concerned primarily with majorities. In short, "the rebel vote is better than the loyal vote, if on the right side." The North hopes for the reorganization of the states and desires an end to the use of the war power. However:

If it [the vote] is not on the right side, then I fear those States are incapable at present of re-organization; the proper power of the Union Government is not restored; the people of those States are not yet prepared to assume their original functions with safety to the Union; and the state of war still exists, for they are contumacious and disobedient to the just demands of the Union, disowning the just conditions precedent to re-organization.

Andrew now makes certain remarks on the nature of leadership, based on his own experience and what he has seen of Southern men since the war—assertions which he has already made in the letters to Sumner and Bokum. "The capacity of leadership is a gift, not a device. They whose courage, talents, and will entitle them to lead, will lead." The foremost public men in the South (in a word, men of the governing class) are still the ones who will have to guide the people back to the Union. No one knows what they can do, but no choice exists for the North but to try them. Those with the courage and judgment necessary for leading the people in a wrong cause are the ones most able and likely to lead them in a right one. Weak men, with less hold on the public confidence (e.g., the "Ten Per Centers"), are powerless to do what has to be done. But the strong men will not stay rooted in the past, or in an institution that they know is dead.

Negro suffrage, which in some form is one of the requirements Andrew deems indispensable, now becomes itself the subject of certain observations. Would it be wise to put this into effect in advance, in order to have the Negro vote in the reorganization? It would be wiser to have the Negro vote conferred by the rebel vote: the question here becomes as much one of statesmanship as of law; the Union desires justice but not chaos and violence. But does the conferral of suffrage thereby become an exclusive and untouchable right of the states? No: the Union is still not dealing with fully reorganized states, but with conquered states. If emancipation could be one of the incidents of conquest, so also may enfranchisement. As for specific suffrage qualifications, a certain latitude should be permitted. A perfectly reasonable test is literacy, but the test should be universally applied. In any case, without such stipulations for the freedmen, the guarantee of a republican form of government will not have been met. Congress must deal with the whole people, and Congress, now seeing new people with new rights, must have the power to stipulate for them too, if it is not to abandon the power to carry out its guarantee. The nation cannot pretend to have governments fully republican in both form and substance "unless it can look all the *people* in the face, and declare that it has kept its promise with them all."

The Governor now with infinite tact proceeds to say what he takes to have been the course of President Johnson up to that moment. Knowing the wishes of his audience, it is as though his greatest care is to interpret the President's intentions at all points in such a light as to deprecate any likelihood of conflict: it is as though such likelihood has never been allowed to invade his mind. All doors to harmony remain as widely open as ever, and his courtesy borders almost on blandness as he says of the President,

He seems to me to have left to Congress alone the questions controlling the conditions on which the rebel States shall resume their representative power in the Federal Government. It was not incumbent on the President to do otherwise. He naturally leaves the duty of theoretical reasoning to those whose responsibility it is to reach the just practical conclusion.

Andrew prefers to regard the President not primarily as the fountain-head of pardon, but as the commander-in-chief, perfectly justified in acting on his own discretion in the absence of positive law. He might have governed by wholly military methods if necessary, and that itself would have been proper (though the unnecessary oppression of an enemy is unjust); as it is, he has actually helped the people reorganize local government. Here, too, he has acted judiciously; "though his method may be less regular than if an act of Congress had prescribed it, still, it has permitted the people to feel their way back into the works and ways of loyalty, to exhibit their temper of mind, and to 'show their hands.' " It proves the government is not "drunk with power."

But the hard, thin line of warning once more shows itself amid the amiable construction which Andrew puts upon the President's acts. Though the states now have their elected legislatures, and though the state seals are now in the hands of elected governors, none of this means that the commander-in-chief has abdicated; his generals are still in the field. What will he do now? That will depend upon what the people of those states do, or fail to do; and in any event, Andrew "assumes"

that, until the executive and legislative departments of the national government shall have reached the *united* conclusion that the objects of the *war* have been fully accomplished, the national declaration of *peace* is not, and cannot be made.

The acts of the drama so far have not gone for nothing, and the Governor does not presume to criticize them. But they are not the whole drama: there are more acts to come. What shall they be? That cannot be decided without the assistance of Congress.

Should any of these various measures prove somehow "impracticable," then Congress still has the right to refuse readmission until appropriate amendments to the Federal Constitution have been passed (the Southern people could hardly object; they, in their own chosen time, broke the original compact); the states, if need be, can wait. After certain warnings about the right and wrong ways to reapportion the South's representation,[21] Andrew now directly addresses his own state:

21 "The scheme to substitute legal voters, instead of population, as the basis of representation in Congress, will prove a delusion and a snare. By diminishing the representative power of the Southern States, in favor of other States, you will not

We might wish it were possible for Massachusetts justly to avoid her part in the work of *political* reorganization. But, in spite of whatever misunderstanding of her purpose or character, she must abide her destiny. She is part of the nation.

Then, quoting Lincoln's "malice toward none" peroration, the retiring Governor takes his leave.

The disillusionment of John Andrew, private citizen, came painfully soon. He spent the critical weeks of late February and early March, 1866, in Washington. There, he saw everyone of consequence—friends of the President, influential Southerners, and members of Congress. By then it had become very clear that the President regarded his own policy, formulated long before, as definitive and final; by then, the inevitable rupture between him and Congress had taken place. All was confusion and uncertainty.

Andrew had little choice but to look matters full in the face, and to reappraise them now for what they were. He saw a total failure of confidence among Northern businessmen and other public men with regard to future prospects in the South, now in so unsettled a state. While still declining, in a letter to Frank Howe, to judge the wisdom of Johnson's policy, he recognized that that policy meant among other things the end of present hopes for the Land Company. Moreover, a profound change had come over the Southerners themselves. The same men who had seemed so reasonable the summer before were now intransigent; they were convinced by this time "that the rebellious South is mistress of the situation."

Last May such men contemplated the early enjoyment of political rights by the colored freedmen. But now the same men resist and resent the bare idea of the protection of the civil or human rights of the same freedmen by national legislation. They declare, and I find many Northern men expect, that our Government will soon receive Senators and Representatives from all the Rebel States, will withdraw nearly all the troops, will curtail the action of the officers of the Freedmen's Bureau; will leave the colored man, loyal emigrants from the North, and the few constantly loyal whites of the South, to the substantial government and control of the "reconstructed" Rebels. With this idea prevailing, there is little hope of our procuring investments to be made in the South,—certainly not for the present.[22]

----

increase Southern love for the Union. Nor, while Connecticut and Wisconsin refuse the suffrage to men of color, will you be able to convince the South that your amendment was dictated by political principle, and not by political cupidity." On this point see also below, pp. 332–33, 336–38.

[22] Andrew to Frank Howe, Mar. 10, 1866, Andrew MSS; Pearson, *Andrew*, II, 314–15.

In March, 1866, Andrew was pressed by Montgomery Blair and Francis P. Blair, Sr., to preside at a Johnson meeting to be held in Boston, the purpose of which was to denounce Sumner and Stevens and rally support to the President's cause. Andrew's gentle but decisive rebuff to the Blairs was a second valedictory to public life. The country, as he saw it, was unanimous in its conviction that the South could not come back without certain arrangements made necessary by the rebellion. Since the President and Congress had apparently not disagreed on that much, in principle, then no man had the right to dogmatize and impose his own personality on a mere difference of method. "Now, if one set of men get up meetings for Paul, another set will get up meetings for Apollos. The result will be, antagonism, not patriotism, and the intensifying, and exaggerating the importance and value of the relatively unimportant, chance utterances of individuals in controversial moods, which ought, if possible, to be forgotten." Congress, now deliberating on a policy, must take longer than the President took to arrive at his ("He had only to agree with himself"); meanwhile, Andrew saw no good whatever coming from anything he himself might do. The important thing above all else was Northern unity. "While the congressional debate is going on, therefore, *I*, for one, desire not to encourage popular excitement, most of all not to aid in making any. I desire not to act at all, in political, still less, in partizan ways. . . ."[23]

In 1867 the Blairs were still, as ever, busily at work. They were urging a reform of Johnson's cabinet, as they had done unremittingly from the moment of Johnson's accession two years before. John Andrew would be an excellent choice, they thought, for Secretary of State. The President, however, "could not see the point," though he later admitted that either Andrew or Oliver P. Morton (the war governor of Indiana) "would have been a tower of strength."[24] Neither man, by then, would have dreamed of accepting such a place. But that little incident may still serve as a symbol of a hundred lost opportunities.

John Andrew himself, by 1867, had resumed a law practice which had grown most lucrative. The state of his health, though it had given his family and friends moments of concern, did not seem alarming;

23 Andrew to F. P. Blair, Sr., Mar. 18, 1866; F. P. Blair, Sr., to Andrew, Mar. 11, 1866; Montgomery Blair to Andrew, Mar. 13, 1866, Andrew MSS; Pearson, *Andrew*, II, 311–13.

24 Benjamin C. Truman, "Anecdotes of Andrew Johnson," *Century*, LXXXV (January, 1913), 438–39.

while he was not then engaged actively in politics, he was not by any means committed, at forty-nine, to staying out of public life forever. Indeed, we see him in September of that year discreetly assisting in some of the Republicans' election efforts in the Southern states; he is praising the "patriotic fidelity" of General Grant ("pure gold, no political trickster nor self-seeker"); and he appears not at all unresponsive to political movements being made in his own behalf by others. He deplores the talk, now current everywhere, of impeaching President Johnson. Still, he is not sorry that the President's behavior has prolonged Southern restoration. "If it takes a state as long to work its way back as it spent in trying to fight its way out, I do not think it can grumble much about it."[25] What John Andrew's own plans may have been, as he followed the fortunes of his party, we cannot know, for on October 29 he suffered a sudden stroke of apoplexy, and died the following day.

II   WADE HAMPTON, ARISTOCRAT

One of John Andrew's insights had been that the peace eventually to be made between North and South must be more than a military peace. It must be a peace between two peoples whose respective leadership would have been more or less in the thick of things from the very beginning—first in war and first in peace, as it were; the leaders in the one were the likeliest to become leaders in the other. The North must have an understanding with the South through the South's men of influence, and this would of course require private arrangements with persons who had the power to carry out their end of them. A great deal would depend upon terms which were clear enough and free enough from ambiguity that things might proceed— once they were understood—simply on the assumption of the word and integrity of honorable men.

The third Wade Hampton, grandee of South Carolina—the man who had been Lee's chief of cavalry—was exactly the type that Andrew had in mind. There is no record of their ever having met. But if they had, we might at least imagine that as men of affairs, as men of great authority and great influence, and as gentlemen, they would have understood each other. Each knew exactly what the war had meant for his side, and if a real settlement were to be made, it would have to be mediated through all that these two men between them represented. These two embodied, in the most reasonable and *negotiable* form, the range of opposites that somehow had to be brought to-

[25] Pearson, *Andrew*, II, 317–23; Andrew to John Binney, Sept. 10, 1867, *ibid.*, p. 320.

gether. Here was the quintessence of North and South: the best that Massachusetts and South Carolina could produce. Wade Hampton, in 1865, like John Andrew, was looking for a settlement. Hampton may somehow serve as the opposite number for Andrew in a kind of allegory of peacemaking—one which must remain, unfortunately, no more than an allegory.

Wade Hampton III was born in 1818, the same year as John Andrew. He was born into authority, in all the ways that counted most. He was the eldest son of an eldest son, heading the third generation of one of the South's wealthiest families. His grandfather had been a lieutenant colonel of cavalry in the Revolution—later, for a time, brigadier general in the United States Army—and by the end of the eighteenth century had through his own enterprise accumulated a fortune in Carolina cotton. He also extended his holdings into the Gulf lands of Louisiana and Mississippi. He served two terms in Congress. The second Wade Hampton served as a staff officer with the rank of colonel under Andrew Jackson in the War of 1812. He built Millwood, the great family estate in South Carolina; there he bred fine racing horses and collected one of the finest private libraries—about 10,000 volumes—then known. He was something of a Warwick in South Carolina politics, seldom serving publicly but exercising great unofficial influence. Many distinguished Americans visited Millwood while his eldest son was growing up.

The third Wade Hampton was trained from the very first on the assumption that he would some day inherit the vast family properties. He was educated at South Carolina College in the 1830's—while LeConte, Lieber, and Thomas Cooper were all there—during that institution's most enlightened period. As a student he was competent but apparently not exceptional. He studied law as part of his preparation for both politics and business affairs, though his chief outside interests in those days were probably riding and hunting. He married young, and his own first son was christened Wade. Under the guidance of his father he gradually assumed the management of the estates. A few years after his first wife died, he married Mary McDuffie, daughter of the former governor and senator, George McDuffie. Hampton was an Episcopalian churchman, prominent in the affairs of Trinity parish, to whose founding his grandfather had been an important contributor.

Wade Hampton was elected to the South Carolina legislature in 1852, where he served two terms in the lower house, thereupon going into the state senate. His politics, in view of the reigning tone of the fifties in South Carolina, were moderate. There was much talk in those years of reopening the slave trade, a proposition which Hampton flatly opposed as un-Christian. He had often, like Jefferson, spoken of his hatred of slavery in principle, and in the exemplary treatment of his own slaves he was something of a model for the antebellum South. He conceded the constitutional "right" of secession but urged his fellow legislators not to resort to it. He was absent in Mississippi when South Carolina seceded; he received the news with no pleasure, and regarded Governor Pickens as rather a fool, having already said so on more than one occasion. But when his state went, Hampton promptly offered his services, and was commissioned a colonel.

In his personality, Wade Hampton represented a type which is extinct today, having largely gone out of existence about two generations ago, and being, therefore, somewhat difficult to re-create and appreciate now. It was not a "democratic" type at all, nor was it quite that of the European aristocrat: the gentry of the antebellum South, flourishing amid a growing democratic culture, was, to say the least, *sui generis*. In character, Hampton reminds us a little of George Washington. He was so situated and so trained from infancy to habits of responsibility for the lives of large numbers of people that he could not properly be said to have had much of a private "self." He was accused by some, whose own station in life was a good deal more fluid, of haughtiness. But it would doubtless be better to assume that that aspect of him which was "public"—belonging, as it were, to others—was featured by correctness, great reserve, and sound judgment. It was perhaps no paradox that the habit of command—or, more accurately, of obedience—was a habit which made possible a soft-spoken courtesy and an unfailing consideration for his hundreds of dependents, both white and black. For there was no question, as would be the case with men more commonly situated, of his possessing great power; he was free at any point to be concerned instead with the responsible way of using it. In his personal habits he was abstemious; he was not a dandy in dress, and he shrank from any personal ostentation: these were things that his very position rendered unnecessary. He was tall, robust, handsome, tremendously strong, and a superlative sportsman. The hospitality at Millwood, with its parks and groves, great library, fine horses, and choice cellar, was magnificent. But here, by the same token, were things which he did not need to act out in his every *personal* gesture—they were simply there: they were his, and everyone knew it. Everything in his background, which was actually one of great depth, conspired to make Wade Hampton a reasonable man; the functioning side of what was once rather accurately called "breeding" decreed that he should be one who deplored excesses of almost every sort. Even excessive praise disturbed him. Perhaps he had his foibles, but his latest biographer has not been able to discover them. It is sociologically quite possible that Hampton himself could not afford very many. Actually, it may be just as well to accept Wade Hampton pretty much on the terms in which history brings him to us: as a man who did everything his culture asked of him and who deserved, for the most part, that which he became in the annals of South Carolina, a legendary and heroic figure.[26]

Hampton in war made as solid a record of distinction as any commander of the Confederate army. At the beginning of the war he organized, largely at his own expense, "Hampton's Legion"—six companies of infantry, four troops of cavalry, and a battery of artillery—for which the young men of South Carolina's best families volunteered with enthusiasm. He led it with merit at the first battle of Bull Run. He was made a brigadier during the Peninsular Campaign, and a major

[26] C. Vann Woodward, in his *Origins of the New South,* has expressed the opinion that Wade Hampton could still use a biography, despite the fact that various phases of the man's career have been treated at fair length by a number of writers. The question of just what ought to characterize the over-all attitude from which such a work would be written—or even whether it ought to be written by a Southerner—the present writer does not presume to pass upon. At the same time, one cannot help noticing several sorts of attitudes throughout the work on Hampton that is available, attitudes sufficiently idiosyncratic as to make one wonder if any one of them would be fully trustworthy as a guide through all of Hampton's life and the culture and traditions he represented. The most complete, and probably the most serviceable, is Manly Wade Wellman, *Giant in Gray: A Biography of Wade Hampton of South Carolina* (New York: Charles Scribner's Sons, 1949), but the book is unfortunately marred by a lost-cause sentimentalism which in the long run does a disservice to the author's very worthy subject. Hampton Jarrell, *Wade Hampton and the Negro* (Columbia: University of South Carolina Press, 1949), deals with the post–Civil War phase of Hampton's public life. It is a very humane Southerner's effort to be fair on the perennial Negro problem, and to exhibit the Hampton version of *noblesse oblige* as a conservative model for Southern conduct in race relations. On the other hand, William Arthur Sheppard, *Red Shirts Remembered: Southern Brigadiers of the Reconstruction Period* (Atlanta: Ruralist Press, 1940) is an account of the same period from a violently anti-aristocratic, redneck viewpoint. In it, Sheppard abuses Hampton for his efforts to thwart and soften the popular impulse toward "redemption" on a full white-supremacy basis in South Carolina. Alfred B. Williams, *Hampton and His Red Shirts: South Carolina's Deliverance in 1876* (Charleston: Walker, Evans & Cogswell, 1935) is a very lively and detailed series of recollections by a South Carolina newspaperman covering the 1876 campaign. The technique is that of straight reporting, and the author's assumption is the simple and limited one that Hampton's principal function was ridding South Carolina of Negro and carpetbag rule. In addition to these works, there are several dealing with Hampton's military career, outstanding among which are: Douglas S. Freeman, *Lee's Lieutenants: A Study in Command* (3 vols.; New York: Charles Scribner's Sons, 1942–44); Edward L. Wells, *Hampton and His Cavalry in '64* (Richmond: B. F. Johnson, 1899); Frank M. Myers, *The Comanches: A History of White's Battalion . . .* (Baltimore: Kelly, Piet, 1871); John Esten Cooke, *Wearing of the Gray . . .* (New York: E. B. Treat, 1867); and "Sketches of Hampton's Cavalry," in Ulysses R. Brooks (ed.), *Stories of the Confederacy* (Columbia: State Co., 1912).

general after Gettysburg. In July, 1864, he was placed in full command of Lee's cavalry, and in January, 1865, he was commissioned a lieutenant general. He fought with the Army of Northern Virginia until early in 1865, when he was transferred to South Carolina to aid in resisting the advance of Sherman. He was wounded five times. In the fighting before Petersburg in 1864, Hampton saw his son Preston—then serving on his staff—shot down in battle, and he held the boy in his arms while he died.[27]

Hampton's attributes as a commander were not drawn from prior military experience, for he had had none; unlike most of Lee's top officers he was without benefit of professional training. Being in his middle forties, moreover, he was older than most other cavalry leaders. He had none of the love of battle that "Jeb" Stuart had; Stuart's flamboyancy, dash, and visions of glory found little counterpart in Wade Hampton. But Hampton's qualities of unostentatious courage, easy judgment, and instinctive leadership of men, all flowed into his earliest battle experiences in such a way as to bring him a competence and distinction which grew as the war went on. He took risks when necessary, but always so employed his forces as to get the most possible advantage out of every operation. He was peculiarly sensitive, above all, to the cost in lives of everything he did; he tried, whenever possible, to put every man he had at the point of operation. "The advantage of this style of generalship was soon apparent," one of his officers later wrote, "for while under Stuart stampedes were frequent, with Hampton they were unknown, and the men of his corps soon had the same unwavering confidence in him that the 'Stonewall Brigade' entertained for *their* general."[28] Wade Hampton was the natural cavalry commander for 1864; the period of his independent command, from July, 1864, to April, 1865, was not a time for bravado. He had, moreover, come fully into his own by then as a seasoned professional soldier.

Hampton's military career brought the marked paternal qualities of his character to a kind of fruition. From earliest youth he had been expected to assume responsibility—a responsibility on which many lives depended—and it had been quite natural, a number of years before when his own father died, that he should have written to his unmarried sisters to say that he must now become their father as well as their brother. He accepted his role as military commander in much the same way. Every description of Hampton in wartime shows him as the

[27] Wellman, *Giant in Gray*, pp. 160–62.

[28] Myers, *The Comanches*, p. 291; Freeman, *Lee's Lieutenants*, I, 94; III, xxiv, 639; Cooke, *Wearing of the Gray*, pp. 58–63.

father of his troops, and like a father he had a concern for their welfare which was quite personal. The trust which his officers and men placed in him was testimony to their full awareness of this. This quality is doubtless one of the significant keys to the man's great postwar influence.[29]

By the time the war ended, all that Hampton had represented was in ruins. He had intended to continue the fight in the lower South after Lee's and Johnston's surrenders, until his own wife, with the assistance of General Joseph Wheeler, persuaded him to give up. Millwood had been destroyed by Sherman's men, most of his fortune was gone; Columbia was burned and his native state laid waste. But Wade Hampton came home to a position of virtually unlimited influence and prestige. He and Robert E. Lee—the *Nation's* correspondent said in the fall of 1865—were "the two most popular and best loved men in the South today." The South could be reached quickest, this writer thought, "through the medium of such men as R. E. Lee and Wade Hampton."[30] Hampton's stand against secession in 1860, his reputation as a conservative, his family, and above all his gallant war record, the destruction of his home, and the sorrow of his son's death—all this made him a symbol of everything the South had loved and venerated in its culture.

To view what Hampton did with his influence in the months following the war is to see him at every point as the man of responsibility. Informed of a Brazilian colonizing venture, he wrote for publication a letter urging South Carolinians not to emigrate but to "take the oath of allegiance to the United States government," to work for the restoration of law and order in South Carolina, and to aid in rebuilding the state. He favored a qualified Negro suffrage and urged that the freedmen be dealt with fairly. He did his best to come to terms with his own former slaves and to re-establish decent working arrangements with them; in this respect the officials of the Freedmen's Bureau in South Carolina were much impressed by Hampton's generosity and patience.[31] In the fall of 1865 he was put forward as a candidate for

[29] Edward L. Wells, who served with Hampton, wrote that "with his stately figure in front—and there it always was—the men said and felt, 'It's all right!'" *Hampton and Reconstruction* (Columbia: State Company, 1907), pp. 109–10. The letter to Mary Fisher Hampton is quoted in Wellman, *Giant in Gray*, pp. 32–33.

[30] Wellman, *Giant in Gray*, pp. 180–89, 193–207; *Nation*, I (Oct. 26, 1865), 524.

[31] A Freedmen's Bureau officer stationed at Columbia wrote to the wartime governor of Michigan, Austin Blair: "Genl Wade Hampton is here now. He is a gentleman, a *true* friend to all freedpersons, and the *Bureau!*" John Williams to Blair, Mar. 15, 1866, Blair MSS, Detroit Public Library.

governor, an office to which he could have been elected almost unanimously. He did not consider it wise, however, that a man of his rank in the army should intrude himself into such prominence so soon, and refused to campaign. He even found it necessary to insist that his friends and the people of his home district not vote for him; as it was, the election was so close that James L. Orr, who was finally declared the winner, was very reluctant to assume office on so questionable a mandate.[32]

What it came to was that Wade Hampton, despite much initial bitterness toward the Union, stood ready to do what he could toward the achievement of a settlement, even to the point of refusing a clear call to public office when he thought the best interests of the South and his state required his remaining in the background. As for the terms of peacemaking, he accepted in good faith what Benjamin F. Perry, Johnson's provisional governor, told him. Perry, whom he knew well, had talked with Hampton in July and convinced him and other leading men of the state that Johnson, speaking for the North, intended a conciliatory policy toward the South. Hampton took Perry and Johnson at their word. The governing principles of the peace would be those provided by the Constitution; the cues would henceforth come from the President and the provisional governor; and Hampton himself more than adjusted to what he assumed would be the North's terms.

But the months went by, and peace did not seem to be coming any closer. By 1866, with growing anger and confusion, Hampton was reading of debates in Congress and utterances in Northern newspapers that had reached a new pitch of bitterness toward the South. He was no longer quite sure that there had been a settlement at all. If there had been, then either the North was not abiding by its terms or else the terms themselves were unclear. Hampton's behavior during this period lacks the precision that it had the previous summer and fall; he was both bewildered and incensed by Northern attacks on the South; he was full of resentment and confusion at what looked like the North's breaking faith. He could not understand why the North now seemed to be expecting further concessions, and why the present agreement (though he himself was not exactly certain what it was) should not be kept:

It is full time that some voice from the South should be raised to declare that, though conquered, she is not humiliated; that though she submits, she is not degraded; that she has not lost her self-respect, that she has not

---

[32] Wellman, *Giant in Gray*, pp. 197–202; Jarrell, *Wade Hampton and the Negro*, pp. 7–9.

laid down her arms on dishonorable terms; that she has observed these terms with the most perfect faith, and that she has a right to demand the like observance of them on the part of the North.[33]

Hampton's confusion, and that of most other Southerners in his position, grew basically out of Johnson's version of what the reconstruction process really meant. Superficially, Johnson's policy looked like a political settlement whose terms had presumably been more or less cleared in the North before the South received them. But according to Johnson, it was not a political settlement at all; it was simply the self-evident constitutional way of restoring the state governments. Yet even here, there was deep perplexity. If this was the constitutional way (rather than an *ad hoc* understanding), then what justification was there for requiring the states to ratify the Thirteenth Amendment *before* readmission?

Of all the inconsistencies of which the North has been guilty—and their name is legion—none is greater than that by which she forced the Southern States, while rigidly excluding them from the Union, to ratify the constitutional amendment abolishing slavery, which they could do legally only as States of the Union. But the deed has been done; and I, for one, do honestly declare that I never wish to see it revoked.[34]

If Johnson's procedure *was* "constitutional," then why did the North not simply recognize it, and stop attacking the South for abiding by the terms? Hampton's instincts were still all for conciliation, but it was becoming more and more difficult to be conciliatory when Northern newspapers and Northern politicians were abusing his people daily.

Of course Hampton had no choice but to support Johnson. No self-respecting Southerner, after hearing Johnson's conditions—even though it should later turn out that the President had not been authorized to present them in the first place—could henceforth be prepared to listen to any others. Moreover, such had been the way in which Johnson's authority had been represented to Hampton that the latter fully assumed and believed, with most other Southerners, that Johnson would win in the 1866 elections. Hampton supported the National Union movement in South Carolina in the summer and fall of 1866, assuming this to be the great middle way, the key to the great heart of moderate Northern sentiment. He still imagined that this was the moderate way to behave; he still wanted a peace between two peoples.

[33] Jarrell, *Wade Hampton and the Negro*, pp. 9–16; Wellman, *Giant in Gray*, pp. 203–14. The quotation is from a speech made by Hampton at Cashier's Valley, S.C., in the fall of 1866; *ibid.*, p. 210.

[34] Wellman, *Giant in Gray*, p. 210.

What Wade Hampton had wanted all along was clear terms—and only after it was too late did he realize that there had not been any. Indeed, everything the man does from this point on, not excluding his most heroic efforts, seems to have a "too late" quality hanging over it, a quality which always seems, now, just a little beyond his control. True, the results of the 1866 elections, though shocking, cleared the air and revealed the true state of things for the first time. The Reconstruction Acts of the following March ended all illusions of an easy restoration. Hampton saw that the Negro was due to become a factor in politics, and he saw that it was necessary for him and his class to make a strong bid for Negro support. Accordingly, he launched great efforts to organize the Negroes for the Democratic party. Though disfranchised himself by the Reconstruction Acts, he addressed many Negro meetings, urging that the blacks would be wiser to accept the leadership of their former masters, whom they knew and could trust, than to risk the dangers of following outside adventurers.[35]

But by then, the appeal of the old planter class must have seemed rather tame compared to the flamboyant promises, the secret clubs and rituals, and the general attentions being offered to the Negroes by carpetbag politicians. Hampton and his friends fought two last rearguard actions, late in 1867 and early in 1868, to prevent the adoption of a radical constitution in order that the state might remain under the infinitely preferable military government. His efforts to defeat the holding of a convention, and later to have the constitution voted down, met with failure. This virtually marks the retirement of Wade Hampton from public affairs for the duration of reconstruction. Upon that subject he had, for the time being, nothing more to say that would be of any positive influence.[36]

[35] *Ibid.*, pp. 216–18; Jarrell, *Hampton and the Negro*, pp. 16–18; Hampton to John Mullaly, Mar. 31, 1867, *Family Letters of the Three Wade Hamptons, 1782–1901*, ed. Charles E. Cauthen (Columbia: University of South Carolina Press, 1953), pp. 141–43. In this letter Hampton said: "Now all the dirty work is taken off our hands by this Sup. Bill, and it seems to me that but one hope is left to us and that is to direct the Negro vote. I advocate a warm protest from the South against all this legislation of Congress, but protests can do us no good. We must meet it, as a *fact;* one we have to deal with and on the solution of which depends the very existence of our country. . . . If we cannot direct the wave it will overwhelm us. Now how shall we do this? Simply by making the Negro a Southern man, and if you will, a Democrat, anything but a Radical. Beyond these motives for my action I have another. We are appealing to the enlightened sense and the justice of mankind. We came forward and say, we accept the decision rendered against us, we acknowledge the freedom of the negro and we are willing to have one law for him and for us. We are making up our record for posterity and we wish no blot or flaw to be found there."

[36] Jarrell, *Hampton and the Negro*, pp. 19–25; Wellman, *Giant in Gray*, pp. 218–21.

Hampton's return to public life in 1876 as governor of South Carolina was surrounded by such circumstances as to make it profitable for us to have one final look at the man and his career. Hampton's conduct at this time greatly deepens the sense of "lost opportunity" which pervaded the peacemaking efforts of a decade before. For one thing, the behavior of Wade Hampton in the election campaign of 1876 and in his subsequent governorship shows "moderation" at the absolute maximum degree which the conditions of the late seventies permitted. For another, we can see Hampton here in a role denied him ten years earlier—that of the responsible negotiator, prepared to make complex arrangements both in his own state and with the federal government, and now having the authority, as well as the sense of honor, to give his word and abide by it. And finally, we may see the governorship of Wade Hampton as the twilight of *noblesse oblige* in South Carolina.

The Southern radical carpetbag governments had all but run their course by 1876, both in the South itself and in the eyes of the Northern public. The implacable energy, tinged with violence, of the white "Redeemers" of the Democratic party had reached high tide; and the political position of the Southern Negro—more and more deserted by his carpetbag allies—was, needless to say, in a desperate state. There was still, however, enough of a balance in South Carolina—where one of the last of the carpetbag regimes still hung on—to require much delicacy on the part of anyone assuming to lead a united Democratic party back to power. The party in 1876 was split between "compromise" and "straight-out" factions. The Republican governor, Daniel Chamberlain, had become something of a conservative reformer, and had much support among the moderate Democrats. This group wanted an arrangement whereby Chamberlain would be supported for re-election as governor (with a Democrat as lieutenant governor and with the remaining slate consisting also of Democrats); after the election, Chamberlain would then be sent to the United States Senate. The other group, however, would have nothing to do with compromises, insisted on a "straight-out" Democratic ticket, and was prepared to resort to violence. In such circumstances the only way to unite the party was to run a conservative Democrat on a "straight-out" ticket. The logical candidate was Wade Hampton.[37]

Hampton was thus faced with problems extremely complex. To win, he would have to unite the entire white population and either

[37] Jarrell, *Hampton and the Negro*, pp. 41–58.

persuade from 16,000 to 18,000 Negroes to vote for him or persuade twice that number not to vote at all. This would require a campaign sufficiently aggressive to unify the whites, weaken the carpetbaggers' confidence in their own power (which was still formidable), and impress the Negroes with the inevitability of a Democratic victory. But it would all have to be done without violence, because violence, with a presidential election also at stake at the same time, would mean certain intervention by federal troops, with the likelihood of the entire election being declared fraudulent.

Hampton's strategy was twofold. On the one hand, to control the great numbers of fanatics among his own followers who were bent on force, he organized them into quasi-military groups ("Hampton's Red Shirts") who could march about and make a show of strength but whom he was able to control by insisting on strict military discipline and abstention from violence.[38] On the other hand, he put himself on record in pamphlets and speeches to Negro voters pledging that they would have complete equality before the law with any white man in South Carolina as long as he was governor and that they would receive better facilities for education than they had ever had before. Hampton's strategy succeeded. The whites went as a unit, some 16,000 Negroes voted Democratic, and by dint of ceaseless efforts Hampton prevented the use of open violence by his followers.[39] Even so, his success was delayed some five months while the radicals tried to have the election declared illegal and to install Chamberlain for another term as governor. At one point, only Hampton's own appearance before a mob prevented the storming of the radical-held State House. His personal authority, dignity, and restraint impressed the North, and Chamberlain's support began to evaporate.[40]

Meanwhile Hampton in 1877 had opened his negotiations with the new President, Rutherford B. Hayes. The terms consisted, on the one hand, of Hayes's final arrangements for removing the federal troops from South Carolina and, on the other hand, of Hampton's word that there would be no disorders which might require the troops' return and that his own campaign promises toward the Negro would be kept. A later agreement was made whereby the federal government would

[38] For a discussion of Hampton's "force without violence" formula, and its success despite the incendiary setting of South Carolina in 1876, see *ibid.*, pp. 58–85.

[39] *Ibid.*, pp. 58–88. Again and again, Hampton stressed the equality theme in order that the record of his promises might be made up in advance. For the record, see *House Misc. Docs.*, 44 Cong., 2 sess., No. 31, "Recent Election in South Carolina," Part 1, pp. 306–10.

[40] Jarrell, *Hampton and the Negro*, pp. 103–20.

drop all further Ku Klux prosecutions, and South Carolina would prosecute no more carpetbaggers for fraud. The Hayes-Hampton correspondence is a model of diplomatic negotiation between men of authority who could count on each other's word. The first letters are cold and formal, but precise; as the two men learn to trust each other the letters take on a more cordial tone and finally show true mutual regard.[41] A world of difference might have been made had similar channels of communication been open a dozen years earlier.

Wade Hampton carried out his pledges to the Negro, though in the face of formidable opposition from the straight-outers. He set up a two-mill tax for the education of both races and appointed Negroes to many minor offices. To demands for a disfranchisement program, he declared: "I would give my life for South Carolina but I cannot sacrifice my honor, not even for her."[42] "You may quote me," said the Republican Negro postmaster of Charleston, "as expressing absolute confidence in Governor Hampton and entire satisfaction with his course. . . . He has kept all his pledges."[43] Hampton, stated J. J. Wright, a radical Negro leader, "has kept every pledge he has made, and on the seventh of next November he will be re-elected Governor almost unanimously. . . . There is not a decent negro in the state who will vote against him."[44] Another Negro leader, a Dr. Cooke, told a convention of Northerners in Charlotte, North Carolina, that "in no state at the North do the colored people enjoy superior rights to those enjoyed by them at present in South Carolina."[45]

Wade Hampton was elected to the Senate in 1879, and his direct personal influence was thereupon removed from state politics. The position of the Negro began crumbling very soon, and in 1882 the franchise was greatly reduced by the passage of the baffling "Eight-Box Law."[46] A new and meaner class of white-supremacy

[41] *Ibid.*, pp. 132–39; the Hayes-Hampton correspondence, from the originals at the Hayes Memorial Library at Fremont, Ohio, are reproduced in an appendix to *ibid.*, pp. 170–87.

[42] *Ibid.*, p. 143; see also George B. Tindall, *South Carolina Negroes, 1877–1900* (Columbia: University of South Carolina Press, 1952), pp. 19–29.

[43] Jarrell, *Hampton and the Negro*, p. 130.

[44] *Ibid.*, p. 139.   [45] *Nation*, XXVIII (Jan. 2, 1879), 1.

[46] This was a voting law with many complex provisions designed to confuse the Negro voter and to make for a very high likelihood that either his registration or his ballot would be disqualified. Among such provisions was one which required the depositing of separately marked ballots in each of eight separate boxes. See Jarrell, *Hampton and the Negro*, pp. 158–59.

politicians was then coming to the fore, men who could without compunction capitalize on the festering sense of injustice born of reconstruction that had already come to form a new morality for the South.[47] That morality, which still persists, seems to have had more than a little connection with the peace that was *not* made in 1865. Negroes did continue to vote in South Carolina until 1895. But the year 1890 had already witnessed the triumph of Ben Tillman as governor, shortly followed by the final retirement of Wade Hampton. Hampton, after eleven years of distinction as a United States senator, was displaced by the candidate of a Tillman-controlled legislature. He lived twelve more years after that, wreathed in veneration and countless honors, though bankrupt politically and much embarrassed financially. He died in 1902 at the age of eighty-four. It is said that his last words were, "God bless all my people, black and white."[48]

[47] The man who became their leader, "Pitchfork Ben" Tillman, according to Hampton's biographer, "had a half-crazy zest for the use of edged weapons. 'I like to cut living flesh with the knife,' he once told his fellow-butchers at a hog-killing." Wellman, *Giant in Gray*, p. 313.

[48] *Ibid.*, p. 333.

Part Two: **1866**
AND AFTER

Chapter 9

Joint Committee on Reconstruction

1 DECEMBER, 1865: THE FIRST ASSEMBLING OF THE POSTWAR GOVERNMENT

By December 4, the opening day of Congress, nearly seven months had elapsed since the ending of the Civil War. Following Lee's surrender there had been a delay of thirty-four weeks—during which time a new President had come to office—before the government of the United States in all its branches could function fully and act concurrently on the immense problems left by the conflict. A new Executive and a new legislature were coming face to face for the first time.[1]

As the members of the Thirty-ninth Congress assembled at Washington, the Republican majority, which supposed itself responsible in the months to come for the formation of government policy, was preoccupied with a growing and dominant concern—the unity and solidarity of the party. This concern over party unity contained two virtually antithetical elements which served for a time to balance each other off. One of them was a general determination that, come what might, Congress must have a major voice in the formation of reconstruction policy and that the process of completing such policy should not be complicated by the presence of Southern members. The feeling that the President's course so far might mean future obstacles to that process caused much uneasiness. But the other element was in its way equally potent: a great reluctance to break with the President. Sustain-

---

[1] Members of the Thirty-ninth Congress had been elected in the fall of 1864 and were now meeting for their first session.

ing this reluctance was the assumption, still widely held, that the presidential policy had been conducted "experimentally";[2] it was thus quite plausible to hope that Johnson would make powerful efforts of his own to maintain harmony with the party that had elected him. In short, there was as yet nothing irrevocable in the relationship, still very fluid, between legislative and executive power. So far as anyone knew, there might be just as much danger to party unity in a split between the two branches of government as in the immediate readmission of Southerners—and among Republicans the latter danger was one about which there was next to no disagreement.[3]

These two preoccupations—desire for legislative-executive harmony, and determination that legislative should share with executive power in the process of reconstruction—showed in two significant developments of the session's opening days. One was the reaction, generally favorable, to President Johnson's first annual message. The other was the speedy formation of the Joint Committee on Reconstruction.

Johnson's message, upon which he had labored for many weeks, was ready before the congressmen arrived, and it was submitted to them on December 5, the second day of the session, immediately after the organization of both houses. What people wanted to find in it, judging from the response throughout the country, was not a series of points upon which to oppose the President but rather points of harmony in the interests of a sensible reconstruction. What they did find, for one thing, was high literary merit. Inherent in its lofty language was a statesman-like moderation, and it was this air of high-mindedness that gave men much reason to hope for adjustment and concord. "In its temper, simplicity, and patriotic fidelity," asserted *Harper's Weekly*, "the Message is a model, and has been received with unprecedented unanimity of approbation." "This," George Templeton Strong, a New York Republican, wrote approvingly, "is what our *tailors* can do."[4]

[2] See above, pp. 76 ff. *Harper's Weekly* in its editorial of December 2 (IX, 754) still maintained this position. "That policy, as now appears, was simply an experiment to ascertain if the late insurgents could be trusted; and the result is before the country."

[3] "There is, unquestionably, among really loyal men outside of Congress, no difference of opinion as to the justice and policy of not rushing frantically into the embraces of the Representatives of the States that voluntarily resigned their title to national representation nearly five years ago." This is from a December 15 editorial of the New York *Times,* one of the strongest of the pro-Johnson Unionist papers.

[4] *Harper's Weekly,* IX (Dec. 23, 1865), 802; Allan Nevins and Milton H. Thomas (eds.), *The Diary of George Templeton Strong* (New York, 1952), IV, 56. The New York *Tribune* (Dec. 6, 1865) and the *Nation* (I [Dec. 14, 1865], 742) also gave strong praise to the message. Congressional reaction seems to have been very favorable. "The message is much better than we expected," commented Garfield, "and I hope that we will be able to work with the President." "Aside from the worst radicals," according to

The dominant note in the response was praise and optimism. But there were matters of substance in the message, apart from its tone, that still gave cause for concern; there were aspects of its reception, moreover, that showed how delicate the balance was. The climax of reconstruction, in Johnson's mind, appeared to be ratification of the Thirteenth Amendment; no provision had been made, in the reasoning of the message, for any subsequent phases of a legislative nature through which the reconstruction process might have to go. The message began with expressions of deference to the dead Lincoln and an acknowledgment of Johnson's own need for confidence and support in discharging the awesome duties he had undertaken. There was praise of the Constitution, the founding fathers, and the principles of indissoluble Union. The President discoursed upon the mutual relations of states and the nation; he declared that the states had no power to dissolve the Union, though states with proper limitations were essential to the existence of the Constitution. "The whole cannot exist without the parts, nor the parts without the whole." Finding the states suffering from the effects of a civil war, the President had had to decide whether or not they were to be held as conquered territory. His decision had been to restore, instead, the vitality of the states ("gradually and quietly, and by almost imperceptible steps"), rather than to incur the great dangers of indefinite military government. That vitality had not been destroyed but only impaired; the states' acts of secession were constitutionally not real but pretended, null and void from the first. After reciting his "almost imperceptible steps"—the appointment of provisional governors, the arranging of conventions and elections, and the careful exercise of the pardoning power—the President took up the new constitutional amendment and made of it a kind of culmination:

The adoption of the amendment reunites us beyond all power of disruption. It heals the wound that is still imperfectly closed; it removes slavery, the element which has so long perplexed and divided the country; it makes of us once more a united people, renewed and strengthened, bound more than ever to mutual affection and support.

The amendment to the Constitution being adopted, it would remain for the States, whose powers have been so long in abeyance, to resume their

---

Representative Shelby Cullom, "the message pleased everyone." James Garfield to Burke A. Hinsdale, Dec. 11, 1865, in *Garfield-Hinsdale Letters*, ed. Mary L. Hinsdale (Ann Arbor, 1949), p. 76; Shelby M. Cullom, *Fifty Years of Public Service* (Chicago: A. C. McClurg, 1911), p. 144. It was not known, until William A. Dunning discovered the fact some fifty years later, that Johnson had had the literary assistance of George Bancroft, the historian and former Democratic cabinet officer under President Polk, in the preparation of his message. See Dunning, "A Little More Light on Andrew Johnson," *Proceedings of the Massachusetts Historical Society*, 2d ser., XIX (1905), 395–405.

places in the two branches of the national Legislature, and thereby complete the work of restoration. Here it is for you, fellow-citizens of the Senate, and for you, fellow-citizens of the House of Representatives, to judge, each of you for yourselves, of the elections, returns, and qualifications of your own members.[5]

Readers of the message could, if they thought about it, construe these words to mean that the President did not deny the power of Congress to take a hand in reconstruction and that the matter was being left open.[6] But the President could just as well be saying that with ratification of the antislavery amendment, by now all but consummated, it remained only for Congress to readmit the Southern members "and thereby complete the work of restoration." Congress was not yet ready to do that; it would take more than ratification of the amendment to qualify the states for restoration. Should the message be construed broadly or narrowly? George William Curtis, of *Harper's Weekly*, inclined toward the former, though in his otherwise laudatory editorial he allowed himself doubts on a point in the President's logic. It was "not competent for the General Government," according to the President, "to extend the elective franchise to the several States." But if the public safety required the states, as a "pledge of perpetual loyalty and peace," to assent to a constitutional amendment, why should the government not be competent to require their assent to a modified suffrage, if the public safety should also demand that?[7] James G. Blaine, admitting the "moderation in language and the general conservatism which distinguished the message," thought that there were important aspects bearing on the states' readiness for readmission that had not been dealt with; "the most partial friend of the President could hardly claim that he frankly communicated the

[5] Richardson, *Messages and Papers*, VI, 353 ff.; *Congressional Globe*, 39 Cong., 1 sess., Appendix, pp. 1–2.

[6] For example: "The subject of reconstruction is left where it properly belongs, with Congress, and we therefore conclude the President will approve its action in the premises." *Bureau County* (Ill.) *Republican*, Dec. 14, 1865. Again: "It would appear from the President's Message that his convictions are that the question of reconstruction belongs to the law-making power of the country, and he is willing that there the responsibility should rest." *Ibid.*, Dec. 28, 1865.

[7] *Harper's Weekly*, IX (Dec. 23, 1865), 802. Similar reservations were expressed by the New York *Tribune* (Dec. 6, 1865) and the *Nation* (I, [Dec. 14, 1865], 742); but in each case such reservations appear, at this time, as minor afterthoughts counterpointing the dominant note of praise. It is as though the President were being reassured that he had been more justified than he himself supposed in his use of arbitrary government power and that he could exercise more if conditions warranted it. The *Nation* roundly rebuked Charles Sumner for comparing the message to the "whitewashing message of Franklin Pierce with regard to the enormities in Kansas." *Nation*, I (Dec. 28, 1865), 801; *Cong. Globe*, 39 Cong., 1 sess., p. 79.

proceedings or the spirit of the Southern conventions and legislatures. He chose to ignore that subject, to hide it by fluent and graceful phrase from public criticism, and thus to keep from the official knowledge of Congress the most important facts in the whole domain of reconstruction. It was a great mistake in the President to pass over this subject in silence."[8]

In the last analysis, however, it was not afterthoughts about its logic that undermined the beneficial effects of the message's reception. What really turned the affair sour was the high praise lavished upon the message by the Copperheads. The normal speeches and resolutions of approval in Congress had been preceded on December 18 by a viciously radical attack on the President's policy by Thaddeus Stevens. Representative Henry J. Raymond of New York thereupon prepared a speech designed both as a defense of the administration and as an answer to Stevens, which he planned to deliver on the twenty-first. On that day, to Raymond's chagrin, William E. Finck of Ohio, a Vallandigham Democrat, and Daniel Voorhees, an even more prominent Peace man from Indiana, got the floor ahead of him. Voorhees offered resolutions which lauded the message as "an able, judicious, and patriotic state paper" and tendered Congress' pledge to the President "to aid, assist, and uphold him in the policy which he has adopted to give harmony, peace, and union to the country."[9] Finck followed with a long speech in support of the President and his message, urging immediate readmission of Southern states to representation and attacking the doctrines of Charles Sumner and Thaddeus Stevens.[10] The mortified Raymond then tried to dissociate his own sentiments from those of Finck by sneering at the latter's belated conversion to Unionism, but the defense of Johnson which he then launched did not sound very different from Finck's; in fact it went over much the same ground in its constitutional theory and opposition to Stevens. In the course of it, Raymond got into several sharp arguments over the question of Southern representation with John A. Bingham of Ohio, one of the most conservative men on the Republican side of the House. The proceedings did not, on the whole, add any strength to Johnson's position,

---

[8] Blaine, *Twenty Years of Congress* (Norwich, Conn.: Henry Bill, 1884–86), II, 115–16.

[9] *Cong. Globe*, 39 Cong., 1 sess., p. 115. When the subject was taken up again on January 9, Representative Bingham offered a much restrained substitute: "That this House has an abiding confidence in the President, and that in the future, as in the past, he will cooperate with Congress in restoring to equal position and rights with the other States in the Union all the States lately in insurrection." *Ibid.*, p. 159. Both Voorhees' resolutions and Bingham's substitute were referred to the Joint Committee on Reconstruction.

[10] *Ibid.*, pp. 117–20.

and Raymond's own political effectiveness was henceforth tarnished by a certain amount of suspicion within his own party.[11]

Of a more dramatic nature, the other development which marked the pre-holiday proceedings of Congress went back to the first day of business on December 4. This was the decision to form the subsequently famous Joint Committee on Reconstruction. The scenes of opening day in the House, dominated by the saturnine Stevens, have been described many times. Edward McPherson, the Clerk of the House and a political beneficiary of Thaddeus Stevens, had already announced his intention a number of weeks before to omit the names of the Southern members-elect from his roll. Johnson, for his part, had hoped that the credentials of Horace Maynard, a loyal Unionist member of the Tennessee delegation, would be sufficiently sound to allow Maynard's being seated—thus clearing the way for the seating of other loyal claimants.[12] Amid mounting excitement the calling of the roll proceeded, according to the prearranged plan, without the names of anyone from the seceded states. Maynard at the appropriate moment arose to challenge the omission of his name, but through brisk parliamentary legerdemain by Stevens and McPherson, Maynard's protest was set aside, unrecognized.[13] Johnson's test case had been a failure, and the House was organized without the Southern members-elect.

The House, on another motion by Stevens, thereupon re-elected Schuyler Colfax of Indiana as Speaker, and Stevens was then free to proceed with the plan—also arranged in advance—[14]

that a joint committee of fifteen members shall be appointed, nine of whom shall be members of the House and six members of the Senate, who shall inquire into the condition of the States which formed the so-called confederate States of America, and report whether they or any of them are

[11] *Ibid.*, pp. 120–25. "It was a great misfortune," wrote Richard Smith, of the Cincinnati *Gazette*, to James Garfield, "that a Copperhead was not elected from New York in place of Raymond. He is the most unreliable of men." R. Smith to Garfield, Jan. 14, 1866, Garfield MSS, Library of Congress.

[12] Gideon Welles wrote on December 3: "The President . . . said they [the plans to exclude Southern members] would be knocked in the head at the start. There would be a Representative from Tennessee who had been a loyal Member of the House since the War commenced, or during the War, who could present himself, and so state the case that he could not be controverted." Welles, *Diary*, II, 387.

[13] *Cong. Globe*, 39 Cong., 1 sess., pp. 3–4.

[14] A full description of the caucus meetings at which the decision was made to form the Joint Committee was published in the New York *Herald* on December 11. Various details of the plan had appeared in the newspapers before that time, however; Johnson and Welles were acquainted with it by the third. See Benjamin B. Kendrick, *The Journal of the Joint Committee of Fifteen on Reconstruction* (New York: Columbia University Press, 1914), pp. 138–40; Welles, *Diary*, II, 387.

entitled to be represented in either House of Congress, with leave to report at any time by bill or otherwise; and until such report shall have been made and finally acted upon by Congress, no member shall be received into either House from any of the said so-called confederate States; and all papers relating to the representation of the said States shall be referred to the said committee without debate.

He introduced a joint resolution to that effect despite the protest of James Brooks, a Democrat from New York, who insisted that the House should await the reception of the Executive message before transacting any further business on so important a subject. The House voted, however, to receive the Stevens resolution, and it was adopted by a vote of 133 to 36.[15]

The manipulations of Thaddeus Stevens thus seemed to set the whole tone of the first day of the first session of the first reconstruction Congress, and indeed, the man's work and the notoriety of his name were to cast shadows over the entire history of reconstruction. But it would be wrong to suppose, from this, that Congress in December, 1865, was abandoned to radical madness. The formation of the committee was actually a more routine decision, less of an extreme step, than was implied in the flamboyant circumstances amid which it was done. The trappings of intrigue and wire-pulling, though certainly there, could hardly have made the difference between doing it and not doing it. In all likelihood the business would have been transacted anyway; the same essential project, a day or so later, might just as plausibly have been fathered by almost any Republican in the House as by Thaddeus Stevens. Conflict with the President was not, so far as most men were concerned, implied in the existence of such a committee. Even here a strong moderate balance prevailed.

For one thing, the resolution to establish it passed with great ease—without a fight, without amendments, and by a great majority. Stevens or no Stevens, most moderate Republicans thought it a perfectly proper and necessary thing.[16] Moreover, the Senate, while accepting

15 *Cong. Globe*, 39 Cong., 1 sess., p. 6. The above quotation is the actual text of the Stevens resolution.

16 A good key to this sentiment might be the actions and words of Henry J. Raymond, who continued to support the administration long after most of his Republican colleagues had deserted it. Raymond, as a member of the preorganization caucus committee, had voted for the plan to set up a Joint Committee on Reconstruction and subsequently defended it in the New York *Times*. He saw "no reason to fear any undue influence or prejudice to the main question, from its action." *Times*, Dec. 5; Francis Brown, *Raymond of the Times* (New York: W. W. Norton, 1951), pp. 283–84. The fact that Raymond later attacked Stevens and the joint committee has led some writers to assume that Raymond had been tricked. See Kendrick, *Journal*, p. 141; Milton, *Age of Hate*, pp. 265–66. Raymond may have been deceived about Stevens' full purposes, but his taking for granted the apparent reasonableness of creating such a committee was presumably what made such "trickery" possible in the first place.

the idea itself, did not do so without debate and without important qualifications. There were to be no infringements upon the Senate's exclusive rights over its own membership. The committee itself was picked with great care, and influence within it was so located that the balance of power was decidedly on the conservative side. Its chairman was a personage of great solidity and distinction, William Pitt Fessenden, the senator from Maine.[17]

II THADDEUS STEVENS: THE MARGINAL POLITICIAN COMES INTO HIS OWN

One of the most coercive of all images in connection with the overthrow of presidential reconstruction is that of Thaddeus Stevens as the evil genius. Cynical old Machiavelli, clubfooted, cadaverous, and malignant, "lashing the others with a whip of scorpions,"[18] full of parliamentary tricks, jamming his measures through by plotting and craft: it is as though nature, obedient to the profoundest demands of art, had with Thaddeus Stevens outdone herself in the presentation of so superb a villain. Stevens, the debauched old reprobate, has succeeded in imposing himself and his personality on an entire era of American history.[19] Nearly every writer confronting that picture has found himself stepping back, seized for the moment with a kind of perverse relish, before its very perfection. "In surveying the career of this Pennsylvania Caliban," exclaims George F. Milton, "it is hard to repress a feeling of admiration for his brutal realism."[20]

One has only to follow the day-to-day proceedings of the Thirty-ninth Congress to be convinced that the picture has much truth in it. Stevens' alertness to take advantage of every opening is very impressive, and it deeply impressed his own contemporaries. Freshman congressmen such as Rutherford B. Hayes were convinced that the old

[17] The members of the Joint Committee were: For the Senate: William P. Fessenden (R., Maine), James W. Grimes (R., Iowa), Ira Harris (R., New York), Jacob M. Howard (R., Michigan), George H. Williams (R., Oregon), and Reverdy Johnson (D., Maryland). For the House: Thaddeus Stevens (R., Pennsylvania), Elihu B. Washburne (R., Illinois), Justin S. Morrill (R., Vermont), John A. Bingham (R., Ohio), Roscoe Conkling (R., New York), George S. Boutwell (R., Massachusetts), Henry T. Blow (R., Missouri), Andrew J. Rogers (D., New Jersey), and Henry Grider (D., Kentucky).

[18] Milton, *Age of Hate*, p. 265.

[19] Such is the prevailing assumption. "One of the controlling elements in the whole reconstruction story," asserts the late Professor Randall, "was the fact that in party counsel and in congressional action the votes of hundreds of men, affecting the happiness of millions of people, were swayed by the domineering force of this hater of the South." J. G. Randall, *The Civil War and Reconstruction*, p. 723.

[20] *Age of Hate*, p. 262.

man held the House in the hollow of his hand; Stevens, according to Blaine, was "recognized as the leader of the majority."[21] The power of his scathing wit alone has taken on legendary qualities with the passage of years—a wit capable, it would seem, of performing prodigies. "So smarting were his rebukes," Milton was asserting two generations after Stevens' death, "that most of the members of Congress would endure almost any contumely rather than offend or cross him."[22] Whenever it is a question of reconstruction, the name of "grim old Thaddeus Stevens" is not invoked even today without something of a shudder.[23]

And yet Thaddeus Stevens and his doings, taken in themselves as a principle of explanation for the events of the period, leave all manner of difficulties and do not end by "explaining" very much. Why should history have designated such a man as Stevens to be the architect (if such he was) of radical reconstruction? Why should it have been a mere congressman from Pennsylvania (that office was the only national one he ever held, and it was not as though he had not tried for higher ones); where did his power come from? Here was an old man in his seventies, a man who had been in public life for nearly forty years; why should success have come so late in his career? Had he been, perhaps, a secret power in Pennsylvania politics all this time? No: he had always been a troublemaker but never a power. If the man were emerging as a power now, then what kind of power? What aspects of his past career and personality had prepared him for the role he seemed to be stepping into now?

Fame first came to Stevens on a macabre note, after a season of poverty and near-failure as a young lawyer in Gettysburg, when in 1817 he brilliantly defended a mad murderer who had all but decapitated his victim with a scythe; much business came to him thereafter, and during the 1820's he invested his earnings in choice real estate and charcoal iron. By 1827 he had more taxable property than anyone else in town. He experimented with politics, served in local offices, and went to the legislature in 1833. He seems to have conceived an abysmal detestation of Democrats just about the time when Andrew Jackson's star (and that of many a career politician) was on

21 *Diary and Letters of Rutherford Birchard Hayes*, ed. C. R. Williams (Columbus: Ohio State Archaeological and Historical Society, 1922–26), III, 9–10; Blaine, *Twenty Years*, II, 112.

22 *Age of Hate*, p. 264.

23 While the Civil Rights Bill of 1957 was being debated in Congress, Thaddeus Stevens' name was brought up a number of times, both in newspapers and in the speeches themselves, as an ancient symbol of malevolence.

the rise in the late twenties—a detestation which also paralleled the rise of Stevens' contemporary, rival, and later fellow townsman, James Buchanan.[24] It was an animus that impelled and sustained him all his life, through times when political sustenance of a more nourishing sort was not to be had.

There is much that remains unclear in the private character of Thaddeus Stevens. Just how and where did he get his reputation as libertine, trickster, cynic, and misanthrope? The evidence grows dimmer the closer one looks at it—until one is inspired to fix the eye of suspicion on the old farceur himself. Nature and fortune seem somehow to have left off in the midst of great promise, and Stevens, like Walt Whitman, took over the job of creating a "stock personality" for himself, much of which had its being in the realm of illusion. There was a slightly mad virtuosity, with a touch of the unworldly, about the result.

Life's principal bounties were handed to him in heavily clipped coin. His mother—to whom Thad was inordinately devoted and who made great sacrifices to send him to Dartmouth from their hardscrabble Vermont farm—was a model of industrious piety; his father was a worthless trifler. Young Stevens was a good student and a sharp debater, but was rather unpopular; his penchant for deviltry got him blackballed from Phi Beta Kappa. He was tall, good-looking, and robust, but clubfooted; this handicap had kept him from boyish sports and it may have deterred him from becoming a town beau in young manhood, assuming he had wanted to be one—and the evidence for that is very scanty. He acquired wealth, but lost much of it through both ill-fortune and inattentive management. An attack of typhoid in his thirties left him bald; he wore a grotesque chestnut wig for the rest of his life. That wig, often askew, may have represented the appeal of the bizarre to a man of great intelligence who was willing to take life's limits and add a flourish to them. For all his reputed irregularity of habits, there is much of the perversely deliberate—a kind of sardonic aesthetic discipline—in the legend which he allowed to grow up around himself.

[24] Stevens and Buchanan, nearly the same age, had careers which paralleled each other very closely—except that Buchanan's was a story of success nearly all the way and Stevens' one of more or less consistent failure. Buchanan, with a very successful law practice in Lancaster, was elected to the state legislature in 1814, made a good record there, went to Congress in 1820 as a Federalist, shifted to Andrew Jackson in the mid-1820's, and by 1828 was recognized as one of the most effective Jackson men in Pennsylvania. From that point on, his rise in the councils of the Democratic party was steady and uninterrupted. He was minister to Russia from 1831 to 1833; senator, 1833–45; Secretary of State under Polk, 1844–49; minister to England, 1853–56; and was elected President in 1856.

The studied indifference, for instance, to rumors of the confirmed bachelor's sex morals strikes us as a little odd for the times. His ménage with the circumspect Lydia Smith, his devoted and devout mulatto housekeeper, was somewhat too picturesque, and it is very unlikely that there was anything irregular in the connection, despite the lascivious gossip which surrounded it.[25] The only other scandal that ever came near him was a fraudulent damage suit—proved baseless—brought against him by the idle father of a dissolute girl. Nothing specific was ever revealed of Stevens' fabulous peccadilloes; indeed, it would not have been unlike him to let it be imagined that he satisfied desires which he may seldom, if ever, have had. "Was there some quirk of his personality," muses one of his biographers, ". . . that made him glad to be damned for the vices of a manly man?"[26] He did, at any rate, steer clear of houses with marriageable daughters.

Nor does Stevens, in other respects, fit the picture of the voluptuary. For all his means, he lavished few luxuries upon himself. He was a teetotaller and deplored alcoholic excesses in others; his only real private vices were gambling and reading in bed. He was not a man of avarice. Although some of his early business operations are said to have been a bit sharp, he does not appear to have inflicted personal damage knowingly in all his lifelong dealings. His affairs at Caledonia Iron Works might run in the red for years at a time, but he took excellent care of the 250 families he employed there; he performed innumerable acts of charity and was known, both at Gettysburg and later at Lancaster, as the town almoner. He took a gruff fatherly interest in his orphaned nephews and always saw to their welfare. He was, according to Blaine, "fond of young men," and though he made a great show of discouraging aspirants from reading law with him ("You have too honest a face"), he was a good teacher and would sometimes have nine or ten apprentices studying in his office at once.[27] To be sure, there was not much tenderness in Old Thad, in the usual sense of the term, so it would be too simple to hustle him off with the old

[25] Ralph Korngold takes a short chapter in his *Thaddeus Stevens* (New York: Harcourt, Brace, 1955), to cast doubt on the Lydia Smith story. His argument is fairly convincing (see pp. 72–76). A fine new biography, much superior to Korngold's but published too recently to allow the present work to profit fully from it, is Fawn M. Brodie, *Thaddeus Stevens: Scourge of the South* (New York: W. W. Norton, 1959). Mrs. Brodie, unlike Korngold, tends to credit the story. The nature of her own evidence, however (see pp. 86–93), simply reinforces this writer's suspicion that Old Thad was not above pulling the leg of Clio, the muse of history.

[26] Richard N. Current, *Old Thad Stevens* (Madison: University of Wisconsin Press, 1942), pp. 300–301.

[27] Blaine, *Twenty Years*, I, 325; Current, *Old Thad Stevens*, p. 115.

saw about a heart of gold beneath a gruff exterior. But there were always those who, even while believing the whole lurid legend, thought they saw in Stevens a soul well worth saving.[28]

Actually, it is Thaddeus Stevens' public, political personality that must set the terms for his ultimate role in history; it was here that most of his aggressions against other men found full expression. The keynote of that personality was cynicism, craft, and vindictiveness. But here too there are many paradoxes. Some men have built careers upon an elaborate public devotion to all mankind, while their private dealings were characterized by selfishness, egotism, and contempt for their closest associates, all under the cloak of a larger benevolence. Thaddeus Stevens' adjustment to life seems in some ways to have been a grotesque reversal of that principle; he faced mankind in the abstract convinced of its worthlessness and not caring who knew it. To articulate this he was fiendishly well equipped with a keen mind, much learning (which, unlike Sumner, he never wasted on ornament), a sharp wit, and a vicious tongue.

His conception of politics was that of a low business, full of fools and gamesters. For his own role, he fancied himself as a super Machiavelli, full of schemes and tricks. He was a very adroit parliamentarian for short-term objects; he loved manipulation and was fond of turning the neat stunt for its own sake. He was good enough at all this to achieve just about the reputation which he seems in some way to have desired and relished. But over the long run, in this conception—this role of the master schemer, of Stevens the politician who would build power through craft and wield it by manipulation—there was just one gaping flaw: he was a terrible failure at it. His political career, all the way into old age, is a long comic sequence of devilish schemes which, one after another, kept blowing up in his face.

It was certainly hard for any non-Democrat in the period between 1830 and 1860 to arrive at a very precise formula for what a good party man should be. But Thaddeus Stevens tried a bit of everything. After his very early Federalist leanings, he flirted with Anti-Masonry, Prohibitionism, and Know-Nothingism (all the while nominally a Whig); he took up antislavery in the 1830's, and came into the Republican party at its beginnings. His hatred of the South, of slavery,

---

[28] Stevens' friend, the Reverend Jonathan Blanchard, would often exhort him to take consideration for his soul's rest. "At present, in every part of the United States," Blanchard once wrote him, "people believe that your personal life has been *one prolonged sin;* that your lips are defiled with blasphemy! Your hands with gambling!! And your body with women!!!" Stevens was attended, at his death, by two ministers and two colored Sisters of Charity. One of the nuns administered rites of baptism. Current, *Old Thad Stevens,* pp. 300, 317–18.

and of Democrats gave a certain theme of unity to much of his political activity, but by blasting away at the Democratic party from one narrow and idiosyncratic partisan position after another he left far too many hostages each time to let him establish many permanent or stable party connections of his own. In short, he was a picturesque and adroit politician, but a very limited one.

Some of his schemes were rather funny, and deserve mention. There was the series of crafty strokes which culminated in Pennsylvania's delightful "Buckshot War" of 1838. As president of the Canal Board, Stevens thought he had so thoroughly covered the state during that summer, through the skilful letting of contracts and the use of other techniques, that the Whigs and Anti-Masons could not possibly lose —but they lost. Then his efforts at Harrisburg to rally the anti-Democrats to form a rump, hang onto the state government, and have the election declared fraudulent attracted a furious mob outside the state house, all screaming for the blood of Thaddeus Stevens—whereupon the lone genius saw that his most prudent move was out the back window. His power in Pennsylvania politics for the next decade remained about zero. With the Whigs' presidential victory in 1840 Stevens counted on a cabinet post, to which, abstractly speaking, his claims were fairly good—except that Clay and Webster, who were calling the party tune, would not touch him. Stevens had glittering visions of himself as a president-maker, but found himself, as steadily as could be, on the wrong side. He kept promoting Winfield Scott for the nomination, exulting in Scott's appeal as a military hero—but in 1844 it was Clay who got it. Offered amends by the Clay men, Stevens at the last moment began stumping vigorously for Clay—and Clay lost. In 1848 the nomination did go to a military hero—but not Stevens' military hero. Scott was nominated at last in 1852—and made a dreadful showing in the campaign, which was the *coup de grace* for the whole Whig party. We see Stevens again in 1856, maneuvering ever so slyly to divide Pennsylvania's electoral ticket to keep his old enemy Buchanan from getting the state's electoral vote. Buchanan gathered in that vote handily. Stevens was at the Chicago convention in 1860 but failed to get on the Lincoln bandwagon—and the old trickster was subsequently outmaneuvered by Lincoln every time he angled for a cabinet post. It is almost an anticlimax to add that Stevens in 1864 opposed the nomination of Andrew Johnson as Vice-President.[29]

[29] *Ibid.*, pp. 56–72, 73–76, 76–79, 82, 94–95, 103–6, 132–33, 200. Korngold disputes Current's version of Stevens' behavior at the 1860 convention, claiming that the latter switched to Lincoln on the third ballot. *Thaddeus Stevens*, pp. 111–12.

Stevens fared just as badly in his efforts at his own advancement, being elected to Congress in 1848 but losing the nomination in 1852 through his own intraparty factionalism. He did not regain his seat until 1858. He thought, in 1857, that he had really made a coup in managing the election of Simon Cameron as the first Republican senator from Pennsylvania. But he soon had every reason to regret it, for the treacherous Cameron proved to be no creature of his. The first Republican boss of Pennsylvania was, alas, not Thaddeus Stevens but Simon Cameron.[30] Stevens would have loved to go to the Senate himself (he was still trying the year of his death), but Cameron, Curtin, and their minions would have none of him. The political legend which Thaddeus Stevens fashioned for himself was borne out no more than half way by the facts of his career, even with the Civil War and reconstruction eras thrown in. He was in fact one of those caricature types which American politics, with a certain credulous indulgence, cherishes in its folklore—the trickster seemingly capable of accomplishing anything, and reveling unabashedly in his trickery. But the type is seldom seen in life—Stevens himself existed to no small degree in the realm of the fabulous—and our politics almost never allows such a prodigy, no matter on what plane he may exist, to manage its majorities.

After all is said, however, it must be admitted that the Stevens legend was given a powerful impetus—and the man's own career a new lease on life—by the quasi-revolutionary crisis of 1861. By the summer of that year, when Congress met after the firing upon Sumter, the intransigent no-compromiser was now splendidly situated. His kind of drive seemed at last in line with the needs of the hour. He nominated Galusha Grow as Speaker; Grow was elected, and Stevens was rewarded with the most powerful of the committee chairmanships, that of Ways and Means, which gave him extensive floor privileges. He spoke with fire, in August, 1861, for the freeing of all slaves and laid down for the first time his "conquered provinces" principle. Now approaching seventy, he became a grim old dynamo, and this initial burst of energy amid the irresolution of men still numbed by the suddenness of the crisis was quite dazzling enough to make Blaine refer to Stevens, in after years, as the "natural leader" of the House.[31]

And yet the Stevens influence cannot be said to have held up over time, except in the oblique sense that some of his advanced positions—

[30] Current, *Old Thad Stevens*, pp. 106–7.

[31] Blaine, *Twenty Years*, I, 325.

such as those on emancipation and the use of Negro troops—were taken over and promoted by more moderate men. He was influential, for instance, in getting the Confiscation Acts through, but they fell far short of his pet projects for elaborate confiscation of Southern property. He certainly did not rule his own committee in financing the war. The Cooke brothers, Henry and Jay, who had a high stake in the committee's business, told each other, "he is of comparatively little importance"; it was such men as Spaulding, Horton, and Morrill who were making the committee's real decisions. Stevens got into various difficulties, having to explain away some of Cameron's dealings in war contracts (and those of one of his own Pennsylvania protégés); his part in the quashing of Elihu Washburne's Illinois canal project antagonized the powerful Chicago *Tribune* and many Illinoisans; and he annoyed everyone by his efforts to get conscientious objectors exempted from money payments under the Draft Act. "Old Thad is stubborn and meddlesome and quite foolishly mad," wrote James Garfield to one of his Ohio friends early in 1864, "because he can't lead this House by the nose as has been his custom hitherto."[32]

Thaddeus Stevens in wartime was always prominent, always in the forefront of things, and certainly entitled to be called one of the wartime radical leaders. But his effectiveness was of an essentially marginal sort: the effectiveness of the parliamentary tactician, not that of the party strategist. The last thing Stevens could be was a dictator. Men of his type seldom have a large share in the making of party policy, except in matters toward which large numbers of men are moving already. Stevens' wartime reputation has something to do with the fact that prosecuting a total war, in which the enemy must be made to surrender unconditionally, requires by its very nature a certain agility, a certain asperity, and decisions of a more or less "radical" character. Thaddeus Stevens was well equipped by temperament to act as a goad for doing what had to be done. He did a great deal in hurrying a number of such decisions along, but that is not the same as saying that he actually made very many of them himself.

What, then, is to be said of Stevens as the whiplash of reconstruction? The situation of late 1865 and early 1866 was not unlike the one he had stepped into in 1861—a situation coalescing toward strong and decisive action and calling for a tactician who knew all the angles. Here is where he makes his grandest and most flamboyant splash. Amid

[32] Current, *Old Thad Stevens*, pp. 173, 162–64, 165–66, 187, 194; *Life and Letters of James Abram Garfield*, ed. Theodore C. Smith (New Haven: Yale University Press, 1925), I, 366.

the fixed determination of Congress to take hold of reconstruction for itself—but rather less certain as to means—his role could hardly be clearer. The parliamentarian comes once again to the fore, full of caustic wit, vindictiveness, and sardonic self-assurance: who could challenge the old man now? Newcomers gaped; it was as though he held the House hypnotized—and in a way he did. Stevens' energy was that of a man absolutely convinced, and in a sense rightly, that he and history were for the moment in perfect step. Some men wait all their lives for such a moment. The events of the next six months were, to all intents and purposes, more than enough to establish Thaddeus Stevens as the bête noire of reconstruction.

The story of Thaddeus Stevens would not be complete without its postscript, which consists, once again, of afterthoughts strongly tinged with suspicion. The question creeps in once more of just how much he deserves of both what he was credited with and what he was damned for. It seems plausible enough, in the political history of the period, to paint Old Thad in satanic colors and attribute to him marvels of manipulation. But, upon combining politics and biography, one discovers that the effort to make him either a great man or a great devil will begin somehow to break apart; there are too many doubts either way. There is really not much in his background to justify the picture of Stevens dictating to an entire party for more than limited day-to-day purposes. For when extremism becomes the majority position, it is not enough—considering the nature of democratic politics—to attribute such a development to the early extremists. Something more, much more, is needed. One has to do, in this case, with a whole party on the move, and not at the beck and call of Thaddeus Stevens. One suspects that large numbers of men do not permit themselves to be pushed about by such a man unless they are headed pretty much in his direction already. When large numbers do, it is, of course, quite a temptation to make folklore on the spot and point to the evil genius—and many, even then, did just that. And for those who relish the spectacle of revolutionary doings, there is something compelling in the image of Old Thad as the original Jacobin. Georges Clemenceau, who shared some of Stevens' attributes, was greatly taken with the old skirmisher.[33] But America was not France; the political culture for sustaining such a type did not exist here. Stevens was of great use to

[33] See Georges Clemenceau, *American Reconstruction, 1865–1870, and the Impeachment of President Johnson*, ed. Fernand Baldensperger and trans. Margaret MacVeagh (New York: Dial Press, 1928), pp. 124–26, 224–27.

his party during the crisis, but not many men really thanked him for it; too many of them were just downright annoyed by his shenanigans.

Thaddeus Stevens must, no doubt, be allowed his hour. But the attributes of prime-movership to be accorded him must be measured out with a good deal of care and no little parsimony, for the really solid work in the process of taking over reconstruction from the Executive during the first session of the Thirty-ninth Congress was done by others. The pivotal figures were men of impeccable standing in the Republican party, men whose integrity and motives were quite above suspicion, men not accustomed to being managed by anyone. They were men, moreover, who did not have much use for the old man from Pennsylvania.[34]

It is all too true that by the time the Thirty-ninth Congress met for its second session in December, 1866, its proceedings and deliberations would be dominated by what may well be called the "spirit of Thaddeus Stevens"; its work, culminating in the Military Reconstruction Acts of three months later, now saw Stevens in the forefront of everything. But by that time, changes of the most prodigious sort had been effected in the relations between the executive and legislative branches as well as in moderate sentiment, both of which had been undermined and demoralized. It would be most misleading—indeed, simply wrong —to think of those changes as having been the work of Thaddeus Stevens.

III   MR. REPUBLICAN: WILLIAM PITT FESSENDEN

Topmost among the Republican party's senior statesmen, as Congress met in 1865, was the man who would shortly assume the chairmanship of the Joint Committee on Reconstruction. He was William Pitt Fessenden, the flint-faced senator from Maine. Fessenden was not an uncommon type, in the sense that a small group, at least, of men of his sort may at almost any time be found in the United States Senate—men who may be counted on to meet virtually any counsels of heat and passion with a certain chilly distaste. They tend to function as a kind of balance wheel, even at those times when the government must steer through the most trying crises of state. Such men, usually of unexceptionable standing in the public confidence and often wasp-

[34] "President Johnson must see," declared *Harper's*, "that the Union party can not accept the indiscriminate support of all his views and measures as the test of constitutional fidelity; and he makes a profound mistake if he regards the situation as a struggle between himself and Mr. Thaddeus Stevens. When he sees those who have as little respect for Mr. Stevens's wisdom as he himself gravely questioning his course, it is a fatal delusion if he sees only Mr. Stevens." *Harper's Weekly*, X (Apr. 14, 1866), 226. See also the letter of Calvin Day to Gideon Welles quoted below, pp. 312–13.

ishly sensitive to the cares and prerogatives of senators, may not always move in the direction of ultimate wisdom, but they seldom move in haste. Few major decisions are made without their leadership—or, at the very least, their concurrence—and their veto in the last analysis can kill almost anything. They will serve as the pivot upon which policy must turn: as the barometer, so to speak, against which the decisions of real consequence must be tested in advance.

The office of senator hardly confers automatic qualities of statesmanship on a man. Indeed, it would be fair to say that those who come fully up to the mark are always a very select minority. And yet of all the roles that are available in American government, that of senator does seem to come closest to providing the maximum incentives and privileges conducive to serious deportment. For those who do attain it, the office usually represents the highest point of a career (the Senate is not often a steppingstone to the presidency), and election to that office, perhaps more than to any other, is normally assumed to be the reward of long years of responsible public service. Such are the conditions of holding the office, at any rate, that there are always those who will take its duties with the utmost gravity. Those who do so behave, moreover, are far more likely to be effective as models, and to exert decisive influence on the setting of policy, than is the case with their counterparts in the less august, less exclusive, and more democratic House of Representatives.

Such a group was most certainly to be found in the Senate at the assembling of the Thirty-ninth Congress. There was Lyman Trumbull of Illinois, who had served as assemblyman, Illinois secretary of state, judge of the Illinois supreme court, and member of Congress; a senator for ten years, he had since 1861 been chairman of the Senate Judiciary Committee.[35] James W. Grimes of Iowa had been a member of both the Iowa territorial and state assemblies, had served as governor, built up the original Republican party in that state, and had gone to the Senate in 1859; he served as chairman, during the war and after, of the Committee on Naval Affairs.[36] John Sherman of Ohio, brother of the general, had been in Congress virtually since youth, going to the House at the age of thirty-one; he was re-elected three times, served

[35] The standard biography of Lyman Trumbull (1813–96) is that by Horace White, *The Life of Lyman Trumbull* (Boston: Houghton Mifflin, 1913). It has the advantage of having been written by a man who knew Trumbull intimately for many years. Trumbull's papers in the Library of Congress are extensive.

[36] The only life of Grimes (1816–71) available is William Salter, *Life of James W. Grimes* . . . (New York: D. Appleton, 1876). Grimes, Trumbull, and Fessenden were later among the seven "recusant Senators" who refused to vote for conviction at President Johnson's impeachment trial.

there as chairman of Ways and Means, and succeeded Chase in the Senate in 1861; he had been a key figure in Civil War financing, both as member and as chairman of the Finance Committee. Sherman's career in the top councils of government (including the secretaryships of Treasury and State) was destined to last over another generation.[37] These were the men from whom the solid Republican journals tended to take their cues during this period, and Republicans everywhere who thought of themselves as men of calm and conservative sentiments (men of the type represented by Samuel Bowles, Hamilton Fish, and George Templeton Strong) looked to this group to bear out their own notions of the right ordering of things.

No one more aptly embodied these judicious standards than did William Pitt Fessenden himself.[38] Fessenden had all the qualifications, including a certain puritanical testiness, for filling out the proper picture of what a senator was supposed to be. He had been one for over a decade, having served before that in the House of Representatives and in the Maine legislature. He had been a leader of the Maine bar, as had his father, and had been prominent in the councils of the Whig party there for many years. Daniel Webster had been his godfather. Fessenden had been elected to the Senate on an antislavery ticket and was a charter member and leader of the Republican party in his state. As chairman of the Senate Finance Committee, Fessenden acquired

[37] On John Sherman (1823–1900), see his own *Recollections of Forty Years in the House, Senate, and Cabinet: An Autobiography* (2 vols.; Chicago: Werner, 1895), also Winfield S. Kerr, *John Sherman: His Life and Public Services* (2 vols.; Boston: Sherman, French, 1908); and *The Sherman Letters: Correspondence between General and Senator Sherman from 1837 to 1891*, ed. Rachel Sherman Thorndike (New York: Charles Scribner's Sons, 1894). There is a very rich collection of Sherman papers in the Library of Congress.

[38] "Among the living statesmen of this country there is none who commands profounder popular confidence than William Pitt Fessenden, Senator from Maine. Absolute integrity, a certain antique severity of character . . . , and a singularly clear and concise oratory, are qualities which are apparent to every man who watches his career. . . . In the Senate debates Mr. Fessenden is always conspicuous for an incisive good sense. . . . In opposition he is always reasonable, speaking to the merits of the special case, and not planting himself upon abstractions. Quick to defend and explain the prerogative of the body in which he sits, he neither traduces nor defies his opponents. . . . Unquestionably, Mr. Fessenden represents the patient common sense of the Union party in this country." *Harper's Weekly*, X (Apr. 7, 1866), 210.

Francis Fessenden, *Life and Public Services of William Pitt Fessenden* (2 vols.; Boston: Houghton Mifflin, 1907), is a very poor biography from the viewpoint of organization. Another has recently been written, Charles A. Jellison, Jr., "William Pitt Fessenden, Statesman of the Middle Ground" (Ph.D. diss., University of Virginia, 1956). Fessenden's political correspondence is in the Library of Congress, and there is a collection of family letters, full of valuable information, at Bowdoin College. Fessenden's letters to his "Cousin Lizzy" (Mrs. Elizabeth Fessenden Warriner), to whom he was very close, are especially illuminating for the political confidences which they impart.

great knowledge and competence in financial affairs and was instrumental in the success of the Treasury's war program. Upon Lincoln's insistence, he succeeded Chase as Secretary of the Treasury in 1864,[39] though he resigned in March, 1865, in order to go back to the Senate.

Fessenden was capable of extreme stuffiness when it came to orderly procedure. He was an exceptional debater, known for frequent shortness of temper, but his very feeling for order gave him an infinite respect for the co-ordinate nature of government. His very sensitivity to the Senate's prerogatives made him acutely conscious of the problems of harmony with the other branches as well as within the party. Thus, though in many ways an austere man, he was by inclination and temperament a negotiator—as illustrated by his behavior with regard to the Confiscation Act of 1862. The bills of both houses had been severe enough to meet the opposition of many conservatives; Fessenden himself thought them unconstitutional. But he knew that a confiscation bill in some form would be sure to pass and that the President would certainly veto the ones then being considered. Accordingly he set to work to get a bill so modified as to meet the major objections and organized the necessary support to pass it—activity which included some careful negotiating with the President himself. Fessenden was denounced by extreme radicals and extreme conservatives alike, but the bill passed, and that wing "under the lead of Collamer, Fessenden, and others," according to Fessenden's biographer, "usually controlled the action of the party from that time on."[40]

Infringements upon the Senate's dignity, from both without and within, pained him unspeakably. The harangues of Charles Sumner not only stretched Fessenden's patience but offended his sense of propriety. "If I could cut the throats of about half a dozen Republican Senators," he once confided to his cousin Lizzy, ". . . Sumner would be the first victim, as he is by far the greatest fool of the lot."[41] He was equally pained by the verbosity of Garret Davis, the proslavery senator from Kentucky, but he opposed an effort in 1862 to expel that

[39] Reaction to Fessenden's appointment was exceptionally favorable for that of a new cabinet officer. The incoming Secretary was described by the Washington *Chronicle* as "A Senator who never left his post, never made a speech without a purpose, and always sharp, clear, brief in debate . . . , a positive, daring statesman . . . of purity and whiteness"; and by the Democratic New York *World* as "Unquestionably the fittest man in his party for that high trust. . . ." Quoted in Jellison, "Fessenden," p. 324. Over the weekend following Fessenden's appointment, long-term government bonds went up as much as two and a half points. *Ibid.*, p. 325.

[40] Fessenden, *Fessenden*, I, 275.

[41] Fessenden to Elizabeth Fessenden Warriner, June 1, 1862, Fessenden MSS, Bowdoin College.

senator for disloyalty: such an effort was unworthy and undignified.[42] Encroachments, actual or contemplated, upon the Senate's freedom of action found him implacable. Debating the admission of senators from Arkansas in 1864, he declared:

I am of the opinion, and have been for some time that the question of reconstruction as it is called, the question of what is and what is not a State entitled to be represented here, should properly be settled by Congress, and can not be settled by any other power but Congress in any possible way.[43]

William Pitt Fessenden was thin and spare in all ways. Though he was not yet quite sixty at the opening of the Thirty-ninth Congress, it was already one of his conceits to picture himself as an old man. With his record of past service, his reputation for stiff-necked rectitude, and his undoubted position of leadership in the Senate, Fessenden was the ideal choice to head the most important congressional committee ever formed. Thaddeus Stevens was a member—but it was not Stevens' committee, it was Fessenden's; the reins were firmly in the hands of the chairman, who had no intention of relinquishing them to anyone.[44]

Fessenden was thus so strategically and pivotally located that his problems and his experience over the ensuing four months can serve admirably as a paradigm of the experience of an entire party. One discovers a great deal more about the government crisis that was precipitated in the winter and early spring of 1865–66 by following the course of things along *his* angle of vision—and that of his colleagues Trumbull, Grimes, and Sherman—than by following the philippics of Charles Sumner and Thaddeus Stevens.

[42] Fessenden, *Fessenden*, I, 276.

[43] *Cong. Globe*, 38 Cong., 1 sess., p. 3364.

[44] See below, p. 277. Typical of Fessenden's touchiness on all such matters were the words he used on December 12, 1865, in debating Stevens' proposed joint resolution on reconstruction: "I have no idea of abandoning the prerogatives, the rights, and the duties of my position in favor of anybody, however that person or any number of persons may desire it." *Cong. Globe*, 39 Cong., 1 sess., p. 27.

Chapter
10

*Johnson's Break
with the Party*

I   FIRST PHASE, DECEMBER 4, 1865–
FEBRUARY 23, 1866: THE FREEDMEN'S BUREAU BILL

The critical period of President Johnson's relations with Congress may be said to have terminated on April 6, 1866, with the successful repassage of the Civil Rights Bill over the President's veto. This period properly falls in two clearly marked phases, the first of which began with the opening of Congress and came to an end with the veto of the Freedmen's Bureau Bill and its immediate aftermath. The entire period, however, was one in which an accommodation with the President on the problem of reconstruction was not only fully possible but was anxiously desired by a majority in Congress and by the public at large. During that time, efforts by Republican leaders—among whom Fessenden, Trumbull, Grimes, and Sherman were outstanding—to negotiate such an understanding with Johnson were pressed with the utmost persistence and energy. For a full appreciation of these efforts, a close attention to chronology now becomes of great importance.

The first phase, from December 4 to February 23, was characterized for the most part by high hopes for a harmonious settlement. Stevens, with his resolution for creating a joint committee on reconstruction, may have been the man of the hour on opening day, but on succeeding days things ground more slowly in the Senate, where members desired more time to make up their minds. The House resolution was not taken up on the fifth, nor (in spite of Sumner's ardor for getting the matter settled) was it considered on the sixth, Fessenden having announced: "I think it had better lie over until we meet again."[1] Five days later, on December 11, a Senate Republican caucus voted to amend the House

[1] *Congressional Globe*, 39 Cong., 1 sess., p. 12.

[274]

resolution in certain important particulars. Despite the wishes of the House, the Senate refused to bind itself against admitting any Southern members until the committee had reported; nor would it agree that all papers pertaining to representation (Southern credentials and related material) should necessarily be turned over to the committee without debate. The point at issue was not the need for such a committee, there being no difficulty on that point; it was rather that the Senate would accept no infringements on its prerogatives, not the least of which was simply that of exercising moderation. For a touch of insurance against danger from another quarter the caucus then made it a concurrent resolution, which, unlike a joint resolution, did not require the President's signature.[2] The amended resolution passed the Senate the next day, with all the Republican senators except Doolittle, Cowan, and Dixon voting for it.[3]

Such was the initial moderate counterbalance to the first impulsive action of the House. This was spelled out by Senator Fessenden, who acted as spokesman for the amended statement on congressional policy. The committee was necessary, and he had approved the idea from the first,

simply for this reason: that this question of the readmission . . . of these confederate States, so called, and all the questions connected with that subject, I conceived to be of infinite importance, requiring calm and serious consideration, and I believed that the appointment of a committee, carefully selected by the two Houses, to take that subject into consideration, was not only wise in itself, but an imperative duty resting upon the representatives of the people in the two branches of Congress.

Still, he had not been "prepared to act upon that question at once," since he felt that "the resolution perhaps went a little too far" and required amending to the form presently being considered. Fessenden particularly emphasized that no quarrel was being sought with the President:

That I am disposed and ready to support him to the best of my ability, as every gentleman around me is, in good faith and with kind feeling in all that he may desire that is consistent with my views of duty to the country, giving him credit for intentions as good as mine, and with ability far greater, I am ready to asseverate.

[2] Benjamin B. Kendrick, *The Journal of the Joint Committee of Fifteen on Reconstruction* (New York: Columbia University Press, 1914), pp. 145–46.

[3] *Cong. Globe*, 39 Cong., 1 sess., p. 30. James R. Doolittle of Wisconsin, Edgar Cowan of Pennsylvania, and James Dixon of Connecticut were the three Republican senators who attached themselves to President Johnson and who, virtually from the first, acted with the Democrats on most matters pertaining to reconstruction. See also above, pp. 80 ff. They were subsequently joined by Senator Daniel S. Norton, of Minnesota.

But he made it clear that the Senate was itself a part of the administration, "and a very important part of it."

I have a great respect, not for myself, perhaps, but for the position which I hold as a Senator of the United States; and no measure of Government, no policy of the President, or of the head of a Department, shall pass me, while I am a Senator, if I know it, until I have examined it and given my assent to it; not on account of the source from which it emanates, but on account of its own intrinsic merits, and because I believe it will result in the good of the country. That is my duty as a Senator. . . .

Such was the reasonable minimum basis, so far as Fessenden was concerned, for a moderate approach to the problems of reconstruction. "It is an imputation upon nobody; it is not anything which any sensible man could ever find fault with, or be disposed to do so."[4]

When the membership of the Joint Committee was announced by Speaker Colfax for the House on December 14, and by President pro tempore Lafayette Foster, of Connecticut, for the Senate on December 21, its balance of power was noticeably on the moderate side. "It is not often," wrote Blaine, "that such solicitude is felt in Congress touching the membership of a committee as was now developed in both branches. . . . Both in Congress and among the people the conviction was general that the party was entitled to the services of its best men. There was no struggle among members for positions on the committee; and when the names were announced they gave universal satisfaction to the Republicans."[5] The leading Republican moderates on the committee were men of high prestige whose opinions carried much weight—Fessenden, Grimes, and Bingham—while the core of professed radicals, Stevens, Boutwell, and Howard, were somewhat less secure in the public esteem. Of the three Democrats, Senator Reverdy Johnson of Maryland had long enjoyed a position of leadership in his party.[6] With such a balance, there was much reason to expect a tone of moderation in the sessions of the committee. Thaddeus Stevens' sarcasm and parliamentary adroitness would be of limited effect in this setting; if he could not persuade Fessenden and Grimes—neither of whom liked him —to his extreme views, he would have to give up all hopes for a two-thirds majority in the Senate. Blaine's assertion, moreover, that there had been no competition for membership on the committee was not entirely correct, for it appears that Charles Sumner had very much wanted to be not only a member but the chairman as well. Sumner's

[4] *Ibid.*, pp. 26–27.

[5] James G. Blaine, *Twenty Years of Congress*, II, 127.

[6] For the Committee's membership, see above, chap. ix, n. 17.

hopes had been foiled by the more or less general preference for Fessenden, a fact which seems to have afforded Fessenden himself no little gratification.

Mr. Sumner was very anxious for the place [he wrote to Cousin Lizzy], but, standing as he does before the country, and committed to the most ultra views, even his friends declined to support him, and almost to a man fixed upon me. Luckily I had marked out my line, and everybody understands where I am. I think I can see my way through, and if Sumner and Stevens, and a few other such men do not embroil us with the President, matters can be satisfactorily arranged—satisfactorily, I mean, to the great bulk of Union men throughout the States.[7]

All in all, from Fessenden's point of view, there appeared to be good grounds for this initial optimism. Although a good deal of radical passion was being aired in the House, the Senate had shown so far that it had ample resources for dampening extremism. The President should thus be able to perceive with clarity where his own hopes for a moderate settlement lay; should he fail to co-operate with Fessenden, Trumbull, Grimes, and Sherman, then so far as anyone could tell, he would have nowhere else to go.

Congress reconvened on January 5, after a two-week recess for the holidays. On that day, the first serious efforts toward a legislative program on reconstruction were initiated when Lyman Trumbull introduced two bills in the Senate. One was titled "An act to amend an act entitled 'An act to establish a Bureau for the relief of Freedmen and Refugees,' and for other purposes," and was henceforth referred to, in congressional debate and elsewhere, as the Freedmen's Bureau Bill. The other, "An act to protect all persons in the United States in their civil rights, and furnish the means of their vindication," was known as the Civil Rights Bill. The immediate stimulus for these measures had been the feeling that federal action of some sort was needed to halt the Southern legislatures in their work of Negro code-making. Public awareness of this legislative trend in the South had become general during the month of December, and Northern reaction to the Southern codes had been unusually hostile; many bitter words were spoken during that period about slavery being enacted all over again. Opinion thus urged federal steps that would bring order to a state of things still apparently out of control—steps for protecting the freedmen in a position currently fluid and precarious, and for stabilizing that position, if possible, against the time when such matters as Negro rights would be entirely under the domination of restored and readmitted Southern

[7] Fessenden to Elizabeth F. Warriner, Dec. 24, 1865, Fessenden MSS, Bowdoin College.

states. Senator Trumbull, concerned to get such measures afoot, and anxious also to preserve and promote harmony with the President, had been careful to clear his plans with Johnson before introducing the bills. Then when the bills were printed (before their consideration in committee), Trumbull furnished the President with copies, and the two men had a number of conversations which convinced Trumbull that they were in full accord.[8]

The Freedmen's Bureau Bill was designed both to extend the life of an act passed during the last month of the Lincoln administration and to expand the functions of machinery presently in existence under that act. The Freedmen's Bureau, the agency created by the original act, operated under the jurisdiction of the War Department, and its officers in the Southern states were charged with problems of relief for ex-slaves and other refugees both colored and white, dispossessed through conditions created by the rebellion. The Bureau also concerned itself with the disposition of abandoned lands, and under the act General Sherman had settled several thousand freedmen upon such lands in order to give them employment, although occupancy was understood to be of a temporary nature.[9] The original act was to have expired one year after the end of the war, and the new measure contemplated its extension until otherwise terminated by law. The powers of the Bureau under existing law were felt to have become inadequate for meeting the problems now facing it, and Trumbull's bill was designed to supplement certain of those powers. The Bureau's administrative structure, geographical jurisdiction, and functions relating to relief, abandoned lands, asylums, and schools were all restated and redefined in the first six sections of the bill. But the sections which would eventually come under greatest debate were the last two, in which, under certain conditions, the Bureau was given power to protect ordinary civil rights. Cases of discrimination, on account of color or prior servitude, against such rights were to come under military courts consisting of Bureau officers and agents and were punishable by fine or imprisonment or both. Such jurisdiction in any state was to cease upon restoration of that state to its constitutional relations to the Union.[10]

[8] *Cong. Globe*, 39 Cong., 1 sess., p. 1760; Horace White, *The Life of Lyman Trumbull*, p. 272. See also below, pp. 292, 316–17.

[9] On the problem of abandoned lands see Oliver O. Howard, *Autobiography* (New York: Baker & Taylor, 1908), II, 189–205, 229–44. General Howard was head of the Freedmen's Bureau. A very valuable modern monograph is George R. Bentley, *A History of the Freedmen's Bureau* (Philadelphia: University of Pennsylvania, 1955).

[10] "An act to amend an act entitled 'An act to establish a Bureau for the relief of Freedmen and Refugees,' and for other purposes," in McPherson, *Reconstruction*, pp. 72–74.

Trumbull's other measure, the Civil Rights Bill, was an effort to give permanent, explicit, and general application to certain principles implied both in the Freedmen's Bureau Bill and, presumably, in the Thirteenth Amendment. It conferred citizenship (in language similar to that of the first section of the later Fourteenth Amendment) upon "all persons born in the United States and not subject to any foreign power, excluding Indians not taxed," and confirmed such citizens in all states and territories "of every race and color, without regard to any previous condition of slavery or involuntay servitude," in the right

to make and enforce contracts; to sue, be parties, and give evidence; to inherit, purchase, lease, sell, hold, and convey real and personal property; and to full and equal benefit of all laws and proceedings for the security of person and property as is enjoyed by white citizens, and [such persons] shall be subject to like punishment, pains, and penalties, and to none other, any law, statute, ordinance, regulation, or custom to the contrary notwithstanding.

The district courts of the United States were to have jurisdiction over all crimes and offenses committed under the act.[11]

These two bills—neither of which in the intention of their author necessarily contemplated suffrage—would be of great importance, as it turned out, in defining the relations between Congress and the President.

Three days after Trumbull's introduction of the Freedmen's Bureau and Civil Rights bills (supplemented, as the senator conceived it, by negotiations with President Johnson), the Joint Committee on Reconstruction opened its own first negotiations with the President. On January 8 a very conservative-appearing subcommittee called upon Johnson (it consisted of Fessenden, Senator Reverdy Johnson, and Representative Elihu Washburne) to request that further Executive action on reconstruction, unless imperatively necessary, be deferred until some action had been taken on that subject by the committee. The "honest brokers" emphasized the committee's desire to avoid collision between Executive and Congress and expressed the hope that there would be mutual forbearance. Johnson assured them that he too desired harmony of action between the two branches. He hoped that the matter of reconstruction would proceed as fast as the public interest permitted, but "it was not his intention to do more than had been done for the present."[12]

[11] *Ibid.*, pp. 78–80; *U.S. Statutes at Large*, XIV, 27.

[12] Kendrick, *Journal*, pp. 39–41.

Fessenden, full of hopes for harmony, yet testy over rumors of conflict, wrote to Cousin Lizzy:

In addition to all other difficulties, the work of keeping the peace between the President and those who wish to quarrel with him, aided as they are by those who wish him to quarrel with us, is a most difficult undertaking. The fools are not all dead, you know. I hope we shall be able to put things upon a sound basis. That *must* be done, quarrel or no quarrel, but I hope to avoid the necessity.[13]

Harper's Weekly and the New York *Tribune* expressed high confidence, assuring their readers that no basic differences existed between Congress and the President. The *Tribune* editorialized:

We spent the latter part of last week at Washington, anxiously inquiring into the political situation, and seeking to measure the probability of the rumored breach between the President and Congress touching Southern "restoration" or "Reconstruction;" and we believe that most of our readers will share the satisfaction with which we announce our conclusion that there need be, and probably will be, none. What maladroit, or malignant, or tale-bearing intermeddlers may achieve, we cannot foretell; but we are confident that there is no necessary incompatibility between the views and purposes of Congress and those of the President, and no desire—at least, no preponderant desire—on either hand to create such incompatibility. And we feel sure that frank, earnest, kindly conferences between the Capitol and the White-House will speedily and almost certainly remove any obstacles which may seem to exist to a cordial and thorough cooperation.[14]

Insisting that Johnson did "not assume to dictate in any least degree to Congress," *Harper's Weekly* spoke in similar vein. "It seems to us that the perpetual distrust of the President which appears in some quarters is wholly unjustifiable. His purpose is certainly beyond suspicion."[15]

Fessenden now, on January 23, made a calculated effort to formalize the relationship of Congress to the President on the highest plane and in its most moderate light. His speech in the Senate on that day was ostensibly a defense of Trumbull's Freedmen's Bureau Bill (soon to be voted on), but the speech had actually been designed to serve a more general purpose: he envisioned for it something in the nature of a self-fulfilling prophecy. As for the bill itself, Fessenden perceived none of the threats to the Constitution which certain of the Democratic members (Hendricks of Indiana and Saulsbury of Delaware) saw in it. He said that the government's powers, in the aftermath of such a crisis as the late war, certainly included whatever was necessary to care for the

[13] Fessenden to Elizabeth F. Warriner, Jan. 14, 1866, Fessenden MSS, Bowdoin College.

[14] New York *Tribune*, Jan. 9, 1866.

[15] "The President's Position," *Harper's Weekly*, X (Jan. 20, 1866), 34.

slaves emancipated as a result of that crisis; neither the expense entailed, nor the absence of written provisions in the Constitution for feeding men, women, or children seemed proper grounds for presuming the measure illegal. He therefore intended to vote for it. Fessenden thereupon proceeded to the more general question of Congress and President, and their mutual relations.

What followed was a set of conciliatory cues, in the form of interpretive predictions regarding the behavior of the President and the duties of Congress. There had been much talk among Democrats of an impending collision, "all idle, ridiculous rumors, without the slightest foundation except the wish of those who invent them and give them currency. . . . I have not, as yet, seen the slightest indication of it, and I do not expect to see it." Even if there were differences of opinion over the most proper time or manner of accomplishing the work of reconstruction, that would hardly be the same as a collision. "Why? Because the President has done nothing that his friends complain of, and his friends in Congress have done nothing that he can complain of." The President's authority for what he had done so far flowed from his duties as commander-in-chief: it was his duty in this case to control the rebellious states and restore order. If, in the course of it, he had wanted to give those states provisional governors and other kinds of assistance, that was his perfect right: "I might have done differently if I had been President, but I might probably not have done so wisely as he did." When should those states be fully returned to the Union? "I think they should come in at the earliest possible moment that they can come with safety. So he thinks."

No man, Fessenden declared, had "a greater respect for the Constitution or a more profound respect for the rights and privileges of the coördinate branches of this Government than the President of the United States." The President would thus have no reason for complaint if Congress, in its turn, did what it had every right and duty to do—to act on its judgment and sense of propriety, taking whatever time should be needed to deliberate upon the common object, which was that "when it can be done safely, at the earliest possible moment, all the States should be restored to their position in the Union." With such an object, there should be no reason to expect disharmony.[16]

Fessenden's aim had been to define a position on middle ground and to give it whatever authority, in speaking for his colleagues, his own utterances might carry (which was considerable); more important, he wished to have his speech serve as a communication to the President.

[16] *Cong. Gobe,* 39 Cong., 1 sess., pp. 364–67.

He was thus setting up a basis on both sides for negotiations and an understanding. That such had indeed been his intention he made clear in a letter to Cousin Lizzy:

I made some remarks a few days since in which I undertook to define his position with regard to Congress. It was a bow drawn at a venture and had two objects,—one to allay the fears of our friends, another to suggest what should be his position. I am inclined to believe that good has been done in both directions, but I shall know more about it to-morrow.[17]

In the most basic sense, Fessenden had indicated to Johnson that if the latter wanted allies in Congress he could have the most powerful ones there were. Fessenden's own great influence was available to him, and the Executive presumably now knew—if he had not known already— the terms on which he might have it. The outcome, at any rate, was an invitation to confer with the President at the White House.[18]

Meanwhile, two developments were emerging. On the twenty-fifth, the Freedmen's Bureau Bill had been passed in the Senate with every Republican senator—even Dixon and Doolittle—voting for it.[19] In the House, at the same time, a full-scale debate was in progress over the first recommendation of the Joint Committee on Reconstruction. Fessenden and his committee had decided that the problem of a new basis for Southern representation (now that the three-fifths provision no longer applied) was one of great urgency; a resolution embodying a proposed constitutional amendment had accordingly been devised by the committee (passing by a 13–1 vote on the twentieth), and was offered to the House on the twenty-second.[20] It was against the background of these developments, then, that Fessenden, on Sunday morning, January 28, called upon the President.

The events of that Sunday apparently proved to be something of an embarrassment for the senator in his hopes for harmony. He and Johnson "spent several hours most satisfactorily," according to Welles, going over the measures then pending; Fessenden, according to his own biographer, "came away with the conviction that the President

[17] Fessenden to Elizabeth F. Warriner, Jan. 28, 1866, Fessenden MSS, Bowdoin College. Fessenden saw the President on the morning of the twenty-eighth, so he evidently wrote this letter the night or day before.

[18] Senator Grimes breakfasted with the President on the twenty-seventh, "and spent two hours with him discussing all subjects in full and most satisfactorily." In the course of their talk, Johnson asked Grimes to arrange for a similar meeting the next day with Fessenden. Gideon Welles, *Diary*, II, 448.

[19] *Cong. Globe*, 39 Cong., 1 sess., p. 421.

[20] *Ibid.*, p. 351; Kendrick, *Journal*, pp. 53, 200. See also below, p. 337.

would act with Congress and there would be no rupture."[21] His optimism must have been heightened still more when Secretary Stanton told him on Monday that "there was no senator in whom the President put so much confidence."[22] But then it turned out that after Fessenden had left, Johnson saw another senator and expressed views which added up to something noticeably different from the impression which Fessenden himself had come away with. Grimes came to Fessenden next day with a newspaper account describing an interview between the President and a "distinguished Senator," and wanted to know if this was his understanding of what Johnson had said to him. The President, according to this story, had declared himself opposed to any further constitutional amendments:

Propositions to amend the Constitution were becoming as numerous as preambles and resolutions at town meetings called to consider the most ordinary questions connected with the administration of local affairs. All this, in his opinion, had a tendency to diminish the dignity and prestige attached to the Constitution. . . .

Nor did the President like the agitation then current for Negro suffrage in the District of Columbia; he thought such agitation "ill-timed, uncalled for, and calculated to do much harm." Fessenden, after reading these things, replied that he had had no such conversation with Johnson; he and Grimes eventually ascertained that the senator in question had been Dixon of Connecticut, a man who at that time exerted next to no influence.[23]

Thaddeus Stevens made an occasion of reading the newspaper story in the House of Representatives on Wednesday (calling it a "proclamation" and remarking that "centuries ago, had it been made to Parliament by a British king, it would have cost him his head");[24] and Fessenden's annoyance was probably about equally divided between Stevens and Johnson. Yet his hopes appear not to have been seriously jarred by the incident, for on February 3 he wrote to his friend George Harrington:

One of my duties (unwritten) is to keep the peace, if possible, between the President and Congress—a matter of some difficulty as you can well

21 Welles, *Diary*, II, 428; Francis Fessenden, *Life and Public Services of William Pitt Fessenden*, II, 34.

22 Fessenden, *Fessenden*, II, 34.

23 New York *Herald*, Jan. 29, 1866. Dixon's low standing at home was commented upon by Welles in an entry for February 15 regarding political affairs in Connecticut. Welles, *Diary*, II, 433.

24 *Cong. Globe*, 39 Cong., 1 sess., pp. 536–37.

understand, when there are many desirous of making a break, and others who have not sense enough to hold their tongues, when talking will do harm. The President's views differ with those of Congress somewhat as to the early admission of the States to their old relations. . . . We think it wise to move slowly and cautiously. This difference does not necessarily involve a quarrel, but Copperheads, ultra abolitionists and rowdies are very anxious to make it one. . . . From all I have seen, the President desires, and means, to stand by those who elected him, and I am resolved to keep him there, if it can be done consistently with the best interests of the country, as I think it can.[25]

On February 6, the House voted on the Freedmen's Bureau Bill and approved it by a great majority. There, too, virtually every Republican favored it, including the outstanding Johnson supporter in the House, Representative Raymond.[26]

The two-week period ending on February 19 seems to have been a time of developing rumors and portents, marked by a growing state of nerves. Behind much of the activity of this period were efforts to arrive at some sort of bargain with the President, one side of which would be his approval of the Freedmen's Bureau Bill, the equivalent being the readmission of Tennessee. Such, at any rate, was the way Gideon Welles understood it, Welles himself having been privy (doubtless involuntarily) to some of these efforts. It was generally assumed that Johnson would sign the Freedmen's Bureau Bill, and nearly all the Republicans thought he should;[27] it was likewise generally supposed that Congress would soon readmit Tennessee, and many newspapers thought that it ought to—and yet back of all that was still a great deal of doubt and misgiving.[28] No one was really quite

[25] Quoted in Charles A. Jellison, "William Pitt Fessenden, Statesman of the Middle Ground" (Ph.D. diss., University of Virginia, 1956), p. 353.

[26] *Cong. Globe*, 39 Cong., 1 sess., p. 688.

[27] According to the Boston *Advertiser*, "there is the best authority for stating that the President some time ago expressed his hearty concurrence in the general principles of the bill. . . ." "The principles of the Freedmen's Bureau bill having already been endorsed by the President," announced the Albany *Journal*, ". . . we can see no reason for the apprehension expressed in some quarters, that it will meet Executive disapproval." And from the Cincinnati *Commercial*: "His approval can hardly be delayed, and perhaps has already been given." Boston *Advertiser*, Feb. 14, 1866; Albany *Journal*, Feb. 12, 1866; Cincinnati *Commercial*, Feb. 16, 1866.

[28] The New York *Tribune*'s Washington correspondent reported on February 17 that there were good arguments on both sides of the Tennessee question. "As to Tennessee, there is, no doubt, an almost universal feeling in favor of the individuals sent by the people of that State to represent them in Congress. As loyalists they are esteemed, and as men they are popular. And this feeling of sympathy for the individual representative predisposes many to look upon Tennessee as an exceptional case, . . . and a variety of good features are discovered in her history and present condition, which, it is

sure what was going to happen. Much would depend on how the President himself saw these developments. Was it a trade? Was he being bribed? Did he even conceive the thing as a negotiable subject at all? One notices a certain tightening-up on both his part and Senator Fessenden's during this period.

It is possible to chart, within a day or so, the President's deliberations on the bill. General J. H. Fullerton, who had been directed to investigate the operations of the Freedmen's Bureau, submitted to Johnson on February 9 a report containing several objections to the pending measure, and Fullerton's estimate of expense, submitted on the twelfth, predicted that the reorganized Bureau would cost $20,000,000 annually to operate.[29] Johnson told Welles on the thirteenth that "he should experience difficulty" in signing the bill. They discussed it again on the sixteenth. "I expressed myself without reserve," wrote Welles, "as did the President, who acquiesced fully in my views. This being the case, I conclude he will place upon it his veto. Indeed, he intimated as much." It may thus be supposed that Johnson had made up his mind by the fifteenth or sixteenth at the latest; perhaps he had even begun on his message already, for Welles adds, "Desired, he said, to have my ideas because they might add to his own, etc."[30] But then nothing, of course, was known for certain at the time regarding the President's final intentions.

Various moves were meanwhile afoot with a view to the early read-

---

urged, entitle her to a different treatment." This view was held by Speaker Colfax and a number of others. On the other hand, "The opponents . . . reply that, Union soldiers were furnished by other Rebel States also; that, if Tennessee is entitled to immediate readmission by having established a Union government and ratified the Constitutional Amendment before the surrenders, so is Louisiana, now one of the most rancorous Rebel States; that although Tennessee is indeed the home of President Johnson, Mr. Johnson would never have been elected Vice President if it had depended upon . . . Tennessee. . . . It is argued, in addition to this, that the account given of the condition of things in Tennessee by the Governor of that State as well as the Union Central Committee, is such as to show how small a share the Union element would have to maintain its official ascendancy in the State if those restrictions were removed which serve as inducement for good behavior. But above all, it is asked: If Tennessee be readmitted, unconditionally, without having given any further guaranties, on what theory . . . are you going to justify the keeping out of the other Rebel States, however disloyal, until they shall have given further guaranties?" New York *Tribune*, Feb. 19, 1866.

[29] Fullerton to Johnson, Feb. 9 and 12, 1866, Johnson MSS, Library of Congress. It seems, according to George Bentley, that Johnson already knew in advance what sort of recommendations he would get from Fullerton at the time he asked for them. During this period Fullerton, though serving with the Freedmen's Bureau as Howard's adjutant, had apparently been doing all he could to curry favor with the President by undermining the Bureau's effectiveness. Bentley, *History of the Freedmen's Bureau*, p. 118.

[30] Welles, *Diary*, II, 432–33.

mission of Tennessee, in the hope that Johnson might be encouraged to sign. Grimes, Bingham, and Grider, acting as a subcommittee of the Joint Committee on Reconstruction, had been investigating Tennessee conditions since January 25 and had gathered the impression that the Union cause there would be encouraged by readmission. On February 15, Bingham offered a resolution in committee to readmit Tennessee without qualifications. No decision was reached that day, however, and discussion was postponed until two days later.[31] Welles wrote in his diary on the sixteenth:

> There is an apparent rupturing among the Radicals [Welles is by now applying this term to the entire Republican party], or a portion of them. They wish to make terms. Will admit the representation from Tennessee if the President will yield. But the President cannot yield and sacrifice his honest convictions by way of compromise.
>
> Truman Smith came to see me yesterday. Says the House wants to get on good terms with the President, and ought to; that the President is right, but it will be well to let Congress decide when and how the States shall be represented. . . . I have an impression that Truman called at the suggestion of Seward, and that this matter of conceding to Congress emanates from the Secretary of State, and from good but mistaken motives.

And again, on the seventeenth:

> Governor Morgan [Edwin D. Morgan, a moderate senator from New York who had ties with Seward and Weed] called this morning on matters of business. Had some talk on current matters. He says Tennessee Representatives will be admitted before the close of next week; that he so told Wilson and Sumner yesterday, whereat Sumner seemed greatly disturbed. From some givings-out by Morgan, intimations from Truman Smith, and what the President himself has heard, I think there is a scheme to try and induce him to surrender his principles in order to secure seats to the Tennessee delegation. But they will not influence him to do wrong in order to secure right.[32]

When the Joint Committee met on the seventeenth, the whole Tennessee plan was very much on the knife edge. Johnson himself had still given no hints on the Freedmen's Bureau Bill. Did anyone present suspect what Welles already knew? How closely had Welles held his tongue with Smith and Morgan? There is no specific evidence. But the moderate position, to say the very least, had nothing from the President on which it might draw for sustenance, and the committee meeting did not go harmoniously that day. Fessenden was no longer disposed to admit Tennessee unconditionally (if, indeed, he ever had been; no evidence exists for that either), and he cast the deciding vote

[31] Kendrick, *Journal*, pp. 63–64, 225–26.
[32] Welles, *Diary*, II, 434.

against Bingham's resolution, thus splitting with his close friend Grimes. Fessenden thereupon appointed a new and more radical sub-committee (composed of Williams, Conkling, and Boutwell) to draw up a new resolution with revised conditions of readmission.[33] But if Fessenden's state of mind had, for any reason, undergone modification on the Tennessee question, the scale was still apparently inclined toward the favorable side, for he wrote that night to Cousin Lizzy:

I ... have just come from a four hours' session of the reconstruction committee, in which nothing was concluded, though progress was made. I think we shall conclude to admit Tennessee in some shape. I hope so as to make a valuable precedent. Whether the President will be easy there I cannot tell; but though I will do something to keep the peace, I will not vote away one inch of the safeguards necessary in this terrible condition of affairs.[34]

All the elements began precipitating out on Monday morning, February 19. The Joint Committee met at 10:30 and heard the resolution which had been prepared by Representative Conkling on the readmission of Tennessee. It was full of conditions: Tennessee had to promise never to assume any rebel debt, never to repudiate the federal debt, never to attempt secession again, and active rebels must remain disfranchised for a five-year period. Bingham did not like the part about disfranchisement and moved to have it struck out; Boutwell wanted to have Tennessee put Negro suffrage into its constitution; and Fessenden did not think it necessary to say anything about the federal debt. In the end nothing at all was done about the resolution; it was not even voted upon, and the committee adjourned until the following day.[35]

At that same hour, the President was addressing his cabinet and telling the members why he was sending Congress the veto message which he had just read to them. He was "emphatic and unequivocal in his remarks," according to Welles, and "earnest to eloquence" as he warmed to a review of matters upon which he had apparently been brooding for some time. There were radical intrigues in Congress, and he saw the Joint Committee on Reconstruction as a kind of radical cabal—a "council of fifteen which in secret prescribed legislative action and assumed to dictate the policy of the Administration."[36] The veto

---

[33] Kendrick, *Journal*, pp. 64–67, 226–27.

[34] Fessenden, *Fessenden*, II, 26.

[35] Kendrick, *Journal*, pp. 68–69, 233.

[36] Welles, *Diary*, II, 434–35. It has been assumed, in one of the studies on this episode, that the committee's new and more stringent plan on Tennessee was actually the cause of Johnson's decision to veto the Freedmen's Bureau Bill (see Beale, *Critical Year*, pp. 81–83). This could hardly have been the case, however, since Johnson could not even

message on the Freedmen's Bureau Bill was released that afternoon. Its effect, both in Congress and throughout the nation, was immediate, and the aftermath was one of great agitation and turmoil.

The message began with the observation that there was "no immediate necessity for the proposed measure," since the previous act establishing the Bureau had not yet expired. The President then went on to say that in any case he thought the bill unconstitutional, both because of the great extension of military power which it contemplated in peacetime and because of the invasion of civil judicial functions which would result from the Bureau's efforts to protect freedmen in the exercise of their civil rights. Examining the bill in detail, the President recited a number of specific objections. The original Bureau had been called into being in wartime to assist in the military destruction of slavery, but now that the rebellion had been ended and slavery eliminated, the agency in its present shape should certainly be adequate for the protection of freedmen and refugees. "If I am correct in these views, there can be no necessity for the enlargement of the powers of the Bureau, for which provision is made in the bill." Moreover, the Constitution never contemplated a "system for the support of indigent persons in the United States," and any legislation for the ex-slaves not based on the expectation of their reaching self-sufficiency "must have a tendency injurious alike to their character and their prospects."

There were still further objections. The new Bureau would require large appropriations of money, and although the condition of fiscal affairs was encouraging, the President thought it necessary "that we practice not merely customary economy, but, as far as possible, severe retrenchment." He also thought that the bill would "take away land from its former owners"; it would "keep the mind of the freedman in a state of uncertain expectation and restlessness"; and to the whites it would be "a source of constant and vague apprehension." It would create a huge system of federal patronage with a pernicious concentration of federal power. The freedman should undoubtedly have protection, but it should come from the civil authorities; his condition was

---

have known about the plan. He had already called his cabinet together and was reading them his message *before* the revised Tennessee resolution made its appearance. The committee met at 10:30 on the day the resolution was introduced (which was also the day of the veto) and adjourned after a short session without acting on it; Johnson's cabinet meeting began at 10:00 and did not adjourn until about 1:00 P.M. In any case, the substance of the message had in all likelihood been set for some days. It is obvious from Welles's account that Johnson's decision to veto the bill was not influenced one way or the other by the Tennessee discussions. Indeed, it is not impossible that the reverse was true, assuming that any hint of Johnson's feelings about the Freedmen's Bureau Bill had leaked out in advance.

actually "not so exposed as may at first be imagined," since the need for his labor would induce each state (because of "its own wants and interests") to do what was necessary and proper "to retain within its borders all the labor . . . needed for the development of its resources." The laws of supply and demand would regulate wages, and it was hoped that the freedmen themselves, "instead of wasting away," would "establish for themselves a condition of respectability and prosperity" —possible only "through their own merits and exertions."[37]

Such was the first part of the President's argument, and that part alone aroused much antagonism. The constitutionality of the measure, as well as the need for it, had been duly examined by the Judiciary Committee of the Senate, whose chairman was still addressed in Illinois as "Judge Trumbull." The bill's support, moreover, had been considerable. "We need not say," observed the Philadelphia *Bulletin*, "that we regret that he has made an issue with Congress on a measure which, after very mature consideration, had passed both Houses of Congress by very large majorities."[38] By taking no notice in his message of the Southern Negro codes and the spirit of their enactment, the President had implied that they created no special need for federal protection. This was particularly irritating. "The President refuses to give his consent to a measure so just and necessary," complained the Chicago *Republican*. "He will give the luckless freedmen, no matter though they may have borne arms and suffered wounds for the nation, no other protection than that of the ferocious clutches from which they have but just been snatched. They shall have no safeguard, no law, no administration of justice, except such as the Rebel States will afford them."[39]

But it was the second part of the veto message, containing an argument which went much beyond the bill in question, and in fact had only indirect bearing on it, that was most offensive to the bill's supporters. Here, the President seemed to be saying that no legislation touching the Southern states should be passed if they themselves were not allowed to be present and vote on it. "At the time . . . of the consideration and the passing of this bill," he asserted, "there was no Senator or Representative in Congress from the eleven States which are to be mainly affected by its provisions. The very fact that reports were and are made against the good disposition of the people of that portion of the country is an additional reason why they need and should have

[37] Richardson, *Messages and Papers*, VI, 398–403.

[38] Quoted in New York *Tribune*, Mar. 3, 1866.

[39] *Ibid.*

representatives of their own in Congress to explain their condition, reply to accusations, and assist by their local knowledge in the perfecting of measures immediately affecting themselves." Such exclusion was against the letter and spirit of the Constitution. The President disclaimed all intention of interfering with the right of Congress to judge the qualification of its own membership. Yet he went on to declare that "that authority can not be construed as including the right to shut out in time of peace any State from the representation to which it is entitled by the Constitution." The President's closing point appeared to be his basis for a claim superior to that of Congress for pronouncing the final word on reconstruction:

The President of the United States stands toward the country in a somewhat different attitude from that of any member of Congress. Each member of Congress is chosen from a single district or State; the President is chosen by the people of all the States. As eleven States are not at this time represented in either branch of Congress, it would seem to be his duty on all proper occasions to present their just claims to Congress.

And as for the word itself:

It is hardly necessary for me to inform Congress that in my own judgement most of those States, so far, at least, as depends upon their own action, have already been fully restored, and are to be deemed as entitled to enjoy their constitutional rights as members of the Union.[40]

There was a pained and angry response from all parts of the North. "The Message of the President," predicted the Dubuque *Times*, ". . . will be read with sorrow by every enlightened and justice-loving citizen." "Since the assassination of President Lincoln," the *Delaware State Journal* asserted, "no public event has more deeply saddened the hearts and called forth the condemnation of the Union men of the State of Delaware than the recent veto." Said the Cleveland *Leader*: "The news of the Veto Message has awakened throughout the North a feeling of indignation in every loyal breast, only equaled by the joy manifested by every Copperhead." And from the New Brunswick (N.J.) *Fredonian*: "We regret it in every aspect in which it can be viewed." "It is not the fact that he refuses to sign Mr. Trumbull's bill that will startle and paralyze the people," declared the Washington *Chronicle*,

But when he appeals, nay demands, that the States, now almost as rebellious as they were a year ago—certainly as filled with hate of the great Congressional majorities and of the loyal masses of the American people—

[40] Richardson, *Messages and Papers*, VI, 403-5.

shall be at once rehabilitated, he will send a thrill of dismay to every loyal heart throughout our wide domain.[41]

Representative John Lynch of Maine wrote home to Governor Israel Washburn:

It is not, as you will see by reading the "veto Message," simply a question as to whether *this* particular bill shall become a law, but whether Congress is a part of the Govt. Notice the monstrous and arrogant assumption, that the Members of Congress represent only localities (as though the aggregate did not completely represent the whole) while the President is the representative of the whole people, and the peculiar guardian of the rights, and interests of the unrepresented States. This is modest for a man chosen to preside over the Senate, and made President by an assassin.[42]

When the Joint Committee met on February 20, the day after the veto, the members (except for the three Democrats) were no longer in much of a mood to act on the Tennessee question, and Conkling's resolution, together with the proposed amendments of the day before, was laid aside. Instead, the Republican members voted unanimously to adopt a concurrent resolution, prepared by Thaddeus Stevens, covering the entire question of representation:

Be it resolved, by the House of Representatives, the Senate concurring, that in order to close agitation upon a question which seems likely to disturb the action of the government, as well as to quiet the uncertainty which is agitating the minds of the people of the eleven states which have been declared to be in insurrection, no senator or representative shall be admitted into either branch of Congress from any of said states until Congress shall have declared such state entitled to such representation.[43]

On that same day, in the Senate, Lyman Trumbull made a long speech, with a sharp point-by-point defense of the bill which the President had vetoed, and declared in closing,

The President believes it unconstitutional; I believe it constitutional. He believes that it will involve great expense; I believe it will save expense.

[41] These extracts are taken from a compilation of opinion on the veto made by the New York *Tribune* and printed in the issue of March 3, 1866. There are editorial excerpts from twenty-three Republican newspapers: the Boston *Advertiser*, Boston *Transcript*, Springfield *Union*, Hartford *Press*, Rochester *Democrat*, Troy *Times*, New Brunswick *Fredonian*, Baltimore *American*, Philadelphia *Bulletin*, Delaware *State Journal*, Washington *Chronicle*, Pittsburgh *Gazette*, Cincinnati *Gazette*, Sandusky *Register*, Cleveland *Leader*, Chicago *Tribune*, Chicago *Republican*, Springfield *State Journal*, Detroit *Advertiser and Tribune*, *Missouri Democrat*, Racine *Advocate*, Dubuque *Times*, and Davenport *Gazette*. The Democratic papers without exception supported the veto.

[42] Lynch to Washburn, Feb. 21, 1866, in Gaillard Hunt, *Israel, Elihu and Cadwallader Washburn: A Chapter in American Biography* (New York: Macmillan, 1925), p. 119.

[43] Kendrick, *Journal*, pp. 71-72, 233-34.

He believes that the freedman will be protected without it; I believe he will be tyrannized over, abused, and virtually reenslaved without some legislation by the nation for his protection. He believes it unwise; I believe it to be politic. I thought, in advocating it, that I was acting in harmony with the views of the President. I regret exceedingly the antagonism which his message presents to the expressed views of Congress. . . . I shall rejoice as much as any one to have those States restored in all their constitutional relations at the earliest period consistent with the safety and welfare of the whole people.

Disavowing "any unkind feeling toward the Executive, with whom I should be glad to agree," Trumbull then called for a vote on repassage. But since five Republican senators now reversed the position they had taken at the time of the bill's first passage, the bill fell short of the necessary two-thirds. In the House that day, meanwhile, the joint committee's concurrent resolution was passed, 109 to 40. Fessenden the following day made great efforts to have the resolution brought to a vote in the Senate, but its consideration was postponed until after the Washington's Birthday holiday.[44]

President Johnson's sensational performance of the twenty-second may be regarded as the high point of the post-veto excitement. Up to this time the people of the United States had not actually been given a very complete picture of their President as a human being, and the speech he made that evening, in response to the crowd of serenaders gathered outside the White House, was the fullest glimpse they had yet had of him since his inauguration as Vice-President. The transports of passion to which the Executive abandoned himself on this occasion gave rise to a wave of wonder and dismay. Some of his best friends were appalled.[45] But what they saw and heard was Andrew Johnson the man, fully true to the fundamental themes of his career and character. It is quite likely that the disapproval greeting his action of the previous Monday had been received by him with a certain incredulity. Rather than interpret it to himself as a sign of popular sentiment (the same imperviousness had been the secret of his survival in wartime Tennessee), he seems instead to have persuaded himself that Thaddeus Stevens, with the connivance of Charles Sumner, had been laying plans to assassinate him. And now, to have before him such a providential audience, a mass meeting to indorse his veto and to do him honor, must have affected his head like a great gust of air from the East Tennessee mountains. All the old themes were acted out once more: the out-

[44] *Cong. Globe*, 39 Cong., 1 sess., pp. 936–43, 950, 954–57.

[45] Hugh McCulloch, *Men and Measures of Half a Century*, p. 393; Welles, *Diary*, II, 439.

sider's brooding suspicions of conspiracy, the intense self-preoccupa-
tion (he used the word "I" 152 times),[46] the need of anchoring himself, his mind, and his sense of rightness to abstractions whose nature
was immovable and eternal—a pristine Constitution, untouched by rebellion, and a nameless People. The driving urgency under which he
labored, throughout a discourse abnormally long for such an occasion,
was not so much that of explaining government policy as of demanding vindication for Andrew Johnson, the man.

After invoking the spirits of Washington and Jackson, and calling
to mind their devotion to the principles of Union, Johnson reminded
the audience of his own devotion to those same principles and how he
had suffered for them during the rebellion. But now that the rebellion
had been suppressed, and now that the traitors had repented, his policy,
following "the example set by the holy founder of our religion,"
would be forgiveness.

What was His example? Instead of putting the world or a nation to death,
He went forth with grace and attested by His blood and his wounds that
he would die and let the nation live. (Applause.)

But now a new rebellion had manifested itself, and there were those
who plotted to subvert the Constitution in another way, to keep the
nation divided, exclude the now-penitent South, and "concentrate the
power of the government in the hands of a few":

We find that, in fact, by an irresponsible central directory, nearly all
the powers of government are assumed without even consulting the Legislative or Executive departments of the government. Yes, and . . . that
principle in the constitution which authorizes and empowers each branch
of the legislative department to be judges of the election and qualifications
of its own members has been virtually taken away from those departments
and conferred upon a committee, who must report before they can act
under the constitution and allow members duly elected to take their seats.

There were men of the North today whose disunionist designs were
just as treasonable as those of "the Davises and Toombses, the Slidells,

---

[46] The personal pronoun ("I," "me," "my," "myself," "Andrew Johnson, he,") was
used 210 times in a speech of about 6,000 words, which at the rate of 85 words a minute
meant that the Chief Executive referred to his person on the average of three times a
minute for an hour and ten minutes. A rather striking comparison, for what it is worth,
may be made with Lincoln's last speech, the circumstances of which were in many
ways analogous: it was also an informal response to a serenade, also on the subject of
reconstruction, also marked by a recognition that certain of the speaker's acts on that
subject had met with disapproval, and also requiring, consequently, a greater than
ordinary use of the first person singular. Lincoln, however, managed to make his point
using "I," "me," etc., 32 times in a 1,700-word speech, or in about half the ratio to the
total as in Johnson's speech. The text of the Johnson speech used here is that which
was printed in the strongly pro-Johnson New York *Herald* on February 23.

and a long list of others" whom Johnson himself had fought in the South. A voice called, "Give us the names."

A gentleman calls for their names. Well, suppose I should give them. . . . *I say Thaddeus Stevens, of Pennsylvania*—(tremendous applause)—*I say Charles Sumner*—(great applause) *I say Wendell Phillips and others of the same stripe are among them.* (A Voice—"Give it to Forney.") Some gentleman in the crowd says, "Give it to Forney." I have only just to say that *I do not waste my ammunition upon dead ducks.* (Laughter and applause.)

The next section of the address, though disjointed owing to the speaker's growing excitement, contains two themes moving in and out in a kind of counterpoint of martyrdom. One involves the words of Stevens—the old man's sardonic comment about King Charles losing his head after usurpations similar to Johnson's[47]—and the other, an appeal to Johnson's public record. "What usurpation has Andrew Johnson been guilty of? ('None, none.')" He recited his past career, including that of tailor ("always punctual with my customers and always did good work"), and going all the way up to the presidency. Andrew Johnson, the man who never "acted otherwise than in fidelity to the great mass of the people": here was the "Presidential obstacle" the plotters were designing to get out of the way. Then follows what the speaker had apparently intended as his peroration:

I make use of a very strong expression when I say that I have no doubt the *intention was to incite assassination* and so get out of the way the obstacle from place and power. . . . Are they not satisfied with the blood which has been shed? Does not the murder of Lincoln appease the vengeance and wrath of the opponents of this government? Are they still unslaked? Do they still want more blood? . . . If my blood is to be shed because I vindicate the Union and the preservation of this government in its original purity and character, let it be shed; let an altar to the Union be erected, and then, if it is necessary, take me and lay me upon it, and the blood that now warms and animates my existence shall be poured out as a fit libation to the Union of these States. (Great applause.) But let the opponents of this government remember that when it is poured out "the blood of the martyrs will be the seed of the Church." (Cheers.)

After preparing to retire on this sanguinary note, the President changed his mind and proceeded to talk about half an hour longer. The imagery became less painful, and the keynotes broader and more abstract: the Constitution, the People, and himself. According to the Constitution, no state should be deprived of its representation; he would adhere to that principle and oppose all who were trying to

---

[47] See above, p. 283.

break up the government by amendments to the Constitution. He exhorted all to join him: "Let us stand by the constitution of our fathers though the heavens themselves may fall." And finally, the old mystical sense of Andrew Johnson and the People:

I am your instrument. Who is there I have not toiled and labored for? . . . They say that man Johnson is a lucky man, that no man can defeat me. I will tell you what constitutes luck. It is due to right and being for the people. . . . Somehow or other the people will find out and understand who is for and who is against them. I have been placed in as many trying positions as any mortal man was ever placed in but so far I have not deserted the people, and I believe they will not desert me.

The affair occasioned great mortification among Republicans everywhere. (A friend of Senator Sherman wrote to ask, "Was he drunk?"[48]) Part of the impact was simply due to the President's extravagant personal behavior, and a great deal was said about his offensive language, the vulgar display of himself before a mob, all very unbecoming to a Chief Magistrate, and so on. But this in itself was something less than damning. The sympathetic eye might see that the President had been provoked. Actually the most striking aspect of the incident was probably not Johnson's lapse in personal taste so much as the things he had done with the power of the presidency itself. Some elements of that power he had consistently overrated; others he had never fully grasped. By naming names and calling attention, in such emphatic language, to a deep division of conviction between himself and the Legislative branch, he had done something which was beyond the power of any other single individual to do: he had accorded official recognition to a split in the government. The split had acquired a formal and legitimate existence which, despite every sign, all the Copperhead editors of the country had been unable to give it before that time. The President, by the act of saying a word, could make certain things true that were not true before he spoke; this was a principle well enough understood by Johnson's predecessor to keep him from ever saying that word.[49] The other thing that Johnson accomplished, by the same token, was to confer a peculiar increment of power upon Thaddeus Stevens. By publicly deigning to bestow Executive notice

[48] James H. Geiger to Sherman, Feb. 24, 1866, John Sherman MSS, Library of Congress.

[49] For a most instructive essay on this point, see David Donald, "The Radicals and Lincoln," in *Lincoln Reconsidered*, pp. 101–27. Lincoln's careful effort to provide an official, public act of unity with Sumner (i.e., his and Sumner's appearance together at the Inaugural Ball), even though their political relations had become very strained over the Louisiana issue, and with the air being filled with gossip about an imminent rupture between them, furnishes a perfect example.

upon the congressman from Pennsylvania and his capacity for mischief, the President had made him bigger; it was a boon which the old knave did not hesitate in his own way to acknowledge.[50]

When the Senate met again on the twenty-third, Senator Fessenden was especially determined to get on with what he had begun two days before. He thought it especially important that the pending concurrent resolution (not to admit any Southern states to representation until Congress had declared them entitled to it) should be considered and voted upon, and the principle settled. Senator Sherman was a bit apprehensive. Since there was no doubt in his mind that Congress already did have the power being claimed for it in the resolution, he wondered if it might not be as well to postpone discussion of it for a few days. In view of recent events, the Senate was perhaps not in its best frame of mind for deliberating with calmness. Fessenden replied that although other senators might be "in a state of excitement and wrath," he himself was too old not to be able to get over such feelings with a night's sleep. He thought that on the whole the Senate could be relied upon to conduct itself with propriety, whereupon he proceeded to make a few remarks. He wanted to make his opinions clearly understood regarding the position and status which President Johnson, in his recent utterances, had apparently marked out for Congress, and to clarify the legitimacy of the "irresponsible central directory" for which he, as chairman, was responsible.

"Charges have been made," he said, "with reference to the committee of which I have the honor to be a member . . . and I feel compelled not only to vindicate that committee, but to vindicate the action of Congress with reference to it." The President's opinion had been that the states should be readmitted "when they have given sufficient evidence of their loyalty, and . . . can be trusted." Everyone agreed, and it was for inquiring into this very question that the committee had been appointed.

Is any committee, either joint or special, which is appointed, anything more than the mere servant of Congress? Can any member of it, or the whole of it, set up its will for a single day or a single hour or a single moment against the will of the body which constituted it? We were appointed for a special purpose, to make inquiries, and report to Congress the result of our inquiries; and for what reason? . . . Simply that neither

---

[50] On March 10, Stevens, with elaborate mockery, declared that the entire report of the speech was a gigantic Copperhead lie: "we all know he never did utter it." He concluded, "Now, sir, having shown my friends that all it is built upon is fallacious, I hope they will permit me to occupy the same friendly position with the President I did before. [Laughter.]" *Cong. Gobe*, 39 Cong., 1 sess., pp. 1308–9.

branch, acting without sufficient information, might take a course from which the other branch would differ. . . . Under those circumstances, is it quite fair to designate the committee of fifteen as a central directory, as a power assuming to judge and to decide questions which belong to the bodies which the committee represents? . . . I am unwilling myself, individually, to rest under such an imputation.

As for the veto message, Fessenden said he had not been fully attached to all parts of the Freedmen's Bureau Bill itself and might even have voted to sustain the President's veto of it. But not after the *obiter dicta* about Congress:

At any rate, I did not mean to put myself in the position of indorsing, or being supposed for a single instant to give my assent to the closing parts of the veto message. What do I understand by the closing parts of that message? Simply that, in the judgment of the President, Congress, as at present organized, has no right to pass any bill affecting the interests of the late confederate States while they are not represented in Congress.

If the President, Fessenden declared, "can veto one bill upon that ground, he will and must, for the sake of consistency, veto every other bill we pass on that subject." The states must do certain things to demonstrate their fitness for readmission—but the President was in effect announcing, "I am the person to decide upon whether those things have been done. . . ."

And yet throughout his remarks Fessenden made it repeatedly clear that he had no intention of casting disrespect upon the President; he was not impugning his patriotism or his devotion to the Constitution:

No man has shown a greater attachment to it than he has; and I wish to speak of him respectfully and kindly. But whether he means it or not, when he advances opinions and lays down principles which, in my judgment, strike at the very existence of this body as a power in the government, I cannot but enter my solemn dissent to it, and call upon Congress to assert its own rights and its own position with reference to all these questions.[51]

[51] *Cong. Globe*, 39 Cong., 1 sess., pp. 984-87. As for his private views, however, Fessenden confided to Cousin Lizzy: "As certainty is preferable to surprise, the President's recent exhibitions of folly and wickedness are also a relief. The long agony is over. He has broken the faith, betrayed his trust, and must sink from detestation into contempt. The consequences I cannot foresee, but they must be terribly disastrous. I see nothing ahead but a long indecisive struggle for three years, and, in the mean time great domestic convulsions, and an entire cessation of the work of reform—perhaps a return to power of the Country's worst enemies—Northern Copperheads. For these calamities we are indebted in great measure to such miserable toadies as Doolittle and Dixon, who have made it their business to flatter our weak President, and make a party for him against the views and wishes of the great body of their political friends. . . . Gov. Morgan of New York is little better, and has sold a good name and honorable reputation for a meal of very poor pottage." Fessenden to Elizabeth F. Warriner, Feb. 25, 1866, Fessenden MSS, Bowdoin College.

II SECOND PHASE, FEBRUARY 23–APRIL 6, 1866:
THE CIVIL RIGHTS BILL

Despite the sharp bursts of exasperation which greeted the President's acts of February 19 and 22, the breach with Congress, though now open, was still by no means so wide as to eliminate all hopes of closing it. Indeed, those hopes remained considerable. There was still quite enough at stake, for the Republican party as well as the country, there was enough resiliency in congressional and public feeling, and the resources of the party's leadership—especially in the Senate—were still at hand in a measure quite sufficient to make another effort at compromise not only highly desirable but altogether feasible. The renewed signs of such an impulse, after no more than a day or so for recovery, began showing themselves immediately.

It was true that Johnson's veto message (and Thursday evening's informal gloss on it), together with Trumbull's and Fessenden's replies, gave the remaining chances for an understanding a fairly narrow margin. The inclination of leading senators to continue acting as honest brokers was itself a good deal less free and uncritical than before. Some, of course, were already disqualified; Dixon, Cowan, and Doolittle, as deeply committed in their way as Sumner and Wade in theirs, were thus no more available for that role than they. But the margin existed; the inclination was still there, and the outstanding figure still least committed in either direction was probably Senator John Sherman of Ohio. Sherman at this point is seen to move a little downstage, a little closer center.

John Sherman's present position and future prospects were such that he had now become the man with the best chance to effect a stable reconciliation between President and Congress, if a chance existed at all; and if he should be successful, the personal advantages thereby gained would be brilliant. The influences that played upon him all served to mark out a role full of promise. He himself had an inherently cautious temperament, further moderated by conservative family connections in a state whose political equilibrium was very uncertain. His older brother William was the nation's number two general, and the Ewings were a family that had in the past been of considerable weight in Ohio affairs; William T. Sherman and Thomas Ewing, Sr. (William's father-in-law),[52] were both strong Johnson supporters and

[52] Thomas Ewing, one of the ablest members of the Ohio bar, had had a distinguished career of his own in Whig politics, having served from 1830 to 1836 as United States senator, later as Secretary of the Treasury under Harrison and Tyler, and under Zachary Taylor as first Secretary of the Interior.

would so continue. Their opinions added up to a political position which seemed for the time being to make good sense for a state chronically on the verge of falling into Copperhead control,[53] and John never ceased to receive these opinions with the utmost respect. William Tecumseh Sherman, in a letter to John written on February 14, 1866, spelled out his younger brother's opportunity for him in sage words which could not have failed to intrigue the latter's ambition: "You are classed universally as one of the rising statesmen, above mere party rules. And whilst you should not separate from your party, you can moderate the severity of their counsels. . . ."[54]

John Sherman had the further advantage of a solid position in the Ohio Republican (or Union) party. He had an excellent public record, plus the security of having just been re-elected senator by a substantial majority in the Ohio legislature.[55] He had been Ohio's choice over Robert C. Schenck, a man of pronounced radical sentiments. Here, then, was Sherman's chance to play the role of statesman. Even a man less sensitive and less ambitious could not have missed the meaning which success in such an effort might conceivably have had for a senator from the most populous state in the Midwest.

The basis for Sherman's support was the Republican majority in the Ohio legislature, with whom he maintained a close and regular correspondence. This correspondence served him in a dual function; it was a very responsive barometer of opinion in the state as well as a very accurate indicator of how he himself was doing. There were various significant elements in it. One such element was irritation with the Freedmen's Bureau veto, but a willingness to accept it if a further *modus vivendi*—based on the Civil Rights Bill and a constitutional amendment on representation—could be achieved. Ohio was not prepared to damn the President out of hand simply over the Freedmen's Bureau. Another element was a good deal of annoyance with the extreme radicals, whose ill-mannered treatment of the President might eventually contribute to the full break which Ohio Republicans greatly wished to avoid. Throughout the correspondence runs a tone of deference toward Sherman himself, which seems to indicate that these leaders may have been concerned not only with instructing their senator but also with the management of a very valuable piece of political property. E. B. Sadler writes to Sherman on February 16:

[53] See above, pp. 26 n., 44–45.

[54] *The Sherman Letters*, ed. Rachel Sherman Thorndike, p. 262.

[55] The senatorial election had been held January 18, 1866.

The general feeling among the Union members is, that the rebel states should be readmitted to representation, so soon as it can safely be done, and not *before*. It is my opinion that if congress should pass the bills of Trumbull protecting all people in their civil rights, and should this and the Freedmen's Bureau Bill, be signed by the President, and then if the constitutional amendment, before referred to be adopted, the union people of Ohio would generally be satisfied to the readmission of the southern states to representation.

And again on the nineteenth:

I have learned with regret that Prest Johnson has vetoed the Freedmen's Bureau Bill. I know not what especial reasons he may have for this, if any, but if he has vetoed it on general principle, the union members of the legislature will generally condemn his act. I shall wait to see his reasons before *swearing much*.

James H. Geiger wrote on February 20:

The veto is received here I understand with mixed feelings. . . . The Radicals denounce it, but there are a great many conservative union men who stand by it. I am informed that the copperheads intend calling a meeting for Thursday night to endorse Johnson. Praise from such knaves ought to lead even the Saviour to rigid self-examination. . . . I congratulate you upon the determination of the senatorial question. It was a good thing to get it out of the way and enables you to act without a halter around your neck.

Sherman was provided with a kind of summing-up on February 21 by Warner Bateman, a lawyer of Glendale and one of the ablest members of the legislature:

The breach between the President and congress is distinctly widening and perhaps already irreparable. The veto is a strong plausible and temperate document touching many of the strongest sentiments of the popular mind. . . . Its effect—immediate—however was with us favorable to Congress and last evening there was greater unity and a stronger disposition to concentrate in action among the union members of the General Assembly than at any time since it met. Thus we are anxious to confirm and if possible consolidate fully the whole strength of the union party here.

. . . It is in vain however to secure their united support to congress or even to maintain the ascendancy of the Union party in Ohio unless congress shall pursue a course more temperate. If it is to be carried along the furious tide with Stevens and Sumner, it is to compromise its high position and great work by a game of epithets and testy retaliation with the President. . . . I felt sure this morning on reading Stevens resolution in the house, disappointed and that congress had lost half the advantage it had. . . . If the admission of Tennessee was proper before the veto was it not proper afterwards or does the policy of reconstruction vary with the capricious spites of the hour.

Our party is now in the hour of its trial and it needs to gain strength

by prudence and wisdom rather than prodigally wasted by the very extravagance of rashness. We can never maintain ourselves against the President or anybody else upon a policy of indefinite and unconditional exclusion of the Southern States, establishing a Hungary or Poland in the midst
of the Republic. We must rather in my judgment offer immediate admission to the rebel states upon terms clear distinct and announced and show
to our people that it is not revenge but safety that we want.

Bateman's letter seemed to represent a consensus of sorts, for it was
indorsed by three other leading members.[56] On that same day, the
twenty-first, a set of Republican resolutions was reported from committee and a copy transmitted to Senator Sherman:

Resolved, That the President, Andrew Johnson, . . . wisely inaugurated
the necessary measures of reconstruction, that can only be completed by
Congress and the States by the adoption of a further constitutional amendment apportioning representation in Congress among the States according
to the number of those . . . who, by the laws of such States, have a voice
in such representation; and that while the safety of the nation and justice
to all its parts require that these States should be admitted only with such
representation, we deem it inexpedient and unnecessary to press upon
them other conditions to a full restoration to their place and rights in the
Union.

Resolved, That we deem it the duty of Congress to provide by just and
prudent but effective legislation for the protection of the freedmen.

Resolved, That we respectfully and earnestly urge upon Congress and
the President to waive extreme opinions, and that in the discharge of the
great trust confided to them by the nation they harmoniously provide for
us the ways of future concord and the moderate but effectual measures of
a lasting reconstruction.[57]

Sherman's position, for the ensuing three weeks or so,
was rather like that of a tightrope walker, with all the dangers of a
misstep with either foot. To maintain his own effectiveness in his
efforts to preserve a moderate state of feeling, he had to convince the
party majority and all those within the range of his influence that the
President was still amenable to reason without selling the party and
public opinion short. The first move in this direction had been his at-

[56] Preceding correspondence all in John Sherman MSS. E. B. Sadler wrote: "Mr.
Bateman has read to me the foregoing letter and I most cordially endorse its sentiments." P. B. Cole used substantially the same words, and William Henry Smith, the
Secretary of State, added: "I think Mr. Bateman has made an admirable statement of
the political situation, and if we can have such action as he suggests, we shall go safely
through the breakers."

[57] These resolutions, plus a portion of Bateman's letter of the twenty-first, were
quoted by Sherman in the speech he made in the Senate on February 26. See *Cong.
Globe,* 39 Cong., 1 sess., Appendix, p. 132.

tempt on February 23, in the interests of a cooling-off, to delay consideration of the new concurrent resolution on reconstruction.

Now, I appeal to Senators [he had urged] whether it is not better and wiser to allow this matter to lie over for a few days. Is the mind of any one here likely to be changed by a little delay? Is it not a proper occasion for us at least to postpone this for a little reflection and for a little consideration?[58]

Three days later, on February 26, he made a major speech in the Senate. In it, he once more expressed great misgivings over the pending resolution. He did not say he would not vote for it—in fact, he rather intimated he would[59]—but he was preoccupied with things that went beyond the resolution. His major concern now was conciliation and the directing of all energies toward a postive plan for early reconstruction. If the resolution were simply a statement of the right of Congress to legislate on this subject, then there should be no difficulty at all, for that right was unquestionable under constitutional law. But then why stop to say so—why not just exercise it? If the purpose were to "close agitation," then the speaker had his doubts. What if the two houses failed to agree? The states might remain unrepresented indefinitely.

Therefore I say that the measure proposed does not meet the real difficulty in the case. What we want is a plan of action by which these States may, upon such terms and conditions as are consistent with the public safety, come back into this Union.

Sherman followed with a long recital of the President's acts in reconstructing the various states, comparing them with the intentions of Lincoln and presenting all in the most favorable possible light. He referred to the Washington's Birthday speech, which he deeply regretted ("I think there is no true friend of Andrew Johnson who would not be willing to wipe out that speech from the pages of history"); he had seen nothing in the conduct of the Joint Committee to justify any attack on that body; and he thought it especially unfortunate that the President should have named his enemies and charged them with plotting to assassinate him. But even a President has feelings of manhood; the President thought he was repelling personal insult, and the "mantle of charity" should be cast over his remarks. As for the Freedmen's Bureau Bill, Sherman himself had voted for it twice, would do so "over and over again," and was surprised that anyone should see anything objectionable in it. But the President's duty, which he had fulfilled

[58] *Ibid.*, p. 981.

[59] "If this resolution would tend to promote these great objects, I would vote for it much more cheerfully than I will...." *Ibid.*, Appendix, p. 125.

conscientiously, was to examine the bill; some of his grounds for vetoing it may not have seemed very reasonable (Sherman gave several
examples), but he certainly had the constitutional right to do what he
did. The President expressed, in any case, full agreement with Congress that the freedmen should be made secure in their rights. "While
he stands by that declaration, . . . I will not quarrel with him about the
means."

The Union party demanded certain things of the President and certain things of Congress. The President must adhere in good faith to the
party whose nomination he had accepted for the vice-presidency. It
was the duty of Congress, on the other hand, to produce a reasonable
plan for restoring the rebel states, and an amendment for establishing a
new system of representation "upon a safe foundation," as promptly
as possible. Above all, there must be harmony within the government,
and Sherman closed his speech with eloquent praise for the President
as "one of the moral heroes of this war."[60]

The response of Sherman's well-wishers in the Ohio legislature was
most encouraging, and the refrain, in letter after letter, was that of conciliation in the interest of party unity. "I have read it [the speech] with
great interest," wrote the judicious Bateman, "and like it very much."

> You have in it achieved that rare distinction of Congressional speech mak-
> ing of maintaining through a long speech the most admirable equity and
> kindliness of temper without remitting anything in your principles. . . .
> I can . . . assure you I think of the approval of the great majority. With
> the authority of Congress fully asserted in prompt and moderate measures
> of reconstruction . . . I think we can consolidate the Union party and
> secure its future power.

A. B. Butler's enthusiasm bordered on excess: "You have . . . so perfectly expressed what I *know* to be the universal sentiment of our friends
here, and your views have met with so much assent even from the radicals themselves, that I feel now, that there is almost a certain prospect
of entire harmony before long." "I wish the President had thought and
done differently," wrote Frank Sawyer, "but I am not in favor of a
breech with him and thus, by dismembering the party, to throw the
government into the hands of the copperheads." Fred H. Oberklem
echoed: "Conciliation is what we want at present in the Union party,
not furious declamation, personal abuse and mutual crimination. The
union party cannot afford to be divided; it must be upheld for the sake
of our country and liberty." And again, the soft voice that beckoned
to ambition: "I trust that your public efforts of the future," wrote

[60] *Ibid.*, Appendix, pp. 124–33.

Charles Davenport, "may be guided by the same amount of discretion, [inasmuch] as (if you will permit me) I do not know of any one, who stands so fairly as yourself, for the office of next standard bearer of the union party of the nation."[61]

The consensus, then, among high-ranking Republican politicians of Ohio—whose conservative instinct for party unity led them to reach automatically for formulas of conciliation—was fervent approval of Sherman's efforts. But what did the people think? E. B. Sadler admitted, ". . . everything is now *mixed* and *uncertain*," but there are occasional items in Sherman's papers that already show glimpses of an unruly state of mind.

The Republican people here [wrote a local functionary from Woodsfield] regard the conduct of the Executive more in sorrow than in anger, and a good deal of anger is expressed also. Those who take the most favorable view of his conduct say that he made a wrong start in his *hasty* reconstruction, that he ought to have called Congress together and ought to have shown some little respect for the People and their Representatives in the Senate and House.

For my humble self I try to keep my temper down. But when the Executive gets a knot of red handed and arrogant traitors from Richmond around him or gets a motley and ruffian crowd collected in the street and then describes us the Republican people, as fierce, vindictive, cruel and desirous of the humiliation of the south, the task becomes a hard one. . . . Of course we are human beings and liable to error and mistake. But *we know* what is passing in our own minds, and we know that our motives in opposing the executive policy are not such as he asserts and that his censures are unjust and undeserved. . . . But as he was utterly deaf to the voice of the people and determined to proceed without the assistance of congress, whose advice would have been so timely and so valuable, of course argument, remonstrance began. . . . Wrath, strifes, contentions have become hot and the quarrel seems likely to become inveterate, so that very good and wise men despair of seeing permanent peace restored in this generation. Now if any civil wisdom had lived at the West end of the Avenue, all this might have been easily prevented, for a people more generous, more humane or more placable than the conquerors in the late civil war never looked up at Gods sun.[62]

[61] Warner Bateman to Sherman, Mar. 4; A. B. Butler to Sherman, Feb. 27; Frank Sawyer to Sherman, Feb. 28; F. H. Oberklem to Sherman, Feb. 28; C. Davenport to Sherman, Mar. 1, 1866, John Sherman MSS.

[62] E. B. Sadler to Sherman, Feb. 28; Edward Archbold to Sherman, Mar. 9, 1866, John Sherman MSS. Sherman had written to Archbold requesting several names for his consideration in the filling of a vacant local office, probably the postmastership. It should be stated as a general principle that such letters as these in the political correspondence of the times (letters of trusted local lieutenants to their congressmen) probably provide the most dependable basis available for ascertaining local opinion. The very maintenance of such a man's position would put a constant premium on accuracy: much would depend on keeping the congressional patron provided with as clear a picture as possible of the way people were feeling and talking in that community.

One crotchety old veteran of the War of 1812 did not seem to care a bit for either the unity of the Republican party, the cautiousness of its politicians, or the equivocations of Sherman's speech. "I had read a synopsis of it that came by Telegraph," he grumbled; "I did not like the synopsis and I like the speech less. It is good Lord good Devil with you; first on this side, then on that, and being neither hot nor cold you will be spewed out by the people. . . . Do you think that they can look upon a person with the least bit of allowance that undertakes to white-wash the southern traitors to make them patriots?" Assemblyman Sadler had, to be sure, warned Sherman. "Your speech will of course be approved by some and censured by others. No man can take both sides without offense. . . ."[63]

Four days after the speech John Sherman, still walking the tight-rope, had to take his next step, as it were, with the other foot. The con-current resolution on readmission of the Southern states, which had provided the nominal occasion for his speech, was voted upon in the Senate on March 2. Among all those now acting consistently with the Republican party, Sherman was the warmest remaining defender of the President. But John Sherman, by the same token, was nothing if not a party man: whatever effectiveness he hoped to exert either way depended on it. The resolution passed, 29 to 18, and prominent among those voting "yea" were William Pitt Fessenden (who had taken the lead in getting it to a vote in the first place), James W. Grimes, Ly-man Trumbull, and John Sherman.[64]

The critical item in the balance, meanwhile, had come to be Trum-bull's other measure for protecting the freedmen. If the mutual con-fidence which Sherman was laboring to re-establish was still possible, everything would now depend on the fate of the Civil Rights Bill. The bill had passed the Senate on February 2 (of the three "Administration Senators," Dixon had favored it, Cowan opposed it, and Doolittle had been absent), and was finally passed in the House on March 13.[65] The measure was generally approved as moderate and sensible, and most of Johnson's supporters hoped he would sign it. James Gordon Ben-nett, who in the previous spring had appointed himself the President's New York spokesman, took it for granted that Johnson would seize the chance to outflank the radicals and open the way for an early restoration. Bennett editorialized to this effect in his New York *Herald:*

[63] John M. Pease to Sherman, Mar. 14; E. B. Sadler to Sherman, Feb. 28, 1866, John Sherman MSS.

[64] *Cong. Globe*, 39 Cong., 1 sess., p. 1147.

[65] *Ibid.*, pp. 606–7, 1367.

As we can find in it nothing conflicting with the constitution as it now stands, and nothing in conflict with the declared opinions and policy of President Johnson, we have no doubt that he will approve the measure. . . . This Civil Rights bill we regard, accordingly, as a practical, just and beneficent measure, and one which the President will cheerfully approve. . . . The President is entitled to great credit in bringing Congress from the vagaries of its Reconstruction Committee to this practical bit of legislation, and with its approval we dare say the radical scheme of the continued exclusion of the late rebel States for several years to come will soon be found to be utterly out of the question.[66]

Sherman himself held substantially the same conviction and publicly gave his own support to the bill in two speeches in Connecticut on the weekend of March 17. Those speeches represented Sherman's final effort to achieve an understanding. In them, he dealt with the Civil Rights Bill as the center position to which both sides would have to come if any settlement were still to be made; he heaped warm praise on the President, and predicted that he would approve the bill.

Let me tell you [he announced at Bridgeport], as the solemn conviction with which I address you to-night, that Andrew Johnson never will throw the power we have given him into the hands of the Copperhead party of the United States. . . .
On Thursday, the day that I left Washington, we sent to him a bill which secures to all the colored population of the southern states equal rights before the law, the civil rights bill. . . . That bill is now in the hands of the President. If he sign it, it will be a solemn pledge of the law-making power of the nation that the negroes shall have secured to them all these natural and inalienable rights. I believe the President will sign it.[67]

At this very time, another Republican leader of the Midwest appears on the scene after a brief and very temporary withdrawal from affairs. He turned up in Washington about the time Sherman was in Bridgeport, and apparently spent no more than a few days there. But they were very decisive days, and they included an interview with the President. The man was Oliver P. Morton, the war governor of Indiana, who was very different in personality from John Sherman but whose political situation at home rather resembled Sherman's. This meant that there were certain political needs which the two held in common. Morton's opportune return early in March from a three months' stay in Europe; his subsequent trip to Washington directly after meeting and talking with Senator Sherman; and Governor Morton's own tremendous influence both at home and in

[66] New York *Herald*, Mar. 17, 1866.

[67] New York *Times*, Mar. 19, 1866; John Sherman, *Recollections of Forty Years ...*, II, 368–69.

Washington—all this and its background gives much importance to the experience which Morton underwent at this time.

If Sherman's Ohio had its Vallandigham, Morton's Indiana had its Voorhees. Oliver P. Morton had had to fight off the Peace Democrats all through his governorship in a state even more doubtful than Ohio— and where popular sentiment on the Negro question, especially in the southern counties, was of a decidedly racist character. Morton had been one of the Republican founders in Indiana and was a party man clear through. The Indiana Copperheads had fomented secret treason in wartime; they had even wielded majorities in the legislature against the state's war effort. The Democratic party was the great lurking enemy. Thus Morton stood, day and night as it were, watching, sniffing the wind, his suspicious eye forever reviewing the ranks of his own party to spy out weaknesses, vulnerable gaps, internal sedition. With the war over and the unifying issue gone, the danger to party solidarity and to Morton's own position became even greater. Morton, who cherished senatorial hopes and perhaps even grander ambitions, had a slender majority to protect and could be counted upon to move with decision against any influence that threatened to undermine it. The party must present no targets for Copperheads to fire at.

As Morton saw things in the fall of 1865, the threat of a premature return of Southerners to national power may have been somewhere in the background, but for him that background must at the time have seemed a bit abstract and remote; his problem was Indiana. It happened that the immediate threat was a man of much disruptive influence in his own state and within his own party—Morton's old political enemy George Washington Julian, the Negro suffrage doctrinaire. The Democrats professed, not without some basis, to discern a Republican party split between Morton and Julian factions during this period; Democratic newspapers gloated over the putative schism and did what they could to exploit it.[68] Morton, for his part, was determined

---

[68] The Indianapolis *Sentinel* (renamed the *Herald* after October, 1865), declared on November 20, 1865, in an editorial entitled "The Julian and Morton Factions of the Republican Party," that there was great bitterness between these two groups and then proceeded to scourge them both. "If there was a difference between them upon any principle or measure affecting the welfare of our country, unhappy under Republican party rule, we should gladly step forward and unite with that division which held out any assurance of being truly for the Union. . . . But as neither wing of the party disavows the propositions that our flag is a flaunting lie [etc.] . . . we can side with neither of the factions of that party, which, before any Southern rebellion occurred, really broke up the Government by practically abrogating the Constitution by which it was formed." Julian's own unmanageability may be construed from his own words. In his autobiography he dwelt with satisfaction on various vain efforts by Morton lieutenants to bring about a reconciliation. "If I had been willing to subordinate my political con-

that the Democrats should not be allowed to get the "nigger-party" label pinned on the Republicans.

As spokesman for the "Conservative" Republicans of Indiana, Morton accordingly took his cue: to ally his position with that of President Johnson, to support a mild Southern policy, oppose Negro suffrage, and thus both freeze out Julian and take the Democrats' main issue away from them. He attracted nationwide attention with a speech which he made on September 29 at Richmond, Indiana, wherein his purposes were given ample expression.[69] He praised the Executive's reconstruction measures, comparing Johnson's policy with that of Lincoln and vigorously denying the principle of "conquered provinces." Most of the speech dealt with the problem of Negro suffrage. Morton denounced the views recently expressed by Charles Sumner on that subject,[70] he invoked the specter of Negro governments, and declared that a period of probation was needed before the Southern freedmen would be qualified to exercise the vote. The Democratic Indianapolis *Sentinel* rather malevolently hinted that the speech was a "Yankee trick," actually designed to clear the way for imposing universal Negro suffrage after getting the South's guard down—a scheme secretly cooked up between Morton and Sumner himself.[71] Julian was angered at Morton's words for different reasons. But the speech evoked warm praise from President Johnson.[72]

His health impaired by a stroke of paralysis, Morton determined in November, 1865, to go abroad and seek a cure at the hands of a renowned physician of Paris. After delivering a message to the legislature, in which he once more urged support of President Johnson's policy, he left the executive affairs of the state in the hands of the lieutenant governor and departed. He went by way of Washington.

---

victions to his ambition," Julian asserted virtuously, "peace could at once have been restored; but as this was impossible, I was obliged to accept the warfare which continued and increased, and which I always regretted and deplored. I only make these statements in justice to the truth." George W. Julian, *Political Recollections*, p. 267.

[69] See William D. Foulke, *Life of Oliver P. Morton*, I, 446–52.

[70] Sumner had made an elaborate Negro suffrage speech on September 14, 1865, at the Massachusetts Republican State Convention at Worcester. See *Works of Charles Sumner*, IX, 437–88.

[71] Indianapolis *Herald* (formerly *Sentinel*), Nov. 9, 1865.

[72] "He was very earnest and eloquent in his condemnation of Mr. Sumner," wrote Julian bitterly, "for proposing to give the ballot to the negroes and disfranchise the white Rebels, but his moral vision failed to discern anything amiss in his own ghastly policy of arming the white Rebels with the ballot and denying it to the loyal negroes." Julian, *Political Recollections*, p. 267. Johnson, on the other hand, said Morton's speech was "the ablest defense of his policy yet made public." Foulke, *Morton*, I, 451.

At his rooms there he received over three hundred callers. He had a cordial interview with the President, who intrusted him with a secret mission to Louis Napoleon, and he proceeded to New York in a private car furnished at government expense. He embarked for Europe early in December, doubtless convinced that in the affairs of the nation, despite sundry small portents, all would be well. He did not return until the first week in March. He was thus out of the country during the most critical period in the relations between his party and the President, and came back at the very moment when matters were shaping toward a climax.[73]

Morton arrived back in the United States on March 7 and remained in New York for about a week before going on to Washington. He was not long in discovering the changed condition of political affairs. During that time he had a talk with Senator Sherman, probably on the fifteenth or sixteenth.[74] Hastening to the capital, he called upon President Johnson and had a long interview with him—an interview which marked a profound turning point in Morton's political career. Morton now made it plain that Johnson's approval of the Civil Rights Bill, then pending, was indispensable to harmony in the government, and that unless he signed it, "this would be the rock upon which the President and the Republican party would separate." Johnson, "laboring under great emotion" and with "beads of perspiration" on his brow, gave Morton to understand that he was "unwilling to do so," and

[73] Foulke, *Morton*, I, 454–62.

[74] The conjecture on dates is based on Foulke's account, supplemented by a typed memorandum in the papers of W. R. Holloway (Indiana State Historical Society), a close political associate of Morton's in Indiana. The paper was written by Holloway himself for a series of reminiscences later published in one of the Indianapolis newspapers. This is the source which identifies Foulke's "Republican senator" (I, 466) as John Sherman. Sherman (we know from other sources) left Washington on Thursday, March 15, and was back in the Senate again on Monday the nineteenth. During this long weekend he made his Bridgeport speech of the seventeenth and presumably saw Morton in New York. The same memorandum (titled "President Johnson and the Civil Rights Bill") intimates that Morton may have terminated his European sojourn earlier than he intended, upon receiving pleas from his Republican friends to come home and help them restore peace with the President: "Prominent congressmen and senators wrote to Morton urging him to return as soon as possible, as he had been on excellent terms with the President before he left and was out of the country during the quarrel, being therefore in a position to talk to him." After seeing Sherman, Morton appears to have proceeded to Washington immediately, which would place his momentous interview with Johnson about March 19 or 20. This interview and its consequences for Morton himself, tallying as it would with subsequent events, leads to the conjecture that Morton's role in the shift of party strategy that occurred during that week (the unseating of Stockton) was much more critical than heretofore thought. He left Washington for home, according to Robert Dale Owen, on the twenty-sixth. Owen to N. P. Banks, Mar. 25, 1866, Banks MSS, Essex Institute. See also below, pp. 319–20. Miss Lila Brady of the Indiana State Library gave the author some very valuable assistance on this problem.

talked of a new party, which he thought he was strong enough to build. Morton told him flatly that nothing of the sort was possible, that the issues must be fought out between existing parties, and that "all roads out of the Republican party led into the Democratic party." There was the President's choice. And should he persist in his determination not to sign, then Morton felt that the two of them "could not meet again in political fellowship."[75] Such was the way in which Oliver Morton, under great stress and against all his prior inclinations, had also had to make *his* choice. If there were now to be a split in the party, it would be with the Doolittles and Johnsons, not with the Julians and Sumners.

Before that day was over, Morton had communicated his impressions to several members of Congress. One of them may have been John Sherman, for two or three days after his return from Bridgeport, Sherman was writing to his bother William in a most gloomy frame of mind, strikingly at odds with the serene tone of his recent speeches. "Johnson is suspicious of every one," he admitted, "and I fear will drift into his old party relations. If so he will carry with him but little force & prestige, and will soon be in deserved disgrace.[76]

While Johnson was making up his mind whether to sign the Civil Rights Bill, examining the alternatives and weighing the consequences, he was able to draw upon the widest range of opinion to assist him in coming to his decision. Naturally he could not be expected to pay much attention to those men who, like Stevens and Sumner, were by now his avowed enemies. He need hearken only to his well-wishers, who were still numerous. Fessenden, Grimes, and Sherman had all indicated their version of a basis (if one did remain) for unity. Morton had made his position clear. Trumbull had been rebuffed once; everything for him would now depend on the fate of his other bill. The President was not in the dark about where any of these men stood.

There were many others, hoping for the success of his administration, who urged their views upon him. Henry Ward Beecher wrote, "The passage of this bill will in a great degree frustrate the influence of those who have sought to produce the impression that you had proven untrue to the cause of liberty and loyalty."[77] Governor Jacob

[75] Foulke, *Morton*, I, 467.

[76] John to William T. Sherman, Mar. 20, 1866, W. T. Sherman MSS, Library of Congress.

[77] H. W. Beecher to Johnson, Mar. 17, 1866, Johnson MSS.

D. Cox of Ohio, who, like Beecher, had already got into trouble for too warmly supporting the President,[78] urged the latter that "if you can find it in accordance with your sense of duty to sign the bill, it will with our Western people make you fully master of the situation, and remove the possibility of any such opposition in the Union ranks on other measures as would prove at all embarrassing to your administration." Cox added, somewhat diffidently: "For similar reasons I believe it would assist us greatly in holding together our State organizations. . . ."[79] Such circumspect journals as the *Nation* and *Harper's Weekly* praised the bill and did not suppose the President would see any objections to approving it.[80] The New York *Herald* also thought it a wise measure.[81] Republicans of temperate views, that is, took it for granted that the President's course was so clear that he himself would not fail to perceive it. Senator Stewart of Nevada, after supporting the Freedmen's Bureau veto, was certain that Johnson would not issue another such paper.[82] Rutherford B. Hayes wrote to his uncle: "He now seems to feel that he was misled and is really anxious to conciliate. If he signs . . . , the chances are that a complete rupture

[78] General Jacob D. Cox had been elected governor of Ohio in 1865 on a conservative pro-Johnson program at a time when the entire party supported the President. But as early as that summer he had antagonized the Negro suffrage advocates of the Western Reserve and elsewhere by a public paper (his celebrated "Oberlin letter") in which he urged a colonization policy for Negroes. From this point on, he was a target of suspicion in radical quarters, a suspicion which deepened at every utterance he subsequently made in support of Johnson. See below, pp. 315–16.

[79] J. D. Cox to Johnson, Mar. 22, 1866, Johnson MSS. Cox also had a personal interview with Johnson a little over three weeks before (Feb. 26), which he described publicly in such effusive terms as to raise many false hopes. In a letter to the New York *Herald* he declared, "if you could meet his straightforward, honest look, and hear the hearty tones of his voice, as I did, I am well assured that you would believe, with me, that although he may not receive personal assaults with the equanimity and forbearance Mr. Lincoln used to show, there is no need to fear that Andrew Johnson is not hearty and sincere in his adhesion to the principles upon which he was elected." New York *Herald*, Feb. 27, 1866.

[80] "The Civil Rights bill has passed both Houses, and a more important bill—one calculated, if but fairly enforced, to effect more important changes in American society —has never come before Congress. . . . None of the main objections which the President made to the Freedmen's Bureau bill lie to it. We trust he will leave the question of its constitutionality to the Supreme Court, which only is competent to decide it." *Nation*, II (Mar. 22, 1866), 353. "The bill passed both Houses of Congress by enormous majorities. . . . and we see no reason to suppose that the President will dissent. We hope indeed that by the time this paper is issued the bill may have been approved by him and have become a law." *Harper's Weekly*, X (Mar. 31, 1866), 194.

[81] See above, p. 306.

[82] Stewart claimed later that Johnson actually promised to sign it. Whereas there may have been some grounds for that impression, it is likelier that Stewart simply deceived himself. *Reminiscences of Senator William M. Stewart, of Nevada*, ed. George Rothwell Brown (New York: Neale Publishing Co., 1908), p. 199.

will be avoided. Otherwise, otherwise."[83] James Garfield had also predicted that the bill would be signed. To that, one of his local lieutenants replied, "I hope so. . . . Well: we will wait and see. If he vetoes it, you have no alternative but to . . . give him the hot end of the poker."[84]

Every member of the cabinet, except Welles, hoped that Johnson would see his way clear to signing the bill.[85] Of the three secretaries most strongly attached to Johnson and his policy (Welles, Seward, and McCulloch), two of them turned over documents to the Executive which should have been of some assistance in determining the state of popular opinion. Thurlow Weed had informed Seward on March 6 of strong radical sentiment in New York, saying that the radicals would carry the people "if any serious mistakes are committed." A California correspondent of Hugh McCulloch told how he had tried in vain among Sacramento Unionists to moderate anti-Johnson feeling after the Freedmen's Bureau veto and the Washington's Birthday speech, even though prior sentiment had been very favorable.[86] On the other hand, Gideon Welles, whose papers contain a remarkably full picture of political affairs in Connecticut, does not seem himself to have grasped very accurately the meaning of what his correspondents told him, and thus could not have communicated much of that picture to the President. In Welles's diary and letters one sees a mind strikingly similar to Johnson's own. Welles, who of all Johnson's advisers was the one most fiercely committed to the President's policies, actually anticipated most of Johnson's decisions simply by virtue of having already come to similar ones himself. Moreover, like Johnson, he had the habit of dismissing most evidence of opposition as the fruit of malignant radical intrigues. He so interpreted much of the political news that he got from home. But Calvin Day, one of Welles's regular correspondents, finally told him in a burst of exasperation:

It seems to me to be mere bosh to say that this Congress are tools in the hands of Stevens, Sumner, or any other ten or twenty men in Congress, & such charges whether put forth in the babbling at the White House, or in the Editorials of the New York Times or Hartford Times or C are simply childish, and are put forth simply on the principle of crying "Mad dog." I have too much respect for the office held by Mr Johnson to say

[83] R. B. Hayes to S. Birchard, Mar. 4, 1866, *Diary and Letters of Rutherford Birchard Hayes*, ed. Charles R. Williams (5 vols.; Columbus: Ohio State Archaeological and Historical Society, 1922–26), III, 280.

[84] W. C. Howells to Garfield, Mar. 26, 1866, Garfield MSS. Howells (father of the novelist) was chairman of the Union Club Committee of Jefferson, Ohio, and editor of the Jefferson *Sentinel*.

[85] Welles, *Diary*, II, 463–64.

[86] Weed to Seward, Mar. 6; Ned F. Miller to McCulloch, Mar. 6, 1866, Johnson MSS.

he is only a tool in the hands of Weed, Blair, or Raymond, but it appears to me quite evident that for some cause he has changed his opinions & conduct & associations strangely since he left Nashville. I have never seen more *unity* or *decision* of feeling in the ranks of the Great Union party on any subject that exists to day, that the course of the President on reconstruction is hasty, unwise, & if carried out will be of lasting & incalculable injury to the country. . . .[87]

Amid the flood of advice and counsel being received by the President at this time and upon which he might draw prior to taking action on the Civil Rights Bill, the only sector of opinion that really indicated clear, unequivocal, and virtually unanimous approval for everything he had done, and was likely to do, lay in the Democratic party. Fernando Wood assured Johnson that the New York Peace Democracy was "well disposed," and Jeremiah Black told him that his Freedmen's Bureau veto had "made millions of good hearts glad and grateful." The Pennsylvania Democracy, the President was informed by R. H. Kern, "will endorse your veto and Reconstruction policy." Likewise the Illinois Democracy ("with extraordinary enthusiasm"), according to Representative Samuel S. Marshall; the President's loyal Democratic followers in that state asked only that he withdraw a little of his patronage from disloyal Republicans and give it to them. Edwards Pierrepont of New York declared with brutal candor, "The leading men and the great body of the Republican party are not with you and they never will be," and in effect gave Johnson a Democratic version of the same advice that Oliver P. Morton would give him from the Republican side—that "all roads out of the Republican party led into the Democratic party." Pierrepont intimated that an excellent bridge between them would be the appointment of a Democrat as Collector at the Custom House.[88]

Another letter, dated March 6, 1866, eventually made its way to the President's desk, though perhaps not soon enough to influence him much one way or the other on the Civil Rights Bill, for it had had to come all the way from San Antonio, Texas. From a delegate to the Texas constitutional convention, it assured Johnson ingratiatingly that the only men there who opposed him and supported Stevens and Sumner were those who had opposed secession—"What was called Union men." "But I can repeat what I said to you in Washington,

[87] Calvin Day to Welles, Feb. 26, 1866, Welles MSS, Library of Congress.

[88] Fernando Wood to Johnson, Feb. 24; Jeremiah Black to Johnson, Feb. 20; R. H. Kern to Johnson, Mar. 2; S. S. Marshall to Johnson, Mar. 2; Edwards Pierrepont to Johnson, Mar. 13, 1866, Johnson MSS.

that there is not a secessionist in the state of Texas who is opposed to you or your policy. . . .[89]

When the President was finally ready to act, he had presumably arrived at his decision in full knowledge of all the alternatives. The spirit of that decision was perhaps best reflected in a scene which took place about this time between the President and his private secretary, Colonel Moore. The two were in the President's chamber one evening, the latter pacing the floor in deep thought. Suddenly Johnson stopped and, fixing his eye upon Moore, declared: "Sir, I am right. I know I am right, and I am damned if I do not adhere to it."[90] It was in some such intrepid spirit that he prepared to cut John Sherman's tightrope.

Johnson delivered his veto of the Civil Rights Bill on March 27. He said in his message that if it were necessary to declare Negroes citizens it would not be "sound policy" to take such a step with eleven of the states concerned still unrepresented in Congress. The conferring of such citizenship, moreover, would discriminate in the Negro's favor against worthy foreigners, who had to wait five years before themselves becoming citizens; it might be better for the ex-slave, "unfamiliar with our institutions and our laws," to "pass through a certain probation." The President felt that the bill would enact "a perfect equality of the white and colored races," imposing federal law on a subject wherein it had "frequently been thought expedient to discriminate between the two races." When the act presumed to punish instances of civil rights being infringed under the color of local law, ordinance, or custom, it invaded the immunities of legislators, judges, and peace officers. Putting all such cases under the jurisdiction of federal courts showed that the bill's actual intention was to strike at state judges who, acting on their responsibility and conscience, gave decisions contrary to it. Such a judge was thus a judge no longer, but "a mere ministerial officer, bound to decide according to the will of Congress." The President thought that if any one of the rights enumerated in the first section of the bill[91] happened to be denied in any state, the federal courts then could and would take away all state jurisdiction in all civil or criminal cases involving Negroes. The machinery which was specified for carrying out the bill's provisions (the powers of arrest conferred on commissioners of the Freedmen's Bureau, the setting-up of courts in more than one part of

[89] Sackfield Maclin to Johnson, Mar. 6, 1866, Johnson MSS.

[90] George F. Milton, *Age of Hate*, p. 310.

[91] See above, p. 279.

a district when needed, and so on) implied "a permanent military force . . . to be always at hand, . . . whose only business is to be the enforcement of this measure." The bill was not only "fraught with evil" in its details, but in its general scope and purpose it exceeded all constitutional bounds:

In all our history, in all our experience as a people living under Federal and State law, no such system as that contemplated by the details of this bill has ever before been proposed or adopted. They establish for the security of the colored race safeguards which go infinitely beyond any that the General Government has ever provided for the white race. In fact, the distinction of race and color is by the bill made to operate in favor of the colored and against the white race. They interfere with the municipal legislation of the States, with the relations existing exclusively between a State and its citizens, or between inhabitants of the same State— an absorption and assumption of power by the General Government which, if acquiesced in, must sap and destroy our federative system of limited powers and break down the barriers which preserve the rights of the States.[92]

It was thus that the key leaders of the Republican party who had worked for compromise over the past sixteen weeks saw their last ground cut out from under them. Fessenden and Grimes had no more to say. It was virtually impossible for the influential Republican journals that had labored for conciliation to continue their support of the President after this point.[93] John Sherman, whose efforts in that direction had failed and whose predictions of harmony had proved baseless, now found his own position (and that of his fellow Ohioan, Governor Cox) decidedly exposed. Sherman's monitor in the legislature, the sage. Warner Bateman, sent him the word on March 30:

Diversity of opinion is rapidly disappearing. . . . It is not now so much a difference . . . as to whether we will or will not support Johnson but as to how we shall deprive his evident defection of its power of mischief. His abandonment of his professed purpose to protect the freedmen is conceded by everybody around except Mr. Cox and Baber. . . .[94] I do not doubt Mr.

[92] Richardson, *Messages and Papers*, VI, 405–13.

[93] E.g., the Springfield *Republican*, having refrained from joining the chorus of disapproval over the Freedmen's Bureau veto, now declared: "It is the feeling of this necessity [for positive federal legislation to protect the freedmen], and the determination that it shall be met, that makes the president's course a disappointment and a grief to all Christian and humane men in the North, and at the same time enlists in his sympathy and support the substratum of the unterrified democracy, the men who mob and murder negroes from sheer madness of prejudice." Springfield *Weekly Republican*, Mar. 31, 1866.

[94] R. P. L. Baber of Ohio was associated closely with Senator Doolittle in the Johnson movement that culminated later that summer in the National Union Convention at Philadelphia.

Cox's entire uprightness but his superserviceable zeal in behalf of Johnson and his policy has I fear fatally compromised his influence with his party. . . . I have lost faith entirely in the President. He intends in my judgment to betray us. . . . I cannot but regard his vetoes as an escape from all his promises of protection to the freedmen on the hypocritical pretence of constitutional objections. His last message hands the Freedman over helplessly to the tender mercies of state legislation and his exasperated master. So we go.[95]

Lyman Trumbull made his case, and that of the Republican party, in the Senate on April 4. After a long analysis of Johnson's objections (during which he icily observed "that the President's facts are as bad as his law"), Trumbull recited with damning precision the course of his own efforts to come to terms with the President. This part of Trumbull's speech constitutes an important source document for one of the most unusual cases of alienation in our political history, a case almost without parallel in the effectiveness with which Executive and Legislative departments were to become for a time sealed off from each other. It is especially significant coming from one of the few Republican senators who would later vote against a general and concerted effort to throw Johnson out of office.

Congress, in the passage of the bill under consideration, sought no controversy with the President. So far from it, the bill was proposed with a view to carry out what were supposed to be the views of the President, and was submitted to him before its introduction into the Senate. I am not about to relate private declarations of the President, but it is right that the American people should know that the controversy which exists between him and Congress in reference to this measure is of his own seeking. Soon after Congress met it became apparent that there was a difference of opinion between the President and some members of Congress in regard to the condition of the rebellious States, and the rights to be secured to freedmen.

. . . All were anxious however, for a reorganization of the rebellious States and their admission to full participation in the Federal Government as soon as these relations could be restored with safety to all concerned. Feeling the importance of harmonious action between the different departments of the Government, and an anxious desire to sustain the President, for whom I had always entertained the highest respect, I had frequent interviews with him during the early part of the session. Without mentioning anything said by him, I may with propriety state that, acting from the considerations I have stated, and believing that the passage of a law by Congress, securing equality in civil rights when denied by State authorities to freedmen and all other inhabitants of the United States, would do much to relieve anxiety in the North, to induce the southern States to secure these rights by their own action, and thereby remove

[95] Warner Bateman to Sherman, Mar. 30, 1866, John Sherman MSS.

many of the obstacles to an early reconstruction, I prepared the bill substantially as it is now returned with the President's objections. After the bill was introduced and printed a copy was furnished him, and at a subsequent period, when it was reported that he was hesitating about signing the Freedmen's Bureau bill, he was informed of the condition of the civil rights bill then pending in the House, and a hope expressed that if he had objections to any of its provisions he would make them known to his friends, that they might be remedied, if not destructive of the measure; that there was believed to be no disposition on the part of Congress, and certainly none on my part, to have bills presented to him which he could not approve. He never indicated to me, nor, so far as I know, to any of its friends, the least objection to any of the provisions of the bill till after its passage. . . .

And yet this is the bill now returned with the President's objections, and such objections! What are they? That—

"In all our history, in all our experience as a people, living under Federal and State laws, no such system as that contemplated by the details of this bill has ever before been proposed or adopted."[96]

It has been assumed by most writers, following the lead of Gideon Welles, that such misunderstandings as those experienced by Fessenden, Grimes, Sherman, Trumbull, and others were traceable to Johnson's habit of listening politely and then making his own decisions.[97] Such an assumption is doubtless essentially correct. With routine callers, that very habit has been the traditional (indeed the only possible) refuge of President after President. But senators who are the leaders of the President's own party constitute a very different sort of case. Senators are not normally routine callers petitioning for favors. Nor do they customarily present themselves for the purpose of providing the President with information upon which he may or may not act; they know that he has other and more systematic ways of obtaining facts. They have come for the transaction of government business. They are there for the planning of policy, for determining those areas within which joint action is possible, and for developing the necessary strategy whereby such action may be effected. Such a process is essentially one of negotiation, whose minimum requirement is that the principals must at least understand one another; that process, re-enacted over and over, has underlain the history of every successful administration known to the American party system. So it was with the calls

---

[96] *Cong. Globe*, 39 Cong., 1 sess., pp. 1755–61. "Without being what is called radical," commented the Springfield *Republican* on April 14, "Mr. Trumbull is true to the theory of his party and ready to follow it to its logical results, and the leading position given him in the questions now at issue, we believe he has the courage and coolness to maintain in such a way as shall promote the welfare of the country and the interests of Republican politics."

[97] Beale, *Critical Year*, p. 25.

made by Republican senators upon President Johnson at various times during the winter of 1865–66; they were made for the purpose of inviting negotiations out of which, it was assumed, a successful line of policy might issue. What Fessenden and Trumbull and the others could not have known, however, for all their experience and lore, was that Andrew Johnson at no time actually assumed negotiations to be going on. The President apparently never understood that he was expected to bargain with leading senators at all.

At last virtually all of them came to realize that policy would have to be made from this point on without the anchor post customarily provided by the Executive office. Indeed, the effectiveness of political discourse in the ensuing election campaign would depend upon the very thoroughness with which the Republicans as a party had cut themselves loose from that post. Shortly after Oliver Morton returned home, he called a meeting of leading Indiana Republicans so that decisions might be made on the line the party should take in the months to come. The declaration of principles which the committee prepared was not to his liking ("We don't want a political essay"); whereupon he himself extemporized a statement of views which was eventually to find expression in an address to the citizens of Indianapolis. It was one of the first, one of the most famous, and possibly the most hair-raising of all the speeches ever made on the theme of treason and the bloody shirt. The man who made it was the same man who, a little more than six months before, had been acknowledged (and had so seen himself) as the leader in his state of "Conservative Republicans."

Every unregenerate rebel lately in arms against his government [hissed Morton] calls himself a Democrat.

Every bounty jumper, every deserter, every sneak who ran away from the draft calls himself a Democrat. Every "Son of Liberty" who conspired to murder, burn, rob arsenals and release rebel prisoners calls himself a Democrat. John Morgan, Champ Ferguson, Wirtz, Payne and Booth proclaimed themselves Democrats. Every man who labored for the rebellion in the field, who murdered Union prisoners by cruelty and starvation, who conspired to bring about civil war in the loyal states, . . . calls himself a Democrat. . . . Every wolf in sheep's clothing who pretends to preach the gospel but proclaims the righteousness of man-selling and slavery; every one who shoots down negroes in the streets, burns up negro school-houses and meeting-houses, and murders women and children by the light of their own flaming dwellings, calls himself a Democrat; every New York rioter in 1863 who burned up little children in colored asylums, who robbed, ravished and murdered indiscriminately . . . called himself a Democrat. In short, the Democratic party may be described as a common sewer and loathsome receptacle, into which is emptied every element of treason North and South, every element of inhumanity and barbarism which has dishonored the age.

And this party ... proclaims to an astonished world that the only effect of vanquishing armed rebels in the field is to return them to seats in Congress, and to restore them to political power. Having failed to destroy the constitution by force, they seek to do it by construction, with ... the remarkable discovery that the rebels who fought to destroy the constitution were its true friends, and that the men who shed their blood and gave their substance to preserve it were its only enemies.[98]

March 27 was a day marked not only by the President's veto but also by the completion of a very questionable transaction in the Senate—the unseating of John P. Stockton, Democratic senator from New Jersey. The sole object in this case was to get rid of one Democratic vote. The august United States Senate was not looking quite so august by now; something had happened to poison the Olympian air of December and January. Though Stockton had been elected senator early in 1865 by methods dubious enough to arouse a petition of protest by disaffected members of the legislature, the Senate under normal conditions would not have taken the extreme step of going behind the returns. In fact the Judiciary Committee had already reported in Stockton's favor on January 30 with only one member dissenting, which ordinarily would have been tantamount to closing a contested election case. But on March 22 the matter was suddenly brought out and made the subject of a four-day debate.

One may well wonder about the crude haste with which the affair was prosecuted, to say nothing of why it should have been revived at all, inasmuch as the Senate normally would not have touched a thing of this sort. It is, and was at the time, well understood that the general aim was to guarantee a two-thirds Republican majority. Men thought such a majority important enough by then that they were willing to sweat over every vote. But the Stockton business had a peculiar urgency; otherwise it would not have had such support; and the upright Fessenden, along with Grimes and Sherman, was conspicuously active in it. This is something that needs to be pinpointed. It has much the appearance of a spontaneous reflex, and it could not in all likelihood have been launched three days earlier. The shock that stirred the Senate into action—and conferred a shaky legitimacy on what they were about to do—seems to have been the sure knowledge on good

98 Foulke, *Morton*, I, 468–78. By this time, according to the malicious Julian, Morton had his henchmen out tracking down and burning every copy of Morton's Richmond speech of the year before that they could lay their hands on. Julian, *Political Recollections*, p. 269.

authority, by about March 20 or 21, that Johnson was planning another veto. The authority was probably Oliver P. Morton, and the news may very well have been carried among senators by the erstwhile peacemaker, Sherman.[99] At any rate, furious activity was launched on the twenty-second in preparation for the veto which would shortly have to be overridden—preparation, many senators thought, for a state of siege. A whole set of nicer scruples—like the honorable gentlemen's frock coats—seems to have been peeled off and laid aside while the gentlemen got ready for a dirty, disreputable brawl.

The details and background of the Stockton case were so complex that to summarize them with any brevity is very difficult. The situation in the New Jersey legislature during the early months of 1865, as the war drew to a close, had been rife with trickery. Neither side had a monopoly on it, except that the Republicans, as things turned out, found themselves out-tricked by the Democrats. Senator John C. Ten Eyck's term was due to expire on March 4, 1865, and it was thus necessary to elect a successor. The rules of the New Jersey legislature required that a senator be elected by a joint meeting of both houses, which in turn could only be convened by a majority vote in each. The party balance was most delicate; there was a 13-8 Democratic majority in the Senate but a 30-30 division in the lower house. The Republicans' dilemma was thus particularly painful. If a senator were to be elected at this time, he would probably be a Democrat and would be irrevocably on hand for six years, whereas with the war moving to a successful close, the fall elections of 1865 would in all likelihood bring Republican majorities in both houses. Thus if the Republicans could maneuver a delay until fall, they stood a good chance of sending a Republican senator to Washington after all.[100]

---

[99] See above, pp. 309–10. The rumor of Johnson's plans, moreover, had spread across a good part of the country. One encounters numerous references to it in the correspondence of these days. E.g., the federal marshal at Springfield, Illinois, a correspondent of Trumbull, wrote on March 22: "Telegrams here say he will veto the civil rights Bill. I hope he will not. I want to support him. I cannot if he takes grounds against his party, for I deem that as taking grounds against the best interests of the country." George Templeton Strong on March 23 referred in his diary to an expected veto. Thurlow Weed in a note to Seward on the twenty-fifth seemed to take a veto for granted. W. C. Howells, writing to Garfield on the twenty-sixth from Jefferson, Ohio, had read of it in the newspapers. D. L. Phillips to Trumbull, Mar. 22, 1866, Trumbull MSS, Library of Congress; Strong, *Diary*, IV, 75; Weed to Seward, Mar. 25, 1866, Johnson MSS; Howells to Garfield, Mar. 26, 1866, Garfield MSS. Welles on March 21 had told two prominent Connecticut Republicans that his "impressions were the President would disapprove of it." Welles, *Diary*, II, 459.

[100] Charles Merriam Knapp, *New Jersey Politics during the Period of the Civil War and Reconstruction* (Geneva, N.Y.: W. F. Humphrey, 1924), pp. 142–48; see also David M. DeWitt, *The Impeachment and Trial of Andrew Johnson, Seventeenth President of*

By February, however, the Republicans had found themselves forced to vote, despite misgivings, to convene a joint meeting. This was principally in deference to public pressure for electing someone, and they were induced to risk it by the knowledge that Stockton, the Democratic candidate, was by no means secure in his own party. It was thus that they hoped, if not actually to squeeze by with Ten Eyck, at least to prevent the majority election of a Democrat and through a deadlock to delay the election until more favorable times. A resolution by Democratic State Senator Daniel Holsman requiring a majority vote to elect was accordingly supported by substantial numbers of Republicans, though for reasons different from those of the Democrats supporting the same resolution. For the Republicans it was a means of preventing Stockton's election by a plurality; for the Democrats—then seeing no chance of electing a Democrat at all unless everyone voted for the party choice—it was a means of pushing the bolters into line. The election itself was then postponed twice while the two sides jockeyed for position.

The Democrats meanwhile discovered that there was still enough anti-Stockton feeling within their own ranks[101] to render his election by majority out of the question, and unless the Republicans could be outsmarted, Stockton's cause (or that of any Democrat) was lost. And yet at the joint meeting of March 15, amid much turmoil, they managed to rush through a vote to rescind the Holsman resolution by a margin of one and proceeded to ballot, after a desperate Republican move to adjourn sine die had been lost by the same margin of one. Stockton was thereupon elected by 40 to 37, and the meeting hastily adjourned. The Republicans had no chance to protest against this changing of the rules in mid-election, since they obviously could not

---

the *United States* (New York: Macmillan, 1903), pp. 66–88. The original report of the Senate Judiciary Committee is printed in *Cong. Globe*, 39 Cong., 1 sess., pp. 1564–65, the New Jersey protest in *ibid.*, p. 1565, and Stockton's able defense of his own position —in the course of which he introduced the journal of the New Jersey joint meeting—in *ibid.*, pp. 1668–76.

101 Such feeling was fairly bitter, if that of former Democratic Senator James W. Wall is any indication. Writing to former President Buchanan two months after the election, Wall raged: "For the last fifteen years, ever since Commodore Stockton and that imbecile Wright connected themselves with the Democracy, the Legislative bodies have become mere auction blocks, where the Senatorial office has been put up for sale to the highest bidder. . . . The Camden & Amboy R. R. Company paid as high as $40,000 to elect the Commodore's son." And again, a month later: "Our best Democrats were disgusted with the exhibition of corruption last winter, when the Commodore boasted, that he would have the office for his son if it cost $50,000." James W. Wall to James Buchanan, May 22 and June 29, 1865, Buchanan MSS, Pennsylvania Historical Society. That Wall himself was an aspirant to the senatorship should no doubt be laid in the balance against this jaundiced testimony.

get a majority vote in both houses to reconvene the joint meeting. Had they themselves been able to elect Ten Eyck by the same method, or by any other, they would no doubt have leaped at the chance. But having been outmaneuvered, their only recourse was to present a petition, in an attitude of injured virtue, to the United States Senate.[102] When Congress met in December, Stockton was provisionally seated and the petition referred to the Judiciary Committee. The committee reported on January 30, all the members except Senator Clark of New Hampshire having voted to accept Stockton's election as valid. The report was laid before the Senate, where nothing was done about it for seven weeks—Stockton meanwhile exercising all the privileges of a senator.

When the matter was brought out for debate on March 22, Fessenden took up Clark's argument and declared that the joint meeting, in changing the rules contrary to all established prior law and without referring the result back to the legislature, had not acted legally as a legislature in accordance with the Constitution. Exciting scenes ensued, with even absent sick men playing crucial roles.[103] The first vote came on Friday the twenty-third. The first roll call showed 21–20 in favor of Stockton's retaining his seat. Thereupon Morrill of Maine asked to have his name called, producing a 21–21 tie. Stockton's New Jersey colleague, Democratic Senator Wright, being in bad health, had made a pair with Morrill some seven weeks previously, against the possibility of his own absence when the case should come to a vote. Two days before, on Wednesday the twenty-second, Morrill (after consulting with Fessenden and Sumner) had advised Stockton to inform Wright that he no longer felt obliged to maintain the pair. Thereupon Stockton, angered, arose and cast his own vote in his own behalf, thus compromising a case which he might otherwise have won. Even Trumbull, who had voted in Stockton's favor, thought it improper that the latter should have voted on his own case. The question was reopened again on Monday, after a resolution not to count Stockton's vote. A second and final vote on the original resolution was taken on Tuesday the twenty-seventh, despite a telegram from the ailing Wright pleading for two more days' delay so that he himself might

---

[102] Knapp, *New Jersey Politics*, pp. 144–45.

[103] *Cong. Globe*, 39 Cong., 1 sess., pp. 1567–68. Wright of New Jersey and Dixon of Connecticut were both ill; each wanted to be present and each was forbidden by his physician to attempt it. Foot of Vermont was on the point of death. Morgan of New York was prevented by illness from being in the Senate on Monday the twenty-sixth, but he was on hand for the final vote the next day, voting with the minority.

be present. The unfortunate Stockton was thereupon unseated, 23 to 20.[104]

It had been a petty, hair-splitting business. Things were now at such a pass that William Pitt Fessenden, instead of acting the statesman, had reverted for the occasion to the Yankee lawyer searching for, and finding, the flaw in the title. "It is all important now," Fessenden observed to his son with a touch of grimness, "that we should have two-thirds in each branch."[105]

It was by the margin of a single vote that the Senate, on April 6, overrode the veto of the Civil Rights Bill. It was the first time such a thing had ever been done with a major piece of legislation.[106] Two of the Republican doubtfuls, Stewart and Morgan, came over to the majority, and when Morgan voted "yea," the galleries cheered. That senator had planned to sustain the veto (and was thus the last of the regular Republicans remaining with the administration), but a final effort by him to work out a compromise with Johnson found the President immovable, thereby leaving Morgan without a choice.[107] Lane of Kansas voted "nay" despite much pressure from

[104] *Ibid.*, pp. 1564–73, 1589–1602, 1635–48, 1666–79. Fessenden, Grimes, and Sherman voted for ousting Stockton. Trumbull and the other members of the Judiciary Committee stuck by their original decision. Clark, the original dissenter, was also consistent, voting with the majority. See also Blaine, *Twenty Years*, II, 154–60.

[105] Fessenden to William H. Fessenden, Mar. 31, 1866, Fessenden MSS, Bowdoin College. The remark had special reference to the Stockton case. "It was a hard fight over Stockton, but we killed him at last. . . ." The same day Fessenden wrote to his father: "Up to this time we have been able to accomplish very little towards securing the country from future dangers. Nominally, we have a majority of more than two thirds in both branches of Congress, and ought to pass such laws as we deem necessary, in spite of vetoes. In all such bodies, however, there are always found weak and unreliable, if not corrupt, men. I think, however, we are daily growing stronger." Fessenden to Samuel Fessenden, Mar. 31, 1866, Fessenden MSS, Bowdoin College.

[106] Only six bills of any kind had previously been passed by both houses over a presidential veto. The first was a bill on revenue cutters and steamers vetoed by President Tyler; the other five were internal improvements bills all vetoed and repassed during the Pierce administration. See Edward C. Mason, *The Veto Power* (Boston: Ginn, 1891), pp. 147–49.

[107] *Cong. Globe*, 39 Cong., 1 sess., p. 1809; Morgan to George Dawson, Mar. 29; Morgan to H. H. Van Dyck, Mar. 31; Morgan to John D. Terry, Apr. 1; Morgan to John Sherman, Apr. 2; Morgan to Ransom Balcom, Apr. 3, 1866, Morgan MSS (Letterbook), New York State Library. "Three days before we came to the vote on the Civil Rights bill," Morgan wrote to Weed, "I made . . . most earnest efforts with Mr. Fessenden and with the President to have a Compromise bill agreed upon and passed. It looked hopeful for a time but failed. The difficulty really was the Presidents objections to the first section of the bill. It was then *this* bill or *nothing*. I believed something should pass both Houses of Congress, and *this* will." Morgan to Thurlow Weed, Apr. 8, 1866, Weed MSS, University of Rochester Library. See also James A. Rawley, *Edwin D. Morgan, 1811–1883: Merchant in Politics* (New York: Columbia University Press, 1955), pp. 219–22. The day after Morgan wrote Weed, the bill passed the House.

both his constituents and his colleagues. Tormented by great anguish and by many doubts, and later by a flood of terrible vituperation, the distracted man went home, where, as Blaine wrote, "his mind gave way and on the eleventh of July, 1866 he committed suicide."[108] The Civil Rights Bill became law when it was repassed in the House of Representatives on April 9. The announcement of the Speaker to that effect, in the words of the congressional reporter, "was received with an outburst of applause, in which members of the House, as well as the throng of spectators, heartily joined, and which did not subside for some moments."[109]

The Joint Committee on Reconstruction had receded into the background of attention during this period, its activities having been temporarily overshadowed by more exciting doings. But the committee, taking testimony and weighing this scheme and that in its search for a satisfactory program of reconstruction, had been anything but idle. Its work would be substantially completed by the end of the month, and its report,[110] in the form of a proposed constitutional amendment and two pieces of legislation, would be presented to Congress on April 30.

Among the many who awaited the report with keen anticipation was Judge Godlove S. Orth, who represented the Eighth Congressional District of Indiana in the House of Representatives. Neither he nor Representative Shelby Cullom of Illinois could really be quite resigned to a permanent break between Congress and President, and neither had much taste for extreme radicalism. Accordingly, about this time (the exact date is not known) the two decided to see if they themselves could do anything about a general reconciliation and to explore this possibility in a talk with the President. "I will never forget that interview," Cullom wrote many years later. "It was at night. He received us politely enough, and without mincing any words he gave us to understand that we were on a fool's errand and that he would not yield. We went away, and naturally joined the extreme radicals in the House, always voting with them afterwards."[111]

On April 29, the day before the committee's report was to appear, Orth wrote home to a friend in Indianapolis. The President, he told

[108] Blaine, *Twenty Years*, II, 185.

[109] *Cong. Globe*, 39 Cong., 1 sess., p. 1861.

[110] Not to be confused with the formal report of the committee prepared by Fessenden and submitted to Congress by him on June 8.

[111] Cullom, *Fifty Years of Public Service* (Chicago: A. C. McClurg, 1911), p. 153.

his friend, had "beyond all controversy designed the destruction of our Party," and had it not been for "the firmness of the loyal men in and out of Congress" and the "important issues at stake," he might have suceeded. Much was due the people, whose voices had "sustained us in every effort we made, and cheered [us] in every step we took." As it was, the President had failed to crush Congress, "and of course he will fail to crush the party. The people have made too many sacrifices to give up the fruits of victory at his bidding. If the rebels under the misguided and mischievous policy of the Prest. could obtain control of the Govt. all will be lost. *But they will not succeed.*"[112]

Judge Orth's language seemed to ring with decision and finality. But even this late the case is not quite closed; the all but smothered spark of possibility reappears once again at the close of his letter. "I believe this report will receive the almost unanimous support of the Union men in both Houses, and also of our friends at home," he writes. "If Johnson approves it, *then* the Party will be a unit, if he vetoes it, we shall pass it over his veto, and then the Party will be a unit *minus Andy.*"

112 G. S. Orth to Stephen Neal, Apr. 29, 1866, Orth MSS, Indiana State Library.

11

The
Fourteenth
Amendment

I THE NATURE OF THE AMENDMENT-MAKING PROCESS

With the repassage of the Civil Rights Bill over the President's veto on April 6, 1866, the Senate in effect gave notice that it would not accept the Executive version of reconstruction. For Congress, the paramount problem thereupon became that of preparing a definitive program of its own, and to a fuller extent than ever before the responsibility for it now fell upon the Joint Committee of Fifteen. To a degree more comprehensive than anticipated in the beginning, numerous lines were now converging upon a constitutional amendment that would embody all the major remedies.

It had been recognized from the very opening of the session that the problem of altering the Constitution, in conformity with the various consequences of emancipation, was a matter that required some sort of settlement. It was not to be solved until more than six months later, and even then, as it turned out, the solution would be a good deal less than definitive. The problem acquired all sorts of implications in the course of this time, and the result—the Fourteenth Amendment to the Constitution—was an odd contraption that few men viewed with wholehearted gratification. The Amendment would never be operative in the fullest sense, and its flat rejection at the outset by every Southern state except Tennessee was, to say the least, an unpromising start for an unpromising career. It was not to serve as a reconstruction program after all; not until the Military Reconstruction Acts of 1867 would the states be started on their way back into the Union.

Such circumstances have placed immense difficulties in the way of writing and thinking about this very complex transaction. Although a great deal has been said about the Amendment and its framing, a primary difficulty has always been the fairly crude one of fixing upon a clear point of departure for organizing the subject and giving it some sort of unity. How are we to characterize the process whereby the Amendment evolved, and make it comprehensible? The unifying themes are certainly not easy to pick out of all that was going on during those six months. The fact that the process underwent considerable qualitative change in the minds of those most involved in it hardly makes the problem any simpler.[1]

Nor is there much enlightenment to be found in subsequent events.

[1] The great body of writing on the Fourteenth Amendment falls into several main categories, representing several quite distinct lines of interest in the subject, only one of which is of concern in the present essay. One of them has to do with the use subsequently made of Section 1 of the Amendment in construing the constitutional rights of corporations as legal persons. The claim of Roscoe Conkling, in arguing a case before the Supreme Court in 1882, that the Joint Committee specifically intended to include corporations in framing the due process clause of that section, constitutes the point of departure for items such as the following: Charles and Mary Beard, *The Rise of American Civilization* (New York: Macmillan, 1927), II, 111–13; Howard Jay Graham, "The 'Conspiracy Theory' of the Fourteenth Amendment," *Yale Law Journal*, XLVII (January, 1938), 371–403, and XLVIII (December, 1938), 171–94; Louis Boudin, "Truth and Fiction about the Fourteenth Amendment," *New York University Law Quarterly Review*, XVI (November, 1938), 19–82; and Andrew C. McLaughlin, "The Court, the Corporation, and Conkling," *American Historical Review*, XLVI (October, 1940), 45–63. Ignoring the narrowly "conspiratorial" overtones of the framing, and dealing with the more general problem of broad judicial interpretation, are Howard Jay Graham, "Justice Field and the Fourteenth Amendment," *Yale Law Journal*, LII (September, 1943), 851–89, and "Procedure to Substance—Extra-Judicial Rise of Due Process," *California Law Review*, XL (Winter, 1952–53), 483–500; Charles Fairman, "Does the Fourteenth Amendment Incorporate the Bill of Rights? Original Understanding," *Stanford Law Review*, II (December, 1949), 5–139; Stanley Morrison, "Does the Fourteenth Amendment Incorporate the Bill of Rights? Interpretation," *ibid.*, II (December, 1949), 140–73; and J. E. Greenbacker, "The Fourteenth Amendment Challenged," *Georgetown Law Journal*, XXXVI (March, 1948), 398–411. A quite different line of inquiry, self-evident from the title, is Jacobus Ten Broek, *The Antislavery Origins of the Fourteenth Amendment* (Berkeley: University of California Press, 1951). Still another, in which the Amendment's very validity is questioned in view of the coercive aspects of its ratification, is W. J. Suthron, Jr., "Dubious Origins of the Fourteenth Amendment," *Tulane Law Review*, XXVIII (December, 1953), 22–44.

The problem to be dealt with in these pages, however, is the Amendment's framing, as it proceeded amid the political exigencies of formulating a congressional policy on reconstruction and in the setting of the Republican party's growing estrangement from President Johnson. The principal works which deal with the Amendment from this angle are Horace E. Flack, *The Adoption of the Fourteenth Amendment* ("Johns Hopkins University Studies in Historical and Political Science," Vol. XXVI [Baltimore: Johns Hopkins Press, 1908]), largely superseded by Benjamin B. Kendrick, *The Journal of the Joint Committee of Fifteen on Reconstruction* (New York: Columbia University Press, 1914), and Joseph B. James, *The Framing of the Fourteenth Amendment* (Urbana: University of Illinois Press, 1956). It is not expected that another essay on this subject will add anything to the excellent scholarship of the last-named. It is, however, hoped that a perspective not fully realized in prior work may emerge if the chronology of the amendment-making process is developed on the assumption that the framers had little notion at the beginning how the process would turn out, that a wide range of alternatives existed until very close to the end, and that the narrowing of those alternatives cannot be understood apart from the behavior of the Executive.

We have already noted earlier that military reconstruction still looms as the great coercive fact in the whole epoch of which this was still barely the beginning. With that came a ruthless scrapping of all elements of the presidential effort since May, 1865, to be followed by a train of evils for which the North is still held accountable. It might thus seem good logic to consider the Fourteenth Amendment a sort of midpoint on the relentless road to the 1867 triumph of radicalism. Such an approach has much to commend it as a strategy for considering the twelve-year span of reconstruction as a whole; yet it is full of liabilities for an analysis of any single phase of reconstruction, particularly this one, since that phase represented by the framing of the Fourteenth Amendment is in many ways the most critical of all. It was during this time that the most profound changes took place in the development of a governmental attitude on what reconstruction ought to consist of. The apparent precision of hindsight, therefore, makes for a certain amount of deception when applied to the Fourteenth Amendment.

Even Benjamin B. Kendrick, whose treatment of this phase is admirable in its detachment—compared with later treatments highly charged with feeling—found himself dogged throughout by that whole dismal aftermath of reconstruction which was consuming so much attention at the time he wrote. An underlying tone of ill-humor was scarcely avoidable at the high tide of the Dunning era of reconstruction scholarship; indeed, it is hard to imagine such a tone ever fully disappearing. Few American scholars, it may be supposed, will ever find very much to praise in Radical Reconstruction. But to admit this is hardly to settle the question of how close a connection should be made between Radical Reconstruction and the Fourteenth Amendment.

For Kendrick, in his *Journal of the Joint Committee*, the dominating fact throughout the making of the Fourteenth Amendment was a kind of insistent hammering toward ends ever more punitive. Here was an approach to organizing the subject that could be serviceable enough if left at that—and Kendrick himself more or less did so leave it. His is still one of the best and most useful monographs we have on the entire period. But later writers found themselves unable to maintain Kendrick's sense of balance; they took off from his work, but in the least promising direction. By Howard K. Beale's and George F. Milton's time, the attitude itself had come to dominate a whole subject matter; without the discipline of Kendrick's feeling for detail, circumstance, and chronology, an irritating canker had become a general inflammation.

The picture drawn by these later writers leaves an aftereffect of perplexity when one considers the cumulative function of scholarship —when it becomes a question, that is, of where one goes from *their* work. A basic technique of explanation has been that of the "plot": the Fourteenth Amendment was deliberately designed to be rejected in order to give warrant to, and prepare opinion for, the measures that followed. The long preliminaries—especially the work of the Joint Committee—could in no true sense be considered a judicial proceeding, but rather (to use Professor Beale's words), "a great American Court of Star Chamber sitting for conviction of the South in an *ex parte* case. The Committee sought not to learn the truth about the South, but to convince the people of the efficacy of the Radical program."[2] The true objective was to construct a Republican political platform for the 1866 election.

As method alone, the "plot" formula has an inherent shortcoming; one is never quite certain whether a thing is being defined or explained. A wide range of transactions—once we know how they turned out— can be called the result of a successful plot, and the statement becomes "true" by definition. But the use of the "plot" terminology as definition makes it very misleading as explanation: in the case of the Fourteenth Amendment a foreordained quality is imparted to the picture, and a clear line of intention that is warranted only by starting with the outcome and reading backward. There were far too many people privy to this "plot" to endow its conspiratorial aspect with very much meaning, and there were far too many alternatives along the way that were in no sense foreordained. To recognize this will do much to help us reconsider this problem. It could turn out to be one of those cases, no stranger to history, where with impeccable orthodoxy we have to start at the beginning and work through.

In any case, the making of the Fourteenth Amendment has a developmental character which ought to be brought to the foreground. That in itself is complicated enough, simply from the viewpoint of detail, but with it must somehow be synchronized a parallel line of development—the evolution of the President's relations with Congress. Most Republicans were painfully reluctant to accept those relations as fixed and irrevocable, even in the face of growing appearances to the contrary. The making of the Amendment, in short, was a week-by-

2 Beale, *Critical Year*, p. 94.

week development; a full accounting of it must include both the range of alternatives and how they were narrowed.

The making of the Amendment was only in the most nominal sense "judicial" in nature. It was primarily a political process. But there should be a way of saying this without recourse to the language of conspiracy, in order to emphasize the protracted effort that was being made all during this time to strike a balance among numerous divergent positions within the Republican party. The result could be called "a mere political platform"; or it could be called a program of reconstruction, one of whose primary requirements was acceptability to as wide a range of Northern public opinion as possible. It could boil down to the same thing, but a case might still emerge for the effort to play it straight. Throughout the whole process, chronology itself functions as a heavy balance wheel. The process took time; when it was finished, many things were no longer as they had been at the beginning, and in all likelihood there was no one involved who had with any accuracy foreseen the outcome.

That aspect of the preliminaries which involved the taking of testimony was not really judicial, because the South had been convicted already. By the time the hearings began in January, 1866, the demand for guarantees of some kind had come to be taken more or less for granted, and most men had a more or less general idea why. The committee did take voluminous testimony relative to maltreatment of Negroes, persecution of Unionists, and harassment of Yankees, and all this had its importance. But "assessment of evidence" was hardly what the committee had in mind; in that sense the "evidence" was loaded. What the inquisitors were after, and what they got, was just that much more of what they were convinced of already. Whether it was loaded in all ways, however, is another matter. To say that the testimony consisted of lies would be dubious; one does not get nearly the impression of flamboyance in reading it that one gets in reading about it. In itself, the material is very detailed and very circumstantial. It was just that the committee was interested in only one side of the story, and most of the informants were summoned because of their special knowledge of that particular side.

What the informants told was more of the same kind of thing Northerners had been reading in the newspapers for six or eight months. The stories of persecution were substantially the same as those which congressmen had been getting in their mail all along from Southern Unionists, and these were the people, along with the Negroes, whom the congressmen had a peculiar interest in protecting. What the committee wanted now were details, as many as could be heaped together, in the effort to make it all "official," and to be put right with a candid world. Were the stories true? For the special aspects of Southern life with which they dealt, they probably were. At any rate, the "trial" was a great success, having turned out just about the way everyone assumed it would. All the transcripts were collected and classified by states and were included with Senator Fessenden's final report; the report, distributed in printed form, served many a party orator that fall as a manual for ready reference.[3]

[3] *Report of the Joint Committee on Reconstruction at the First Session Thirty-ninth Congress* (Washington: Government Printing Office, 1866). This document consists of Fessenden's report and four major sections, mostly testimony: Part I, Tennessee (subcommittee: Grimes, Bingham, Grider), 128 pp.; Part II, Virginia, North Carolina, South Carolina (subcommittee: Howard, Conkling, Blow), 294 pp.; Part III, Georgia, Alabama, Mississippi, Arkansas (subcommittee: Harris, Boutwell, Morrill), 187 pp.; Part IV, Florida, Louisiana, Texas (subcommittee: Williams, Washburne, Rogers), 167 pp.

It would serve no purpose here to argue the merits of this testimony one way or the other for the purpose for which it was gathered, since it is conceded that the purpose was primarily to prepare an indictment of the South. And yet this very fact has prevented its ever being analyzed for any other purpose. The present writer is convinced that, properly weighted and classified, the material constitutes an extremely valuable body of source documents for judging the state of Southern feeling at this period, quite aside from the "badness" or "goodness" of that feeling. Certain categories of witnesses may be assumed to have had special biases, but the problem then becomes one of assessing just how those biases may have affected their answers taken one by one rather than whether their testimony should or should not be considered lies. They were, after all, under oath.

For example, of the 145 witnesses (about a half-dozen of whom submitted their testimony in writing), 35 were Union army officers, over half of them generals, not counting officers of the Freedmen's Bureau. Some level of dependability has to be imputed to such witnesses as a class, and it becomes a problem of seeing how the replies to specific types of questions tally with other replies from other witnesses: this is the plane upon which correlation will yield whatever meaning is to be got out of the material. Or take the Freedmen's Bureau officers, of whom there were 17, most of them having been on army duty. To the extent that their testimony involves their own administrative experience, it should be taken for the information it contains, regardless of what it did or did not do for the over-all case which the committee was making.

Or, take the Southerners themselves, of whom there were 71, including 7 Negroes and not counting anyone who had lived in the South less than 20 years. The biases of the 13 who were avowed ex-Confederates should be easy enough to assess. The rest either reported themselves Unionists of one shade or another, or said they had remained aloof from the war. The federal officeholders among them (6) would have had one kind of bias (they seemed very interested in federal protection); the state officeholders —19 in all, including 13 members-elect to Congress—would presumably be interested in restoration. The biases of the Negroes, and of the white Unionists who reported personal sufferings and persecution (two dozen or so) would also be clear enough: they were the result of experience. The same would be true of the 10 Northerners living in the South. But what about that experience? Just as experience alone it ought to be worth something. Of the 12 Northern travelers, there is some problem of how selective a bias was involved in simply being a Northerner, when it came to answering any specific question.

In short, there should be some alternative to ignoring this evidence—some sensible

And yet this aspect of the work of amendment-making was still, all told, something of a side line, not having in itself a very direct relationship to the major decisions which were made in the long course of the process. It is actually the political nature of the amendment-making procedure that should receive the primary emphasis. It amounted to a political compromise, based for one thing on the general conviction that there had to be something (public pressure was to become more and more insistent as time went on), and, for another, on the need to strike a balance within the party on a number of key items. Certain of those items should now be noted.

One of them involved the general question of Negro suffrage and Negro rights. General agreement prevailed throughout the party on the need for federal protection of civil rights, though it was not at first clear whether such protection needed to be written into a constitutional amendment. On the question of suffrage, however, there was much disagreement on how much prominence suffrage should be given as an issue. On the one hand, Charles Sumner and his friends were determined that Negro suffrage should receive explicit guarantees, but, on the other, there was a widespread desire among political leaders, especially those in the Midwest and Middle Atlantic states, to avoid the issue on the ground that it would injure them politically. It was this side of the matter, not Sumner's side, that was favored by Thaddeus Stevens, and Stevens belabored Sumner for his intransigence on more than one occasion.

A question of transcendent importance was that of Southern representation. All agreed that the South should not be permitted, without further safeguards, to gain representatives as a result of emancipation. The three-fifths compromise was no longer operative, and to avoid ambiguity a change in the Constitution seemed urgent; the South would have about a dozen more representatives if Negroes were fully counted as a basis for representation, and some eighteen less were they not to be counted at all. But as to how such a change was to be managed there was no agreement, and the question was debated down to the very last. Men from the Midwest tended to favor a plan of representation based on qualified voters; that is, the greater the extent to which the Negro population was enfranchised in a state, the greater

technique for dealing with all of it on its merits, and for determining both the extent and the limits of those merits. To do so would yield a great deal of information about the quality of loyalty in the South, the effect of the President's policy, the treatment of Unionists and Negroes, the state of feeling regarding the debt, the Negro, the Yankee, and numerous other questions.

would be the number of representatives to which that state was entitled. Even the President had in January expressed himself as not hostile to such a plan, though he preferred no plan at all. On the other hand, spokesmen for New England went on record very early against the scheme, arguing that under it their own representation—because of a smaller percentage of voters per capita than in the states farther west—would actually be in danger of reduction. As a result, the Joint Committee was eventually to recommend representation based on population, with proportional reduction of some kind if any males over twenty-one were disfranchised for racial reasons. This amounted, in effect, to a compromise not only between the two positions on representation but also between the two positions on suffrage.

A further item had to do with disfranchisement of former rebels and disqualification of Southern leaders for officeholding. Stevens and his radical followers wanted the most drastic possible reduction of Southern political power; they would disqualify and disfranchise as many ex-Confederates as they could, and the more the better. But there was sentiment equally strong within the party for a general amnesty that would exclude only a few notorious rebels—a plan which had such advocates as Horace Greeley, Senator Stewart, and Governor Andrew—and in between these two positions, there was many an intermediate shade. This, too, was not settled until the very end.

A final problem, which never emerged as an open issue and which became of far greater consequence later than it did at this time, was that of a definitive versus a provisional settlement. Stevens, Sumner, and certain other radicals, realizing that the country was by no means prepared for universal suffrage or general confiscation, were anxious to avoid a final settlement, in the hope that majorities might eventually be obtained for measures of a more Spartan nature. But the majority sentiment throughout the winter, spring, and summer of 1866 favored offering the South a clear settlement that could be accepted or rejected. The general feeling was for a re-establishment of the Union upon principles mutually recognized, and though some alternative to Johnson's terms (generally recognized as unsatisfactory) was required, it was certainly not expected that the alternative should be to do nothing at all. As it turned out—whatever the intention had been—matters were so arranged that each could think what he wanted to think. But the side which took for granted that the Amendment contained the final terms was still the majority side all through, until events made the question an academic one. There is thus every reason to suppose that if there had been any incentive to make an issue with Stevens during the campaign, the latter's position (which depended on avoiding explicitness) would simply have evaporated.

Another aspect of the amendment-making which is now problematical, but which should be considered in connection with the alternatives that remained open down to the end, is the question of what would have happened if President Johnson had himself taken a part in the process. What if the President's influence had gone into the striking of the final balance? Was it not too late—say, after March 28—for any sort of compromise?

In spite of all that had happened already, it was not by any means too late. The point which now meant everything to the President (though great numbers of men were still loath to believe it) was the point that the Southern states had to be represented before Congress could take any action pertaining to them; to yield on that point alone would reopen a whole range of possibilities for the Executive position. Refusing to yield, on the other hand, meant nothing substantive any longer, for on that aspect of the President's position, Congress—with majorities all over the North—had no choice. Congress would act as a legislative body on matters of reconstruction whether the President thought it had the right to do so or not. But had the President decided to participate in the normal way in the making of the constitutional amendment—by establishing communication with his party leadership, letting his inclinations be known, and thus having something to say on what the amendment should consist of—he would have created a sensation. The advantages all around would be considerable, not only in terms of presidential leverage, but for the general well-being of the party itself. This was quite generally recognized at the time, and it might be well, in this connection, to view briefly some of the alternatives.

Politically, a settlement with Johnson, for most Republican politicians, would still be all to the good if it could be managed. It would still be the best single guarantee of a Union victory in the fall. In the spring of 1866 such a victory could by no means be seen as an open-and-shut certainty. Quite the contrary; for one thing there was still a sizable bloc of voters, so far as anyone knew, who might follow Johnson if forced to a clear choice. This was a particular hazard in such large pivotal states as New York, Pennsylvania, Ohio, and Indiana. Moreover, no one yet knew what the effects might be of a substantial loss of federal patronage. Conceivably, such patronage might be turned over to the Democrats in amounts sufficient to result in serious damage to the Republican effort.

There were certain items upon which neither the Joint Committee nor Congress as a whole could do any basic compromising. These were: federal guarantees of civil rights, limits on Southern representation, and guarantees of the federal debt. But the President's own position had never really been closed on any of these items. His annual message had recognized, at least in principle, the civil rights problem; even his two veto messages had left certain loopholes which did not entirely foreclose federal action.[4] His published interview with Senator Dixon in January had given explicit recognition to the principle of limiting representation.[5] And with regard to the debt, there was no disagreement anywhere, except for the most extreme Copperheads.

At the same time, however, there was the widest room for negotiation, maneuver, and compromise on the remaining items at issue. This was particularly the case with the problem of Negro suffrage, which would never, even in the Amendment's final version, be made the subject of hard and fast conditions. One solution to that question, in which many men concurred, was inherent in Johnson's own views on representation. As for disqualification and disfranchisement, the extreme seesawing which took place here was more than proof that no clear majority commitment existed in advance. With regard to immediate readmission once the amendment was ratified, this was precisely the arrangement which—despite the Stevens position—was favored by the majority. The public assumed that such would indeed be the under-

[4] The President had said in his annual message: "But while I have no doubt that now, after the close of the war, it is not competent for the General Government to extend the elective franchise in the several States, it is equally clear that good faith requires the security of the freedmen in their liberty and their property, their right to labor, and their right to claim the just return of their labor. I cannot too strongly urge a dispassionate treatment of this subject, which should be carefully kept aloof from all party strife." *Congressional Globe,* 39 Cong., 1 sess., Appendix, p. 3; Richardson, *Messages and Papers,* VI, 360. Senator Trumbull in his speeches of February 20 and April 4, 1866, called attention to these expressions of Executive sentiment. *Cong. Globe,* 39 Cong., 1 sess., pp. 936, 1760. Subsequently, in his Freedmen's Bureau veto message, Johnson said: "I share with Congress the strongest desire to secure to the freedmen the full enjoyment of their freedom and property and their entire independence and equality in making contracts for their labor. . . ." Richardson, *Messages and Papers,* VI, 398. Senator Sherman, speaking on February 26, quoted this passage in support of his plea that despite the veto, harmony with the President was still possible. *Cong. Globe,* 39 Cong., 1 sess., Appendix, p. 130. Even the Civil Rights veto, otherwise much sharper than that on the Freedmen's Bureau, contained the words: ". . . I will cheerfully cooperate with Congress in any measure that may be necessary for the protection of the civil rights of the freedmen . . . , by judicial process, under equal and impartial laws, in conformity with the provisions of the Federal Constitution." Richardson, *Messages and Papers,* VI, 413.

[5] New York *Herald,* Jan. 29, 1866; *Cong. Globe,* 39 Cong., 1 sess., p. 537.

standing; with the President's influence behind the express position that it was final, it is difficult to see how Congress could refuse to make the matter explicit. As things turned out, of course, this was never brought to a test.

A final set of alternatives would have to do with the other side of the case—with a presidential refusal either to take an actual part in the process of amendment-making or to endow it with any sort of Executive sanction. A general and pervasive result of such a refusal would certainly be to confer an increment of authority, energy, and decision upon the extreme side of every question that was not there before. It is not sound to assume that the result would have been what it was no matter what the President did; the very discrediting of his rigid position, on the other hand, would give added sanction to the extremist impulse for punishing the South. In the second place, so far as the committee and its deliberations were concerned, if there were no negotiable Executive position to which the members had to adjust, the President's opinions would cease to make any difference. And finally, whatever else the Amendment's ultimate version might be, it would at least have to constitute a secure platform upon which the party's candidates could stand in the fall elections. The committee's moderates were quite solid on this point. With presidential influence removed, therefore, and with incentives to resist extremist energy considerably reduced, the crucial argument for settling a clash on anything would tend more and more to come down to the question: *"Will it win or lose us votes in November?"*

II   THE FIRST TRIAL PERIOD: DECEMBER 5, 1865–MARCH 27, 1866

A number of tentative ventures at writing an amendment had already occurred before the Civil Rights veto, which meant that there had been a certain amount of opportunity to test alternatives.

The concept of representation based on the number of qualified voters in a state—a notion which would later take on rather conservative connotations—was first proposed by Thaddeus Stevens himself, who offered it as a resolution in the House on December 5.[6] The idea met with some favor, and was discussed in committee early the follow-

[6] *Cong. Globe*, 39 Cong., 1 sess., p. 10. The resolution was as follows: "Representatives shall be apportioned among the States which may be within the Union according to their respective legal voters; and for this purpose none shall be named as legal voters who are not either natural-born citizens or naturalized foreigners. Congress shall provide for ascertaining the number of said voters. A true census of the legal voters shall be taken at the same time with the regular census."

ing month, at which time Stevens was supported by Roscoe Conkling. The speech of James G. Blaine on January 8, however, did much to crystallize—if not to settle—congressional sentiment on this point. New England, itself standing to lose representation on such a basis, thereafter constituted an opposition formidable enough to cause Stevens and Conkling to abandon their plan, even though interest in it was to continue for some time thereafter.[7]

Meanwhile, the Joint Committee on Reconstruction had worked out its own version of an amendment on representation. The committee's recommendations, in the form of a resolution, was passed on January 20; it was thereupon reported to the Senate by Fessenden on the twenty-second and to the House by Stevens on the same day:

Representatives and direct taxes shall be apportioned among the several States which may be included within this Union according to their respective numbers, counting the whole number of persons in each State, excluding Indians not taxed: *Provided,* That whenever the elective franchise shall be denied or abridged in any State on account of race or color all persons of such race or color shall be excluded from the basis of representation.[8]

The resolution reported was one of two which had been debated in committee. The other, which Fessenden had favored, would have required the states, flatly and unconditionally, to provide in their constitutions for an impartial suffrage.[9] It should be noted that the committee's resolution was more severe than the comparable section in the completed Fourteenth Amendment, since any abridgment of voting rights for reasons of color would automatically remove from the basis of that state's representation the total number of the race so discriminated against. The resolution passed the House on January 31 (after "direct taxes" was struck out), but it failed of the necessary two-thirds vote in the Senate, owing in no small part to the opposition of Charles Sumner.[10]

[7] Kendrick, *Journal,* pp. 41–42; facts and figures relative to representation were presented by Blaine in his speech of January 8 and by Conkling in more systematic form in his speech of January 22. *Cong. Globe,* 39 Cong., 1 sess., pp. 141–42, 354–59. Governor Andrew of Massachusetts also attacked the scheme in his Valedictory on January 5.

[8] *Cong. Globe,* 39 Cong., 1 sess., pp. 337, 351.

[9] Kendrick, *Journal,* p. 50. The alternative resolution, defeated in committee, read: "Representatives and direct taxes shall be apportioned among the several States within this Union, according to the respective numbers of citizens of the United States in each State; and all provisions in the Constitution or laws of any State, whereby any distinction is made in political or civil rights or privileges, on account of race, creed, or color, shall be inoperative and void."

[10] *Cong. Globe,* 39 Cong., 1 sess., pp. 538, 1289. Fessenden wrote home on February 3: "You see I am in better spirits, and I need to be, for our constitutional amendment is

A wide range of sentiment was explored in the course of the Senate debates. Senator Doolittle, offering a substitute amendment on February 6, revived the representation-according-to-legal-voters scheme originally promoted by Stevens, and Sherman, speaking on a different subject later in the month, also expressed preference for that plan.[11] Sumner, much to the angry chagrin of Fessenden, delivered two lengthy and ponderous attacks on the committee's measure, one on February 5 and 6, and the other on March 7. Such an explicit distinction among citizens on grounds of "race or color" as was admitted in the resolution, according to Sumner, would not only defile the text of the Constitution but would hold out an unworthy bribe to the former slaveholder which the latter's cunning would find the means to circumvent anyway. Sumner's own formula was a simple resolution declaring what he construed the Constitution to contain already, now that slavery had been abolished: equal civil and political rights for all.[12] Fessenden, in his defense of the resolution on February 7, declared that he was not concerned with abstractions, that his constituents had not sent him there to philosophize but to act, and that the main question was, "What can pass?" Another plan was proposed by Senator Howard on February 19: suffrage for all Negroes over twenty-one years of age who had served in the army or who could read and write or who owned $250 in property. A similar proposition had been recommended by President Johnson to Governor Sharkey the previous summer.[13] The Democrats attacked the committee resolution on various grounds, all based upon their opposition to any kind of reduction in Southern representation.[14] Before the resolution came to a final vote,

coming up on Monday, and Mr. Sumner says he shall put his foot on it and crush it. Well, the amendment is the committee's and not mine. I shall make a half hour's speech on it, and be followed by Sumner with a printed oration which he says will take two days. He is waiting for this opportunity to show the country the difference between a great orator and a mere talker. We shall see how it ends." Francis Fessenden, *Life and Public Services of William Pitt Fessenden*, II, 25–26.

[11] *Cong. Globe*, 39 Cong., 1 sess., p. 673, Appendix, p. 131.

[12] *Ibid.*, pp. 673–87, 1224–32.

[13] *Ibid.*, pp. 702–8, 915. Johnson, in a telegram to the provisional governor of Mississippi on August 15, 1865, had suggested the same qualifications for suffrage. *Senate Executive Documents*, 39 Cong., 1 sess., No. 26, "Provisional Governors," p. 229.

[14] The arguments of the Democrats included the following points: (1) that voting should not be linked to representation, since a representative represents not simply the voters but the entire population; (2) that the amendment violated the "no taxation without representation" principle; (3) that as long as so much stress was put on human rights, consistency required the Republicans to enact female suffrage; (4) that with the disparagement of the state sovereignty and state equality principles, consistency also required changing the composition of the Senate; and (5) that the states to which the amendment applied were not being consulted until after its passage. These arguments are summarized in Kendrick, *Journal*, pp. 207–10.

Sumner made the second of his two assaults on it, and Fessenden delivered a blistering reply which made Sumner writhe and which occasioned deep satisfaction to members on both sides of the chamber.[15]

There was a sense, however, in which Sumner had been right. His harangues, despite their bloated doctrinaire quality, had managed to encompass the major objections to the proposed amendment and to anticipate the grounds for its failure. It did fall between two stools of a nice moral dilemma which Fessenden himself could hardly have failed to appreciate; the guarantee of equal rights implied in it was indirect, left-handed, and questionable, and at the same time the penalty for disregarding it was crassly punitive. What it all demonstrated was that there was no pattern of clarity in sentiment throughout the party and that nobody at this point controlled party opinion, least of all Thaddeus Stevens. Indeed, Stevens' grip had become about as precarious during this period as it had ever been; and one could very well speculate about what might have been the effect of a presidential decision to intervene in a positive direction, instead of rendering the political atmosphere murky with his Freedmen's Bureau veto and subsequent pronouncements. In any case, Sumner's own activities had served to highlight the cross-purposes within the party, and Stevens did not hesitate to let him know it.[16] In a conversation with Welles on March 9, the day the committee's resolution was defeated in the Senate, James W. Grimes in a sour mood pronounced a plague upon them both.[17] The committee would have to try again; its first effort had been a failure.

In the House, meanwhile, another problem had come up. Representative Bingham had been convinced all along that Congress ought to have constitutional power to protect civil rights, but he did not think that such power as yet existed (this was the basis for Bingham's opposition to the pending Civil Rights Bill); and accordingly he introduced on February 26 a proposed constitutional amendment which would remedy the defect. He had already introduced his resolution once before, but at Stevens' suggestion he had agreed to let it be re-

15 *Cong. Globe*, 39 Cong., 1 sess., pp. 1275–81. This speech was delivered on March 9; later in the day the amendment came to a vote and was defeated. It did, however, give Fessenden some satisfaction to vent his aggressions: "I believe everybody was gratified with the whipping I gave Sumner. . . ." Fessenden, *Fessenden*, II, 55; see also James, *Fourteenth Amendment*, p. 74.

16 Gideon Welles, *Diary*, II, 441; Richard N. Current, *Old Thad Stevens*, pp. 236–37; C. W. Wardwell to T. Stevens, Mar. 3, 1866 [endorsed by Stevens to Sumner], Sumner MSS, Harvard College Library. Stevens told Sumner he hoped "that if we are to be slain it will not be by our friends."

17 Welles, *Diary*, II, 447–48. Grimes, according to Welles, called Stevens "a pretty unscrupulous old fellow, unfit to lead any party," and Sumner "a cold-blooded, selfish, dangerous man."

committed. The resolution met with various kinds of opposition, but its principle, significantly modified, would ultimately reappear as Section 1 of the completed Fourteenth Amendment. It would be difficult at this point to characterize the proposal as either "radical" or "conservative." Bingham himself was hardly a radical; indeed, the New York *Herald* (the President's advocate) declared that such an amendment was unnecessary, since the power already existed. But the opposition is interesting: most of it was based on the fear that the resolution conferred unduly centralized powers on the federal government.[18]

The question of representation was taken up again in the Senate on March 12, now on a different tack. On that day, Sumner and Grimes introduced resolutions which were not only virtually identical in their effect but which came to about the same thing as the subsequent Section 2 of the Fourteenth Amendment. The principle which had now come to the fore was that of proportional rather than total reduction of representation for failure to accord equal political rights.[19] Again, one finds no way to characterize this proposal within either radical or moderate categories. It was certainly milder than the committee's original scheme for representation, and Wendell Phillips did not think it was any improvement.[20] Did it involve Sumner himself in a change of front or a compromise of principle? Probably it did not; it omitted, unlike the committee resolution, the words "race or color," which may have gratified Sumner's partiality to abstractions. Support for

[18] *Cong. Globe,* 39 Cong., 1 sess., pp. 813, 1033–34; New York *Herald,* Feb. 15, 1866; James, *Fourteenth Amendment,* pp. 81–87; Kendrick, *Journal,* pp. 213–20. The amendment had been adopted in committee on February 3 by the narrow margin of 7–6; it was favored by Howard, Williams, Washburne, Morrill, Bingham, Boutwell, and Rogers; those opposed were Fessenden, Grimes, Harris, Stevens, Grider, and Conkling. Kendrick, pp. 60–61.

[19] *Cong. Globe,* 39 Cong., 1 sess., pp. 1320–21. Grimes's resolution was as follows: "Representatives may be apportioned among the several States which may be included within this Union according to their respective numbers, counting the whole number of persons in each State, excluding Indians not taxed; but whenever in any State the elective franchise shall be denied to any portion of its male citizens above the age of twenty-one years, except for crime or disloyalty, the basis of representation of such State shall be reduced in the proportion which the number of male citizens so excluded shall bear to the whole number of male citizens over twenty-one years of age."
And Sumner's: "Representatives shall be apportioned among the several States which may be included within this Union according to their respective numbers, which shall be determined by taking the whole number of persons, and excluding Indians not taxed: *Provided,* That whenever male citizens of the United States over the age of twenty-one years shall be excluded from the elective franchise of any State, except for participation in the rebellion, the basis of representation therein shall be reduced in the proportion which the number thus excluded bears to the whole number of male citizens of the United States over the age of twenty-one years in such State."

[20] James, *Fourteenth Amendment,* p. 92.

direct guarantees of suffrage, moreover, had not up to this time been very promising. Actually, Sumner did not adhere to this latest inspiration very long anyway.

A fresh new turn was given to the entire question of reconstruction by a series of resolutions offered by Senator William M. Stewart of Nevada on March 16. These resolutions constituted the most dramatic proposal so far, and occasioned considerable stir. Stewart's "universal amnesty and universal suffrage" plan was conceived not as a constitutional amendment but as an immediate settlement that could be offered by Congress and accepted—or not—by the South in good faith. Its several parts were as follows:

The Southern states could have their representation in Congress immediately restored upon amending their constitutions to do away with discriminations of color on civil rights, to repudiate the rebel debt, to renounce all claims to compensation for emancipated slaves, and to make no discriminations in the suffrage on grounds of color or prior servitude.

Be it resolved [etc.], 1. That each of said States, whose people were lately in insurrection . . . , shall be recognized as having fully and validly resumed its relations with this Government, and its chosen representatives shall be admitted into the two Houses of the national Legislature whenever said State shall have so amended its constitution as, first, to do away with all existing distinctions as to civil rights and disabilities among the various classes of its population by reason either of race or color, or previous condition of servitude; second, to repudiate all pecuniary indebtedness which said State may have heretofore contracted, incurred, or assumed in connection with the late unnatural and treasonable war; third, to yield all claim to compensation on account of the liberation of its slaves; and fourth, to provide for the extension of the elective franchise to all persons upon the same terms and conditions, making no discrimination on account of race, color, or previous condition of servitude: *Provided*, That those who were qualified to vote in the year 1860 by the laws of their respective States shall not be disfranchised by reason of any new tests or conditions which have been or may be prescribed since that year.

A general amnesty would be proclaimed after the ratification of these conditions by a popular vote.

2. *Resolved*, That after the aforesaid conditions shall have been complied with and the same shall have been ratified by a majority of the present voting population of the State, including all those qualified to vote under the laws thereof as they existed in 1860, a general amnesty shall be proclaimed in regard to all persons in such State who were in any way connected with the armed opposition to the Government of the United States, wholly exonerating them from all pains, penalties, or disabilities to

which they may have become liable by reason of their connection with the rebellion.

The states of the North should also incorporate such provisions into their constitutions.

3. *Resolved,* That in view of the importance of the thorough assimilation of the basis of suffrage in the various States of the Union, all other States not above specified be respectfully requested to incorporate an amendment in their State constitutions respectively, corresponding with the one above described.

And finally, these conditions were not to be regarded as coercion, but as an understanding.

4. *Resolved,* That in the adoption of the aforesaid resolutions it is not intended to assert a coercive power on the part of Congress in regard to the regulation of the right of suffrage in the different States of the Union, but only to make a respectful and earnest appeal to their own good sense and love of country, with a view to the prevention of serious evils now threatened, and to the peaceful perpetuation of the repose, the happiness, and true glory of the whole American people.

At the conclusion of Stewart's explanation there was great excitement in the Senate, and for a week or so thereafter the plan had wide and enthusiastic support. Sumner impulsively exclaimed: "Sir, I welcome with open arms the Senator from Nevada." Sumner's Massachusetts colleague, Henry Wilson, declared:

I desire simply to say that I thank the Senator from Nevada for offering this proposition. I have no doubt it will receive the serious consideration of the committee to which he proposes to refer it, of the Senate, and of the country. I am for one, and I believe the country are, willing to settle this whole question on the basis of universal liberty, universal justice, universal suffrage, and universal amnesty.[21]

A good omen for the plan was the generous welcome it received. There were even influential Southerners who were much impressed; Henry S. Foote of Mississippi favored it, and Alexander Stephens said that "it would be the best possible settlement." Former Governor Andrew of Massachusetts wrote Stewart to express his "satisfaction and interest" in the latter's proposals and to declare his "hearty sympathy with the general design and plan they indicate." Horace Greeley of the *Tribune* indorsed the plan with enthusiasm, as did the *Nation* and the New York *Sun;* even the radical *Independent* recognized its justice. Stewart, in fact, claimed that his plan had been supported "by every leading Union newspaper throughout the North." Welles im-

[21] *Cong. Globe,* 39 Cong., 1 sess., pp. 1437–38.

plied in his diary on March 20 that President Johnson himself regarded it with favor. The fact that Stewart was known at this time to be on good terms with the President made his plan look very attractive all the way around: it might serve as middle ground for a real compromise, especially with Stevens currently having such a hard time keeping his followers in line in the House.[22]

And yet the whole thing died a relatively quick death, and the name of William M. Stewart—despite the bright promise of an hour—now brings no echoes down the corridors of history. The senator was pushed off the stage; what killed his plan was Johnson's veto of the Civil Rights Bill on March 27. The vulnerable feature all along had naturally been the "universal amnesty" provision, and after the veto its entire spirit had been rendered out of date. But the enthusiasm and relief with which the plan had initially been welcomed showed that, for a time at least, here was something that, given judicious pump-priming, was negotiable. When Johnson cut the ground from under him, Stewart became his enemy for life.[23] When Stewart tried to bring his resolutions to a vote on April 4, Lyman Trumbull, now implacable, shouldered him aside in his own brusque determination to demolish the President's veto message, which he then proceeded to do. That was virtually the last of the Stewart plan. Stewart appeared before the Joint Committee on April 16 with a final plea for his resolutions, but by then there was no further disposition to act upon them.[24] The Stevens spirit had been given a new lease on life.

III   THE OWEN PLAN AND THE COMMITTEE PLAN

The next trial period—the period between the Civil Rights veto and the completion of the Joint Committee's final recommendations—was marked by the clear emergence of two related elements. One was the realization that some kind of omnibus arrangement would be the most auspicious framework for settling the problems now pending, and the other was a narrowing of the field of alternatives to the search for a party compromise, now that the President's own connections with the Republican party had been made so tenu-

[22] George R. Brown (ed.), *Reminiscences of Senator William M. Stewart of Nevada* (New York: Neale Publishing Co., 1908), pp. 215–18; Kendrick, *Journal*, pp. 252–55; J. A. Andrew to Stewart, Mar. 20, 1866, Andrew MSS (Letterbook), Massachusetts Historical Society; James, *Fourteenth Amendment*, pp. 96–97; *Cong. Globe*, 39 Cong., 1 sess., p. 1754; Welles, *Diary*, II, 457.

[23] *Reminiscences*, pp. 198–200.

[24] *Cong. Globe*, 39 Cong., 1 sess., pp. 1753–55; Kendrick, *Journal*, p. 82. Stewart had by this time changed the form of his proposal to a constitutional amendment.

ous. The "party compromise" aspect—the reconciliation of divergent positions among Republicans themselves—had of course always been there; but so long as the President remained a factor in congressional deliberations, the problem had retained a scope that went a good deal beyond simply the health and well-being of the Republican party. Such well-being had now, however, come to assume paramount importance.

The necessity for bringing the work to completion was sharpened by the growing pressures of public opinion. In his Civil Rights veto message, Johnson had reiterated his opposition to any major enactments touching the Southern states so long as those states remained unrepresented, and at no time during the coming period of drafting— from about the last week in March to April 30—was he to give any indication that he had changed his mind. The extent, therefore, to which action would be taken with an eye to either the President's approval or disapproval, was henceforth much reduced; incentives for adjusting to the Executive views had lost much of their reality. What was, on the other hand, becoming more and more of a reality was the likelihood that the final arrangement would not only be opposed by the Executive but would also have to serve as a secure platform upon which Johnson and his supporters might themselves be opposed in the fall elections. The final arbiter now, public opinion—already running against Johnson—had meanwhile become just that much more insistent that Congress itself should act positively and soon. The keynote was sounded by the *Nation* as early as March 22:

The more people reflect, the better satisfied they are that Congress, . . . which is from its very nature in closer contact with the country and better informed of its thoughts and feelings from day to day than the Executive can possibly be, is the branch which has and ought to have most to do with such a work of reorganization as is now before us. . . .
. . . But then it was assumed that Congress would have a policy. It has now, however, sat for nearly four months, and has nothing of the kind. We hear a great deal of the President's policy; it is something definite, determined, capable of being set down in black and white and discussed in all its bearings; but we never hear of the policy of Congress, because there is no such thing. The people are ready to keep the South out until it complies with certain conditions, but they want to know what these conditions are. . . . The Reconstruction Committee has produced several valuable measures, each of them meeting some great want of the crisis, but not forming part of any well-defined plan. . . .

More serious work than we have yet had must now begin. If it does not . . . we greatly fear the coming fall will find the public thoroughly out of patience with Congress and quite ready to let the President and his friends have their own way. He would be a bold man who should venture to predict what would then happen, or to calculate how much of the fruits of our victories would be left us.

On April 12, the *Nation* emphasized the other side of the case, the importance of due deliberation. "But," it reiterated, returning once more to the theme of urgency,

we beg Congress not to accept this view as an excuse for procrastination. The time has arrived at which it must visibly begin to shape a policy. The people are not always as patient as they should be. They want some tangible proposition. Congress can agree on some plan now with a clear understanding that it will be vetoed. If it can be passed over the veto, well; but if not, let it be something upon which we can go to the country with firmness and confidence.[25]

This phase took as its point of departure a new set of proposals, this time offered by an outsider. Robert Dale Owen, whose name (as well as that of his father) had been connected with numerous reform projects, came to Washington in the latter part of March "greatly exercised," as he put it, over the lack of action by Congress, and bearing with him a plan of his own. He sought out Oliver Morton, who had not as yet departed for home, and found an approving listener; he then called upon Thaddeus Stevens, whom he counted among his friends, and read the plan to him. Stevens' response was immediate and gratifying:

"I'll be plain with you, Owen. We've had nothing before us that comes anywhere near being as good as this, or as complete. It would be likely to pass, too; that's the best of it. We haven't a majority, either in our committee or in Congress, for immediate suffrage; and I don't believe the States have yet advanced so far that they would be willing to ratify it. I'll lay that amendment of yours before our committee to-morrow, if you say so; and I'll do my best to put it through."

Fessenden, more guardedly, told Owen that his proposal was "the best that had yet been presented"; and more or less similar approval was expressed by every Republican member of the committee. All recognized it as the closest approach so far to meeting all the requirements which now faced them.[26]

The Owen plan, which was formally introduced in committee by Stevens on April 21, consisted of a five-part amendment to the Consti-

25 *Nation*, II (Mar. 22, Apr. 12, 1866), 358–454.

26 Robert Dale Owen, "Political Results from the Varioloid," *Atlantic Monthly*, XXXV (June, 1875), 662–64; Richard W. Leopold, *Robert Dale Owen: A Biography* (Cambridge, Mass.: Harvard University Press, 1940), pp. 367–72. It should be added that at least as late as March 23 (four days before the Civil Rights veto) Owen had supported the Stewart plan. Owen to J. A. Andrew, Mar. 23, 1866, Andrew MSS.

tution, together with a supplementary enabling act. The amendment, section by section, was as follows:

Section 1 provided for equal civil rights:

No discrimination shall be made by any State, nor by the United States, as to the civil rights of persons, because of race, color, or previous condition of servitude.

Section 2 required, after 1876, an impartial suffrage in all states:

From and after the fourth day of July, eighteen hundred and seventy-six, no discrimination shall be made by any State nor by the United States, as to the enjoyment, by classes of persons, of the right of suffrage, because of race, color, or previous condition of servitude.

Section 3 provided that discrimination in suffrage on grounds of race or prior servitude *before* 1876 would mean a reduction in representation up to that time:

Until the fourth day of July, eighteen hundred and seventy-six, no class of persons, as to the right of any of whom to suffrage discrimination shall be made by any State, because of race, color, or previous condition of servitude, shall be included in the basis of representation.

Section 4 forbade the payment of either the rebel debt in any form or compensation for emancipated slaves:

Debts incurred in aid of insurrection, or of war against the Union, and claims of compensation for loss of involuntary service or labor, shall not be paid by any State or by the United States.

And Section 5:

Congress shall have power to enforce, by appropriate legislation, the provisions of this article.

The enabling act provided for full readmission as soon as the amendment had been ratified and incorporated into the Constitution, with only three limited classes of persons from the erstwhile Confederate states being ineligible for congressional office. (This was the next thing to Stewart's "universal amnesty" idea.) Even that disability would be removed after 1876.

That whenever the above-recited amendment shall have become part of the constitution, and any State lately in insurrection shall have ratified the same and shall have modified its constitution and laws in conformity with the first section thereof, then and in that case all laws, or parts of laws, confiscating the property of any of the inhabitants of such State, or imposing on any of them pains, penalties, and disabilities because of their participation in the late insurrection, shall be deemed and held to be repealed and of no effect, so far as the said inhabitants are concerned. And

[27] Owen, "Varioloid," p. 662.

the senators and representatives from such State, if found duly elected and qualified, shall, after taking the usual oath of office, be admitted as such. *Provided,* That no person who, having been an officer in the army or navy of the United States, or having been a member of the thirty-sixth Congress or of the Cabinet in the year one thousand eight hundred and sixty, did afterwards take part in the late insurrection, shall be eligible to either branch of the national legislature until after the fourth day of July, 1876.[28]

What happened to Owen's plan? Its prospects looked excellent for several days, and indications to that effect leaked out to the public through the Chicago *Tribune* (which heartily approved of the plan) and other newspapers.[29] By April 25, however, it began to be noised about that trouble had developed, and by the time the committee was through with it three days later the final result did not bear much resemblance to Owen's original scheme. The manner in which it was amended constituted a spelling-out of the compromises which were felt necessary in order to satisfy conflicting interests within the committee and within the party.

The major decision was to evade the issue of Negro suffrage. Section 2 of Owen's amendment, which extended a direct guarantee of impartial suffrage, was struck out, and the indirect expedient of proportional reduction came once again to the fore as a compromise between the direct guarantee principle of Section 2 and the total reduction principle of Section 3. Sentiment developing in several directions at once may account for the committee's decision not to make the matter explicit. In the first place, several large state caucuses held during the week had concluded that direct Negro suffrage would be a very risky issue in the coming elections—conclusions that were immediately known, of course, to the committee.[30] In the second place, a good many public men were convinced that the South would give the Negro the vote anyway, rather than have its representation reduced. Benjamin C. Truman, whose report on Southern conditions was submitted on April 9, had given this as his opinion; Johnson's own thinking had in fact been grounded on just such an assumption when he gave his interview to Senator Dixon on January 28.[31] And finally, it was beyond doubt Thaddeus Stevens himself who tipped the balance

28 *Ibid.,* pp. 663–64.

29 Chicago *Tribune,* Apr. 24, 1866; James, *Fourteenth Amendment,* pp. 108–9.

30 James, pp. 109–10; Owen, "Varioloid," p. 666.

31 Truman in his report had said, ". . . if the politicians of the south have the absolute certainty laid before them that in 1870 their representation in Congress will be diminished largely in consequence of the non-enfranchisement of the negro, they will see to it before that time that the proper reform is introduced. They will convince their constituents that it is necessary and proper to allow the negro to vote, and he will be allowed so to do." *Sen. Exec. Docs.,* 39 Cong., 1 sess., II, No. 43, "Report of Benjamin C. Truman," p. 11.

on this question. Being none too keen on direct enactment of Negro suffrage—he fully appreciated the misgivings of the state caucuses over suffrage as an election issue—Stevens could not in any case have thought Negro suffrage by 1876 worth bartering for such an exceedingly generous policy of amnesty and readmission as was contemplated in Owen's enabling act. Stevens, consequently, was by no means candid with Owen when he told the distressed reformer afterward that Fessenden's illness had provided just enough margin of delay for Midwest politicians ("hang their cowardice!") to make their influence felt in the committee and thus force a reconsideration of the vote. It had, as a matter of fact, been Stevens himself who made the motion to strike out that section.[32]

On civil rights, Owen's Section 1 was extended by Bingham's more comprehensive definition, which included the "due process" and "equal protection" principles. The President's Civil Rights veto had made everyone a good deal more sensitive to this problem than previously, and though the bill itself had been repassed over Johnson's veto, the only guarantee against the Democrats' repealing it, should they once again command majorities, would be to write its basic features into the Constitution.[33]

A disfranchisement section was put into the committee's proposed amendment which had had no counterpart at all in Owen's amendment. Prior to 1870, all persons who voluntarily participated in the rebellion would be ineligible to vote in federal elections. This, presumably, would give Southern Unionists an advantage in federal elections up to that time, and would guarantee a Republican President for 1868.

The disqualification-for-federal-officeholding principle, which in a token sense had been included in Owen's enabling act, was much extended in the supplementary legislation proposed by the committee. The categories of ineligible persons were greatly widened.

Finally, on the matter of readmission, a significant alteration of wording was made in the Owen version. Upon ratification of the amendment, and upon the amendment's incorporation into the Constitution, Owen's enabling act had provided explicitly for the readmission of Southern representatives, if duly qualified. Upon the motion of Senator Fessenden, however, the word "shall" was changed to "may [be admitted]."[34] Fessenden was no doubt fully aware of what he was doing, though it is more than likely that this alteration later assumed

[32] Owen, "Varioloid," pp. 665–66; Kendrick, *Journal,* pp. 101, 302.
[33] Kendrick, p. 106.   [34] *Ibid.,* p. 107.

a significance far greater than it had in the minds of those who voted for it at the time.

The result was the Joint Committee's plan of reconstruction, reported on April 30 by Fessenden and Stevens to the Senate and House, respectively,[35] and consisting of a five-part constitutional amendment and two bills.

SECTION 1. No state shall make or enforce any law which shall abridge the privileges or immunities of citizens of the United States; nor shall any State deprive any person of life, liberty or property without due process of law; nor deny to any person within its jurisdiction the equal protection of the laws.

SEC. 2. Representatives shall be apportioned among the several States which may be included within this Union according to their respective numbers, counting the whole number of persons in each State, excluding Indians not taxed. But whenever in any State the elective franchise shall be denied to any portion of its male citizens not less than twenty-one years of age, or in any way abridged, except for participation in rebellion or other crime, the basis of representation in such State shall be reduced in the proportion which the number of male citizens shall bear to the whole number of such male citizens not less than twenty-one years of age.

SEC. 3. Until the 4th day of July, in the year 1870, all persons who voluntarily adhered to the late insurrection, giving it aid and comfort, shall be excluded from the right to vote for Representatives in Congress and for electors for President and Vice-President of the United States.

SEC. 4. Neither the United States nor any State shall assume or pay any debt or obligation already incurred, or which may hereafter be incurred, in aid of insurrection or of war against the United States, or any claim for compensation for loss of involuntary service or labor.

SEC. 5. The Congress shall have power to enforce by appropriate legislation the provisions of this article.

The first of the committee's two bills was the enabling act for readmission:

Be it enacted [etc.], That whenever the above recited amendment shall have become part of the Constitution of the United States, and any State lately in insurrection shall have modified its constitution and laws in conformity therewith, the Senators and Representatives from such State, if found duly elected and qualified, may, after having taken the required oaths of office, be admitted into Congress as such.

SEC. 2. . . . That when any State lately in insurrection shall have ratified the foregoing amendment to the Constitution, any part of the direct tax under the act of August 5, 1861, which may remain due and unpaid in such State may be assumed and paid by such State; and the payment thereof, upon proper assurances from such State to be given to the Secretary of the Treasury of the United States, may be postponed for a period not exceeding ten years from and after the passage of this act.

[35] *Cong. Globe*, 39 Cong., 1 sess., pp. 2265, 2286–87.

The other bill defined those persons ineligible to hold federal office:

1. The President and Vice-President of the Confederate States of America, so-called, and the heads of departments thereof.

2. Those who in other countries acted as agents of the Confederate States of America, so-called.

3. Heads of Departments of the United States, officers of the Army and Navy of the United States, and all persons educated at the Military and Naval Academy of the United States, judges of the courts of the United States, and members of either House of the Thirty-Sixth Congress of the United States who gave aid or comfort to the late rebellion.

4. Those who acted as officers of the Confederate States of America, so-called, above the grade of colonel in the army or master in the navy, and any one who, as Governor of either of the so-called Confederate States, gave aid or comfort to the rebellion.

5. Those who have treated officers or soldiers or sailors of the Army or Navy of the United States, captured during the late war, otherwise than lawfully as prisoners of war.[36]

IV THE FINAL PHASE: MAY 1–JUNE 13, 1866

The response to the committee's efforts, both in Congress and on the part of the public, was marked by no great enthusiasm. There seemed to be a general willingness in Congress to accept the plan, but there was also a decided undertone of disappointment. Some, like Garfield, were distressed that suffrage could not have been given a direct guarantee (Garfield would also have eliminated the disfranchisement section); Stewart did not like either the section on disfranchisement or that on representation; Bingham, Trumbull, and Colfax thought that as soon as a state ratified, it ought to be readmitted without waiting for the necessary three-fourths. The *Nation* was dubious about the amendment's success ("If adopted, it will only be from fear of doing worse") and showed disappointment over the committee's failure to take hold of the suffrage problem directly. The Chicago *Tribune* felt that while the amendment would probably encounter little outright opposition in the North, it would meet with no particular favor either. "It is not exactly what any of us wanted," Grimes admitted, "but we were each compelled to surrender some of our individual preferences in order to secure anything."[37]

As for the response of the President himself, now that the new plan was out in the open, the question might once more be raised whether at this late date such response would make any difference. It would

---

[36] *Ibid.*, pp. 2286–87.

[37] *Nation*, II (May 18, 1866), 578; Chicago *Tribune*, May 1, 1866; Fessenden, *Fessenden*, II, 62; William Salter, *Life of James W. Grimes* (New York: D. Appleton, 1876), p. 292; James, *Fourteenth Amendment*, pp. 117–20.

indeed make a difference, even now. The committee's work was done, but the result had hardly taken the country by storm: too much trimming had had to be done for anyone to be sure how the thing as a whole would carry. A change of heart on the part of the President, at such a juncture, might have tipped matters in almost any direction. The possibility of such a change had still not entirely departed from Fessenden's mind; ". . . the President," he wrote hopefully, "is, I think, beginning to see that he is not the government."[38] Bingham's effort to make the readmission of any state automatic upon ratification, regardless of what other states did, was generally recognized as a move to make the amendment acceptable to Johnson—who, if nothing else, was still capable of doing it much mischief.[39] Were the Executive, on the other hand, to accept the inevitability of a constitutional amendment on reconstruction, and at the same time make positive efforts of his own to influence the result, this would be the very point—a time of considerable fluidity—where those efforts might still matter a great deal.

Johnson, however, made his decision immediately: He would have nothing to do with any of it. He would oppose the entire business flatly and unequivocally and would trust the people to vindicate his stand in the coming election. He called a meeting of his cabinet on May 1 and insisted that each member take a position for or against the amendment. He spent considerable time denouncing it himself, and in fact declared that "the government could be restored without a resort to amendments." Johnson then released the story in an officially prepared version to the press, and the same report, verbatim, was used in all the newspapers.

The President was earnest in his opposition to the report of the committee, and declared himself against all conditions precedent to the admission of loyal representatives from the Southern States in the shape of amendments to the constitution, or by the passage of laws. He insisted that under the constitution no State could be deprived of its equal suffrage in the Senate, and that Senators and Representatives ought to be at once admitted into the respective houses as presented by law and the constitution. . . . He remarked, in general terms, that if the organic law is to be changed at all, it should be at a time when all the States and all the people can participate in the alteration.[40]

It was a declaration of war on the men who had drafted and supported the committee's amendment, and that was how it was understood in

---

[38] Fessenden, *Fessenden*, II, 62.

[39] New York *Times*, May 2, 1866; New York *Herald*, May 2, 1866.

[40] New York *Herald*, May 2, 1866.

the Senate. "I suppose," said Senator Grimes the next day, as he held up the morning paper, "that this is the antagonist proposition that is put forth from the White House in opposition to the report of the committee . . . on reconstruction—the immediate unconditional admission, without any terms, without any conditions, of the representatives of those States and of the people of those States."[41] Johnson's conditions for his co-operation (surrender of the Fourteenth Amendment and six months' work) were such that his own influence for modifications of any kind was explicitly removed. As a result, the problem now became, with greater clarity than ever, that of writing an amendment that would keep the party together in the face of a hostile President. The party would have to operate as a unit—as Judge Orth had put it three days before—*"minus Andy."*

It took only three days after the opening of debate to get the committee's amendment through the House, though its passage was not marked by much enthusiasm. Those who objected to the disfranchisement section were for the most part agreed that the rest of the amendment was satisfactory; there were those, on the other hand, who thought that the disfranchisement section was the only part worth voting for. "Without that," declared Thaddeus Stevens, "it amounts to nothing." The amendment itself passed the House on May 10, and consideration of the accompanying bills was postponed pending the action of the Senate.[42]

Such postponement was not to the liking of Representative Bingham, who very much wanted to get an enactment by Congress specifying in clear terms that the Southern states were entitled to readmission upon ratifying the constitutional amendment. He had on May 1 proposed a modification of the committee's enabling act which would allow any Southern state to ratify and be admitted without waiting for the others. There had been a good deal of enthusiasm for Bingham's proposal at the time, and it was reported that Bingham had the support of Fessenden in the Senate.[43] But that had been before the President's cabinet meeting; afterward, the sentiment for immediate action in this direction appears to have cooled considerably. On May 15 Bingham tried to get the House to take up the enabling act, either amended or in its current form, but was sharply rebuked by Stevens.

[41] *Cong. Globe*, 39 Cong., 1 sess., pp. 2333–34. There was much denunciation of Johnson in the House on May 5; see *ibid.*, pp. 2399 ff.

[42] *Cong. Globe*, 39 Cong., 1 sess., pp. 2544, 2545.

[43] *Ibid.*, p. 2313; New York *Times*, May 2, 1866.

"When the Senate shall have concurred in our action on the constitutional amendment," rasped the old man, "it will be time enough for us to go on and pass the bill reciting the action of both branches of Congress." The motion to postpone was supported by a number of Democrats.[44]

The Fourteenth Amendment reached what in substance would be its final form between May 23, when debate opened in the Senate, and May 29, when the Senate Republican caucus committee, having taken account of the debates, presented its revised draft. Most of the debate centered upon the disfranchisement section, and it was recognized from the first that this section had next to no support; the section would have to be eliminated and something else substituted. Sentiment developed very quickly, led by Senator Clark of New Hampshire, for a disqualification section to put in its place. Wilson of Massachusetts suggested that Clark's substitute, which embraced only federal officeholding, be extended to include state officeholding as well. Senator Wade thought that the meaning of "citizen" in Section 1 should be defined explicitly, and that guarantees of the federal debt should be added to repudiation of Confederate debts. For all such changes, support was more or less general. Direct Negro suffrage died reluctantly, though Stewart made another effort to revive it along with a general amnesty. A final attempt was made by Senator Sherman to bring back representation based on voters, and as Republican senators met in caucus over the weekend of May 26 and 27, there were actually rumors that Sherman's proposal might possibly replace both Sections 2 and 3, but nothing came of them.[45]

The Senate caucus, after two unsuccessful meetings, finally appointed a five-man committee, headed by Fessenden and composed of the Republican members of the Joint Committee on Reconstruction, to put in final written shape what appeared to them to be the sense of the caucus and of the Senate. What Fessenden emerged with next day was a set of changes consisting of the following:

1. A first section with a definition of citizenship added.

2. Elimination of the disfranchisement section.

3. A new third section on disqualification, now no longer in a bill (as specified in the Joint Committee's April 30 report) but, in a form more severe than originally planned, incorporated in the amendment

---

[44] *Cong. Globe*, 39 Cong., 1 sess., pp. 2599–2600.

[45] *Ibid.*, pp. 2768–70, 2798–2803. For a discussion of these debates see James, *Fourteenth Amendment*, pp. 135–39, 140–41; Kendrick, *Journal*, pp. 310–15; *Cong. Globe*, 39 Cong., 1 sess., p. 2804; New York *Times*, May 26, 1866.

itself. The disabilities could, however, be removed by a two-thirds vote of Congress.

4. An added guarantee for the federal debt in Section 4.

5. The enabling act would be changed to allow immediate readmission as soon as a state ratified.

6. Tennessee, having already complied with the requirements set forth in the amendment, would be readmitted at once.[46]

From that point on, the party voted as a unit and the present Fourteenth Amendment was passed by the Senate on June 8. The Senate's version was concurred in by the House on June 13.[47] And yet when Congress finally adjourned six weeks later—though the state of Tennessee had meanwhile been readmitted to the Union—there was still no enabling act. How might the rest of the states come back? Most of the members assumed, apparently, that what applied to Tennessee would in a general way apply to the others, but Congress had still made no hard and fast commitments. That last margin of reluctance represented, in effect, the last of a long series of compromises in a long and exhausting season of disillusionments and political warfare.

Article XIV

Section 1. All persons born or naturalized in the United States, and subject to the jurisdiction thereof, are citizens of the United States and of the State wherein they reside. No State shall make or enforce any law which shall abridge the privileges or immunities of citizens of the United States, nor shall any State deprive any person of life, liberty, or property, without due process of law; nor deny to any person within its jurisdiction the equal protection of the laws.

Sec. 2. Representatives shall be apportioned among the several States according to their respective numbers, counting the whole number of persons in each State, excluding Indians not taxed. But when the right to vote at any election for the choice of electors for President and Vice-President of the United States, Representatives in Congress, the Executive and Judicial officers of a State, or the members of the Legislature thereof, is denied to any of the male inhabitants of such State, being twenty-one years of age, and citizens of the United States, or in any way abridged except for participation in rebellion, or other crime, the basis of representation therein shall be reduced in the proportion which the number of such male citizens shall bear to the whole number of male citizens twenty-one years of age in such State.

Sec. 3. No person shall be a Senator or Representative in Congress, or elector of President and Vice-President, or hold any office, civil or military, under the United States, or under any State, who, having previously

[46] New York *Times*, May 26, 30, 1866; New York *Herald*, May 28, 1866; Kendrick, *Journal*, p. 316.

[47] *Cong. Globe*, 39 Cong., 1 sess., pp. 3042–3149.

taken an oath, as a member of Congress, or as an officer of the United States, or as a member of any State legislature, or as an executive or judicial officer of any State, to support the Constitution of the United States, shall have engaged in insurrection or rebellion against the same, or given aid or comfort to the enemies thereof. But Congress may by a vote of two-thirds of each House, remove such disability.

Sec. 4. The validity of the public debt of the United States, authorized by law, including debts incurred for payment of pensions and bounties for services in suppressing insurrection or rebellion, shall not be questioned. But neither the United States nor any State shall assume or pay any debt or obligation incurred in aid of insurrection or rebellion against the United States, or any claim for the loss or emancipation of any slave; but all such debts, obligations, and claims shall be held illegal and void.

Sec. 5. The Congress shall have the power to enforce, by appropriate legislation, the provisions of this article.

V AFTERMATH AND CONSEQUENCES

Public response to the Fourteenth Amendment, though perhaps more favorable than it had been to the committee's plan, was still rather lukewarm. The Amendment was generally recognized for what it actually was—a compromise that commanded no overwhelmingly fervent support from any particular viewpoint. Most Unionist journals, however, thought it was weighted on the moderate side— enough so that it constituted a secure platform on which to go to the country that fall. Even the pro-Johnson papers did not consider the Amendment's terms unreasonable. Indeed, both the New York *Times* and the *Herald* thought that the Senate caucus had brought the final result so close to the President's own position that little further ground remained for conflict. Raymond of the *Times* declared on May 31 that the Senate's action was "in the direction of harmony and conciliation."

The exclusion from office of men who added perjury to treason is certainly not severe, either as a penalty or a precaution, and no one can object to declaring the national debt inviolate. To every one of these propositions, presented on its own merits, we presume the President himself would not object.

The South, Raymond added on June 2,

will have little reason to complain of harshness, especially inasmuch as it is provided that Congress may by a two-thirds vote remove the disability in exceptional cases as they arise. As thus modified, the amendment is really a compromise, which the South may be asked to consider with some likelihood of acceptance. And by the change, the Union majority in the Senate have taken an important step toward the vindication of their party from the disgrace and the weakness inflicted upon it by Mr. Stevens' intemperate malignity.[48]

[48] New York *Times*, May 31, June 2, 1866.

The *Herald* even claimed that Congress had stolen Johnson's own program, and Editor Bennett praised Fessenden both for his "masterly report" and for "reducing the crude and impracticable reconstruction scheme of Thaddeus Stevens to a practical shape."

This is, we say, a strong platform upon which to go to the people of the Northern States. There is nothing here obnoxious to public opinion in the way of negro suffrage, while the alternative suggested will be satisfactory to the North. There are no vindictive penalties here against rebels and traitors, but conditional exclusions, which cannot be resisted successfully before the people who put down the rebellion. . . . The republican supporters of President Johnson, as against Congress, can make no fight against this platform, for it is the President's own policy. It is a compromise platform against which Johnson republicans cannot even quarrel with the radicals before the people, although the hatred of the radicals against Johnson may continue.[49]

It might be supposed that the prospect of harmony between Congress and the Executive, so many times shown to be a mirage, should by this time have been dissipated once and for all. And yet somehow the spark of hope persisted. That hope was expressed once more by *Harper's Weekly* on June 16:

It is true that the President may refuse all accommodation. He may insist that he has required all that is needful, all that is constitutional. He may declare that he will stand or fall without moving an inch from his present position. He has indeed virtually said as much. But he said it under other circumstances. . . . He said it before the mature decision of Congress had been declared. If after that declaration . . . the President should insist that the representatives of the loyal people are to have no voice in the settlement of the victory which those people have won, then the issue will indeed be made, and the final appeal taken to the country.

But surely all those who believe as we do, that the division of the Union party . . . would be incalculably disastrous to the cause of true liberty and civilization, will not passionately insist that such division, with all its consequences, is inevitable. . . .

It is to secure the gains already made; to intrust the completion of the work of restoration to the hands which defeated rebellion, that it is the imperative duty of the President, of Congress, and of all loyal men, to maintain the ascendancy of the Union party until its work is accomplished.[50]

[49] New York *Herald*, June 12, 1866.

[50] *Harper's Weekly*, X (June 16, 1866), 370. Reports of the Republican caucus meetings during the last week in May were full of references to senatorial hopes that the amendment's final version would be satisfactory to the President. A speech by Secretary Seward at Auburn, New York, on May 22 had intimated that there was still a possibility of reconciling presidential and congressional views. See New York *Herald*, May 23, 1866; James, *Fourteenth Amendment*, pp. 139–41.

Johnson, however, did not lose much time in making his position clear and removing any doubt that may have remained. The modifications had done nothing to alter his stand, and he sent Congress a message on June 22 reiterating his opposition to the Amendment, dissociating himself from all the work of Congress, expressing doubt that such work was "in harmony with the sentiments of the people," and letting it be understood by North and South alike that in his opinion the Southern states had no obligation to ratify.

Waiving the question as to the constitutional validity of the proceedings of Congress upon the joint resolution proposing the amendment, or as to the merits of the article which it submits through the executive department to the legislatures of the States, I deem it proper to observe that the steps taken by the Secretary of State in transmitting it to the several states . . . are to be considered as purely ministerial, and in no sense whatever committing the Executive to an approval or a recommendation of the amendment to the State legislatures or to the people. On the contrary, a proper appreciation of the letter and spirit of the Constitution, as well as of the interests of national order, harmony, and union, and a due deference for an enlightened public judgment, may at this time well suggest a doubt whether any amendment to the Constitution ought to be proposed by Congress and pressed upon the legislatures of the several States for final decision until after the admission of such loyal Senators and Representatives of the now unrepresented States as have been, or may hereafter be, chosen in conformity with the Constitution and laws of the United States.[51]

Later that month, moreover, the President gave notice that he would work for the defeat in the fall elections of all Republican candidates who opposed his policy. On June 25, a call for a "National Union" convention, prepared with Johnson's active assistance, was sent out to organize a campaign for this purpose. Before the current session of Congress closed, another Freedmen's Bureau bill was passed, and on July 16 the President—despite the sharp public response to his action on the first bill back in February—sent in another veto. This time, however, there was no difficulty in repassing it.[52] Even when his long-cherished hope of having the Tennessee delegation back in Congress was about to be realized at last, Johnson, though he signed the resolution of readmission, lectured Congress on the theoretical basis upon which the thing was being done. He thought that the Tennessee members should have been admitted without such a resolution and without the state's having to ratify the constitutional amendment first.[53]

[51] *Cong. Globe*, 39 Cong., 1 sess., p. 3349.

[52] *Cong. Globe*, 39 Cong., 1 sess., pp. 2878, 3413, 3524, 3562, 3838–42, 3849–51; McPherson, *Reconstruction*, pp. 147–151.

[53] *Ibid.*, pp. 151–54; *Cong. Globe*, 39 Cong., 1 sess., pp. 4102–3.

The response of the remaining ten Southern states to the Fourteenth Amendment that fall and the following winter was in any case most decisive. All of them rejected it, three unanimously and two others with only one contrary vote each. The greatest number of votes the Amendment received in any state was in North Carolina, where ten members of the lower house favored ratification.[54]

A final problem in connection with the Fourteenth Amendment and the aftermath of its passage in Congress, is what various writers have dealt with as the problem of intention. It has come to be assumed not only that the Amendment itself was framed in such a way as to guarantee its non-acceptance but also that in top party councils it was never seriously assumed that the Amendment should constitute the final terms of readmission at all, even if the Southern states had been willing to ratify it. Thus the "plot" theme, in its most formidable and baffling manifestation, emerges once more.

As for the acceptability of the Amendment to the South, both Beale and Kendrick, referring to Section 3, have pointed out quite correctly the extreme repugnance felt by Southerners toward anything that would disqualify so great a number of their best leaders from holding office. And yet it would not be well to consider this as evidence of a design on anyone's part to have the Amendment so framed that it could not be ratified. Indeed, the final version of Section 3—substituted as it had been for the general disfranchisement of voters contemplated in the committee's plan—was generally recognized as a moderate compromise. Henry J. Raymond, the President's leading supporter in the House, who had opposed the first version in toto, not only voted for the final version but called it a move "in the direction of harmony and conciliation."[55] Having been with the problem so long and having had to focus more and more exclusively on the task of fashioning something acceptable to the Republican party, even the moderates could

[54] McPherson, *Reconstruction*, p. 194. The ten ex-Confederate states rejecting the Amendment did so as follows: Texas (Senate, unanimous; House, Oct. 13, 1866, 5 yeas, 67 nays); Georgia (Senate, Nov. 9, 1866, unanimous; House, Nov. 9, 1866, 2 yeas, 131 nays); Florida (Senate, Dec. 3, 1866, unanimous; House, Dec. 1, 1866, unanimous); Alabama (Senate, Dec. 7, 1866, 2 yeas, 27 nays; House, Dec. 7, 1866, 8 yeas, 69 nays); North Carolina (Senate, Dec. 13, 1866, 1 yea, 44 nays; House, Dec. 13, 1866, 10 yeas, 93 nays); Arkansas (Senate, Dec. 15, 1866, 1 yea, 24 nays; House, Dec. 17, 1866, 2 yeas, 68 nays); South Carolina (Senate, unanimous; House, Dec. 20, 1866, 1 yea, 95 nays); Virginia (Senate, Jan. 9, 1867, unanimous; House, Jan. 9, 1867, 1 yea); Mississippi (Senate, Jan. 30, 1867, unanimous; House, Jan. 25, 1867, unanimous); Louisiana (Senate, Feb. 5, 1867, unanimous; House, Feb. 6, 1867, unanimous).

[55] Beale, *Critical Year*, pp. 201–5; Kendrick, *Journal*, pp. 348–51; for Raymond's course see *Cong. Globe*, 39 Cong., 1 sess., pp. 2502–3, 2545, 3149, and New York *Times* editorial, May 31, 1866.

not have retained much sensitivity, as the process neared completion, to what would or would not please the South. Apparently few if any Republicans appreciated the possible effect of this section, especially having just eliminated something a good deal more severe.[56]

Of a far more serious nature is the assumption that the Amendment as a whole was never intended as a final settlement with the South. It is actually rather hard to see the case in any other light, since, as things turned out, the Amendment would not in fact constitute the final terms. Stevens and Sumner certainly did not intend that it should—not if they could have their way. But then Stevens and Sumner were not the party. It would be wrong to assume that a majority of Congress or even a considerable part of it, to say nothing of the country at large, had any intention of letting them have their way.

Kendrick, whose version of the "plot" is the most reasonable and most convincing, has used four principal tests for the question: Fessenden's formal report, the failure of Congress to pass an enabling act, the restoration of Tennessee, and public statements by leading figures. The first—the report prepared by the Joint Committee's chairman—is properly disposed of as being somewhat inconclusive either way. On the one hand, the committee concluded that

the so-called Confederate states are not, at present, entitled to representation in the Congress of the United States; that before allowing such representation, adequate security for future peace and safety should be required; that this can be found only in such changes of the organic law as shall determine the civil rights and privileges of all citizens in all parts of the republic, shall place representation on an equitable basis, shall fix a stigma upon treason and protect the loyal people against future claims for the expenses incurred in support of rebellion and for manumitted slaves, together with an express grant of power to Congress to enforce those provisions.

But on the other hand, the committee did recommend the passage of a restoration bill. The report might be construed as a recommendation that the states be readmitted after meeting certain conditions; it may also be taken simply as a campaign platform. It certainly was the latter; undoubtedly it was both.[57]

The fate of the committee's enabling act, which specified the terms of readmission, constitutes weighty evidence of a plot; indeed, there appears to have been an understanding that no effort would be made to bring the bill to a vote. Kendrick asserts that "the majority of the

[56] The two New York pro-Johnson Unionist papers serve as a good test of this point. See above, pp. 355–56.

[57] *Report of the Joint Committee*, p. xxi.

Republican party were at no time willing to promise unreservedly to restore the Southern states upon their ratifying the fourteenth amendment.[58] The assertion, so far as it goes, is correct. As long as the original committee version of the Amendment stood, with its disfranchising section, even Thaddeus Stevens appeared not unwilling to see a restoration bill enacted, but then all during May—with the disfranchisement section more and more clearly doomed—a number of variations were proposed, revealing a persistent divergence of views. Bingham wanted automatic readmission, state by state; Boutwell proposed amending the act to apply only to Arkansas and Tennessee (and only after those states enacted Negro suffrage); Stevens himself on the twenty-eighth proposed a bill not unlike the later Reconstruction Act of 1867. Representative Kelley offered a similar bill on June 11. Wilson of Iowa said he would vote for whatever he could get but hoped it would not be Bingham's bill. Windom of Minnesota thought the original bill should be passed. Julian of Indiana was for keeping all the states out until they provided for Negro suffrage.[59] In the Senate, Williams of Oregon on May 2 suggested a plan whereby Arkansas and Tennessee might be admitted immediately after ratifying and whereby, after March 4, 1867, all other ratifying states would be readmitted whether the Amendment had as yet become part of the Constitution or not. This greatly annoyed Fessenden, since Williams, a member of his committee, was thereby openly breaking ranks.[60] Sumner proposed, on May 29, the inclusion of Negro suffrage in the committee's bill. But for some reason, nothing more was heard in the Senate about a restoration bill after that. The Senate caucus had apparently promised Sumner, in return for his support of the new amendment without disfranchisement (or perhaps simply as the price of his silence), that no further attempt would be made to press the enabling act.[61] In the House, the committee's restoration bill was finally tabled on July 20; and on the twenty-eighth Stevens' own bill, which envisioned a thoroughgoing reconstruction, underwent a similar fate despite a moving and eloquent plea for it by its author. And there things rested.[62]

[58] Kendrick, *Journal,* p. 327.

[59] The positions of these congressmen as stated in the above paragraph are to be found in the *Congressional Globe* (39 Cong., 1 sess.) as follows: Bingham, pp. 2598–99; Boutwell, p. 2313; Stevens, p. 2858; Stevens' reconstruction bill is summarized in *Nation,* II (June 5, 1866), 712; Kelley, p. 3090; Wilson, pp. 2947–49; Windom, pp. 3166–75; Julian, pp. 3208–11.

[60] *Ibid.,* pp. 2332–33.

[61] On this point see Kendrick, *Journal,* p. 333; James, *Fourteenth Amendment,* p. 170.

[62] *Cong. Globe,* 39 Cong., 1 sess., pp. 3981, 3303–4, 4304.

Some further light may possibly be shed on this impasse by the convenient ratification by Tennessee of the Fourteenth Amendment. The governor of that state, the embattled Brownlow, had accomplished the business by virtual coercion, and Brownlow's telegram to the Senate on July 19 raucously announced the result:

We have fought the battle and won it. We have ratified the constitutional amendment in the House—43 votes for it, 11 against it, two of Andrew Johnson's tools not voting. Give my respects to the dead dog of the White House.[63]

A resolution admitting Tennessee was carried next day in the House, its passage being managed by Representative Bingham. In the Senate, a preamble was attached to the resolution by Trumbull's Judiciary Committee, intended to make it clear that there were numerous other evidences of Tennessee's loyalty besides its having ratified the Amendment. Fessenden during the debate let it be understood that in his opinion Tennessee was a special case, and that this was not necessarily a precedent for readmitting the others before the Amendment became part of the Constitution. The resolution was passed on the twenty-first, and before the session closed, Tennessee's representatives were seated in Congress.[64]

It could thus be said that the readmission of Tennessee had been seized upon as a release from all the embarrassments of non-action in committing Congress on the other states. Even Trumbull and Fessenden were parties to the plot. It could now look as though Congress, while not binding itself to the letter of anything, had at least given certain assurances in spirit.

But there is still the question of whether "plot" is a very useful touchstone for discovering specific majority intentions. The Republican party conspired (doubtless behind closed doors) to refrain for the time being from coming to any further decisions. Or, to put it another way with rather less sinister echoes: if the party found itself unable in the end to agree on a definitive arrangement for restoration, the least odious solution might very well have been simply to let things slide until after the election, after having settled the main thing, the framing of an amendment. Nor might it have seemed such a bad bargain at the time. On the one hand, there were at least three positions (not counting the marginal variations) on restoration. One of them

---

[63] *Ibid.*, p. 3957; see also E. Merton Coulter, *William G. Brownlow, Fighting Parson of the Southern Highlands* (Chapel Hill: University of North Carolina Press, 1937), pp. 311–14. Brownlow had foiled a movement to prevent a quorum in the legislature by having two fleeing members arrested and forcibly detained in the capitol building while the vote was taken.

[64] *Cong. Globe*, 39 Cong., 1 sess., pp. 3932, 3966, 3980–81, 3987–4008.

(Bingham's) was restoration immediately upon ratifying; another (Fessenden's) was restoration only after three-fourths of all the states had ratified; and a third (Sumner's) was restoration only upon direct provision for Negro suffrage. And on the other hand, there was the question of a constitutional amendment with a severe disfranchising section, or one with a less severe disqualifying section. Conceivably the best that could be had all around was to get the Amendment through—in its milder form—in return for leaving the restoration question open, and with Tennessee thrown in as a vague earnest of good faith. No irrevocable step had been taken either way. Here was something upon which, despite its liabilities, both William Pitt Fessenden and Thaddeus Stevens could for the time being agree, while their party girded itself for a stormy campaign in which the stakes (as both knew all too well) were to be exceptionally high.

Such an understanding constituted, in any case, a loose enough fit to accommodate many different speakers and writers during the coming summer and fall—and at the same time the theme that tended to predominate throughout such discourse was the assumption that ratification would, in fact, mean readmission. Sumner and Theodore Tilton denied it and made no secret of their conviction that the Amendment as it stood was not enough. As for the majority, however, the impression prevailed that "the Republican party," as the *Nation* put it, was "substantially committed to a certain policy in respect to this matter."

If enough Southern States [the *Nation* announced] ratify the amendment before January to make its final passage secure, and do this in a spirit manifesting good faith, we believe that they will certainly be restored to their places in Congress. . . . The Republican party is generally fighting its battles upon the basis of the amendment, and on the assumption that it contains the terms of reconstruction. Certainly no State convention and no national committee have authority to bind the whole party to any particular course of action; but as a matter of fact, a sufficient number of candidates for Congress are committing themselves to this policy to make it certain that it will be carried out, if the South is shrewd enough to present the question in a practical form.[65]

The one challenging aspect of this problem of Republican intentions is an aspect which has little to do with the problem's actual settlement one way or the other; events overtook it in such a

---

[65] *Nation*, III (Oct. 4, 1866), 270. For general opinion on this point, see James, *Fourteenth Amendment*, pp. 172–74. Representative John M. Broomall of Pennsylvania, who did not agree with the prevailing sentiment, wrote, "I regret that the public press persisted in putting forth the Constitutional Amendment as the terms of reconstruction. I never assented to that proposition." Broomall to Thaddeus Stevens, Oct. 27, 1866, Stevens MSS, Library of Congress.

way that it could not be settled then and cannot be now—not when formulated in terms of "intentions." The real question is why the problem should have existed in the first place. Why should the historian really have to accept it in that form? Were it not for Andrew Johnson, President of the United States, we would not have the question to puzzle over; no one would have thought of asking it. If there is any single factor to which we may look for an explanation of why the Fourteenth Amendment should have made such a puzzle, it would be the flat refusal of the President, at any time during the process of making and ratifying that Amendment, to exert his own great influence for positive purposes in determining the outcome. Thaddeus Stevens himself said as much the day the Amendment was passed, and the old man's words, even with their overtones of irony, are not entirely without point. "We might well have been justified," he said, "in making renewed and more strenuous efforts for a better plan could we have had the cooperation of the Executive. With his cordial assistance the rebel States might have been made model republics, and this nation an empire of universal freedom."[66]

[66] *Cong. Globe*, 39 Cong., 1 sess., p. 3148.

Campaign
Preparations

On February 11, 1866, an editorial appeared in the
New York *Herald* under the title: "A Great Conservative National
Party Should Be Organized." In order to give full expression to the
true sentiment of the country, the editorial argued, and to circumvent
the proscriptive fanaticism of the radicals in Congress, all true conservative men who supported President Johnson's administration and
policies should form "a grand national organization." That same editorial, in one form or another, had appeared in the *Herald* a number of
times already. It was the work of the *Herald*'s proprietor, James Gordon Bennett, whose support of Andrew Johnson for about a year and
a half following the latter's inauguration was, for Bennett, a marvel of
faithfulness.

Of all Johnson's supporters there was probably none whose views
reached the public more widely or more often than did those of Bennett. No one was more persistent in giving advice to the President than
he; no one was more fertile in schemes for strengthening the President's position; hardly a week went by that did not bring, in the editorial columns of the *Herald*, some new design for promoting the well-
being of the administration. Although Bennett kept contradicting himself over and over, consistency not being his strongest point, nevertheless the man had much energy, and in the end there were few angles
that Bennett had failed to think of at one time or another for spreading
havoc and confusion in the ranks of Johnson's enemies.

James Gordon Bennett was doubtless not the most solid sort of person to have on one's side. He was, in fact, one of the gamiest characters
ever to appear in the world of New York journalism. He had begun
his career in Grub Street amid dreadful poverty, ready to do any job
and willing to write anything about anyone. He had literally made his
way up out of a damp cellar—where the *Herald*'s first office was lo-

cated in the middle 1830's—by defaming the reputations of others. He would let himself be horsewhipped month after month for his libels, blasphemies, and pornographic stories, and with little shame and much relish he would describe each thrashing in next day's paper. Though personally despised almost everywhere, James Gordon Bennett was ultimately successful in getting the *Herald* circulated more widely than any other New York journal. Sheer circulation, therefore, ought to have counted for something in the way of influence.[1]

Since Bennett's political allegiances were never very dependable, his support of Andrew Johnson, lasting as long as it did in the face of such unpopularity as the President came to acquire, may actually have set something of a record. There is evidence, moreover, that Johnson appreciated Bennett's support.[2] It is somewhat less certain how impressed he was with Bennett's advice. Some of it he took; most of it he ignored.

Among Bennett's various plans for the President, as noted above, was the formation of a conservative third party, "a grand national organization." Another course which the *Herald* repeatedly urged upon Johnson was the use of federal patronage in such a way as to reward his friends, punish his enemies, and consolidate his personal following. "Let the official guillotine be set to work forthwith," exclaimed Bennett on April 23, 1866, as he demanded the removal of all "contumacious and hostile radicals":

Let the places be given to conservative Union administration men, and our word for it there will be such a revolution by next fall that the radical disorganizers will be defeated in the election, and the Johnson party thus formed may hope to be the party of the future.

A recurrent theme in Bennett's editorials was the need for Johnson's views to be presented directly to the people, without being clouded and distorted by radical officeholders, politicians, and members of Congress; there was the assumption, in the *Herald's* thinking, of an essential rapport between the convictions of the President and the true

[1] The two chief sources on Bennett's life and works are Don C. Seitz, *The James Gordon Bennetts, Father and Son: Proprietors of the New York Herald* (Indianapolis: Bobbs-Merrill, 1928), and Oliver Carlson, *The Man Who Made News: James Gordon Bennett* (New York: Duell, Sloan and Pearce, 1942).

[2] "This letter . . . is . . . simply to tender you my thanks for the able and disinterested manner in which you have defended the policy of the Administration since its accession to power. It is the more highly appreciated because it has not been solicited. . . .

"Now is the time for the principles upon which the government is founded to be developed, discussed and understood. There is no man in America who can exercise more power in fixing the government upon a firm and enduring foundation than you can. With such aid the task will be made easy in the performance of this work. . . ." Johnson to Bennett, Oct. 6, 1865, quoted in Seitz, *James Gordon Bennetts*, pp. 198–99.

feelings of the people. Thus when the Chief Executive began his speaking tour in August, 1865, the *Herald* thought it a pity that the trip should be confined to points between Washington and Chicago. It should be extended to all parts of the country; the President should keep on going into the Northwest, then proceed down the Mississippi to Louisiana, through the South and back by way of Richmond, spreading "the influence which he exercises in such a magnetic manner over the people":

We put it most earnestly to Mr. Johnson not to forego this grand opportunity, but to avail himself of it in the interests of the nation; and we run no risk in predicting that, when he gets back to Washington, he will have given the death blow to the radicalism which has proved so disastrous to the reunion and the prosperity of the States.[3]

There were, finally, certain economic items to which Bennett reverted from time to time. How seriously he may have taken them as campaign issues is not easy to judge, but he does seem to have thought that at least something should be made of them. He opposed, for instance, an overhasty contraction of the currency. A sudden resumption of specie payments, he thought, would bring "a terrible crisis," to the ruin of all debtors. "Universal bankruptcy would necessarily follow. . . . [The] rich would become richer and the poor poorer, relatively." He took a jaundiced view of the national banks, and saw no reason why their note issues should not be replaced by greenbacks. Bennett also grumbled occasionally about business monopolies. He thought that the Senate's willingness, in its internal revenue bill of 1866, to let gas companies charge extra rates to cover the federal tax had shown a "disposition to assist monopolies." In June, 1866, the tariff bill about to be passed by the House drew a burst of wrath, and Bennett made it a symbol for all the jobbing and extravagance of which he thought the Thirty-ninth Congress had been guilty:

Monopolies and capitalists receive special favors from their hands, and any project, however unjust, that furnishes a good market for distribution is pushed through in hot haste. From this record the issue must be made at the coming elections, and a Congress elected which will pay more attention to the interests of the public and less to special jobs, or ruin and repudiation will soon be forced upon us.[4]

Some of these items, championed editorially as they were by Johnson's advocate, James Gordon Bennett, have been taken up by scholars of a later time and given a great deal of emphasis. It has been suggested

[3] New York *Herald*, Apr. 23, 1866 (see also Apr. 25, 1866); Sept. 1, 1866.

[4] *Ibid.*, Sept. 14, 1866; Mar. 15, June 23, Aug. 27, Sept. 3, Sept. 10, Sept. 14, 1866; June 23, 1866; June 30, 1866.

that Johnson did not do what might have been done in exploiting them. It would be well, therefore, to consider some of the choices that may or may not have been open to the President during the critical election campaign of 1866—the alternatives which might conceivably have made a difference in the strength of Johnson's position before the country.

I   ECONOMIC ISSUES

About a generation ago when scholarly interest in the Johnson era was at its height, one writer gave a very provocative turn to historical thought by declaring that Johnson missed an excellent chance to make political capital out of various kinds of dissatisfactions that were beginning to make themselves felt by 1866, especially in the Midwest. It should have been possible, according to Howard Beale, for Johnson to exploit these dissatisfactions, which were of an economic nature, in such a way as to minimize the importance of reconstruction as an election issue and to recruit support for himself on grounds other than reconstruction. "By training and instinct," Professor Beale wrote, Johnson "was an enemy of bondholders, national banks, monopolies, and a protective tariff. Had he . . . followed his bent and launched into the campaign an attack upon the economic views of the Eastern wing of the Radical party . . . he could have marshalled all the latent discontent of the West to his support, and could have split the Radical party at one blow."[5] This viewpoint—that there were economic issues before the country which, properly managed, might have made a powerful difference in the 1866 campaign—is not one with which the present writer can agree. But such a viewpoint at one time commanded considerable respect, and some attention should therefore be given it before examining other features of the campaign. The important problem here is not so much whether these matters—currency, tariffs, monopolies, and the like—were subjects of dissatisfaction, for in some sense they all were. The really pertinent question has to do with the political setting within which they were to be handled. Were they of such a nature as to be available as party issues? Was it possible to use them as opposition items in a political campaign? How, and to what extent, could these economic questions be organized politically at all?

There were certain difficulties in the very character of such issues that raise doubts about what, if anything, could have been made of them in 1866, when economic suffering was not a major problem. For one thing, it is very hard to see how they could have been organized

---

[5] Howard K. Beale, *The Critical Year*, p. 299.

sectionally; the Midwest was certainly not a unit, for or against, with reference to any of them. An anti-tariff campaign in Ohio or Michigan, for example, could hardly have made much more headway than in New York or Pennsylvania. But the really hopeless obstacle lay in the fact that these issues themselves, as a group, had no natural unity.[6] A man might with perfect consistency favor any combination of the pro and anti positions on any of them, depending on his own particular interests. He might (like Samuel J. Tilden) favor contraction of the currency as well as a low tariff; or (like Thaddeus Stevens), he could favor high tariff, railroad subsidies, and greenback currency. Such differences might be found within the same party and in the same part of the country: Pennsylvania ironmasters and Pennsylvania bankers (Democrats or Republicans) might agree on a high tariff and be worlds apart on currency. They might also agree on government subsidies to railroads, unless a particular banker happened to have an interest in Union Pacific, in which case there would be a good chance of his being against federal aid to any more transcontinentals. Commercial interests in New York might agree with Illinois agrarians on tariff but probably not on currency. What it came to politically was who should be organized against whom, and how. In the Populist period a generation later, these economic questions did come to acquire enough cohesiveness to warrant the organizing of political activity around them, but there is not much evidence that many people saw the urgency of such activity in 1866. The issues had not as yet achieved that degree of sharpness, and it is doubtful, this early, that they would have under any circumstances—even were the country not already occupied with one of the most vital issues ever to come before it, political reconstruction. The likelihood is that Andrew Johnson or anyone else at this time would have brought greater difficulties upon himself by raising these economic issues than by leaving them alone. A closer look at some of them seems to confirm this suspicion.

Had the administration favored inflation, or had it even taken a stand on Sherman's middle-of-the-road views, opposing both further inflation and contraction, the deflationist demands of Morrill and other leading Radicals could have been used to organize a powerful political opposition to them that would have split the Radical Party.[7]

[6] For a thorough discussion of this point see Stanley Coben, "Northeastern Business and Radical Reconstruction: A Re-examination," *Mississippi Valley Historical Review,* XLVI (June, 1959), 67–90. Mr. Coben argues very convincingly that the diverse economic interests of Northern businessmen can hardly tell us much about the political behavior of those same men (in their character as good Republicans) with regard to reconstruction.

[7] Beale, *Critical Year,* p. 244.

The campaign strategy suggested by the above passage assumes a sentiment for inflation sharply enough focused that under energetic presidential leadership effective political use might have been made of it. There is no doubt that support for inflation had begun by 1866 to makes itself felt, and that opposition to Secretary McCulloch's policy of currency contraction had by the spring of 1866 gained a good deal of headway, especially in the Midwest. There is considerable doubt, on the other hand, that such sentiment was strong enough to be organized in any way by either party, and there is even less likelihood that it stood a chance either of replacing reconstruction as the key issue or of "splitting" the Republican party. It is important to note, in fact, that such sentiment where it existed was actually of a nature quite different from the popular "greenbacker" impulse of a few years later, and it would be a great mistake to suppose that the "money of the people" angle on legal tenders had much meaning in 1866. Those were not at all the terms in which men thought about problems of currency and finance in the year or two following the Civil War. The most basic attitude that can be identified with regard to government policy in this area was simply the impulse to tidy up after four years of clutter and disorder—an impulse that came to be qualified, as time went on, by certain afterthoughts.

The leading economic facts of 1865 and 1866 bearing on problems of currency and finance were high prices, heavy wartime taxes, and an unwieldy public debt. The country, that is, had had plenty of inflation already (there were few voices to be heard seriously calling for more), and in addition to that there was a tax structure which made next to no sense for peacetime, as well as a public credit whose condition was disorderly in the extreme. Over $400 million in greenbacks issued during the war were still outstanding, and the national debt, a hodgepodge of notes and bonds, totaled more than $2.75 billion. The natural reaction of most people to this state of things was a more or less undifferentiated desire—common sense at low tension, it might be called—to retrench and get back to normal. That meant a little of everything, not all of it necessarily consistent as economic policy per se: lower prices, lower taxes, lower government expenditures, reorganization of the debt, and an effort to stabilize the currency—an effort which would require a certain amount of contraction (not inflation) in the circulation of greenbacks. Secretary McCulloch submitted a report on December 4, 1865, which envisioned just such a program and which was received with great enthusiasm everywhere. The House of Representatives on December 18 gave the report an almost unanimous vote of confidence. At the level of theory, in short, a virtually perfect harmony prevailed.[8]

But when the time actually came for carrying out the program of retrenchment, it turned out to be less easy in practice to retrench at specific points than it had seemed in theory to retrench everywhere. A comprehensive system of tax reform had been recommended by a Treasury-appointed commission headed by David Wells in January, 1866. The commission's report was widely praised; the many reductions in the 1866 Internal Revenue Act might be said to have reflected in some degree the general spirit of the report. But instead of being written in accordance with the principles of rational planning envisioned by Wells and embodied in his report, the act represented instead the aggregate pressures of numerous special (though non-partisan) interests.[9] As for government expenditures, while the outlay for warmaking was of course no longer required, for peacetime retrenchment there were few clear standards by which to be guided. The agonies of cutting back were aptly symbolized in two celebrated items of the Civil Appropriations Bill of 1866. On the one hand, a $100 bounty voted to the soldiers entailed considerable expense but was widely criticized for not amounting to more; on the other hand, a salary increase for members of Congress, whose added expense to the people was trifling, probably drew more complaints than anything else in the bill. In each case, however, the measures were thoroughly bipartisan in nature, and it would have been more than embarrassing to fix responsibility on either party.[10]

[8] "*Resolved*, That this House cordially concurs in the views of the Secretary of the Treasury in relation to the necessity of a contraction of the currency with a view to as early a resumption of specie payments as the business interests of the country will permit; and we hereby pledge cooperative action to this end as speedily as practicable." The vote on this resolution was 144 to 6. *Congressional Globe*, 39 Cong., 1 sess., p. 75. On the wartime program of taxation, currency, and finance, see Davis R. Dewey, *Financial History of the United States* (10th ed.; New York: Longmans, Green, 1928), pp. 271–330.

[9] "Report of the United States Revenue Commission," *House Executive Documents*, 39 Cong., 1 sess., VI, No. 34; *Nation*, II (Feb. 8, 1866), 167; Dewey, *Financial History*, pp. 391–95; New York *Herald*, Aug. 1 and 28, 1866; *Cong. Globe*, 39 Cong., 1 sess., Appendix, pp. 339–66.

[10] The proposal to increase salaries was offered by a Democrat, Senator Riddle of Delaware, and an amendment for reducing mileage allowance from 40 cents to 20 cents (ultimately adopted) was introduced by Senator Henderson of Missouri, a Republican. The votes on these amendments reveal no pattern of party division. For the debates on both the salary and bounty items in the bill see *Cong. Globe*, 39 Cong., 1 sess., pp. 4074–76, 4143–45, 4258–59, 4287; the entire act is printed in *ibid.*, Appendix, pp. 412–17. Johnson did make an issue of this in his "Swing around the Circle," but in doing so he did not attack one party or the other, but Congress *in toto*. "But let me tell you what Congress has done," he exclaimed at Detroit, after announcing that his

Secretary McCulloch's greenback retirement policy encountered similar difficulties. McCulloch's approach to the entire problem was quite resolute; he was convinced, along with hundreds of Americans of all classes, that greenbacks were basically immoral—that the issuance of paper money had been a wartime expedient from which the government was in honor bound to disengage itself as soon as possible and return to a specie basis. In principle there was general and widespread agreement on this, particularly (it should be noted) among the Democrats, whose suspicion of Treasury tinkering dated well back into the war. But although McCulloch's contractionist policy, as set forth in his December report, met with wide approval, there was a good deal less unanimity on how fast the Secretary in his ardor should be allowed to carry it out. Prices did begin to lower somewhat by the spring of 1866, credit began to grow a little tighter, and the prospect of an over-hasty contraction came to assume certain dangerous overtones: it might, under the circumstances, turn out to be very bad for business. On the whole, however, when Congress took up the matter in March, 1866, the currency policy embodied in the Loan Act passed at that time was still decidedly on the contractionist side. In the act provisions were made for refunding the public debt and for conferring upon Secretary McCulloch, with certain limitations and restrictions, the authority to launch a program of retiring greenbacks.[11]

The vote on this bill, in March and April, 1866, actually shows all the wrong things, considered either from the viewpoint of a subsequent populist-greenbacker logic or from that of a resourceful President who may have contemplated becoming the political champion of inflation. All but one of the Democrats in the House voted for the bill (that is, for contraction), whereas the Republicans were about

---

own salary had not been increased. "They changed their pay since they came into power. Yes! this Congress that has assailed and attacked me for faithful discharge of my duty . . . yes, this immaculate, this pure, this people loving, this devoted Congress finds it convenient while they had the chance, while they were in power, to increase their pay nearly double. . . . Yes, this immaculate Congress increased their pay nearly double, while at the same time they were magnanimous to vote $50 for the brave two year veterans of the war; $50 bounty for the men who shed their blood. . . ." New York *Herald*, Sept. 5, 1866. The $50 bounty referred to by the President was for two-year veterans; three-year veterans were given $100. These were over and above all other bounties.

[11] Don C. Barrett, *The Greenbacks and Resumption of Specie Payments, 1862–1879* (Cambridge, Mass.: Harvard University Press, 1931), pp. 161–67; Dewey, *Financial History*, pp. 334–44; *Cong. Globe*, 39 Cong., 1 sess., Appendix, p. 317. The idea of a specie currency as a matter of morality was earnestly (though not eloquently) set forth by Secretary McCulloch in a speech at Fort Wayne, Indiana, in October, 1865, some of which is reproduced in McCulloch's memoirs. See Hugh McCulloch, *Men and Measures of Half a Century*, pp. 201–3.

evenly divided. Those most vigorously opposing the bill (the "populists," as it were) included such inveterate radicals as Thaddeus Stevens, William Kelley, John Broomall, and George W. Julian. The measure passed the Senate with only seven opposing, but among the seven were Ben Wade, Zach Chandler, Jacob Howard, and John Sherman.[12] We might well imagine that Johnson, had he decided at this point to turn inflationist, would have gained nothing but confusion. He would have reversed the policy of his own administration and probably made himself even less popular than he already was. He might have picked up the one inflationist Democrat in the House (whom he had anyway), but he would have alienated, by the same token, large numbers of Democrats already committed to him on reconstruction—not to mention his most formidable eastern supporters, such leaders of the National Union movement as Belmont, Tilden, Dix, and Raymond. Whether he would thereby have swung Stevens, Wade, Chandler, and Julian to his side is more than dubious. One can only conclude that on currency and finance, at least, Johnson was best off doing just what he did: supporting McCulloch. There were actually few items in the policy of his administration, all things considered, that commanded greater unity than this one.[13]

The point, again, is whether this was an issue that stood any chance of being used politically to get the voters' minds off reconstruction. If it had been, and if any group on hand were likely to perceive this, one should suppose it would be the Democrats—not August Belmont's Democrats, but rather, let us say, the Democrats of the Midwest. The most apt test of this point is provided by the Ohio Democratic convention of January, 1867. On that occasion Washington McLean, editor of the Cincinnati *Enquirer*, tried to get a soft-money plank put into the party platform but was briskly overridden by a majority led by such party notables as Vallandigham, Thurman, and George H. Pendleton—a Pendleton who had not yet thought of his "Ohio Idea" for greenback inflation, or even remotely dreamed of it. The convention adopted Vallandigham's platform, announcing in effect that the big

[12] McCulloch himself felt that the bill did not go far enough in giving him the authority to contract that he thought he should have; but those who opposed the bill in Congress (including Senator Sherman) did so on the grounds of its contractionist features. McCulloch, *Men and Measures*, p. 210; John Sherman, *Recollections of Forty Years*, I, 373–76; *Cong. Globe*, 39 Cong., 1 sess., pp. 1608–14, 1845–54.

[13] It is not without significance that one factor in the growing inclination to place limits on McCulloch's contraction powers was not really economic but political; McCulloch, along with Seward and Welles, was a leading cabinet exponent of President Johnson's policy on reconstruction. On this point see Barrett, *Greenbacks and Resumption*, p. 164.

issue before the people was still reconstruction. This was after the Democrats had been soundly beaten on that very issue, only three months before; they recognized, even now, that they still did not have a better one. In fact Pendleton himself, who would subsequently gain some notoriety as an inflationist, opened the 1867 campaign in April, declaring that the country had been cursed with too much inflation already.[14] The currency question did, indeed, become a potent political issue later on. But it is hard to find much warrant for reading it back into the politics of 1866.

Regarding the tariff, the things to be said of that item's viability as a political issue are quite analogous to those bearing on currency and finance. Here again it has been claimed that Johnson's inscrutability prevented the solidarity of the Republican party from being shattered over the tariff:

Had he or the Philadelphia Convention vigorously attacked it, and launched in the West a campaign of repeated public iteration that a desire to maintain the protective system was an important factor in Radical opposition to Johnson's Southern policy, the Radicals would have found themselves facing a hopeless dilemma. . . . a tariff issue would have split the Radical Party, and won many converts to Conservatism.[15]

Once again, the key question is practical: whether Johnson would have gained or lost votes by an effort to stir the people up over the tariff. There is little evidence that it would have done him any good either way, and even less to indicate that the tariff, presented as a national issue, would have touched deep chords in the national bosom amid the storms of reconstruction. The vote on the House tariff of 1866, which was the most concrete test available at the time, showed

[14] Chester McA. Destler, "The Origin and Character of the Pendleton Plan," *Mississippi Valley Historical Review*, XXIV (September, 1937), 171–84; Horace Samuel Merrill, *Bourbon Democracy of the Middle West, 1865–1896* (Baton Rouge: Louisiana State University Press, 1953), pp. 36–39. Early in 1867 the Republican business tycoon N. B. Pennypacker wrote to the radical congressman John M. Broomall, "Our paper Government dollar carried us through the war, and prospered all branches of industry, sunk oil & salt wells opened new coal mines—& mines of gold & silver put in motion Iron mills factories &c beyond any period heretofore. . . . If money or currency is made scarce and men of moderate means must be cruelly shorn to get money no enterprises would be thot of.

"No, let the N. York brokers rave. They ought not to overturn the whole settled future of business so as to compel the laborer to work all day for a gold dollar instead of two paper dollars.

"My humble opinion is all this vaporing is in the interest of the copper heads." N. B. Pennypacker to J. M. Broomall, Feb. 28, 1867, Broomall MSS, Pennsylvania Historical Society.

[15] Beale, *Critical Year*, p. 297.

95 for, 52 against, and 35 not voting.[16] If this corresponded even in the roughest way to popular sentiment in the North, the inference would be that taking a strong stand against protection was to take a distinctly minority position. It is in the nature of tariffs as an issue that pro-tariff sentiment is traditionally more concentrated and purposeful than anti-tariff sentiment, and in this case there was almost twice as much of it. (Could it be that protection might really have been a better angle for Johnson than its opposite?) But the political problem, in any event, would have had to be geared to those states which were strategic for a Republican defeat or victory in the election. Those states where the margin would be closest included New York, Pennsylvania, Ohio, Connecticut, and Indiana. Yet, with the exception of Indiana, these were all strong pro-tariff states. One hesitates to think, for instance, of what would have happened to any Johnson man who might venture into Pennsylvania campaigning against the tariff: Pennsylvania, split on reconstruction, would have returned a bipartisan landslide for protection. He would also have been wise, by the same token, to stay out of Ohio or Michigan—to say nothing of New England, from which not a single vote was cast in the House against the tariff of 1866.[17]

Actually, there was in the Midwest (ruling out Ohio and Michigan

[16] *Cong. Globe*, 39 Cong., 1 sess., p. 3725.

[17] It would of course be foolish to deny that a majority of the South entertained anti-tariff views, or that Southern readmission would mean future difficulty for protectionist elements in the United States Congress. But there is a long and dubious step between establishing this general fact and equating it with any sort of hypothetical campaign strategy on reconstruction. E.g., there is a table in Howard K. Beale's *Critical Year* (p. 294) on certain tariff bills considered during the 39th Congress, with conjectures on what would have happened (defeat) if the Southern representatives had been there to vote on them—the intention being to show why it was in the obvious interests of protectionists to keep the South out. The other part of the reasoning is that mobilizing Northern anti-tariff sentiment would have "split" the Republican party in 1866 and induced substantial numbers of Republicans to join the Democrats in working for Southern readmission, in order to kill the tariff. But this seems rather like trying to add apples and pears: (1) It does not explain the failure to arrest the subsequent course of nineteenth-century protectionism *after* readmission (freezing too many variables in the table itself might have something to do with this; i.e., failing to analyze the "not voting" column, which contained many Republicans, and assuming that every Democrat, North and South, was by nature an anti-protectionist, which was simply not the case); and (2) It assumes a no-compromise attitude on tariff everywhere—that men were ready to do anything if they could only get their way on that issue, whereas presumably they were quite willing to temporize on reconstruction. Actually something like the opposite was closer to the truth. In short, if the principal point to be settled is the viability of tariff as an item in the campaign strategy of 1866, then there is no choice but to conclude that it made little difference. For other purposes the tariff may have mattered a great deal to a great many people, but not in this setting: the issue upon which men happened to be voting was of such a nature as to override their sentiments, for or against, on just about everything else, and it is doubtful how much would have been changed by any amount of additional public enlightenment on the subject of tariffs.

for the purpose as "un-midwestern") a good deal of anti-protection feeling, especially in Illinois. But the congressional leaders of the Republican party, even without the threat of an anti-tariff rampage by President Johnson, did what politicians have always done in such cases, especially with tariffs: they adjusted and compromised. There is no evidence that they would not have done so even more decisively had it been necessary. The House bill of 1866, when it got to the Senate, was simply buried. One set of recommendations in the above-mentioned Wells report was a series of modifications in the tariff schedules, including many reductions, and in 1867 a bill prepared by Wells himself was passed in the Senate as a substitute for the House bill of the previous session.[18] The most powerful anti-tariff state was Illinois. But the anti-tariff pressures there—Illinois was heavily Republican—were exerted within the party, and the adjustments were intra-party adjustments rather than occasions for political warfare. No better example for Illinois may be found than that of Joseph Medill, as a test for the question of anti-protection versus reconstruction as an election issue. Medill, editor of the Chicago *Tribune*, was as strong against the tariff as any man in the state; yet no newspaper ever flogged Andrew Johnson with less mercy over reconstruction than did the Chicago *Tribune*.[19]

It may indeed be that the President's desire for a low tariff was so

[18] Wells's bill passed the Senate in January, 1867, by a comfortable majority of 27–10, and was favored in the House 106–64. The House vote, however, fell short of the two-thirds necessary to suspend the rules and to pass the bill before the short session ended. *Cong. Globe*, 39 Cong., 2 sess., pp. 931, 1658; F. W. Taussig, *The Tariff History of the United States* (8th ed.; New York: G. P. Putnam's Sons, 1931), pp. 171–78. Meanwhile, the longer the war rates continued, the more settled became the habit of looking at them as a permanent protective system.

[19] Although the *Tribune* was solid in its support for the re-election of Lyman Trumbull, Elihu Washburne, and all other Republican members of Congress from Illinois, this did not prevent Medill and Horace White (also of the *Tribune*) not only from attacking the 1866 tariff editorially but also from putting great private pressure on Republican congressmen to smother it. It should be noted that this was not necessarily a manifestation of free-trade doctrines; indeed, according to Professor Taussig, "There was at that time no free-trade feeling at all . . ."; it was rather a question of doctrinaire and uncompromising protectionism versus enlightened and reformed protectionism. Commissioner Wells's bill was in the latter class, and Medill himself was a protectionist. "Mr. Medill, the oracle of the Protectionists of the west," wrote White to Trumbull, "has written the most pressing letters to his fellow Protectionists in the House telling them that the bill must be killed or both Protectionism and Republicanism will be killed in Indiana, Illinois, and Iowa. I have written as strongly as possible on this subject to Senators Fessenden and Wilson." Tariff, in short, was one of those problems upon which the party could afford internal divisions, and in fact had them. Such was not the case with reconstruction, upon which the party was united. White to Washburne, July 13, 1866, Washburne MSS, Library of Congress, Taussig, *Tariff History*, p. 177; Chicago *Tribune*, June 22, 26, 28, July 3, 1866; White to Trumbull, July 5, 1866, Trumbull MSS, Library of Congress.

intense that he saw his only true course and took it. Only with the Southern states back in the Union would there have been much real chance of sweeping the protectionists from the field, and in such a case the most prudent course for the President would have been to keep his design a secret, and to work for restoration against the day of a final triumph for free trade. We are inclined to doubt, however, that such was the President's true motive for remaining silent on this subject. Indeed, as one searches for a hypothetical apostle to persuade the American people away from their protectionist errors, it is hard to imagine a man less likely to succeed in that work than Andrew Johnson.

As for that ancient democratic bogey, monopoly, no one—not even Professor Beale—has ever made a very serious case for the use of such an item as a national campaign issue in the period of the sixties. Invoking the specter of monopoly had been a favorite ceremonial feature of campaign rhetoric since the time of Jackson, but it is difficult to see what sense it would have made on a more literal level in Andrew Johnson's time—say, with regard to the railroads. To have taken any specific "monopoly" by the throat, as Old Hickory did with the Bank, would have brought down upon Johnson the wrath of both parties. The most sensational monopolists whose doings were in any way aired during the year 1866 appear, indeed, to have been Democrats. The evil genius of the Camden and Amboy was Commodore Stockton, who was said to have bought a seat for his son in the United States Senate with C.&A. lucre, and John P. Stockton thereupon became New Jersey's Democratic martyr when he was unseated to get rid of one Johnson vote.[20] John A. Dix, president of Union Pacific, was one of the pillars of the Johnson movement in New York, as was Samuel J. Tilden, whose monopolistic machinations with the Chicago and North Western railroad furnished rich matter for the early muckraking pamphleteer, James Parton. Parton, a fire-eating Republican radical, was an ardent friend and follower of Benjamin F. Butler.[21]

[20] See above, chap. 10, n. 101.

[21] Parton's pamphlet, which he published in the fall of 1866, was called *Manual for the Instruction of "Rings," Railroad and Political, with a History of the Grand Chicago and North Western "Ring."* As the Thirty-ninth Congress prepared to convene, an Oregon businessman high in the councils of the Democratic party in that state wrote to Senator Nesmith: "I do not want favors of you Congressmen, except the passage of that Railroad bill granting lands to the 'California and Columbia River Railroad Company.'. . . This is no personal favor to me, but I advised the survey, and have made speeches in favor of it and wrote in favor of it, and the people on the West side of the river look to me and Barry to see that the Bill is passed; and if it was not passed, would suspect that I had not acted in good faith." J. Barton to Nesmith, Oct. 26, 1865, Nesmith MSS, Oregon Historical Society.

If any of these several problems, serious though they might all some day become, actually entered the President's mind with the approach of the 1866 campaign, he seems to have decided, in a rare flash of prudence, to renounce them as political issues and not to throw away what remaining political support he had. The truth was that he, together with political leaders of all factions, Republican, Democrat, and "National Union"—men whose business it was to know what were, and what were not, viable campaign issues for 1866—all agreed that the principal issue was just what everyone said it was, political reconstruction. Seldom has there been greater unanimity on exactly what was at stake in an election.

In short, while we can belabor President Johnson for a great many things, it would hardly be fair to tax him for this. In the years to come, problems of tariff, currency, and monopoly would indeed become acute and pressing; it is even possible that something of their nature might have been foreseen as early as the middle 1860's had there not been matters more acute and more pressing still. But we cannot make a Populist of Andrew Johnson twenty years too soon. The whole question, indeed, could be turned squarely around. Since the Republican party was so solidly united on the problem of reconstruction, why should we not speculate on how the President, had he been so minded, might best have used that unity in the interest of such ends as a rational tariff program, an intelligent policy on money, and a judicious federal regulation of corporate enterprise? To have co-operated with Congress and the party on reconstruction might really have made President Johnson a figure of towering moral authority on a sweeping range of other matters. Thus fortified, upon what great objects might he not have shed his enormous prestige? What vistas might not have been open to him then, in the work of making this disorderly Republic a model of economic enlightenment?

II PATRONAGE

A further reason for the collapse of the Executive position in 1866, according to Johnson's well-wishers both then and now, was the President's failure to take full advantage of his appointive powers. Many times during his first eighteen months in office Johnson was implored to grasp the patronage firmly and wield it as a club to enforce discipline. With the power of appointment and removal he might suppress recalcitrance and create a corps of loyal officeholders who could be counted upon to strengthen administration doctrines among the nation's voters. "Let the President . . . use all the legitimate means at his command, in the dispensation of patronage," pleaded Bennett's New York *Herald*, "to strengthen his position and encourage his supporters within the lines of the Union war party. The Johnson republicans everywhere, under this encouragement, can go into the Congressional contest with every assurance of success."[22]

Such reasoning rested, and still rests, upon certain widely held assumptions regarding the mysterious and magical power of patronage. Party men, especially minor ones, are in politics simply for the emoluments of office. For the sake of their places, officeholders may thus be expected to use all their energies and the influence of the office to promote in their locality the interests and doctrines of the party and its leaders. Therefore the final check on the system is the power of appointment and removal. The man who controls the patronage, should he find his policies and interests not being properly supported by certain officeholders, may simply cause those delinquents to be removed and replaced by others more agreeably disposed.

If this were the whole story on the workings of patronage, then it should follow that Andrew Johnson missed a great opportunity to repair his authority in time for the 1866 elections. The federal bureaucracy had been greatly extended during the course of the war, which made for a corresponding enhancement of Executive powers. In not wielding the patronage until it was too late, Johnson failed to take hold of an instrument which might have done much to guarantee and solidify the party's loyalty to himself in every corner of the country that could be reached by a federal bureau. By irresolute delays he allowed the party, local and national, to fall into unfriendly hands. When at last he did become aroused to his danger and began making more or less general removals about the early part of September, he committed the gross error of appointing to office an inordinate number of actual Copperheads. Thus the sufferings of Johnson's Unionist supporters during the campaign of 1866 presumably included a certain degree of plain undernourishment.[23]

For all his unfamiliarity with the Republican organizations, it was not as though the President lacked for experienced politicians to advise and assist him. There were the Blairs—Montgomery Blair had been

[22] New York *Herald*, Apr. 25, 1866.

[23] Applying these principles to Johnson's case, Howard Beale wrote, "However strikingly they agreed with Johnson's policies, politicians could not afford to support him as long as his opponents controlled the plums of office. However strenuously they objected to Johnson, politicians would have had to support him if he had made officeholdings dependent upon loyalty to him." *Critical Year*, p. 117.

Lincoln's Postmaster-General; Secretary Seward owed his position to the power he had wielded in New York politics; Henry J. Raymond had been national chairman for the 1864 campaign; and most notably there was the sage political wizard Thurlow Weed. In New York Johnson had, through Weed, a patronage network inherited virtually intact from Lincoln's time, and the apparatus was used energetically in Johnson's behalf all through the 1866 campaign. But it still did him very little good, even though New York was one of the great pivotal states. How, then, is one to account for the President's apparent ineptitude in realizing the potentialities of this vast power?

Actually, there remains a very large question of just how heavily Johnson ought to be censured for anything he did or did not do with the patronage to help his cause along. In all likelihood patronage would have done him little good no matter how he had used it. There is even evidence that he would have done himself the least damage by leaving it entirely alone. The President had already challenged the Republican party on reconstruction, which was the main reason for the position he was now in; to challenge it further on patronage would—and in fact did—only serve to hasten his downfall. Moreover, the very nature of the patronage system was such as to place sharp limits on the kinds of things that could be done with it and on the extent to which it could be manipulated without side effects more severe than the evils being purged.

Certain axioms on patronage might be derived from the precedents and practices of the Lincoln administration. As a matter of training, instinct, and principle Abraham Lincoln had handled the patronage with great care and delicacy. He appeared to understand that it had both its possibilities and its limits. The patronage could be as a set of silken threads useful for binding his organization more securely, assuming it were also securely knit in other ways. Those threads could be used for drawing key men along desired paths, assuming those men were not already determined to follow other paths. Patronage was certainly an adjunct of power, but hardly a perfect synonym for it.

The cardinal principle was that bestowal of office was a reward for services, past and future, rendered to the party. It was in a real sense a ritual of recognition, a proclamation of merit in which fitness for the specific duties of the office counted for something but was subordinate to the primary criterion of the man's value to the organization. To award the office on any other basis, despite the occasional sacrifice of administrative efficiency, was to risk alienation of local support and disharmony in the party. Lincoln's party in 1861 may have been assuming power for the first time nationally, but yeoman labor in the states over a period of several years had created a deserving corps of the faithful and true. There was thus a sense in which the organization, even at the beginning—was already there.[24]

Another axiom was that the chain of command should be scrupulously observed. Important positions within a state were to be filled only after consultation with the Republican senator or senators from that state. Fourth-class postmasterships were cleared through the congressman representing the district in which the post offices were located; indeed, it was announced at the very outset that applications would be acted upon quicker if sent directly to the congressman concerned. If the representative of a given district happened to be a Democrat, then the local Republican boss would be consulted. Advice was taken at all times, of course, from governors and other individuals of influence. Only in limited classes of cases would Lincoln take decisions into his own hands—cases which arose from a division of the party in some local area. But even here it was not a matter of disregarding the rules but rather of applying other rules. If he discriminated against one group, it would be for reasons of that group's appointments having met with dissatisfaction, having become unpopular, or some similar grounds, all of which in another sense was an assessment and recognition of the two factions' relative strength. In many cases he simply tried to effect compromises between them.[25]

Lincoln recognized, finally, the very limited usefulness of the patronage in waging a personal vendetta. Salmon P. Chase had already

[24] A sense of the richness of background which the "new" party had already accumulated, and of the obligations which it had already incurred, is afforded by the case of Lewis Clephane, upon whom was bestowed the postmastership of Washington. "Few persons had given such untiring service to the party as Clephane, former business manager of the antislavery organ, the Washington *National Era*, whose pages had first run Harriet Beecher Stowe's *Uncle Tom's Cabin* serially before its appearance in book form. While still associated with the *National Era*, in disseminating antislavery propaganda, Clephane formed in 1855 a small club known as the Republican Association of Washington. Acting for this organization, Clephane prepared the 'call' which was issued for the meeting of anti-Democratic leaders at Pittsburgh that in turn made arrangements for the first Republican National Convention in 1856. He likewise had rendered indefatigable service in support of the Lincoln-Hamlin campaign. Few influential leaders contested Clephane's right to the Washington post office, and Lincoln himself even refused the position to Nathan Sargent, whom he referred to as 'my old friend,' in order to reward Clephane." Harry J. Carman and Reinhard Luthin, *Lincoln and the Patronage* (New York: Columbia University Press, 1943), p. 73. Lincoln's sense of the extreme importance of patronage was such that he spent time on it in the spring of 1861 which many felt should have been devoted to the developing war crisis.

[25] *Ibid.*, pp. 70–71, 228–29, 265–66, 333.

built himself a powerful machine in the Treasury Department by the time his opposition to Lincoln became fully manifest. Lincoln would not, however, strike at Chase through his appointees. He made removals in New York, for example, only after Chase himself was out of the way as a threat to Lincoln's second candidacy, and in recognition of a new balance of party power in that state. At no time did Lincoln make a removal lightly—knowing how many other disbalances would automatically be created in the process—and he hoped, after his re-election, that he would not have to make any more removals at all. "To remove a man is very easy, but when I go to fill his place, there are *twenty* applicants, and of these I must make *nineteen* enemies."[26]

Lincoln's management of the patronage, following as it did a more or less orthodox pattern, thus warrants certain generalizations which can apply to the political practice of an entire era prior to civil service reform. The dispensation and acceptance of patronage involved intricate standards, a recognized punctilio, and a special morality of its own which was not lightly breached. It would be a little too crass to think of a patronage office simply as a "job"—a species of cumshaw whose price was the exaction of routine labors for the party. It was that, of course, but it was also much more: The award of an office was a symbol of how a man rated in the local organization; it had its aspect of "honor," not unlike military rank. If the insignia meant little without the emoluments, then the same principle applied in reverse.[27] The office, in short, not only maintained a man and his family; it marked a point on the curve of a man's career, serving as an indicator of past services and future prospects. The system of pre–civil service patronage, whatever else it may have been, at least functioned as a carefully graded and recognized system of institutional standing.

In view of the heavily political orientation of community life in nineteenth-century America, it is perhaps understandable that the patronage should bear a direct relationship to both the party organization and the centers of authority and influence in the community. In

[26] *Ibid.*, pp. 231–33, 261–67, 278–81, 300. The quotation is from some remarks Lincoln was reported to have made to Senator Clark of New Hampshire shortly after the 1864 election.

[27] During World War II it was taken as axiomatic throughout the army that whenever a man felt called upon to declare, "It isn't the stripes I want, it's the money," he was lying. In Sonya Forthal's *Cogwheels of Democracy: A Study of the Precinct Captain* (New York: William Frederick Press, 1946), p. 21, there is a story about a woman who, being asked why she went on doing precinct work year after year, answered slyly that she was in it "for the graft." (Actually the perquisites of her particular position involved next to no "graft.") She, too, was lying: she was ashamed to admit that she was in politics simply because she loved it.

no local community can a system of influence be created overnight, and it would be misleading to think of a local public more or less passively receiving waves of "influence" emanating from the local officeholders. It was more likely to have worked the other way around: the officeholders, rather than being the creators of influence, were picked in recognition of their affinity to the influence system already in operation. Thus the full effectiveness and meaning of patronage would depend on a fully functioning organization with a solid local base that had to be present to start with. Since much of the value of a local office was inherent in public recognition of a man's standing in local politics,[28] conversely, to hold the office without such local recognition and without the favor of the local leaders would be to possess something that was not worth very much to anyone—to either the man conferring it or the man receiving it. An office held under such conditions—appointive office being normally an incident of influence, rather than a cause of it—might be worse than useless; it might be an actual liability to a man's political future.

Thus the limits of maneuverability in the use of patronage were a great deal narrower in actual practice than they may have seemed in theory. The "bludgeon" metaphor was really all wrong; patronage was not a club that could be swung about with abandon. Indeed, the tiniest bit of fiddling could mean shaking a complex system of connections and careers, possibly with very dangerous and disruptive consequences. Patronage could be used to great effect, but for limited purposes and within recognized rules—for instance, to help tip the balance between contending factions. This would assume, of course, that a real balance was there to tip. If, on the other hand, one faction was clearly of little account, then patronage in its hands could be the next thing to worthless; it would be like bestowing commissions, no matter how high, in an army about to be destroyed. And it would violate the punctilio of the political community; it would be proclaiming, in effect, that there was influence in quarters where everyone knew none existed. In short, the last thing possible was to "create" a new organization with patronage, or even to build one up that had only limited standing in the community to start with. Putting in men contrary to the wishes of the local people would be in effect to staff the offices with carpetbaggers and scalawags, and with nothing but local good will to protect them.

[28] The same principle could be applied to the control of appointments as well as to the receiving of them. The ability to control patronage represented a great deal more than the chance to lay a few people under obligation and tribute; it, too, was a measure of standing and influence in the confidence of both the institution and the community at large; here again was an item whose value went beyond money.

These principles applied very directly to the situation of Andrew Johnson and blocked him at every turn. The effectiveness of the patronage in Johnson's hands depended on a certain rapport with the party leadership. As long as the President's influence continued, his appointments of course carried the full prestige of party recognition. But should his right to speak for the majority be challenged, then everything he did on patronage would affect the entire network, all the way down to the appointee himself. The new appointee would have to make his choice, to decide whether his own future and that of the party lay with Johnson or with those challenging him. The choice would be influenced profoundly if it were clear that he could accept the office only in the teeth of local contempt. (This was something more than a crass calculation on "holding his job.") The old appointee, on the other hand, might find it a distinct political advantage to have been turned out of his place under such auspices. Moreover, the leaders of the district—the men whose recommendations had normally been tantamount to appointment—would be irrevocably alienated. To strike at a man's patronage in almost any degree was, politically speaking, to bring a knife rather close to his throat. And finally, should the principal local supporters of Johnson turn out to be Democrats, then Johnson, if he were going to make any changes at all, would have no choice but to turn over the patronage to them.

Johnson had engaged, it appears, in a certain amount of experimental tampering with the patronage almost from the first of the session, though judging from the scattered evidence this was not done in a particularly systematic way. Yet each instance was like touching a nerve. The patronage of Representative William ("Pig-Iron") Kelley of Pennsylvania seems to have been partially if not wholly withdrawn as early as January, 1866.[29] Senator Henderson of Missouri was similarly served, according to a complaint made by that senator in April.[30] The erratic handling of patronage was especially irritating in Illinois. For instance, in April and May, 1866, the President struck back at Representative Ebon Ingersoll for the latter's anti-Johnson speeches in such a way—by removing the Internal Revenue Collector and the Peoria postmaster—as to stir up an anti-Johnson hor-

[29] John Lynch to Israel Washburn, Feb. 1, 1866, in Gaillard Hunt, *Israel, Elihu and Cadwallader Washburn: A Chapter in American Biography* (New York: Macmillan, 1925), p. 118. Lynch was Representative from the First Congressional District of Maine; Washburn, formerly war governor of that state, was at this time serving as Collector of Customs at Portland.

[30] *Cong. Globe*, 39 Cong., 1 sess., p. 2308.

net's nest in Ingersoll's district. The man whom Johnson nominated as collector did not even want to take office under the circumstances, since he considered himself a good Republican; he had not sought the appointment and would be—in fact was already—accused of having sold himself for an office. "I think I see how the matter stands," he wrote to Trumbull. "While the senate would not refuse to confirm me if compelled to act, I think they prefer not to be obliged to choose in the dilemma, and I do not blame them. They do not wish to be the President's instrument to execute his spite upon Ingersoll. . . ."[31] The mail of Trumbull and Washburne all through this period was full of complaints over capricious removals, and there were even indications that Senator Doolittle of Wisconsin (one of the three Johnson Republicans in the Senate) was dabbling with the federal appointments for northern Illinois.[32] These exasperations occurred with sufficient frequency that Trumbull and others, by mid-April, were in a state of smoldering ill-humor over the entire subject of appointments.

All this came to a head in an acrimonious Senate debate which went on for more than three weeks over an amendment to the Post Office Appropriation Bill for 1866. During this period, from April 18 to May 11, the air was full of rumors—in addition to the many complaints over removals already made—to the effect that the President was preparing to use his patronage powers to declare open war on all who would not support his policy. The subject of patronage and the subject of reconstruction were debated together, with the Senate's presiding officer making no effort to separate them, and the entire ground was gone over with some thoroughness. It was at this time that the Republican party considered the alternatives and formulated its policy on patronage.

The central issue was that of what measures, if any, should be taken to limit the President's powers of removal during the recess of Con-

[31] John H. Bryant to Trumbull, May 24, 1866, Trumbull MSS; Peoria *Transcript*, May 24, 1866. When Bryant first heard of the appointment, he had written to Trumbull: "While I feel it a duty to treat Mr. Johnson with all the respect due to his exalted position I want him to understand, that I am not now and never have been a believer in, or supporter of his policy on Reconstruction, and should the senate see fit to confirm the nomination I suppose they will do it understanding my position to be that of a friend and supporter of the right and duty of congress to control the settlement of the restoration of the rebel states in such manner as they in their wisdom shall see fit." May 16, 1866, Trumbull MSS. The other affair, that of the postmastership, was described (along with related matters) in letters to Trumbull from Gershom Martin (editor of the *Transcript*), Apr. 19, 1866, and A. P. Bartlett, Apr. 20, 1866, Trumbull MSS. There was similar difficulty over the assessorship at Cairo. John Olney to Trumbull, Apr. 19, 1866; Cairo Unionist Committee to Trumbull, May 3, 1866, Trumbull MSS.

[32] Anson S. Miller to Elihu Washburne, June 20, 1866, Washburne MSS.

gress. Foremost among those favoring positive action was Lyman Trumbull. Trumbull promoted with considerable energy a provision which would hold up the salaries of all offices requiring Senate confirmation if appointments were made to them after the Senate adjourned, except in cases where the President had filled vacancies caused by death, resignation, or expiration of term. In the early stages of discussion the fiction was preserved—though somewhat thinly—that the amendment was required simply to give greater explicitness to accepted practice and that it was not directed specifically at President Johnson; but as the debates grew intense, there were many flare-ups, and a number of senators came out and said what was on their minds. Henderson of Missouri threw off the mask on May 1, blurting that no one could be sure what Johnson intended to do with his "vast power of patronage" and revealing at the same time that his own influence over appointments in Missouri had been taken away.[33] By this time the newspapers were regularly predicting imminent decapitations, and on May 2 Howe of Wisconsin rose and read one such dispatch in the Senate; a few days later he read another which was more specific, an item from the *Wisconsin Union* about an interview which a Democratic congressman from Wisconsin claimed to have had with the President:

Mr. Eldridge . . . alleges that he and a number of others of his party were at the White House on yesterday evening, and that the President assured him that every Federal office-holder in Wisconsin who does not sustain the President's policy will be removed and those who sustain him put in their places.[34]

Reference was also made during that week to a very unsatisfactory condition of things in New Jersey. After Stockton's expulsion, one Scovel, a member of the legislature who held the deciding vote for convening the two houses to elect a new senator, had been induced by Johnson's supporters to use his vote in blocking the joint meeting, thus preventing an election. His reward was a voice in the federal appointments for New Jersey. Scovel's use of his new powers had been a source of festering resentment among Republicans in Congress.[35]

33 "I have nothing to ask of the present Executive in the way of patronage; and I can safely express the opinion here that if I had the President would not grant it. I am satisfied from various appointments that have been made in my own State, and from appointments that I understand are to be made in that State, that nothing I could say would have any influence whatever." *Cong. Globe,* 39 Cong., 1 sess., p. 2308.

34 *Ibid.,* pp. 2337, 2453.

35 "Now, what would you think," demanded Senator Henry Wilson on May 8, "of a letter written by a public officer to another public officer in New Jersey saying, 'The Secretary of the Treasury directs me by the order of the President to say to you that

Senator Poland of Vermont was not convinced that passing Trumbull's amendment would be the most judicious course for the party to take and on May 7 made a long argument against it, whereupon the exasperated Trumbull contributed some information of his own about things going on in Illinois and elsewhere.[36] In effect the Senate, as tempers waxed hotter, was conducting a kind of dress rehearsal for the Tenure of Office Bill which would be enacted the following year.

In the end, however, Trumbull's amendment was voted down. Some of the Republican party's most authoritative voices urged its defeat on grounds of both expediency and principle, and their arguments contained significant items of theory on the workings of patronage. Sherman did not think that patronage would do the President any good if he should try to use it in the interests of his policy: "He would lose more votes by the exercise of a power of that kind . . . than he would gain."[37] Poland spelled out the point with great completeness when he urged his party that there was no need to resort to desperate expedients. He explained that during times when popular feeling on public questions was no more than perfunctory, a set of busy officeholders circulating among the people might make a great deal of difference in turning things one way or the other at election time; but in the present state of concern over national issues the principle no longer held. The party's apprehensions showed a "mistaken lack of faith in the people," who in their own insistence on guarantees of Southern loyalty had actually as much reason to fear the effect of patronage on Congress as Congress had to fear for them:

---

you must remove a certain man in your employment, and in filling his place consult Mr. Scovel?' It is well known and understood that Mr. Scovel struts over New Jersey claiming to control the public patronage in that State, and we have nominations before the Senate now of his dictation." *Ibid.*, p. 2452. On the Scovel affair see David M. DeWitt, *Impeachment and Trial of Andrew Johnson*, pp. 79, 158.

[36] "But the Senator tells us he has no knowledge that the President designs making any removals. . . . Well, sir, I have some knowledge that removals are being made throughout the country. It is not proper to speak here of removals which have been made and are now pending in executive session; but if it was, I think I could bring to the notice of the Senator quite a number of cases. But, sir, outside of executive session, I have seen it stated in the newspapers of the country that the marshal of the western district of Pennsylvania has been removed, that the collector of internal revenue in the district of Pittsburg has been removed, that the postmaster in Pittsburg has been removed. Sir, I have heard of a number of removals, which are also noticed in the papers of my own State. Yes, sir, I have heard of a letter written to a man holding an insignificant office in Illinois from one of the Departments, informing him that, having taken part in a meeting which passed resolutions sustaining Congress, he would have an opportunity to explain the matter. The Senator seems not to have heard of any of these things." *Cong. Globe*, 39 Cong., 1 sess., p. 2420.

[37] *Ibid.*, p. 2280.

Now, Mr. President, what luck do you suppose some postmaster, or marshal, or assessor, made by the President out of a copperhead, or limping Republican, would have among these people arguing for the immediate and unconditional admission of the rebel States?

Fessenden, who at first had sided with Trumbull, changed his mind after the arguments of Sherman and Poland and decided to oppose the amendment. Henry Wilson of Massachusetts, who also opposed it, declared three days before the final vote was taken, "I tell Senators, and I tell the President, that the American people are in no condition to be bought and sold by Government patronage. . . ." On May 11, the amendment was rejected, 23 to 16, with 10 not voting.[38]

The essential correctness of the Poland thesis appears to have been well borne out all along, and would so continue up to election time, by the response of the officeholders themselves to threats of dismissal. The punctilio of local and party honor was all duly acted out by men who were either about to be, or already had been, removed for their acts and utterances against the Executive policy. A dominant theme that runs through the political correspondence of the period from postmasters, assessors, and other federal officials is a certain grim relish in being persecuted for loyalty to Congress and the party. "I have had to work very hard the past year," wrote one of them to Washburne, ". . . but I expect that Mr. Johnson will release me ere long of my labors but I shall try to live without it. I shall have the satisfaction of knowing that I have not sacrificed my *principles* for *position*. . . ."[39] An Illinois postmaster accepted his dismissal philosophically when he heard that others were meeting the same fate. "I would have felt badly," he told Trumbull, "if it had been based on charges. I aimed to do my duty but all the Post Offices in Illinois could not buy me to the support of A. Johnson."[40] A newly removed assistant assessor from the Eleventh Illinois District voiced much the same sentiment: "I suppose the President has decided that it will not do to continue in office an Inspector who will travel over the district and have his expenses paid who is opposed to 'my policy.' I submit cheerfully to the mandate and return to *private life*."[41] Horace Beebe, assessor for the

38 *Ibid.*, pp. 2418, 2447, 2449, 2559.

39 B. F. Baird to Washburne, May 18, 1866, Washburne MSS.

40 H. S. Thomas to Trumbull, May 19, 1866, Trumbull MSS. "If it is the purpose of the President to remove me on political grounds," wrote the Internal Revenue Collector of the Nineteenth Ohio District to Garfield, "of course I have nothing to say, but if for other cause I would like to be heard." Henry Fassett to Garfield, June 15, 1866, Garfield MSS, Library of Congress.

41 Peter Smith to Trumbull, June 7, 1866, Trumbull MSS.

Nineteenth Ohio District, described to Garfield how at Ravenna the local Johnson men had circulated the National Union call; ". . . it was presented to me," he said, "for the purpose of having me refuse (& in that they were gratified) and now Gillett & Cotter are saying that I will loose my head & seem to exult over it—Well if I must die I will die with my harness on. I will not desert my friends to hold any position."[42] "The Republicans in office," one of Washburne's lieutenants proudly reported, "mostly face the music like men."[43]

There were even those who perceived that dismissal could be a decided asset to them. "I think it would be for my future advantage, at least," wrote a nephew of John Brown to Washburne, "to be turned out of the office I hold in a good degree through your kindness." Another, already turned out, was almost Machiavellian in his glee over the results:

> You have been informed ere this of my removal, and also who my successor is. It is having a beneficial effect in this Co. on the Nov. election, and if any of my friends or yourself should wish to change the appointment even back to myself I would suggest the propriety of keeping quiet until after the election. . . . As a matter of policy I . . . think that no move, nor complaint ought to be made in the matter until after the election for it can be used (the appointment) against the Copper Johnson party.[44]

Hannibal Hamlin, who held one of the most lucrative of all federal offices, the collectorship of Boston, resigned his post in August because he could not support the National Union Johnson movement. "With such a party as has been inaugurated, and for such purposes," he wrote loftily to the President, "I have no sympathy, nor can I acquiesce in its measures by my silence. I therefore tender you my resignation. . . ."[45]

[42] Horace Beebe to Garfield, July 26, 1866, Garfield MSS. "I had rather never hold an office in my life," insisted a correspondent of Trumbull, "than to be even suspected for a moment of having any sympathy or favor for 'my policy.'" He closed his letter by exhorting Trumbull himself to "Stand fast in the faith." I. H. Howe to Trumbull, Apr. 23, 1866, Trumbull MSS. Even as early as January, an old stalwart from Ogle Station told Washburne, "I had rather be a door keeper in the Republican Party than to dwell in the White House with Andy, or like Moses of old, I had rather suffer afflictions with the Union Party than to enjoy the pleasure of his bread and butter for a season." C. C. Royce to Washburne, Jan. 4, 1866, Washburne MSS.

[43] M. B. Brown to Washburne, Sept. 7, 1866, Washburne MSS. An employee in the First Auditor's Office at Washington wrote: "The report is current here that all of us are to be turned out, who refuse to support 'My Policy.'. . . So I suppose I shall have to walk, for unless I can see some reason why I should change I shall remain where I am. I intend to be consistent . . . and not subscribe in any way to that which I think is not right. I am opposed to 'my policy' and shall have to hear some good reason before I can change my views." George C. Rice to Washburne, Aug. 24, 1866, Washburne MSS.

[44] Frederick Brown to Washburne, June 19, 1866; A. C. Jackson to Washburne, Sept. 7, 1866, Washburne MSS.

[45] Hamlin to Johnson, Aug. 28, 1866, in Charles Eugene Hamlin, *The Life and Times of Hannibal Hamlin* (Boston: Houghton Mifflin, 1899), p. 507. The United States Attor-

Against those, on the other hand, who might accept the proffered offices, community opinion could invoke the "scalawag" principle with an effect just as deadly in a Northern as in a Southern community. "Patronage can buy the venal and corrupt who may be bold enough to meet the scorn of the whole people," observed Warner Bateman, thus adding a corollary to the Poland thesis, "but its very possession will excite distrust and any zeal in behalf of the President will degrade the officeholder below the position of the slightest influence. The Union party is now safe. Its power with prudence is most certainly assured. Johnson's position out of its confidence is in the last degree pitiable."[46] Even Washburne himself came under a bit of suspicion, since as it happened no removals from Treasury offices were made in his district until September, and there were a few mutterings among the people at home that perhaps this was because Washburne had come to some dishonorable understanding with Johnson. He was warned by one of his henchmen that "some of the Republicans go so far as to assert that there has been a bargain and sale between the President and E. B. and in proof of it say that E. B. says that there will be no removals from office in his district."[47]

Actually, the President does not seem to have followed more than a halfway policy on removals until late in the summer. Perhaps he realized by then that for his purposes there could be no such thing as judicious local replacements, since such a course of harassment was earning him nothing but more hostility. Some time late in August or early September it must have dawned on him that there had to be all-

---

ney at Pittsburgh offered his resignation for similar reasons about this time. R. B. Carnahan to Johnson, Aug. 7, 1866, Johnson MSS, Library of Congress.

46 Warner Bateman to William Henry Smith, Apr. 10, 1866, Smith MSS, Ohio Historical Society. Bateman was a member of the Ohio state senate and a trusted adviser of John Sherman; Smith was the secretary of state of Ohio and a prominent figure in Republican state politics. In another letter to Smith on September 22, Bateman described with scorn how an erstwhile local Republican had been induced through his own cupidity to support Johnson and appear on the same platform with the Copperhead George Pendleton. It was as though the most profound depths of defilement had at last been plumbed. Of the Pennsylvania Republicans John Forney wrote: "With scarcely an exception they refuse to sacrifice themselves for the filthy bribes of [Mr. Lincoln's] false successor. In many counties valuable offices have been proffered for months to such Republicans as would support My Policy, and generally when men are found willing to take these places they are without influence, integrity or capacity." Forney to Zachariah Chandler, Aug. 14, 1866, Chandler MSS, Library of Congress.

47 C. K. Williams to Washburne, Sept. 14, 1866, Washburne MSS. Secretary McCulloch wrote Washburne on September 14 that although no Treasury removals had been made in his particular district up to then, the Secretary could give no further guarantees: ". . . in the present canvass there is so much violence and excitement that there are influences at work to compel changes in office which the Secretary cannot control, and which it would be very difficult for the President himself to resist." Washburne MSS.

out war or nothing. During his "Swing around the Circle" he made a public declaration:

How are these men to be got out ... unless your Executive can put them out, unless you can reach them through the President? Congress says he shall not turn them out, and they are trying to pass laws to prevent it being done. Well, let me say to you, if you will stand by me in this action—(cheers)—if you will stand by me in trying to give the people a fair chance, soldiers and citizens, to participate in these offices, God being willing I will kick them out. I will kick them out just as fast as I can.[48]

But even all-out war—if, indeed, it ever really did come to that—was of no avail.[49] If we may judge from an exchange of letters between the Secretary of the Treasury and Senator Fessenden about this time—up to and after the Maine election—the whole business of patronage was turning into a bad dream for the President's cause. Though McCulloch and Fessenden were by then far apart in their political views, their personal relations remained quite unimpaired and it was still possible for them to deal more or less matter-of-factly with each other on questions of Treasury appointments. On August 15, Fessenden asks McCulloch's assistance in protecting several officeholders from removal. Then he adds: "Turning our friends out of office any where only unties their tongues, and intensifies the activity of energetic and influential men. If the President will do it to gratify such flunkies as Doolittle and Cowan, he must take the consequences." On August 17 he warns McCulloch about the way in which Johnson, in spite of himself, would be brought to the point of filling the offices with Democrats:

Sweat, the Copperhead candidate for Congress in this Dist. with others of his kidney, will probably try to persuade Mr. Johnson that if he can control the offices in this Dist. he can be elected and will support him. Let not the President be deceived. Sweat is totally untrustworthy. We shall whip him to death with ease, and all the worse if the President makes a change in the offices. He may take my word for it, if he pleases.

[48] This speech was made September 8 at St. Louis. New York *Herald*, Sept. 10, 1866.

[49] If anything, the removals were actually beneficial (as noted above) to the Republicans. The fact of their having been made was used as a reason for added assessments for campaign funds—e.g., the following excerpt from a circular letter of the Michigan State Republican Committee to all candidates: "Heretofore the State Committee have mainly depended on assessment of Federal office holders to meet the unavoidable expenses of an election contest. But now, while the illustrious A. J. is 'Swinging around the Circle,' cutting off the heads of Republicans, and 'kicking' them out of office because they remain loyal to the principles of the loyal party, the usual resources of the Committee are no longer available, except as to candidates for office. The Committee has, therefore, levied an assessment against you...." W. S. Wood to Austin Blair, Sept. 13, 1866, Blair MSS, Detroit Public Library. Blair was one of Michigan's war governors, now running for Congress.

He acknowledges, on August 29, the Secretary's reply, in which the latter has apparently told him that the President had no choice but to accept Democratic support. "I can only regret," Fessenden answers, "that the President finds himself compelled . . . to remove faithful and competent officers, and to fill their places with copperheads and flunkies. He must take the consequences. We can only accept them." Fessenden's predictions of the seventeenth apparently materialized, for he reports on September 7:

A few men here . . . are acting as the President's friends and putting the offices up for sale—asking only that the recipients will agree to support Sweat [the Democratic candidate] for Congress. Their offers are spurned with contempt. . . . You will see the result in a few days of this miserable attempt to corrupt the American people by an appeal to their cupidity. I shall continue to believe that you have nothing to do with it.

The fall elections—in line with the custom of holding them early in Maine—took place on September 10, and even Fessenden was taken a little aback by the decisiveness of the Republican victory. The first reason he mentions, in attempting to account for it, involves the use of the patronage:

. . . the fact that a few very contemptible and effete politicians . . . who have no support from any party, have been permitted by the President to put the offices up for sale has both dispirited and enraged all decent men, while it has made the President no supporters except among those whose support is an injury. I warned him that he had much better leave Maine as it was.

And a final post-mortem on the fifteenth:

The election is now over. No further changes can produce the least effect, except to exchange good officers in whom the people confide for bad ones, where appointments will disgust thinking men of all parties. My advice to the President is to turn a deaf ear to those fellows whom they leave about him, talking of support. All they mean by it is the necessity of supporting them out of the Treasury—not caring how odious they make the President and the Secretary.[50]

The things at issue in the struggle between the majority party and the Executive, as the elections of 1866 approached, were sufficiently basic that no conceivable mode of altering the balance of power with patronage was possible. Patronage, no matter how skilfully handled, must in this case represent so much watered stock in an essentially defunct corporation. The point may be given a final illus-

50 Fessenden to McCulloch, Aug. 15, 17, 29, Sept. 7, 11, and 15, 1866, McCulloch MSS, Library of Congress; McCulloch to Fessenden, Sept. 11, 1866, Fessenden MSS, Library of Congress.

tration in the experience of Thurlow Weed, whom the fortunes of politics had made a leading stockholder in the Johnson concern in New York state. The nineteenth century furnishes no more accomplished technician in the arts of the cloakroom and lobby than Weed; yet in spite of a long career full of experience, rich lore, and a course of lessons well learned, this master spoilsman—once known as the "Dictator" —was to find himself at the final accounting holding a handful of worthless securities.

The presidential campaign of 1864 had constituted something of a pinnacle for the partnership of Weed, Seward, and Raymond, a combination which had thrown all its energies into the winning of New York for Abraham Lincoln. The battle, however, left deep fissures within the Republican organization of the state itself, for Lincoln had found it necessary to discriminate against a strong Chase faction—out of which would grow the Fenton-Conkling machine—in order to bestow the appropriate rewards upon the Seward-Weed group. Thus although Weed by early 1865 controlled a heavy share of the federal patronage in New York, the death of Lincoln in April was to leave his and Seward's position peculiarly vulnerable and somewhat at the mercy of the rising radical faction at Albany in charge of the governorship. The only choice open to Seward and Weed, therefore, and from all indications it seemed hardly a bad choice at the time, was to link their fortunes with those of Andrew Johnson. But such was the nature of the choice—Fenton's group having already declared war not so much on Johnson as upon Seward and Weed themselves—that no matter what happened, there could be no turning back.[51]

From about the fall of 1865 on, the influence of Thurlow Weed began to decline steadily. Although he had made his power felt through "masterly maneuvering and the use of federal patronage," as his biographer put it,[52] in the New York state convention that summer, it was not long before his "masterly maneuverings" began to take on a certain air of unreality. We catch glimpses of him during this period flirting with the War Democrats and conjuring up new align-

---

[51] Glyndon G. Van Deusen, *Thurlow Weed, Wizard of the Lobby* (Boston: Little, Brown, 1947), pp. 307–12; Thurlow Weed Barnes (ed.), *Memoir of Thurlow Weed* (Boston: Houghton Mifflin, 1884), pp. 444–52; Carman and Luthin, *Lincoln and the Patronage*, pp. 243–47. See also Sidney David Brummer, *Political History of New York State during the Period of the Civil War* (New York: Privately printed, 1911), pp. 390–96, 443, 447; and Homer A. Stebbins, *A Political History of the State of New York, 1865–1869* ("Columbia University Studies in History, Economics, and Public Law," Vol. LV [New York: Columbia University Press, 1913]), pp. 24–28, 59–80.

[52] Van Deusen, *Thurlow Weed*, p. 312.

ments, thus earning the suspicion of the regular Democratic organization, while being already in bad odor among the Republicans. After the New York Custom House collectorship was vacated in November, Weed's letters show him imagining that his purposes might best be served by the appointment of a Democrat. By February, 1866, he had decided that a Republican might be better after all ("*That* will confound the Enemy, and with that we can inaugurate a triumphant future"), though he continued to nourish schemes of some sweeping new conservative coalition.[53] The collectorship, filled in April by a Weed man, presumably augmented the forces who were to do battle for Weed and the administration cause.[54] All through the spring and summer of 1866 we see him tirelessly scheming—marshaling recruits for the grand conservative gathering at Philadelphia, busy with the many details of mobilization, girding for the final effort at the polls.

But there were so many breaches in the breastworks that the old general could not possibly repair them all. He knew the signs too well; with the coming of the fall, he could no longer conceal from himself the extent to which things were deteriorating all along the line. Complaints kept coming in from besieged local headquarters; on the one hand, such and such a district was hopelessly radical: "Our office holders are all Radical, our press is Radical and the influence of each is used to procure a Radical victory."[55] On the other hand, when removals were made, so many of the replacements in spite of all Weed's precautions were turning out to be Copperheads. "If I may be allowed to advise in the matter of removals," pleaded the collector of the Nineteenth District, "I would say no more copperhead appointments at present." "The Democracy in this section," wrote D. H. Cole from Albion in tones of desperation, ". . . are endeavoring *secretly* to produce changes and then fill them with Democrats. *This wont do* and is only effectually destroying the influence of Republicans who wish to strengthen your self and Gov. Seward as old friends. . . ."[56] How much of this was due to Weed and how much to Johnson himself is not easy to say. Weed, however, had taken alarm by the end of October and was telling Seward that removals were actually costing votes for the President's cause:

[53] Weed to Seward, Jan. 28, 29, Feb. 28, Mar. 12, 1866, Seward MSS, University of Rochester Library.

[54] New York *Herald*, Apr. 18 and 19, 1866.

[55] Henry T. Munson and others (Jefferson County delegation to state National Union convention) to Weed, Sept. 11, 1866, Weed MSS, University of Rochester Library.

[56] George W. Ernst to Weed, Oct. 2, 1866; D. H. Cole to Weed, Oct. 17, 1866, Weed MSS.

In many cases where unwise Appointments have been made the lines are drawn between the Loyal and Disloyal men, with, unhappily, the Disloyal faction in favor of the President.

I know how plausibly these Removals are urged, but I do hope that we shall be spared further mischief of this sort until the Election is over.[57]

But then how could it be helped? By far the majority of the President's suporters were Democrats; Weed himself had promoted an ex-Democrat, John A. Dix, for governor;[58] and the time had now come when any Democrat who came to Johnson saying that he stood a fair chance of carrying his district, if only he were given the disposal of this or that office, must have sounded pretty convincing.[59]

The power of Thurlow Weed was broken more or less decisively by the 1866 elections. There is a note of reminiscence in one of his communications to Seward the following year which might be taken as something of a political swan song: "I took too [many] trusting Friends with me to the block last fall. . . . I followed [the President] into the ditch. In working for a Democrat for Governor I destroyed the consistency of a long political life. . . . He [the President] could have overwhelmed the Radicals. But he has thrown it all away.[60]

III   THE NATIONAL UNION MOVEMENT

The most serious effort that was to materialize for the promotion of President Johnson's reconstruction policy—an effort that reached a relatively high phase of planning and articulation—was the National Union movement of 1866. This movement represented the final fruition of several months' urging and endeavor by Johnson's chief supporters to launch some sort of political vehicle for electing congressmen who would stand back of the President's position. "What we want just now, amidst the chaos of political elements that are float-

[57] Weed to Seward, Oct. 27, 1866, Seward MSS. Such a policy, in strong Unionist districts, was bad even for the Democrats. A Democrat from San Francisco wrote to Samuel J. Tilden: "For the present at least, *no Democrat should be appointed to any offices*, by the admin. The bare *report of* two such appointments in this city, showed by the effect produced, the evil consequences of the reality. The admin. is anything but fortunate in either its old or *new* appointees in this city: but Democrats would certainly have made bad infinitely worse. I hope you will impress on friends at Washington the necessity of the *utmost caution* in all matters here." E. Casserly to Tilden, Sept. 9, 1866, Tilden MSS, New York Public Library.

[58] When Dix, a War Democrat, failed to be nominated, Weed then went the whole way and supported the regular Democratic candidate, John T. Hoffman.

[59] Johnson was heavily besieged, especially after the Philadelphia convention. Some of the delegations came straight from there to Washington to see him in person, having as a major object changes in the federal offices of their state. Cf. *Nation*, II (Aug. 23, 1866), 141; New York *Herald*, Aug. 18, 20, 21, 1866.

[60] Weed to Seward, Sept. 15, 1867, Seward MSS.

ing about," insisted James Gordon Bennett early in February, "is a new party organization founded upon the vital question of the time—that is, upon President Johnson's policy for the earliest restoration of harmony and the enjoyment of equal political privileges by every section and State of the Union."[61] Organized in the late spring of 1866 in an atmosphere of optimism and hope, the National Union movement gathered momentum during the summer and reached the high point of its power and influence with the meeting of the National Union Convention at Philadelphia in mid-August. From that time on, however, its influence with Union Republican voters declined, until by October it had come to be considered as little more than a "front" organization for the Democratic party.

The possibility of inept management as a cause of the movement's failure naturally presents itself, having occurred not only to historians but also to some of Johnson's own contemporaries. There was feeling, even at the time, that perhaps the President had not moved soon enough in lending his own sanction and support to the organization. By the time he did so move, the support of such conspicuous conservative figures as Trumbull, Sherman, and Morton—assuming that such support might have been available earlier—was most certainly no longer to be had. Senator Doolittle, himself a leading spirit in the organizing of the convention, tended to share this feeling.[62] Even the irrepressible Bennett, by the time the formal call was issued on June 26, could not respond with quite the unmitigated enthusiasm which he might have showered upon such an enterprise two or three months earlier.[63] Then there was the odd irresoluteness of such key men as Seward and Raymond on making the full commitment to a third party. They could not quite bring themselves to a formal severance from the Union party,

[61] New York *Herald*, Feb. 11, 1866.

[62] Doolittle felt that a reorganization of Johnson's cabinet would have provided an important focus of solidarity for the Executive position and that his delay in so doing might deprive the National Union movement of some of its appeal. Such a reorganization was constantly urged in the editorial columns of the New York *Herald*. See also Gideon Welles, *Diary*, II, 556, on Johnson's slowness of decision to strengthen the power of his office.

[63] "We would have preferred to see this movement practically inaugurated in Congress, and thence extended naturally to the people at the fall elections. But our advice was not followed by the leaders of the Congressional factions, and at this late day . . . it is with mingled amusement and interest that we see them endeavoring to atone for the errors of the past and the present by planning great combinations for the future." New York *Herald*, June 29, 1866. The *Herald* did, however, support the movement. An observer on the West Coast wrote to Samuel J. Tilden, "Could the President have seen his way clear to do at the first, say right upon his 'dead duck' speech, what he has been forced to do at last,—make a distinct party break with the Radicals,—the present situation would be very much better." E. Casserly to Tilden, Sept. 9, 1866, Tilden MSS.

though they had already done so in all but saying the final word. Conceivably, therefore, the movement stopped just enough short of the ultimate step—resolute and unequivocal separation from both parties—to deprive itself of that last little ounce of momentum which could make the difference between failure and success.[64]

But was this final failure of energy circumstantial and factitious, or was it due to something more fundamental? How would we locate politically the key people in the movement, in relation not only to their principles but to their careers? Did they all have the same kind of party in mind? Would such figures as Trumbull and Sherman have been any more available for such a movement in December, 1865, than in June, 1866? What is there in the logic of two-party majority politics, aside from considerations of principle, that relates to the forming of third parties?

It is generally recognized that the logic of "two-ness" in American national politics is directly related to the unobtrusiveness of ideology and special principle. The system has always been one of majority politics rather than of coalition politics, and the prevailing choices have been in the simple terms of "for and against," "one or the other," and "in versus out," rather than a multiple struggle of contending factions each organized around a special and continuing ideological position. The system does not seem to permit success on any other terms. This is hardly to say that principle has gone for nothing in American politics, but rather that the premiums on principle have been consistently lower than on the institutional claims of party and career. Men change parties from time to time, but only under extreme conditions do they try to form new ones.

It is true that the supreme effort to organize a third party of principle is occasionally called forth. But its only chance of success—as with the Republican antislavery party—seems to depend on its ability to break down or swallow up one of the two majority parties and to become a majority party itself. As a matter of history and practice, that process has worked more often in reverse. Every institutional interest of the two major parties will inspire them figuratively to turn upon the third and suck away its life. As for the individuals who go

[64] "A party had stood ready made. But its natural leaders remained inactive while for six months Johnson merely defended a tiresomely immutable policy, leaving all aggression to the Moderates. Inactivity lost the Moderates much of the advantage of their original position." Beale, *Critical Year*, p. 123. "The array of moderate men was imposing; but notable Moderates of a few months earlier were conspicuously absent—stumping for the Radicals: Morton of Indiana, John Sherman of Ohio, Trumbull of Illinois, ex-Governor Andrew of Massachusetts, men who in January would heartily have supported the movement." *Ibid.*, p. 132.

into such movements, they will turn out in a great many cases to have been politically displaced persons—men who, for a variety of reasons, can no longer count upon clear futures in the regular organizations. Conversely, those solid in their regular party connections seem consistently able to resist the call of special principle.

Inherent, then, in the very launching of a third party is the activation of forces that work to sap its energy. Elements within the new movement may even be observed to strain back, in spite of themselves, toward their original components in the major parties. Such at least would seem to be the inferences we are entitled to draw from the National Union movement of 1866. Inept management and poor timing were very minor items, if they were items at all, in the movement's failure.

It appears that the initial impulse for a Johnson movement came in large part from men with uncertain prospects in the regular parties who were seeking new political arrangements for themselves. Weed, Seward, and Raymond (as already noted) had been all but read out of the Republican party. The same was true of the Blairs and of Senators Cowan, Doolittle, and Dixon.[65] J. H. Geiger, R. P. L. Baber, and Lewis D. Campbell, all of Ohio, had a standing in the Unionist circles of that state which was hardly more than marginal.[66] Some of the War Democrats of New York—such as John A. Dix, Edwards Pierrepont, and even Dean Richmond—found the Copperhead influence in the regular organization somewhat too strong for

[65] The Blairs' search for a new political home, which began even before Johnson's accession to the Presidency, has already been noted. Doolittle's support in Wisconsin had become so precarious after the Freedmen's Bureau veto that the legislature by early March was already considering asking him to resign as senator. After he ignored a resolution urging him to support his party on the Civil Rights Bill, the legislature finally, on April 10, passed by substantial majorities a joint resolution "Declaring it to be the duty of Senator Doolittle to resign." E. W. Keyes to Doolittle, Mar. 1, 1866; Horace Rublee to Doolittle, Mar. 6, 1866, Doolittle MSS, Historical Society of Wisconsin; James L. Sellers, "James R. Doolittle," *Wisconsin Magazine of History*, XVIII (September, 1934), 27; *Journal of the Senate of Wisconsin, 1866*, pp. 992–93, 1026, 1034. A note in Doolittle's papers, dated July 3, 1866, and signed, "Four fifths of Wisconsin," reads as follows: "I have supported you untill I can do it no longer. You have turned *traitor* to your State and gone over to Johnson and the rebels. I think you had better do as Lane of Kansas has done, come home and put a *ball* through your *rotten* head. Any *decent* man would leave after being instructed out, by the legislature as you have been. Now resign & come home, you *poor devil*, don't stay any longer where you aint wanted."

[66] One of Garfield's lieutenants, in a letter reporting the solidarity of pro-Congress, anti-Johnson feeling in the 1866 Ohio state Republican convention, remarked: "True[,] that distinguished *trio* Campbell, G[e]iger & Baber were present but utterly harmless." Abner Kellogg to Garfield, June 25, 1866, Garfield MSS.

their own political comfort and wished to stay clear of it. Dix in particular was in an equivocal position, being not at all solid with either party and being at the same time aware that his own chief political value was as possible bait for a conservative coalition.[67] Editorial support to the movement was given by James Gordon Bennett, who was the sort of "independent" who had nothing to lose in the way of personal influence, and conceivably something to gain, by experimenting with a new political venture.

But why should there not have been more conservative Republicans of high standing connected with the National Union movement? Oliver P. Morton, for example, had expressed strong sentiments of support for Johnson in the fall and early winter of 1865. But in terms of political reorganization, Morton could hardly have had much more in mind than a slightly altered Union coalition in which some War Democrats might possibly be exchanged for a few of the more obnoxious radicals, such as Julian and Sumner. There is nothing in Morton's wartime or postwar career to suggest any thought of a basic rearrangement which should include substantial numbers of Democrats (whose behavior, in Morton's Indiana experience, had been the next thing to treasonable). When Johnson raised such a possibility to Morton in March, 1866, the latter brushed it contemptuously aside. Neither Morton, Andrew, Sherman, Fessenden, nor Trumbull were in any political sense marginal men. They were all figures of solid prominence in the Republican party who at no time had anything to gain through a new movement organized outside the party or even on its outer fringes. Their support of Johnson in the first place had been on the assumption that he occupied a center position, that his purposes and those of the party majority were in essential harmony. Any other state of things from their point of view could represent only danger: if Johnson's position should ever take such form that it had to be separately organized, it could only operate as a threat to the unity of the party. They did not have much use, to be sure, for the likes of Stevens and Sumner. But not only is there no evidence that they were willing to risk party disunity in order to get rid of such men, but the political disputes of 1866 were of such a nature as to draw them all closer together rather than farther apart. Much the same principle, indeed, held for the regular Democrats. A number of them would flirt with the new organization, but on the basis of an essentially limited commitment. Most of them assumed that it was, or could be turned into, a kind of expanded Democratic party.

[67] Stebbins, *Political History of New York*, pp. 100–101.

The only possible principles for such an organization were of course President Johnson's conditions for reconstruction, and the first positive steps were taken strictly on grounds of principle. The first general signal seems to have been the repassage of the Civil Rights Bill on April 9 over Johnson's veto. A few days afterward the "National Union Executive Committee," a forerunner of the organization to be launched formally some two months later, arranged for a soldiers' and sailors' serenade of the President to be held on April 18. The speech with which the President responded on that occasion, though less publicized than the one he had made on February 22, resembled the other in all particulars, with the possible exception that this time the personal note, the sense of persecution, was even less controlled than before. His only terms were still what they had always been: immediate and unqualified readmission of the Southern representatives to Congress. The entire problem had been reduced by Johnson to a desire of Northern "traitors" to destroy his influence with the people:

. . . I think I have given some evidence that I am sincere and earnest; and now I want to know why it is that the whole train of slanderers, and calumniators and traducers have been barking and snapping at my heels? Why is it that they array themselves against me? . . . Where were they during the rebellion? In the Senate I raised my voice against it; and . . . did I not leave my place in the Senate—a place of emolument, ease and distinction, and take my position where the enemy could be reached, and where men's lives were in danger? While I was thus exposed personally and publicly, and in every way, some of my present traducers and calumniators were far from the foe, and were enjoying ease and comfort. But I care not for them; I care not that slander, that foul whelp of sin, has been turned loose against me. I care not for all that. . . . They have turned the whole pack loose to lower me in your estimation. Tray, Blanche and Sweetheart, little dogs and all, come along snapping and snarling at my heels. But I heed them not.[68]

Immediately after the serenade, the National Union Executive Committee (also known as the "Union Pure Andrew Johnson Club") held a meeting and drew up a platform. The platform denied both the right of secession and the right of the federal government to exclude a state from the Union or to govern it as a territory; it affirmed the right of each state to regulate its local institutions, subject only to the Constitution of the United States; and it declared that each state was entitled to prescribe its own terms of suffrage. All states had the right to representation, and loyal members duly elected were entitled to admission—subject only to the right of each House to be the judge

[68] New York *Herald*, Apr. 19, 1866.

of its own members' qualifications. There should be no compromise with traitors by "bartering universal amnesty for universal suffrage"; the national debt was declared inviolate; and gratitude was expressed to the soldiers and sailors. Two days later the President, when this platform was presented to him, gave it his indorsement.[69] These principles, together with the words of the President's speech, added up to a single meaning: the fundamental condition of any Johnson platform would have to be immediate and unqualified readmission of the Southern states.

From the viewpoint of organization, there was a certain ominous note in connection with the trial balloon sent up by the Washington Johnson club. That organization did not want to be confused with another Johnson group in the same city, the "Intelligencer Club," because the latter was heavily tinged with Copperheadism. And yet the principles of each were virtually the same.[70] Here was a theme which in one form or another would do a great deal to undermine the entire enterprise, since it involved a distinction between Unionist and Copperhead which in this queer setting was painfully hard to maintain; the principles of any Johnson movement actually made very little sense outside the Democratic party. Unqualified readmission meant that reconstruction was at an end, and had been for some time. No conditions, such as the Fourteenth Amendment, could be expected without voluntary Southern co-operation, and as things stood this was not very likely. So if Congress were denied the constitutional right to impose any prior conditions, then the chances of getting substantial numbers of Republicans to indorse such principles would become very slight indeed. Thus it was more than likely that even though most of the organization's "front" men might be nominally Unionist, the main source of recruitment would have to be the Democratic party. And since the Democrats themselves were the minority party in the North and in Congress, the new organization's leadership could not afford to be too particular about what kind of Democrats were let in. There was not much guarantee, in short, that the scene would not be alive with Democratic adventurers of every kind.

Why was not all this clear to such experienced politicians as Seward, Weed, and Raymond? In the light of simple political self-preservation, why did they not foresee the perils that awaited them? The career of a Thurlow Weed, and of many another like him, reminds us a little of the career of a public performer whose talent, and even his experience, are meaningless without his audience. A man must retain his

[69] *Ibid.*, Apr. 20 and 23, 1866.   [70] *Ibid.*, Apr. 19, 1866.

following in order to hang onto his skill; let him lose that and he loses everything. With a wrong guess, a missed cue, or a flat performance he may figuratively hit the skids; he has lost his touch. It was apparently something of this sort that had already happened by 1866 to the seasoned concern of Seward and Weed in New York. Surrounded by their hundreds of enemies, accumulated through a lifetime on the circuit, they had about played out the string by the end of the war and seem subsequently to have carried a number of their associates—including Henry J. Raymond—down with them. We cannot identify with exact precision the moment at which Seward and Weed had been jarred out of tune with the general harmonies;[71] still, it happened, and by 1865 their position in New York politics was already vulnerable. This, plus their early commitment to Johnson, seems to have carried them beyond the point of no return before they ever quite realized it. The initial state of confidence in the Johnson administration throughout the North had provided a certain warrant for that commitment and may to some extent explain (though only partially) how it could have retained its plausibility for them until after it was too late.

The Seward-Weed-Raymond appraisal of their own position did have running through it, in the early stages of the Johnson administration, a vein of soundness and common sense. When Congress met in December, 1865, it was more than plausible that they should picture their position as a central, controlling one: they might play a major role in the final liquidation of the war. They could count on the full energy and prestige—and therefore presumably the full and active political co-operation—of the President in bringing the country back to normal. It was not unreasonable, moreover, to imagine the Union party moving closer to an attitude of conservatism on reconstruction: therein would lie the best hope of retaining the Northern War Democrats and perhaps of adding some conservative support from the South. Here Lincoln himself had seemed to point out the direction, and the mass of Union voters certainly seemed to want, other things being equal, a return to peaceful ways. As prominent figures in the conservative wing of the Union party, therefore, in all good logic Weed and his friends stood to gain in influence as the party moved toward conservatism. The logic would hold just so long as the party did not move toward radicalism instead.

The nightmare of rising radical influence by March and April, 1866, added an element of desperation for the Weed-Seward-Raymond po-

---

[71] Serious trouble was already brewing for Weed in New York Unionist circles by the spring of 1863. See Brummer, *New York during the Civil War*, pp. 290 ff.

sition, though perhaps not necessarily one of hopelessness. With the unfolding of events, there were two "conservative" ways in which men might conceive the relationship of Johnson and the Republican party. For those of moderate views who were at the same time solid party men (e.g., Sherman and Trumbull), it was the party that tended to be seen as the stable item in the equation, with the President moving ever farther toward the outside edge, and eventually outside altogether. But for Weed and Raymond, whose fortunes were now more closely tied to Johnson than to the party at large, the picture had to be reversed. The party must keep being redefined in such a way that Johnson remained always in the center of it, no matter how uncompromising Johnson's own position might become. Rising radical influence would thus have to be defined as "abnormal." Vigorous measures could still conceivably save the Unionist Johnson supporters, though for strategic purposes such measures might have to be launched outside the *regular* Republican organization, since that organization was now "abnormally" dominated by radicalism.

Indeed, the idea of striking off at something of a tangent had its attractive side. To the continuing popular wish for a peace settlement could now be added a desire that the frustrating struggle between President and Congress be brought to an end. The issues of protection for the Negro and readjustment of Southern representation still seemed not utterly beyond compromise. Even though the President favored unqualified Southern readmission, there should surely be some reasonable way of promoting this position with an energetic Johnson movement. Might it not be possible to get the Southerners, informally, to make certain voluntary concessions, such as ratifying the Fourteenth Amendment and enacting legislation for the freedmen? Why could not such an organization bring in the greatest variety of elements: vast numbers of peace-loving Northerners, co-operative Southerners, loyal Northern Democrats, conservative Republicans? It was an admirable scheme; once under way, why should not the thing just grow and grow? Why might not such a new national coalition dominate American politics for a generation?[72]

But a final aspect of the Seward-Weed-Raymond version of a

[72] Weed was busily scheming along these lines by March, 1866, and perhaps earlier. He refers to "the *new* Organization" in a letter to Seward on March 12; in another on the seventeenth he reports a meeting he has had with the Democratic leader Dean Richmond. "We have sketched a plan of political operations for our own State—a plan which with the support of the Administration, will give a healthy, vigorous and triumphant result." Seward MSS. Raymond in June was still trying to persuade Republicans in Congress to join him in a great effort to "nationalize" the Union party along the lines laid down by the President. See his speech of June 18, 1866, *Cong. Globe*, 39 Cong., 1 sess., p. 3250.

Johnson movement contained the Achilles' heel of the whole affair. These men could not admit that what they had in mind was really a third party, and they kept pretending to the world and to themselves that it was something else. They could not see themselves just going over to the Democrats, who very possibly would not have had them anyway; nor could they fully re-enter the bosom of the Union party, from which they had been all but excommunicated. But since they could not bear the thought of close proximity with Copperheads, they had to imagine that the Union party itself might be cleansed and puri-fied. Here the reasoning becomes a little hazy. The movement should not really split off formally from the Union party; that would cut them adrift entirely. It should be under the control of Union mod-erates, *they* being the true "moderates." Therefore those Democrats who came in must co-operate by submerging not only their partisan interests but also their party name. This would all work in the greater interest of a victorious moderate program—and of new life for Seward, Weed & Co.

There were three ponderous difficulties in this otherwise hopeful logic. For the scheme's success, a majority of the Union party would ultimately have to accept Weed's and Raymond's "everyone-out-of-step-but-us" definition of true Unionism. But then since virtually the entire Democratic party accepted Johnson's principles, there were actually no dependable criteria for discriminating among Democrats in matters of purity. And finally, there was no evidence that the Democratic party would have anything to gain by effacing itself in all this. Indeed, what was there in the final accounting to prevent the Democrats' absorbing it, rather than its absorbing the Democrats?

Preparations for the Philadelphia convention and the launching of a full national organization began to take shape in the late spring of 1866. Specific origins are not easy to trace with precision; diverse streams had by that time begun flowing into a more or less common channel. Local organizations would have been the logical outgrowth of the various Johnson meetings, held after the President's first veto and similar inflammatory events which thereafter occurred with some regularity. Such an organization, doubtless typical of oth-ers, was formed in New York as early as mid-February;[73] something

[73] A full description of the New York effort was given in a letter from P. M. Wet-more to Hugh McCulloch, Feb. 26, 1866, McCulloch MSS. Similar activity in Pennsyl-vania was referred to by William A. Wallace, writing to William Bigler, Mar. 28, 1866, Bigler MSS, Pennsylvania Historical Society. Wallace was chairman of the Pennsylvania Democratic Committee and a state senator; he was later to become, in 1875, U.S. Sena-tor from Pennsylvania. Bigler was a former governor of that state.

important was also afoot in Pennsylvania by March. In Washington, Alexander W. Randall, the Assistant Postmaster-General, and Montgomery Blair finally effected a merger of the pro-Johnson clubs of that city some time during the late spring.[74] One of the first acts of the resulting "National Union Club" was to arrange a serenade of the President's cabinet officers, to be held on May 23, in order to smoke out their views. The serenade was not a success: Seward, Harlan, and Speed did not appear; Welles responded with curt brevity that he approved Johnson's policies; Stanton and Dennison made ambiguous speeches; and only McCulloch spoke with emphasis and vigor in support of the President.[75]

Thurlow Weed had been negotiating all during this period with Dean Richmond and other New York Democrats with an eye to forming some sort of conservative Johnson coalition in his state.[76] Weed's activities and those of Seward had been enough in evidence that Welles—who on general principles was suspicious of them both— came to feel that their connection with the movement had been undertaken for devious and dubious purposes.[77] Senator Doolittle, for many weeks prior to the issuing of the call on June 26, had been busy rounding up all possible support for the formal launching. Doolittle, as much as any one individual, was the workhorse of the movement.

On the evening of June 11, 1866, a group of Johnson Union congressmen and other gentlemen called upon the President for the first of several talks out of which final plans were to emerge. Present on that occasion were Senators Cowan and Doolittle, Representative Green Clay Smith of Kentucky, Charles Knap, Samuel Fowler, Walter Burleigh, Randall, and Orville H. Browning.[78] Johnson seemed very anxious to strike at the radicals in Congress. According to Browning's account,

[74] Robert W. Winston, *Andrew Johnson, Plebeian and Patriot,* p. 353; Montgomery Blair to S. J. Tilden, Apr. 15 and June 14, 1866, Tilden MSS. See also William E. Smith, *The Francis Preston Blair Family in Politics,* p. 360.

[75] New York *Herald,* May 24, 1866; see also George Fort Milton, *Age of Hate,* pp. 332–34, and Welles, *Diary,* II, 512–13.

[76] Henry W. Raymond (ed.), "Extracts from the Journal of Henry J. Raymond," *Scribner's Monthly,* XX (June, 1880), 278; Weed to Seward, Mar. 17, 1866, Seward MSS.

[77] Welles, *Diary,* II, 530–35, 538–40.

[78] Knap and Fowler were prominent members of the Johnson organization in Washington; Randall was shortly to be appointed Postmaster General upon the resignation of William Dennison on July 11; Burleigh was territorial delegate from Dakota; and Orville H. Browning, former senator from Illinois, would soon (July 27) succeed James Harlan as Secretary of the Interior.

To rescue the power from their hands, and avert such a calamity he was willing to put in all the capital he had. He would give $20,000 in cash, and all the influence he had as Chief Executive. The patronage of the government and the Presidency for the next term could be used by the true friends of the country to accomplish the desired results, &c. We all thought a convention of the friends of the country should be called at an early day.[79]

Four days later, on the fifteenth, Doolittle saw Welles and got his support, whereupon the two went to the President for further consultation, and it was agreed that Doolittle should draft the call.[80]

Throughout the following week Doolittle worked on his draft, and in the course of its preparation he received the advice of Browning, McCulloch, Seward, Welles, Cowan, Randall, Raymond, and the Blairs. It was arranged in final conferences with Johnson and others on June 21 and 23 that the call should be signed by Cowan, Dixon, Norton, and Doolittle in order to give the impression that it originated with the Union members of Congress. Additional signers would be Democratic Senators Nesmith and Hendricks, as well as Randall, Browning, and two leading members of the Washington club, Knap and Fowler. It was thought by some that the cabinet members should also be asked to sign, but Welles objected on grounds of propriety, whereupon it was agreed that after the call appeared, Welles, Seward, and McCulloch would write letters of approval to Senator Doolittle.[81]

The main stress was once more placed upon the South's right to immediate representation, and the principles of the call were essentially the same as those in the National Union Executive Committee's platform of two months before.[82] Much to the bitter disappointment of Welles, who wanted to take a stand of open and outright opposition to the Fourteenth Amendment, it was agreed that the amendment should not be mentioned—thereby avoiding, it was hoped, the unnecessary alienation of moderate Unionists.[83] There was further agreement that the Democrats should for the time being play a secondary role and that the extreme Copperheads should so far as possible be

[79] James G. Randall (ed.), *Diary of Orville Hickman Browning* (Springfield: Jefferson Printing and Stationery Co., 1933), II, 79.

[80] Welles, *Diary*, II, 528.

[81] Welles, *Diary*, II, 533–35, 538–40; Raymond, "Journal," pp. 276–77; Browning to Thomas Ewing, June 26, 1866, Ewing MSS, Library of Congress.

[82] The call was published in all leading newspapers on June 26, 1866. The text of it is printed in McPherson, *Reconstruction*, pp. 118–19.

[83] Welles, *Diary*, II, 529–31, 534, 539.

excluded.[84] When the call was published it was hailed by Henry J. Raymond in the New York *Times* as an effort to place the Union party, as Lincoln himself would have wished it, on a fully national rather than a sectional foundation. "The basis thus presented," he asserted hopefully, "is sufficiently broad to meet the expectations of Union-loving men everywhere."[85]

The difficulties, however, in the way of maintaining a predominantly Unionist tone for the enterprise began manifesting themselves almost from the moment the call was issued. The most immediate response from Unionist spokesmen and the Unionist press was, as might have been expected, one of unequivocal hostility. The New York *Tribune* declared that the movement was simply a bolt from the Union party, engineered to restore rebels and Copperheads to power; *Harper's Weekly*, hopeful as late as June 23 that a compromise might still be effected between Johnson and Congress, now denied the right of the Philadelphia convention or its sponsors to speak in any way for the party; while the *Nation* treated the call as little more than a trick to confuse the minds of Union voters.[86] A Republican congressional caucus was held on July 12 which denounced the convention as a scheme to break up the party, and the caucus virtually excommunicated anyone who had anything to do with it. A resolution to this effect passed with only one dissenting vote. Raymond, who was present, came in for much abuse which he repelled as best he could.[87]

There were already signs, among Johnson Republican elements themselves, of a certain sapping of energy. Raymond's own behavior was rather symptomatic. To Judge Ransom Balcom, an upstate Republican leader, Raymond on July 17 wrote a peculiarly equivocating letter (later published) about the coming convention in which he tried to cover himself from all sides. On the one hand, he said, there seemed to be a "substantial unanimity of the Union party" against the Convention, but on the other hand, the convention "should not disturb the integrity or ascendancy" of the party; on the one hand, it looked as though the convention might be "mainly in the hands of the Copperheads"; on the other hand, "it may possibly exclude the extreme Copperheads and Rebels, and lay down a platform which shall com-

[84] This was easier said than done; Doolittle himself was not unaware of the difficulty. See below, p. 407.

[85] New York *Times*, June 27, 1866.

[86] New York *Tribune*, June 29, 1866; *Harper's Weekly*, X (July 14, 1866), 434; *Nation*, II (June 28, 1866), 817.

[87] Raymond to Weed, July 12, 1866, in Raymond, "Journal," p. 276. Barnes, *Memoir of Thurlow Weed*, p. 452.

mand the respect of the whole country." On the one hand, the radicals had throughout the winter said many "rash things" and urged many "crazy schemes"; but on the other hand, the proposed constitutional amendment was in itself "reasonable, wise, and popular," and the President had "made a great mistake" in taking a stand against it. As for what he himself planned to do about the convention, Raymond was not quite prepared to say: "I shall be governed in my course toward it by developments."[88] Thurlow Weed, meanwhile, was having his own troubles among his henchmen throughout the state. Many of the Weed appointees, though not specifically refusing to co-operate, had their reservations about the Philadelphia convention and, by one excuse and another, were letting the Boss know how reluctant they were at getting unduly involved in it.[89]

The Democratic party now represented one of those problems that would not let itself be talked out of existence; it soon became apparent that the Democratic tail was growing bigger and faster than the Unionist dog. With the bulk of support coming from Democrats, there was no way either to prevent them from becoming increasingly influential or to discriminate—in the face of the Democrats' own unwillingness to do so—in culling out the extreme Copperheads. Doolittle and Raymond had already rehearsed this impasse between them even before the call was issued. Doolittle, taking his draft to Raymond for final suggestions in mid-June, had been told by the latter that the call should try to exclude all those disloyal during the war and all who had sympathized with them. But this would hardly have brought many Southerners to Philadelphia; and Doolittle pointed out, in effect, that the only applicable test was loyalty now. In short, virtually no one would be excluded.[90]

[88] Augustus Maverick, *Henry J. Raymond and the New York Press* (Hartford: A. S. Hale, 1870), pp. 173–74. Raymond published the letter in the *Times*, Oct. 15, 1866.

[89] "I am not so fully posted as to the purposes and prospects of the proposed New Organization as I could wish," wrote Alonzo Hawley from Hinsdale, "and do not know what would be expected of me if I should identify myself with it. . . . An open demonstration on my part would I think render me powerless for doing good in this district." A. Hawley to Weed, July 15, 1866, Weed MSS. William S. Lincoln, running for Congress in the Twenty-sixth District, wanted to assure Weed of his loyalty but hoped Weed would understand why he was having to run on the radical Republican ticket. "I am running on the Radical ticket and as none but a Radical can be elected in that district I want you should see to it that I have *fair play* and I will duly appreciate same." He also remarked, with surprising matter-of-factness, that his vote might be cut down by accusations that he was "a friend of Messrs Weed & Raymond." W. S. Lincoln to Weed, Sept. 2, 1866, Weed MSS.

[90] Raymond, "Journal," p. 276. But though the call itself could not discriminate, the managers still tried to discriminate in practice. "They would have only what they called War Democrats," *Harper's* observed, "and reactionary Republicans from the

From the Democrats' own point of view there was no such dilemma. Their position was actually quite free and flexible, having a "take it or leave it" quality which allowed them to move whichever way local circumstances should define as the more expedient. The "take it" side, if that should be the party's pleasure, had a logic which was not easy to answer: we are the only ones who really support Johnson; how can you keep us out? "It is plain enough—this question of supporting the President," wrote A. E. Burr, a Democratic leader of Connecticut:

The Democratic voters to a man, are with him. The Republican voters, by a large majority are against him, and with Stevens and Sumner. Unite all the friends of the President and he could carry almost all the Northern States, or at least a majority of them. But if he depends upon his friends within the Republican party and there alone, he will certainly be defeated at every point. He has enemies in his own cabinet and nearly all the offices all over the country are filled by his opponents.[91]

The Copperheads had not the least intention of standing back; some of the state Democratic delegations to Philadelphia were even planning to go under their regular party organizations.[92]

Equally feasible was the "leave it" side of the Democratic logic. The Democrats, to be sure, had everything to gain by going into the movement if it were run on terms to their liking; also clear, however, was the little they had to lose by staying out if it were not. The Democrats could have it both ways. They could go in or stay out, or they could just temporize. "You ask to know my views," wrote the Illinois state Democratic chairman to Cyrus Hall McCormick, "with regard to the position of the Democratic Party of Illinois in relation to the Philadelphia Convention. Simply masterly inactivity."[93] The Penn-

---

North, and those who had not been conspicuous rebels from the South. This was an impossible distinction at the North; for the last party platform of the Democracy was that made at Chicago, which was the work of Vallandigham, and was equally supported by the Peace Democrats and the War Democrats. . . . The line which divided them as Peace and War Democrats was invisible when compared with that which united them simply as Democrats. Moreover, as a matter of fact, the Democratic party was the party of opposition to the war. It acted as a unit in the election of 1864 during the war, and at the State elections of 1865 after the war was over. It, therefore, could not submit to being divided in 1866 by any external authority." In short, from the Democrats' viewpoint it was all or nothing; and the managers deluded themselves if they imagined that they had very much choice in setting the terms; the movement could not have lasted twenty-four hours without the Democratic party. *Harper's Weekly*, X (Aug. 25, 1866), 530–31.

[91] A. E. Burr to Welles, July 8, 1866, Welles MSS, Library of Congress.

[92] John A. Dix to Doolittle, July 23, 1866, in Duane Mowry, "Some Political Letters of Reconstruction Days Succeeding the Civil War," *American Historical Magazine (Americana)*, IV (May, 1909), 335.

[93] Isaac R. Diller to C. H. McCormick, July 23, 1866, McCormick MSS, Historical Society of Wisconsin.

sylvania Democrats initially regarded the movement with some suspicion: "The programme for new party is all right if confined to their organization," the chairman of that state's committee had written when he first heard of it, "but must not be permitted to affect us—and we can afford to encourage their movement if we are *forewarned* of their purposes."[94] But as things turned out, the Johnson Republicans in Pennsylvania agreed to support the regular Democratic candidate for governor, and the Democrats quite obviously had nothing to lose. Their attitude was comfortably summed up in a letter to James Buchanan from a Democratic worker about to make his way to Philadelphia: "There may be some trouble with some extreme friends sent from the South or the West, but in every respect in which I can view things at this time I am led to think the convention may do good and cannot well do harm."[95]

Whatever the Democrats did, in any case, they would make no move to jeopardize their own party, and the reasons were exactly analogous in reverse to those of the regular Republicans for *their* decision to stay clear of the movement entirely. The Democrats' chances of victory in the coming election, like those of the Republicans, would be at a maximum with the full power of their party machinery behind them. The unusual Republican strength which was then developing throughout most Northern states might indeed cut into Democratic totals, but even so, the Democrats' prospects were as good as they had been in years. There was little reason why they should water down those prospects, either by submerging their extreme Copperhead element or by abandoning any part of their integrity as an organization.

There was, moreover, the matter of principle. Few elections would ever be fought out on such clear differences of principle as the one shortly to take place, and the Republicans' principles were not the only kind. In wartime great numbers of peace-loving men, faced with the horror of hundreds of thousands of kindred Americans destroying one another, could conscientiously espouse what the Republicans were calling "Copperheadism." A majority of the Democratic party had in

94 W. A. Wallace to W. Bigler, Mar. 28, 1866, Bigler MSS.

95 David R. Porter to Buchanan, July 21, 1866 (also Sept. 16), Buchanan MSS, Pennsylvania Historical Society. The Johnson Republicans' support of Clymer was not accorded, however, without some soul-searching. The Copperhead tinge hung about the candidate with sufficient persistence that emissaries from the National Union committee tried late in August to buy him off with a foreign mission, by authority of President Johnson, in order to let a more solid Unionist be nominated in his place. Clymer, with the support of persons high in the regular Democratic organization, indignantly spurned the bribe. W. A. Wallace to W. Bigler, Aug. 28, 1866; Hiester Clymer to Bigler, Sept. 6, 1866; E. M. Clymer to Bigler, Sept. 17, 1866, Bigler MSS.

effect set itself against the Republicans' conception of total war, and that commitment had been solidified by a process that went quite beyond the ordinary. Principles had been tested, as it were, through fire and adversity, and men had suffered together for them. "I have never known any good to come to the Democratic party from hiding or suppressing their principles for the sake of expediency," wrote former President Buchanan from his retirement. "A bold avowal and maintenance of them can alone insure its triumph."[96] By many Democrats those principles had been advocated in extreme form, but then it is seldom easy to rebuke excessive zeal in a holy cause. As the major parties girded for new battle, the Democrats would be no more willing to repudiate their extremists than were the Republicans to repudiate theirs. There was thus a peculiar sense in which each party had tacitly accepted the label pinned on it by the other; the Republicans had become the Radical party, the Democrats the Copperhead party.

Here, then, was the setting in which disaffected Unionists were trying to organize a "third force"—a setting of grim warfare about to break loose between the major parties. If that "force," defenseless and irresolute between the two armies, could not decide what it was and where it belonged, then there was more than a little likelihood of its being either shredded to bits or swallowed up by one side or the other.[97]

With the meeting of the Philadelphia convention, despite the optimism which marked the occasion and its aftermath, the sapping process became irresistible. For all the apparent determination

[96] Buchanan to George Leiper, Nov. 30, 1866, Buchanan MSS. Buchanan in this letter was apparently passing judgment on those of his party brethren who may have compromised their party principles during the campaign. "It is certain," he said, "we have not made much by our alliance with Johnson republicanism." Indeed, one of former Governor Bigler's friends in Pennsylvania, a Peace Democrat from Mercer, was fully convinced that by 1866 the party's old purity in his district had been subverted by trimmers. "The leaders of the Democracy here are not Democrats at all," he wrote morbidly. "They were nearly all in the Union party after the war commenced for from 1 to 2 yrs and bellowed as loud for coercion and war as any abolitionist in the country." He gave the names of two such men, "the 1st a man of no principle who many a time said that such men as you and I ought to be in Fort Warren and the latter a young squirt who edited a paper at the beginning of the war which advised that such men as we are ought to be hung. . . ." R. M. DeFrance to Bigler, July 21 and Aug. 6, 1866, Bigler MSS.

[97] "The . . . Philadelphia Convention can not change the real aspect of the situation. It may be a convenient gate for discontented Unionists to enter the Democratic fold; but the great contest will still be fought out by the Union and Democratic parties. There will not in this State, for instance, be three differing parties at the autumn elections; and even should there be apparently three, two of them will be merely allies against the other." *Harper's Weekly,* X (Aug. 25, 1866), 531.

that was pushing the movement forward, there were at the same time forces now in full motion working from both within and without to drag it back and to keep it from acquiring a separate and distinct organizational character. This sapping of will and energy was a process that worked both on the organization and on the men.

The Unionists' partial capitulation to the Southerners, after being much harassed by them, was a feature of the preliminaries that removed any last claim which the new organization might have had to "Republican" principles. Henry J. Raymond had finally been persuaded, after great reluctance, to take an active part in the convention and to deliver its main address. This address had to be very closely connected with the Declaration of Principles to be presented to the convention, and the same Committee on Resolutions—of which Raymond was a member but upon which Southerners predominated[98]—was to pass upon both. There was very little operating margin in these committee meetings; the atmosphere was far too tense.

Raymond read his first draft to the committee, and there were a number of things in it to which the Southerners made hot objection. He had touched ever so indirectly on the pending Fourteenth Amendment by suggesting that perhaps "some enlargement" of the government's powers "in the respects covered" by the amendment "might be desirable." The reaction to this was immediate; the committee would have none of it. Any hint that the amendment met with the convention's approval, even tacitly, had to be struck out. When Raymond finished reading his draft it was quite clear to him that the touchy Southerners just did not like the tone of it. Why must he keep using such words as "rebellion" and "insurrection"? Why did he have to say so much about the destructive effects of slavery on prewar politics? Actually Raymond needed both these items, the first for his constitutional logic, and the second to underscore the intersectional harmony which should prevail now that slavery had been done away with. Raymond, working hard for a "harmony" which was not really there, did what he could to placate the late enemy by censoring out as many offensive words as possible. A similar difficulty arose over one of the resolutions, in which the "American soldier" was praised for his courage (references to his "patriotism" and his "stay-at-home neighbor" had already been struck out) and which the Southerners felt should

---

[98] This was Raymond's own assertion; it is not clear whether he meant in terms of numbers (there were supposed to be two members on the committee from each state), or of initiative. Perhaps he exaggerated. His exact statement was: "Southern delegates preponderated on this Committee, and were mainly strong men." Raymond, "Journal," p. 279.

apply to both Union and Confederate soldiers. In order to prevent the committee's adjourning without passing any resolutions at all about the soldiers, Raymond offered a last-minute proposal; The federal government should recognize the soldiers' services by paying off "their just and rightful claims." This proposal, which was adopted, was as far as the committee would go.[99]

Then there was difficulty with the Northern Democrats. Although the delegations abounded with Copperheads, the Unionists' already shaky equanimity was not quite proof against the appearance of such notorious personages as Fernando Wood and Clement L. Vallandigham. Pre-convention feeling was thus further confused over the problem of what, if anything, ought to be done with them. Raymond wrote in his journal:

The Democrats felt that it would hardly answer to desert members of their own party, and Southern men thought their constituents would not approve of their consenting that men from the North should be ejected for having been their friends during the war. The collision of sentiment gave rise to the usual turmoil and heat which attends the outside discussions of such a body.

After considerable pressure, which must have struck many of the delegates as ungracious and unseemly, these two Democratic zealots were persuaded to withdraw.[100]

The sessions of the convention, opening on August 14 and lasting three days, were very orderly; but neither the physical nor the parliamentary arrangements were conducive to very much real exuberance. There were throngs of delegates from everywhere, great numbers of them from the South; the Southerners represented, according to the *Herald*, "all classes of society, from general officers to resurrected politicians." But the hotel accommodations were all located about three miles away from the convention hall itself, which was a huge, damp, half-finished, hastily constructed wooden building situated out in a northwestern suburb. "Any decent Indian would be ashamed to have it as a wigwam," complained the *Herald* reporter, who then added that "a better building and a better site would have been provided but for the intrigues of local radicals." Officials of the city railway system (themselves tinged, perhaps, with radical malice) neglected to put on extra cars, so that there was much jamming and crowding, and the sweating delegates riding back and forth afforded abundant game for the local pickpockets. Heavy showers the first day forced several thousand people, after adjournment, to remain for some time inside the

[99] *Ibid.*, pp. 279–80. [100] *Ibid.*, p. 278.

queer structure until the weather cleared up. As for the business of the convention, the managers had so arranged things that there should be no impromptu oratory from the floor. All resolutions were to be reported without debate to the appropriate committees, and each day's session—none of which lasted more than a few hours—was devoted mainly to set speeches and reports.[101]

The most dramatic event was a prearranged scene which occurred at the very outset on opening day. After the spectators and delegates had all assembled and seated themselves, Postmaster-General Randall, who was on the platform, arose, peered down the aisle, and cried out: "Gentlemen of the Convention, I have to announce to you the approach of the delegates from Massachusetts and South Carolina, arm-in-arm." Thereupon ensued the triumphant entry of Governor James L. Orr of South Carolina, a man of great stature and bulk, drawing along with him a very small Yankee, General D. N. Couch of Massachusetts. Following after them, similarly paired off, were the rest of the delegates from the two former enemy states. Unsympathetic observers made sport of the episode, though sympathetic ones reported that it was very affecting to witness a scene so symbolic of reconciliation.[102]

But this rehearsed quality, the note of careful discipline and order, permeated the entire proceedings. Real spontaneity, improperly controlled, could reveal all sorts of very unharmonious and non-fraternal sentiments, and the managers could at no point afford to let the delegates say everything that was on their minds. A real flare-up might possibly wreck the whole affair.[103] So the margin of chance was wisely kept as narrow as possible, and men generally stayed on their best behavior. Even the band music was judiciously graded, with a due number of renditions of "Dixie" interspersed with "Yankee Doodle" and

101 The present account is based primarily on the reports of the convention in the New York *Herald*, August 15, 16, and 17, 1866. The item on the Southerners appeared August 11. Pictures of the Philadelphia "wigwam," both inside and out, are shown in *Harper's Weekly*, X (Sept. 1, 1866), 545–46.

102 New York *Herald*, Aug. 15, 1866; New York *Times*, Aug. 15, 1866. Nast's terrible caricature of the "Arm in Arm Convention" appeared in *Harper's Weekly* in the issue of September 29, 1866 (X, 617). An earlier one, by another artist, appeared in the same magazine on September 1 (X, 551). "Postmaster-General Randall knew perfectly well that Massachusetts could enter his Convention only in the person of a man like John A. Andrew," a *Harper's* editorial asserted. "If he staid away Massachusetts was not there" (X, 547).

103 "The Convention was ostensibly intended to afford opportunity for consultation and frank expression of opinion between fellow-citizens long alienated," *Harper's* pointed out. "But no expression was permitted. The way in which the managers controlled the proceedings showed that they feared to allow general debate" (X, 546).

"Rally round the Flag, Boys." The major item of interest the first day was a speech by the temporary chairman, General Dix, whose principal points no one disputed. The convention had assembled to "vindicate and restore" the Constitution; with ten states still unrepresented the country was not living under the government which the fathers had formed; there was no likelihood that the proposed constitutional amendment would be ratified, and Congress had no right to prescribe it as a condition of readmission anyway; and finally: "When the President of the United States declared that armed resistance to the authority of the Union was over, all the States had a right to representation in Congress."

The second day was largely a matter of committee reports and referrals; Senator Doolittle assumed the convention's permanent chairmanship and made a speech, whose theme was harmony and reunion. If the entire people of the United States could look in upon this scene, he said, "our work would be already done. . . . If they could have seen this body, greater in numbers and in weight of character and brain than any convention that ever yet assembled on this continent under one roof, melted to tears of joy and gratitude to witness this commingling [of Massachusetts and South Carolina], there would be no struggle at the polls in the coming election."[104]

The third and final day of the convention was devoted to the reading of Raymond's address (in its censored form) and the Declaration of Principles. The culminating note of the address was immediate and unqualified readmission of the South, and the arguments, arranged in a precise, able, and orderly manner, were familiar to all. The country was at peace and the convention was not there to deal with any but peaceful matters. The government's victory had settled two things: that slavery existed no longer and that the right of secession had never existed at all. The real character and purpose of the war had been the government's effort to maintain its authority, not to gain new powers for itself; the Constitution had not changed, and there could still be no such thing as "conquered provinces" or abrogation of the states' equal suffrage in Congress. Raymond then enumerated and repelled what he considered to be certain false and erroneous allegations. It had been claimed that the states voluntarily forfeited their right of representation; but representation was a duty as well as a right, and duties could not be forfeited. Some argued that the rights presently being claimed by Congress flowed from the rights of war; but it had been an insurrectionary uprising, not a war. Constitutional changes, some said, were

[104] New York *Herald*, Aug. 15 and 16, 1866.

necessary in order to secure certain guarantees; but the Constitution could only be amended in the proper way by the full participation of all the states. Finally, it had been asserted that the rebellious states could not safely be readmitted without guarantees of their future loyalty; but they were now clearly loyal—there was no further inclination to rebel against the authority of the Union. Therefore, he concluded,

We call upon you in every Congressional district of every State, to secure the election of members, who, whatever other differences may characterize their political action, will unite in recognizing the RIGHT OF EVERY STATE OF THE UNION TO REPRESENTATION IN CONGRESS. . . .[105]

Throughout the convention there had been only two breaches of discipline, but those two breaches were gravely symptomatic. They underscored the basic liability which would prevent the entire movement from achieving anything like an independent organizational character. On the second day, the leader of the Ohio delegation moved that Vallandigham's letter of withdrawal be read to the convention, and the chairman's efforts to prevent it were drowned amid cheers, applause, and shouts of "Read! Read!" The letter was thereupon read; contained in it was a resolution of loyalty to Vallandigham which had been passed by his delegation:

Resolved unanimously by the Ohio democratic delegation, That we recognize the right of Hon. Clement L. Vallandigham, a duly elected delegate from the Third Congressional district of Ohio, to hold a seat in that Convention; that we should regard his exclusion from such seat as an unjust and unreasonable infringement of the rights of the democracy of said district, and are ready to stand by him in the assertion of his rights and the rights of his constituents; that we endorse most cordially the purity and patriotism of his motives, and his fitness in every way to a seat in said Convention; yet for the sake of harmony and good feeling in the same, and in order to secure the great ends for which it is called, we consent to his withdrawal from a seat in the Convention if in his judgment his duty to his constituents shall justify such withdrawal.

The letter then states, in accents of dignity, Vallandigham's desire "that there shall be no pretext from any quarter for any controverted question or disturbing element in the Convention to mar its harmony," and accordingly he would decline to take his seat. In closing, the martyr pronounced his blessing upon the convention's work, and thereby had the last word, after all, in the case of *National Union Convention* v. *C. L. Vallandigham.*[106]

The other disturbance was created by S. S. Hayes, another Demo-

[105] Maverick, *Raymond*, p. 458; New York *Herald*, Aug. 17, 1866.
[106] *Ibid.*, Aug. 16, 1866.

crat from Ohio, who objected violently to the plan of allowing no open deliberation or debate on the resolutions until the convention should be at last permitted to vote upon them. Before he was finally squelched, Hayes declared:

The general platform of the Convention should not, in my opinion, impinge on the opinions of the party to which I belong upon points in regard to which the Union and democrat party have differed. When I came here, in response to an invitation made to democrats, I naturally expected that the Convention would do nothing and say nothing in their platform, to which I, as a constitution loving and Union loving democrat could not subscribe. I know the sentiment of the democratic party of this country. I, sir, am proud to be a member of the democratic party, and I believe that if there ever was a patriotic party in the world, it has been the democratic party.[107]

"If the Philadelphia Convention should make separate nominations," commented *Harper's Weekly* afterward, "it will be with the simple intention of attempting to divide the Union vote in favor of the Democratic candidate. This is the sole practical result of the Philadelphia Convention, and this was obvious from the beginning."[108]

Whether or not the National Union movement actually did divide the vote very much, after all was said and done, is dubious. The Democrats accommodated themselves to the movement by simply gobbling it up, a process nowhere more evident than in the National Union "stronghold," New York. There, a state "National Union" convention, called for nominating state officers, took place several weeks after the Philadelphia convention and was under the full management of the Democrats. Thurlow Weed, who had at first nurtured high hopes for the outcome, soon found his plans pushed badly askew. The original idea had been to nominate Weed's candidate for governor, John A. Dix, on a National Union platform. But that had rested on a somewhat tenuous understanding with the state Democratic leader, Dean Richmond, and it is doubtful that Richmond had ever been very heartily committed to Dix anyway.[109] In any event, with Richmond's sudden death shortly before the convention, Weed's

---

[107] *Ibid.*   [108] X (Sept. 1, 1866), 546.

[109] Dorothy Dodd, *Henry J. Raymond and the New York Times during Reconstruction* (Chicago: University of Chicago Libraries, 1936), p. 60. It was even claimed by some that Richmond's real candidate was Henry C. Murphy of Brooklyn, though Weed had not so assumed. Stebbins, *Political History of New York*, pp. 100, 112; New York *Times*, Oct. 9, 1866. "Up to the time of Mr. Richmonds death," wrote Tilden to Hugh McCulloch, "the arrangement for the State nominations was that the Democrats should take the Governor, and the Republicans the Lieut. Governor. The only chance

schemes began to crumble. When the gathering convened at Albany on September 11, it was overrun by Tammany men and became, in effect, the regular Democratic state nominating convention. The Republicans by that time had already nominated Governor Reuben E. Fenton, a thoroughgoing radical, and the regular Democrats thereupon saw no further point in flirting with pale-faced "moderates." Weed's position had deteriorated to little more than that of an ineffectual dilettante. He and Dix were brusquely shouldered aside as the Democrats, all pretenses gone, proceeded to nominate one of their own—John T. Hoffman, a good Tammany regular, comfortably tinged with copper. "Thurlow Weed is an old, played-out stump," exclaimed one of the delegates with callous joviality, "and he cannot shove any old-time granny like Dix on the Democratic party! No! not if the Court knows itself, which she thinks she does."[110]

The National Union "party" of 1866, which had never had a chance to become a party at all, was just about drained of its life and energy by election time. As a matter of personal experience, the same might be said of the men who had attached themselves to this movement, hoping to find a true third alternative for themselves in the expression of a political position. The principle of withdrawal in the face of divided loyalty may give the best clue to what became of their energy.[111] Strictly speaking, the movement had never made sense to

_____

that Dix had was in a movement which was originated by me. It was contingent on events which could not be controlled, and on the failure of which, it was only to be persisted in under such circumstances which could not be prudently defied." S. J. Tilden to McCulloch, Sept. 17, 1866, Tilden MSS.

110 Stebbins, *Political History of New York*, p. 104 n.; New York *Tribune*, Sept. 12, 1866. A description of the entire affair is in Stebbins, pp. 99–112.

111 Here is how the principle has been stated in a study of political behavior made in our own time:

"How are interest and cross-pressures inter-related? Remembering that controversy often makes issues exciting, we might expect that those for whom the decision is difficult would become most involved with and concerned about the election. But that would leave out of the reckoning a basic pattern of human adjustment. When people desire and shun a course of action in about equal degree, they often do not decide for or against it but rather change the subject or avoid the matter altogether. For many clashes of interest, the easy way to get out of the uncomfortable situation is simply to discount its importance and to give up the conflict as not worth the bother." Paul F. Lazarsfeld, Bernard Berelson, and Hazel Gaudet, *The People's Choice* (New York: Duell, Sloan & Pearce, 1944), pp. 61–62. In a footnote to this passage, the authors call attention to the psychological "Field Theory" of Kurt Lewin. "In developing that theory, Lewin showed, for example, that if a child is acted upon by a psychological force drawing him toward a goal and [is] at the same time acted upon by an equal and opposite force pushing him away from that goal, he would 'solve' the problem by moving away from both forces rather than in the direction of either. In other words, the 'resultant' leads out of the field."

any but stranded Unionists in the first place, whose dilemma was that of trying to be "Unionists" with fully certified Democratic principles —and of standing aside, at the same time, from the full implications of associating with wartime Democrats.

The National Unionist was in the present-day sense a "fellow traveler"—a man taking a position of limited involvement in preference to the full commitment—and he was thus subject to all the agonies, as the time for action approached, of being brought closer and closer to a choice which he had never really visualized and to a decision which he had hoped, deep down, never to have to make.[112] We have a few glimpses, in personal letters of the time, of men undergoing just such torments. These unfortunate persons, about to find themselves face to face with real-life Copperheads, were having to make up their minds. Would they smother their misgivings and go ahead and work with these men—or would they simply get out? There was the case of General James T. Pratt, a Johnson Republican of Connecticut who in July was preparing to take a leading part in the state National Union convention to be held at New Haven on August 4. Writing to Gideon Welles on July 19, Pratt expressed all the appropriate sentiments; he denounced Congress and the radicals and affirmed: "That we shall have a respectable gathering I have no doubt." But the note of dead-heartedness robs the words of all vigor:

When the call for the Convention was first published it was pretty generally well received by all except a few Thad Stevens disciples: but the endorsement of the "democratic" M.Cs. set back a good many. Those who sustained the Govt. during the rebellion have a horror of Copperheads: and I must confess, I cant fellowship with them until they repudiate their war record, declare the Chicago platform, at least, a mistake, and agree to behave in future.[113]

Pratt did go to the convention, but the sight of his new associates there was too much for him. "Gen Pratt left the Convention in a formal manner," Welles was told by another correspondent. "His ostensible reason was, the election of Cleveland as a delegate—but he has not been satisfied for some time. He wanted an exclusive party, from which Burr, Osborne, etc. should be omitted. . . . I do not know where he will go or what he will do now."[114] Such cases were reported with

[112] Much of the energy of the Wallaceites in the 1948 campaign was sapped by the realization that they were having to associate with actual Communists.

[113] Pratt to Welles, July 19, 1866, Welles MSS.

[114] James F. Babcock to Welles, Aug. 5, 1866, Welles MSS. The withdrawal of another delegate (for similar reasons) was given in the same letter. Another description of Pratt's withdrawal was given in a letter from A. E. Burr to Welles, Aug. 13, 1866,

gloomy frequency by the lieutenants of Thurlow Weed, often as excuses for their own flagging zeal. One of the reasons "why Republicans dont take hold of this Convention," according to the federal marshal at Brooklyn, was "the excessive haste and zeal displayed by Democrats heretofore distinguished as violent Copperheads who are giving out what they are going to do and stigmatising the Republicans who dont follow them. And it is this that is distasteful to our people in the matter of the Philadelphia Convention."[115] " 'Our people' have a great aversion to associating with Copperheads," wrote a worker from Albany to Frederick Seward. "We will be troubled to send the right sort of delegation from 'our district.' "[116] Another from Syracuse told Weed that "the rush of pilgrims from the disloyal democracy to Phila. renders it again doubtful whether we can go there."[117] Even in England, Charles Francis Adams, one of the founders of the Republican party in Massachusetts who now favored Johnson's position on constitutional grounds, was all too unhappily aware of the choices now confronting him:

My own situation . . . becomes a painful one, the moment I shall be called to take a side. For I cannot help seeing that my friends will generally be against me, and I shall find myself thrown among those with whom I have had heretofore little sympathy. The only way open to me to avoid this difficulty is to remain here for the present, and on my return home to hit the moment when I can return to private life without observation.[118]

These Unionists, trying to steer an "independent" course, were not only being undermined by their own revulsion at the presence of persons whose political associations offended their taste; they were also subjected to the most punishing moral pressures from both political camps. For the most fully revealing of all such experiences, one comes back again to the case of Henry J. Raymond, some particulars of

---

Welles MSS. "Still," Burr asserted, "no great harm will follow—the Convention was all right, and regarded principle rather than personal preferences."

115 Anthony F. Campbell to Weed, July 10, 1866, Weed MSS.

116 Hugh Hastings to Frederick Seward, July 11, 1866, Seward MSS.

117 V. W. Smith to Weed, July 19, 1866, Weed MSS. "Our people as you are aware are very radical," Weed heard from Albion, "and though very many of them do not approve the action of Congress but do approve the policy of the President, yet they have a terrible fear that the convention will fall under the control of men who opposed the war and sympathized with the rebels." D. H. Cole to Weed, July 19, 1866, Weed MSS. And from Homer: "The Conservative men of our section have a great horror of going over to the Copperheads. . . ." Samuel Smith to Weed, Aug. 23, 1866, Weed MSS.

118 Charles Francis Adams, "Diary," July 25, 1866, Adams MSS, Massachusetts Historical Society.

which have been mentioned already. We may imagine that whatever resilience Raymond still retained by August must have been about wrung out of him in the course of being pushed into line at Philadelphia; just how he felt on the way home can remain a matter of conjecture. But there were still further blows awaiting him. Raymond had been chairman of the National Committee during the victorious Union campaign of 1864, and technically he still held that position in 1866. The cruel test came, however, when four members of the Union Republican National Committee took matters into their own hands and called an illegal meeting to be held at Philadelphia on September 3. Raymond himself promptly called another meeting of the same committee, to be held the same day in New York. Seven members showed up at Raymond's meeting; fifteen others went to Philadelphia, and the Philadelphia meeting—though having no quorum—proceeded not only to oust Raymond as chairman but also to eject him and two other Johnson members from the committee entirely. Their action was ratified by the New York Republican convention then in session at Syracuse. Meanwhile the New York *Times* had lost about a third of its readers over Raymond's unpopular editorial policy, incurring losses which, according to the editor's own estimate, amounted to upwards of $100,000.[119]

The so-called National Union convention at Albany, where the regular Democrats of the state had jubilantly wrecked the National Union movement and made the affair their own, was apparently the last straw for Henry J. Raymond. He had recommended that all good "Philadelphia men" should support it (though he himself did not attend), and he even went through the motions afterward of indorsing the Hoffman nomination. But this state of shock lasted no more than two or three days. On September 15 Raymond published an open letter to his constituents announcing his decision not to run again for Congress: "I shall best consult my own self-respect, as well as the sentiments of my constituents and the interest of the Union cause, by withdrawing my name from the canvass altogether." At the same time, Raymond repudiated the Hoffman ticket. Two weeks later, he repudiated Andrew Johnson.[120]

[119] Stebbins, *Political History of New York*, p. 85; Dodd, *Raymond*, pp. 59–60, 63. Tilden in a letter to McCulloch noted the drop in the *Times's* circulation. S. J. Tilden to H. McCulloch, Sept. 17, 1866, Tilden MSS.

[120] Maverick, *Raymond*, pp. 174, 186–90; Dodd, *Raymond*, p. 63.

Johnson
and the
Election Campaign
of 1866

In the issue which was fought out in the fall elections of 1866 there was an extraordinary absence of vagueness and ambiguity. It was a case in which a political party found itself campaigning against its own President and in which the President took a savagely personal part in campaigning against his party. In effect, a victory for the party's opposition would be a victory for him. The issue in this election was the immediate and unqualified readmission of the Southern states to congressional representation, and it had been reduced by then to a degree of clarity and simplicity that hardly anyone would have thought possible a few months before.

In less than a month after the Philadelphia convention, it had become obvious that everything was going one way, and that President Johnson was getting all the worst of it. Many of the Unionist supporters whom the President might still have claimed in the early summer—such men as Henry J. Raymond, Jacob D. Cox, and Henry Ward Beecher—had by this time either deserted him or lapsed into neutrality. The Maine election early in September was an emphatic show of Republican power which pointed rather clearly to a Republican sweep everywhere.

Historians have in general tended to identify three major aspects of the campaign, in addition to those already discussed, that contributed most prominently to the deterioration of the Executive position. They are the New Orleans riot of July 30, in which some two hundred Negroes and white Unionists were killed or wounded; Johnson's "Swing around the Circle," in the course of which the Chief Magistrate came in for unprecedented popular abuse; and the influence of a radical press upon public opinion generally.

I   THE NEW ORLEANS RIOT

The bloody affair at New Orleans in July, 1866, involved the most questionable behavior on every side, but the very circumstances of its origin were such that no matter how judiciously the responsibility was allocated, the Republican party stood to profit in the eyes of the public, and Johnson was pretty much bound to come out the loser.

By the spring of 1866 the Louisiana government of J. Madison Wells had come to find itself in precarious straits. Wells the year before had curried favor with ex-Confederate elements, had discriminated against native radicals, and had given vigorous public support to the policies of Andrew Johnson. But although Wells was re-elected governor in November, 1865, the honeymoon very quickly faded in the wake of an election which gave the state a Democratic lieutenant governor and brought the legislature under the virtually unanimous control of ex-Confederates. This legislature passed a black code for Louisiana—one of the severest anywhere—early in 1866, and Wells found his personal machine about to fall apart following the passage of legislation for local self-rule which removed a major share of the governor's patronage. After receiving what amounted to a direct order from Johnson, Wells reluctantly permitted an election for a mayor of New Orleans, and the man elected was John T. Monroe, an unpardoned rebel whom Johnson thereupon pardoned. Parish elections brought overwhelming Democratic majorities. The position of the Louisiana Unionists—virtually Wells's only source of support by this time—was thus desperate. The most promising solution to their dilemma that they could now think of was to reconvene the constitutional convention of 1864, under a reconvoking clause—whose legality, after all this time, was dubious to say the least—and to have the convention disfranchise ex-Confederates and enact Negro suffrage.[1] Similar steps had been taken in wartime Tennessee under the Johnson regime. But there were differences; this was peacetime, and Johnson, now President, had pronounced the state of Louisiana fully reconstructed.

At a caucus of convention members held on June 26, 1866, it was found that since not more than thirty or forty of the original delegates

[1] Willie Malvin Caskey, *Secession and Restoration of Louisiana* (University, La.: University of Louisiana Press, 1938), pp. 165–204, 211–14; Johnson to J. Madison Wells, Mar. 2, 1866, Johnson MSS ("Telegrams"), Library of Congress.

were likely to turn up for a new meeting, it would be necessary to elect some fifty more in order to have a quorum. Judge Edmund H. Durrell, who had been the convention's president, did not want to issue a call, since he could see no legal authority for doing so, whereupon Durrell was deposed and a call issued anyway. Wells, while managing to take no direct part in these proceedings, still co-operated with the movement, signing a call for the election of new delegates to be held on September 3. Meanwhile the convention rump, with faint prospects of success in an open election, decided to hold their meeting on July 30, quorum or no quorum.[2]

The Democratic officials of the state—most prominent of whom were Lieutenant Governor Albert Voorhies and Mayor Monroe—thereupon made up their minds that the convention meeting had to be stopped, come what might. Monroe wrote to General Absalom Baird, the local commander, on July 25 saying that an unlawful assembly was about to be held, "calculated to disturb the public peace," and that if the meeting did not have the sanction of the military he planned to have the delegates arrested. The following day Baird replied that he neither sanctioned nor forbade the meeting, since the government's policy was to keep the military aloof from the state's political affairs, but that Monroe himself hardly had the right to undertake such a decision on his own authority. He said that the meeting's legality was a matter for the courts to decide. If the mayor thought there was a likelihood of violence, and if he felt that his local police were not adequate for controlling it, then as many troops would be furnished as might be needed.[3]

Two messages went out to Washington from New Orleans on July 28. One was from Lieutenant Governor Voorhies to the President, reporting a radical pre-convention mass meeting in the city, composed of large numbers of Negroes, during which incendiary speeches had been made. He said that Governor Wells was siding with the radicals but that he, Voorhies, and the attorney-general were planning to arrest the convention delegates under a process from the criminal court. "Is the military," he asked, "to interfere to prevent process of court?" Johnson sent a brisk reply the same day: "The military will be expected to sustain, not obstruct or interfere with, the proceedings of

---

2 Caskey, *Secession and Restoration*, pp. 214–18.

3 Monroe to Baird, July 25, 1866, and Baird to Monroe, July 26, 1866, *House Report*, 39 Cong., 2 sess., No. 16, "Report of the Select Committee on the New Orleans Riots," pp. 441–42; also in Johnson MSS ("Telegrams").

the courts."[4] Johnson also wired Wells, demanding to know why he had called such a convention; Wells replied that he had not signed the convention call but only the call for an election.[5] The other message was the famous unanswered telegram from General Baird to Secretary Stanton:

A convention has been called, with the sanction of Governor Wells, to meet here on Monday. The lieutenant governor and city authorities think it unlawful, and propose to break it up by arresting the delegates. I have given no orders on the subject, but have warned the parties that I should not countenance or permit such action without instructions to that effect from the President. Please instruct me by telegraph.[6]

Baird got no reply from Stanton and refused to allow the civil authorities to go ahead with their plans, even after Voorhies had shown him the telegram which he himself received from Johnson. He thought that if the convention were indeed illegal, there would be ample chance for the courts to say so later.

The night before the convention was to meet, the police were called from their beats and armed. About noon on July 30, Voorhies—apparently more anxious than Monroe to avoid violence—now decided that it would be better to have troops on hand after all and called upon Baird to ask for them. Baird thereupon set about making the necessary arrangements to bring the troops into the city but wasted a good deal of time doing so, and by the time they arrived on the scene it was too late to prevent the massacre that had meanwhile taken place. Large numbers of Negro partisans of the convention in the vicinity of the Mechanics' Institute, some of them armed for the purpose of guarding the hall, were assaulted by a mob; and the bloodshed that followed was primarily the work of the police, whom the city authorities made no effort to control. According to the surgeon's report, all but one of the killed and wounded were Negroes and white Unionists, with ten policemen "wounded slightly."[7]

[4] Voorhies and A. J. Herron to Johnson, July 28, 1866; Johnson to Voorhies, July 28, 1866, Johnson MSS ("Telegrams"); "New Orleans Riots," pp. 21, 49. The most inflammatory of these speeches appears to have been one made by Dr. A. P. Dostie, a particularly desperate local radical; for this speech see Walter L. Fleming, *Documentary History of Reconstruction* (Cleveland: A. H. Clark, 1906), I, 231–32. The mob on July 30 wreaked a terrible vengeance on Dostie.

[5] Johnson to Wells, July 28, 1866; Wells to Johnson, July 28, 1866, Johnson MSS ("Telegrams"); "New Orleans Riots," p. 472.

[6] Baird to Stanton, July 28, 1866, Johnson MSS ("Telegrams"); "New Orleans Riots," p. 443.

[7] "New Orleans Riots," pp. 12–16. Cf. Caskey, *Secession and Restoration,* p. 297 n. Caskey's great efforts to excuse the New Orleans authorities for the butchery itself,

All of the political repercussions of the affair fell upon the President, who had put himself, as it turned out, in such a position as to incur criticism either way, and whose subsequent behavior aroused a wave of anger in the North. Secretary Stanton later explained his own failure to answer Baird's message by saying:

There was no intimation in the telegram that force or violence was threatened by those opposed to the convention, or that it was apprehended by General Baird. Upon consideration, it appeared to me that his warning to the city authorities was all that the case then required. . . .[8]

As an excuse for not replying, or for not turning Baird's message over to Johnson, this is not very convincing. It is more than likely that the devious Secretary of War just did not want Johnson to do what Stanton knew he would do if he had received the message—namely, give orders to suppress the convention without waiting for a judicial decision. By insisting that the state was already fully reconstructed, Johnson had forfeited all right to interfere in its internal concerns, but his message to Voorhies and Wells made it clear that he did not intend to be restrained in this case by any such niceties.[9]

General Baird was himself not free from blame. Although Baird did not appear to show any partiality in the affair, and though he claimed to have misunderstood the time of the meeting,[10] he was certainly not as alert as he might have been in getting his troops there. On the other hand, he had no way of knowing how the police were going to behave,

---

when the evidence and testimony seem to go all to the contrary, make that part of his study somewhat unreliable. On the casualties, for instance, he calls it a "fact" that forty-two policemen were "killed or wounded," relying only on a claim later made by Mayor Monroe and ignoring the reports of the surgeon and coroner, which were checked at the time with the hospital and police headquarters and which were very detailed in their figures, even describing the wounds of each patient. They are given in the House committee's report on the riots (pp. 12–16) and show only ten policemen wounded. Caskey does not use this 596-page document at all, taking for granted that it was "biased" and therefore worthless. Actually the House report—as is usually the case with similar documents of similar length—contains a great many internal checks on its own reliability; it contains both a majority and a minority statement on the evidence; both Democrats and Republicans examined witnesses; all the relevant papers are printed in full, with index and summaries; and everyone connected with the affair on all sides was permitted to have his say and to have his testimony printed. In short, it contains, to all intents and purposes, an immense amount of fairly valuable and trustworthy information.

8 "New Orleans Riots," p. 546.

9 Johnson also sent a message to the attorney-general, A. J. Herron, telling him to ask General Sheridan "for sufficient force to sustain the civil authority in suppressing all illegal or unlawful assemblies, who usurp or assume to exercise any power or authority without first having obtained the consent of the people of the State." Johnson to Herron, July 30, 1866, Johnson MSS ("Telegrams").

10 "New Orleans Riots," pp. 443–44.

and in any case he was obviously most reluctant to get himself caught in what was bound to be a very sticky political complication. As for Governor Wells, he was not even on the scene, having absented himself when he heard that bloody work was afoot.[11] Voorhies and Monroe were determined to stop the convention, and were fortified in the knowledge that they had the President's sympathy. Monroe in particular was far more concerned about this than he was about keeping order, and in the investigation that followed, there were few who made much effort to defend his suspicious failure to control the police. The police themselves, as the statistics showed, were clearly out for blood; their principal interest was in killing Negroes.[12] An effort was made to fix the blame on radical members of Congress, and although no evidence was uncovered to prove that congressmen were in touch with the Louisiana Unionists, one may still suppose that they would have been pretty poor radicals had they held aloof from such an excellent chance to stir up trouble within the state. The Unionists, as the minority report later insisted, must have been getting some kind of encouragement for supposing that their work would receive congressional approval.[13]

But it was, after all, the President's behavior that everyone watched. General Sheridan, investigating the riot, sent a report to General Grant two days after it occurred, which was published in the New York *Times* with the key passage suppressed. The dispatch, with the censored portion in italics, is as follows:

You are doubtless aware of the serious riot which occurred in this city on the 30th. A political body, styling itself the convention of 1864, met on the 30th, for, as it is alleged, the purpose of remodelling the present constitution of the State. The leaders were political agitators and revolutionary men, and the action of the convention was liable to produce breaches of the public peace.

I had made up my mind to arrest the head men, if the proceedings of the convention were calculated to disturb the tranquillity of the department; but I had no case for action until they committed the overt act. *In the mean time, official duty called me to Texas, and the mayor of the city, during my absence, suppressed the convention by the use of their police force, and in so doing attacked the members of the convention and a party of two hundred negroes, and with fire-arms, clubs, and knives, in a manner so unnecessary and atrocious as to compel me to say that it was murder.* About forty whites and blacks were thus killed, and about a hundred and

[11] *Ibid.*, p. 438.

[12] For scenes at police headquarters while the police were being armed and instructed in the work they were expected to do, see *ibid.*, esp. pp. 142–47, 201–4.

[13] *Ibid.*, p. 438.

sixty wounded. Everything is now quiet; but I deem it best to maintain a military supremacy in the city for a few days until the affair is fully investigated. I believe the sentiment of the general community is great regret at this unnecessary cruelty, and that the police could have made any arrests they saw fit without sacrificing lives.[14]

Sheridan was much incensed at what he called "this breach of military honor" in tampering with his report.[15] The *Times* correspondent testified that the dispatch was obtained by him at the White House from the President's private secretary, after receiving the President's permission.[16] Henry Ward Beecher, up to that time a strong Johnson supporter, was greatly disillusioned over this incident and said so in a public letter.[17]

Even more decisive for Johnson's position was the President's September 8 speech in St. Louis on the subject of the riot. He expressed no regret over the bloodshed but launched instead into a jumbled tirade against both the New Orleans radicals and radical members of Congress. By not condoning the acts of the police he presumably condemned them; but it was as though he were saying that the radical agitation in Louisiana made the massacre inevitable. After what the police had done, and considering Sheridan's messages, and in view of the rebel antecedents of the Louisiana civil authorities, Johnson's belligerent defense of those authorities had the worst possible effect on Northern public opinion.[18]

14 New York *Times*, Aug. 3, 1866; Sheridan to Grant, Aug. 1, 1866, Johnson MSS ("Telegrams").

15 "New Orleans Riots," pp. 352–53. Besides his first telegram on the riot, Sheridan sent three others: to Grant, Aug. 2 and 3, 1866, and to Johnson, Aug. 6, 1866, all in the Johnson MSS ("Telegrams").

16 "New Orleans Riots," pp. 474–75. This correspondent, W. W. Warden, did not see the document; it was read to him by Johnson's secretary while he took down the words. The paper from which the secretary read is still in the Johnson collection, and one may observe that the controversial passage is marked off in pencil with brackets. The original intention appears to have been to suppress also the sentence following—the one giving figures of killed and wounded—and the bracket was first marked there. It was, however, rubbed out and moved back to include just the passage that the *Times* did in fact omit in its published report. There is further testimony on the incident in *House Reports*, 40 Cong., 1 sess., No. 7, "Impeachment Investigation," pp. 535–40, 635–43.

17 New York *Times*, Sept. 8, 1866. "The perversion and mutilation of Sheridan's despatches needs no characterization. I do not attribute this act to him. Yet it was of such a criminal and disgraceful nature that not to clear himself of it by the exposure and rebuke of the offending party, amounted to collusion with crime after the fact."

18 *Ibid*. "Mr. Johnson's haste," Beecher declared, "to take the wrong side at the atrocious massacre of New-Orleans was shocking." Another riot, also involving Negroes and local police, had occurred in Memphis on April 30 and May 1 It had not made nearly as great an impression on the public as did that of New Orleans.

II "SWING AROUND THE CIRCLE"

The "Swing around the Circle" is the name given to the President's speaking tour between Washington and Chicago, made in late August and early September, 1866, with an entourage that included a number of high officers of the government.[19] The official purpose of the trip was to assist at the dedication of the Stephen A. Douglas monument at Chicago, but the President's primary object was to make speeches to the people along the way in defense of his Southern policy. A number of his friends advised him not to go. They felt that it was beneath the Executive dignity, and they were already aware of Johnson's proneness to vulgarity in extemporaneous discourse. Johnson refused to listen to such advice. He was convinced that if only he might meet his fellow citizens face to face, he would be able to win their sympathy for himself and his cause.[20] The trip, which began on August 28 and did not end until September 15, turned out disastrously. At some places the angry crowds would not even let the President talk; at other places he abused them for their discourtesy and argued with individual hecklers; throughout the tour he kept saying the same things over and over and denouncing Congress for opposing what had now become a derisive Republican byword: "My Policy." Chided on the scene for his undignified language, he shouted that he cared nothing for dignity; members of the presidential party, meanwhile, suffered agonies of humiliation.[21] All in all, as a triumphal progress, the thing could hardly have turned out worse.

[19] Among the dignitaries accompanying the party were Secretaries Seward and Welles, Postmaster-General Randall, Senator Doolittle, Generals Grant and Custer, and Admiral Farragut.

[20] J. G. Randall (ed.), *Diary of Orville Hickman Browning*, II, 91; Thomas Ewing to Henry Stanbery, Aug. 27, 1866, Ewing MSS, Library of Congress; Doolittle to Johnson, Aug. 29, 1866, Johnson MSS; *Autobiography of Thurlow Weed*, ed. Harriet A. Weed (Boston: Houghton Mifflin, 1883), pp. 630–31; Gideon Welles, *Diary*, II, 647. "President Johnson," Welles afterward wrote, "always heard my brief suggestions quietly, but manifestly thought I did not know his power as a speaker." *Ibid.*, p. 648.

[21] The *Herald* correspondent wrote in his dispatch of September 6: "It is reported that General Grant has said: 'I am disgusted with this trip. I am disgusted at hearing a man make speeches on the way to his own funeral.'" Welles said that although Grant behaved with great tact throughout the trip, it still gave the General much pain to hear Copperhead John Hogan bellow out his introductions at every stop: "Mr. Hogan, the Representative of St. Louis District, accompanied us, by invitation of the President, on our way from St. Louis to Washington. . . . It gave him pleasure with his strong lungs to introduce the President and his associates to the crowds at the stopping-places. General Grant told me at Cincinnati that it was extremely distasteful to him to be introduced . . . by Hogan, who was a Copperhead. . . ." New York *Herald*, Sept. 7, 1866; Welles, *Diary*, II, 591–92. The morning after the terrible Cleveland fiasco (at which point Grant appears to have drowned some of his ennui in liquor), the busy *Herald* reporter, who was up bright and early, commented on the "Condition of the

Johnson's enemies made much of the manner in which the dignity of the presidency was debased during the tour, and beyond doubt the Chief Executive's performance did shock people. But there were deeper reasons for the fiasco. Later Presidents have made speaking tours without killing themselves politically, and the fact that the "Swing around the Circle" happened to involve the first modern campaign train should not be held against Andrew Johnson. Nor might it so have been, even then, had the President been on top of his subject. He was not in a position to know that it was a subject which had by that time passed out of his control. It is possible that the critical element in this picture was less a question of Johnson's own particular idiosyncrasies, or his choice of technique, than of the general conditions under which men speak and communicate themselves successfully to audiences any time, and of what may happen to a man when something critical is missing from those conditions.

Andrew Johnson was essentially a stump speaker rather than a polished orator. This need not have been a bad thing in itself; indeed, for Johnson's own career it had been a tremendous asset. But such a technique is a special art with very special requirements. For stump speaking there must be an extra degree of rapport with the audience; there is an immediacy about it which is not demanded in the case of a prepared address. The speaker's powers must function at top vitality throughout and must be renewed continuously through this very sense of communion with the audience. Stump speaking is essentially a spell-binding and conjuring operation, and the element of extemporaneity is what carries it. Most speakers have had occasion, at one time or another, to recognize the "all or nothing" quality that seems to inhere in extemporaneous or semiextemporaneous talk. A man either has all his powers, which can mean great clarity and agility—he is possessed of the spirit—or else the vital something is simply not there. He feels muffled, inarticulate, unreal, and he discovers that he is talking to himself. Such a slipping of the wheels, from all we know of Andrew Johnson, had seldom befallen him back in Tennessee. Before a campaign, he could compose one good speech and deliver it with inspired variations

---

Party": "The President did not appear to be in the best of health. Admiral Farragut was not in his usual spirits. Postmaster Randall looked as if something had occurred that did not please him. Senor Romero was eloquent on mosquitoes. Senator Patterson appeared gloomy." By the time the entourage reached Chicago, the correspondent, in explaining "The President's Purpose in Speaking So Much," wrote: "He thinks he can convince them that he is right and Congress wrong. Many of his friends, however, think he is only furnishing ammunition to his enemies, and while increasing their bitterness is also spurring them to redoubled exertions." New York *Herald*, Sept. 5 and 7, 1866; Howard K. Beale, *The Critical Year*, pp. 307–8.

everywhere. It was somehow the extras, and the tricks he could do with them, that carried it. In short, the thing was a *performance*.

Consequently, Johnson was not accustomed to think of a speech as a statement that would be reported throughout the nation and that a man went "on record" with. It was rather something mystical that happened principally between him and the people in front of him, which meant in effect that each new occasion was a new speech, even though the words would be more or less the same. He seems to have expected, judging from the reported texts, that the "one speech with variations" technique would be good enough for the "Swing around the Circle," despite the presence of a trainful of reporters taking down every word.[22]

On the first few occasions, going through Pennsylvania, New Jersey, and into New York—states where, as it happened, he still had a good deal of support—the President spoke well and things did not go at all badly. Bennett's *Herald*, on the basis of the initial speeches and their reception, predicted a glorious success for the whole enterprise.[23] But then, as the trip extended itself across New York state and as Johnson began repeating himself, his arguments lost whatever freshness they may originally have had, a process whose demoralizing effects were apparently accelerated by the thinning patience and mounting hostility of Johnson's audiences. Which came first is hard to say; the one undoubtedly hastened the other. In any case, the repetitions became grotesque, the variations hollow and mechanical.[24]

He would begin a typical speech by declaring that he had not come to make a speech, and would then proceed to make one.

In being here to-night it is not for the purpose of making a speech, in the common acceptance of the term [Albany, Aug. 30].

You are aware that it is not my purpose to make a speech, but I am constrained to express in a few words the gratification and pleasure which have been afforded me by the demonstrations of the people of New York [Schenectady, Aug. 31].

[22] On this point see Welles, *Diary*, II, 590, 647–48. For a very thorough recent analysis of the "Swing around the Circle" from the viewpoint of a professor of speech, see Gregg Phifer, "Andrew Johnson Takes a Trip," *Tennessee Historical Quarterly*, XI (March, 1952), 3–22; "Andrew Johnson Argues a Case," *ibid.* (June, 1952), pp. 148–70; "Andrew Johnson Delivers His Argument," *ibid.* (Sept., 1952), pp. 212–34; and "Andrew Johnson Loses His Battle," *ibid.* (Dec., 1952), pp. 291–328.

[23] New York *Herald*, Sept. 1, 1866.

[24] Actually Johnson's basic speech, with its themes of persecution, etc., was familiar to the country before the tour even began. He had first delivered it on February 22, 1866, and again on April 18. See above, pp. 292 ff., 399.

Language is inadequate to convey in any degree the feelings and emotions that are produced on this occasion; and in being welcomed here to-day, and in acknowledging that welcome in the deepest sincerity of my heart it will not be for the purpose of making a speech . . . [Auburn, Aug. 31].

But if I were disposed to make a speech, and time would permit me to do it . . . [Buffalo, Sept. 1].

In being introduced to you to-night, it is not for the purpose of making a speech [St. Louis, Sept. 8].[25]

As the President repeatedly disclaimed his intention to speak, and as he marveled at the spontaneous expressions of popular enthusiasm being shown to himself, the crowds became rather less polite. Interrupted by some ribald query while arguing at Westfield, New York, that he was not going to make a speech, the President shouted back: "Keep quiet till I have concluded. Just such fellows as you have kicked up all the rows of the last five years."[26] And at Indianapolis:

FELLOW CITIZENS: (Cries for Grant.) It is not my intention—(Cries of "stop," "Go on,")—to make a long speech. If you give me your attention for five minutes—(Cries of "Go on," "Stop." "No, no, we want nothing to do with traitors." "Grant, Grant," "Johnson," and groans.) I would like to say to this crowd here tonight—(Cries of "Shut up! We don't want to hear from you. Johnson! Grant! Johnson! Grant! Grant!")

The President paused a few moments, and then retired from the balcony.[27]

The President did not understand why he was being denounced as a traitor; he had gone up to the top through all the available offices he could occupy, and thus had no further personal ambitions.

Let my enemies slander me as they will, let a subsidized and mercenary press vilify me as it will. . . . What have I to gain now? From the office of Alderman up to that of President of the United States I have filled all positions [New York City, Aug. 29].

I have filled every office in the government, and for what reason would I play the traitor? I have acquired all that could be acquired [Buffalo, Sept. 3].

And . . . having occupied most positions, from an Alderman up to the Chief Magistracy of the United States . . . and at last having been charged with being a traitor . . . I say what have I to gain . . . ? [Silver Creek, New York, Sept. 3].

I have filled all offices in the gift of the people, and my ambition is satisfied. Why should I turn traitor . . . ? [Cincinnati, Sept. 12].[28]

25 New York *Herald,* Aug. 31, Sept. 1, 4, 10, 1866.

26 *Ibid.,* Sept. 4, 1866.

27 *Ibid.,* Sept. 11, 1866.   28 *Ibid.,* Aug. 30, Sept. 4, 13, 1866.

He was being attacked, he declared, because of his policy of pardon and forgiveness. Jesus had been persecuted for the same policy; Johnson, too, was willing to sacrifice himself if the nation's welfare should require it.

The Son of God, when he descended and found man condemned under the law, instead of executing the law, put himself in their stead and died for them. (Applause.) If I have erred in pardoning, I trust in God I have erred on the right side [New York City, Aug. 29].

I say to you if the worst comes to the worst, if it is blood they want, let them take mine if it be necessary to save the country, for I would freely pour forth my blood as a last libation for its safety and security [Utica, Aug. 31].

But they say I have pardoned some men here and there. . . . I understood that when the Saviour of men came and found them condemned, instead of putting the world to death He died and shed His own blood that the world might live. I thank you for this sincere manifestation of your regard to me . . . [Buffalo, Sept. 3].

Yes, the Saviour of man came on earth and found the human race condemned and sentenced under the law, but when they repented and believed, he said let them live, instead of executing and putting the whole world to death. He went upon the cross, and there was nailed by unbelievers, then shed his blood . . . [St. Louis, Sept. 8].

If I have pardoned traitors I have only obeyed the injunction of scripture—to forgive the repentant. . . . Hang eight millions of people! Who ever heard of such a thing? Yet because I refuse to do this, I am called a traitor. If more blood is needed, erect an altar, and upon it your humble speaker will pour out the last drop of his blood as a libation for his country's salvation [Cincinnati, Sept. 12].[29]

The President on a number of occasions sought to repel, with further allusions to Scripture, charges that instead of having performed these Christ-like deeds, he had in fact played Judas Iscariot:

. . . I have been maligned; I have been called Judas Iscariot, and all that. . . . Judas Iscariot! Judas! There was a Judas once, one of the twelve apostles. Oh yes; the twelve apostles had a Christ. (A Voice, "And a Moses, too!") (Great laughter.) The twelve apostles had a Christ, and he never could have had a Judas unless he had had twelve apostles. If I have played the Judas, who has been my Christ that I have played the Judas with? Was it Thad Stevens? Was it Wendell Phillips? Was it Charles Sumner? [St. Louis, Sept. 8].

I vetoed the Freedmen's Bureau bill twice in the interest of the people, and I will do it forty more times if need be. (Cheers.) For this I have been denounced a traitor, and even a Judas; but why a Judas? Because I dared

29 *Ibid.*, Aug. 30, Sept. 1, 4, 10, 13, 1866.

stretch out my hand in defence of the people? Judas betrayed Christ. Have I done any such thing? Are the radicals my Christ? [Cincinnati, Sept. 12].[30]

A figure used constantly by the President was that of the Union as a "magic circle." But the imagery seemed always to get a little tangled up with what, in Tennessee idiom, the President was himself doing: "swinging 'round the circle."

There I have stood. I was determined that when this great circle of the Union—this great magic circle of Freedom—was attacked, whether from the North or the South, my business was, as far as in me lay, to protect and defend it [Buffalo, Sept. 3].

I tell you, my countrymen, I have been fighting the South . . . and now, as I go around the circle, having fought traitors at the South, I am prepared to fight traitors at the North [Cleveland, Sept. 3].

I fought the battle on the Southern extreme, and now, when the circle is going around, we find men attacking the Union on the Northern verge [Detroit, Sept. 4].[31]

And finally, the President concluded every speech with the same formula, with minor variations:

I leave the constitution and the Union of these States in your hands, you must take care of them, and so, goodby [Schenectady, Aug. 31].

In parting with you I leave the constitution and the Union in your hands, where I am satisfied they are safe [Fonda, Aug. 31].

I turn the constitution and Union over to you, the people, in whose hands I believe they will be safe [Little Falls, Aug. 31].

I will say that I shall leave the constitution in your hands, and I shall place along with it the Union of the States . . . [Auburn, Aug. 31].[32]

At Buffalo, the President added the national flag to the gifts which he was leaving with the people at each stop:

I hand over this flag of your country to you, not with twenty-five stars, but with thirty-six stars upon it. I hand over to you the Union of these States; not a semi-circle; no, but a complete circle of States, and along with them the constitution [Buffalo, Sept. 3].

I leave the constitution and the flag which you have unfurled yonder, not with twenty-five but with thirty-six stars on its folds, and the Union which it represents, in your hands, where I know they will be safe [Silver Creek, N.Y., Sept. 3].

[30] *Ibid.*, Sept. 10, 13, 1866.

[31] *Ibid.*, Sept. 4, 1866; McPherson, *Reconstruction*, p. 135; New York *Herald*, Sept. 5, 1866.

[32] *Ibid.*, Sept. 1, 1866.

And now, in parting, I leave in your hands the constitution, the Union and the glorious flag of your country, not with twenty-five but with thirty-six stars [Toledo, Sept. 3].[33]

By the time the President got into Michigan and Illinois, there were many stops at which the populace was so unfriendly that the President's final benediction was cut short by what appeared to be the conductor's haste in moving his train away from scenes of danger:

Before the President had an opportunity of saying anything more than "I leave the constitution in your hands," the train moved off [Lemont, Ill., Sept. 7].

He said to those who were disposed to create a disturbance that he was on the "line" with General Grant contending for the Union of the States. Before he could say more the train resumed its way [Bloomington, Ill., Sept. 7].

In the midst of the cheering a voice cried out, "Three cheers for Congress." The whistle was blown, the train moved away and the response was unheard [Atlanta, Ill., Sept. 7].[34]

"Isn't Andy doing finely?" gleefully wrote Garfield's friend W. C. Howells. "Who ever heard of such a Presidential Ass," exclaimed a dignitary of Olivet College, "—and I am sure his visit to Mich will help our majorities largely. . . ."[35]

The punishment which the President was bringing upon himself all along the way provided rich material for the spoofing of "Petroleum V. Nasby," who represented himself as a grateful Copperhead traveling with the presidential party:

UTICA. . . . He introdoost here the remark that he didn't come to make a speech; that he wuz goin to shed a tear over the tomb uv Douglas; that, in swingin around the circle, he hed fought traitors on all sides uv it, but that he felt safe. He shood leave the Constooshn in their hands, and ef a martyr wuz wanted, he wuz ready to die with neetness and dispatch.

ROME. . . . He menshuned to the audience that he had swung around the Southern side uv the cirkle, and wuz now swingin around the Northern side uv it, and that he wuz fightin traitors on all sides. He left the Constitooshun in their hands, and bid em good bye. . . .

[33] *Ibid.*, Sept. 4, 5, 1866.

[34] *Ibid.*, Sept. 8, 1866.

[35] W. C. Howells to Garfield, Sept. 13, 1866, Garfield MSS, Library of Congress; James B. Porter to Austin Blair, Sept. 13, 1866, Blair MSS, Detroit Public Library. "We have all heard," complained the *Missouri Democrat*, "that Mr. Johnson was once an Alderman; that he stands on the Constitution and the flag; and delivers them to his hearers whenever two or three are gathered together. It is very kind of him to give to the people what belongs to them already. We have seen him swing round that weary circle, until we are ready to pardon much in consideration of his dizziness." Sept. 7, 1866, quoted in Phifer, "Andrew Johnson Delivers His Argument," pp. 212–13.

LOCKPORT. . . . Ez for himself, his ambishn wuz more than satisfied. He hed bin Alderman, Member uv the Legislacher, Congressman, Senator, Military Governor, Vice President, and President. He had swung around the entire circle uv offises, and all he wanted now wuz to heal the wounds uv the nashen. He felt safe in leavin the Constooshn in their hands. . . .

Finally we reeched Detroit. This bein a Democratic city, the President wuz hisself agin. . . . He gathered together in one quiver all the sparklin arrows he had used from Washington to this point, and shot em one by one. He swung around the cirkle; he didn't come to make a speech; he hed bin Alderman uv his native town; he mite hev been Dicktater, but woodent; and ended with a poetickal cotashun wich I coodent ketch. . . .

YPSILANTI. . . . He asked em, ef he was Judis Iskariot who wuz the Saviour? Thad Stevens? If so, then after swingin round the cirkle, and findin traitors at both ends of the line, I leeve the 36 States with 36 stars onto em in yoor hands, and—

The train wuz off amid loud shouts uv "Grant! Grant!" to which the President responded by wavin his hat.

ANN ARBOR. . . . The air their band wuz playin, "Hail to the Chief," was appropit, ez he wuz Chief Magistrate uv the nashen, to wich posishen he hed reached, hevin bin Alderman uv his native village, U.S. Senator, etsettry. The crowd hollered "Grant! Grant!" and the President thanked em for the demonstration. It showed him that the people wuz with him in his efforts to close his eyes on a Union uv 36 States and a flag uv 36 stars onto it. Ef I am a traitor, sed he, warmin up, who is Judis Iscariot? Ez I'm swingin around the cirkle, I find Thad Stevens on the one side and Jeff Davis on the—

The conductor cruelly startid the train, without givin him time to finish. . . .

KALAMAZOO. . . . Grant! Grant! The President responded, saying, that in swingin around the cirkle, he hed bin called Joodis Iskariot for sacrificin uv hisself for the people! Who wuz the Saviour? Wuz Thad Stevens? No! Then cleerly into yoor hands I leave the Constitution uv 36 stars with 36 States onto em, intact and undissevered.[36]

The rapport which the stump speaker needed was gone, and by the time Johnson had reached Buffalo there were few of his efforts that did not deteriorate into a rout. His worst experience—quite comparable to that of Robert La Follette at Philadelphia in 1912, after the belligerent Wisconsin campaigner had about used up his supporters' patience—apparently came at St. Louis, where he babbled on and on in virtual incoherence:

"Yes, yes; they are ready to impeach [me]—(Voice—'Let them try it'), —and if they were satisfied they had the next Congress by as a decided majority as this, upon some pretext or other they would vacate the Executive department of the United States. (A voice—'Too bad they don't im-

[36] Petroleum V. Nasby [David Ross Locke], *"Swingin Round the Cirkle"* (Boston: Lee & Shepard, 1867), pp. 210–11, 213, 215–17.

peach him.') But as we are talking about this Congress let me call the soldiers' attention to this immaculate Congress. Let me call your attention. Oh, yes; this Congress that could make war upon the Executive because he stands upon the constitution and vindicated the rights of the people, exercising the veto power in their behalf. Because he dared to do this they can clamor and talk about impeachment. And, by way of stimulating this increasing confidence with the soldiers throughout the country, they talk about impeachment. So far as offenses are concerned—upon this question of offenses, let me ask you what offenses I have committed? (A Voice—'Plenty, here, to-night.')"[37]

Andrew Johnson, like La Follette, had not lost his "reason"; he had simply lost touch with his audience, and the demons of unreality that are in the air when a man no longer knows what he is saying were all round about Andrew Johnson that night. It was not necessarily his method; it was rather the issue, an issue which overwhelming numbers of his hearers had already decided for themselves. The "Swing around the Circle" still merits contrast with the almost magical energy and heroism with which the same Andrew Johnson had spoken for the Union in Tennessee back in 1861: he had had a losing issue there, too, but it was at least a viable one; he could still make many converts with it. In 1866 things were quite different. More than one man has made a fool of himself trying to talk before groups to whom his arguments are no longer comprehensible and to whom—for either just or unjust reasons—the very sight and sound of him has become odious.

During the first few days of the trip, Johnson was welcomed by the highest dignitaries of the places where he stopped, including the radical governor of New York, as an accepted incident of the nonpartisan honors which are due any time to the President of the United States. But then it quickly became clear what use Johnson was making of these privileges. While demanding that the people "rise above party," "do away with party," and declaring that he himself "cared nothing for party," he would then, in great passion, proceed to denounce the Republican Congress and say things which in general pleased only his Democratic listeners. It was in such a setting that more and more of Johnson's receptions were broken up by Republican hotbloods and local rowdies.[38] The result was that mayors and governors began flee-

---

[37] New York *Herald*, Sept. 10, 1866.

[38] Most accounts of the tour place stress on the fact that a number of these occasions were disrupted by "organized hecklers." This is certainly true enough as a reported fact; as the key, however, to a sequence in causation it is rather more dubious. The presence of such elements will hardly do as an explanation for the failure of the tour itself, since a more basic problem seems to be that of explaining the hecklers. What sort of pass have things come to, when heckling—"organized" or otherwise—is allowed to proceed at all, let alone disrupt with impunity the welcome being given to a President

ing at the approach of the presidential train, leaving to private groups of Democratic citizenry and Union-Johnson men the chore of getting up some sort of welcome.[39] Thus the mayor of Pittsburgh explained to the local committee on arrangements:

I should be pleased to assist in doing honor to the Chief Magistrate of the United States, if I had a reasonable expectation he would refrain upon the occasion ... from stigmatizing those whose views of reconstruction coincide with my own, as traitors on the Northern side of the line. The speeches made by Andrew Johnson in other cities prevent me from believing that he will. I am therefore constrained, from motives of self-respect, to decline your invitation.[40]

Johnson professed to be gratified at such snubs, since they gave an opportunity for "the people" to make spontaneous demonstrations in his honor:

A welcome to Pittsburgh by the people, the masters of those who refused welcome to a fellow citizen and to the Chief Magistrate, a welcome from their masters, I repeat, is peculiarly gratifying to me (the noise below continued), and in being here to-night I will say in the few words to which I intend to give utterance. ... [The President was able to make little progress with his speech, being forced to retreat amid shrieks, groans, whistling, and loud cheers for Admiral Farragut and General Grant.][41]

But when the bedraggled survivors finally made their way back into Washington, the mayor of that "non-partisan" city came out, welcomed them with soothing words, and gave thanks for their safe return. In his reply the reeling President, by this time doubtless functioning on instinct, announced:

Let me say to you that through that tour the demonstrations and manifestations of the popular heart were unmistakeable. I tell you that the great mass of the American people are being moved, and that the popular heart is going to respond to the demand that the constitution, the Union, and the laws of the United States are making upon it.[42]

As for locating the "effect" of the "Swing around the Circle," it is probably fair to say that few truly confirmed Johnson partisans were likely to have changed their minds as a result of it, dig-

---

of the United States? Normally on occasions of such importance a crowd which is enthusiastic, or even respectfully polite, will have the amplest resources for dealing with would-be hecklers in its midst. It should also be remembered that such heckling did not begin until the President had gone nearly all the way across New York state—that is, after the country had had a week in which to observe his performances.

39 Welles, *Diary*, II, 592–94.

40 New York *Herald*, Sept. 14, 1866.

41 *Ibid.*   42 *Ibid.*, Sept. 17, 1866.

nity or no dignity. Yet the problem for Johnson was not simply that of keeping what following he had but also of persuading large numbers of not yet fully hardened Unionists to make the decision of deserting to him. Not only did the tour fail in this function for the doubtfuls, but for great numbers of those that remained it seemed to have provided the perfect excuse to throw away all lingering reservations and to do what they were already on the point of doing—return to the Republican fold for good. It was then that they could insist, while having no more use for Thad Stevens than ever, that they could not support a man who had so debased the dignity of the presidency as had Andrew Johnson. Here are the words of men who had begun going through the process of detaching themselves from further support of the President:

[James Gordon Bennett:] At Cleveland he had words with some fellow who called him a traitor, and said, "if you could see that man's face you would find cowardice and treachery in it." When accused of a want of dignity he exclaimed, "I care not for dignity," and proceeded to denounce his enemies as "subsidized gangs of hirelings and traducers." ... Wherever cheers on the route would be proposed for Congress he would stop and argue the case between himself and Congress, as if he were upon an electioneering stump canvass in some remote Western Congressional district.

But it is unnecessary to prolong the catalogue of these painful quotations. It is mortifying to see a man occupying the lofty position of President of the United States descend from that position and join issue with those who are draggling their garments in the muddy gutters of political vituperation.[43]

[Henry J. Raymond:] President Johnson, in his speech at Cleveland remarked that "he did not care about his dignity." In our judgment this is greatly to be regretted. The American people care very much about it and can never see it forgotten without profound sorrow and solicitude. ... The President of the United States cannot enter upon an exchange of epithets with the brawling of a mob, without seriously compromising his official character and hazarding interests too momentous to be thus lightly imperiled.[44]

[Henry Ward Beecher:] What shall I say of the speeches made in the wide recent circuit of the Executive? Are these the ways of reconciliation?[45]

[43] *Ibid.*, Sept. 26, 1866.   [44] New York *Times,* Sept. 7, 1866.

[45] *Ibid.*, Sept. 8, 1866. "As to politics," wrote a friend of Henry L. Dawes, "since Johnson went to Chicago—I am more afloat than ever—I had thought I belonged to his *party,* as well as to his *policy*—but as he has receded Westward I dont think 'distance has lent any enchantment to the views!'" Charles Delano to Dawes, Sept. 22, 1866, Dawes MSS, Library of Congress.

III PRESS AND PUBLIC

A final explanation for the failure of the President's cause in the 1866 campaign might possibly be found in the activities of the press—"a subsidized and mercenary press," as Johnson had put it in his speeches. There may be something to be said for this "control of the media" argument (as it would later be called); a systematic campaign of vilification and abuse against the President by a radical-dominated press was bound in the end to have its effect. Newspapers, one writer has suggested, were dependent on advertising, and "Radical manufacturers, business houses, and other large advertisers boycotted Johnson papers." Thus radical propaganda, based on half-truths, came to dominate all channels of communication and ultimately Northern public opinion in general. "Basing their ideas on scant and unreliable information from party-prejudiced sources, newspaper editors became a great power for good or evil. It was these editors and their papers that the Radical minority in the Republican Party controlled."[46] The picture thus appears to be that of a majority manipulated by a minority through the latter's domination of the press.

The fact is that by the summer of 1866 the American people actually had at their disposal an extraordinary amount of information upon which to make up their minds about any political issue, probably as much as would ever be the case in comparable circumstances. But something should still be said about the "power of the press" argument on its merits. It implies a theory of influence that is actually somewhat crude and primitive for dealing with opinion in a democratic political society. The press is undeniably capable of exerting considerable "influence," but it should be recognized that "influence" is, even at its simplest, a two-way affair. In the equation of "press" and "public," both must be taken as variables, not just one of them; it is an error to think of "the public" as in any sense a passive quantity, a *tabula rasa* upon which the press may write what it pleases. On such a basis the election of 1866 would be incomprehensible. On the contrary, the public might even be considered the more dynamic of the two. Quite aside from the element of active choice in the kind of paper a person wants to be "influenced by"—virtually every community in 1866 had, after all, both Republican and Democratic newspapers[47]—it is very

---

[46] Beale, *Critical Year*, pp. 316, 328.

[47] E.g., the two major newspapers in northern Illinois were the radical Chicago *Tribune* and the Copperhead Chicago *Times*. "To give you some idea," wrote the postmaster of Mount Carroll to Elihu Washburne, "of the interest taken by the people in

likely at a time of high feeling that the state of public opinion actually has a great deal more effect on the formation of editorial opinion than the reverse. The great journals of "influence" in those days did not, as a matter of fact, depend primarily on advertising; they depended on subscriptions, and thus in a very real sense they were at the mercy of their readers. There is a limit on the extent to which newspapers can "manufacture" opinion at any time, and there are even greater limits to what they can do to effect reversals of opinion on matters of deep popular conviction. In such cases "coercion" and "manipulation" tend to come, as it were, from the other direction. Newspapers in critical times can enjoy relatively little margin for the luxury of deviant opinions but must accommodate themselves to the majority views of the public and function as reflectors of these views.[48]

Only in such terms can one understand the capitulation and reversal of the two great Johnson-Unionist dailies of New York, the *Herald* and the *Times*. By the fall of 1866, each was faced with a final choice that could no longer be deferred—a choice between Johnson and Congress—and the choice in each case was to support Congress. The explanation is not very complicated. Their readers would no longer stand for their pro-Johnson attitude, and so both journals "sold out" to public opinion.

---

the struggle between congress and the president I give you the number of papers taken in '64 and now:

Tribune in 1864—63 copies weekly
Tribune in 1866—136 copies weekly, to present time and increasing
Chi Times 1864   52   "   "
Chi Times 1866   3   "   "

The people support My Policy, don't they." R. J. Tomkins to Washburne, July 7, 1866, Washburne MSS, Library of Congress.

[48] For instance, Julius W. Pratt, in his study of the business press at the time of the Spanish-American War, found the country's leading commercial and financial newspapers uniformly opposed to expansionism. Most of them, however, reversed themselves entirely once the national adventure against Spain had got under way. While this does not tell us much about the connection between "business" and "imperialism"—except that, other things being equal, American businessmen did not seem to be very interested in imperialism—it tells us a great deal about "public opinion." These editors undoubtedly made their switch not in their character as business spokesmen but simply in their more inclusive character as enthusiastic American citizens. See J. W. Pratt, "American Business and the Spanish-American War," *Hispanic American Historical Review*, XIV (May, 1934), 163–201. Much the same thing might be said of Professor Beale's "radical" businessmen in 1866. Indeed, from a "rational" business viewpoint, it could very well be argued that the sooner peace, reconciliation, and stability were re-established—"other things being equal"—the better. But "rationality" of this sort does not appear to have much of a show against the "blind prejudice" of a groundswell of democratic popular sentiment. On the other hand, the opponent of such sentiment—checked, of course, by the very values of his culture from being really against "the people"—has to seek sinister and obscure reasons for it, e.g., Johnson's "subsidized and mercenary press."

The *Herald*, as previously mentioned, had the greatest circulation of any paper in the nation. James Gordon Bennett, though a nominal Unionist, took special pride in his independence from the claims of "party." Actually, he enjoyed a great deal more independence than most publishers. There were all sorts of things about the *Herald*—a superbly efficient general news coverage, as well as numerous special features such as the full reporting of sports events and spicy stories of low life—that made the paper unusually attractive and thus gave Bennett a great deal of leeway for political adventuring and idiosyncratic opinions on the editorial page. As with the New York *Daily News* of today, great numbers of working-class readers could derive immense enjoyment from the lively *Herald* while paying relatively little attention to the editor's private fancies.[49]

As for rabble-rousing techniques, few editors could match Bennett in sheer scurrility. It is difficult to find radical editors anywhere at this time abusing Johnson with half the gusto employed by Bennett in abusing radicals. Nor was this confined to the editorial page. The news reports, for example, of the Northern and Southern Loyalist convention held at Philadelphia in September, 1866, were introduced each day during the sessions under the headline, "Disunion," followed by such choice subheads as: "First Grand National Convention of Nigger-Worshippers at Philadelphia," "Renegade Southerners on the Rampage," "Blacks and Whites, Free Lovers, Spiritualists, Fourierites, Women's Rights Men, Negro Equality Men and Miscegens in Convention," "Negro Insurrection to be Incited," "The South to be a St. Domingo," "Drunken Orgies at the Hotels," "Horrible Blasphemy of the Delegates," "Twaddling Tilton Likened unto Jesus Christ," "The President Compared to Satan," "Midnight Debauch of the Delegates," "Jack Hamilton Weak in the Flesh," etc.[50]

And yet even Bennett, with bigger and better techniques for "mass manipulation" than those of any other newspaper in the country, and with no scruples about using them, found himself back-tracking later in September as popular opinion manifested itself more and more plainly with regard to the approaching election. He had already advised the South to accept the Fourteenth Amendment and was meanwhile imploring Johnson himself to accept it in the interests of har-

---

49 A considerable portion of New York's lower-class citizenry in those days were Irish immigrants, preponderantly Democratic in their political behavior; and it is possible that Bennett, with a newspaper which catered to all sorts of instincts not of a political nature even though his own editorial opinions were nominally anti-Democratic, had in such a group of readers an extra margin of safety for his political "independence."

50 New York *Herald*, Sept. 4, 5, 7, 12, 1866.

mony and to call off his personal feud with Congress. The Maine election looked like an unmistakable sign. "We regard the contest between the President and Congress as virtually decided by Maine. We bow to the judgment of the mighty North, and we trust that the President will shape his course accordingly."[51] The *Herald* thereupon served notice on Johnson, both in its editorials and in private correspondence with him, that its further support required his yielding to "public sentiment." The election results of November were obviously decisive, and the *Herald* said so. But the President did not yield, and consequently he found the *Herald* no longer among his partisans.[52]

The case of the *Times* has already been narrated. The agreement between Raymond and the *Times*'s publisher and chief stockholder, George Jones, had stipulated that whatever editorial policy Raymond might see fit to pursue was solely the concern of the editor and would not be interfered with. Jones, though his own views did not coincide with Raymond's, never did interfere, and the two men maintained harmonious relations throughout. And yet all this must have weighed with some oppressiveness upon Raymond's conscience as he and the forbearing Jones watched the paper lose thousands of dollars as the subscription list dwindled and dwindled. Such developments appear to have had more than a little connection not only with Raymond's support of Andrew Johnson but also with the "popular will." When Raymond finally abandoned that support, and trimmed a little closer to the "popular will," the *Times* once more prospered.[53]

The thing that must in the long run be accounted for is the "popular will" itself. No amount of manipulation, plotting, wirepulling, or "propaganda" can really do much toward explaining such a manifestation as that of 1866, except by way of plucking about its fringes. The problem is still the same one that faced Raymond, Bennett, Beecher, Cox, and everyone else in their position who saw the

---

[51] *Ibid.*, Sept. 14, 1866.

[52] W. B. Phillips to Johnson, Oct. 7 and Nov. 8, 1866, Johnson MSS. "Mr. Bennett makes everything—yes, the public welfare and everything else—subordinate to what he supposes may promote his interests as proprietor of the paper," Phillips wrote Johnson on January 25, 1867. "Besides," he added farther down in his letter, "the Herald always endeavors to go with the strongest party or side when its editor discovers which is or is not going to be the strongest." Johnson MSS.

[53] Dorothy Dodd, *Henry J. Raymond and the New York Times during Reconstruction*, p. 62; Augustus Maverick, *Henry J. Raymond and the New York Press*, pp. 193, 204; James C. Derby, *Fifty Years among Authors, Books, and Publishers* (New York: G. W. Carleton, 1884), p. 364; New York *Times* "Jubilee Supplement," Sept. 18, 1901. See also *ibid.*, editorials of Oct. 11, 25, Nov. 8, 9, 17, 1866.

ground being steadily cut out from under them. They were all confronted by the solidarity and sense of moral certainty, not of a designing minority, but of the Republican party as a whole and of the mass electorate that supported it.

There were all sorts of things that the party, a few months before, had not been unanimous on or certain about. Back in the spring, victory could by no means be assumed as a foregone conclusion. As for the precise nature of terms to the South, the question of whether the Fourteenth Amendment should or should not constitute the final ones, a satisfactory compromise with the Executive, how soon the states should be readmitted, and so on—on all these matters there were many differences, and during the late winter and spring party leaders had felt a great deal more responsibility about them than they felt now. Yet there was one thing they all did agree on, which was simply that, in the way of further conditions, there had to be something. And the developments which had by now occurred were all such as to make it clear beyond doubt that there was no longer anything else they did have to agree on. Johnson himself had done all that was needed to clear the air and to unite party and people. He had so narrowed the choices that it had to be just one thing or the other. He had formalized everything; he had told the people that they had to choose between their elected representatives and himself, that their own choice was between "reconstruction" and a "restoration" already accomplished, and that so far as he was concerned it was either immediate and unqualified readmission or nothing at all. He had swept away a whole range of qualifications, a boon which is very seldom handed to any party by the opposition at election time; Republican candidates needed do no more than take up the issue exactly as he had thrown it down to them. Johnson had thus left himself not the slightest margin for compromise, and now that men looked back, this was what he had been spelling out in ever clearer terms—despite their initial reluctance to recognize it—ever since December, 1865. Now, with the issue so clear and the choice so simple, it should scarcely be a matter of wonder that all the uncertainties and dissensions of the winter and spring should at this point have been removed and replaced by great unity, by an irresistible surge of determination that a full sweep be achieved everywhere.

There is no better example of how it all worked than in the dubious and marginal state of Ohio.

The Republican grip in that state was considerably less strong than the size of its delegation in the Thirty-ninth Congress might seem to indicate, since the representatives of that delegation had been elected at the crest of the military and presidential victory wave of 1864. Actually the balance throughout had been most precarious. In 1862, at a time of military stalemate and with the Emancipation Proclamation as an issue, the Democrats had won fourteen out of nineteen congressional seats; and in the state and gubernatorial elections that would be held in 1867, just a year after the ones presently being considered, the Democrats would win control of both branches of the legislature, and the Republican nominee for governor, Rutherford B. Hayes, would barely squeak through by a margin of just under three thousand out of nearly half a million votes cast.[54] So Ohio was anything but a solid Republican state. Nor had the party itself been very solid internally all through the previous year. There was an extraordinary amount of bad feeling, for instance, over the Negro question. While there had been much agitation for Negro suffrage in a number of the Western Reserve districts, the same subject was anathema downstate, where, in the past ebb and flow of political fortunes, white-supremacy Democrats had been accustomed to making many profitable incursions. In February, 1866, the Republican caucus of the legislature had passed a resolution praising the Ohio congressmen for supporting the Freedmen's Bureau Bill, but the caucus still hesitated to go specifically on record against the President himself even after he had vetoed the Civil Rights Bill a month later. Even in May, when local conventions were held, the question of supporting or opposing the President was still touchy enough to be generally bypassed. Meanwhile, Governor Jacob D. Cox did all he could to keep the party together and to avoid any possible splits over Johnson, his policy, Negro suffrage, and other matters. The Democrats and Johnson Unionists, consequently, had good reason for optimism in the late spring of 1866, and R. P. L. Baber wrote Johnson in June that he thought eight or ten radical congressmen would be defeated.[55]

As the time approached for the Republican state convention to be held at Columbus on June 20, the party workers had a good many misgivings over the difficulties that seemed sure to arise when men of such divergent views tried to achieve some basis for unity in the coming campaign. Moderate men expected trouble from Reserve radicals, and

[54] Comparative figures may be found in the *Tribune Almanac*, II, 1863, 55–56; 1865, pp. 56–58; 1868, 45–46; see also George H. Porter, *Ohio Politics during the Civil War Period* (New York: Privately printed, 1911), pp. 100–109, 238–48.

[55] Porter, *Ohio Politics*, pp. 220–25; J. D. Cox to Cincinnati *Commercial*, published in New York *Herald*, Feb. 27, 1866; Cox to Johnson, Mar. 22, 1866; R. P. L. Baber to W. H. Seward, Mar. 30, 1866; Baber to Johnson, June 28, 1866, Johnson MSS; Cox to Garfield, Apr. 10, 1866, Garfield MSS.

the radicals were afraid of appeasement and trimming from the men of the lower counties. "Columbus will swarm with Copperheads, Administration partisans and place seekers," wrote a gloomy radical from Chardon, "and a three days commingling with such elements would lead a man to despise humanity, detest democracy and doubt the wisdom of Deity."[56]

But when the delegates all gathered on the appointed day, and met each other face to face, it dawned upon them that something miraculous had occurred: they were not divided at all. From one end of the state to the other the party was a solid unit. Differences were thereupon composed in a twinkling; the Reserve delegates agreed to bury Negro suffrage for the time being and the downstaters agreed to support the Fourteenth Amendment. Whether or not the amendment represented the North's final terms could now be ignored; each man in his particular district was free to say what he pleased about it.[57] "There was much more unanimity & good feeling than I had anticipated," now admitted the doubter from Chardon. "There was apparently but little of the Johnson element in the Convention." Abner Kellogg of Jefferson was likewise impressed: "We found the convention composed of gentlemen of intelligence, and almost with one accord sustaining the action of Congress, against the President, indeed so far as any effort to sustain the President was concerned he seemed to have no one to speak for him. . . ."[58] Something close to euphoria seems to have enveloped the proceedings. "You ask as to the temper of the State Convention," wrote one of Garfield's lieutenants. "I cannot better answer, than by saying that every man felt *good*. . . . 'Andy' was not in the convention and nothing but a sense of propriety prevented shouts of applause when Granville Moody prayed, '*God bless our noble Congress*.'" "There never in the history of the Union party (nor any other party,)" exulted William Stedman, "has assembled a convention in Ohio marked with such unity of feeling & confidence in measures to be adopted. . . . I am ready for the contest. Victory is already ours."[59]

---

[56] M. C. Canfield to Garfield, June 4, 1866, Garfield MSS.

[57] Porter, *Ohio Politics*, pp. 226–27. Cf. Benjamin B. Kendrick: "In the political campaign that ensued, the fourteenth amendment was spoken of by Republican politicians, as a finality in reconstruction, or a mere step toward 'complete justice,' partly according to the temperament of the speaker, but principally according to the nature of the constituency which he represented." *The Journal of the Joint Committee of Fifteen on Reconstruction*, p. 353. It should be added, however, that in the case of Ohio most of the candidates assumed that the Amendment constituted final terms, and said so.

[58] M. C. Canfield to Garfield, June 22, 1866; A. Kellogg to Garfield, June 25, 1866, Garfield MSS.

[59] P. Hitchcock to Garfield, June 26, 1866; W. Stedman to Garfield, June 22, 1866, Garfield MSS.

And off they all went, in a great surge of energy, to launch the campaign.

Governor Cox did not abandon his efforts, even after the convention, to patch things up between the party and the President. He wrote to the President the following day, assuring him of his continued support for what he agreed was "the true theory of restoration"—though "asking only what is the most truly wise mode of reaching the desired end." His initial speech in the campaign was another plea for harmony in which he still insisted that the President's purposes and those of the Union party were really basically the same.[60] Shortly, however, the full bankruptcy of Johnson's position, late in August and early in September, was demonstrated before the country, and when the President visited Ohio during the latter part of his tour his reception was dismally inauspicious. Meanwhile the Republican campaign in that state, as an Ohio historian remarks, "was quite spirited," reaching unusual heights of enthusiasm, energy, and vitality: there was a sense in which "the people" had taken it over.[61] One of Garfield's friends wrote that it gave him deep satisfaction to see the people "turn out in full" for their primary township meetings. "This," he declared, "they really should do every year," and then they would get good government. "When they neglect this duty, they are at fault for all the mischief political wireworkers may occasion." Another wrote from Geneva after "about two thirds of all the voters in town" had turned out for the primary meeting there:

The magnitude of the questions under consideration . . . has so awakened the public mind to the necessity of having "the right man in the right place," that delegates cannot *now* be elected simply by some one calling out the names and everyone taking it as being all right and electing the whole squad by acclamation.[62]

Whatever it was that had happened in Ohio, the Governor himself had somewhere along the way come to see and acquiesce in the trend of things. We see him next at Pittsburgh on September 24, having just accepted the permanent presidency of the radical Soldiers' and Sailors' Convention meeting in that city, launching into a vigorous and (for him) fiery speech:

With many of us it was a sore trial to believe that any man who had done good service in camp or in political action in civil life, during this

[60] Cox to Johnson, June 21, 1866, Johnson MSS; Porter, *Ohio Politics*, pp. 232–33.

[61] *Ibid.*, p. 233.

[62] B. F. Hoffman to Garfield, Aug. 17, 1866; Asa Lamb to Garfield, July 7, 1866, Garfield MSS.

struggle of four years, could prove false to his principles. . . . It was not pleasant to find ourselves brought face to face with this fact; but now, seeing that the fact is so, seeing that we are pledged to recognize the truth, that it has entered into the minds of some to exalt the Executive department of the government into a despotic power, and to abase the representative portion of our government into the mere tools of despotism—learning that this is the case, we now, as heretofore, know our duty, and "knowing dare maintain it."[63]

In November, when all the Ohio returns were counted, the Republicans had carried the leading state offices by over 40,000 votes and had won seventeen out of nineteen congressional seats. Elsewhere in the North it was pretty much the same. In every state where a governorship was contested, it was the Republicans who won it; every state legislature was carried by Republicans; and every Northern delegation to Congress was dominated by Republican majorities.[64]

[63] New York *Herald*, Sept. 26, 1866. This convention, in addition to a Johnson "Soldiers' and Sailors' Convention" which met at Cleveland on September 17, and those already mentioned (the Philadelphia "National Union" convention and the Philadelphia "Northern and Southern Loyalists'" convention), brought the total number of such national gatherings that summer to four.

[64] *Tribune Almanac*, II, 1867, pp. 49–67.

Military Reconstruction, 1867

The sweeping character of the Republican victory in the 1866 fall elections, together with the decisive finality of the Military Reconstruction Acts which became law only a few months later, in March, 1867, ought to lead rather naturally to the conclusion that the entire business had been more or less settled by the elections. The elections had represented, in effect, a final mandate for unfettered radicalism; there now remained little to prevent drastic punitive action against the South. With the last barriers of reason and responsibility removed—as they now apparently were—only four months of hammering by Thaddeus Stevens and his radical cohorts, backed by great majorities, would be required to produce the logical consummation.

Such reasoning has the advantage of striking for the shortest distance between two points. Yet there are certain important things which it leaves out. It leaves out the question of whether President Johnson still had another chance, after the election was over, to regain some of his influence in the Republican party by modifying his no-compromise position on reconstruction and making a closer accommodation to the interests of the party majority. There is also the question of whether the way still remained open for the South to get a settlement substantially milder than the one which it eventually did get. Actually, neither of these possibilities was in any way closed as Congress prepared to meet in December, 1866. Congress, so far as either the country or the Republican majority was concerned, was by no means dominated by extremism, and the party was still a long way from committed to the reconstruction policy represented by Thaddeus Stevens. If anything, the elections had alleviated passions rather than increased them, and the second session of the Thirty-ninth Congress, like the first a year before, was full of possibilities and alternatives.

As things turned out, however, Johnson not only made no move to seize his final chance but positively did all he could to prevent the South from accommodating to the terms embodied in the Fourteenth Amendment. Meanwhile the South, whose salvation depended at the very least on taking these terms seriously, not only failed to do so but rejected them decisively out of hand. The President's advice had a very great deal to do with this. In addition, the Northern Democratic party played a role of considerable importance, marked by an irresponsibility at least equal to that of the most extreme elements in the Republican party. The Democrats' every effort was directed toward producing not a settlement but a stalemate. The consequences of such a line of effort upon Southern fortunes were apparently given very little consideration; the main idea was that it would split the Republican party into fragments. Thus, on the one hand, Democratic organs, in effect representing themselves as monitors of Northern political sentiment, ceaselessly exhorted the Southerners to stand fast. On the other hand, the Democrats in Congress quite knowingly co-operated with Thaddeus Stevens in his efforts to block a moderate compromise —such a compromise having remained a distinct possibility to the end. In the South, meanwhile, incident after incident involving atrocities upon Negroes and Unionists occurred with mounting frequency.

It was in the setting created by all these developments, in the two or three months following the 1866 fall elections, that the still-moderate inclinations of substantial numbers of Republicans were swept away and replaced by the conviction that matters as they then stood could only be righted by measures of the most drastic kind.

I   PROSPECTS FOR A MODERATE SETTLEMENT

In a negative sense the issue of the election had been Johnson's policy of immediate and unqualified readmission of the Southern states. But standing back of this was the positive function of the election as a referendum on the Fourteenth Amendment. A great majority of the Northern public and of Republican party leaders in the various states assumed that the Amendment was Congress' alternative to the Johnson policy and that it represented Congress' terms to the South. "Congress, it is true, is not bound to anything," insisted the *Nation*, "but it would, nevertheless, disappoint a majority of those who are now supporting it, if, after the South had fully accepted the amendment, it were suddenly to announce that it was still not satisfied, and that its last word had still to be spoken. . . ."[1] These terms, sup-

1 *Nation*, III (Nov. 1, 1866), 350.

ported by the Republican party and opposed by the President, were being placed before the people and the people's verdict would constitute the ultimate authority. "If the elections are against us," wrote Rutherford B. Hayes to a friend in the South, "we shall submit. If they are *for* us, the Democracy will submit. We shall be united in any event. Do not be again deceived with the hope of Democratic help in a further struggle. I hope you will give the Congressional plan a fair hearing. If we succeed you must adopt it, if you regard your own welfare. . . . My last word," Hayes admonished his friend in closing, "is, don't let Andy Johnson deceive you."[2]

Consequently, the elections, whose results were so unequivocal as to remove a multitude of lingering fears and doubts, produced a mood of general satisfaction and relief. The people had spoken and the primary decision on reconstruction had thus been placed beyond dispute for the first time since the end of the war. The Union was to be restored, but there would have to be terms. Even President Johnson, conceivably, was no longer quite the scoundrel he had seemed beforehand; ". . . the strong feeling against the President," according to *Harper's,* "has been in great degree placated by the elections."[3] The President himself should now see the direction of popular sentiment. Despite remaining overtones of bitterness toward Johnson over his indiscriminate use of the patronage just before the election, the general feeling was that he had been taught a lesson. Moreover, the Democrats had been badly beaten and the South had been shown in the clearest terms that the Republican party, supported by a Northern majority, was a unit behind Congress. And now if Johnson and the South were to accept the decision and support the Amendment, the entire tangle of reconstruction might be straightened out once and for all and at last there would be peace.

There was thus, with the approach of winter and the year's end, a very good set of circumstances in which reason might once more prevail in the national capital. Moderate Republican leaders seemed to express a generally shared feeling when they said they expected no special trouble in the forthcoming session of Congress. "We are getting along quietly thus far," wrote Senator Grimes to his wife early

[2] *Diary and Letters of Rutherford B. Hayes,* ed. Charles R. Williams (Columbus: Ohio State Archaeological and Historical Society, 1922–26), II, 32–33.

[3] *Harper's Weekly,* X (Nov. 17, 1866), 722. The New York *Tribune* said: "Mr. Johnson, in his message, may, as he has a perfect right to do, accept the decision of the people as his guide, and yet suggest to Congress another plan for carrying it out in fidelity. We desire that Congress shall take no steps to renew unnecessary dispute, but that it shall consider that the elections have established peace in the Government till it is known whether war is meant." Dec. 3, 1866.

in December, "and the indications are that we shall have an easy-going session." *Harper's* declared: "Unless . . . the President shall exasperate and alarm the country, we do not believe that in the present condition of public opinion he will be impeached. . . . Nor do we anticipate at this session of Congress the proposition of any severer conditions of restoration than the adoption of the Amendment."[4]

The point has already been made in a previous chapter that by no means all Republicans were satisfied with the Amendment as constituting final terms. For that reason the matter had been left open at the time of the measure's final passage in the summer.[5] Moreover, the South's case was hardly helped by the fact that when Congress met in December, 1866, three of the former rebel states had already rejected the Amendment.[6] Nor were matters improved by the President's Second Annual Message, which was transmitted to Congress on December 4. In it, despite many high hopes to the contrary, the Chief Executive gave no indication that his views on the Amendment had in any way changed. Indeed, although everything now depended on the Amendment, Johnson did not so much as mention it.[7] The Democrats were already beginning to exult over a "dead-lock."

There was consequently a certain impetus for radical energy from the very beginning of the session. On December 4 Sumner announced

[4] J. W. Grimes to Mrs. Grimes, Dec. 5, 1866, in William Salter, *Life of James W. Grimes* (New York: D. Appleton, 1876), p. 308; *Harper's Weekly*, X (Nov. 17, 1866), 722. "As for Butler or impeachment, you need not fear we shall follow the one or attempt the other," Senator Sherman wrote to his brother. "Johnson ought to acquiesce in the public judgment, agree to the amendment, and we shall have peace. The personal feeling grows out of the wholesale removal of good Union men from office." John Sherman to William T. Sherman, Dec. 3, 1866, *The Sherman Letters*, ed. Rachel Sherman Thorndike (New York: Scribner's, 1894), p. 284. "We are inclined to believe . . . that the effect of the late vote of the North on Mr. Johnson has been 'chastening,'" said the *Nation*, "and that he is now in . . . a 'subdued frame of mind.'" *Nation*, III (Oct. 25, 1866), 321. Much, of course, depended on the President's forthcoming attitude. Welles noted in his diary on November 17: "Senator Grimes writes me that if the President does not take the present terms, harder ones will be proposed—that never was more leniency shown to conquered by conquerors. These are the sentiments and views of our prominent legislators and statesmen." *Diary of Gideon Welles*, II, 618.

[5] See above, pp. 361–62.

[6] Texas and Georgia had rejected the Amendment in October and November, respectively; Florida did so on December 3, the day Congress assembled. During the critical month of December, four more states would refuse to ratify. See above, chap. 11, n. 54.

[7] The New York *Tribune*, whose editorial tone only the day before had been calm and reasonable (see above, n. 3), now bitterly declared: "We believe that there was no feeling of resentment to the President, not even in the hearts of the most Radical members of Congress, that would not have given way before the slightest tendency of the President to harmonize the country. In his Message he shows no such tendency. He clings to his dogmas with as much tenacity as when he hoped to carry the country in the late election." Dec. 4, 1866.

that he intended to offer resolutions which would declare the existing governments in the rebel states illegal, exclude them from congressional representation, and bar them from voting on constitutional amendments.[8] On the same day John Broomall introduced a resolution to more or less the same effect in the House.[9] Thaddeus Stevens on December 19 declared his wish to take up once again the reconstruction bill which he had introduced late in the previous session.[10] The moderate James G. Blaine, noting on December 10 that every Southern state except Tennessee which had so far considered the Amendment had refused to ratify it, said he did not think the Amendment provided the necessary protection for Unionists and Negroes. The latter required, he said, "the gift of free suffrage."[11] Representative Rufus Spalding of Ohio, on the other hand, wanted it spelled out in so many words that Congress did intend to readmit the Southern states upon ratification. His resolution, offered on December 10, was referred to the Joint Committee on Reconstruction and never heard of again.[12]

Nevertheless, the Republican commitment to the Fourteenth Amendment as the terms for readmission was about as strong as it could well have been at this time, given the party's unwillingness, as a body, to go the length of a full, explicit, and categorical promise. It was sufficiently strong, at any rate, that a number of top Republican leaders felt morally bound by the commitment, and said so. Benjamin F. Wade, in heated debate with Sumner on December 14, accused the latter of misleading the Southern states by his original vote in favor of Amendment:

If the Senator did not intend that they should have the benefit of what we had done by compliance with the terms on their part it seems to me there was something wrong. I intended to let them in on the terms prescribed. . . . Certainly, I am as much for colored suffrage as any man on this floor, but when I make such an agreement as that I stand by it always.
. . . Of course they must send loyal men; they must send men who can take the oath; but all these conditions being complied with they should be received. If we did not mean that, I do not know what we did mean.[13]

John Sherman said virtually the same thing. "I know I voted for th[e] amendment with that understanding. I felt that I would be bound

[8] *Congressional Globe*, 39 Cong., 2 sess., p. 7.

[9] *Ibid.*, p. 11.

[10] *Ibid.*, p. 209; Kendrick, *Journal of the Joint Committee of Fifteen on Reconstruction*, pp. 358–61.

[11] *Cong. Globe*, 39 Cong., 2 sess., p. 53.

[12] *Ibid.*, p. 48; Kendrick, *Journal*, p. 356.

[13] *Cong. Globe*, 39 Cong., 2 sess., pp. 124–25.

by that action." He added, "The people of the State of Ohio, at least, understood that if any State in the South accepted this constitutional amendment its Senators and Representatives should take their seats by our side."[14] The *Nation* insisted on December 20:

We think there can be little question that, as a matter of fact, the mass of the party, in Congress and out of it, did understand that when the amendment was proposed its acceptance was the only necessary condition of readmission, and the elections were carried on this understanding in all the Northern States. If this was a misconception, the Radical leaders are to blame for not having spoken out more loudly before the vote. So far as we know, no organ of that wing of the Republican party, except the *Independent*, gave the slightest intimation that there was any doubt about the matter.[15]

John Bingham was maintaining this position as late as January 16, even though protection for Negroes and Unionists, together with Southern recalcitrance about ratifying, had by then erupted into issues of the most intense sort. "I stand upon the proposition," he declared in the House, "that the Congress . . . did give out this amendment to the people of the United States as the future basis of reconstruction. . . ."[16]

14 *Ibid.*, p. 128. The remarks of both Wade and Sherman were incidental to a debate then in progress over the admission of Nebraska to statehood. The principle involved was whether Congress had the right to change the terms of admission (or, in the case of the South, readmission) after terms based on prior arrangements had been complied with. Sumner opposed the admission of Nebraska because the latter's constitution contained the word "white" in its qualifications for voting, despite the fact that the congressional enabling act of 1864 for Nebraska had made no conditions on this point. By the same token he did not feel bound by the Fourteenth Amendment as terms of readmission for the South, despite the general understanding to that effect, since it did not specifically provide for Negro suffrage. The Nebraska bill, however, was passed in January, 1867, then repassed early in February over the President's veto. An effort at the same time to bring in Colorado failed, that territory having then less than 30,000 population. McPherson, *Reconstruction*, pp. 160–66.

15 *Nation*, III (Dec. 20, 1866), 485. The net balance of sentiment may have been more or less accurately expressed by Senator Fessenden on December 19. On the one hand, Fessenden denied that Congress had committed itself unconditionally to readmit states upon ratification; on the other hand, he let it be understood that such evidences of good faith as a disposition to ratify would find him personally very receptive. ". . . I say now, as I have said before, I am as desirous as any man can be that this unhappy controversy should be ended; I am as desirous as any man can be that all these rebellious States should be back again in the Union on a perfect equality with those that are there now, and I will do everything in my power to bring it about, and I will not be too stringent as to conditions; I am willing to yield much and to suffer much; but I will not yield under any circumstances the guarantees we have insisted upon up to this date, and such further ones if necessary—I do not say now that any others are necessary—as will secure the Union against a recurrence of a disaster such as we have suffered." *Cong. Globe*, 39 Cong., 2 sess., p. 193. The context of these remarks was a short and rather acid reply which Fessenden was making to an argument of Senator Doolittle, who had claimed that if a state were legally capable of accepting a constitutional amendment, it was automatically entitled to perform all the other functions of a state as well.

16 *Cong. Globe*, 39 Cong., 2 sess., p. 500.

Up to early January, moderate Republicans had some grounds for optimism in their hopes of achieving a settlement. They had made a variety of efforts in the weeks following the election to convince individual Southerners privately, and the South at large publicly, that they would get no better terms than those represented by the Amendment and that in their own best interests they would do well to ratify.

In at least two key states, Virginia and Alabama, these counsels during the month of December appeared to be having a certain effect. General Schofield, commanding the Department of the Potomac, was in constant touch both with Republican congressmen and with members of the Virginia legislature, and strongly advised the latter to accept the Amendment. Virginia "would thus be restored at once to her full privileges as a State in the Union." Schofield had the assurance from leading Republicans, "so far as it was in their power to give it, that such would be the result," and had reason to think "that the amendment would be speedily ratified."[17] Alexander Sharp, a federal appointee in Richmond, had much the same impression after sounding out a number of the legislators. "Now they look much more favorably on it," he wrote to Elihu Washburne in mid-December. "Changes are daily taking place. . . . [Mr. Pendleton] is on the Committee to whom this question has been referred, and speaks very hopefully of its passing."[18] And yet in the end, according to Schofield, "other influences, understood to come from some source in Washington (probably President Johnson), finally prevailed; the amendment was rejected; and Virginia was thus doomed to undergo 'congressional reconstruction' in company with her sister States."[19]

Efforts in Alabama by General Swayne similar to those of Schofield in Virginia appear to have had, up to a point, a fairly persuasive effect. Governor R. M. Patton, who had initially advised the legislature not to ratify, subsequently changed his mind and on December 6 transmitted a special message urging "favorable action upon the proposed

[17] John M. Schofield, *Forty-six Years in the Army* (New York: Century, 1897), pp. 394–95.

[18] Alexander Sharp to Elihu Washburne, Dec. 19, 1866, Washburne MSS, Library of Congress.

[19] Schofield, *Forty-six Years*, p. 395. After the rejection, Sharp again wrote to Washburne apologizing for having misled him as to sentiment in Virginia. "The intention," he explained, ". . . was to not act on it until the end of the session—about the 4th of March. I am told that some members votes were influenced by threats that the President would dispose of Congress summarily etc. etc. Of this however I have no knowledge myself. But am surprised at a number who did *not vote at all* but dodged the question." A. Sharp to E. Washburne, Jan. 10, 1867, Washburne MSS.

amendment to the Constitution," and declaring: "We should look our true condition full in the face."[20] Meanwhile Swayne had written to Sherman, "Give us a little time, and we will be all right on the Amendment. . . ."[21] Certain circumstances, however, forced a premature vote on the question. A dispatch from former Provisional Governor Lewis E. Parsons, who was then in Washington, emphatically opposed ratification. It was widely believed that Parsons' telegram had been directly inspired by the President, and under the excitement created by it nearly every member on December 7 fell into line in voting the Amendment down. Yet Governor Patton, by now convinced that the state would never get any better terms, that Congress would settle for nothing less, and that the legislature ought therefore to reconsider, decided to campaign vigorously during the Christmas recess in favor of the Amendment. He appears to have made substantial headway, and the legislature was about to take a new vote when another telegram arrived from Washington on January 17, strongly asserting that no purpose would be served by a reconsideration. The Amendment was thereupon doomed in Alabama. No one in the state was by then in much of a position to dispute this latest message, since its author was President Johnson.[22]

II INCEPTION AND GROWTH OF A RADICAL POLICY

Stevens, Sumner, Broomall, and other radical congressmen were determined from the beginning of the session to impose a program of radical reconstruction on the South. They were quite naturally disposed to interpret the election as a mandate for strong measures, even though such a view did not initially correspond with the general post-election feeling.[23] For Stevens this meant a certain

[20] Patton said that his original convictions still held, in principle, but added: "The necessity of the case, I am now constrained to think, is different." For Patton's two messages to the legislature, see *American Annual Cyclopaedia, 1866*, pp. 11–12.

[21] Wager Swayne to John Sherman, Dec. 5, 1866, John Sherman MSS, Library of Congress.

[22] Swayne to S. P. Chase, Dec. 10, 1866, in "Diary and Correspondence of Salmon P. Chase," *Annual Report of the American Historical Association, 1902* (Washington: Government Printing Office, 1903), II, 516–17; Beale, *Critical Year*, p. 402 n. Johnson's telegram of January 17 was sent to former Provisional Governor Parsons (now back in Alabama), who immediately made its contents known. Walter L. Fleming, *Documentary History of Reconstruction* (Cleveland: Arthur H. Clark, 1906), I, 237–38; Fleming, *Civil War and Reconstruction in Alabama*, pp. 394–97; McPherson, *Reconstruction*, pp. 352–53.

[23] E.g., *Harper's* in its editorial of November 17 vigorously disclaimed being among those "who suppose that the elections have given Congress *carte blanche*, authorizing it to do whatever eccentricity or extravagance may propose. . . . Those who persistently reason of the people of the United States to-day as if they were the French Revolution-

degree of actual confiscation; for Sumner and most of the others it meant a minimum program of universal Negro suffrage and wide disfranchisement of ex-Confederates. What they all did agree on, however, was that the existing state governments in the South—with the exception of Tennessee's—must be set aside and replaced for the time being by direct federal rule. Typical of this sentiment was the resolution offered in the House by Broomall on opening day:

Resolved, That the Committee on Territories be instructed to inquire into the expediency of reporting a bill providing territorial governments for the several districts of country within the jurisdiction of the United States, formerly occupied by the once existing States of Virginia, North Carolina, South Carolina, Georgia, Florida, Mississippi, Alabama, Louisiana, Arkansas, and Texas, giving to all adult male inhabitants, born within the limits of the United States, or duly naturalized, and not participants in the late rebellion, full and equal political rights in such territorial governments.[24]

The argument for an enlarged congressional policy along some such line as this grew progressively more convincing as time went on. The existing state governments, it was held, could not really be considered legal. Virtually no Republican congressman ever had, in fact, considered them fully constituted governing entities. They had been organized by the President without consulting Congress, so that neither the President nor the states themselves seemed to have any true grounds for claiming that they were automatically entitled to congressional representation. With every week bringing fresh indications that these states would never voluntarily accept even the minimum terms Congress had offered, the South's stolid insistence meanwhile on its "rights" could hardly have failed to generate a spreading poison in Northern feeling.

Added to this was the fact that steady persecutions of Unionists and Negroes in the South were coming more and more to occupy the forefront of Northern attention. Their very regularity made them hard to ignore. A government with any claim to legitimacy, so went the argument, must at the very least be able to maintain law and order. The only remedy, it began to seem, was direct federal intervention.

---

ists of 1793 will probably see nothing but a reign of terror in the assembly of 'a Radical Congress.' But such persons have neither faith in popular government nor in any other principle which requires confidence in the public good sense." *Harper's Weekly,* X (Nov. 17, 1866), 722.

[24] *Cong. Globe,* 39 Cong., 2 sess., p. 11. See also the remarks of Sumner on December 4 and 5, and those of Stevens on January 3, *ibid.,* pp. 7, 15–16, 250–53. The argument for this whole general viewpoint was fully and eloquently, if somewhat floridly, expressed by Representative Hamilton Ward of New York on December 13. *Ibid.,* pp. 115–18.

Stories of atrocity incidents and miscarriages of justice had of course been drifting northward all during the past year and a half. But whether such incidents were or were not happening any oftener now, men became much more sensitive to them; the stories seemed to take on a new, heightened, and more sinister meaning once it became quite clear that the fall elections and their results were making no difference in the behavior of Southern communities. Letters of besieged Union men to members of Congress were full of woe. "If Congress will only *destroy these bogus governments,*" implored J. C. Emerson from Fernandina, Florida, "they may leave us to take care of ourselves for years while they reconstruct if they choose. But as it is now we are bound hand and foot in the tender mercies of the rebels."[25] Redress even from the military was apparently very hard to come by in the face of local police and judicial practice. "We can arrest under the present laws of Congress," complained the federal commander at Little Rock to General Howard, "but we can not hold any one in the face of the writ of habeas corpus. . . . I had some half dozen murderers in confinement who were arrested by my order for murders—principally of union men and freedmen—but they sue out writs of habeas corpus and before I am aware of it are released by one of the *Union* judges of the present State government. . . ."[26] By January, 1867, a number of North Carolina newspapers were complaining of bands of ruffians and murderers roving through certain counties of that state. Governor Jonathan Worth experienced a variety of clashing emotions, particularly since these editorials were appearing in papers otherwise friendly to his administration. In the many letters which the harassed Governor wrote during this period he would, all at one and the same time, declare that state assistance should have been called for, that the local officers were "grossly negligent in pointing out and bring[ing] malefactors to justice," that all such reports were doing the state "incalculable mischief" and furnishing "rich material

25 Rev. J. C. Emerson to Col. Liberty Billings, Dec. 21, 1866, Charles Sumner MSS, Harvard College Library. Emerson was a former army chaplain currently doing missionary work in Florida. His letter, which Billings passed on to Sumner, described some of the legal and judicial persecutions practiced on Union men in local Southern courts. As for himself, he said: "I would not live here for another year at the risk of my life, & pay costs, & other expenses to meet the common rights of citizens for all the property here."

26 Gen. E. O. C. Ord to Gen. O. O. Howard, Dec. 31, 1866, Sumner MSS. "I hope General," urged Ord, "you will use your influence in trying to secure me more troops in this Dept. especially cavalry—now I have none and the outlaws are well mounted—in some instances the agents of the Bureau write me that less than 25 mounted men need not be sent to arrest the bands of murderers—these bands are more or less numerous in about half the counties of the State—and I have but five hundred footmen to protect the union men and freedmen."

to the Radicals," and that, indeed, the stories were basically lies and should never have been printed at all. Most revealing, in terms of both the state of the Southern mind and the state of law and order in North Carolina, was the Governor's remark that the real evil was "not want of power in the State nor counties—but the cowardice of the people wronged."[27]

Two incidents in particular—one in South Carolina and the other in Virginia—had recently been given wide attention because of the Executive Department's intervention on behalf of murderers convicted by military commissions. The first case involved six South Carolinians who had killed three Union soldiers on guard duty in the fall of 1865. They had been given a lengthy military trial; four were found guilty; two were condemned to hang and the other two sentenced to life imprisonment. After appeals and much publicity the condemned prisoners' sentences were commuted to life imprisonment in the Dry Tortugas. The prisoners were then, however, directed by the President to be transferred to Fort Delaware instead. Upon their arrival, the commander at that place was served with a writ of habeas corpus from a federal district judge of Delaware. The writ was complied with; there was a hearing in mid-November before the judge, who ordered the prisoners released on the grounds that the civil courts of South Carolina had been open at the time the crime was committed. The freed culprits upon their return to South Carolina were given a grand welcome and no effort was subsequently made to bring them to trial.[28]

The other case concerned a Dr. James L. Watson, of Rockbridge County, Virginia, who in November, 1866, had by his own admission pursued, shot, and killed a local Negro of acknowledged good character for having accidentally inflicted about fifty cents' worth of damage on his carriage while passing it on a narrow road. (The act of passing was considered an insult to the doctor's wife and daughter, who were on their way to church.) An "examining court" of five justices of the peace tried and acquitted Watson, whereupon General Schofield in pursuance of the congressional act of July 16, 1866, extending mili-

---

[27] "In the language of Vance, 'people who allow themselves to be pressed upon without resentment, cannot expect the laws to protect them.'" Worth might have added—though it was psychologically impossible for him to do so—that the "cowardice" of such people was likely to continue so long as the entire weight of local community sentiment was exerted to discourage them from seeking redress. See *The Correspondence of Jonathan Worth*, ed. J. G. de Roulhac Hamilton (Raleigh: North Carolina Historical Commission, 1909), II, 867–82.

[28] *House Reports*, 39 Cong., 2 sess., 1866–67, No. 23, "Murder of Union Soldiers." With some distaste the Secretary of War, uncertain about the implications of the Milligan decision, recommended compliance with the writ. See testimony of E. M. Stanton in *ibid.*, pp. 34–36.

tary jurisdiction over a variety of cases involving freedmen, ordered Watson tried by military commission. The commission found the defendant guilty of murder. President Johnson on December 21 ordered the commission dissolved and the prisoner released. The previous trial by the local examining court was to be regarded as final.[29]

These incidents, *causes célèbres* though they were, need not have proved anything conclusive about the "lawlessness" of the Southern population in 1866 and 1867. But they did, and do, illustrate a very basic principle of American justice, which is that such justice positively requires co-operation and a working consensus at the local level or it cannot work at all. It was not even so much a matter of unwillingness on the part of higher judges and officials to do their duty; it was rather an all-but-total reluctance of local courts and local police to proceed in the face of community sentiment. The federal commanders in the South, Generals Thomas, Schofield, Wood, Sickles, and Baird, all testified to this effect, each saying that in his opinion neither the Unionist or Negro could expect justice in the Southern courts:

GENERAL WOOD. . . . When cases come into the higher courts some of the better classes of judges are more disposed to do justice, and to have the laws fairly executed; but my observation during the time I held command in Mississippi has been that justice cannot be administered, with the public sentiment of the people of the State such as it remains, against the black people, and against Union men.

Q. Was that machinery so utterly defective . . . as to make the courts entirely unreliable?

A. Yes, sir; I should call it unreliable. That is a very good word.[30]

[29] *Sen. Exec. Docs.*, 39 Cong., 2 sess., 1866–67, No. 29, "Violations of the Civil Rights Bill," pp. 17–37. From the testimony and records of both these cases it appears that special efforts were made to provide the prisoners with a full and impartial trial. Owing to the grave implications of each case, the commanding generals of the departments concerned (Sickles and Schofield) had felt it necessary to give much personal attention to the proceedings. The criticisms made against these trials, indeed, were not concerned with their fairness (to which there was very little objection); they rested rather on the argument that military commissions could not be resorted to when the civil courts were open. Taking into account the special congressional legislation which had been enacted to meet the then current conditions in the South (Freedmen's Bureau and Civil Rights Acts), this was, to say the least, a moot question.

[30] "Murder of Union Soldiers," pp. 29–30. General Sickles said: "I think the judges of the higher courts . . . have respect for the law, and will declare it as they conscientiously believe it to be. But the men you would have on a jury in the case of a Union man . . . would not heed the court or the law. . . . To have justice done, the arrests must be made; the ministerial officers of justice must be vigilant and honest in their desire to arrest the party; the inferior magistrates must issue warrants promptly on proper information, must put them into the hands of a zealous and efficient officer, and see that he does his duty; the sheriffs must be active and vigilant; and then the offenders must be securely confined in jails until the time of trial. All this is very seldom done, nor anything like it." And General Baird: "I believe the judges, who are men of edu-

The general effect of all such reports, coming when they did, was to discredit the legitimacy of the Southern state governments. Not only did these governments lack *de jure* sanction, being unrecognized by Congress, but they did not even seem operative in a *de facto* sense, inasmuch as they could not provide protection for loyal citizens.

The time would very quickly come when this was no longer simply an argument for radicalism but seemed the observation of common sense. "None—not the most moderate," the New York *Times* was saying by early February, 1867, "—has declared himself content with matters as they are. Not one has denied the need for some further interference to prevent the outrages that are now perpetrated with impunity, and to afford more effective guarantees to the loyal portion of the community."[31]

III THE DEMOCRATS AND THE STRATEGY OF "DEAD-LOCK"

The Democrats' losses in the fall elections were sufficiently crushing that they could not afford to think in terms which went much beyond shoring up their immediate organizational position. For political tactics they now seemed more dependent than ever on harassment and sniping for short-term purposes; they could overlook no opportunity that might enable them to pick up a few votes for the next state and local elections or to maneuver an office or two away from the local Republicans. "Unable to see beyond a post-office, custom-house, or the next election," a taunt whose essence was familiar enough in American politics, applied with exceptional pertinence to the Democratic party of 1866 and 1867. The Democrats had fallen upon evil days; they were in bad moral odor with a large section of the public; and they were living, as it were, on their wits.

In the national government, though technically the Democrats "held the balance of power" and were capable of many sorts of mischief, they were less than ever in a policy-making position. They were in a position which required that all emerging problems be converted more or less automatically into issues that had a chance of hamstringing or somehow confounding the Republican majority. Thus with regard to

---

cation, would be more frequently disposed to do justice, but I am satisfied that they would be unable to procure justice in a suit between a white man and a black man or a Union man and a rebel." General George H. Thomas, asked if he thought the ordinary courts of justice in Georgia were sufficient for the protection of Negroes and Unionists, replied, "Not as administered now by these people." *Ibid.*, pp. 13, 28, 32. The above-quoted testimony was given to a House committee in January, 1867.

[31] New York *Times*, Feb. 11, 1867.

Southern affairs, despite the overwhelming importance of such affairs, the Democrats' operations could not be expected to produce much in the way of statesmanship, considering how difficult it now was for the party to function in the normal sense as a responsible opposition. It is therefore in this setting, with a severe dearth of talent in Congress, and unduly dominated by those negative requirements of day-to-day skirmishing which so shorten the vision, that the Democrats' behavior during this period has to be understood.

The Democrats were no longer interested primarily in ending the difficulties of reconstruction; they apparently assumed that restoration of some kind was not far distant anyway. Rescuing their Southern brethren now came second to their willingness to prolong, if it seemed worthwhile, an issue that had a chance of discrediting the Republican party. Thus one major item in their strategy, with the opening of Congress, was to do everything they could to prevent or sabotage any sort of rapprochement between President Johnson and the Republican majority. Before the contents of the President's Annual Message were known, the Democrats were touchy, fearful that Johnson might feel called upon to do some compromising, and they were most anxious to keep hostilities going. "It is for our interest," confided a highly placed operative of the New York Democracy to Manton Marble, "to precipitate this fight with the Radicals, and I am apprehensive J. will so manage as to postpone it. I have inspired Cox to set things in train (if he can do it so covertly as not to seem officious) for launching some sort of a thunderbolt immediately on the reading of the message, to set the Radicals on fire and kindle a conflagration."[32] They were actually quite willing to turn upon Johnson himself if they could get any advantage out of it. "If the Prest. does not give us an opportunity to fight the Radicals in *his* interest, we must fight both them and him in our own."[33]

The principal issue was the Fourteenth Amendment, whose great danger to the Democrats was the possibility of terms. The party there-

[32] "J. C." to Manton Marble, Dec. 2, 1866, Marble MSS, Library of Congress. Marble was editor of the New York *World*, spokesman for the Democratic party in New York. "J. C." was at this time staying at Willard's in Washington; the "Cox" to whom he refers was S.S. ("Sunset") Cox, originally an Ohio Democrat who had moved to New York in 1865 after being promised by the New York Democrats that they would do what they could to elect him to Congress from that state.

[33] "We must have a fight with them *anyhow*; and if they fall back on the message, we must either dislodge them from their stronghold or *blow it up.*" *Ibid.* This feeling—that Johnson, should he compromise in some way with the Republicans, would be a liability to the Democratic party—was strong enough early in December that Tammany at one point decided to withdraw its support from him. As matters turned out, of course, the Democrats need not have worried.

fore labored mightily to prevent either Johnson or the South from
making any sort of adjustment on that issue, and in the final stages of
debate on the Reconstruction Act in February they tried to tie up a
developing movement toward a settlement, all in the hope of initiating
a groundswell of popular reaction against the Republicans in the
North.

Their rallying cry was "dead-lock." With regard to the Amendment the election had settled nothing; let the South refuse to ratify,
and the Republican party would be rendered impotent. "There is no
power in the government to punish a State for refusing to ratify
amendments to the Constitution." The Republicans would not dare to
impose harsher measures such as territorial governments or military
rule, since the Supreme Court would then "declare such legislation
void, and the whole subject [would] revert into its present shape." No
matter what the Republicans did, they were paralyzed. Let Congress
put forth a sterner plan, suggested the Detroit *Free Press:* "Who cares
if it does?" Let the Republicans try impeaching the President, jeered
the *World:* the effect "would be to fill the public mind with uncertainty and precipitate a commercial revulsion." Ultimately the peace-loving masses of the North were certain to tire of disunion. Their patience exhausted, they would then turn upon the Republicans and
throw them out of office. Thus, reasoned the *World,*

every hour this dead-lock is prolonged does no harm to the South beyond
the continuance of its present deprivations. But to the Radicals the prolonged dead-lock is ruin. They must do something. They are responsible
for disunion; they can only rid themselves of the responsibility by permitting the Union to restore itself.[34]

These notions had certain corollaries in strategy. For one thing, the
South and the Democrats could, and should, stand still. By the same
token, the Democrats reasoned, if the issue should remain deadlocked,
the Republicans might either have to surrender entirely or else take
such drastic measures—disfranchisement and Negro suffrage—as to
drive a large contingent of moderate Republicans into the Democratic
party and bring the Democrats great numbers of moderate votes. Extreme reconstruction measures were certainly bruited about from the
very first, though from all indications the Democrats never quite believed, until almost the last minute, that the Republicans would really
and truly resort to them. This may help to explain why the Democrats,

[34] These excerpts, in the order quoted, appeared in the New York *World,* Nov. 17
and Dec. 6, 1866; Detroit *Free Press,* Nov. 15, 1866; New York *World,* Nov. 14 and
Dec. 1, 1866. The "dead-lock" theory was worked out at great length in the editorial
columns of the *World,* particularly during the weeks following the election. See esp.
(in addition to those cited) editorials of Nov. 8, 9, 19, 20, and 30, 1866.

with a kind of hypnotic fascination, were actually rather disposed to encourage radical schemes in order to see just what might happen to them.[35]

The main thing, in any case, was that all efforts to arrive at a compromise must be blocked. The Democratic Chicago *Times*, trying to take a larger view of the problem, suggested in November that the Southern states might do well to enact a qualified Negro suffrage so that the North might be better disposed to an early termination of military rule. Most of the country's other Democratic newspapers were furious. The *Times* was widely attacked for cowardice and trimming.[36] As late as February, when a rumor spread briefly to the effect that Johnson was considering some sort of understanding with Congress, the Democrats were again thrown into a frenzy. "Would the President improve his personal position by yielding?" demanded the *World*. No, the Republicans, who hate him now, would despise him then. "But if *they* do not think better of him for yielding, who will?"[37] A. E. Burr, a Democratic functionary in Connecticut, wrote agitatedly to Gideon Welles that he hoped the rumor was untrue. It would be very bad, he said, for the Democrats in the Connecticut spring elections.[38]

[35] E.g., the Detroit *Free Press* suggested at the beginning of the session that it would be a good idea for the Democratic members of Congress to protest but not to put up any actual opposition to radical plans as such plans were brought forward and developed. The absence of Democratic resistance would allow the inevitable factional splits (or so the Democrats imagined) to develop between conservative and radical Republicans. "Let them, unimpeded, have their own way, and we are mistaken in our judgment of the American people if the divisions in the Republican ranks do not turn out, after all, to be the best security for our institutions." Detroit *Free Press*, Dec. 6, 1866. This rather suicidal conception did much to govern the Democrats' behavior all during the session.

[36] Chicago *Times*, Nov. 12 and 13, 1866. On these days the *Times* broached its suggestion that the Democratic party "cut loose from the administration of Andrew Johnson, and leave that hybrid concern to float on the sea of public contempt into which it some time since entered" and that it cut the ground from under the Republicans by supporting impartial Negro suffrage for the South. The *World* would have nothing to do with the idea; the *Free Press* in shocked horror denounced it as a "bold but unprincipled proposition." New York *World*, Nov. 19 and 20, 1866; Detroit *Free Press*, Nov. 16, 1866. The *Times* on Nov. 16 admitted that its proposal had met with considerable opposition from the rest of the Democratic press. The Cincinnati *Enquirer* had declared: "The democracy will not adopt the miserable heresy of negro suffrage, of making this a mixed black and white government, but it will ever maintain that as this is the white man's country, it should be ruled by white men pure and exclusive." Nov. 14 and 18, 1866. Of the major Democratic newspapers, the Chicago *Times* and Boston *Post* were virtually the only ones that advocated impartial suffrage. It is significant that both were located in strong radical Negro suffrage areas.

[37] New York *World*, Feb. 14, 1867.

[38] "A dispatch today . . . says the Evening Post has information from Washington, reliable, that 'the President will meet Congress more than half way in reconstruction, and that he will not oppose any measure embracing the proposed Constitutional Amend-

The Northern Democratic party could not hope, in view of its recent disasters, to make much positive difference in the formation of national policy. But the influence which its spokesmen could and did exert in the South was quite another matter. In some ways the most interesting and least appreciated aspect of the Democrats' activity during this period was how they undertook the tutelage of an audience truly captive by circumstance, and set themselves up as bellwether for the South of political developments in the North.

The chief organ for this was the *World*, official voice of the New York Democracy and acknowledged leader of Democratic opinion throughout the North. Other Northern Democratic newspapers generally followed the cues given out by the *World*; and especially remarkable was the fact that Southern journals hung upon every pronouncement which the *World* saw fit to make throughout the period. That paper, it would be quite safe to say, came regularly to the desk of nearly every editor in the South.

Amid the thousands of words directed at its Southern constituency, the *World* played variations upon two major themes. In the first place, the Amendment was a fraud and a swindle. It was stultifying and humiliating to the South; there was no guarantee that Southern representatives would be readmitted even if it were accepted; and in any case the states would have to come in with reduced representation if they were then unwilling to barter their honor for Negro suffrage in accordance with Section 2 of the Amendment.[39]

The other theme was that the South had "nothing to fear." Congress had already done its worst. Here was the "dead-lock" theory as it applied to the South: no law could force a state to ratify a constitutional amendment against its will; territorial rule or new penalties for

ment.' I hope this is not true. It would injure us were the President to countenance that tyrannical Amendment in any way." A. E. Burr to Gideon Welles, Feb. 11, 1867, Welles MSS, Library of Congress. In the same letter Burr reflected the other general aspect of Democratic strategy when he said: "Let the Radicals go on. . . . The more extreme the measures of the radicals . . . the sooner they will be whipped so they will stay whipped."

39 "As it is actually offered, it is a question whether the South will ratify a hostile and humiliating amendment on its merits, and trust, with confiding verdancy, to the mercy of a Radical Congress afterwards. So long as this remains the state of the question, we advise the South to commit no such gratuitous folly as to subject itself to certain loss without any counterbalancing gains." New York *World*, Oct. 25, 1866. "What would they [the Southern states] gain by doing so? Admission to Congress, perhaps— but of that they have no promise—with a diminished representation." *Ibid.*, Nov. 8, 1866. "The true interpretation . . . is, that the Republican leaders know that the amendment was a dishonest sham, which, having served its purpose, they desire to bury out of sight. . . . They never meant it as a plan of settlement, but only as a piece of electioneering claptrap." *Ibid.*, Nov. 20, 1866.

treason were unconstitutional and would be voided by the Court; and to impeach the President would be to cause a financial panic. Meanwhile the Northern Democrats would never indorse the Amendment. With the President, the Supreme Court, and the Democratic party all standing firm to protect the South, the radicals were blocked and the South need not budge. "When, therefore, it shall be made to appear that the Union cannot be restored by extorting from the South ratifications which it would not give, a reaction will set in against the Radicals."[40]

The leading Democratic arguments, which for the South represented the line of least resistance, were naturally picked up in most of the leading Southern newspapers. Democratic success, warned the *World*, required that the Southern states stand firm. "This is good advice," responded the Augusta *Daily Press*, "and will be followed by the people of the South."[41] The South would not assist in its own disfranchisement, announced the *World*. "The New York *World* correctly states the feeling among us," responded the Richmond *Enquirer*.[42] There was no way to force the South to ratify, said the *World*; and the Jackson *Clarion*, in the same words the *World* itself had used on November 17, demanded on the twenty-fifth: "Where is 'the power in the government to punish a State for refusing to ratify amendments to the Constitution?' A few mad fanatics may threaten, but where is the authority to execute?"[43] The South had "nothing to fear," said the *World*. "We counsel our readers," echoed the *Clarion*, ". . . not to be frightened by Radical blusterers nor be persuaded to give up our inalienable rights by the weak-kneed of our own section."[44] And the Richmond *Times* stoutly promised: ". . . we will neither be intimidated nor made to aid in our own degradation and dishonor."[45]

The image of the "dead-lock"—with the President, public opinion, the Constitution, and the Supreme Court all protecting the South, and with Congress at the end of its rope, having already gone as far as it dared—was fatally subversive to Southern thinking and Southern judgment. Despite all evidence to the contrary, Johnson must still be seen as the South's bulwark against the radicals. "Turn where they will, he is found with his heel upon the constitutional landmarks; and until he is deposed for refusing to obey despotic laws—and that will be the most

[40] *Ibid.*, Oct. 25, Nov. 8, 9, 17, 30, Dec. 1, 6, 1866.

[41] Augusta (Ga.) *Daily Press*, Oct. 19, 1866.

[42] Richmond *Enquirer*, Nov. 1, 1866.

[43] Jackson (Miss.) *Clarion*, Nov. 25, 1866; cf. above, p. 462.

[44] *Ibid.*   [45] Richmond *Times*, Dec. 1, 1866.

perilous undertaking of all—we see but little prospect of a Radical triumph over the people of the South."[46] "You may reject members of Congress but [you] cannot get the people to endorse your nefarious constitutional amendments. Congress may be Republican, but it cannot alter the present form of government without the consent of the people."[47] "The sensible men of the North desire peace as well as we," the Richmond *Enquirer* told itself, "and enough of them will refuse to concur in this new programme of distraction and turmoil, to throw the agitators into a minority. So we believe."[48] "The awful threats, bellowings and maledictions which the Radicals have been hurling at the South to coerce the adoption of the (un)constitutional amendment," calmly announced the Richmond *Times*, "are simply a part of that bluff game which the Yankees play upon every one who is fool enough to be victimized by this species of Chinese warfare. . . ."[49] In a series of editorials in December, the *World* employed lengthy legal exegesis and quoted weighty precedents—a technique which the Southern mind had few resources for resisting—to "prove" that territorializing the South was constitutionally impossible and would be struck down by the Court. These "exceedingly able articles" were greeted in the South with a chorus of praise.[50]

By mid-February the reconstruction bill was nearing completion. Everyone knew what it contained and the temper of Congress, by that time, was only too clear. Yet on February 22 the Jackson *Clarion*, still in its fool's paradise, confided:

The New York *World* thinks that the Radicals have committed a great error in declaring war against the Supreme Court, and that if this bill . . . pass the Senate it will be the greatest blunder the Radical party has yet made. It will enable the President to send in a veto message more crushing in argument, and more telling in its exposure of dangerous designs than any State paper ever published either in England or America. It is such an opportunity as Mr. Johnson has every reason to covet.

The *World*, meanwhile, could no longer hide from itself the realization that military reconstruction was going to be an actuality. On the twenty-third it reversed itself and advised the South to reorganize under the new bill. Moreover, it would be better to hurry so that Southern votes would be available for the 1868 presidential election. Its

[46] Jackson *Clarion*, Nov. 18, 1866.   [47] *Ibid.*, Nov. 28, 1866.

[48] Richmond *Enquirer*, Dec. 4, 1866.

[49] Richmond *Times*, Jan. 9, 1867.

[50] E.g., Richmond *Times*, Dec. 15, 1866; New Orleans *Picayune*, Dec. 16, 1866; Charleston *Courier*, Dec. 29, 1866.

previous advice, the *World* blandly added three days later, had been wrong. But then no one could have predicted the depths to which the radicals would sink; "it was not supposed or supposable that such a stretch of perfidy or inconsistency could be ventured upon."[51] The *World* might also have added that if anything had been needed to guarantee the inevitability of what was now happening, it was the very policy which the Northern Democratic press, led by itself, had been recklessly urging for the past four months.

The South began at last to realize that it had been duped, that Congress was, in fact, supported by the Northern public after all, and that the "great popular revulsion" against the radicals was nowhere in sight. "Those who have induced us to believe otherwise," bitterly observed the Augusta *Daily Press*, "have deceived themselves and us."[52]

IV THE SOUTH AND "MASTERLY INACTIVITY"

There were, of course, other voices in the North besides that of the Democratic party to which the South had been free to listen in the months following the election. Provincial Southern editors and their rural readers were understandably oppressed by the resentments of defeated and impoverished communities; they were only too ready to listen to anyone who encouraged them in their bitterness; and largeness of vision concerning the true and proper course of action for the South was not likely, at this particular time, to grow spontaneously out of the current popular feeling. And yet the South was presumably not without its men of judgment and responsibility. There were still Southern leaders capable of discriminating between true and false counsels without entirely giving way to popular passions. Such men had access to higher, more direct, and more official sources of information than were available to the common run of local spokesmen. At federal military headquarters, for instance, they could find commanders who were as a rule men of circumspection, committed to peace and order, and who had no wish to see the South unduly heaped with fur-

---

[51] New York *World*, Feb. 23, 26, 1867.

[52] "Whatever we may do . . . we will do well to bear in mind that public opinion at the North approves the Congress which has just expired, and will approve its more advanced and progressive successor, and that so far as our present troubles are concerned, to look for a 'revulsion of feeling at the North' is like waiting for the sky to fall to catch larks." Augusta *Daily Press*, Mar. 9, 1867. The *Press* on March 2 had recalled the post-election advice of the Chicago *Times* and remarked that the South would have done better to listen to it rather than to that of the majority of the Democratic press. As early as February 25 the Richmond *Times* was saying that the Northern Democrats, who had simply used the South for their own party advantage, were no longer to be depended on. Nor was it likely that much could be expected from the Supreme Court either.

ther humiliations. By the same token there were a number of Republican congressmen, anxious for a peaceful settlement, whose records were quite free of extremism. There was in fact a degree of private interchange, by no means inconsiderable, between highly placed Southerners and official persons of this sort whose word on Northern opinion and the trend of affairs at Washington ought to have been well worth heeding. Indeed, as previously noted, advice from such sources was not wholly without its effect.

It is not always possible, however, to predict "rationally" what sort of action will result—or whether action will result at all—when strong advice is coming from two opposing directions. The result in this case was paralysis. There was, it should be added, still another source of advice and counsel whose influence was probably decisive in producing such an effect. This was Andrew Johnson, who, despite all that had happened, still occupied the nation's highest post of authority. It was still virtually impossible for any Southerner to perceive that Andrew Johnson's voice and views could never again be regarded as "official," so long as they remained at such variance with those of the Republican majority.

The fall elections of 1866 had plunged the South into heavy gloom, which was only natural. Many leading Southerners had supported the National Union movement, and they felt that they had gone as far at Philadelphia as honor would allow. Their gestures of reconciliation had in effect been rejected; their hopes of speedy readmission were abruptly ended. They were thus not in the best position to make fine discriminations in "moderate" Republican sentiment— where their best hope lay if it lay anywhere in the North—or to resist the South's being made a pawn in Northern partisan politics. The very notion of "moderate" had lost a great deal of its meaning for them.

This mood of apathy might have passed fairly soon after the election, as it later would, quickly enough, with the passage of the Reconstruction Acts. But for the time being, the main thing which the conflicting pressures from the North did to most Southerners was to demoralize them. The warnings of Republican moderates that Congress was not bluffing did, it was true, make a certain impression. But to take these warnings with full seriousness would have required a painful and unavoidably unpopular adjustment. On the other hand, to have resisted what they were daily told by the Northern Democratic press, when it coincided in every particular with what they most wanted to believe anyway, would have required an almost superhuman effort of self-denial. The result was that Southerners to a remarkable extent withdrew from the problem altogether. They said "no" to every effort they were asked to make in their own behalf, and trusted that the future would vindicate a present policy of "masterly inactivity."[53]

If the South's most responsible leaders had their doubts about the wisdom of such a policy, they tended to resolve them by turning to the one figure in the national government whom they supposed they could fully trust, President Johnson. The manner in which these men responded to Johnson's views and feelings during this period was in many ways reminiscent of the summer and fall of 1865. From the election until mid-February every cue, formal and informal, given out by the President reflected his strong desire that the South should stand fast in its unwillingness to ratify the Fourteenth Amendment. It would be well to review some of these expressions, since their importance and effect appear to have been considerable.

In the period prior to the election Johnson had already given a number of indications of his flat opposition to the Amendment.[54] In October, during the closing weeks of the campaign, Secretary of the Interior Orville H. Browning wrote a long political letter to two Illinois friends setting forth various objections to the Amendment; this letter, which was released for publication, was generally taken as the official statement on the Administration's position. It was discussed with great animation in the Democratic press both North and South.[55]

[53] "Masterly inactivity," which needs no definition, was an expression well known to the vocabulary of mid-nineteenth century American politics. The term was especially pertinent to the attitude of the South during the post-election months of 1866–67 and was widely used in referring to it. See also above, chap. 12, n. 111.

[54] E.g., his press statement of May 1 on the report of the Joint Committee and his message of June 22 to Congress (see above, pp. 351 and 357), as well as his speeches during the "Swing around the Circle."

[55] O. H. Browning to Col. W. H. Benneson and Maj. H. V. Sullivan, Oct. 13, 1866, published in the New York papers on Oct. 24, 1866. The letter had been read by Browning to Johnson on Oct. 20 and the President was especially anxious that it be published. *Diary of Orville Hickman Browning*, ed. James G. Randall (Springfield: Illinois State Library, 1933), II, 101. Being a campaign document, however, the letter did not necessarily have to be taken as expressing an absolutely irreversible position. In fact the major reason for Johnson's desire to make it public may not have been so much what it said about the Amendment, but rather the extravagant praise ("pure patriotism," "courage and heroism equally sublime," etc.) which it lavished upon himself. Be that as it may, the letter was seized upon everywhere in the South as a sweeping repudiation of the Amendment—e.g., Richmond *Enquirer*, Oct. 27, 1866; Jackson *Clarion*, Nov. 1, 1866; Charleston *Courier*, Nov. 1, 1866. "It shows," exulted the *Courier*, "that Mr. Johnson stands to-day, as heretofore, opposed to the proposed constitutional amendment. . . ."

For a time after the election, however, Johnson's position was left in some doubt. There were indications early in November that the President was wavering. He contemplated a conciliatory message announcing his readiness to co-operate with Congress, and even went so far as to prepare a draft of such a message. Yet by mid-November he had changed his mind and resumed his former position. The views expressed in the message which he did deliver—that the Southern states should be readmitted without further conditions—were in no way different from those he had held all along.[56]

Nevertheless, the extent to which Johnson was prepared to go in positively discouraging the Southern states from ratifying was as yet not known, especially in the North.[57] The inside advice which former Governor Parsons gave to the legislators of Alabama as a result of his talk with Johnson early in December was doubtless based on sound impressions, but it was not accompanied by a specific statement in the President's own words. By then the President's desires must have been perfectly clear in his own mind, and those persons with whom he conferred could not have had much difficulty in deciphering them, but the Chief Executive was understandably reluctant to have it publicized that he was involving himself in the internal politics of Southern states.

And yet the time was bound to come when the President's private promptings to Southern visitors would become a subject of notoriety, public gossip, and distinct embarrassment to himself. Shortly before Christmas a Colonel T. C. Weatherly, member of the South Carolina legislature then in session, made a hurried trip to Washington. He had been specially deputized by a caucus of his fellow legislators to find out as much as he could regarding what action South Carolina ought to take on the proposed Amendment. On the one hand, he spoke with a number of Republican congressmen; they assured him that if South Carolina should ratify, all obstacles to the state's readmission would be removed. On the other hand, the Colonel had a long talk with President Johnson, who apparently discouraged him from taking such promises seriously or doing any real negotiating with the enemy. The

[56] This interesting fact was discovered by Howard K. Beale in the course of his research for *The Critical Year* (see pp. 399–406 of that book for details). The draft of Johnson's original message is in the Johnson papers at the Library of Congress. It is possible that Johnson was dissuaded from any waverings he may have experienced by such of his intimates as Doolittle, Browning, and the Blairs, though it was not likely that he required much dissuading. But the letter from "J. C." to Marble (see above, n. 32) indicates that as late as December 2 the Democrats were not entirely certain what Johnson would do. Montgomery Blair had assured "J. C." that Johnson would "come out right in the end," but the latter was still quite dubious about believing this.

[57] He did not specifically refer to the Amendment at all in his Annual Message. See Richardson, *Messages and Papers*, VI, 445 ff.

President "expresssed the hope that the Southern States would remain firm in their position as regards the constitutional amendment, and steadfastly reject it. . . ."[58]

The story of this interview, which was obtained by "Leo," the Washington correspondent of the Charleston *Courier*, was of course printed everywhere. The President angrily denied it. The *Courier*, however, gloated over the accuracy of its information, while Weatherly himself, though much embarrassed, would not contradict the basic truth of "Leo's" facts. In any case, the Colonel had wasted no time in getting off a dispatch of his own to the South Carolina legislature right after the interview, and it was acted upon instantly. The Amendment was rejected with only one dissenting vote.[59]

Johnson was finally forced out in the open by the apparent headway which Governor Patton was making in Alabama toward getting the legislature of that state to reconsider its earlier vote on the Amendment. Patton was one Southern leader who had been convinced, despite Johnson's advice, that further stubbornness would mean nothing but trouble for his state and who was currently engaged in speaking his mind. In a series of speeches he declared that "he loved his State and his people, and rather than see the State reduced to a territorial condition, he would sacrifice office and everything else," but he thought it better to ratify the Amendment now "rather than fare worse" later on.[60] The Governor was listened to respectfully everywhere he went and he had reason to hope, as the legislature met again in January to reconsider the question, that his pleas had been successful. At this point former Governor Parsons sent the following telegram to President Johnson:

January 17, 1867

Legislature in session. Efforts making to reconsider vote on constitutional amendment. Report from Washington says it is probable an enabling act will pass. We do not know what to believe. I find nothing here.

The same day he received a reply:

[58] Charleston *Courier*, Dec. 25, 1866.

[59] "Leo's" first dispatch was carried in the Charleston *Courier* of December 21, 1866, and a second appeared on the twenty-second. The *Courier* published another story about Weatherly's mission on December 25, and on January 5 rejoiced that its facts were borne out by the investigations of other journals including the New York *Tribune*. The Chicago *Times* of December 29 reported Johnson as saying that he "gave no advice whatever on the subject, but [was] desirous that the southern legislatures act without influence from any source." The New York *World*, paying no attention to Johnson's denial, printed an account of the affair on January 10, 1867, which substantially corroborated "Leo's" story. The *Courier* on January 14 carried a long summary and recapitulation of all developments in the matter up to that time.

[60] Report of speech made at Huntsville, Dec. 31, 1866, Jackson *Clarion*, Jan. 5, 1867.

What possible good can be obtained by reconsidering the constitutional amendment? I know of none in the present posture of affairs; and I do not believe the people of the whole country will sustain any set of individuals in attempts to change the whole character of our government by enabling acts or otherwise. I believe, on the contrary, that they will eventually uphold all who have patriotism and courage to stand by the Constitution, and who place their confidence in the people. There should be no faltering on the part of those who are honest in their determination to sustain the several coordinate departments of the government in accordance with its original design.[61]

Late in January, 1867, the President appears to have had some misgivings over the paralysis which he himself had done so much to encourage among the Southern leaders. Some time during this period a proposed substitute for the Fourteenth Amendment was drawn up by some members of the North Carolina legislature. Under it, a general amnesty would be accompanied by a qualified Negro suffrage similar to that suggested in Johnson's telegram to Governor Sharkey of Mississippi in July, 1865. In addition, certain prominent ex-Confederates would be prohibited from holding federal (though not state) office. Johnson gave the plan his approval, recommending that it be submitted to the other Southern states by North Carolina.[62]

Details of the "North Carolina plan" were published during the first week in February, before any Southern legislature—including that of North Carolina—had done anything about it. But by then there was little energy or inclination in the South for taking any sort of initiative at all. The Republicans in Congress had long since made it clear that they would listen to no terms short of their own Fourteenth Amendment; the military bill, moreover, was already well on the way to completion. Northern Democrats gave no support to the plan, and one Democratic senator declared contemptuously that he thought it would be disapproved by "one million eight hundred thousand Democrats in the non-seceding States." The majority of Southerners themselves sensed that such schemes had already been rendered out of date and that the states might as well rest in their "masterly inactivity" until it was clear what Congress intended to do with them. Having a belated

[61] McPherson, *Reconstruction*, pp. 352–53; Fleming, *Documentary History of Reconstruction*, I, 237–38. For a summary of this episode see Fleming, *Civil War and Reconstruction in Alabama*, pp. 394–97.

[62] For the full text of the plan, see McPherson, *Reconstruction*, pp. 258–59, and Fleming, *Documentary History of Reconstruction*, I, 238–39. There is a copy of it in the Johnson papers with suggested alterations penciled in by the President. Gideon Welles refers in his diary to Johnson's having consulted him about the plan on January 31. Welles showed no enthusiasm for it. Welles, *Diary*, III, 31–33.

gesture thrown back in their faces would be just another unnecessary humiliation. North Carolina's own governor had next to no interest in the "North Carolina plan," suspecting, as he confided to one of his friends, that those who had encouraged it "only want to make us ridiculous."[63]

It was rumored—though the rumor was never substantiated—that Johnson's wavering had by mid-February led him to initiate talks with some of the Republican congressmen, offering at last to co-operate in some sort of compromise which would re-establish the long-defunct harmony between Congress and the Executive. The *World's* comment on this was superbly crass:

If the President is capable of yielding, it would have been better to save the country from this turmoil by yielding long ago. By his vigorous opposition he has exasperated the Radicals, and educated the South into stubbornness. At an earlier stage, the South would have submitted more easily, and Congress have been less exacting. . . . He should either not yield at all, or have yielded sooner and saved all this gratuitous mischief.[64]

V   HOW THE RECONSTRUCTION ACTS WERE
PASSED: DECEMBER, 1866, TO MARCH, 1867

The foregoing amounts to a series of approximations to the problem of military reconstruction and may suggest a composite of the angles from which the problem as a whole should be viewed. These can now be fitted into the chronology of the bill's actual passage. Like the Fourteenth Amendment—the unsuccessful previous effort to devise an omnibus reconstruction plan—the Military Reconstruction Act was a development, a product of intense and extended debate, the results of which were not anticipated at the beginning nor the implications entirely appreciated even at the end.

No single mind was responsible for the Act, not even that of Thaddeus Stevens. A comprehensive military bill was not contemplated by most men when the session began. Even after the need for such a measure had become more or less generally accepted, very wide alternatives remained open to the end. The nature of these alternatives was not fully clear even to those who debated them. Simple military rule

---

63 Saulsbury of Delaware, speaking on Feb. 6, 1867, *Cong. Globe*, 39 Cong., 2 sess., p. 1047; *Correspondence of Jonathan Worth*, II, 893. The *Nation* on February 7 said skeptically: "It remains to be seen whether the proposition will even be entertained. For that matter, it remains to be seen whether it will ever even be made. It may be a weak invention of the reporters." "But the country which requires more than the provisions of the pending [Fourteenth] amendment," asserted *Harper's*, "will hardly stop long to consider one which demands less." *Harper's Weekly*, XI (Feb. 23, 1867), 115.

64 New York *World*, Feb. 14, 1867.

was considered, and rejected as being too radical, whereas this in practice would undoubtedly have been the least disruptive and most merciful course that could have been taken in the circumstances, and it would probably have been ended relatively soon. Inasmuch as the majority favored a bill which would incorporate provisions for eventual readmission, the other major choice was whether or not the existing state governments would be allowed to take the initiative in reconstructing themselves. The Act of March 2, 1867, was supposedly a compromise between radical and moderate viewpoints; a far more moderate compromise, however, had been killed in the final stages by extreme radicals with the assistance of the Democrats. Not until after passage of the completed Act did it dawn upon congressmen that the measure had not really placed the initiative anywhere.

It is not unknown to the American legislative process that a complex measure long and bitterly debated, many times amended, and painfully compromised may in the course of its development cause even those most closely involved to lose track of the changing implications as more and more effort is directed into simply patching up something that will hold together long enough to pass. In this case it was necessary to pass another act later in the month to untangle the meaning of the first. The supplementary act prepared the way for carpetbag-scalawag-Negro reconstruction.

The entire process may be marked out roughly in three main phases. The first phase lasted from the opening of Congress in December, 1866, through the Christmas recess; the second, from January 3 to February 7, 1867; and the third, from February 7 to March 2, 1867.

December 3, 1866–January 2, 1867.—The two and a half weeks between the opening of Congress and the Christmas recess was an exploratory period in which sentiment was tested, alternatives examined, and positions tentatively marked out. Although no major piece of legislation was debated in December, there were certain side issues—Johnson's message, suffrage in the District of Columbia, and the admission of Nebraska to statehood[65]—which served to mark out what sorts of divisions existed in Congress on reconstruction and what their relative strengths were.

Three—and possibly four—general positions emerged during this period. There were the extreme radical Republicans, who were deter-

[65] The Negro suffrage bill for the District of Columbia was passed December 14, 1866. It was vetoed January 7, 1867, and repassed the same day in the Senate and the following day in the House. See McPherson, *Reconstruction*, pp. 154–60. On Nebraska, see *ibid.*, pp. 164–66; also above, n. 14.

mined to liquidate Johnson's work entirely, to put the South under military rule, and to reorganize the Southern governments under Unionists and Negroes. There were the Democrats, who continued to oppose the Fourteenth Amendment and to insist that Southern representatives be readmitted immediately and unconditionally. The moderate Republicans might have been divided into two groups. A number of them maintained explicitly and with virtually no qualification that the Amendment represented Congress' pledge of terms to the South. Others, probably a substantial majority, had accepted the Amendment as a campaign issue and assumed that Southern ratification would have meant immediate readmission, but were quite unwilling to hold the offer open indefinitely in the face of Southern intransigence.

By the middle of December, several things became clear that had still been uncertain when Congress first met. For one thing the entire Republican party, radical and moderate, had become profoundly exercised over the stories of Unionists and Negroes being abused in the Southern states. At the same time the Democrats, apparently all unchastened by the elections, proclaimed to their public that the majority party was "dead-locked," helpless, and afraid to go any farther on the road to reconstruction than it had gone already. An atmosphere was thus created in which all legislation on Southern affairs was automatically defined as emergency business. Moreover, the Republican party's commitment to the Amendment, provisional as it was, simply would not hold up against continued Southern rejections. Some, like Sherman and Bingham, would continue to stand pat. But those who, like Blaine and Fessenden, constituted the majority assumed that this commitment depended on a speedy and businesslike ratification by the Southern legislatures. These legislatures, therefore, would have to act immediately and decisively if Congress were to be persuaded not to intervene directly in the affairs of the Southern states. This, of course, they failed to do.

On the day Congress adjourned for the holidays, Senator Ross of Kansas offered a resolution laying down the lines which Congress was to pursue after the recess:

Whereas the amendment to the Constitution . . . not having been accepted by a constitutional majority of the States, and certain sections of the country lately in rebellion being deemed thereby in danger of falling into a state of anarchy, by reason of their having no legitimate civil government: Therefore,

Be it resolved [etc.] . . . That the joint committee on reconstruction be directed to inquire into the expediency of establishing such regulations for the government of such districts lately in rebellion against the United

States as shall have refused or may hereafter refuse to adopt the said proposed amendment, as may be found necessary for the preservation of the peace and the protection of society and the interests of the Government in those districts.[66]

January 3–February 6, 1867.—During this next phase, all the Republican moderates came to accept the necessity of some form of military rule for the South. At the same time, they were able as a group to defeat Stevens' initial plan for turning the Southern governments over to the Unionists and Negroes.

On January 3, the day Congress reconvened, Thaddeus Stevens spoke on behalf of his reconstruction bill.[67] He called attention to the desperate conditions of existence for Union men in the South; something should be done immediately, he declared, "to protect these people from the barbarians who are now daily murdering them; who are murdering the loyal whites daily and daily putting into secret graves not only hundreds but thousands of the colored people of that country. . . ." He denounced the recent Supreme Court decision on the unconstitutionality of military commissions in places where the civil courts were open; he restated his "conquered provinces" doctrine, denied the legality of all that had been done under the Johnson governments, and insisted that it was necessary to give the Negro the vote and to place the rebel states "under the guardianship of loyal men."[68]

The moderate Republican position—that the Amendment alone con-

---

[66] *Cong. Globe*, 39 Cong., 2 sess., p. 211. Ross would later be one of the "recusant senators" who, along with Fessenden, Grimes, and Trumbull, voted against the impeachment of Andrew Johnson. The above resolution, accompanied by a speech, was offered on December 20, 1866.

[67] The text of the Stevens bill is given in *ibid.*, p. 250; see also Kendrick, *Journal*, pp. 358 ff. According to this measure, the Confederate states had forfeited all their rights and could only be restored by Congress; the present governments had been illegally formed and were to be placed under military rule; Confederate officers of all ranks, civil and military, would forfeit their citizenship for at least five years; and the new state constitutions, to be approved, must provide for Negro suffrage. There was no guarantee in the bill that a state complying with these terms would be readmitted, and even a readmitted state which later violated them would again forfeit its right to representation. This speech was the one in which Stevens made his famous remark: "Another good reason is, it would insure the ascendency of the Union party. Do you avow the party purpose? exclaims some horror-stricken demagogue. I do. For I believe, on my conscience, that on the continued ascendency of that party depends the safety of this great nation."

[68] *Cong. Globe*, 39 Cong., 2 sess., pp. 250–53. The decision Stevens referred to was that of *ex parte Milligan*. "That decision," he said, "although in terms perhaps not as infamous as the Dred Scott decision, is yet far more dangerous in its operation upon the lives and liberties of the loyal men of this country. That decision has taken away every protection in every one of these rebel States from every loyal man, black or white, who resides there." In view of the special conditions of local justice then prevailing in the South, Stevens' argument was not without its points.

stituted Congress' terms and that the elections had been carried on that assumption—was expressed in a speech by Rufus Spalding of Ohio on January 5. Spalding urged that the South be given until March 4 to ratify; after that time, he said, he would be willing to support the Stevens measure. Thus Stevens' main theme was "speed," that of Spalding, "delay"; but even Spalding was unwilling to wait indefinitely.[69]

Representative John A. Bingham, also of Ohio, was the most energetic spokesman for the moderate viewpoint during the ensuing fight over the Stevens measure. His immediate effort was to get the bill referred to the Joint Committee, where he hoped to bury it; Stevens, however, wanted it considered by the committee of the whole, maintaining that it was not a new bill but a substitute for one already introduced in the previous session. The ensuing debate was nominally over the issue of recommittal; in reality it covered the whole ground of reconstruction.

Bingham on January 16 launched a bitter attack on the Stevens bill. He pointed out that it had the sanction of no committee, that it was in direct contradiction to the work of the Joint Committee on Reconstruction, and that it violated the spirit of the Republicans' campaign statements on the Fourteenth Amendment. He denied Stevens' claim that the Southern states were fully out of the Union; he wanted the Amendment declared ratified when three-fourths of the loyal states had agreed to it, and he urged that the Southern states be admitted to representation as each ratified the Amendment.[70]

Bingham's argument, though able and vigorous, was at certain points quite vulnerable. He was unable to deny the numerous breakdowns of law and justice in Southern communities or the possible need for federal action to protect the Negroes and Unionists. His constitutional argument required a general conviction in the North—one which was by this time noticeably ebbing—that the Southern governments were legitimate in at least a *de facto* if not a *de jure* sense. The South's persistent refusal to have anything to do with the Amendment, together with continued harassment by the Democrats on their "dead-lock" formula, made it difficult for Bingham either to counter Stevens' demand for speed or to persuade even the most moderate of his colleagues to accept a proposal involving indefinite delay. On being challenged to tell the House how many of the states had already rejected the Amendment, Bingham lamely replied, "If they have all rejected it, it does not follow that they will not all yet accept it."[71]

[69] *Ibid.*, pp. 288–91.   [70] *Ibid.*, pp. 500–505.   [71] *Ibid.*, p. 505.

By January 28 it was becoming apparent that any reconstruction plan which permitted the delay required for the South to reconsider the Amendment had no chance of success.[72] But it was equally apparent that the moderates had a good chance of getting together enough votes to have the Stevens bill referred to the Joint Committee. At this point George W. Julian of Indiana suggested a rather shrewd compromise. In an effort both to satisfy the growing desire for speedy assertion of congressional authority and at the same time to remove the objectionable features of the Stevens plan, Julian proposed a simple bill to extend direct military rule throughout the South.[73]

Stevens was unwilling to accept the new plan until he had tested his own strength in the House, but a vote of 88–65 on Bingham's motion to recommit his original bill convinced him that he had no choice. The bill was referred to the Joint Committee, which refused to accept it, and Stevens thereupon agreed to have George H. Williams of Oregon introduce the Julian bill in the Senate on February 4. The new bill was then sent back to the committee, and after some amendments were made in it Stevens was asked to report it in the House. The state of mind of the Joint Committee on Reconstruction thus reflected that of Congress at large. The members were convinced of the need for emergency action, and though unwilling to support the Stevens plan, they were equally unwilling to let matters ride.[74]

Stevens introduced the Julian bill on February 6 and asked for immediate action on it. He seems to have persuaded himself that if the South could once be placed under full military rule, he could then argue the new Fortieth Congress into reconstructing the rebel states along the lines desired by himself and Sumner. Yet it is quite likely that on this point Stevens was mistaken. Should the sense of crisis generated by the atrocity stories be once allayed by the imposition of military government, the new Congress, though more radical than the current Thirty-ninth, would in all probability have settled for simply keeping the Southern states out until after the 1868 presidential election. This would certainly have been a more popular, and thus politically a safer, program than radical reconstruction. But subsequent events, including

[72] E.g., Henry J. Raymond, attacking the Stevens bill on January 24, had proposed a compromise whereby the Amendment's punitive clause would be eliminated and the Amendment adopted when three-fourths of the loyal states had ratified it. These suggestions, designed to mollify the South, met with little interest among the Republican members. *Ibid.*, pp. 715–20.

[73] Julian's speech was made on January 28. *Ibid.*, Appendix, pp. 77–80.

[74] The text of the unamended bill, as introduced by Williams, is in Kendrick, *Journal*, pp. 380–82; for the committee's deliberations on it and the Stevens bill, see *ibid.*, pp. 122–29.

moderate moves which had unanticipated consequences, rendered Stevens' miscalculation harmless.

Bingham, fuming at previous slurs which he thought Stevens had cast upon his personal honor, prepared on February 7 to make a furious attack on the new bill. His colleagues, fearful of an irreparable split in the party, thereupon deserted the House and prevented a quorum. By early afternoon the angry Bingham had calmed down. During the luncheon recess he had been persuaded that military rule of some sort was, at least for the time being, absolutely essential. This ended all Republican opposition to the principle of immediate congressional action in the South. At the same time, the way was opened to a whole range of new perplexities.

February 7–March 2, 1867.—It was during this final period that moderate efforts to soften military rule, together with Democratic efforts to split the Republican party, set the stage for radical reconstruction.

Bingham, addressing the House on the afternoon of February 7, asked that the preamble of the military bill be so amended as to guarantee readmission when the Southern states had met certain specified terms.[75] James Garfield, speaking on the eighth, showed his great annoyance over the South's rejection of the Amendment but indicated that he too was reluctant to vote military rule without providing the Southern states with a way of ending it on their own initiative. Nathaniel P. Banks of Massachusetts brought up the question of whether it might still be possible to work out a compromise which would win the support of President Johnson. Stevens, pressing for immediate action, accused Banks of carrying on secret negotiations with the President, which Banks denied.[76] Stevens tried to force a vote by calling the previous question but was defeated by a margin of 81–62. The Democrats voted with the moderate Republicans, as they had previously done on the motion to recommit Stevens' first bill, and it was thus apparent that as long as radicals and moderates acted in opposition, the Democrats could tip the balance either way.

[75] *Cong. Globe,* 39 Cong., 2 sess., pp. 1080–83. Bingham did not state explicitly what these terms should be; Kendrick assumes that ratification of the Amendment was all he had in mind. Kendrick, *Journal,* pp. 395–96.

[76] *Cong. Globe,* 39 Cong., 2 sess., pp. 1104–5. This exchange occurred on February 8, just after a visit of Southern governors to confer with Johnson on a possible Southern substitute for the Fourteenth Amendment. There were, moreover, persistent rumors during the ensuing week to the effect that talks were taking place between Johnson and some of the moderate Republicans. Whether such talks ever really occurred, or who took part in them if they did, is, so far as the present author knows, still a mystery.

On February 12 James G. Blaine offered an amendment to the military bill, momentous for the turn which it gave to subsequent debate. The Blaine amendment was designed to allow the Southern states to regain their representation once they had ratified the Fourteenth Amendment and guaranteed a general Negro suffrage. It assumed local initiative and would commit Congress to specific terms for ending military rule. Garfield supported Blaine's proposal; Stevens and Boutwell vigorously attacked it; and on the thirteenth Stevens again tried to cut off debate with the previous question. Again the House refused to support him. Bingham also defended the Blaine amendment, having come some distance since his speech of January 16 (and even that of February 7), on the ground that it would enable the South to do its own reconstructing. The Democrats were thus given ample opportunity to see what the united moderate position now was.[77]

Blaine then moved that the entire bill, with his amendment, be referred to the Judiciary Committee with instructions to report it out immediately. At this point the Democrats, sensing a growing unity in Republican ranks, deserted the moderates and voted with the radicals. A vote was taken on ordering the motion—one step before voting on the motion itself—but the result found Stevens, even with his new allies, still in the minority.[78]

Stevens now launched the supreme effort to win over a few waverers, and his speech of the thirteenth, as Kendrick put it, "may be placed as one of the few ever delivered in Congress that have resulted in the changing of votes." It was quite a masterpiece. In elegiac tones the old man grieved over the inactivity of the nation's lawmakers while thousands of loyal men suffered in unregenerate rebel communities. He lamented the fate of his previous bill and declared that the new one, should it too be recommitted, was likewise doomed. The Blaine amendment, which represented "universal amnesty and universal Andy-Johnsonism," would throw away everything; it would let in "a vast number of rebels" and shut out nobody. Presuming upon his age, the speaker tearfully beseeched the "young gentlemen" around him to rise to the occasion, "without bickering, without small criticisms," to promote "the great cause of humanity and universal liberty."

[77] *Ibid.*, pp. 1182–84, 1206–13.

[78] *Ibid.*, p. 1213. Halfway through the vote, the Democrats, having intended at first to vote with the moderates for the amendment, changed their minds and voted with Stevens. The New York *World* on Feb. 14 explained the switch by saying that it was made in order "to force the dominant party to show their colors or retreat again, as they have for days past, in a demoralized condition." From the *World*'s news story and editorials of that day it was apparent that the Democrats did not want a settlement.

The plea was a success; the Pennsylvania Commoner detached enough votes from the moderate majority to defeat Blaine's motion for referral. And again the Democrats gave him their gleeful assistance.[79]

It was at this point that the pseudo-Machiavellianism of the Democrats first began falling apart. Stevens was now able to force a vote on the unamended military bill and to carry it, 105–55. Continuing their strategy of "dead-lock," the Democrats deserted Stevens and voted against the bill, expecting that the moderates would vote with them. In this they were much mistaken. The moderates had hoped for an amended bill, but they were quite unwilling to end the session with nothing at all. They would take a military bill rather than allow the opposition to achieve a stalemate.

It is ironic to reflect that, despite all the fury in the House up to this time, either of the alternatives debated on February 13 would have given the Southern states a substantially easier reconstruction than the one they eventually got. But the pulling and hauling between House and Senate during the following week over an amended versus an unamended bill, bringing Congress ever closer to its March adjournment, resulted in a last-minute "compromise" which must have brought vast relief to Old Thad Stevens.

Debate on the reconstruction bill opened in the Senate on the fourteenth. Williams, who took charge of the measure, agreed to add the Blaine amendment after being convinced by Senate moderates that it would not pass otherwise. The next day he withdrew the amendment, having in the meantime been equally convinced by House radicals that the House would not concur in an amended bill. The conflicts and disagreements which thereupon erupted in the Senate and continued for the next two days made it begin to look as though Congress would get no bill at all. Under this peril an emergency committee was appointed by a party caucus on February 16, charged with amending the bill in such a way as to make it acceptable to a majority of Republican senators. The chairman of this committee was John Sherman. The result of its work was the so-called Sherman substitute—which, except for slight alterations, amounted to about the same thing as the Blaine amendment. This new bill was passed by the Senate in the early morning hours of the seventeenth, while Charles Sumner made no effort to control his rage and disappointment.[80]

The Sherman substitute occasioned another day of debate in the

[79] *Cong. Globe*, 39 Cong., 2 sess., pp. 1213–15.
[80] *Ibid.*, pp. 1303–4, 1360–61, 1364–98, 1440–69; Welles, *Diary*, III, 46–47; Kendrick, *Journal*, p. 407.

House on February 18, being attacked by Boutwell and defended by Bingham. On the nineteenth the Democrats, ignoring all the portents, once more voted with the radicals to refuse concurrence. They still did not seem to realize that all delay from here on was to the advantage of the radicals, since no matter what happened, and regardless of the apparent disunity in Republican ranks, the latter were at least united in their determination to pass something before adjournment. If the present measure failed, the South would certainly get nothing better and would in all likelihood be given something worse. Meanwhile, the Senate considered a House request for a conference and finally voted to refuse it. The House, now faced with another vote on the Sherman bill, met that evening. As it became apparent that the moderates had enough strength to carry the measure, the Democrats used delaying tactics to prevent a vote, and still another day was gone.[81]

The breaking point came on February 20. Two amendments were offered in the House, one by James Wilson of Iowa, the other by Samuel Shellabarger of Ohio, and these turned out to make all the difference. Under Wilson's, all persons excluded from officeholding under the Fourteenth Amendment were barred both from serving as delegates to the new state constitutional conventions and from voting in elections to choose such delegates. The Shellabarger amendment extended the same principle to *all* officeholding and declared that prior to readmission any civil governments should be deemed "provisional only, and in all respects subject to the paramount authority of the United States at any time, to abolish, modify, control, or supersede the same. . . ." The bill, with the Sherman, Wilson, and Shellabarger amendments, passed the House by a vote of 126–46. On the same day the Senate concurred in what the House had done.[82] Since the Thirty-ninth Congress was about to dissolve forever, President Johnson might have smothered the bill with a pocket veto. Instead, the President chose to stand squarely on principle as usual and send in a veto message, which he did on March 2. It was, of course, promptly overridden.[83]

---

[81] *Cong. Globe*, 39 Cong., 2 sess., pp. 1316–38, 1340, 1356–58, 1555–70.

[82] *Ibid.*, pp. 1399–1400, 1625–45.

[83] McPherson, *Reconstruction*, pp. 166–73, 191–82; Richardson, *Messages and Papers*, VI, 498–511. Two other significant enactments became law on that day. One was the Tenure of Office Act (discussed in chap. xv below); the other was an Army Appropriation Act with a section which required the President to issue all his orders through the General of the Army, whose headquarters were not to be removed from Washington without Senate approval. The fact that Johnson and Grant remained on harmonious terms until early in 1868, however, and that neither was at all fond of Secretary of War Stanton, makes it impossible for the author to judge how much difference this Command of the Army provision made in the subsequent course of reconstruction.

The great fact for the Republicans was that they had at last a reconstruction bill. But concerning all the potentials in it, they were considerably less clear. Each succeeding addition and amendment, with the thousands of words of debate which accompanied them as time grew ever shorter, had actually done much to cloud the entire undertaking in confusion. The basic act, for which Stevens had pleaded and hammered without success, would simply have suspended Southern local political life and placed the governments under military supervision until Northern animus should spend itself and give way to a general demand for ending the entire abnormal business. One tends now to forget that such a reaction would be substantially complete in any case with the election of General Grant in 1868, with its "Let us have peace" theme, and that the commitment to carpetbaggery was to become more and more of a burdensome liability from that time on. That commitment, paradoxically enough, had originally been fastened upon the party as the outgrowth of a stubborn conservative reluctance to cut loose altogether from the principle of local self-rule. The expression of this had been the Blaine and Sherman amendments to the military bill, requiring the Southern governments to enact Negro suffrage and to ratify the Fourteenth Amendment "on their own initiative." How the Fourteenth Amendment, with its disqualifying clause, would affect the then incumbent governments was still very uncertain. Even the Wilson and Shellabarger amendments did not fully clear up this point. As for the disfranchisement provision in the Shellabarger amendment, even that was something of a "sleeper." Sherman, who in the final stage had assumed the leadership in getting Senate concurrence, did not appreciate how effectively such disfranchisement would cripple Southern initiative.[84]

Immediately after passage of the Act, therefore, it was assumed by many that the first efforts at reorganization could still somehow be made by the Southern states themselves. After the initial shock, a wave of "realism" swept over the South. Southern newspapers crackled with exhortations. It was time at last for the South to end its "masterly inactivity," to do the conqueror's will, and to recognize once and for

[84] On February 20 Sherman argued: "The amendment now proposed by the House does exclude a few people from voting, I think unwisely; but how many? It excludes about from six to ten thousand, and when? Only at the first election for delegates to the convention. After that they can vote." *Cong. Globe*, 39 Cong., 2 sess., p. 1626. Such haziness in the mind of a leading senator (and in a mind hardly noted for dullness) may give some idea of how widely it must have been shared. The situation was unprecedented; no one had much of an idea in advance how the bill would work out in practice.

all that there was no choice.[85] By then, unfortunately, it was too late.

The lawmakers of the new Fortieth Congress, meeting immediately upon the adjournment of the Thirty-ninth, were not long in perceiving that the Reconstruction Act would never be operative at all unless it were set into motion by an enabling act, which they proceeded to pass on the twenty-third of March. And this would require the supervisory presence of swarms of federal officials—or as they would shortly come to be called, carpetbaggers.[86]

Thus Thaddeus Stevens, willy-nilly, had got something very close to what he had wanted in the first place, before he came to accept a simple military bill and to press for it with such ferocity. In this, Democratic assistance had been priceless, as nearly everyone recognized.[87] The

[85] This period, during which it was as yet unclear how much initiative the Southerners would actually have under the Reconstruction Act, saw a substantial number of Southern spokesmen urging compliance. They included Governor Patton of Alabama, former governors Joseph E. Brown of Georgia and Albert Gallatin Brown of Mississippi, and many others. The tone of the Southern press changed strikingly. To take a leading example, the hitherto intransigent Jackson *Clarion*, whose editorial chair was taken over at about this time by the prewar secessionist and Confederate congressman Ethelbert Barksdale, now became very vigorous and positive in calling for action. Fleming, *Civil War and Reconstruction in Alabama*, pp. 503–4; Louise B. Hill, *Joseph E. Brown and the Confederacy* (Chapel Hill: University of North Carolina Press, 1939), pp. 269–71; James B. Ranck, *Albert Gallatin Brown, Radical Southern Nationalist* (New York: D. Appleton-Century, 1937), pp. 253–56; Jackson *Clarion*, Mar. 3, 6, 7, 9, 12, 13, 1867.

[86] The First Reconstruction Act of March 2, 1867, may be summarized as follows: (1) The first four sections provide for military government, there being then "no legal State governments or adequate protection for life or property" in the ten Southern states. These states would be divided into five military districts, each under command of a general officer who was authorized to maintain order through the military and to organize military commissions for trying and punishing offenders (though no capital sentence would be executed without the approval of the President). (2) The fifth section (the Blaine-Sherman amendment) specified the conditions under which Congress might readmit the states: ratification of the Fourteenth Amendment and formation of constitutions which provided for universal Negro suffrage. (3) The Wilson amendment appears as a proviso to Section 5: persons disqualified for officeholding under the Fourteenth Amendment were ineligible to vote for, or serve as, delegates to the constitutional conventions which would enact the above provisions. (4) The Shellabarger amendment appears as Section 6: any government formed prior to final readmission would be deemed "provisional only"; meanwhile those persons not qualified under Section 5 were not qualified to vote for, or serve in, *any* state office. The Supplementary Reconstruction Act of March 23 prescribed in detail the procedure of registering voters and holding constitutional conventions in the Southern states. Nonetheless, still further clarification on the mechanics of registration was required, and on July 19, 1867, a Third Reconstruction Act was passed. A fourth and final reconstruction measure, enacted in March, 1868, was made necessary by the difficulties then being encountered in getting the voters to ratify the "carpetbag" constitutions. The new law required only a majority of votes cast, rather than a majority of the registered voters. For a discussion of the legal confusion surrounding all these enactments, see Randall, *Civil War and Reconstruction*, pp. 754–60. *Acts and Resolutions*, 40 Cong., 1 sess., p. 260; *U.S. Statutes at Large*, XV, pp. 14, 41.

[87] "The debt which the Radicals owe the Democratic party is almost incalculable." *Nation*, IV (Feb. 21, 1867), 141. During the debate on the Supplementary Reconstruc-

Democrats themselves, meanwhile, were already turning their thoughts to the 1868 election, somehow hoping that Southern votes might be made available to them in time. But Wade Hampton of South Carolina, observing that "it was *that* party that led us to our ruin and then forsook us," could not be much concerned with presidential elections. Wearily he wrote to a friend in New York:

I have no idea that the Southern States will be allowed to vote for Presdt. *unless the Democrats are willing to fight on that issue.* They have shown that they will not fight for principle, but perhaps they may do so for plunder. When they will stand up fairly for their principles, we will not desert them but now we are fighting for bread and life. . . .[88]

---

tion Bill, James Wilson of Iowa, referring to the last-minute amendments to the first act which now made another act necessary, maliciously observed: "Hence, gentlemen on that side of the House [the Democrats] may thank themselves—their friends of the South may thank them also—for those features of the reconstruction act of the 2d of March. . . ." *Cong. Globe*, 40 Cong., 1 sess., p. 64.

[88] Hampton to John Mullaly, Mar. 31, 1867, in Cauthen, *Family Letters of the Three Wade Hamptons*, pp. 142–43.

Chapter 15

Afterthought: Why Impeachment?

The policy of the United States government toward the South had been settled, despite the opposition of the executive branch, by the decision to undertake military reconstruction. After that time President Johnson apparently had no measurable influence over such policy, and for almost any practical purpose, the presidency as an effective and positive force in the nation's affairs ceased to exist.

But the story cannot be closed entirely without a parting question. Why did the Republican majority then turn upon the President and proceed to impeach him? Why did the Republicans, after binding Johnson hand and foot, try to throw him out of office less than a year before his term was to end anyway, and at a time when his successor's nomination had become all but certain? We may well ask why they bothered. It is hard to find anything in the proceeding that was really necessary; indeed, there was much in it that would seem politically quite risky.

The problem is largely one of interpretation. Most of the details are well known, this having been one of the best-ventilated episodes in American history. Probably few real secrets of fact remain undisclosed, and the excellent narrative account published in 1903 by David DeWitt is not likely to need redoing for some time to come, if indeed ever.[1] Nor is there now much point in trying to "justify" the act of

---

[1] David M. DeWitt's *The Impeachment and Trial of Andrew Johnson* (New York: Macmillan, 1903) is complete, comprehensive, and elegantly written; it constitutes something of a classic. A short account, whose interest derives chiefly from its author's personal role in the trial, is Edmund G. Ross, *History of the Impeachment of Andrew Johnson* (Santa Fe: New Mexican Printing Co., 1896). The chapters in Milton's *Age of Hate* which relate to this phase of Johnson's administration are especially useful. The bulk of the documentary evidence bearing on the affair may be found in two government publications. *Trial of Andrew Johnson* . . . (3 vols.; Washington: Government Printing Office, 1868) contains the record of the trial itself. *Impeachment Investigation Testimony* . . . (Washington: Government Printing Office, 1867), bound together with *House Reports*, 40 Cong., 1 sess., No. 7, "Impeachment of the President," is a massive

impeachment, if in calm reflection there ever was. The case against its justification has been so well made, and made so often, that we need not anticipate any serious effort to reverse it. Men who actually voted for impeachment at the time confessed, in after years, to stirrings of remorse.[2] But the feelings of normally reasonable men still have a claim on our curiosity, even if those of unreasonable ones are no longer interesting, and the question of why so many were willing to support such a proceeding in the first place is still worth asking.

More than one conjecture, each based on the same essential body of evidence, is possible. There is still, for instance, the thesis of the radical plot, in this case well substantiated, to remove the last obstacle from full Republican domination of the South. This was the line taken by DeWitt, and it forms the interpretive basis for his monograph. It is a straightforward and obvious approach, and the most likely point in the entire Johnson administration at which to apply it would be precisely here. Impeachment efforts may not have reached their climax before the late winter months of 1868, but they had been set in motion as early as 1866 in the wake of the fall elections. There was Ashley's resolution in December of that year; efforts were periodically renewed throughout more than a year thereafter; and the most fantastic and unsavory work was done by Ashley, Boutwell, and Butler in trying to connect Johnson with the assassination of Abraham Lincoln. Johnson's "violation" of the Tenure of Office Act was merely the final pretext. The final decision to impeach, in short, was the successful culmination of a long period of labor and planning.

Another line of approach, a variation upon this theme, is a more direct recognition that the removal of Johnson himself would make little objective difference at this stage, but that more general designs of a long-range institutional nature were involved. Here was an opportunity, seldom so aptly presented, for Congress as the legislative branch

collection of miscellaneous testimony given before the House Judiciary Committee in 1867 while that body was still trying unsuccessfully to make up a case against the President.

[2] E.g., James G. Blaine: "The sober reflection of after years has persuaded many who favored Impeachment that it was not justifiable on the charges made, and that its success would have resulted in greater injury to free institutions than Andrew Johnson in his utmost endeavor was able to inflict." George W. Julian wrote: "The attempt to impeach the President was undoubtedly inspired, mainly, by patriotic motives; but the spirit of intolerance among Republicans . . . set all moderation and common sense at defiance." After describing his own part in the scenes, Shelby Cullom concluded: "And thus ended for the first time, and I hope the last time, the trial of a President of the United States before the Senate, sitting as a Court of Impeachment for high crimes and misdemeanors." Blaine, *Twenty Years*, II, 376; Julian, *Political Recollections*, pp. 317–18; Cullom, *Fifty Years*, p. 158.

of the government to seize an added increment of power and to strengthen itself in relation to an executive weakened by the threat of easy removal. The real meaning of the impeachment, therefore, was the opening it gave to profit from the feeling against Andrew Johnson, to readjust the balance of governmental powers, and thus to establish a significant political and constitutional precedent that would favor ministerial responsibility.[8]

Such interpretations, considered theoretically, are certainly not without merit. But here is one point at which the "institutional" approach may actually be less enlightening than it was at earlier stages of the reconstruction struggle, when the entire party could imagine itself threatened with division and defeat. To see the Republican majority acting either as a party or in its character as the legislative branch, fulfilling institutional requirements and reaching out for more institutional power, is to see it in the impeachment episode doing precisely all the wrong things. To think of these men acting in rational pursuance of group interests and objects is to derive a number of somewhat misleading conclusions.

The impeachment of the President, from even the crassest of party motives, was an undertaking fraught with political peril. Indeed, the action of the Republican members on the occasions when they did act as a national party and remained collectively, as it were, in their right mind, demonstrated again and again their clear recognition of this liability. It was only too true, of course, that the establishment of carpet-bag governments—currently giving the Republicans much anxiety—represented the great opportunity for extending the party's power throughout the South with a presidential election pending, and for giving it a solid base in the country at large. But the true keys to party security still lay, after all, in the North. All ambitions of a national character, while full of meaning and importance, could have meaning for individuals only to the extent that the security of their own district organizations was not in question. And this could not be taken for granted for a single moment.

Every Northern state had a Republican majority. Yet the margins of 1866 could not guarantee similar margins for another year on other issues, and several states would, in fact, go Democratic in 1867. If

---

[8] "They [many analysts] have concluded that had impeachment proved successful as a weapon to remove a politically inacceptable President, the precedent would have been established for the removal of any President refusing persistently to co-operate with Congress, an eventuality implying the establishment of a parliamentary form of government with legislative ascendancy." Alfred H. Kelly and Winfred A. Harbison, *The American Constitution: Its Origins and Development* (New York: W. W. Norton, 1948), p. 477.

public opinion were to rally, not necessarily behind Andrew Johnson himself but in support of the executive office and its stability, the Republicans could conceivably lose control of the North. Their Southern foothold would thereupon be rendered worse than useless. For such a foothold to make any real political difference, the party required a visible and fully legitimate working margin in the North. And it goes without saying that even victory in a national election is small comfort, any time, to a Republican senator or representative who happens to have lost his office in a local Democratic sweep. Such is the ultimate liability in a popularly based political system, even in "revolutionary" times, and it has more than a little bearing on, though it assuredly does not clarify, the impeachment of Andrew Johnson.

There is hardly anything new in saying that considerations of morality and reason, or dilemmas created by their absence, have always given at least some measure for assessing men's behavior in our political life. Those considerations have certainly been applied in one way or another to this particular episode, and they may as well be applied again. Perhaps if the impeachment of Johnson were simply thought of as a towering act of abandoned wrath, wholly detached from "reason," it would be surprising to discover how little else was required in the way of explanation. Rather than follow down the trail of the stealthy impeachers, we could, instead, restrict our notice to those occurrences which may have produced such a state of unwholesome madness in the first place.

The final setting was one in which the people had been rendered wholly out of touch with the presidency. It was one in which, for the other branches, the executive was "co-ordinate" only by a kind of inverted mockery. The moral air of the nation's politics, like the air of Hamlet's Denmark, had become heavily poisoned. Knavery and Ben Butlerism seemed to have free play in every committee room; buffoonery had erupted in the War Department; distinguished generals were fleeing from the President's efforts to promote them against their will and make them lay siege to a barricaded Secretary of War. The normally conservative congressman was not simply encouraged in his growing sullenness by the attitude of his radical colleagues; he was, at the final break, egged on by a howling constituency. But why?

Two important considerations bearing on the impeachment could make another look at it very worthwhile. In the first place, much depends on whether the President's role during this period is regarded as an active or a passive one. Johnson had been rendered all but powerless to exercise any functions of real leadership, and we are thereby tempted to think of him as an inert quantity from here on, waiting to be victimized. But that would be a gross misjudgment of Andrew Johnson. For this particular problem Johnson must be seen as a very active force indeed; otherwise the impeachment could not have occurred. A critical aspect of the picture is that of Johnson *taking the initiative*. His actions from June, 1867, to February, 1868, constituted a long series of provocations, including much premeditated spite over his curtailed prerogatives, which served to drive the Republican North into a state of frenzy and loathing. They made such men as the cautious Bingham, momentarily heedless of consequences, yearn for Johnson's head on a pike simply for the immense relief of having his voice silenced. There was a deep psychological need to eliminate Johnson from American political life forever, and it was principally Johnson himself who had created it. During the trial the oratory and editorial rhetoric teemed with intensely surgical metaphors. The presidential incumbent no longer functioned in the body politic except to infect it. Out with the infection! Cut it away![4]

The other requirement for bringing the impeachment into being, besides the President's own initiative, was a widespread faith after February 21, 1868, that Johnson's conviction would be simple and swift. A large Republican majority had been brought to a state of mind in which it could easily persuade itself that the President had on that day broken the law. His celebrated but miserably clumsy attempt to oust Secretary Stanton had been specifically anticipated with the framing of the Tenure of Office Act a year before, and now that he had done just what Congress had tried by legislation to prevent him from doing, congressmen saw no further reason to refrain from doing what they themselves so fervently longed to do. It is now forgotten that the gaping absurdities of that law were hardly so obvious then as they came to seem later; the questionable part of the proceeding could only emerge by demonstration.

Indeed, there was a good deal in the affair that could only emerge by demonstration. The overtones left in history have been those of unworthiness, which is just as well; but while those overtones were certainly there from the first, they were not at the time the ones that predominated. It is right that history's account should be made up more from the aftermath and afterthoughts than from the causes; but it is also well to observe that this is primarily because the impeachment failed. Had it succeeded, we may be very sure that the echoes of the

[4] Or, as Joseph Medill put it to John Logan: "Like an aching tooth, every one [*sic*] is impatient to have the old villain out." Quoted in Milton, *Age of Hate*, p. 518.

affair would have been, if still not exactly sweet, at least very different. And we may also be sure that if the prosecutors had not imagined that they had a simple and safe case, they would never have undertaken it. That they, too, would come to have their afterthoughts is still not part of the story's beginning.

Impeachment, again, was a grave and risky step; only under the greatest stress could the majority members bring themselves to take it. Four times a minority tried to bring impeachment forward; three times it was voted down. Up to the final break, there had been no charges that contained legal substance—a point which was remarked upon by most of the party's leaders and editorial spokesmen. Yet four times a rage for impeachment at any price was reawakened by the President's grim refusal to call off his one-man war against everyone who seemed to be of any importance, while even Johnson's own advisers vainly told him that he was best off keeping quiet and doing nothing.

I FIRST IMPEACHMENT EFFORT: JANUARY–JUNE, 1867

Representative James M. Ashley of Ohio had at some point become obsessed with the feeling that the country was not safe without the President's removal. Ashley's resolution of December 17, 1866, to appoint a committee of inquiry on this subject, however, was smothered when the House refused to vote on it. But as soon as Johnson resumed his vetoing habits (this time with the District of Columbia Negro suffrage bill), Ashley on January 7, 1867, could jump up and say that since none of the older members would offer an impeachment resolution, he would have to do it himself. The resolution passed, though it is not likely that the House took it with very great seriousness. By its terms the Judiciary Committee was to inquire into Johnson's official conduct and determine whether he had done anything impeachable. The assumption seems to have been that the mere existence of such an investigation would serve as a warning and deterrent to Johnson and would be reassuring to all who might doubt the vigilance of Congress.[5]

This investigation, conducted in secret but described daily to the

5 *Cong. Globe*, 39 Cong., 2 sess., pp. 154, 320–21. "According to Mr. Sumner," observed the *Nation*, "the whole North is eager for impeachment; but if we may judge from the press, very few people are eager for it. The Washington correspondent of the Springfield *Republican*, who is generally both sensible and accurate, estimates the chance of impeachment as one in a hundred, and the chance of conviction as one in a thousand, which we think is probably a fair estimate of the extent of Mr. Johnson's risk." IV (Jan. 24, 1867), 61. *Harper's* said: "They [the people] will hear with attention and interest what Mr. Ashley has to say. But if it be a mere repetition of General Butler's speech it will not persuade them that the President ought to be impeached." XI (Jan. 26, 1867), 50.

President by Allan Pinkerton, was a grotesque and clownish business not unlike that of Joseph McCarthy and his 57 Communists. The searchers professed to know of evidence that Johnson had bribed public officers, swung around the circle full of whiskey, plotted to betray Tennessee in wartime, and conspired with Booth to murder Lincoln. On this final item, Ashley, who was not even a member of the committee, volunteered his services and expended much effort. Ashley was an occult mixture of superstition and lunacy. He seems to have had a theory that the deaths of American presidents in office were by nature due to vice-presidential foul play. He was encouraged and assisted in his work by George S. Boutwell of Massachusetts, and the arrival of Benjamin F. Butler in March, 1867, completed as baleful a trio of buzzards as ever perched in the House. Butler made broad hints that pages had been removed from Booth's diary to protect Johnson ("Who spoliated that book?"); and when Jefferson Davis, who was supposed to have shared in the plot, was released on May 13, the already languishing investigation was given some fresh impetus. Supposedly Johnson, involved in both assassination and treason, did not want to try Davis and have all his own secrets revealed.[6]

It soon became apparent that the only high official who had wanted Davis prosecuted was Johnson himself, the government's case having been spoiled by perjurers. It was also discovered that no pages had been torn from Booth's diary, that the President had not been drunk on the "Swing around the Circle," and that none of Johnson's canceled checks had been made out to corruptible public employees. Johnson had clearly done nothing impeachable. A majority of the Judiciary Committee, including Chairman James Wilson, had no further stomach for its mission and voted on June 3, 1867, that no evidence of high crimes and misdemeanors existed.[7]

[6] Ashley, later called before this same committee to testify, was given a *mauvais quart d'heure* by the Democratic members, who pressed him mercilessly regarding just how much he could substantiate these wild imaginings. "I have had a theory about it," he replied. "I have always believed that President Harrison and President Taylor and President Buchanan were poisoned, and poisoned for the express purpose of putting the Vice Presidents in the presidential office. In the first two instances it was successful. It was attempted with Mr. Buchanan, and failed. It succeeded with Mr. Taylor and Mr. Harrison. Then Mr. Lincoln was assassinated, and from my stand-point I could come to a conclusion. . . . It would not amount to legal evidence." *Impeachment Investigation*, p. 1199. Butler tried to stir up the members in a speech made on March 26 in which he broadly hinted that Bingham, as one of the government prosecutors in the Davis case, had tampered with Booth's diary in order to protect some highly placed conspirator who "could profit by assassination." *Cong. Globe*, 40 Cong., 1 sess., pp. 362–64. That Pinkerton was keeping Johnson informed about Ashley's cloak-and-dagger work was discovered by George F. Milton. See *Age of Hate*, p. 411.

[7] *House Reports*, 40 Cong., 1 sess., No. 7, "Impeachment of the President," pp. 59–105.

Impeachment at that point was dead, and would have remained so had the President not in effect taken steps to give it new life.

There is now a general impression that Johnson, though opposed to the Reconstruction Acts, proceeded faithfully to carry them out once they had become law. This is true only in the most strained and nominal sense. In less than three months after their passage, he began interfering with the efforts of the federal commanders to put the acts into practice, particularly with regard to registering voters and dealing with civilian officials. One difficulty encountered by the commanders involved the numerous cases in which the registrants were known by the registrars to be swearing false oaths in order to qualify for voting. To meet this and other problems General Pope issued a set of regulations for his district which included provisions for challenging such oaths. Another difficulty was over the course to be followed with civilian officials who failed to co-operate in administering the law. Pope's orders in this case were that when necessary such persons were removable by military authority, Congress having declared that there were no legal governments in these places and that those existing were to be deemed "provisional only." In such measures Pope and the other commanders had the consistent support of General Grant.[8]

But Johnson on June 20, 1867, issued a set of his own orders, and at no point did these orders bear much resemblance to the way the army was construing the Reconstruction Acts. In a directive embracing a number of questions, he declared that boards of registry had no power to challenge a man's oath, which legally entitled him to vote once he had taken it, and that the only recourse in cases of suspected perjury was to bring suit in the Southern state courts. Participation in rebellion was defined in such a way as to allow the great bulk of white Southerners to qualify in the forthcoming elections. The commanders were said to be without power to remove civilian officials, or to appoint substitutes, or to promulgate decrees having the force of law. The effect of this order would have been to give the existing state governments the most extensive control over the pending elections and to guarantee the largest possible white vote.[9]

[8] *Sen. Exec. Docs.*, 40 Cong., 1 sess., No. 14, "Correspondence Relative to Reconstruction"; *House Exec. Docs.*, 40 Cong., 1 sess., No. 20, "Reconstruction"; *Report of the Secretary of War*, 40 Cong., 2 sess., I, 240–395; Fleming, *Civil War and Reconstruction in Alabama*, pp. 475–80, 488–91.

[9] *House Exec. Docs.*, 40 Cong., 1 sess., No. 34, "Interpretation of the Reconstruction Acts"; Richardson, *Messages and Papers*, VI, 527–31, 552–56.

Feeling against the President once more flared very high. Inspired by protests from the military that proper control was impossible under such an interpretation of the law, Congress met in July and passed another Reconstruction Act. This act defined the "true intent and meaning" of the first two Reconstruction Acts, and in so doing systematically reversed every point in Johnson's June 20 order. Johnson promptly vetoed this bill and in his message denounced the actions of Congress, declared that he would never willingly surrender his constitutional powers, and exhorted the people to remove by ballot the rod of military despotism.[10]

II SECOND IMPEACHMENT EFFORT: JULY–DECEMBER, 1867

Despite the Judiciary Committee's previous arid efforts, it now seemed to become plausible all over again that Johnson might really have been guilty of all those treasonable acts—including the assassination of his predecessor—for which a month before no evidence had existed. On July 11 the committee was instructed to proceed afresh with its labors and be ready to report at the next meeting of Congress. Meanwhile Ben Butler, who had quickly emerged as the stoutest demagogue in the House, was placed at the head of a special committee to plumb the depths of Lincoln's murder. This group became known as the "Assassination Committee." Its members schemed and skulked for the remainder of the summer.[11]

Against the earnest advice of General Grant, Johnson in August began removing various officers who were especially obnoxious to him and who were especially zealous in their efforts to carry out the Reconstruction Acts. He started with the Secretary of War himself on August 5, and before he was through he had removed all but one of the district commanders in the South. He ousted Sheridan from command of the Louisiana-Texas district and Sickles from his command in South Carolina. He added Pope and Ord to his list of removals in December. General Swayne, who was head of the Freed-

---

[10] *Cong. Globe*, 40 Cong., 1 sess., pp. 517–46, 549–58, 569–86, 594–98, 610–15, 617–20, 622, 625–28, 631, 637–38, 640, 729–32, 741–47, Appendix, pp. 43–44; Richardson, *Messages and Papers*, VI, 536–45. House and Senate passed bills on this subject on July 9 and 11, respectively; a mutually satisfactory version was completed July 13; the bill was vetoed July 19 and repassed in both Houses on the same day.

[11] The "instructing" really occurred in a negative sense; the House simply failed to act on the question of discharging the committee. The new "Assassination Committee," composed of Representatives Butler, Shellabarger, Julian, Ward, and Randall, was appointed on July 8. It never made a report. *Cong. Globe*, 40 Cong., 1 sess., 522, 592–93, 656–57, 697–98, 720, 725, 761–63, 765–66; Ross, *History of the Impeachment*, pp. 49–50.

men's Bureau in Alabama and had great influence with the leading men of that state, was removed along with Pope.[12]

Johnson's effort to get rid of the ambiguous Stanton was to drag out for more than six months, during which time the President would manage to shed a certain amount of undeserved luster on an able but very unattractive, unheroic, and devious man. As a result of several changes made during 1866, Johnson now had a cabinet whose members—with the exception of Stanton—he could more or less count on to support his policies. On the other hand, the loyalty of Stanton, who had close ties with the radical group in Congress, had been known for some time to be defective. Stanton had been the only cabinet member to oppose Johnson's order of June 20 or his veto of the July 19 Reconstruction Act, and he had persistently ignored Johnson's well-known desire that he resign.[13]

By August 1 Johnson had finally decided—having meanwhile discovered that Stanton had actually helped write the Act of July 19—that the man must go. On August 5 he asked for the Secretary's resignation, which Stanton refused to give, whereupon Johnson decided to remove him. He had been trying all during this time to persuade Grant to accept the office. Grant was most reluctant to do it, expressing his understanding (one which was quite generally shared) that Stanton was protected by the Tenure of Office Act, a measure which had been passed on the same day as the first Reconstruction Act.[14]

The fashioning of this law had occurred under very complex circumstances, and that section of it which applied to the Stanton case was not a product of the original impetus that had brought the measure into being. The act had grown directly out of the wholesale removals from rank-and-file federal offices made by Johnson both during and after the election campaign of 1866. It was designed primarily to protect Republican officeholders from executive retaliation, which had created a problem of some seriousness, and consequently it had the overwhelming support of Republicans in both houses. The radicals, however, had taken advantage of rising tension over reconstruction in

12 *House Exec. Docs.*, 40 Cong., 2 sess., No. 57, "Removal of Hon. E. M. Stanton and Others"; McPherson, *Reconstruction*, pp. 345–46; Fleming, *Civil War and Reconstruction in Alabama*, pp. 492–93.

13 Richardson, *Messages and Papers*, VI, 584. Gideon Welles's *Diary* is virtually a week-by-week chronicle of the curious relationship between Johnson and Stanton, a relationship in which, behind an elaborate mask of mutual politeness, each was perfectly aware of the other's distrust of himself. This went all the way back to 1865.

14 "Removal of Hon. E. M. Stanton and Others," pp. 1–2; Milton, *Age of Hate*, p. 447; Richardson, *Messages and Papers*, VI, 584.

January and February, 1867, to add a section protecting cabinet members as well. They had Stanton specifically in mind. This passed the House but ran into strong opposition from Senate moderates, John Sherman in particular.[15]

In the final stages of debate a House-Senate compromise was agreed upon which covered cabinet officers during the term of the President who had appointed them, the question of exactly what constituted "appointment" being left somewhat vague. The Senate accepted the bill in that shape. On the one hand, the House members of the conference committee took this as a full victory for their version of protection for cabinet officers, while, on the other, Sherman assumed, or at least so argued in the Senate, that this part of the bill raised no real issues, since a test at the cabinet level was not likely to arise. He would later come to regret these words. But Sherman himself was far more interested in the ordinary officeholders—his mail was full of appeals from his own appointees for protection—and he was willing to include the disputed section rather than hold up the measure any further.[16]

But whatever may have been the reservations of Senate moderates, there was no question in the general view over what that section was intended to do. A substantial number of Republicans, realizing that Stanton was their only remaining access to the executive department,

[15] The bill was debated continuously in the Senate from January 10 until January 18, 1867, on which date it was passed. *Cong. Globe*, 39 Cong., 2 sess., pp. 382–90, 404–12, 433–42, 460–71, 487–97, 517–28, 541–50. The House took it up on February 1, added its own amendment, and passed it the next day. *Ibid.*, pp. 935–44, 969–70. Lyman Trumbull was very much in favor of accepting the House amendment when it arrived back in the Senate but was opposed by Sherman and other moderates. This repeated the pattern of sentiment on appointments which had emerged during the previous session in 1866 in connection with the Post Office Appropriation Bill (see above, pp. 384–87). The Senate on February 6 refused concurrence in the amended House version. *Ibid.*, pp. 966–69, 978, 1039–47. For a summary of these debates, with commentary, see DeWitt, *Impeachment*, pp. 183–99.

[16] E.g., "I am glad to see in the movements of the body of Congress so much temperance and steadiness. I hope we shall have as strong a law as Congress can pass regulating appointments and removals from office and restraining abuse of power in that respect." Warner Bateman to John Sherman, Dec. 7, 1866, John Sherman MSS, Library of Congress. Sherman during this time was besieged by protests over Johnson's removals: J. M. Brown to S., Nov. 7, 1866; E. Forsman to S., Nov. 17, 1866; J. F. Dewey to S., Dec. 4 and 14, 1866; citizens' petitions from 8th and 9th Ohio districts, Dec. 8, 1866; M. Walker to S., Dec. 19, 1866; William Stedman to S., Jan. 3, 1867; petition from members of Ohio legislature, Jan. 26, 1867; petition from citizens of Lima, O., n.d. [No. 25934]; Sherman MSS. The joint conference committee, appointed on February 14, 1867, was composed of Schenck, T. Williams, and J. F. Wilson for the House, and G. Williams, Sherman, and Buckalew for the Senate. The committee's substitute was reported back to the Senate on February 18, to the House on the nineteenth, and was agreed to in both places. The bill was vetoed by the President on March 2 and re-passed in both houses on the same day. *Cong. Globe*, 39 Cong., 2 sess., pp. 1340, 1514–18, 1737–39, 1964–66; Richardson, *Messages and Papers*, VI, 492–98.

wanted very much to keep him there and assumed that this was now guaranteed. A touch of irony lay in the fact that Stanton himself did not at the time approve of the measure, and he probably helped Seward write Johnson's veto message. But Stanton nevertheless allowed himself to be convinced that the country's salvation demanded his remaining at the War Department.[17]

After the events of June and July, therefore, Grant's advice to Johnson—that removing Stanton would be contrary to the way the law was understood by the people—was actually quite sound. Johnson hesitated a few days; then on August 5 two items appeared in the President's mail which settled his mind and drove him to action. One was the information, recently brought out in the trial of John Surratt, that Judge Advocate Holt had never properly shown him the petition for clemency which had been forwarded with the papers of Mrs. Surratt back in 1865. Johnson was convinced that Stanton had been back of this. The other was a letter from Sanford Conover, a very shady person whom the government had at one time employed as a spy in the Jefferson Davis case but who was now in jail awaiting sentence for perjury. Conover described elaborate efforts by Ashley and Butler to get him to cook up "evidence" of Johnson's having been in on the assassination plot. The *quid pro quo* was to have been a pardon for Conover—which Holt had already tried to obtain—but having lost hopes of it from that quarter, Conover was now, in effect, double-crossing the "Assassination Committee" with a direct appeal to the President. Regardless of whether the Secretary of War had himself been involved in any of this, Stanton was Holt's superior and was thus officially responsible for his doings. The President accordingly demanded the Secretary's resignation, and when Stanton refused to give it, Johnson began laying plans to remove him.[18]

[17] Richardson, VI, 587; Welles, *Diary*, III, 50–51, 54. The act's basic provisions were: (1) That any civil officer requiring Senate confirmation should, when confirmed, hold office until a successor had been appointed and confirmed in the same manner; (2) That cabinet officers were to be considered in the same category, except that they were to hold office during the term of the President who had appointed them, and one month thereafter, subject to removal by and with Senate consent; (3) That in cases of misconduct during a Senate recess, the President might suspend the offender, appoint a temporary successor, and report the reasons therefor to the Senate within twenty days after its next meeting; should the Senate refuse concurrence, the offender was to be reinstated; (4) That only in cases of death or resignation might an officer be replaced during a recess of the Senate, and in such cases the successor's commission would expire at the end of the next session; and (5) That violations of the act would be deemed "high misdemeanors," and would be punishable by fine and/or imprisonment. *Cong. Globe*, 39 Cong., 2 sess., Appendix, pp. 198–99.

[18] St. George L. Sioussat, "Notes of Colonel W. G. Moore, Private Secretary to President Johnson, 1866–1868," *American Historical Review*, XIX (October, 1913), 98–

After another week Grant finally agreed to take office on an *ad interim* basis, and on August 12 Stanton was not removed but "suspended," pending a report to the Senate. Thus Johnson, yielding to the reluctance of Grant, remained to the latter's satisfaction within the Tenure of Office Act. Meanwhile Stanton, bowing, as he said, to "superior force," vacated the office to Grant, who thereupon assumed its duties. Johnson hoped and assumed that Grant would ultimately do one of two things: either hold office long enough to let the case be tried in the courts if the Senate refused to concur in the suspension, or else resign in time for Johnson to have someone else in the post by the time the Senate, with its non-concurrence, should force the case to a test. This assumption would later become the subject of a bitter public debate. But for the time being it could remain (like Stanton) in a state of suspension, since Congress was not then in session. Such was the way things stood when Congress met again late in November, 1867.[19]

Between the time of Stanton's suspension and the meeting of Congress, Johnson managed to enrage the Republicans on certain other counts. His removal of Sheridan was made over the vigorous objections of his new Secretary of War *ad interim*, who predicted that it would "only be regarded as an effort to defeat the laws of Congress." In this Grant was right; the removal, not only of Sheridan but of Sickles as well, set off a great public outcry and added measurably to the growing conviction that Johnson was trying to subvert the Reconstruction Acts. In the autumn, moreover, the Democrats made substantial gains in a number of state elections. Johnson seized the occasion to make a "victory speech" to a crowd of serenaders on November 13 in which he announced that his policy had been vindicated by the people. Thomas Ewing had made agitated but vain efforts beforehand to dissuade the President from making any such speech.[20]

---

132. The Conover material, the original of which is in the Johnson papers, was released for publication and appeared in the Washington and New York newspapers on August 10, 1867. The President had actually known for some time, from other sources, about these goings-on. See Milton, *Age of Hate*, pp. 413–14. The exchange of notes regarding Johnson's desire for Stanton's resignation and the Secretary's refusal to give it is in Richardson, *Messages and Papers*, VI, 584, and McPherson, *Reconstruction*, p. 261.

19 "Removal of Hon. E. M. Stanton and Others," pp. 1–3.

20 Grant urged against Sheridan's removal both in conversation and in two letters (Aug. 1 and 17, 1867) which he wrote to the President on that subject. Johnson, it appears, had sought advice everywhere; virtually everyone he consulted advised very strongly against the removal, but he proceeded to go ahead and make it anyway. Even the Chief Justice was sent for. The latter "begged him for his own sake and for that of the country" not to take such a step. ("He does not realize at all the feeling against

It was against this background that the House Judiciary Committee (despite the embarrassments of the Conover fiasco, which had been made public on August 10) decided by a narrow 5–4 vote on November 20 to recommend impeachment. On December 2, 1867, three reports were laid before the House. A majority report recommended that the President be impeached on general grounds of "usurpation of power." The second, a Republican minority report written by Chairman Wilson, attacked the majority report on all counts but recommended that Johnson be "censured" for betraying the confidence of those who had placed him in power. The third was a Democratic minority report which supported Johnson throughout.[21]

The regular second session of the Fortieth Congress convened on the same day, December 2. On the following day Johnson sent in his Third Annual Message. In it, he defiantly declared that "cases may occur in which the Executive would be compelled to stand on his rights, and maintain them, regardless of consequences." The House sweated and heaved, but in a record vote taken on December 7 impeachment was defeated. For all their chagrin and ire, the Republicans had again been forced to recognize that they still did not have a case.[22] Had Johnson stopped there, the momentum could not possibly have been revived: the issue would have been closed. But once again he resumed the initiative.

III   THIRD IMPEACHMENT EFFORT: JANUARY–FEBRUARY, 1868

Johnson gave the members of Congress two more things to reflect upon over the Christmas holidays. On December 12 he sent to the Senate his reasons for suspending Stanton. On December 18 he sent Congress a message on another subject, the motive for which can hardly be diagnosed as other than simple cussedness. Sheridan's replacement, Winfield S. Hancock, a Democratic general who did not approve of the Reconstruction Acts, had recently issued a

---

him in the country," Chase wrote to Garfield.) No one in the cabinet, except the irascible Welles, approved of the removal; in fact, "Mr. Browning's face actually seemed to grow thin at the suggestion." "Removal of Hon. E. M. Stanton and Others," pp. 2–4, 7–8; S. P. Chase to Garfield, Aug. 7, 1867, Garfield MSS, Library of Congress; Welles, *Diary*, III, 149–57; "Notes of Colonel Moore," p. 114. According to the New York *Tribune* on August 27, ". . . the country needs adjustment, security, tranquility, repose, and he persists in keeping it unsettled, distracted, angry, and apprehensive." Johnson's "victory speech" is in *Impeachment Investigation*, p. 1175; Ewing's letter of November 14 against making it is in the Johnson MSS.

21 *House Reports*, 40 Cong., 1 sess., No. 7, "Impeachment of the President."

22 Richardson, *Messages and Papers*, VI, 558–81; *Cong. Globe*, 40 Cong., 2 sess., pp. 67–68, Appendix, pp. 54–65.

military order asserting the supremacy of civil over military government. This was in virtually direct contradiction to the Act of July 19, which Hancock was supposed to be administering in the Texas-Louisiana district. Back in July the House of Representatives had voted special resolutions of thanks to Sheridan, Pope, and Sickles for "able and faithful performance" of duty in their respective districts; Johnson now asked in his message that a similar vote of thanks be tendered to Hancock. The effect of this sally may well be imagined. After the members had gone home, moreover, Johnson proceeded to remove Pope, having already removed the other two.[23]

For the third straight year, congressmen visited with their constituents during the holiday season and came back to Washington in a frame of mind markedly more radical than when they had left. This was no wonder, since in addition to everything else they were now beginning to be flooded with letters from anguished carpetbaggers and Southern Unionists wanting to know what Congress was going to do for them in their efforts—currently meeting numerous obstructions—to set up the new state governments.[24] In a little over three

[23] Richardson, *Messages and Papers*, VI, 583–94, 595–96; *Cong. Globe*, 40 Cong., 1 sess., pp. 500, 504 (July 5, 1867); *House Exec. Docs.*, 40 Cong., 2 sess., No. 58, "General W. S. Hancock." "Mr. Covode. I am anxious to know whether that is genuine or whether it is a hoax. [Laughter.] The Speaker. It is a message from the President." *Cong. Globe*, 40 Cong., 2 sess., p. 264. Eldridge of Wisconsin, a Democrat, thereupon tried unsuccessfully to get the floor in order to offer the requested resolution. This was on December 18. When he finally did offer it on January 6, 1868, Washburne of Illinois promptly moved a substitute: "That we utterly condemn the conduct of Andrew Johnson, acting President of the United States, for his action in removing that gallant soldier Major General P. H. Sheridan. . . ." *Ibid.*, p. 332. Johnson's order of December 28 removing Pope called also for the removals of Ord and Swayne. McPherson, *Reconstruction*, pp. 345–46.

[24] "For some reason," according to DeWitt, ". . . the majority reassembled in a sullen mood. The distinction between conservative and radical seemed to have been obliterated." *Impeachment*, p. 316. There is much material in the correspondence of Sherman, Washburne, and Sumner during this period from workers in the various Southern Republican outposts. These testaments of frustration are vibrant with anger over the disruptive effects of Johnson's removals. "The removal of Gens. Pope and Swayne," C. W. Buckley wrote to Washburne on January 9, 1868, from Montgomery, Alabama, "has taken from the work of reconstruction two able and experienced leaders. Their loss to the union men of this state is irreparable, and their removal is followed by such an outburst of rebel hostility . . . that we are on the very eve of violence and bloodshed." Elihu Washburne MSS, Library of Congress. "Had he [Swayne] remained in command here our work would have been comparatively easy, and success certain. Unfriendly military management has killed us. . . . What next are we to do? . . . We can only look to Congress to come to the rescue." George Ely to Washburne, Feb. 9, 1868. See also W. M. Dunn to John Sherman, Nov. 18, 1867; A. L. Harris to S., Nov. 29, 1867; Foster Blodgett to S., Dec. 30, 1867, Sherman MSS, Library of Congress; W. H. Gibbs to Washburne, Nov. 26 and 29, 1867, Jan. 29, Feb. 3, and 21, 1868; John C. Underwood to W., Dec. 9 and 16, 1867, Washburne MSS; James L. Dunning to Sumner, Dec. 29, 1867; R. R. Williams to S., Jan. 1, 1868; John H. Anxhurst to S., Jan. 1, 1868;

weeks after the recess, the President would be involved in a fresh quarrel, this time with General Grant.

On January 10, 1868, the Senate Committee on Military Affairs issued a report vindicating the suspended Stanton, and on the thirteenth the Senate voted to refuse concurrence in the suspension. On the day after the committee made its report (but before the Senate had acted on it), Grant, by now very uncomfortable, told Johnson that he did not want to stay in office any longer and serve as a test case while violating the Tenure of Office Act. Johnson tried to argue Grant out of his misgivings and managed to exact a half-hearted promise that the General would wait until they had had another talk before taking any action. But Grant, whose peace of mind required that he be shielded from the complicated side of anything, bolted on the following Tuesday after having heard about the Senate's vote the night before. He vacated his office, went back to army headquarters, and washed his hands of all further responsibility for the War Department. Stanton, lurking about the premises, was thereupon free to reoccupy his old office, which he promptly did. Grant then sent a note to the President, again calling attention to the Tenure of Office Act and inclosing a report of the Senate's action, saying that he could no longer serve as Secretary of War *ad interim*.[25]

That same day, Tuesday, January 14, Johnson summoned Grant in before a full cabinet meeting to explain himself, continuing, despite Grant's embarrassed protests, to address him as "Mr. Secretary." He pointed out that Grant had broken their agreement. The General said rather lamely that he had not expected the Senate to act so soon and offered to go personally to Stanton and persuade him to resign. (This he later did, without success.) What followed precipitated another call for impeachment.[26]

Johnson at this point had two alternatives. Although he had caught Grant in a questionable act, he might still retain the co-operation of Grant as General of the Army by simply issuing his executive orders through him and ignoring Stanton. This he was strongly advised to do by Thomas Ewing, and Grant himself was not unwilling to proceed

Thomas W. Conway to S., Jan. 6, 1868; J. Sumner Powell to S., Jan. 20, 1868; Oscar M. Waring to S., Feb. 11, 1868; G. Norton to S., Feb. 13, 1868; W. Dockray to S., Feb. 22, 1868, Sumner MSS, Harvard College Library.

25 McPherson, *Reconstruction*, p. 262; Adam Badeau, *Grant in Peace* (Hartford: S. S. Scranton, 1887), pp. 110–12; "Notes of Colonel Moore," p. 115; Browning, *Diary*, II, 173–74; Welles, *Diary*, III, 259.

26 Welles, III, 259–62; Browning, *Diary*, II, 173–75; "Notes of Colonel Moore," pp. 115–16; McPherson, *Reconstruction*, pp. 283–91.

on such a basis. But in order to preserve this rapport Johnson would have had to let the matter of their disagreement drop; there was nothing now to gain and much to lose by continuing to harp on it. In any case the magnitude of Grant's duplicity had to be measured by the size of Johnson's moral claim on him in the first place—and this in turn had to be defined from the standpoint of Johnson's own designs for testing the Tenure of Office Act, to which Grant had been determined all along not to be a party.

Or, Johnson could do what he in fact did: try to show up the General publicly and demonstrate his own rightness. He released his version of the cabinet interview for publication, which angered Grant and set him to brooding, and thereby inaugurated an exchange of letters all of which found their way into print. Grant, egged on by his friends, wrote the President giving his version of the agreement, which he said did not include his assisting Johnson to get rid of Stanton if it meant breaking the law. The exchange terminated on February 10 with a scathing letter from Johnson, accompanied by statements which the President had obtained from each of the cabinet members saying that he was right and that Grant was in effect lying. Johnson certainly had the better of the exchange, for whatever it might be worth, but he had humiliated and alienated Grant forever.[27]

The fact was that a bargain between Johnson and Grant had never been possible on any but the narrowest of ground—their mutual distaste for Stanton—and to strike any sort of agreement each had had to keep a whole set of reservations strictly in the background. Their views on the two acts of Congress which had caused most of the trouble—the Tenure of Office and Reconstruction Acts—had been miles apart from the first. One of the precipitating reasons for Johnson's desire to replace Stanton was the latter's opposition to his June 20 order and his veto of the July 19 Reconstruction Act. Grant, on the other hand, appears to have thought that if he himself did not accept office Johnson might appoint someone else who would embarrass the army in carrying out the law. Grant would not have been likely to make this plain when he accepted; when he later did say it, Johnson was quite naturally enraged. Johnson, for his part, wanted to use Grant and his immense prestige to get rid of Stanton and to demonstrate, if possible, that the Tenure of Office Act was a legal nullity. Had he insisted on the full

[27] William T. Sherman, *Personal Memoirs of Gen. W. T. Sherman* (3d ed., rev. and corrected; New York: Charles L. Webster, 1890), II, 423; Badeau, *Grant in Peace*, pp. 113–15; Welles, *Diary*, III, 269–76; "Notes of Colonel Moore," pp. 117–18; Browning, *Diary*, II, 178–80. The entire Johnson-Grant exchange is in McPherson, *Reconstruction*, pp. 283–91.

implications of this at the time, Grant would not have accepted at all. The General would only take the appointment within the bounds allowable by the same Act, which he said he intended to obey. Johnson would later deny that *his* agreement to these terms—suspension and *ad interim* replacement, rather than direct removal and reappointment—had implied any acquiescence to the Tenure of Office Act.

These, then, were the bounds within which the General of the Army committed his treachery to the President of the United States. By January, 1868, if not before, Grant had undoubtedly become aware in his rather dull way that he had got himself into a bad scrape, and he was no longer any too particular how he got out of it. And he was dull indeed if he had not begun to suspect that he himself was going to be the next President. He was already receiving a good deal of coaching, and was probably being chided daily for having let himself be drawn into Johnson's schemes for self-vindication in the first place. It may not have been *his* wits that foiled Johnson with a resignation which came too soon for one side of the executive plan and too late for the other, but for all his own political naïveté it could not have failed to occur to him at some point that the more completely he was rid of the business, the better it would be for him. It might be said that Johnson wrestled with Grant's political managers for control of the inert General's scruples, and Johnson lost.[28]

At any rate, documentary evidence now seemed to exist showing that Johnson had tried to plot with Grant to break the law, thus providing some solid ground for impeachment. But the members of the Reconstruction Committee, much as they would have loved to strike, reluctantly voted after much searching of soul not to recommend it.

[28] The present author is assuming that the version of Johnson (that the General had been guilty of deceiving him) was technically correct. Needless to say, Grant himself never so assumed. Grant's own side of the case rests mainly on the emphasis with which he expressed his desire to Johnson, in their interview of January 11, to leave the War Office. Johnson's side depends on the clarity with which it was understood that Grant would remain pending further developments. Badeau, who saw Grant before and after this interview, says that the General was adamant and that Johnson, who "pleaded and argued," was the indecisive one. This is "indirect" evidence, but then so was everything that followed. Seward's statement indicates that there did not seem to be full clarity of understanding between the two men. At the cabinet showdown, on the other hand, Grant, confronted by an angry President with a roomful of supporters, hardly showed to his best advantage. It is on the basis of this episode, and the subsequent epistolary efforts of the President and his cabinet advisers to describe it, that the history of the affair (by DeWitt, Milton, *et al.*) has been written. A more recent biographer of Grant, however, is inclined to dismiss all this evidence as decidedly biased and flimsy, and to assume that Grant's intentions were just what the General said they were. He thinks that Grant, never noted for "courage in battles of words or wars of ideas," simply botched the affair. See William B. Hesseltine, *Ulysses S. Grant, Politician* (New York: Dodd, Mead, 1935), pp. 107–10.

They could hardly impeach Johnson without involving Grant, who had, to say the least, bungled his part of the affair. So once again the impeachment drive was stalled, and again the issue was closed, if Johnson would now let it remain *in statu quo*. Said Thaddeus Stevens in disgust: "I shall never bring up this question of impeachment again."[29]

IV THE FINAL EFFORT: FEBRUARY 21–MAY 26, 1868

Most of Johnson's closest advisers now urged him to ignore Stanton and make no further attempt to remove the barricaded Secretary, who had taken to eating and sleeping in his office at the War Department. But Johnson would have none of this advice. He turned grimly to this general and that, while each fled in dismay from the President's efforts to elevate him to cabinet honors. General Sherman resisted the presidential entreaties and hastily left town; Johnson subsequently tried to get him back by making him a brevet general in command of a new military department, with headquarters at Washington, created for the occasion. Sherman, in fresh alarm, wired his brother John from St. Louis to have the Senate kill the appointment. Johnson tried the same approach with General George H. Thomas, also with the lure of a brevet general's commission, but the Rock of Chickamauga, now weary of strife, managed to excuse himself from this new call to arms. The President thought of making General Thomas Ewing Secretary of War, but old Thomas, Senior—Johnson's otherwise loyal counselor—would not hear of his son's career being ruined. Even the chief clerk at the War Department, John Potts, could not be persuaded to accept the place. At last the President resurrected General Lorenzo Thomas, an aged dandy full of nonsense, who had been languishing for some time in semiretirement, and put the proposition to him. Thomas received the President's plan with much relish. Upon being told that he was expected to "support the Constitution and the laws," he said that he would. He was accordingly given a letter of authority to assume the duties of office *ad interim* on February 21.[30]

[29] The House Committee on Reconstruction, which had taken charge of the impeachment question, voted 6-3 on February 13 to lay an impeachment resolution on the table. New York *World*, Feb. 14, 1868. The Stevens statement is from an interview with the *World's* Washington correspondent. Stevens thought that Johnson and Grant were probably both lying to some extent, "though the President has the weight of evidence on his side."

[30] Browning, *Diary*, II, 182; T. Ewing to Johnson, Oct. 12, 1867, and Jan. 29, 1868, T. Ewing to W. T. Sherman, Jan. 25, 1868, Johnson MSS; Sherman, *Memoirs*, II, 425-33; Thorndike, *Sherman Letters*, pp. 300-307; M. A. DeWolfe Howe (ed.), *Home*

Thomas presented himself to Stanton with his letter on the same day, and Stanton told him he would think it over. The General then left and proceeded to float through the most riotous twenty-four hours of his life. He told half the town how he was going to take office by force the next day; that evening he went off to a masked ball where he waltzed and drank toasts into the small hours; news of the old beau's drunken exploits penetrated even to the darkened executive mansion. Thomas emerged from his bed in the morning to be met by a federal marshal with an arrest warrant which had been sworn out by Stanton during the night; he went and made bail, reported to the White House, and was told to go out and storm the works. But confronted by an adamant Stanton flanked by radical congressmen, the would-be hero, now weak with hunger, proved unequal to his supreme test. He ended his brief Secretaryship of War (*ad interim*) in a surrender ceremony which involved a fresh round of guzzling before breakfast, the whiskey this time being provided by Stanton himself, who was gracious in victory and still, to all intents and purposes, Secretary of War. A faint war cry from Lorenzo Thomas' home state would later come back to haunt him: "The eyes of Delaware are upon you!"[31]

While the nation's military affairs were suspended amid these light doings, the House of Representatives voted to impeach President Andrew Johnson for high crimes and misdemeanors. At that moment there was very little doubt that the crazed members had the support of a majority of their fellow citizens.[32]

With all the combustible matter that Johnson had heaped together for them over the past three years, it is understandable that the impeachers could at last imagine—in the blaze set off by this final spark—that they had a perfect case. It is no wonder that a major-

---

Letters of General Sherman (New York: Scribner's, 1909), pp. 368–74; *Trial*, I, 483–85, 517, 521, 529–30; McPherson, *Reconstruction*, pp. 263, 346; Milton, *Age of Hate*, p. 741 n.; "Notes of Colonel Moore," pp. 119–20; *Trial*, I, 417–18.

31 *Trial*, I, 211, 221, 223–28, 427–37, 509, 515–16; Milton, *Age of Hate*, p. 506.

32 *Cong. Globe*, 40 Cong., 2 sess., pp. 1336–55, 1358–69, 1382–1402, Appendix (see Index to Appendix, "Impeachment of the President," for speeches). The resolution for impeachment, presented to the House on February 22 by the Reconstruction Committee, could not be passed, owing to the flood of oratory that it inspired, until the twenty-fourth. Every Republican state convention that met between that time and the end of the trial strongly supported impeachment. See *American Annual Cyclopaedic*, 1868, pp. 384, 493–94, 542, 604, 619–20, 758, 766. In the showers of letters and telegrams which congressmen received from home, it is typical to find Congress being chided for not having acted sooner: "The people are alarmed . . . by the apparent apathy of Congress"; "Let there be no halting or wavering"; "Security for the future hitherto denied us on

ity could not only desire but fully believe that all would be over in a puff. The eleven articles of impeachment were themselves a kind of hectic mirror of this illusion. The first nine articles, barely distinguishable from one another, all had to do with Johnson's "plot" to violate the Tenure of Office Act; the tenth involved Johnson's "scandalous harangues"; and the eleventh—which in the trial was voted on first—was an effort to encompass in print everything upon which the President could conceivably be condemned. The longer they were debated, the flimsier they looked. The trial, which has been minutely described in many other places, ended for practical purposes on May 16, 1868. On that day the seven "recusant senators" (Fessenden, Fowler, Grimes, Henderson, Ross, Trumbull, and Van Winkle), with their votes for acquittal, left the prosecution with one vote short of conviction. The key man, Ross of Kansas, had been in doubt up to the last. When the Senate reconvened on May 26, only two more articles were voted upon before everyone realized that impeachment had been a failure. The "court" thereupon adjourned sine die.[33]

The impeachment was a great act of ill-directed passion, and was supported by little else. It was rather like an immense balloon filled with foul air, the most noisome elements of which were those most active. But as from a balloon, the air began oozing out fairly early. Most people, including the noblest of the recusant senators, were sick to death of Andrew Johnson and would have given much to see the end of him.[34] But this could be accomplished neither by a popular referendum or by a legislative vote of "no confidence," though either one would have settled his fate in an instant, and in either event the

grounds of expediency is all that we ask of our Senators"; Congress had redeemed itself at last for "the rather disreputable effort heretofore to dodge or give it [impeachment] the go by." T. Foote to Austin Blair, Feb. 24, 1868, Blair MSS, Detroit Public Library; N. Ewing to John Covode, Feb. 27, 1868, Covode MSS, Historical Society of Western Pennsylvania; Frank G. Dounsbery to Charles Sumner, Mar. 5, 1868, Sumner, Mass.; J. Reed to James Garfield, Mar. 7, 1868, Garfield MSS.

[33] Under Article I, Sections II, 5 and III, 6, of the Constitution, the House of Representatives prefers the charges (i.e., does the impeaching); the Senate sits as a court of impeachment to judge the merits of the case and decide whether to convict or acquit the accused; and if the President of the United States is the accused, the trial is presided over by the Chief Justice of the Supreme Court.

[34] E.g., Fessenden frequently expressed his contempt for Johnson in private correspondence, and after the trial wrote to a friend: "It was hard enough to keep down my own strong impulses towards conviction as it was." Shelby Cullom, then a young congressman, said in his memoirs that Trumbull had originally favored impeachment. While the House vote was being taken on the Articles, Trumbull said to Cullom: "Johnson is an obstruction to the Government and should be removed." Fessenden, *Fessenden*, II, 226; Cullom, *Fifty Years*, p. 154.

zeal of Trumbull and Fessenden would have been only too available. But the only form open was that of a judicial trial, and matters had reached such a pass that many men were quite willing to stretch their principles all out of shape, to seize upon any form at all that was plausible, and to face their consciences later. "Not a loyal tongue will wag against impeachment," Representative Blair was assured by a constituent from Flint, Michigan; "The people want rest." Yet political principles were one thing, legal principles quite another. The Tenure of Office Act, thanks to the equivocations of a joint conference committee back in February, 1867, was quite unable to bear the intense legal scrutiny to which it was subjected during the trial of Andrew Johnson. The President's counsel, men of the very highest character and ability, showed rather mercilessly how little protection the Act really gave to Lincoln's holdovers, and they argued most effectively that nothing treasonable could be found in the President's effort to test a law which he considered unconstitutional. The Managers of Impeachment, whose composite personality was a curious blend of demagogue and rascal, were not really able to give them much of a battle. More than one observer must have cringed at the spectacle.[35]

The longer the show dragged on under such circumstances, the less ardent became the general desire to continue it. There was great gnashing of teeth when it was over, since many normally honorable men had been committed to seeing the folly out to the end. But there was also considerable secret and not-so-secret relief. The *Nation*, having hoped all along for Johnson's conviction, had at last had enough; it declared, on May 28: "We shall ... hear no more of impeachment, and we are glad of it."[36]

All of which suggests still another use for the "balloon" metaphor: the principal function of the impeachment was that of a long-needed psychological blow-off. There were still, after all, certain compensations. The extreme step had, at least, been taken, and the impeachers had come very close; they had failed by only one vote. Meanwhile the

[35] George W. Fish to Austin Blair, Mar. 3, 1868, Blair MSS. The Managers of Impeachment—or "prosecuting attorneys"—chosen by the House were Thaddeus Stevens, George S. Boutwell, Benjamin F. Butler, John A. Logan, Thomas Williams, James F. Wilson, and John A. Bingham. The President's counsel were William M. Evarts, Benjamin R. Curtis, Henry Stanbery, and William S. Groesbeck. Evarts, an extremely witty and brilliant lawyer who would later serve as Hayes's secretary of state, did the bulk of the work for Johnson's case. The *Nation*, despite its desire for Johnson's conviction, conceded that "the Managers were overmastered throughout in learning and ability. There is no use now in passing this over without notice. The contrast was patent to everybody throughout the trial and was a constant subject of comment." VI (May 21, 1868), 404.

[36] VI, 421.

people had been rescued from a very questionable act and all its possible consequences; there were not many who really welcomed the thought of Ben Wade as President and Ben Butler as Secretary of State, even for a little while.[37] Legend tells, and quite truthfully, that Fessenden and the others came in for much abuse because of the votes they gave. But it is also true that these men were rewarded, almost from the moment the trial ended, with an audible and growing chorus of praise. The *Nation* was not alone when it affirmed: "We believe, for our part, that the thanks of the country are due to Messrs. Trumbull, Fessenden, Grimes, Henderson, Fowler, Van Winkle, and Ross, not for voting for Johnson's acquittal, but for vindicating . . . the sacred rights of individual conscience."[38] The affair had served, in short, as a catharsis.

Finally, the country had a cheering new object for its attention. Between the first and second votes on impeachment, the Republican national convention had met and nominated Ulysses S. Grant—looked upon everywhere as the man of peace—for the next President. No one could yet foresee, of course, the shoddiness of Grant's own administration, or yet know that it would still require the whole of Grant's two terms to liquidate all the passions and badness engendered by the Johnson regime. But his appearance now, as standard-bearer for the future, was a vast relief. It was miraculous how quickly impeachment was for-

[37] Wade, as presiding officer of the Senate, would have become President in the event of Johnson's conviction. He had already made up a list of his cabinet, headed by the name of Benjamin F. Butler as Secretary of State. Badeau, *Grant in Peace*, pp. 136–37; Milton, *Age of Hate*, p. 603.

[38] "Happily the great body of the party, certainly all the intelligent portion of it, and all its most influential and respected newspapers, made a determined stand against this amazing burst of folly [the attack on Fessenden and the others], and thus saved the party from damnation. . . ." *Harper's Weekly*, VI (May 21, 1868), 404. The Chicago *Tribune*, referring to Republican newspapers in general, declared on May 20: "While there is no difference of opinion among those journals as to the righteousness of impeachment, neither is there any difference as to the impolicy of rending one's garments over the result, or of . . . reading Senators out of the party who have not been able to vote for the conviction of Johnson." *Harper's Weekly* said: "Whoever has read the opinions of Senators Fessenden, Grimes, and Trumbull, however he may regret the conclusions to which they come, will not deny the ability, the dignity, and the candor with which their views are stated." XII (June 6, 1868), 354. *Harper's* quoted the Providence *Journal*, Chicago *Tribune*, Boston *Advertiser*, Hartford *Courant*, Chicago *Post*, Bridgeport *Standard*, Cincinnati *Commercial*, and the Union League Club of New York, all to the same effect. *Ibid.*, XII (May 30, 1868), 339. A present-day scholar goes so far as to say that the "martyr" story on the "recusant senators" was hardly more than a myth from the first. See Ralph J. Roske, "Republican Newspaper Support for the Acquittal of President Johnson," *Tennessee Historical Quarterly*, XI (Sept., 1952), 263–73; and "The Seven Martyrs?" *American Historical Review*, LXIV (Jan., 1959), 323–30.

gotten, as all turned to beam upon the hero.[39] Stanton retired from the War Department; General Schofield, acceptable to all sides, was confirmed as Secretary of War; and the remainder of Andrew Johnson's presidency passed in relative tranquillity.

[39] E.g., Nast's June 6 cover for *Harper's* shows a matronly Columbia benignly pinning a medal (the nation's hopes) on a serene and inscrutable Grant. After this time, there is surprisingly little talk of impeachment in the editorial columns. " 'Impeachment' is dying out," wrote David E. Bayard to John Covode from Uniontown, Pennsylvania, on June 1. "As Andy has but a short time to serve we can 'stand' him his term out." Covode MSS, Historical Society of Western Pennsylvania. Later in the summer a friend of Jacob Howard (one of the more radical senatorial judges) wrote: "Although I would rejoice to see Andrew Johnson deposed it does not strike me now as game worth the candle. These are or were about your views too as I gathered from our last talk. The political situation looks well to me. . . . I believe Grant will really walk over the course." N. G. King to Jacob Howard, Sept. 1, 1868, Howard MSS, Detroit Public Library.

Selected
Bibliography,
with
Notes

The problem of a bibliography has caused me a certain amount of perplexity. A work of this length and proportions ought to have some such apparatus appended to it, if only for the most utilitarian of reasons. The reader is entitled to know at a glance, in some general way, where the author has gone in the course of preparing his work, and students desiring to investigate the subject further should be given some sort of ready reference map of the territory. But certain considerations which I shall mention, besides those of space, have persuaded me that these functions might be fulfilled with something less than a minute and exhaustive bibliography. At the same time, the answer did not seem to lie in a bibliographical essay. I found that I had already done this, in a different way, by diffusing a great many of the obiter dicta normally reserved for such an essay throughout the text and footnotes, so it hardly seemed necessary to repeat the commentary at the end of the book.

Had I not explored this territory from angles of vision different in many respects from those of my immediate predecessors, there would, of course, have been little warrant for my writing this book at all. Yet the fact remains that, with regard to materials as well as subject, it is still basically the same territory. The conditions of manuscript research, it is true, are infinitely easier for the scholar of today than they were for the scholars of thirty years ago, what with microfilming facilities and the generosity of research foundations—both of which were virtually unheard-of then. Even so, with a few marginal exceptions I cannot claim to have exploited materials which were not familiar to Howard Beale and George Milton back in 1930, or to others a generation before them. It is largely a matter of degree. The same assertion applies, with even greater pertinence, to the printed materials. Most of these have been, in every sense, in the public domain for many years.

The compromise which I eventually hit upon was a selected bibliography, accompanied by notes whose emphasis would be rather more on the methodological than on the evaluative or comparative side. There are a great many items in all categories of which I made only passing use. These have been duly cited in the footnotes but will be omitted from the list below. More important than a complete listing is the fact that there were a number of points at which the same materials were seen by me and by other writers in very different lights, and that the uses made of such materials varied accordingly. It struck me, therefore, that the reader might be interested in knowing of the principal places where this occurred.

I COLLECTIONS OF LETTERS AND MANUSCRIPTS

John A. Andrew MSS, Massachusetts Historical Society
William Bigler MSS, Pennsylvania Historical Society
Jeremiah Black MSS, Library of Congress
Austin Blair MSS, Detroit Public Library
James Buchanan MSS, Pennsylvania Historical Society
Salmon P. Chase MSS, Pennsylvania Historical Society
James Comly MSS, Ohio Historical Society
George William Curtis MSS, Harvard College Library
James R. Doolittle MSS, Historical Society of Wisconsin
Thomas Ewing MSS, Library of Congress
William Pitt Fessenden MSS, Library of Congress and Bowdoin College
Andrew Johnson MSS, Library of Congress
Hugh McCulloch MSS, Library of Congress
Edwin D. Morgan MSS, New York State Library
Justin S. Morrill MSS, Library of Congress
William H. Seward MSS, University of Rochester Library
John Sherman MSS, Library of Congress
William Henry Smith MSS, Ohio Historical Society
Thaddeus Stevens MSS, Library of Congress
Charles Sumner MSS, Harvard College Library
Samuel J. Tilden MSS, New York Public Library
Lyman Trumbull MSS, Library of Congress
Benjamin F. Wade MSS, Library of Congress
Elihu Washburne MSS, Library of Congress
Thurlow Weed MSS, University of Rochester Library
Gideon Welles MSS, Library of Congress

1. While it is true that files of political correspondence can be a valuable treasury of miscellaneous information on a great many small points pertinent to general developments, it seems that such information is seldom very systematic and seldom more than fragmentary. It is particularly important, I feel, not to expect that too much of an "inside story" will materialize from such correspondence, or that this sort of material will, by its nature, abound in evidence of secret plans. In this respect I have come to think that the significance of Charles Sumner's correspondence, especially that of 1865, has been rather overrated. Sumner's idiosyncratic character and the simple fact that his papers are so much more complete than those of most other political figures of that period have tempted historians to let these papers dominate much of the period's tone. They have been led to ascribe undue influence to Sumner's opinions, to draw many an injudicious inference about the general state of party sentiment during this time, and to see in Sumner's letters evidence of a powerful scheme to undermine the Johnson administration. Yet as I checked these

assumptions against evidence found in other collections of the same period, I was struck to discover the emphasis which most Republican politicians placed, well into 1866, on the importance of maintaining harmonious relations with the executive branch.

2. In another connection, however, I have been impressed by the unusual number of letters from persecuted Southern Unionists to be found in the papers of both Sumner and Thaddeus Stevens. These letters are seldom if ever mentioned by writers who have dealt with the period. Undoubtedly it has been assumed, owing in some way to Stevens' and Sumner's reputations, that such testaments represent biased evidence. Yet I am not so sure that this is quite reason enough for ruling such evidence out. Had I myself been a persecuted Unionist, I imagine that the first men to whom I would have thought of writing would have been Stevens and Sumner. At any rate, the student who is interested in investigating this problem systematically will find in these papers much hair-raising reading. A similar point could be made with regard to the troubles of harassed carpetbaggers in the fall and winter of 1867–68, as described to Sherman, Sumner and Washburne.

3. The greatest revelation for me in the political correspondence of the time lay in the things it told me about the network of expectations and responsibilities that existed between congressmen and their local constituencies, particularly the district officeholders. With regard to local sentiment, for instance, the most dependable index of this did not seem to be found in letters from "uncommitted" and "disinterested" citizens but rather in those from men attached through patronage to the local party organization and thereby committed to the maintenance of the organization's local health. It was their particular concern to judge with accuracy the local effect of national policy and to report it to their congressional patrons. Nor do I think one need be discouraged to find the correspondence of leading statesmen unduly clogged with items of "mere routine patronage." On the contrary, these very items can be substantively more informative than many a reference to affairs of state which are usually far better reported in the newspapers. In this regard I found the papers of James Garfield, John Sherman, Lyman Trumbull, Elihu Washburne, and Thurlow Weed exceptionally useful. Trumbull's patronage problems, for example, throw considerable light on that senator's behavior during the spring of 1866 and his later support of the Tenure of Office Act. A wonderful case study in local political relationships, moreover, may be found in the town of Ravenna, Ohio, and in the 19th Ohio Congressional District, through the letters of James Garfield.

II PRINTED SOURCE COLLECTIONS AND OFFICIAL DOCUMENTS

American Annual Cyclopaedia and Register of Important Events of the Year 1865 [and succeeding volumes for 1866, 1867, and 1868]. New York: D. Appleton, 1869.

Congressional Documents [see note].

Congressional Globe, 39th and 40th Congresses, 1865–68.

McPherson, Edward. *The Political History of the United States of America during the Period of Reconstruction . . .* Washington: Philp & Solomons, 1871.

Report of the Joint Committee on Reconstruction, 39th Congress, 1st Session. Washington: Government Printing Office, 1866.

Richardson, James D. (ed.). *A Compilation of the Messages and Papers of the Presidents, 1789–1897.* 10 vols. Washington: Bureau of National Literature and Art, 1896–99.

Trial of Andrew Johnson . . . 3 vols. Washington: Government Printing Office, 1868.

Tribune Almanac for the Years 1838 to 1868 Inclusive. Vol. II. New York: The Tribune, 1868.

United States Reports.

United States Statutes at Large.

The character and uses of this sort of material require no detailed comment. Special reference, however, should be made to the congressional documents. These documents, published serially in bound volumes by House and Senate separately, and grouped according to sessions, are indexed by subject at the front of each volume. The major categories are Miscellaneous Documents, Executive Documents (furnished by executive departments in response to congressional requests for information), and Reports of Committees. The latter two in particular are immensely useful. A number of the committee reports which involved the extensive taking of testimony are full of fascinatingly human material. I believe that it is possible, moreover, to consider this testimony much more seriously than has been the practice of previous studies of the period, quite aside from the partisan purposes for which much of it was gathered. No guarantees, of course, have ever been devised to prevent perjury. But the very conditions of testifying provide a number of internal checks on what is said in the course of it, which in turn allows one to draw any number of legitimate inferences about the events concerned. I have already called attention to this point in reference to the Report of the Joint Committee on Reconstruction and the Report on the New Orleans Riots (see pp. 331, 424 n.). It would apply similarly to the testimony of the district commanders on the state of law enforcement and justice in Southern communities (see p. 459 and nn.). On the other hand, the report of the House Judiciary Committee on evidence for impeaching Johnson discredits itself; it is the committee's own members who say so (see p. 499). To take another sort of example, two very different reports on conditions in the South were submitted to the Senate in January, 1866, one written by Carl Schurz and the other by General Grant. I believe that we may take them both on their merits with equal seriousness. Grant's, submitted after a very brief official tour of inspection, concerned the "mass of thinking men" (these were the only ones the General talked to); Schurz, for his part, was rather more impressed by the mass of non-thinking men. In the foregoing study I have given due attention to each category.

III NEWSPAPERS AND PERIODICALS

Augusta (Ga.) *Daily Press*, 1866–67

Boston *Advertiser*, 1865–66

Charleston *Courier*, 1865–67

Chicago *Times*, 1865–67

Chicago *Tribune*, 1865–68

Cincinnati *Enquirer*, 1865–67

Detroit *Free Press*, 1865–67

Harper's Weekly, 1865–68

Jackson (Miss.) *Clarion*, 1865–67

The *Nation*, 1865–68

New Orleans *Picayune*, 1865–67

New York *Herald*, 1865–68

New York *Times*, 1865–68

New York *Tribune*, 1865–68

New York *World*, 1865–68

Philadelphia *Age*, 1865

Richmond *Enquirer*, 1866–67

Richmond *Times*, 1866–67

Springfield (Mass.) *Republican*, 1865–68

Washington *National Intelligencer*, 1865–68

1. In addition to the many other purposes for which I used these materials as different occasions arose, I considered it highly important, in following the course of developments which this story covers, to keep track of what might be called the "middle-of-the-road" position in Republican sentiment. The fact that the "center" kept altering as the conflict with the executive worsened—inasmuch as the party as a whole was led by circumstances to assume an ever more radical attitude—does not change the fact that there continued to be a "center" throughout. By far the most dependable index of this position was to be found in the editorial columns of *Harper's Weekly* (checked at many points with the private correspondence of its editor, George William Curtis) and in those of E. L. Godkin's *Nation*. These two periodicals might be called the counterparts, in journalism, of William Pitt Fessenden and Lyman Trumbull in the U. S. Senate.

2. Another service which the newspaper files (and other kinds of material) performed was in connection with the story's rather complicated chronology. Although chronology is one of the most orthodox tools known to historical analysis, I was still surprised at the results that were yielded at a number of points by a strict application of it. The evolution of the Fourteenth Amendment was an outstanding case. There are, of course, a good many historical events that are best analyzed and understood by hindsight—that is, in terms of their outcome—and there is many a purpose for which "hindsight" is an excellent method. And yet there are other events which are incomprehensible except through the process of development—by starting at the beginning and watching them unfold. I found a number of these in the Johnson administration: sequences of events whose "irrational" outcome was not necessarily prefigured either in their beginnings or in the intentions of the men involved. They had to be correlated with other events occurring along the way.

IV MEMOIRS, DIARIES, LETTERS, PAPERS

BOUTWELL, GEORGE S. *Reminiscences of Sixty Years in Public Affairs.* 2 vols. New York: McClure, Phillips, 1902.

BROWNING, ORVILLE H. *The Diary of Orville Hickman Browning.* Edited by JAMES G. RANDALL and THEODORE C. PEASE. 2 vols. Springfield: Illinois State Historical Library, 1933.

BUTLER, BENJAMIN F. *Private and Official Correspondence of General Benjamin F. Butler.* Edited by JESSIE AMES MARSHALL. 5 vols. Norwood, Mass.: Plimpton Press, 1917.

CAMPBELL, JOHN A. "Papers of Hon. John A. Campbell—1861–1865," *Southern Historical Society Papers*, N.S. IV (October, 1917), 61–74.

CHASE, SALMON P. "Diary and Correspondence of Salmon P. Chase," *Annual Report of the American Historical Association, 1902.* Washington: Government Printing Office, 1903.

CULLOM, SHELBY M. *Fifty Years of Public Service.* . . . Chicago: A. C. McClurg, 1911.

DAVIS, HENRY WINTER. *Speeches and Addresses.* . . . Edited by J. A. J. CRESWELL. New York: Harper & Bros., 1867.

GARFIELD, JAMES. *Life and Letters of James Abram Garfield.* Edited by THEODORE CLARKE SMITH. 2 vols. New Haven: Yale University Press, 1925.

HAMPTON, WADE. *Family Letters of the Three Wade Hamptons, 1782–1901.* Edited by CHARLES E. CAUTHEN. Columbia: University of South Carolina Press, 1953.

HAYES, RUTHERFORD B. *Diary and Letters of Rutherford Birchard Hayes.* . . . Edited by CHARLES R. WILLIAMS. 5 vols. Columbus: Ohio State Archaeological and Historical Society, 1922–26.

JOHNSON, ANDREW. *Speeches of Andrew Johnson, President of the United States.* Edited by FRANK MOORE. Boston: Little, Brown, 1865.

JULIAN, GEORGE W. *Political Recollections, 1840 to 1872.* Chicago: Jansen, McClurg, 1884.

LECONTE, JOSEPH. *Autobiography of Joseph LeConte.* Edited by WILLIAM D. ARMES. New York: D. Appleton, 1903.

LINCOLN, ABRAHAM. *The Collected Works of Abraham Lincoln.* Edited by ROY P. BASLER. 8 vols. and Index vol. New Brunswick, N.J.: Rutgers University Press, 1953–55.

McCULLOCH, HUGH. *Men and Measures of Half a Century: Sketches and Comments.* New York: Charles Scribner's Sons, 1900.

MOORE, W. G. "Notes of Colonel W. G. Moore, Private Secretary to President Johnson, 1866–68," edited by ST. GEORGE L. SIOUSSAT, *American Historical Review*, XIX (October, 1913), 98–132.

PERRY, BENJAMIN F. *Reminiscences of Public Men, with Speeches and Addresses.* Greenville, S. C.: Shannon & Co., 1889.

RAYMOND, HENRY J. "Extracts from the Journal of Henry J. Raymond," edited by HENRY W. RAYMOND, *Scribner's Monthly*, XX, 275–80 (June, 1880).

SCHOFIELD, JOHN. *Forty-six Years in the Army.* New York: Century, 1897.

SCHURZ, CARL. *The Reminiscences of Carl Schurz.* 3 vols. Garden City, N.Y.: Doubleday, Page, 1913.

——. *Speeches, Correspondence, and Political Papers of Carl Schurz.* Edited by FREDERIC BANCROFT. 6 vols. New York: G. P. Putnam's Sons, 1913.

SHERMAN, JOHN. *Recollections of Forty Years in the House, Senate and Cabinet: An Autobiography.* 2 vols. Chicago: Werner, 1895.

SHERMAN, WILLIAM T. *Personal Memoirs of Gen. W. T. Sherman.* 3d ed., rev. and corrected. 2 vols. New York: Charles L. Webster, 1890.

———. *Home Letters of General Sherman.* Edited by M. A. DeWolfe Howe. New York: Charles Scribner's Sons, 1909.

———. *The Sherman Letters: Correspondence between General and Senator Sherman from 1837 to 1891.* Edited by RACHEL SHERMAN THORNDIKE. New York: Charles Scribner's Sons, 1894.

STEWART, WILLIAM M. *Reminiscences of Senator William M. Stewart of Nevada.* Edited by GEORGE ROTHWELL BROWN. New York: Neale Publishing Co., 1908.

STRONG, GEORGE TEMPLETON. *The Diary of George Templeton Strong.* Edited by ALLAN NEVINS and MILTON H. THOMAS. 4 vols. New York: Macmillan, 1952.

SUMNER, CHARLES. *The Works of Charles Sumner.* 15 vols. Boston: Lee & Shepard, 1870–83.

WELLES, GIDEON. *Diary of Gideon Welles, Secretary of the Navy under Lincoln and Johnson.* Edited by JOHN T. MORSE, JR. 3 vols. Boston: Houghton Mifflin, 1911.

WORTH, JONATHAN. *The Correspondence of Jonathan Worth.* Edited by J. G. DE ROULHAC HAMILTON. 2 vols. Raleigh: North Carolina Historical Commission, 1909.

The one special observation which I am inclined to make here is that the period's most complete document in this realm, the *Diary of Gideon Welles,* has been overrated somewhat in the way that Sumner's letters have been, likewise owing in great measure to its very completeness. Welles's personal rectitude and incorruptibility, plus the immense readability and informative usefulness of his *Diary,* have all but obscured the fact that his was actually one of the narrowest and most rigid minds of the entire period. In Welles, political sagacity—and thus in many a sense wisdom—was all but totally lacking. We have no sure way of knowing whether it was Welles's advice that led Andrew Johnson to his political ruin, inasmuch as Johnson seems not to have been much influenced by the views of anyone; still, it very well could have been, and the results would be about the same. To the extent, at any rate, that scholars have relied upon Welles for balanced judgments on the events of the period, such reliance, it seems to me, has been misplaced.

V MONOGRAPHS, BIOGRAPHIES, ARTICLES, AND OTHER WORKS

ALEXANDER, THOMAS B. *Political Reconstruction in Tennessee.* Nashville: Vanderbilt University Press, 1950.

ANDREWS, SIDNEY. *The South since the War, As Shown by Fourteen Weeks of Travel and Observation in Georgia and the Carolinas.* Boston: Ticknor & Fields, 1866.

BADEAU, ADAM. *Grant in Peace.* Hartford: S. S. Scranton, 1887.

BAKER, LAFAYETTE C. *History of the United States Secret Service.* Philadelphia: L. C. Baker, 1867.

BARRETT, DON C. *The Greenbacks and Resumption of Specie Payments, 1862–1879*. Cambridge, Mass.: Harvard University Press, 1931.

BEALE, HOWARD K. *The Critical Year: A Study of Andrew Johnson and Reconstruction*. New York: Harcourt, Brace, 1930.

BLAINE, JAMES G. *Twenty Years of Congress: From Lincoln to Garfield*. 2 vols. Norwich, Conn.: Henry Bill, 1884.

BOWERS, CLAUDE G. *The Tragic Era: The Revolution after Lincoln*. Boston: Houghton Mifflin, 1929.

BRUMMER, SIDNEY D. *Political History of New York State during the Period of the Civil War*. New York: Privately printed, 1911.

BUCK, PAUL H. *The Road to Reunion, 1865–1900*. Boston: Little, Brown, 1937.

BURGESS, JOHN W. *Reconstruction and the Constitution, 1866–1876*. New York: Charles Scribner's Sons, 1902.

CARLSON, OLIVER. *The Man Who Made News: James Gordon Bennett*. New York: Duell, Sloane & Pearce, 1942.

CARMAN, HARRY J., and LUTHIN, REINHARD H. *Lincoln and the Patronage*. New York: Columbia University Press, 1943.

CASKEY, WILLIE M. *Secession and Restoration of Louisiana*. University, La.: University of Louisiana Press, 1938.

CLEMENCEAU, GEORGES. *American Reconstruction, 1865–1870, and the Impeachment of President Johnson*. Edited by FERNAND BALDENSPERGER and translated by MARGARET MACVEAGH. New York: Dial Press, 1928.

COBEN, STANLEY. "Northeastern Business and Radical Reconstruction: A Re-examination," *Mississippi Valley Historical Review*, XLVI (June, 1959), 67–90.

COULTER, ELLIS M. *William G. Brownlow, Fighting Parson of the Southern Highlands*. Chapel Hill: University of North Carolina Press, 1937.

CURRENT, RICHARD N. *Old Thad Stevens: A Story of Ambition*. Madison: University of Wisconsin Press, 1942.

DESTLER, CHESTER McA. "The Origin and Character of the Pendleton Plan," *Mississippi Valley Historical Review*, XXIV (Sept., 1937), 171–84.

DEWITT, DAVID M. *The Impeachment and Trial of Andrew Johnson*. . . . New York: Macmillian, 1903.

DODD, DOROTHY. *Henry J. Raymond and the New York Times during Reconstruction*. Chicago: University of Chicago Libraries, 1936.

DORRIS, JONATHAN T. *Pardon and Amnesty under Lincoln and Johnson: The Restoration of the Confederates to Their Rights and Privileges*. Chapel Hill: University of North Carolina Press, 1953.

DUNNING, WILLIAM A. *Essays on the Civil War and Reconstruction and Related Topics*. New York: Macmillan, 1898.

ECKENRODE, HAMILTON J. *The Political History of Virginia during the Reconstruction*. "Johns Hopkins University Studies in Historical and Political Science," Ser. XXII. Baltimore: Johns Hopkins Press, 1904.

FESSENDEN, FRANCIS. *Life and Public Services of William Pitt Fessenden, Senator from Maine*. . . . 2 vols. Boston: Houghton Mifflin, 1907.

FICKLEN, JOHN R. *History of Reconstruction in Louisiana (through 1868)*.

"Johns Hopkins University Studies in Historical and Political Science," Ser. XXVII. Baltimore: Johns Hopkins Press, 1910.

FLACK, HORACE E. *The Adoption of the Fourteenth Amendment.* "Johns Hopkins University Studies in Historical and Political Science," Ser. XXVI. Baltimore: Johns Hopkins Press, 1908.

FLEMING, WALTER L. *Civil War and Reconstruction in Alabama.* New York: Columbia University Press, 1905.

FOULKE, WILLIAM D. *Life of Oliver P. Morton.* 2 vols. Indianapolis: Bowen-Merrill, 1899.

GARNER, JAMES W. *Reconstruction in Mississippi.* New York: Macmillan, 1901.

GRAHAM, HOWARD JAY. "The 'Conspiracy Theory' of the Fourteenth Amendment," *Yale Law Journal,* XLVII (January, 1938), 371–403, and XLVIII (December, 1938), 171–94.

GRAY, WOOD. *The Hidden Civil War: The Story of the Copperheads.* New York: Viking Press, 1942.

HALL, CLIFTON R. *Andrew Johnson, Military Governor of Tennessee.* Princeton: Princeton University Press, 1916.

HAMILTON, J. G. DE ROULHAC. *Reconstruction in North Carolina.* New York: Columbia University, 1914.

HARRIS, WILMER C. *The Public Life of Zachariah Chandler, 1851–1875.* Lansing: Michigan Historical Commission, 1917.

HESSELTINE, WILLIAM B. *Lincoln and the War Governors.* New York: Alfred A. Knopf, 1948.

——. *Ulysses S. Grant, Politician.* New York: Dodd, Mead, 1935.

JAMES, JOSEPH B. *The Framing of the Fourteenth Amendment.* Urbana: University of Illinois Press, 1956.

JARRELL, HAMPTON. *Wade Hampton and the Negro: The Road Not Taken.* Columbia: University of South Carolina Press, 1949.

JELLISON, CHARLES A. "William Pitt Fessenden, Statesman of the Middle Ground." Ph.D. thesis, University of Virginia, 1956.

KENDRICK, BENJAMIN B. *The Journal of the Joint Committee of Fifteen on Reconstruction.* New York: Columbia University Press, 1914.

KIBLER, LILLIAN A. *Benjamin F. Perry, South Carolina Unionist.* Durham: Duke University Press, 1914.

KNAPP, CHARLES M. *New Jersey Politics during the Period of the Civil War and Reconstruction.* Geneva, N.Y.: W. F. Humphrey, 1924.

MERRILL, HORACE S. *Bourbon Democracy of the Middle West, 1865–1896.* Baton Rouge: Louisiana State University Press, 1953.

MILTON, GEORGE F. *The Age of Hate: Andrew Johnson and the Radicals.* New York: Coward-McCann, 1930.

OBERHOLTZER, ELLIS P. *A History of the United States since the Civil War.* 5 vols. New York: Macmillan, 1917–37. (See Vols. I–II.)

OWEN, ROBERT DALE. "Political Results from the Varioloid," *Atlantic Monthly,* XXXV (June, 1875), 660–70.

PATTON, JAMES W. *Unionism and Reconstruction in Tennessee.* Chapel Hill: University of North Carolina Press, 1934.

PEARSON, HENRY GREENLEAF. *The Life of John A. Andrew, Governor of Massachusetts, 1861–1865.* 2 vols. Boston: Houghton Mifflin, 1904.

PHIFER, GREGG. "Andrew Johnson Takes a Trip," *Tennessee Historical Quarterly*, XI (March, 1952), 3–22; "Andrew Johnson Argues a Case," *ibid.* (June, 1952), pp. 148–70; "Andrew Johnson Delivers His Argument," *ibid.* (September, 1952), pp. 212–34; "Andrew Johnson Loses His Battle," *ibid.* (December, 1952), pp. 291–328.

PIERCE, EDWARD L. *Memoir and Letters of Charles Sumner.* 4 vols. Boston: Roberts Bros., 1877–94.

PORTER, GEORGE H. *Ohio Politics during the Civil War Period.* New York: Privately printed, 1911.

RAMSDELL, CHARLES W. *Reconstruction in Texas.* "Columbia University Studies in History, Economics and Public Law," Vol. XXXVI. New York: Columbia University Press, 1910.

RANDALL, JAMES G. *The Civil War and Reconstruction.* Boston: D. C. Heath, 1937.

———. *Constitutional Problems under Lincoln.* New York: D. Appleton, 1926.

———. *Lincoln the President.* 4 vols. New York: Dodd, Mead, 1945–55. (Vol. IV, subtitled *Last Full Measure*, by J. G. RANDALL and R. N. CURRENT.)

REID, WHITELAW. *After the War: A Southern Tour, May 1, 1865 to May 1, 1866.* London: Sampson Low, Son, & Marston, 1866.

RHODES, JAMES FORD. *History of the United States from the Compromise of 1850 . . . [to 1877].* 7 vols. New York: Macmillan, 1893–1906. (See Vols. V–VI.)

ROSKE, RALPH J. "Republican Newspaper Support for the Acquittal of President Johnson," *Tennessee Historical Quarterly*, XI (September, 1952), 263–73.

———. "The Seven Martyrs?" *American Historical Review*, LXIV (January, 1959), 323–40.

SALTER, WILLIAM. *The Life of James W. Grimes. . . .* New York: D. Appleton, 1876.

SELLERS, JAMES L. "James R. Doolittle," *Wisconsin Magazine of History*, XVII (December, 1933, March, June, 1934), 168–78, 277–306, 393–401; XVIII (September, December, 1934), 20–41, 178–87.

SIMKINS, FRANCIS B., and WOODY, ROBERT H. *South Carolina during Reconstruction.* Chapel Hill: University of North Carolina Press, 1932.

SMITH, WILLIAM E. *The Francis Preston Blair Family in Politics.* 2 vols. New York: Macmillan, 1933.

STAPLES, THOMAS S. *Reconstruction in Arkansas.* "Columbia University Studies in History, Economics and Public Law," Vol. CIX. New York: Columbia University Press, 1923.

STEBBINS, HOMER A. *A Political History of the State of New York, 1865–1869.* "Columbia University Studies in History, Economics and Public Law," Vol. LV. New York: Columbia University Press, 1913.

STRYKER, LLOYD PAUL. *Andrew Johnson, A Study in Courage.* New York: Macmillan, 1929.

TEMPLE, OLIVER P. *Notable Men of Tennessee, from 1833–1875*. New York: Cosmopolitan Press, 1912.

THOMPSON, CLARA MILDRED. *Reconstruction in Georgia, Economic, Social and Political, 1865–1872*. New York: Columbia University Press, 1915.

TROWBRIDGE, JOHN T. *The South: A Tour of Its Battle-Fields and Ruined Cities.* . . . Hartford: L. Stebbins, 1866.

VAN DEUSEN, GLYNDON G. *Thurlow Weed, Wizard of the Lobby*. Boston: Little, Brown, 1947.

WELLMAN, MANLY WADE. *Giant in Gray: A Biography of Wade Hampton of South Carolina*. New York: Charles Scribner's Sons, 1949.

WHITE, HORACE. *The Life of Lyman Trumbull*. Boston: Houghton Mifflin, 1913.

WINSTON, ROBERT W. *Andrew Johnson, Plebeian and Patriot*. New York: Henry Holt, 1928.

To the scholarly merits of many of the above-listed works, despite the ways in which their viewpoints have diverged from my own, I have by my very dependence on them, given implicit and explicit acknowledgment. There are other works, however, which have impressed me in other ways. James Ford Rhodes was a scholar and James G. Blaine was not, and there is much in the work of both with which my own judgment does not concur. But with regard to the particular events which I have written about here, I have discovered an unusual rapport with each of these writers. Leaving aside the dimension of scholarship, which in Rhodes's case is considerable, and the lack of which in Blaine's is counterbalanced by his having been in the thick of things, I find in both these minds elements of practical judgment which seem worthy of much respect. They both recognized that the Johnson episode was at best a sorry business from almost any viewpoint, an insight which is not in itself very hard to come by. But their thinking, unlike that of many another writer, did not stop with simply deploring the general condition of things. Both Blaine and Rhodes seem to have had a highly developed appreciation of the conflicting political requirements which these events involved, a sense of limits, and an understanding of the possible, all adding up to an attitude of mind which I found very helpful in my own efforts to understand why the men of the time behaved as they did.

Acknowledgments

For part of the leisure needed to launch this study, I am indebted to a grant from the Rockefeller Foundation. Another from the Ford Foundation enabled me to undertake research in a number of widely separated places, the expense of which would otherwise have been prohibitive. Typing and clerical assistance in the final stages of preparing the manuscript were provided through grants from the Walgreen Foundation and the Rutgers Research Council. I have been much influenced by the opinions and criticisms of those who have taken the time and trouble to read the manuscript through. For this I want to thank Sigmund Diamond, Kingsley Ervin, Henry Graff, John Higham, William T. Hutchinson, William Leuchtenburg, Sabra Meservey, Walter Metzger, and Wallace Sayre. A particular debt is owing to Richard Hofstadter and C. Vann Woodward, whose criticism, encouragement, and keenness of interest went beyond anything I had a right to expect from either of them. The special role of Stanley Elkins, who gave both time and ideas to the project, partook of the conspiratorial.

Index